Reading
Instruction
for Today

Second Edition

Reading Instruction for Today

Jana M. Mason
University of Illinois, Urbana-Champaign

Kathryn H. Au
Kamehameha Schools, Honolulu, Hawaii

HarperCollins*Publishers*

Credit lines for copyrighted materials appear in the
Acknowledgments section beginning on page 497. This section
is to be considered an extension of the copyright page.

Library of Congress Cataloging-in-Publication Data

Mason, Jana M.
    Reading instruction for today / Jana M. Mason, Kathryn H.
  Au.—2nd ed.
       p.   cm.
    Includes bibliographical references.
    ISBN 0-673-38774-7
    1. Reading (Elementary)   2. Language arts (Elementary)
  3. Reading comprehension.   4. Children—Books and
  reading.   I. Au, Kathryn Hu-Pei.   II. Title.
  LB1573.M376   1990
  372.4—dc20   89-29535
                                                              CIP

   2   3   4   5   6   7—VHJ—95   94   93   92   91   90

Preface

In the second edition of *Reading Instruction for Today*, we have tried to capture the most recent wave of change in the field of reading and language arts. More than half of this textbook has been completely rewritten to incorporate current research and practice in topics such as emergent literacy, writing, reading in the content areas, teaching students with special needs, classroom organization, and voluntary reading. We have given more attention, in particular, to the process of classroom learning, including such instructional techniques and concepts as scaffolding and the gradual release of responsibility.

The book is intended as the main text for a semester-long course on elementary school reading instruction. It is typically used with courses for second or third year undergraduates, or occasionally for returning master's level students, and assumes that prospective teachers have had no other reading instruction courses.

Because of the rich research base, there is more for prospective teachers to know about reading than about any other part of elementary school curriculum. Reading and writing instruction are also complex topics. For these reasons, we have made every effort to organize and present the material clearly. Each chapter begins with a quotation from another author, highlighting an important concept in the chapter. An overview of the chapter and an overarching perspective of the chapter topic follows. Each chapter is then structured around four or more key concepts, which are summaries of the main ideas covered. The key concepts will aid readers in learning and retaining the information presented. Each key concept is introduced with an overview of issues and relevant research. We also add exercises to promote a deeper understanding and a platform for discussing critical issues. We then provide instructional guidelines and activities consistent with current knowledge of the area.

There are two major changes in the organization of this edition. First, writing is no longer the subject of a separate chapter. Instead, we have tried to show throughout the book the many ways in which writing can be integrated with reading instruction. Second, the order of the chapters is changed. The three chapters on comprehension now come right after Chapter 1. We think this approach gives a stronger initial sense of the reading process in general and of reading for meaning. However, because each chapter presents complete coverage of a particular topic, instructors are free to change the order in which the chapters are taught.

Chapter 1 presents an overview of literacy in society, the reading process in general, and children's learning to read; it is best used as the introduction to the book. Chapter 2 introduces the comprehension process, continues the themes introduced in Chapter 1, and outlines principles for effective comprehension instruction appropriate at all grade levels. Chapter 3 focuses on methods for helping students comprehend and write about stories and appreciate literature. In a parallel manner, Chapter 4 focuses on the comprehension of expository texts, study skills, and the writing of research reports.

Chapter 5, vocabulary, provides explanations of word meanings and how they are learned while reading. This chapter serves as the bridge from comprehension into issues especially affecting young literacy learners, particularly word identification. Chapter 6 focuses on introducing reading and writing to kindergarten children and other beginners. Chapter 7 provides an extensive treatment of teaching word identification skills, including phonics, and shows the close connections to both writing and comprehension. Chapter 8 covers the teaching of reading and writing to students with special needs.

Chapter 9 presents a discussion of how teachers can use assessment to guide and support classroom instruction. Chapter 10 provides an overview of reading materials and methods, and Chapter 11 suggests how classrooms can be organized and managed for effective instruction. Finally, Chapter 12 describes reading and writing in the school, home, and community, highlighting the importance of looking at reading beyond the walls of the classroom. This final chapter carries the reader back to the initial chapter by affirming the importance of literacy in everyday life.

This edition includes many descriptions of actual classroom lessons for the purpose of showing the responsive quality of effective teaching. Other features of this textbook the reader should find valuable include definitions of terms that are framed by the text context, chapter summaries, lists of further readings, visual aids, and a complete index. An Instructor's Resource Book is also available.

First and foremost, we wish to thank Taffy E. Raphael and Sam L. Sebesta for the time and thought given in reviewing the drafts of our chapters. We are also grateful for suggestions made by June Barnhart, Patricia A. Herman, and Victoria Chou-Hare. For their continuing influence and support, we are indebted to Richard C. Anderson and William Nagy at the Center for the Study of Reading, and to Alice J. Kawakami, Judith A. Scheu, and Jo Ann Wong-Kam at the Kamehameha Schools. And finally, for their patience and encouragement, we wish to thank Anita Portugal and Christopher Jennison, our editors at Scott, Foresman.

Guiding students toward becoming confident and capable readers and writers is surely one of the greatest challenges facing today's elementary school teachers. We hope the second edition of *Reading Instruction for Today* will prove to be a useful resource to teachers as they seek to meet this challenge.

Jana M. Mason
Kathryn H. Au

Contents

Chapter 3

Developing Children's Appreciation of Literature and Comprehension of Stories
73

Chapter 4

Developing Study Skills and Teaching Comprehension of Expository Text
124

Chapter 12

Reading in the School, Home, and Community   460

Reading and Learning to Read

I learned from the age of two or three that any room in our house, at any time of day, was there to read in, or to be read to. My mother read to me. She'd read to me in the big bedroom in the mornings, when we were in her rocker together, which ticked in rhythm as we rocked, as though we had a cricket accompanying the story. She'd read to me in the diningroom on winter afternoons in front of the coal fire, with our cuckoo clock ending the story with "Cuckoo," and at night when I'd got in my own bed. I must have given her no peace. Sometimes she read to me in the kitchen while she sat churning, and the churning sobbed along with *any* story. It was my ambition to have her read to me while *I* churned; once she granted my wish, but she read off my story before I brought her butter. She was an expressive reader. When she was reading "Puss in Boots," for instance, it was impossible not to know that she distrusted *all* cats.

It had been startling and disappointing to me to find out that story books had been written by *people*, that books were not natural wonders, coming up of themselves like grass. Yet regardless of where they came from, I cannot remember a time when I was not in love with them—with the books themselves, cover and binding and the paper they were printed on, with their smell and their weight and with their possession in my arms, captured and carried off to myself. Still illiterate, I was ready for them, committed to all the reading I could give them.

Neither of my parents had come from homes that could afford to buy many books, but though it must have been something of a strain on his salary, as the youngest officer in a young insurance company, my father was all the while carefully selecting and ordering away for what he and Mother thought we children should grow up with. They bought first for the future.
(Welty, 1983, pp. 5–6)

▋ OVERVIEW

We begin this chapter by viewing reading as a social process and highlighting its importance in our daily lives. We discuss the purposes people have for reading, and the importance of considering not just the text, but the social context surrounding the reading event. Then we examine the reading process as it is seen in mature, competent readers. We show why reading is defined as the process of constructing meaning from text and discuss four aspects of reading as a psychological process. Next, we discuss the teacher's role in fostering children's reading development. The idea is to lead children gradually toward independence. Near the end of this chapter, we look at classrooms at the kindergarten, second, and fourth grade levels, where students are engaged in meaningful reading and writing activities. Finally, we lay out broad goals for the elementary school reading program.

Chapter 1 is organized around the following key concepts:

Key Concept 1: Reading is a social process, one of the means people rely upon to accomplish everyday goals and to make sense of their lives.

Key Concept 2: Reading may be defined as the process of constructing meaning from text.

Key Concept 3: Reading development is fostered when the teacher helps children with tasks too difficult to perform on their own, then gradually releases responsibility for the task to the children.

Key Concept 4: The classroom program should center on reading and writing activities which promote the overall goal of giving students a foundation for lifelong literacy.

▊ PERSPECTIVE
Literacy and Reading

Literacy, or the ability to use reading and writing, plays an increasingly important role in today's world. For example, while at work, people in the United States spend an average of more than two hours a day reading, and the materials they read are usually at the tenth- to twelfth-grade level in difficulty (Mikulecky, 1982). Nearly all adults in the United States read magazines (Monteith, 1981), and about two-thirds read the newspaper daily (Guthrie, 1981). Older adults read an average of almost a book a month (Ribovich & Erickson, 1980). Clearly, literacy is pervasive not only in school but in the workplace, home, and community.

What it means to be functionally literate, to be able to use literacy to meet the basic demands of daily life, varies from society to society. People in some societies may not need to use literacy at all to lead fulfilling lives. However, high levels of literacy are required of people who wish to take full advantage of opportunities offered by societies like the United States.

People can attain different levels of literacy. For example, the U.S. National Assessment of Educational Progress (NAEP, 1987) describes these five levels:

Rudimentary: Able to carry out simple reading tasks, such as following brief written directions or selecting the phrase to describe a picture.
Basic: Able to understand specific or sequentially presented informa-

tion, such as locating facts in uncomplicated stories and news articles.

Intermediate: Able to see the relationship among ideas and to generalize, such as making generalizations about main ideas and the author's purpose.

Adept: Able to understand, summarize, and explain complicated information, such as analyzing unfamiliar material and providing reactions to whole texts.

Advanced: Able to synthesize and learn from specialized reading materials, such as extending and restructuring ideas in scientific articles or literary essays.

Perhaps only 2 percent of all adults in the United States are illiterate, unable to read and write at all (Mikulecky, 1987). From studies conducted by NAEP, we know that almost all 17-year-olds have achieved a basic level of literacy. About 84 percent have achieved an intermediate level of literacy (about the eighth-grade level), and about 40 percent have achieved an adept level of literacy. However, only 5 percent can function at an advanced level of literacy (Applebee, Langer, & Mullis, 1985).

Teachers have the important task of helping their students to become literate. In preparing students to meet the challenges of the future, we will need to take them well beyond basic literacy. Our goal as educators is to lead students toward becoming literate at the adept and advanced levels.

> **Key Concept 1**
>
> Reading is a social process, one of the means people rely upon to accomplish everyday goals and to make sense of their lives.

▮ THE IMPORTANCE OF READING IN EVERYDAY LIFE

When we say that reading is a social process, we mean that reading is one of the means people employ to communicate with one another and to go about their daily lives in our society. In fact, most of us can hardly imagine going through a day without reading and writing. This is because literacy has many different *functions*, and we use it to accomplish so many different purposes (Heath, 1980). Here are some examples: When we check price tags or street signs, we are reading to deal with the practical problems of everyday life. When we exchange letters and greeting cards, we are reading and writing to maintain social relationships. When we peruse the front page of the news-

(1) Make a list of all the ways you have already used reading and writing today, or plan to use reading and writing today.

(2) How many ways did you think of? You might be surprised at the many different ways you use reading and writing in the course of an ordinary day.

(3) How would your life be different if you weren't able to read and write?

Many people report leaving notes for members of their family; making shopping lists; taking notes in class; reading books, newspapers, or magazines; writing letters and sending greeting cards; reading bills and making out checks; and filling out forms. Many of us find it difficult to think of our lives without reading and writing. Participating in activities at school, at work, at home, and in the community seems almost impossible without reading and writing. Literacy has a central role in our lives and is part and parcel of the way we carry out many activities.

paper, we are reading to learn about distant events. And when we curl up with a good book, we are reading for recreation and enjoyment.

Research by Taylor (1983) shows further what we mean when we say that reading is a social process. Judging that this social process had its roots in the family, Taylor set out to learn about young children's earliest experiences with literacy. She looked at six families, each with a child who was successfully learning to read and write. She found that the styles and values of literacy were transmitted to the children by their parents, and in turn were shaped by the personalities and preferences of the children themselves. The process of encouraging children's learning to read and write in the home turned out to be highly dynamic and flexible, with the parents preserving certain aspects of their own experiences (e.g., the reading aloud of storybooks) but deliberately changing others (e.g., making reading more important than it had been in the home when they were growing up).

Taylor discovered "that children learn to organize their environment through the use of print" (p. 54). This is one example:

> Kathy was playing at Bonnie's house, and together they organized a club in which James was a member. Once again, print was used in many of the negotiations. Kathy and Bonnie designed membership forms which included the name, school, and birthdate of each member. Each member filled out the form and received a club pass on which his or her name was written. Kathy and Bonnie also wrote out the club rules. . . . (p. 46)

Taylor observed that the children attended more to the *uses* of print in everyday life than to the print itself. That is, words and letters were not valued for their own sake but were seen as a means to an end. For example, the children used notes to communicate to their parents, just as their parents communicated to them through notes left on the refrigerator. Messages were also written to siblings and friends.

Reading and writing were ways of engaging in and making sense of everyday life. Children learned about the way print could be used to accomplish different purposes *before* they learned about the alphabet and the conventions of writing. As Taylor's work demonstrates, reading is part of the larger process of being literate and participating in a literate society.

We can think of reading as a social process involving different kinds of contexts. Smith, Carey, and Harste (1982) suggest the following three contexts:

> Linguistic context is the written text per se, that which appears visually on the page.
>
> Situational context . . . is the setting in which a reading-event occurs; it includes the linguistic text, the individuals involved (e.g., a student and a teacher), the location (e.g., in a classroom or at home), the expectations (e.g., that a recall test will be given over the material), and all such other factors impinging immediately on the event.
>
> Cultural context is the social/political matrix in which the situation of reading has come about.   (p. 22)

These abstract ideas can be made more concrete by considering an example. Consider the case of a teacher who is reading aloud to a class. The linguistic context is often a story in a children's book. Besides the story, the situational context often includes twenty-five or more students but just one teacher. The lesson takes place in a classroom, which in turn is in a school building. Most of the time, the children sit quietly, facing the teacher and listening.

But how did these students come to be involved in lessons like this every day? To answer this question we must consider the cultural context. It includes such diverse factors as the value the children and their families attach to education, the need for children to be occupied while their parents are off at work, laws requiring children to be in school, and the way schools are organized into grade levels and classes.

Notice, as in Taylor's view, that the printed page itself, the linguistic context, is only one of the contexts or factors to be considered in the act of reading. Since reading is a social process and a form of communication, it is equally important to consider its larger situational and cultural contexts as well.

What it means to be a competent reader or to be literate may vary, depending on these broad contexts. For example, parents may encourage the young child to "read" a favorite storybook by retelling the events without actually repeating the words verbatim (Holdaway, 1979). If the child goes to school the next day and does the very same thing, however, he or she might be scolded by an unsympathetic teacher for "reading carelessly." This might happen because the parent is trying to encourage enjoyment of reading, while the teacher's goal is to call the child's attention to the details of words and letters.

Similarly, there is not just one way to learn to read or to become literate.

For all children, literacy begins at home. That is why it's important for teachers to be aware of children's home experiences with literacy, such as family storybook reading.

This point is clearly established in the work of Scribner and Cole (1981), who studied literacy among the Vai in Liberia. The Vai are a traditional people who in the early nineteenth century invented a syllabic writing system to represent their own language. Scribner and Cole found that many Vai men could read and write using this script. Except for this high rate of native-language literacy, however, the Vai lived in virtually the same way as neighboring groups. One did not become literate in Vai by attending school or by becoming educated, in the sense of having to master a written body of knowledge. Obviously, a young person becoming literate in Vai goes through very different experiences from a young person becoming literate in English in a school in the United States.

There is an important practical implication stemming from the key concept of reading as a social process. As a social process, reading may have a different meaning for different people. Thus, teachers need to be alert to the overall meaning of the reading event to their students. Children have larger lives, outside the school, which may give the situational and cultural contexts 'of reading in the classroom a different definition from that assumed or intended by the teacher.

Young children, in particular, are best taught to read in situations compatible with those of their home culture. Au and Mason (1983), for example, investigated this issue with students of Polynesian-Hawaiian ancestry. Teachers who insisted that Hawaiian children speak one at a time in answering their questions had great difficulty in conducting effective reading lessons. On the other hand, teachers who allowed the children to cooperate or speak together in answering questions could conduct highly effective lessons.

Teachers who used this second style of interaction were teaching in a manner consistent with the rules for talk story, an important nonschool speech event for Hawaiian children. In talk story, speakers cooperate with one another in telling stories. Rather than one person telling the whole story, two or more speakers take turns, each narrating just a small part. Use of a cooperative talk-story style was important to the students, perhaps because it seems to reflect the value many Hawaiians attach to the performance and well-being of the group or family, as opposed to the individual.

In short, the effective teaching of reading depends on the teacher's taking a broad view of the contexts of literacy and learning to read. In the study by Au and Mason, for example, the text itself was not the problem at all. Rather, the barrier to effective instruction was found in the situational and cultural contexts.

In this key concept we stressed the importance of the social context for reading and learning to read. Of course, reading can also be understood as a special kind of thinking occurring in an individual's mind. Therefore, in the next key concept we look at reading as a psychological process and at the kind of mental activity that reading entails.

Key Concept 2

Reading may be defined as the process of constructing meaning from text.

SCHEMA THEORY AND THE FOUR ASPECTS OF READING

Much has been learned about the reading process by researchers investigating *schema theory* (e.g., Spiro, Bruce, & Brewer, 1980). Schema theory is a way of trying to explain how people store knowledge in their minds, how they use the knowledge they have, and how they acquire new knowledge. The term *schema* (the plural is *schemata*) refers to a "packet" or structure of knowledge in the human mind (Rumelhart, 1981).

Figure 1.1
Aspects of the Reading Process

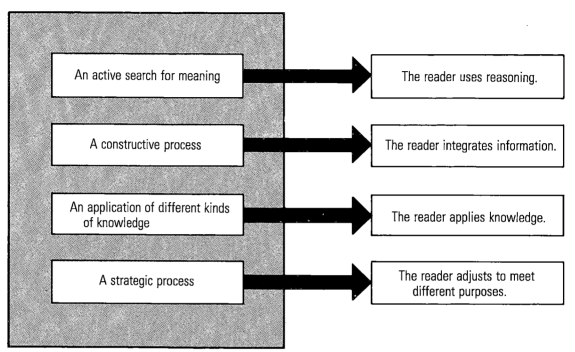

The idea that there is nothing so practical as a good theory certainly applies to the teaching of reading. There should be a close, if not necessarily direct, connection between what we know about the process of reading and how we go about teaching children to read. In this section we discuss four aspects of the reading process as we can understand it from the perspective of schema theory. These four aspects are shown in Figure 1.1. We can define reading as:

1. an active search for meaning
2. a constructive process
3. an application of different kinds of knowledge
4. a strategic process

To make the ideas being discussed more concrete, we include a short exercise illustrating each aspect.

Reading as an Active Search for Meaning

Teachers should always remember that reading requires an orientation to meaning. First and foremost, reading should be seen as comprehension and a special form of reasoning, not word-calling or sounding out. This more scientifically valid view of reading as a search for meaning does not mean ignoring letters and words. Of course, they have to be identified. The identification of letters and words, however, is always subservient to the overall search for meaning. Even beginning readers need to be reminded and allowed to consider the larger meaning of the text.

As evident from the quotations below, this view that reading is a meaning-getting process is not a new one but has long been held by eminent scholars in the field:

Huey (1908): Reading is "thought-getting and thought manipulation."

Thorndike (1917): "Reading is reasoning."

Gray (1925): "Reading is a form of clear vigorous thinking."

Dewey (1938): Comprehension is "an effort after meaning." (from Mason, 1984, p. 26)

What *is* new is that we are now beginning to understand the nature of the reasoning and sense-making people do when they read. In this view of reading as an active search for meaning, we see the importance of the reader as a person. We realize that letters and words do not carry meaning and value in themselves, but take these on as they become the objects of the reader's attention. When we teach children to read, then, we should keep in mind that our job is basically one of helping them learn to use reasoning when dealing with text.

What do we mean when we say that reading is reasoning? To a large degree, we are referring to the importance of *inference*. Inference may be defined as the making of logical connections or the filling in of information from one's memory and experience. In an overview of research pointing to the importance of *inference*, Johnston (1983) writes:

We do not consider readers to have comprehended something if they can give only a rote recall of the elements. We consider that readers have comprehended a text only when they have established logical connections among the ideas in the text and can express these in an alternate form. In this way, inferences are critical acts of comprehension, since they allow us to make various words meaningful, join together propositions and sentences, and fill in the missing chunks of information. (p. 7)

Making inferences itself, Johnston notes, is not a single type of skill. Rather, readers are required to make several different kinds of inferences. For example, not only must they infer the meaning of single words in context, they must also infer a larger framework for understanding the meaning of sentences and the text as a whole.

Here is an example of what we mean by making inferences while reading. Suppose you were to read the sentence, "John put a dime in his piggy bank." What you would probably infer is the following: A male person named John, most likely a child, owns a bank (probably three to twelve inches long, in the shape of a pig and made of metal or pottery) in which he is saving dimes and other coins.

Exercise

(1) Reread the paragraph on page 8 that begins, "Teachers should always remember . . ."

(2) Write in a sentence or two what you got from reading that paragraph.

(3) Now, answer the following questions:

(a) Were you aware of sounding out or stumbling over any of the words?

(b) Were you aware of thinking about the reasons we included this paragraph at this particular point? Refer to what you wrote in response to #2 above.

Let's consider your responses to questions 3a and 3b.

(3a) The chances are that you had no trouble with any of the individual words in the paragraph. In fact, you probably had so little trouble that you were scarcely aware of any particular words at all.

(3b) On the other hand, you probably were quite concerned with getting the overall meaning of the paragraph. If we succeeded in getting our message across, you probably noted that we would be talking about reading as a form of reasoning.

What we hope you have learned from this exercise is that, while words and letters are important in the process of reading, the whole point is to get meaning from text. Moving through the individual words is a means to this end.

Without ever thinking about it, we added a great deal to that one short sentence. We needed to make these additions through inference because without them we would not have had an adequate sense of meaning. Notice that we showed special knowledge in two areas. First, we used our knowledge of the reading process. We made inferences automatically because we know this to be a necessary part of reading. Second, we used cultural knowledge. By growing up in a certain culture, we acquired knowledge of children saving money in piggy banks.

According to the principles of schema theory, we were able to read with understanding because we already had in our minds the necessary schemata, or structures of knowledge, for the reading process and for saving money in piggy banks. This knowledge helped us to reason along the proper lines.

Reading as a Constructive Process

The second aspect we highlight is that of reading as a constructive process during which the reader makes meaningful connections among ideas in a text and to background knowledge. What does it mean to say that reading is a "constructive process"? Langer (1982) explains this idea in the following way:

> Comprehension is not a simple text-based process in which readers piece together what the words, sentences, or paragraphs "say"—as if words themselves have some inherent meaning. Nor is it simply a concept-driven process in which readers begin with a global notion of what the text will be about, and anticipate the larger meanings the text will convey. Rather, comprehension is a process which requires *readers*—real live readers with ideas and attitudes of their own—to interpret what the author is saying. (pp. 40–41)

Smith, Adams, and Schorr (1978) showed how important it is for adults to be able to connect and integrate information as they read. Subjects in their study were first told to read and learn two sentences containing apparently unrelated facts. For example:

1. The banker broke the bottle.
2. The banker did not delay the trip.

Next, some of the subjects read and learned a sentence that allowed them to integrate all of the information. One example of such a sentence is:

3. The banker was chosen to christen the ship.

The other subjects were given a sentence which did not allow them to tie things together, such as:

4. The banker was asked to address the crowd.

The results of the study showed that people required less time to learn sentence 3 than sentence 4 and also remembered it better. The explanation for this finding is that sentences 1, 2, and 3 formed an integrated unit that readers could relate to their own knowledge while sentences 1, 2, and 4 remained unintegrated and less meaningful.

Both Langer and Spiro (1980) point out that the text serves merely as a linguistic "blueprint" which readers must enrich with their own ideas, in this way creating their own meaning for the text. Langer adds:

> This is not to suggest that readers go off into an idiosyncratic world of fanciful meaning but that they alone have the power to create meaning—their meaning is closer to or further from the meaning that the author intended, but reader-generated nonetheless. (p. 41)

A related idea is that the construction of meaning does not occur spontaneously or in a perfectly straightforward way. Rather, the reader gradually constructs meaning from text through a trial-and-error process. This process is that of formulating hypotheses about the text, testing them, and then continuing or rejecting them (Spiro, Bruce, & Brewer, 1980).

During this process of generating and testing hypotheses, the reader appears to be constructing a mental model of the text. Collins, Brown, and Larkin (1980) suggest that the reader is trying to create an overall framework to fit the events and other information described. An initial model is constructed, then revised and evaluated. The authors refer to this process as one of "pro-

Exercise

(1) Place a card or a sheet of paper over the text below so that you will be able to read it just one sentence at a time. After you look at the first sentence, jot down on a sheet of paper what you think the text is about. Then read the second sentence and do the same. Then go on to the third sentence. (Passage and information about responses taken from Collins, Brown, & Larkin, 1980, p. 387.)

Text:

He plunked down $5 at the window.

She tried to give him $2.50, but he refused to take it.

So when they got inside, she bought him a large bag of popcorn.

(2) Think about your responses as you were reading.
(a) What was your first impression of what the text was about?

(b) If your impression changed as you read the second and third sentences, what triggered the change?

Let's consider your responses.

(2a) Some people think the man is at a racetrack window placing a bet, and many others see him at the window of a bank or theater. At any rate, the first sentence is fairly ambiguous.

(2b) Upon reading the second sentence, some people think that "she" refers to a cashier who is trying to give the man change. With this interpretation, it is somewhat puzzling when the man refuses the money. Upon reading the third sentence, most people arrive at the conclusion that the woman referred to in the second sentence is probably the man's date and that they are going to a movie. She wanted to pay for her own ticket but he wouldn't let her, and she then decided to use the money to buy him some popcorn.

The point we would like you to get from this exercise is that of the gradual shaping of meaning as the reader moves through the text. Text is often ambiguous. It does not "tell" us very much and can lend itself to different interpretations. Therefore, to comprehend at all, readers must actively work at developing a mental model of the text.

gressive refinement" in comprehending text. For example, suppose that you were starting to read a mystery. As you read, you gradually develop a picture of the setting and the characters, and you soon become immersed in the plot. The further you read, the more definite your ideas become. Details presented earlier, which at first seemed insignificant to you, suddenly gain a new importance. Slowly, pieces start to fall into place, and once the mystery is solved, you understand how all of the pieces fit together.

As teachers we want to help our students learn to formulate and test their own hypotheses about text. In this process we will be less interested in whether answers are "right" or "wrong" than in the steps children follow in making and checking hypotheses. If their reasoning is sound, and their mental model of the text can account for the information presented, we may accept an unusual interpretation of the text. However, we might also acquaint the children with a more conventional interpretation of the text. In the last exercise, some children might argue that the couple is going to a football game, where the same series of events could have occurred. If so, we would not reject their argument but might offer reasons for the more common movie interpretation.

Reading as an Application of Different Kinds of Knowledge

In discussing the third aspect of the reading process, we look at the different kinds of knowledge the reader must use in formulating and testing hypotheses about the text. We have seen that the reader must *construct* meaning from the text, which serves much like a blueprint. The act of reading with comprehension, then, requires the reader to use knowledge of the world as well as knowledge of text. He must draw upon information already in his mind, gained through life experiences, previous reading, and so on.

This means teachers should keep in mind the following two points: First, children cannot be expected to read with comprehension if they have no way of connecting the new information in the text to their prior or background knowledge (Adams & Bruce, 1982). Second, since no two readers will have had exactly the same life experiences, due to differences in culture and family circumstances, to name just two, teachers should expect differences in the ways students interpret text. Their interpretations may differ from the teacher's and from one another's.

A great deal of research has been conducted demonstrating how background knowledge (also referred to as prior knowledge, preexisting knowledge, knowledge of the world, or scriptal knowledge) influences reading comprehension. Background knowledge can affect comprehension in at least four different ways (Langer, 1982): (1) by influencing the way information is organized and stored in memory; (2) by influencing the type of information brought to mind when reading about a particular topic; (3) by influencing the associations made, due to personal experiences and background knowledge; and (4) by influencing the language or vocabulary applied because of the perspective brought to the task of reading.

Of course, in addition to knowledge of the world, the reader must also apply knowledge of text. The text itself must be analyzed at different levels, from letters and words to its overall meaning (e.g., Rumelhart, 1976).

Another kind of knowledge the reader must apply is that of *text structure*, or knowledge of different types of text (more information on this kind of analysis is provided in Chapters 2, 3, and 4). Readers expect and look for dif-

Exercise

(1) To get some idea of just how powerful the effects of background knowledge can be, read the passage below (taken from Anderson, Reynolds, Schallert, & Goetz, 1977).

Rocky slowly got up from the mat, planning his escape. He hesitated a moment and thought. Things were not going well. What bothered him most was being held, especially since the charge against him had been weak. He considered his present situation. The lock that held him was strong but he thought he could break it. He knew, however, that his timing would have to be perfect. Rocky was aware that it was because of his early roughness that he had been penalized so severely—much too severely from his point of view. The situation was becoming frustrating; the pressure had been grinding on him for too long. He was being ridden unmercifully. Rocky was getting angry now. He felt he was ready to make his move. He knew that his success or failure would depend on what he did in the next few seconds.

(2) What do you think this passage is about?

(3) In the study by Anderson et al., two groups of subjects were asked to read this same passage. One was a group of students majoring in music, and one a group majoring in physical education. The passage was interpreted very differently by the two groups. The music majors thought they were reading about a jail break, while the physical education majors thought they were reading about a wrestling match.

If you look back, you will see that the passage lends itself equally well to both interpretations. Thus, the deciding factor was the subjects' background knowledge, which made it more likely they would see the passage from one perspective rather than the other. In your own case, which interpretation did you arrive at? What factors in your own exerience do you think caused you to arrive at that particular interpretation?

We hope this exercise has helped you see the importance of background knowledge. Again, interpretation depends on what the reader brings to the text, and we can expect this to be different for different readers.

ferent kinds of information based on their knowledge of the type of text they are reading. So, for example, at the beginning of a short story, they seek out information about the setting, because that is likely to be important to their comprehension of later events. When reading an editorial in the newspaper, they identify the stance being taken and the evidence used in support of it. Or, when reading a scientific article, they read carefully when the definition of an unfamiliar but important term is given.

The reader works to construct meaning from text by testing hypotheses using several different kinds of knowledge at once. We can imagine that there is a constant flow of information through the reader's mind, with information of one kind having to be coordinated with all the others. For example, the reader may guess that the text is about a wrestling match but still need visual evidence, at the level of letters and words, to support this idea. Only in this way can a coherent model of the text be developed. Thus, the reader is trying to adjust hypotheses about letters and words, and hypotheses about overall meaning, to be consistent with one another.

A practical implication here is that, when we teach children to read, we need to prepare them to deal with and coordinate different kinds of knowledge and information.

Reading as a Strategic Process

This fourth aspect is also consistent with our focus on the reader as a person who brings his or her own goals and unique store of background knowledge to the task of constructing meaning from text. When we say that reading is *strategic*, we mean that it can be adjusted depending on the reader's purposes at a certain time. Sometimes we will set purposes for students' reading, but we want them eventually to be able to read for purposes they find important and set for themselves. Mature readers do just that. They read for some reason, for example, to entertain themselves, keep up with current events, or learn how to use a new gadget. Having these different purposes might lead them to read in a somewhat different manner.

Reading as a strategic process includes the monitoring of ongoing comprehension activities to see if our purposes are being met (Brown, 1982). In addition to the evidence from our newspaper example in the exercise on page 16, consider the earlier exercise involving the passage about the couple going to the movie. In trying to make sense of that passage, you were probably aware of monitoring your own comprehension and making adjustments to your interpretation.

In constrast, young children often do not monitor their own comprehension processes while reading and seem blissfully unaware that information is not being put together in a sensible way. Small instances of this are often observed. For example, a first-grader might read the sentence, "My mother got a new job today" as "My mother got a new jump today." This might happen if the child is so busy trying to figure out the word on the basis of letter information that she fails to notice that the resulting sentence does not make sense.

Effective readers, unlike poor or beginning readers, are *aware* of what they are doing as they read, and of what they need to do to meet their purposes. Awareness of one's own thinking or cognition is called *metacognition*. A practical implication is that teachers want to help students develop an awareness of their own mental activity while reading.

For example, suppose the child has misread the sentence, as described above. The teacher might ask the child if the sentence makes sense. When the child answers no, the teacher could ask her what could be done to fix the problem. If the child suggests rereading, the teacher could praise her for know-

(1) Reflect upon the habits you have for reading the newspaper. What do you usually do?

(2) Do you read the entire paper through, word for word, from start to finish? Or do you jump around, skipping some parts but not others? Of the parts you do read, do you give them all the same amount of attention? How do you treat some parts differently from others?

We guess that you do not read the paper through with equal attention from start to finish, but skim and skip around. You probably have a number of different purposes in mind, and you vary the way you read depending on those purposes. For example, when one of the authors read the paper recently, she just skimmed the front page, glancing at the headlines and deciding the stories were all too depressing to read after a hard day's work. She did stop to read a page 3 article about a possible teachers' strike. She then turned to the sports section, to read carefully articles about a couple of local teams. She made an effort to remember this information because she knew friends would be looking forward to discussing it the next day. Then she turned to the food section. She scanned the advertisement for the neighborhood supermarket and added a couple of items to her shopping list.

What we hope you have gotten from this exercise is a sense, in daily activity, of how reading is used purposefully and flexibly.

ing a strategy to correct a problem when reading. The teacher could also remind the child to think of what else she knows about the story, that something has happened to cause Mary to move to a new school. Then the teacher could point out to the group that these are two things to do if you run into problems when reading: reread the sentence and think about what you know about the story so far.

By now you have learned quite a bit about the reading process itself, and the kinds of thinking mature readers do to achieve a variety of purposes. Obviously, there is a lot that children must learn if they are to master all the complexities of reading. We look next at the whole concept of instruction and how teachers can help children learn about the reading process and become independent readers.

Key Concept 3

Reading development is fostered when the teacher helps children with tasks too difficult to perform on their own, then gradually releases responsibility for the task to the children.

THE TEACHER'S ROLE IN CHILDREN'S READING DEVELOPMENT

In this key concept we will return to some of the themes introduced in Key Concept #1, where we discussed reading and learning to read as social processes.

The ideas behind this key concept come from the theory developed by Vygotsky (1978). Vygotsky points out that children learn higher level mental processes, such as those involved in reading, through the help of knowledgeable others. Before they come to school, children have parents and other relatives to assist them, and after they come to school, they also have teachers to help them learn to read.

Learning is an external, social process, which takes place during the interactions children have with adults. Talking with students about the reading process and the kinds of reasoning we do with text is very important, because the thinking we do when reading is invisible. For example, when children watch an adult read silently, about all they see is eyes moving back and forth and a hand occasionally turning a page. Nothing can be known about the adult's thinking, unless the adult talks about it. This is why teachers need to talk to children about the thinking processes mature readers use when they read.

Similarly, when children read, their thinking generally is invisible to their teachers. We can, however, find out about children's mental processes by engaging them in discussions. For example, we can ask them questions about the text (What was the problem in the story?), and the processes of thinking they used (How did you figure out that was the problem?). Through social interactions, which may be formal lessons or informal conversations, adults provide children with the help they need.

Of course, not all kinds of help is equally beneficial to children's reading development. It would not be beneficial for a teacher to help a child with a reading task the child could just as well do alone. Nor would it be beneficial for a teacher to present a child with an impossibly difficult task. Rather, the teacher wants to present a task which is just beyond the child's reach, and then provide help so the child can be successful.

In Vygotsky's (1978) terms, a task which is just beyond the child's reach is said to be in the *zone of proximal development*. The zone of proximal development represents the next step forward in mental development. A task in the zone of proximal development is too difficult for the child to accomplish independently, but not too difficult for the child to accomplish if adult guidance is available.

The term *scaffolding* is used to describe the kinds of support a teacher might give a child dealing with a reading task in the zone of proximal development. Using the term *scaffolding* reminds us that the support given is necessary at the time but just temporary (Wood, Bruner, & Ross, 1976). The scaffolding or extra support is to be adjusted, reduced, and finally taken away.

▌ **Figure 1.2**
▌ **A Model of Teacher Scaffolding**

Student 1: My question is, what does the aquanaut need when he goes under water?
Student 2: A watch.
Student 3: Flippers.
Student 4: A belt.
Student 1: Those are all good answers.
Teacher: Nice job! I have a question too. Why does the aquanaut wear a belt? What is so special about it?
Student 3: It's a heavy belt and keeps him from floating up to the top again.
Teacher: Good for you.
Student 1: For my summary now: This paragraph was about what aquanauts need to take when they go under the water.
Student 5: And also about why they need those things.
Student 3: I think we need to clarify gear.
Student 6: That's the special things they need.
Teacher: Another word for gear in this story might be equipment, the equipment that makes it easier for the aquanauts to do their job.
Student 1: I don't think I have a prediction to make.
Teacher: Well, in the story they tell us that there are "many strange and wonderful creatures" that the aquanauts see as they do their work. My prediction is that they'll describe some of these creatures. What are some of the strange creatures you already know about that live in the ocean?
Student 6: Octopuses.
Student 3: Whales?
Student 5: Sharks!
Teacher: Let's listen and find out. Who'll be our teacher?

Source: From "Interactive teaching to promote independent learning from text" by Annemarie S. Palincsar and Ann L. Brown, *The Reading Teacher*, April 1986, p. 771. Copyright © 1986 International Reading Association, Inc. Reprinted with permission of Annemarie S. Palincsar and the International Reading Association.

Figure 1.2, an excerpt from an actual lesson (Palincsar & Brown, 1986), presents an example of teacher scaffolding. In this reading lesson, the teacher and students are engaged in an activity called reciprocal teaching (discussed further in Chapter 2). In earlier lessons, the teacher helped students learn how to ask questions, summarize, and make predictions. By now Student 1, who is leading the discussion, is able to ask a good question: "My question is, what does the aquanaut need when he goes under water?" Student 1 is also able to give a summary: "For my summary now: This paragraph was about what the aquanauts need to take when they go under water."

The teacher lets Student 1 and the other students carry out as much of the discussion as they can, giving assistance only at certain critical points. In this case, the teacher provides scaffolding by asking an additional question about the aquanaut's belt, and by suggesting that another word for *gear* might be *equipment*. Then, when Student 1 cannot think of a prediction to make, the teacher suggests one.

Pearson (1985) refers to the careful adjusting and removal of scaffolding as the *gradual release of responsibility*. This model is shown in Figure 1.3. On the left, we see that instruction begins with the teacher's modeling or showing the students how the task can be accomplished. At this point, responsibility for the task rests with the teacher.

Figure 1.3
The Gradual Release of Responsibility
Model of Instruction

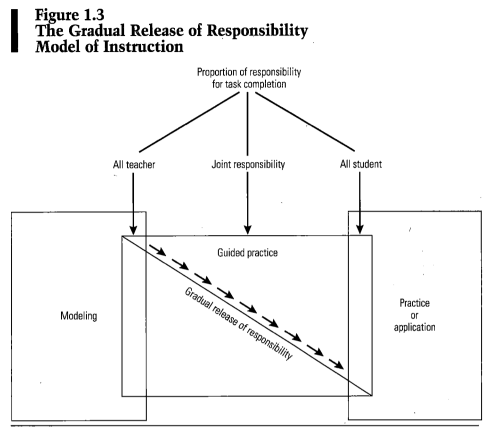

Source: From Pearson and Gallagher, *Contemporary Educational Psychology*, vol. 8, no. 3, 1983. Reprinted by permission of Academic Press, Inc., and P. David Pearson.

In the center of the diagram, the teacher involves the students in guided practice, and the teacher and students have joint responsibility for the task. (The lesson excerpt just presented showed this kind of joint responsibility.) The diagonal line going from upper left to lower right shows how the teacher reduces the scaffolding and gradually releases responsibility for the task to the students. The teacher assumes less and less responsibility, while the students take on more and more.

On the right, we see that the teacher has arranged for the students to practice the task on their own and to apply what they have learned. Now all of the responsibility for the task has been transferred from the teacher to the students.

In brief, we can think of the teacher's role as that of helping students through the zone of proximal development, or helping them to take the next step forward in learning to read. Effective instruction involves proceeding along a continuum in which the teacher gradually releases responsibility to the students. In the end, students will set their own goals and determine for themselves if teacher assistance is necessary (Gavelek, 1986).

Key Concept 4

The classroom program should center on reading and writing activities which foster the overall goal of giving students a foundation for life-long literacy.

▌ A FOUNDATION FOR LIFELONG LITERACY

Reading and Writing Across the Grades

In the first part of this section we look at three classrooms: a kindergarten classroom, a second-grade classroom, and a fourth-grade classroom. In each of these classrooms we highlight the main activities students engage in, and how these activities change across the grades. You will notice that these activities center on important functions of reading and writing.

Kindergarten. To start the day, the teacher writes the following message on the chalkboard:

Today is Monday.
An egg hatched!
We have a baby bird!

By writing the message the teacher shows the children how important information can be conveyed through print as well as through the spoken word. The children struggle to read the message aloud as a group. Then they have all kinds of questions: "How big is it?" "When did it come out?"

After more analysis of the message, the teacher gives the children a chance to do their own writing. First, she asks what they would like to write about. As individuals give their answers ("I want to write about going to my grandma's"), she excuses them to return to their seats. Some children make drawings, some draw and add labels or captions, and some write sentences with invented spellings (for example, GN for *grandma*). The teacher circulates around the room, leading the children to add more information about their topics and helping them to apply knowledge of writing conventions they have learned through work with the morning message (for example, consonant sounds). Later, several children are selected to sit in the Author's Chair (Graves & Hansen, 1983) and share their writing with the class.

After writing time, the teacher reads a storybook to the children. Often, she reads from a Big Book with print large enough for the children to see as

Rather than simply pointing out features of print herself, this kindergarten teacher lets her students show what they have observed about the words and letters in the morning message.

they are seated on the carpet. (Big Books are available from many publishing companies, although in some cases teachers make their own large versions of favorite stories.) The teacher encourages the children to make predictions about what will happen next and to chime in on repeated phrases ("Not I," said the pig). After the story has been read, the children discuss what happened and what they especially liked about the story. Returning to the pages of the Big Book, the teacher points out phrases and words to the children, and the children notice some patterns, for example, that "Not I" appears several times on the same page. The teacher puts the book in the library corner for the children to look at on their own. When she and the children reread the Big Book tomorrow, the children will have the chance to enjoy the story again and to make more observations about print.

At various times during the day, the children can choose to go to the library corner to look at books on their own. Often, two children will share a book, telling the story from the pictures. They scarcely glance at the print, but enjoy the book just the same. Sometimes, a child will be able to read the words in a book previously read aloud by the teacher, and others will gather to listen. Some children have favorite books they return to read again and again. (This description of a kindergarten class is based on Crowell, Kawakami, & Wong, 1986.)

Second grade.   The teacher starts the day by modeling how a writer can add to a piece by drafting a new sentence and then drawing an arrow to show where that sentence should go. One of the boys wants to add information about the bait he used on a fishing trip, so his piece is used as an example. One of the girls shares her newly published book about her gymnastics class. After a brief discussion, most of the children get out their writing books and work on their drafts. A few children recopy their pieces and prepare illustrations for books they are publishing. Meanwhile, the teacher meets with individuals who want to have a conference about their writing.

When writing time is over, the teacher explains the day's assignments and then calls one of the reading groups up for a lesson. Most of the other children in the class begin their reading and writing assignments at their seats, while some children take their turn going to the listening center, the art center, or the library corner.

The children meeting with the teacher share their writing about the basal reader story they started reading earlier in the week. Today, the teacher says they will finish reading the story. The teacher has the children silently read and then discuss the last few pages in the story. She adds to a chart the important story information the children discover. Then they discuss the message the author was trying to convey. Finally, the teacher tells the children to write about the author's message and how it might relate to their own lives.

These children return to their seats to write about the author's message, and the teacher calls up another reading group. In the course of the reading/language arts period, the teacher holds a lesson with each reading group. The children not meeting with the teacher complete their written assignments, participate in activities at the learning centers, and read books on their own. At the end of the period, the children gather for a brief discussion of their accomplishments, as well as any problems encountered, and the teacher reads aloud to them for a few moments.

Fourth grade.   The teacher begins the morning by having the students engage in sustained silent reading. This is a quiet time when students read books of their own choice, and the teacher reads silently too. After about ten minutes, the teacher asks if any students would like to tell the class about their books. Two students volunteer, and their enthusiasm convinces some of their classmates that they would like to read those books, too.

The writing period is next, and the teacher follows procedures similar to those in the second grade class. She conducts a brief lesson, has a student share her work, and then lets most of the students write on their own while she holds individual conferences. These fourth graders are preparing research reports about the exploration of space. They have chosen a wide range of topics, from the astronauts to the planets in the solar system. To gather information, the students read books, the encyclopedia, newspapers, and other sources.

The teacher stops the class briefly to explain the day's assignments, and then she calls up a reading group for a lesson. Each of the groups is reading a different novel. The lesson begins with the students' sharing the summaries of Chapter 3 they wrote the day before. They discuss the strengths and weaknesses of one another's summaries, and the teacher models on the chalkboard how the various strong points might be combined in a single summary. This discussion leads naturally into a review of Chapter 3 and an introduction to Chapter 4. When they return to their seats, the students will read and write about Chapter 4.

In comparison to the second graders, the fourth graders have more responsibility for planning the use of their time. Some of their assignments take a week or more to complete. Some students choose to spend part of their time reading and taking notes for their research reports, while others devote all of their time to reading and writing about their novels. Still others take a few moments to return to the books they chose for recreational reading. Students are allowed to seek the help of others. On this day, students in the first reading group are puzzled about how to summarize the information in Chapter 4 of their novel. The teacher suggests that each student choose a partner and engage in cooperative learning for a few minutes. This way, the students can share ideas, although each is responsible for writing an individual summary. The students gather in pairs to discuss their summary writing. As they begin writing, they continue to consult with one another. Their conversations conclude once they feel able to proceed on their own.

At the end of the period the teacher has the students discuss their progress and raise questions about their work. One student suggests that the table with the encyclopedias should be kept as a quiet writing area for only two students at a time. The teacher agrees, and the students decide that they will have a sign-up system. By the fourth grade, students are starting to be able to use reading and writing for a wide variety of purposes, and they are also aware of how their environment can be structured to support their literacy learning.

In all three of these classrooms, the students are engaged in reading and writing activities interesting and meaningful to them. Some activities, such as the morning message and other lessons, are directed by the teacher. Others, such as the reading of books in the library corner, are directed by the students themselves. The students in these classrooms have many opportunities to learn about the functions of literacy, and to use literacy for many purposes.

Goals of the Classroom Literacy Program

Teachers want to prepare students to use literacy for a variety of purposes throughout their lives. These purposes can be placed in two general categories:

1. Recreational and aesthetic, involving reading for pleasure.
2. Functional, involving reading to meet the demands of everyday life, at work or in the context of the family or community.

Earlier, we discussed the key concept of reading as a social process, one of the ways people communicate with one another and make sense of their world. Mature readers are capable of using reading for a wide variety of purposes, according to many different patterns. For this reason, teachers want to give students the opportunity to develop fully as readers, while being sensitive to their individual tastes and preferences. Thus, the elementary school reading program should be broad in scope, exposing students to many of the ways reading can be useful and enjoyable.

When we think of reading in this broad, multipurpose sense, we see that reading instruction should not be limited simply to use of a commercial program for only a short period each day. We need to call children's attention to the many, many uses of reading within the school and community, to everything from print on the cereal boxes they may see on the table, to the street signs they pass on their way to school, to the teacher's sending notes to the office, to the librarian's reading stories aloud to them, and so on throughout the day. During their elementary school years, we want to give students a view of reading as an integral part of life in a literate society.

We mentioned recreational and aesthetic goals first because one of the best ways to motivate children not already eager to learn to read is by treating them to good literature. Once students have experienced the joys of reading, the teacher's job is made much easier. If in the elementary school children begin to read for the sheer pleasure of reading, they have started to develop a habit that can be a source of enjoyment throughout their lives.

Functional goals are those related to using reading on the job or in the home and community for the tasks of everyday life. Reading on the job may entail everything from scanning memos, to close analysis of technical and scientific articles, to checking bills of sale. In the home family members leave notes for one another on the refrigerator, read the newspaper, sort through mail, and write checks. Thus, in the classroom reading program we want to prepare students to tackle many of these tasks, large and small, simple and complex.

Of course, students' achievement of these recreational and functional goals cannot be the sole responsibility of their elementary school teachers. For one thing, many children receive a good start toward achieving these goals in the home, before they ever come to school. For another, their development of reading abilities will continue for a long period of time, through their secondary school and perhaps college careers. Still, the aim of the elementary school program is to lay a solid foundation for future learning in both broad areas.

In summary, the goals of the elementary school reading program are best thought of in very broad terms. The teaching of reading even from the very beginning, in kindergarten and first grade, should be guided by our vision of children as literate citizens of the future. Such a vision will encourage us to give students a wide variety of lessons and opportunities for exploration in learning to read. Our aim is to create a classroom program designed to show children the power and joy of reading, and to enable them to use reading for the purposes they choose.

∎ SUMMARY

We began this chapter by considering the importance of literacy in our daily lives. In the first key concept we pointed out that reading is a social process, one of the means we use to meet everyday goals. Literacy serves many different functions, and we put it to many different uses. We looked at how, through home experiences, many children grow into a knowledge of the functions, and then the forms, of literacy. Three different contexts for literacy were identified: that provided by the text, by the social situation, and by the larger culture and society. We considered how reading may have different meanings in different cultures, and similarly, how culture may have a powerful influence on learning to read.

In the second key concept we defined reading as the process of constructing meaning from text. In doing so we looked at four aspects of reading as a psychological process. First, reading may be thought of as an active search for meaning, in the sense that the reader must reason and make inferences about text. Second, reading is a constructive process, one which requires the making and testing of hypotheses about text. Third, reading involves the application of different kinds of knowledge, of the real world and of the properties of text. Fourth, reading is a strategic process, being adjusted according to the reader's purposes.

In the third key concept we discussed the teacher's role in fostering children's literacy development. We presented several ideas from Vygotsky. One of these ideas concerned the importance of speaking with children about the reasoning involved in reading. We examined the idea of the zone of proximal development, or the next step forward in mental development. We described how teachers can move children through the zone by providing just the right amount of support or scaffolding. The overall idea is that teachers should gradually release responsibility for the performance of tasks to students. This enables students eventually to take charge of their own literacy learning.

In the fourth key concept we looked at classrooms at three different grade levels. The purpose here was to get a sense of the kinds of reading and writing activities likely to be meaningful to students at different phases of literacy development. These classrooms had certain features in common, in having both teacher-led and student-initiated activities, and involving students in reading and writing for a variety of purposes. Finally, we set out the goals of the elementary classroom program. To prepare students for lifelong literacy, teachers need to help children learn to read both for enjoyment and to meet the demands of everyday life. In this way, teachers can move students beyond basic literacy toward becoming literate at adept and advanced levels.

■ BIBLIOGRAPHY

References

Adams, M., & Bruce, B. C. (1982). Background knowledge and reading comprehension. In J. A. Langer & M. T. Smith-Burke (Eds.), *Reader meets author/Bridging the gap: A psycholinguistic and sociolinguistic perspective*. Newark, DE: International Reading Association.

Anderson, R. C., Reynolds, R. E., Schallert, D. E., & Goetz, E. T. (1977). Frameworks for comprehending discourse. *American Educational Research Journal, 14* (4), 367–381.

Applebee, A., Langer, J., & Mullis, I. (1985). *The Reading Report Card: Progress Toward Excellence in Our Schools*. Princeton, NJ: National Assessment of Educational Progress, Educational Testing Service.

Au, K. H., & Mason, J. M. (1983). Cultural congruence in classroom participation structures: Achieving a balance of rights. *Discourse Processes, 6* (2), 145–167.

Collins, A., Brown, J. S., & Larkin, J. M. (1980). Inference in text understanding. In R. J. Spiro, B. C. Bruce, & W. F. Brewer (Eds.), *Theoretical issues in reading comprehension*. Hillsdale, NJ: Erlbaum.

Crowell, D. C., Kawakami, A. J., & Wong, J. L. (1986). Emerging literacy: Reading-writing experiences in a kindergarten classroom. *The Reading Teacher, 40* (2), 144–149.

Gavelek, J. R. (1986). The social contexts of literacy and schooling: A developmental perspective. In T. E. Raphael (Ed.), *The contexts of school-based literacy*. New York: Random House, pp. 3–26.

Graves, D., & Hansen, J. (1983). The author's chair. *Language Arts, 60* (2), 176–183.

Guthrie, J. T. (1981). Acquisition of newspaper readership. *The Reading Teacher, 34*, 616–618.

Heath, S. B. (1980). The functions and uses of literacy. *Journal of Communication*, Winter, 123–133.

Holdaway, D. (1979). *The foundations of literacy*. Sydney, Australia: Ashton Scholastic (distributed in the United States by Heinemann).

Johnston, P. H. (1983). *Reading comprehension assessment: A cognitive basis*. Newark, DE: International Reading Association.

Langer, J. A. (1982). The reading process. In A. Berger & H. A. Robinson (Eds.), *Secondary school reading: What research reveals for classroom practice*. Urbana, IL: National Conference on Research in English and ERIC Clearinghouse on Reading and Communication Skills.

Mikulecky, L. (1982). Job literacy: The relationship between school preparation and workplace actuality. *Reading Research Quarterly, 17*, 400–417.

Mikulecky, L. (1987). The status of literacy in our society. In J. E. Readence & R. S. Baldwin (Eds.), *Research in literacy: Merging perspective*. Thirty-sixth Yearbook of the National Reading Conference. Rochester, NY: National Reading Conference, pp. 211–234.

Monteith, M. K. (1981). The magazine habit. *Language Arts, 58*, 965–969.

National Assessment of Educational Progress (1987). Levels of reading proficiency, 1984. *The Reading Teacher, 40* (7), p. 700.

Palincsar, A. S., & Brown, A. L. (1986). Interactive teaching to promote independent learning from text. *The Reading Teacher, 39* (8), 771–777.

Pearson, P. D. (1985). Changing the face of reading comprehension instruction. *The Reading Teacher, 38* (6), 724–738.

Ribovich, J. K., & Erickson, L. (1980). A study of lifelong reading with implications for instructional programs. *Journal of Reading, 24,* 20–26.

Rumelhart, D. E. (1976). *Toward an interactive model of reading* (Tech. Rep. No. 56). San Diego, CA: Center for Human Information Processing, University of California.

Rumelhart, D. E. (1981). Schemata: The building blocks of cognition. In J. T. Guthrie (Ed.), *Comprehension and teaching: Research reviews.* Newark, DE: International Reading Association.

Scribner, S., & Cole, M. (1981). *The psychology of literacy.* Cambridge, MA: Harvard University Press.

Smith, E., Adams, N., & Schorr, D. (1978). Fact retrieval and the paradox of inference. *Cognitive Psychology, 10,* 438–474.

Smith, S. L., Carey, R., & Harste, J. C. (1982). The contexts of reading. In A. Berger & H. A. Robinson (Eds.), *Secondary school reading: What research reveals for classroom practice.* Urbana, IL: National Conference on Research in English and ERIC Clearinghouse on Reading and Communication Skills.

Spiro, R. J. (1980). Constructive processes in prose comprehension and recall. In R. J. Spiro, B. C. Bruce, & W. F. Brewer (Eds.), *Theoretical issues in reading comprehension.* Hillsdale, NJ: Erlbaum.

Spiro, R. J., Bruce, B. C., & Brewer, W. F. (Eds.) (1980). *Theoretical issues in reading comprehension.* Hillsdale, NJ: Erlbaum.

Taylor, D. (1983). *Family literacy: Young children learning to read and write.* Portsmouth, NH: Heinemann.

Vygotsky, L. S. (1978). *Mind in society.* Cambridge, MA: Harvard University Press.

Welty, E. (1983). *One writer's beginnings.* New York: Warner Books.

Wood, D., Bruner, J., & Ross, G. (1976). The role of tutoring in problem solving. *Journal of Child Psychology and Psychiatry, 17,* 89–100.

Further Readings

Anderson, R. C., Hiebert, E., Scott, J., & Wilkinson, I. (1985). *Becoming a nation of readers: The report of the Commission on Reading.* Washington, DC: National Institute of Education.

Cairney, T., & Longbien, S. (1989). Building communities of readers and writers. *The Reading Teacher, 42* (8), 560–567.

Clay, M. M. (1979). *Reading: The patterning of complex behaviour.* Auckland, New Zealand: Heinemann.

Davidson, J. L. (1988). *Counterpoint and beyond: A response to becoming a nation of readers.* Urbana, IL: National Council of Teachers of English.

Fishman, A. R. (1987). Literacy and cultural context: A lesson from the Amish. *Language Arts, 64* (8), 842–854.

Winograd, P., & Paris, S. G. (1989). A cognitive and motivational agenda for reading instruction. *Educational Leadership, 46* (4), 30–36.

Chapter 2

Reading Comprehension: General Considerations

If we think of education as an act of knowing, then reading has to do with knowing. The act of reading cannot be explained as merely reading words since every act of reading words implies a previous reading of the world and a subsequent rereading of the world. There is a permanent movement back and forth between "reading" reality and reading words—the spoken word too is our reading of the world. We can go further, however, and say that reading the word is not only preceded by reading the world, but also by a certain form of writing it or rewriting it. In other words, of transforming it by means of conscious practical action. For me, this dynamic movement is central to literacy.

Thus, we see how reading is a matter of studying reality that is alive, reality that we are living inside of, reality as history being made and also making us. We can also see how it is impossible to read texts without reading the context of the text, without establishing the relationships between the discourse and the reality which shapes the discourse. This emphasizes, I believe, the responsibility which reading a text implies. We must try to read the context of a text and also relate it to the context in which we are reading the text. And so reading is not so simple. Reading mediates knowing and is also knowing, because language is knowledge and not just mediation of knowledge.

Perhaps I can illustrate by referring to the title of a book written by my daughter, Madalena. She teaches young children in Brazil and helps them learn to read and write, but above all she helps them know the world. Her book describes her work with the children and the nature of their learning. It is entitled *The Passion to Know the World*, not *How to Teach Kids to Read and Write*. No matter the level or the age of the students we teach, from preschool to graduate school, reading critically is absolutely important and fundamental. Reading always involves critical perception, interpretation, and "rewriting" what is read. Its task is to unveil what is hidden in the text. I always say to the students with whom I work, "Reading is not walking on the words; it's grasping the soul of them."
(Freire, 1985, pp. 18–19)

▌ OVERVIEW

At the beginning of this chapter we discuss the process of reading comprehension and compare it to the process of writing. Then we take a closer look at the critical role of background knowledge in reading. We present a framework for conducting lessons to build students' comprehension ability. A central feature of this framework is that it includes a phase when the teacher leads children to draw upon background knowledge about the topics to be discussed. During text discussion lessons, the teacher can shape students' thinking by developing questions on the basis of their answers. In addition to shaping students' thinking responsively, the teacher can tell students about strategies they can use to improve their comprehension, and teach them these strategies. The teacher can further strengthen students' reading comprehension ability by following a process approach to the teaching of writing.

Chapter 2 is organized around the following key concepts:

Key Concept 1: Reading comprehension lessons should be carried out following an orderly framework, usually involving prereading activities, to access or develop appropriate background knowledge; guided reading activities; and postreading activities.

Key Concept 2: The teacher should mediate or involve students with information and actively engage them in text discussions.

Key Concept 3: The teacher should lead students to become active, strategic readers, able to oversee their own reading comprehension processes.

Key Concept 4: The teacher can strengthen students' comprehension ability by following a process approach to the teaching of writing.

▌ PERSPECTIVE

Functions Involved in Reading Comprehension

While it is obvious that writers construct messages, it is less obvious that readers construct messages. This idea is less apparent because readers are working with texts already in existence. However, as we discussed in Chapter 1, readers must indeed construct messages. Messages or meanings are not conveyed automatically, just because the words are already down on paper. Rather, messages must be constructed by readers who are thinking actively about what they are reading.

What must happen in order for a reader to comprehend a text? In Chapter 1 you learned that reading involves special kinds of thinking. Palincsar and Brown (1984) provide a more detailed picture of the nature of this thinking by suggesting that readers must accomplish the following six functions during reading for meaning.

1. Readers must construct purposes for reading. Only by developing purposes will readers be able to gain the appropriate kind of information while reading. The purpose may just be to find a particular piece of information, for example, in the directions for using a new tape recorder. Or the purpose may be to get the overall gist, as in a newspaper editorial.
2. Readers must activate relevant background knowledge. As you may recall from Chapter 1, most texts leave a lot unsaid and rely on readers to fill in the gaps from background knowledge. This point will be discussed in detail later in this chapter.
3. Readers must allocate attention in order to focus on major content at the expense of trivia. Given our purposes for reading, some information will be important, and other information will be unimportant. A lot of time and effort would be wasted if readers did not direct their attention to the major or important content, glossing over and paying less attention to the minor or unimportant content.
4. Readers must critically evaluate the content of the text. They must determine if the information presented is internally consistent. They must also check to see if the text information is consistent with their own background knowledge and with common sense.
5. Readers must monitor ongoing activities to see if they are actually comprehending the text. It is all too easy to run one's eyes over the words without actually gaining a clear understanding of the text. This is why it is important for readers to check on their own comprehension. Every now and then, they need to pause to ask themselves if they are, indeed, gaining an adequate understanding of the text. They might check their comprehension by asking themselves questions or by mentally reviewing the information just covered.
6. Readers must make and test inferences of many kinds. As you know, readers are constantly filling in gaps and making assumptions while they read. Interpreting, predicting, and arriving at conclusions are all part of the process of reading for meaning. It is important to test these inferences, because it is easy to make incorrect or inaccurate inferences, for a number of reasons. For example, an author might deliberately mislead us in order to set up a surprise ending to a story. Or we might develop an interpretation that fits all the facts up to a certain point, but later come across a fact that does not fit.

This set of functions helps to show just how complex the process of reading comprehension really is. Research conducted by Palincsar and Brown and others demonstrates that the comprehension process cannot be broken down into simple, separate steps or skills. It is possible to speak of the different functions involved in comprehension, as we just did, or of the different aspects of comprehension. However, it should always be kept in mind that there is a great deal of overlap among these functions and aspects, and that it is best to think about the comprehension process in a more global or holistic way.

Insights About Reading Comprehension Gained from Research on Writing

You have learned that reading, like writing, involves the construction of meaning from text. Recent research has revealed other important similarities between the processes of reading and writing, in addition to the idea that both have to do with constructing messages. Understanding these similarities will give you a better sense of the dynamic nature of reading comprehension, or reading to gain an understanding of the text. We will also be discussing writing in detail because writing is as important to literacy as reading, and may be one of the most effective means of strengthening reading ability, as will be discussed in Key Concept #4.

Perhaps the most obvious similarity between reading and writing is that both involve the use of language to communicate with others. As readers, we generally assume that the texts we read have been written by someone who wishes to communicate a message. As writers, we usually put words down on paper in order to communicate a message to others.

However, apart from this obvious similarity, many of us tend to think of reading and writing as quite different from one another. When it comes to reading, we think of dealing with a text that is already in existence. Reading that text is usually quite easy for us. But when it comes to writing, we think of having to create a new text. Writing often requires a great deal more effort than reading and may be quite difficult for us.

The Writing Process

In order to understand other similarities between reading comprehension and writing, it is helpful to know more about the process of writing. This process appears to involve a number of subprocesses, according to research by Graves (1983), Humes (1983), and others. We will use the terms planning, drafting, revising, editing, and publishing for these subprocesses, but other terms are often used as well. For example, some people prefer to use the term prewriting rather than planning.

Planning. Unless a topic has been assigned, the first problem many writers face is that of what to write about. Choosing a topic of interest and importance is central to planning. But planning does not stop once the writer has decided what to write about and has begun to put words down. Writers are actively engaged in planning at all stages of producing a text. They think of the ideas they want to express, gathering materials from external sources as well as their own minds. They organize the ideas, i.e., decide how the text will be structured, and set goals for themselves, i.e., decide what they will work on at that point.

Drafting. Drafting is the act of putting thoughts down as written words. Other terms for the same act are *writing, recording,* and *translating.* Drafting is extremely complex because there are so many different elements the writer must consider at the same time. These range from concrete and relatively straightforward elements, such as spelling and punctuation, to highly abstract elements, such as clarity and the perspective of the audience.

Revising. Revising is the process of making changes in the text and of developing new thoughts about it. Revising often begins with the writer's reviewing the words he has drafted to see if they are conveying the intended message. The writer may make minor revisions, such as adding a new phrase, or he may make major revisions, such as reorganizing the flow of ideas or adding several new sections. Revising gives writers the opportunity to reshape and restructure their work.

Editing. Editing is the process of making corrections and adjustments, often rather minor ones, to prepare the work to be read by others. Editing and revising are similar in that both involve the making of changes. Editing, however, is usually more a matter of polishing than of basic reshaping. For example, editing may include correcting the spelling, grammar, capitalization, and punctuation in a piece of writing.

Publishing. Publishing involves making the work public or accessible to others. Usually, we think of publishing in the sense that a newspaper, book, or magazine is published. Publishing may be much simpler than that, however. The text may be recopied, typed, or otherwise made more legible. It may also be read aloud to an audience or shared in other ways.

As you can see, the writing process is complex and multifaceted. Although it can be said to include different subprocesses, these subprocesses overlap. For example, as discussed above, revision and editing overlap in the sense that both involve making changes to the text. Also, the writer can move freely back and forth between subprocesses. For example, the writer may move from drafting to revising, and then back to drafting again.

Features Shared by Reading and Writing

The descriptions of the reading and writing processes just presented show that both are complex and involve overlapping functions. Tierney and Pearson (1983) identify another basic similarity between reading and writing. They make the point that both are acts of meaning construction or *composing.*

We believe that at the heart of understanding reading and writing connections one must begin to view reading and writing as essentially similar processes of meaning construction. Both are acts of composing. From a reader's perspective, meaning is created as a reader uses his background of experience together with the author's cues to come to grips both with what the writer is getting him to do or think *and* what the reader decides and creates for himself. As a writer writes, she uses her own background of experience to generate ideas and, in order to produce a text which is considerate to her idealized reader, filters these drafts through her judgments about what her reader's background of experience will be, what she wants to say, and what she wants to get the reader to think or do. In a sense, both reader and writer must *adapt* to their perceptions about their partner in negotiating what a text means. (p. 568)

Perhaps you have already guessed about other similarities between the reading and writing processes. Here are the ones Tierney and Pearson highlight.

Both reading and writing involve *planning.* In both cases, planning requires the setting of goals and the calling up of relevant background knowledge.

The notion of *drafting* also applies to both reading and writing. Tierney and Pearson view drafting as the refinement of meaning which occurs when readers and writers work with the print on a page. We are all familiar with the idea of producing a first draft when we write. However, Tierney and Pearson point out that readers must also arrive at a first draft or initial understanding when they read. This is an important first step toward gaining a full understanding of a text.

Another similarity between reading and writing is captured in the term *alignment.* According to Tierney and Pearson, alignment has to do with the stance a reader or writer adopts in order to collaborate or communicate with the author or audience. Readers and writers assume different stances or roles when they approach different texts. For example, a writer may take the role of an advocate, challenging her audience to recognize a problem. Or a writer might address the audience in the kind of casual, relaxed voice used when speaking to close friends. Similarly, a reader might read a text with a sympathetic attitude, a critical attitude, or a neutral attitude. A writer might write from the perspective of one of the characters or as a neutral observer. A reader might read either as if he were one of the characters, involved in the action, or as a neutral observer.

Reading and writing both involve *revising.* Tierney and Pearson argue that revising is just as important to the reader as it is to the writer. They state: "If readers are to develop some control over and a sense of discovery with the models of meaning they build, they must approach text with the same deliberation, time, and reflection that a writer employs as she revises a text" (p. 576). Readers should think of the interpretations developed during reading as drafts, subject to revision. These drafts should be critically evaluated, for example, through rereading with a different alignment. When the

Students in this second grade class engage in open-ended writing about the story they have just read. Activities like this simultaneously improve both reading and writing ability.

reader arrives at a mental model of the text, it should be a "piece" the reader feels satisfied with.

In the case of both reading and writing, *monitoring* entails the coordination of all other subprocesses. The reader or writer must think about what subprocess is required at a certain point, make sure that subprocess is called into play, and then decide what should be done next. For example, at certain points it may be necessary to plan, while at others revising may be required. Another aspect of monitoring is evaluating one's progress with a particular reading or writing task. When the writer has drafted a text, or the reader has arrived at an interpretation, the work done up to that point must be evaluated. Monitoring enables one to decide whether more work must be done, or whether it is all right to relax.

You should now have an understanding of the key similarities between reading comprehension and writing. There are two important practical implications growing from this research. First, because reading comprehension is a complex, dynamic process, it is best taught in rather complex, dynamic ways. Second, because the process of reading comprehension has many features in common with the process of writing, it is beneficial to provide students with lessons and activities which combine reading comprehension and writing. Having knowledge of the writing process can help students to read with greater understanding. This is a point we will discuss further in this chapter under Key Concept #4.

CHANGES IN COMPREHENSION ABILITY AS CHILDREN GET OLDER

We have just reviewed some of the complexities in the processes of reading and writing. It should not surprise you to learn, then, that reading comprehension ability develops gradually in young children (writing ability also develops gradually; see, for example, Clay, 1975). The findings below give a sense of some of the differences that teachers might expect to see between younger and older readers, or less capable and more capable readers.

Testing 8- to 18-year olds, Brown and Smiley (1977) found older students better able than younger ones to distinguish important from unimportant text ideas. The older children, but not the younger ones, also knew how to study selectively, spending their time reviewing important rather than unimportant information. All students, however, recalled the most important information better than the least important.

Older children not only know better how to study text, they also have a sense of what makes text easier or more difficult to understand and remember. Danner (1976) gave children in grades 2, 4, and 6 passages with either well-organized or randomly ordered sentences. All children remembered the well-organized passages better, but only the sixth graders could explain which passages were more difficult and why. The sixth graders were also the only ones who knew that topic sentences, and not other less important ones, would help them remember the rest of the text.

Younger children do not necessarily realize that there are different ways of going about reading a text, that reading activity can and should be adjusted depending on one's purpose. Forrest and Waller (1979) had children in grades 3 and 6 read stories (a) for fun, (b) to make up a title, (c) to skim for just one piece of information, and (d) to study. They found that only the sixth graders varied their approaches to the text for these different purposes.

Another difference between younger and older children has to do with their ability to monitor and repair their own comprehension. If they become aware that they are failing to understand a text, younger children do not know what to do so they will understand it (Myers & Paris, 1978).

As you can see, being able to comprehend and remember text involves complex strategies which take years to develop. Reading comprehension does not come automatically but is learned over time. Strategies for understanding and learning from text, like those described above, are what we need to teach.

Key Concept 1

Reading comprehension lessons should be carried out following an orderly framework, usually involving prereading activities, to access or develop appropriate background knowledge; guided reading activities; and postreading activities.

▮ IMPORTANCE OF BACKGROUND KNOWLEDGE

On the surface, comprehension of text may seem to be simply a matter of (1) paying close attention to the text and (2) knowing how to decode all of the words in it. In fact, no matter how carefully the reader pays attention to the text, or how easy it is for him to say all the words in it, he may still fail to understand its message. The exercise is designed to help make this idea clear.

The purpose of the exercise is to highlight the importance of background knowledge, or knowledge of the world, in reading comprehension. We may be able to read every individual word in a passage, but fail to comprehend, if we are unable to apply the proper background knowledge.

Anderson and Pearson (1984) review a large body of research supporting the idea that an important aspect of reading is to fill in text gaps with inferences drawn from one's own background knowledge. Texts never present a complete picture and would be unacceptably boring if they did. Imagine, for example, how dull the passage below would be if all the trivial steps Mrs. White went through to get ready to go shopping were written in. Because we could easily infer this information (such as the fact that she probably had to open the door to get outside), there is no need for it to be written. Authors expect readers to fill in minor gaps from their own background experience and so focus their writing instead on important or unusual events. In the passage below, take notice not only of what we are told but also of what has been left out:

> One day Mrs. White was going to the market. She put some fruit in a basket. She put on her hat. She walked down the road.   (*Mrs. White's Hat*, 1978, p. 52)

The reader learns that Mrs. White carries some fruit, (Is she going to sell it or is that her lunch?) puts on her hat, (Now, why did the author bother to tell us that rather than that she put on her shoes, coat, or dress?) and walks down the road. (It sounds as though she has no car and lives in the country or a small town rather than the city. Will that turn out to be true?) As experienced readers we assume that the author had good reasons for including certain information, that which we will need to know as we read on, and omitting other information, that which is unimportant. Holding these assumptions, we begin to ask ourselves questions, and this makes the story more interesting.

Prior knowledge not only helps children make inferences about text, it also helps them to learn and remember what they read. For example, Marr and Gromley (1982) showed that prior knowledge of a topic helped fourth grade students remember information from passages they read. Hayes and Tierney (1982) found that prior knowledge of sports and baseball helped high school students interpret and recall texts about cricket matches, itself a topic they knew little of.

Children can learn to use prior knowledge to help them remember text

Exercise

(1) Read the following passage:

The procedure is quite simple. First you arrange things into different groups. Of course, one pile may be sufficient depending on how much there is to do. If you have to go somewhere else due to lack of facilities that is the next step, otherwise you are pretty well set. It is important not to overdo things. That is, it is better to do few things at once than too many. In the short run this may not seem important but complications can easily arise. A mistake can be expensive as well. At first the whole procedure will seem complicated. Soon, however, it will become just another fact of life. It is difficult to foresee any end to the necessity for this task in the immediate future, but then one can never tell. After the procedure is completed one arranges the materials into different groups again. They can be put into their appropriate places. Eventually they will be used once more, and the whole cycle will then have to be repeated. However, this is part of life. (Bransford & Johnson, 1973, p. 400)

(2) Did you feel you were able to comprehend this passage? Were you left with any questions when you finished reading it?

(3) Suppose that you had been given a title for the passage: "Doing Laundry." Read the passage over again, with this in mind.

(4) What differences did you notice while reading the passage the second time?

During their first reading of the passage, most people do not guess that it is about doing laundry. As a result, they find the passage vague and puzzling and do not feel they have understood it. This may have been your experience. When you read through the passage a second time, knowing it was about doing laundry, you probably found that everything fell into place. This is because your background knowledge about the topic was now assisting your comprehension.

The point of this exercise is to illustrate the importance of background knowledge, or knowledge of the world, in reading comprehension. We may be able to read every individual word in a passage but still fail to comprehend. However, once we can apply background knowledge appropriately, we experience the "click" of comprehension.

information. This was confirmed in a study by Stein and Bransford (1979), who asked fifth graders to try to remember sentences such as:

The kind man bought the milk.
The short man used the broom.
The funny man liked the ring.
The hungry man purchased the tie.

As presented, these sentences are not easy to remember, because there is no obvious relationship between the characteristics of the people (e.g., being short or funny) and their actions (e.g., using a broom or liking a ring). However, when the children were taught to elaborate on the sentences so that all the words were tied together in an understandable way (e.g., the kind man was buying milk for hungry children), they had no difficulty remembering the information.

Key Areas of Background Knowledge

Two areas of background knowledge seem particularly important for successful reading comprehension: (1) knowledge of the topic of the text, and (2) knowledge of text structure.

Text topic. Prior knowledge about the topic of the text is important for successful reading comprehension because, as we noted earlier, readers have to fill in gaps in text. Readers construct possible interpretations—hypotheses— and then search the text *and their own background knowledge about the topic* for pieces of evidence which support or contradict their hypotheses. Having an adequate amount of prior knowledge about the topic is essential to the formation and evaluation of hypotheses to guide reading comprehension.

The instructional implication here is that teachers should attend to whether children have the necessary background knowledge of the text topic. If not, knowledge of the topic may have to be taught. Specific methods for doing this are presented in Chapter 4.

Text structure. Readers need knowledge of the *global* or overall organization of various types of text. Think, for example, how different our expectations are, once we know that we will be reading a novel, versus a short story, versus a poem, versus an essay, versus a report. We have expectations about length, type of language, and, given a title, about content. We expect the ideas in a poem to be presented and organized much differently from ideas in a report. Having all this prior knowledge of text structure at a global level allows comprehension to proceed much more efficiently and effectively.

Children need to be given the same opportunity to develop those expectations. They need to read a variety of kinds of texts and to discuss various text structures in reading lessons and the functions served by different structures.

We also need knowledge of text structure at a *local* level, or the level at which phrases and sentences are combined (Halliday & Hasan, 1976). Comprehension is boosted if we can see the links among text ideas at this level. For example, we use our knowledge of conjunctions such as *and, because,* and *or* to learn whether one idea is to be added to another, whether one event caused another, or whether one condition alters another. Children need to learn how these and other devices help readers keep track of information within a text. Instructional activities for both global and local text structures are presented in Chapters 3 and 4.

▌ USING A LESSON FRAMEWORK

In developing students' comprehension ability through guided discussion, you should follow a *lesson framework* likely to prove effective. According to Cunningham, Moore, Cunningham, and Moore (1983), the teacher will generally wish to follow a sequence incorporating these basic steps:

Step 1: Activate or develop background knowledge necessary for understanding the text.

Step 2: Set purposes for reading (i.e., identify information to be searched for, questions to be answered, predictions to be verified).

Step 3: Have students read for these purposes.

Step 4: Have students show in some way (i.e., by answering questions, summarizing, reading relevant information aloud) whether they have met the purposes.

Step 5: Give students feedback about their comprehension performance (i.e., let them know if their reasoning was sound and if their responses were right, wrong, or perhaps incomplete).

The lesson framework or method below is a specific approach for incorporating these steps. It includes recommendations for the teacher's planning, as well as prereading, guided reading, and postreading components. This framework may be used when comprehension instruction takes the form of guided discussion of a particular text. It should be distinguished from methods for the direct instruction of particular comprehension strategies, such as comprehension monitoring, described later in this chapter under Key Concept #3.

Experience-Text-Relationship Method (ETR)

The purpose of this method (Au, 1979) is to give students a general approach to text comprehension, bringing out the importance of background knowledge. Basically, lessons involve the teacher's leading the children in the discussion of text and text-related topics. At the same time, the teacher models for the children the process an expert reader goes through in trying to construct meaning from text. Through repeated experience in ETR lessons, the children should be able to use this overall approach independently. This method works well with basal reader stories and is particularly useful in working with primary grade children.

Planning. Preview the story and identify its central theme, topic, and/or important or interesting points you want the children to grasp. Decide in what way the central theme or points might be made relevant to the children's background experiences. Of course, this requires knowledge of your students as well as of the text.

While previewing the story, look for natural breaks, so that you can divide the story into segments for silent reading. If the story is likely to be easy for the children, the segments can be longer. If the story is likely to be challenging for them, the segments should be shorter (for more information about planning, especially the use of story mapping, refer to Chapter 3, Key Concept #2).

Experience or E phase. Begin the lesson by finding out about the children's background experiences related to the theme or topic of the text. From a general beginning, move the discussion closer to the story about to be read. For example, you might show the children one of the illustrations or tell them the title of the story, making sure they see the connection to the background knowledge activated earlier. Have the students make predictions about the story. Then have them read a portion of the story silently. Remind them of their predictions and set other purposes as well, for example, having them identify the setting, characters, and problems presented in the text.

Text or T phase. When the children have finished reading each segment of text, reopen the discussion by having them talk about their predictions. Have them discuss whether their predictions were confirmed by the text, and have them talk about other information covered in the purposes set for reading. Then have the children make predictions about the section of text to be read next, setting additional purposes as appropriate, to call their attention to important text information. Alternate periods of silent reading and discussion in this manner until the whole story has been read and discussed.

Each day the story is being read, you can give children an assignment to be completed while they are at their seats. For example, you might ask them to write about the story, or to complete worksheets based on story information.

Relationship or R phase. When the story has been completed, be sure to ask questions relating text information to background knowledge and experiences. For example, ask the children what they would have done if they had been in the main character's shoes. Or ask the children if they have ever faced a problem like that of the main character.

Sample Series of Lessons

In this series, based on lessons actually taught in a second grade class, you will see how a teacher combined the teaching of experience-text-relationship (ETR) lessons with the use of seatwork assignments directly tied to the small group ETR lessons. These and other writing assignments are discussed in more detail in Chapters 3 and 4.

The teacher spent five days teaching this story, which was a challenging one for this particular group of students. The instructional cycle for a less challenging story would be much shorter than this.

Overall planning. The teacher previewed the story, "The Secret Hiding Place," in the basal reader. The story is about a baby hippo who wishes to be alone once in a while, especially after he notices that all the other jungle animals have their own hiding places. After several attempts, he finally finds a satisfactory hiding place. The teacher recognized that the story was typical in structure: having a problem, attempts to deal with the problem, and a resolution. She knew her students were already quite familiar with these elements of a story and would be able to use this knowledge of text structure to comprehend their new story. Next, she thought about possible themes in the story and decided upon "solitude is good sometimes," a theme likely to be meaningful to her students.

Day 1—Start of experience phase. The teacher decided to begin the lesson by activating her students' background knowledge of *jungle* through a writing activity to be assigned as seatwork. She had the students do the writing activity, and then meet with her for their reading lesson. During the lesson she questioned students about their writing and wrote their ideas about the jungle on a sheet of chartpaper. Michael read what he had written: "The jungle is filled with wild animals like lions and tigers and snakes and hippos." Jennifer added, "In the jungle there's lots of trees, bushes, vines, and thorns." From the students' writing and responses during the lesson, the teacher concluded that they had enough knowledge of the jungle to understand the story.

Day 2—Conclusion of experience phase and start of text phase. The teacher began the next day's lesson by referring to the chart started the day before. She asked the children, "Why do you think we talked about the jungle yesterday?" After some discussion, Matthew concluded, "We were getting our brain ready for the new story." The teacher had the students open their books and look at the colorful pictures of the jungle. They read the title, "The Secret Hiding Place." Then the teacher asked the children to read the first three pages silently, to see what the title might have to do with a jungle story.

When the students had finished reading, the teacher asked what they had learned about the title. The students identified the story characters and discussed their relationship to Little Hippo. They suggested that the problem was the other hippos' "watching Little Hippo all the time," and that Little Hippo might want a hiding place.

On this day the teacher assigned the children a worksheet designed to help them review the day's reading. She made certain the children knew that the sentences on the worksheet were from their story, and that they would be working with some new words from the story.

Day 3—Text phase. Judging from the Day 2 lesson and the children's completed worksheets, the teacher felt they had a good start in understanding both the content and structure of the story. She began the Day 3 lesson by having the children review the most important point established the day before: the nature of Little Hippo's problem. The children read the answers they had written: "He doesn't want to be watched all the time." "He wishes he could walk by himself." Satisfied that all had grasped the problem, the teacher asked, "What might happen next in our story?" The children predicted that Little Hippo would try to solve his problem. They termed this part of the story "the trying part." "Yes," the teacher replied, "we call the 'trying part' the attempt."

The children read the next three pages to check their prediction. They learned that Little Hippo had run away and encountered different jungle animals in their hiding places. The teacher added the new information to the chart. Near the end of the lesson, she gave the students their next independent assignment, requiring them to match animals with their hiding places.

Day 4—Conclusion of text phase and start of relationship phase. In reviewing the children's finished work, the teacher found that they were continuing to show a good grasp of story events and vocabulary. Their overall familiarity with the structure of stories was aiding their understanding. She made plans for concluding reading of the story, including thinking of ways to lead toward the theme and relate the theme to the children's own lives.

During the lesson, the teacher first had the children discuss how Little Hippo solved his problem. They understood that he would probably use his hiding place from time to time. She led the children to infer the theme, that "solitude is good sometimes." Then the teacher had the children draw relationships between the theme and their own lives. She asked, "What about you? Do you ever like to be alone?" The children answered that they sometimes liked to go, "in my bed, in my room, outside" to be by themselves. They talked about reasons for wanting to be alone, but concluded that usually they liked being with their families.

The teacher gave the children a worksheet requiring them to review the events in the story, according to the structure of problem, attempts, and solution. The worksheet also asked students to "write about times when you like to be alone."

Day 5—Relationship phase. By examining the completed worksheets, the teacher determined that the children had understood the sequence of events and the structure of the story. She saw that they were able to empathize with Little Hippo's dilemma and see relationships between the story and their own lives.

For the last day's lesson, the teacher introduced the children to a tradebook, *My Secret Hiding Place*, which she asked them to read and write about independently. When the children met for their lesson, she led them in a short discussion of the book. Then she asked them to compare the book to the story they had just read. The children arrived at the following summary:

> The story is about a little hippo who lives in the jungle and wants to find a place to be alone once in a while. The book is about a girl who lives at home and has a place to be away from her family sometimes.

In this case, the teacher not only had the children draw relationships between the story and their own lives, she also had the children draw relationships to another story.

The example above is adapted from Scheu, Tanner, and Au (1989). Refer to that article for more details, especially on seatwork assignments. The article also describes ETR lessons taught to fifth graders. Refer to Chapter 3 to learn about similar lessons taught to fourth graders, based on the novel *Sadako and the Thousand Paper Cranes*.

We hope this description of a sample series of lessons has given you a sense of the general pattern of instruction, following the ETR lesson framework. The overall flow is from a prereading or experience discussion, into a guided reading or text discussion, and finally to a postreading or relationship discussion. You saw how writing activities could be used to enhance and reinforce story comprehension during all three phases. You also saw how the relationship phase of instruction could be extended to include the reading of other books and stories.

Key Concept 2

The teacher should mediate or involve students with information and actively engage them in text discussions.

▍ THE CONCEPT OF INSTRUCTION

In Chapter 1 we described the teacher's role as being that of moving students forward through what Vygotsky called the zone of proximal development. We spoke of how the teacher's job is gradually to release responsibility for the reading task to the children. In this section we build upon those basic ideas by exploring the concept of instruction. We draw upon the work of Roehler and Duffy (in press). They define instruction as intentional actions taken to move students toward particular curricular outcomes. In other words, instruction involves the actions teachers take to further students' learning.

Roehler and Duffy divide instruction into two broad categories. In the first category are the actions teachers take when they are giving information to students. These actions are discussed in this chapter under Key Concept 3. In the second category are the actions teachers take when they are mediating or involving students with information. While mediating, teachers take steps which require students to think actively about information. Mediating is the basic instructional action in ETR lessons. For example, the teacher is mediating when she asks students about the relationships they see between text information and their own background experiences.

Mediating

According to Roehler and Duffy, when teachers are mediating, they are helping students to gain new understandings of the text they are reading and of the process of reading comprehension. Mediating is probably a more demanding kind of instruction than giving explanations. This is because the giving of explanations can be planned in advance. In contrast, mediating must be done spontaneously, during the flow of a lesson. Mediating cannot be planned in advance because the teacher's mediating actions depend on what students are thinking and saying.

Roehler and Duffy state that teachers use two main kinds of actions to mediate students' learning. First, they ask questions which build students' understanding. Second, they gradually release responsibility to students, a point we discussed in Chapter 1.

What does it look like when a teacher is asking questions which build students' understanding? An example of this kind of questioning may be seen in the following ETR lesson, conducted with a group of second graders. The students had just finished reading a story entitled "Annie and the Old One" (Miles, 1971). At the beginning of the story, the Old One (Annie's grandmother) announces to the family that she will return to Mother Earth when the rug Annie's mother is weaving is taken from the loom. Annie takes her grandmother's words literally and tries everything she can to prevent the rug from being completed. At the end of the story, the Old One takes Annie out into the desert and helps her to understand the natural cycle of life, death, and rebirth. Notice how the teacher uses questions to shape the students' comprehension of this part of the text.

Teacher: Now grandmother, in a very simple way, tries to explain to her about time. How did she do that? How did she explain to Annie about the dying and about time? What did she compare it to?

Rachel: The sun.

Teacher: Okay, tell me about the sun, Rachel.

Rachel: (*Reads from text*) "The sun comes up from the edge of earth in the evening. Earth, from which good things come for the living creatures on it. Earth, to which all creatures finally go."

Teacher: That's very nice. So what is like the sun?

Kent: Life.

Teacher: Can you tell me now, what—when they say the sun rises, how does that relate to life?

Kent: Um, you get born.

Joey: Someone get born.

Kent: It's like the years passing when the sun finally goes down and you die.

Joey: Sets—sets. And then it comes up again when somebody else is born and [inaudible] it again.

Teacher: That's very nice. I like the way you said that. But she also compared it when she said—

Joey: The cactus.

Teacher: Okay, tell me about the cactus, Joey.

Joey: Oh, I know about the cactus.

Teacher: [What did you find] about the cactus?

Joey: (*Reads from text*) "The cactus did not bloom forever. Petals dried and fell to earth."

Teacher: Okay, what is she trying to tell Annie by using that analogy of the cactus?

Ross: That people die of old age. That people don't just die when they say so.

Teacher: Well, yeah, okay that's—that's true. But what did they mean when they said, "The cactus did not bloom forever?"

Ross: That people, they got to die.

Kent: That means that when it starts blooming a life will start, but when it falls a life will end.

(Au & Kawakami, 1986, pp. 70–71)

At the start of the excerpt, Rachel reads aloud the relevant section of the text, rather than giving an explanation in her own words. Using Rachel's reading as a starting point, the teacher asks questions to get the children to be more specific. For example, she asks, "So what is like the sun?" The teacher's questions lead Kent and Joey to speak about how the Old One compared the sunrise and sunset to birth and death. Notice that the teacher did not tell the students the answer, but used questioning to draw the answer from them.

Then Joey mentions the cactus, showing that he has anticipated the idea the teacher wants the group to explore next. Perceiving that Joey is on the right track, the teacher asks a question to encourage him: "What did you find about the cactus?" After Joey reads the relevant section of text, the teacher asks another question, to see if the children have grasped the significance of the comparison. Ross ventures an opinion, and the teacher asks him to be more specific: "But what did they mean when they said, 'The cactus did not bloom forever'?" Ross just repeats his answer, but Kent then chimes in with a full interpretation of the analogy.

As you can see, the teacher had in mind certain points she thought it important for the students to understand. But she did not lead students to those points by asking a preset list of questions. Instead, she encouraged the students to speak about what they had been able to infer on their own. In each case certain students could identify the relevant section of the text. But it was necessary for the teacher to ask a few leading questions before they could speak clearly about the analogies the Old One had used.

If you have the impression that it takes a lot of practice to be able to teach in this way, you're absolutely right! However, you will find it well worth your while to invest the time and energy required to learn to ask questions to build students' understanding. This kind of questioning can be termed *responsive* questioning because it is done in response to ideas the students present. The teacher listens to what the students are saying and then thinks of a question which will further their thinking. These questions encourage students to think more deeply. As a result, as we saw in the lesson excerpt, they often arrive at surprisingly sophisticated interpretations.

Responsive questioning supports the gradual release of responsibility to students. In responsive questioning, the teacher first attempts to elicit or draw ideas from the students. The teacher tells students ideas only *after* they have shown a lack of understanding. In this way the teacher makes the students themselves responsible for doing as much of the comprehension work as they can.

▌ ENGAGING STUDENTS IN DISCUSSION

In lessons following the ETR framework or other similar approaches, the teacher must actively involve students in the discussion. Teacher mediation, leading to improvements in students' understanding, cannot occur unless the students are giving responses. Hearing students' responses allows the teacher to determine the kinds of comprehension activities they can carry out on their own and the ones they need help with. Here are some guidelines to follow when you want students to participate actively in a discussion.

1. *Aim for a balance between teacher talk and student talk. Create numerous opportunities for students to respond.*

For a discussion to be successful in improving students' comprehension ability, there must be a *balance between teacher talk and student talk.* If the teacher does most of the talking, there will be little opportunity for the give-and-take required to further comprehension development.

2. *In general, elicit responses from students instead of telling them the answer. When an incorrect answer is given, help the student to work out the correct response.*

Research by Au and Kawakami (1984) suggests that effective teachers consistently try to draw answers from children during comprehension discussions. They almost never tell the answer, instead pushing the children to come up with the right answer themselves. They do, however, ask leading questions which make it possible for the children eventually to succeed. That is, they do not simply repeat their original question. Instead, they paraphrase it or break it into two or more easier questions for the children to answer. Then they help the children put the pieces together to answer the original, more difficult question. At a deeper level, these effective teachers are not just con-

Exercise

(1) The next time you give a reading or other lesson to a group of students, make a tape recording of it.

(2) Play the tape back and, using a stopwatch, try to determine about how much time you spent talking versus how much time you allowed the children to talk. There may be times when both you and the children were talking at once, and these should be counted as "overlapping speech." Include in the "silence" category time spent in silent reading or writing. Time for the four categories of teacher speaking, students speaking, overlapping speech, and silence should add up to the total number of minutes in the lesson.

Teacher speaking:	_____ minutes
Students speaking:	_____ minutes
Overlapping speech:	_____ minutes
Silence:	_____ minutes
Total lesson time:	_____ minutes

(3) Consider the results of your analysis. A good goal is to aim for a 50-50 split, with half of the speaking time given to teacher talk and half to student talk. Many teachers find that they are doing almost all of the talking (75% of the time or more!).

(4) Play the tape again, and this time see if you can count the number of opportunities you created for the children to speak. Generally, these will be times when you asked a question and then allowed the children to answer it. Also included in this count would be times when you allowed the children to ask their own questions.

Opportunities for children to speak: _____

(5) Consider the results of this analysis. Do you feel, in view of the time spent, that you gave the children enough opportunities to respond, comment, or ask questions? The number might vary depending on the quality of the opportunities provided for the children. Fewer opportunities might be given if the children were providing lengthy answers. More opportunities should be given, however, if the children are giving short answers of just a word or a phrase.

(6) In future lessons, see if you can increase the amount of time you allow the students to speak. See also if you can create more opportunities for the students to respond.

cerned with right and wrong answers but with guiding children through a process of sound reasoning about text ideas.

Effective teachers tend to ask challenging questions, so it is not uncommon for their students to answer incorrectly. In fact, according to Au and Kawakami, about one out of every five lead-off questions asked may be too difficult for the children to answer correctly on their own. On these occasions, however, the teacher helps them work out the answer, in the manner described above.

Exercise

(1) Using the same lesson tape, try to identify all the times when the students gave an incorrect or incomplete answer to your questions.

(2) In each instance, identify your reaction. Note whether you helped the child work out the answer, had another child answer instead, told the answer, asked another question, and so on. List each of your different reactions and how many times it occurred.

(3) Consider this analysis. In what way might each of your reactions help the students learn? In what way might each tend to prevent the students from learning? What, if anything, do you think you might try to do differently?

While there is no particular teacher response that will work in all instances, here is a procedure you can try to follow when you ask a difficult question which the children are unable to answer correctly. The idea behind using this procedure is that you will be encouraging the children to do as much of the thinking as they can.

1. Begin by paraphrasing the question. If you used difficult vocabulary, try to substitute terms the children would be more likely to know. For example, suppose your original question was, "What was Annie's predicament?" You might rephrase your question as, "What problem was Annie facing?" and tell the children that a predicament is the same as a problem.

2. If this does not work, have the children review the text or background information required to answer. In this case you might ask, "What just happened in the story? Why was everyone in Annie's family so upset?" Keep asking these more specific questions until the information has been covered.

3. Finally, pose your original question again. If necessary, point out to the children how the specific text or background information just discussed should be used in answering your original question. In this case you might say, "Now who can use the points we just discussed, about what grandmother told the family, to answer my question. What was Annie's predicament?"

4. When a child comes up with the correct response, paraphrase it for the group. This allows all of the children to see the elements in a complete and appropriate response. Repeating children's answers also signals that you have recognized their thought and effort.

3. Be aware of the different ways that you can manage talk during discussions. Use methods which involve all students, being careful to use an interactional style which shows respect for the values of the students' culture.

Most of us tend to be unaware as we teach of the way that we are managing talk during discussions. Yet as we teach we decide what students must do to get a turn to speak, which students will win turns, and what they may talk about. These procedures can have a profound effect on how much students learn during lessons.

To understand this subject, consider the importance of the rules for three types of behavior: speaking, listening, and turntaking (Shultz, Erickson, & Florio, 1982). People from all cultures have unwritten rules for these behaviors. These rules have to do with beliefs about the proper behavior to be shown in face-to-face discussions. While we are not generally aware of these rules, even for our own culture, we act upon them all the time. They affect what we do and how we judge the behavior of others.

These unstated cultural rules operate in classrooms, just as they do in other settings. In classroom discussions one of the common rules is that the teacher sets the topic. That is, he or she determines what will be talked about. Usually, the teacher sets the topic by asking a question. Another common rule, this one affecting turntaking, is that the children do not call out the answer but raise their hands. This signals to the teacher that they want to answer. The teacher then chooses one of the children to speak. Usually, a further rule is that no other child but the one called on may speak. After that child answers, the teacher may evaluate the response given, call on another child to answer, or ask another question.

Meanwhile, the usual rule for listening is that all of the children keep their eyes on the teacher, or perhaps look at the child chosen to answer. They are not supposed to look around the room or at other listeners.

This pattern for organizing discussion (see Mehan, 1979) is outlined below:

Pattern #1

Teacher asks question
One child answers
Teacher evaluates child's answer

While you will probably use this pattern quite often, you should be aware of other patterns that may be equally or perhaps more effective for achieving comprehension goals. Four other patterns are outlined below. Think about when you might try them. Remember, of course, to announce to the children any changes in the rules for participation.

Here is a pattern useful if you are working with a small group, want to give many children the chance to answer, and are after a range of different responses.

Pattern #2

Teacher asks a question (often an opinion or open-ended one)
Children are allowed to respond if they have something to say (several
    may be speaking at the same time)
Teacher repeats the highest-quality student responses for the benefit of
    the group

The following pattern can be used if the teacher wants to pick up the pace with an activity involving all of the children. Children who are having difficulty responding can still join in with the group, without the fear of being embarrassed.

Pattern #3

Teacher asks a question (requiring a very short answer)
Children respond in a chorus
Teacher gives group feedback

To encourage children to contribute more, and so to take as much responsibility as they can for the comprehension discussion, you might use the next two patterns.

Pattern #4

Teacher invites or allows children to introduce a text-related topic for
    discussion, or to pose a question for the group to address
One or more children propose topics or questions
Teacher leads group discussion of topics or questions

Pattern #5

Teacher asks an open-ended question
One child answers
Second child reacts to first child's answer
Third child reacts to second child's answer
Children continue to discuss one another's answers
Teacher summarizes or gives feedback to group

Research in classrooms with culturally different children suggests that there may be a negative effect on learning to read if the teacher conducts discussion using a pattern uncomfortable for the children. For example, in research with Hawaiian children, Au and Mason (1981) found the children paid more attention to the text and gave better answers if discussion generally followed pattern #2 instead of pattern #1. As mentioned in Chapter 1, this was because pattern #2 was closer to the rules for speaking, listening, and turn-taking the children followed outside of the classroom in an event called "talk story." The rules in talk story reflected the values of Hawaiian culture, including an emphasis on group rather than individual achievement (for other examples of this idea, refer to Chapter 8).

Key Concept 3

The teacher should lead students to become active, strategic readers, able to oversee their own reading comprehension processes.

COMPREHENSION STRATEGIES AND METACOGNITION

At the very beginning of this chapter, we described some of the functions the reader must accomplish when reading for meaning. These included having a purpose for reading, activating relevant background knowledge, and making and testing inferences. We went on to compare the reading process with the writing process to demonstrate the complex nature of reading comprehension.

How do good readers manage to comprehend what they are reading? Research suggests that good readers have *strategies* for reading. Strategies are mental plans that readers employ, and they use these plans deliberately but flexibly, adapting them to fit different reading situations (Duffy & Roehler, 1987).

For example, suppose that you are about to read a magazine article. You might read the title, glance at the photos, and start to think about what you already know about the topic. Then you might begin to make predictions about the information the article will present. These are examples of prereading strategies, or the plans a reader uses before reading a text.

You can probably think of other strategies you might use once you have begun reading, such as rereading a paragraph that seems particularly important. There are other strategies you might use after you have finished reading. For example, if you want to remember the main points in an article, you might go over them in your mind or jot them down. The exercise will show you about yet another kind of comprehension strategy.

Winograd and Paris (1988) argue that the most important goal of reading instruction may be to develop students' ability to use strategies to enhance comprehension. A first step is to focus on teaching students useful strategies for reading comprehension. But just teaching students strategies is not enough. Another necessary step is to focus on *metacognition*, or students' awareness of the thinking they are doing as they attempt to comprehend text. Metacognition is important because students need this awareness to use strategies in a purposeful, independent manner. They need to be aware of their own thoughts when reading so they can set purposes and decide upon the strategies to follow to meet those purposes.

In the rest of this section we will discuss further how teachers can develop students' metacognition and teach them specific comprehension strategies.

Giving Students Information

In the previous key concept we mentioned that one type of effective instructional action is giving students information (Roehler & Duffy, in press). Roehler and Duffy view information as the raw material students need to construct schemata about reading and about how reading works. In their view, teachers should give students information about reading strategies because

Exercise

Part of being an expert reader is knowing what to do when you experience a failure in reading comprehension. See if you can remember a time when you experienced a breakdown in comprehension.

(1) Do you recall what you were reading? Why do you think you had difficulty comprehending the text?

(2) What did you do when you found yourself experiencing difficulty?

(3) Compare the strategies you used to those suggested below.

Collins and Smith (1980) suggest that expert readers use *repair strategies* when they experience comprehension failures. They resort first to solutions that are the least disruptive to their ongoing reading activity. Moving from least to most disruptive, these solutions might be:

1. ignore the problem and continue reading
2. suspend judgment
3. form a tentative hypothesis, using text information
4. reread the current sentence
5. reread the previous context
6. go to an expert source

This exercise was intended to make you aware of the strategies people use when a failure in comprehension occurs. These are strategies you might want to model and discuss with your students. It might be helpful to let them know that even teachers experience failures in comprehension from time to time!

this information does not always become available to students in the course of everyday events. Teachers can provide information which is useful in dealing with the particular reading task students are facing, and which builds upon what students already know.

One way that teachers can give students information about reading strategies is through *explicit explanations*. Explicit explanations are explanations in which students are given information directly, without having to guess about what the teacher is telling them. Students should be told *what* they should do, or the steps they should take. They should also be told *why* following those steps is useful. Finally, they should be told *when* those steps should be applied.

For example, here is an explicit explanation a teacher might give to teach students about making predictions:

What to do: To make a prediction, you think about what has happened so far in the story, and then you make the best guess you can about what is going to happen next.

Why: Making predictions can help you to read more carefully. When you make a prediction, you have something to think about. You can read to see if your prediction was right or wrong. It's a good way to see if you're understanding the story.

When: You can make predictions just about any time you're reading. You can make predictions when you're reading a story during our reading lessons, and you can make predictions when you're reading a book on your own, even when you're at home.

Roehler and Duffy suggest that it is especially important to explain to students *why* and *when* reading strategies such as predicting should be used.

Another way teachers can give students information is through modeling. Roehler and Duffy define modeling as what a teacher does to show students how to perform a particular task. An especially effective kind of modeling is what Duffy, Roehler, and Hermann (1988) call *mental modeling.* This is a form of modeling in which students are shown the reasoning expert readers use to comprehend a text. The following example shows a teacher using mental modeling to bring out an expert reader's thinking while activating background knowledge:

> *T:* Watch me think out loud while I try to predict what this story is going to be about. The title is *Sign Language Fun.*
>
> [Teacher is looking at the pictures.] Here is a picture of Sesame Street characters and a picture of a lady doing sign language. And the title says it is going to be about sign language. I know something about Sesame Street characters from my past experience. I've seen them do some pretty fantastic things. And the people on Sesame Street teach things to the puppets. Since the lady is doing sign language, maybe she is going to teach the Sesame Street characters how to do sign language. I'm going to guess that in this story the lady is going to teach them how to use sign language.   (Duffy, Roehler, & Hermann, 1988, p. 764)

Mental modeling is a form of "thinking aloud" and a good means of making normally invisible thought processes clear to students.

Modeling Comprehension Monitoring

One way that mature readers show metacognition in reading is by monitoring their own comprehension of text. *Comprehension monitoring* involves keeping track of how well one is understanding the text (Wagoner, 1983). Comprehension monitoring is important because it allows the reader to notice when a particular comprehension strategy should be called into play. As Baker and Brown (1984) point out, children may know how to execute a particular comprehension strategy but not know that the time has come to use it, because they are not monitoring their own comprehension.

Discuss with the children the importance of active thinking while reading (Fitzgerald, 1983). Mention both the importance of checking on understanding and generating hypotheses about the text. Read part of a text out loud and, as you proceed, comment on your mental activity. That is, mention the hypotheses you have about the text, revisions you make to your original hypotheses, anything that strikes you as unclear, and so on.

Start lists on the board with the headings "Know" and "Don't Know." Pause every few sentences to add notes to the lists of what you know and don't know. Explain to the children that you are using the lists to keep track of information in the text.

Conduct follow-up lessons so you can gradually involve the children. The first time, essentially repeat the first lesson but have the children provide the hypotheses and information for the lists. The second time, have the students work in pairs and take turns thinking aloud while reading. Third, have the children practice the technique on their own.

Other activities for encouraging comprehension monitoring and other aspects of metacognition in reading are described in Chapter 4.

Helping Children Learn to Identify the Sources of Information Needed to Answer Questions

As you know by now, reading comprehension requires the ability to use background knowledge as well as text information. Sometimes, children fail to comprehend because they are drawing from background knowledge and ignoring text information. At other times they may fail to comprehend because they are drawing on text information and not using background knowledge. One way of improving children's reading comprehension ability is to make them aware of the different sources of information they should be using when they read. This can be done by teaching them about different kinds of questions and the sources of information needed to answer them (Raphael, 1982).

Pearson and Johnson (1978) suggest that questions may be placed in three categories, depending on the source of information the reader will need to use to answer it (sample text and questions from Wixson, 1983, p. 288):

1. The answer to a *text explicit* (TE) question is explicitly stated in the text. Such a question can almost be answered just by quoting from the text. Often, the answer is contained in a single sentence.

Text: The wheel fell off the car. The car crashed into a tree.
TE question: What fell off the car?

2. The answer to a *text implicit* (TI) question is implicitly present in the text. That is, the answer is hinted at or can be inferred from the text, but is not stated directly. Often the reader must integrate information from several sentences, paragraphs, or even larger portions of the text.

TI question: Why did the car crash into a tree?

3. The answer to a *script implicit* (SI) question comes from the reader's background knowledge (also called scriptal knowledge), not from the text.

SI question: Why did the wheel fall off the car?

The Pearson and Johnson taxonomy of questions is more consistent with our current understanding of the reading/thinking process than other well-known category systems. The idea here is that, if we are interested in improving children's comprehension ability, there is not much point in looking at questions in and of themselves. Instead, we need to look at the interaction of the reader and his background knowledge with the text and the question.

∎ INSTRUCTIONAL ACTIVITIES
QARS

Students' ability to read strategically and to answer comprehension questions can be improved if they understand Question-Answer Relationships or QARs (Raphael, 1986) derived from the Pearson and Johnson taxonomy. Raphael suggests that students be taught straightforward labels for the different QARs.

There are two main types of QARs:

In the Book
In My Head.

In the Book is the label used to describe questions with answers in the text. These questions may be either text explicit or text implicit. In My Head is used to describe questions with answers which are mainly script implicit or rely heavily on the use of background or scriptal knowledge.

Each of the two main types can be further divided into two categories.

In the Book: In My Head:
  Right There   On My Own
  Think and Search   Author and Me

Right There questions are those with text explicit answers. Generally, the answer is located within a single sentence in the text. Think and Search questions have text implicit answers. The relevant information may be drawn from different places in the text, perhaps from sentences within the same paragraph or from a number of different paragraphs. Some teachers prefer to teach their students the label Putting It Together, in place of Think and Search.

On My Own questions are those that can be answered largely from background knowledge alone. An example of such a question is, "Have you ever had to be brave and think of a clever solution to a problem?" Author and Me questions are those requiring the application of both text information and scriptal knowledge. An Author and Me question cannot be answered, and may be difficult to understand, unless you have read the text. An example of such a question is, "How might the story have ended differently?"

All four types of QARs are shown in Figure 2.1. This figure may be turned into a chart or overhead transparency to be used in teaching students about QARs.

Figure 2.1
Illustrations to Explain QARs to Students

In the Book QARs

Right There
The answer is in the text, usually easy to find. The words used to make up the question and words used to answer the question are Right There in the same sentence.

In My Head QARs

Author and You
The answer is *not* in the story. You need to think about what you already know, what the author tells you in the text, and how it fits together.

**Think and Search
(Putting It Together)**
The answer is in the story, but you need to put together different story parts to find it. Words for the question and words for the answer are not found in the same sentence. They come from different parts of the text.

On My Own
The answer is not in the story. You can even answer the question without reading the story. You need to use your own experience.

Source: Excerpts from pp. 517–518 and Figure 2, p. 519, from "Teaching question answer relationships, revisited" by Taffy E. Raphael, *The Reading Teacher,* February 1986. Copyright © 1986 International Reading Association, Inc. Reprinted with permission of Taffy E. Raphael and the International Reading Association.

QAR instruction is appropriate for students in grades 1 through 6. Teachers working with first and second graders will probably introduce only the two main categories of QARs: In the Book and In My Head. Students who have mastered basic labels, or students in grades three and above, may be introduced to the subcategories as well. Some students, including many fifth and sixth graders, may not need systematic teaching of QARs; it may be enough just to tell them about the labels.

Raphael (1986) presents the following instructional suggestions and examples:

Here is an illustration of a typical introductory lesson.

Sample text: Mom put a large plate of meat on the table. Then she went back into the kitchen. She came out with more food. She had a plate filled with carrots. She also had a plate filled with potatoes.
Question 1: What food did mom put on the table?
Question 2: What meal were they eating?

Using the above sample text, the teacher initially presents the text on chart paper, an overhead projector, or the board so all children can see it. The text is then read, and the teacher asks the first question. The dialogue below is taken from a teacher presenting this lesson to a group of third grade students.

Ms. H: What food did mom put on the table?
Student 1: Meat.
Student 2: Potatoes.
Ms. H: How do you know that this food was on the table? Can you prove it in any way?
S3: It says so in the story.
S4: What does it say about the food in the story?
S3: It says there was meat, potatoes, and carrots.
Ms. H: Can you point to where in the story it tells you? (student points to words carrots, meat, and potatoes)
Ms. H: Great! That information was in the story you just read. That is one place you can go to find answers to questions—in the stories and books that you read.

Note Ms. H's emphasis on locating the information using the text, rather than on the accuracy of the answer. In answering the second question, she also emphasizes the answer information source, in addition to its accuracy.

Ms. H: (in response to students saying the text is about dinner) How do you know? Does the text tell you that it is dinner?
Students: No!
Ms. H: Then how do you know?
S1: You don't eat meat with carrots and potatoes for breakfast.
S2: That's what you eat for dinner.
Ms. H: How do you know that? What helped you decide on that?
S3: Because that's what I eat for dinner sometimes.
Ms. H: You used a good source of information for that answer—your own experiences. Many times it is important when we're reading and answering questions to think about information up here (points to her head), in our heads.

When students have a clear picture of the differences between In the Book and In My Head (this takes minutes for upper grade students, weeks for early primary grade students), each category should be developed further (pp. 517–518).

It appears to be most effective to focus on the two sources separately. That is, when ready to expand, select either In the Book or In My Head and teach the two categories in that source. In the sample lesson above, Ms. H eventually expanded the In the Book category as follows:

Ms. H: When you found the information in the text to tell what kinds of foods mother brought in, did you find all the information in the same sentence? Where did you find the information?

S1, 2, 3: (Simultaneously) In the first sentence.
At the end.
In the whole story.

Ms. H: Exactly! You are all partially right. The information is in many places. For a complete answer, you had to think of all the different parts to the answer, search through the text, and put it all together! That's why this kind of QAR is called a Think and Search. Sometimes we can find all the information we need to answer a question right there in the same sentence, but many times we think and search for information that we have to put together to give a complete answer.

Note the continued emphasis on strategies for seeking information, as well as the way Ms. H works the category labels into the instructional explanation. For students to acquire these strategies, it is important for them to see that the goal is not merely to identify question categories but to use these categories as signals for different strategies for seeking information and using their textbook (p. 520).

Training in question-answer relationships can easily be coordinated with ETR lessons. During the experience phase of lessons, the teacher is likely to ask many On My Own questions. During the text phase of lessons, the teacher is likely to ask many Right There and Think and Search questions. Finally, during the relationship phase, there will probably be many Author and Me questions. Thus, during each phase of ETR lessons, the teacher can cue students to identify the QAR and use this information to help themselves answer questions.

Eventually, the teacher will only need to provide cues once in a while, as the students begin to use knowledge of QARs spontaneously. For example, during an ETR lesson given to a group of third graders, one student impatiently said to another, "I don't know why you're still thinking, she only asked a Right There question!" He then pointed to the spot in the other student's book where the answer was located.

Up to now in this key concept, we have discussed how teachers can model comprehension monitoring and how they can teach students about question-answer relationships. Both of these approaches target specific aspects of reading comprehension ability. The next approach, reciprocal teaching, is more general and aimed at improving students' overall comprehension ability.

Reciprocal Teaching

Palincsar (1984) describes a program of instruction shown to be effective in improving children's comprehension monitoring/fostering activities. The program targets these four activities: (1) self-questioning (asking main idea rather than detail questions), (2) summarizing, (3) predicting, and (4) evaluating (identifying and clarifying the meaning of difficult sections of the text). The basic procedure can be adapted for use with small groups of children from the first grade on up.

The method of instruction used for all four activities was *reciprocal teaching*. In Chapter 1, we showed you an excerpt from a reciprocal teaching lesson. In reciprocal teaching, the teacher engages the children in discussion by first modeling an activity. Then the children try to engage in the same activity, with the teacher guiding their performance by providing corrective feedback.

In introducing the reciprocal teaching procedure, begin with a group discussion of why people might sometimes have difficulty understanding reading material. The children are likely to come up with responses such as "hard words." Follow this introductory discussion with instruction in each of the four comprehension monitoring/fostering activities. For example, teach your students some of the summarization rules presented in Chapter 4. Let your students know that these activities will help them focus their attention on the text and gain a better understanding of it. Finally, discuss the content areas, such as science and social studies, where these activities can be used, and how they can help with tasks such as writing reports and taking tests.

In Palincsar's study, the reciprocal teaching procedure was introduced in the following way:

> Students were told that everyone in the group would take turns being teacher during the reading session. It was explained that whoever assumed the role of teacher was responsible for asking the group an important question, summarizing, predicting what might be discussed next in the passage, and sharing anything that he or she found unclear or confusing. The teacher was to call on someone to answer his or her question and was responsible for telling the student whether or not the answer was correct. In turn, the students who were not teaching that particular segment of the passage were to comment on the teacher's question(s) and statements and feel free to contribute to that segment.   (Palincsar, 1984, p. 254)

After working for several days on the information above, have the students begin to follow this procedure. First, give the students an expository passage of about 1,500 words. Shorter passages would, of course, be given to younger students. If you are working with first and second graders, select passages to read aloud to them. If the passage is new to the children, have them make predictions based on the title. If they are already familiar with the passage, ask them to state the topic and the important points already learned.

Then, have the children read a paragraph or two. If the children are just being introduced to the reciprocal teaching procedure, let them know that you will be acting as the teacher for this text segment. If the children are already familiar with the procedure, choose a child to be the teacher.

After the segment has been read silently, ask an important question about it, or have the child teacher ask the questions. The teacher then summarizes and makes a prediction or clarification, if appropriate. If a child is serving as the teacher, Palincsar recommends providing the following kinds of assistance:

> Prompting, "What question do you think a teacher might ask?"; Instruction, "Remember a summary is a shortened version, it doesn't include a lot of detail"; Modifying the activity, "If you're having a hard time thinking of a question, why don't you summarize first?" and by soliciting the help of the students, "Who can help us out with this one?" (pp. 254–255)

Invite the other members of the group to offer comments or additional information to supplement that presented by the child or adult teacher. Provide praise and feedback to the child teacher, using comments such as these:

> "You asked that question well, it was very clear what information you wanted." "Excellent prediction, let's see if you're right." "That was interesting information. It was information that I would call detail in the passage. Can you tell us the most important information in that paragraph?" After this feedback, adult teachers modeled any activity they felt continued to need improvement: "A question I would have asked would be . . ." "I would summarize by saying . . ." "Did anyone else find this statement unclear?" (p. 255)

If the students are familiar with question-answer relationships, they will find it helpful if you use terms from this approach when you model question-asking or prompt them. For example, if a student is having difficulty thinking of a question, you could say, "You might want to look at the sentences again. See if you can think of a question that has an answer 'right there' on the page."

Palincsar reports that it takes most teachers about a week to feel comfortable with modeling the comprehension monitoring activities. She suggests that teachers practice with the materials they plan to use with the students. Teachers may also wonder if their students will really be able to engage in reciprocal teaching. To ensure that the first few lessons will be successful, Palincsar recommends that you select well-structured expository passages, clearly written and with headings. Be prepared to do a lot of modeling and to call on more capable students to act as models for less capable members of the group.

To get an idea of the kind of progress students can make through participation in the reciprocal teaching procedure, refer to Figure 2.2. These are excerpts from the dialogue between a teacher and a student who was a very poor reader. Notice how much help the student required in the beginning, and how he gradually became able to ask questions with less and less help from the teacher.

▌ **Figure 2.2**
▌ **Reciprocal Teaching Procedure**

Day 1:
S: What is found in the southeastern snakes, also the copperhead, rattlesnakes, vipers—they have. I'm not doing this right.
T: All right. Do you want to know about the pit vipers?
S: Yeah.
T: What would be a good question about the pit vipers that starts with the word "why"?
S: No response.
T: How about, "Why are the snakes called pit vipers?"
S: Why do they want to know that they called pit vipers?
T: Try it again.
S: Why do they, pit vipers in a pit?
T: How about, "Why do they call the snakes pit vipers?"
S: Why do they call the snakes pit vipers?
T: There you go. Good for you.

Day 4:
S: No question.
T: What's this paragraph about?
S: Spinner's mate. How do Spinner's mate . . . ?
T: That's good. Keep going.
S: How do Spinner's mate is much smaller than . . . how am I going to say that?
T: Take your time with it. You want to ask a question about Spinner's mate and what he does beginning with the word "how."
S: How do they spend most of his time sitting?
T: You're very close. The question would be, "How does Spinner's mate spend most of his time?" Now you ask it.
S: How does Spinner's mate spend most of his time?

Day 7:
S: How does the pressure from below push the mass of hot rock against the opening? Is that it?
T: Not quite. Start your question with "What happens when?"
S: What happens when the pressure from below pushes the mass of hot rock against the opening?
T: Good for you. Good job.

Day 11:
S: What is the most interesting of the insect-eating plants and where do the plants live at?
T: Two excellent questions! They are both clear and important questions. Ask us one at a time now.

Day 15:
S: Why do scientists come to the south pole to study?
T: Excellent question! That is what this paragraph is all about.

Perhaps you noticed some of the features shared by the procedures recommended by Fitzgerald for modeling comprehension monitoring, by Raphael for QAR training, and by Palincsar for reciprocal teaching. All three approaches emphasize the strategies capable readers use to comprehend text, and students' awareness of using strategic thinking when they read. Effective comprehension instruction targets the process of reading comprehension, and not just the product or correct answer. All three procedures also are intended to lead students toward independence in the use of comprehension strategies.

Key Concept 4

The teacher can strengthen students' comprehension ability by following a process approach to the teaching of writing.

▌ THE PROCESS APPROACH TO WRITING

At the beginning of this chapter we described several important similarities between the process of reading comprehension and the process of writing. We also mentioned that writing could be one of the most effective means for promoting reading comprehension. You will read shortly about five ways that reading and writing can be connected at the classroom level (Blackburn, 1984). To prepare you to understand these connections, we present a brief overview of some of the key features of the process approach to writing. This approach to writing makes it quite natural for students to apply what they have learned about writing to learning to read.

In the writing process approach advocated by Graves (1983a) and others, children take charge of their own development as writers. For example, they select the topics they would like to write about, and they have the opportunity to write every day. They experience all five subprocesses of the writing process described earlier: planning, drafting, revising, editing, and publishing.

At the heart of this approach is the writing conference (discussed in more detail later), when children meet with the teacher or other students to discuss the information in their drafts. As a result of these conferences, children may decide to revise their drafts. Graves (1981) writes:

> When children revise they demonstrate their changing visions of information, levels of thinking, what problems they are solving, and their level of control over the writing process. Revision is not only an important tool in the writer's repertoire, but is one of the best indices of how children change as writers. (p. 23)

Publishing is another important aspect of the approach. In the classroom publishing may take many forms. For example, an individual child may publish a story by printing it neatly, and then adding drawings, in a booklet with a construction paper cover. Or the teacher may type the child's text. Publishing is important because it makes children aware of writing as an act of communication and heightens their sense of audience. Generally, children are encouraged to publish what they consider to be their best work or the work they would most like to share. They learn, as professional writers do, that not every piece should be published, only one's best work. This selectivity tends to lead children to the thoughtful revising and polishing of their writing.

In a brief writing conference with his teacher, this kindergarten child receives help with his draft. The teacher first praises his efforts and then gives him one specific suggestion about how to proceed.

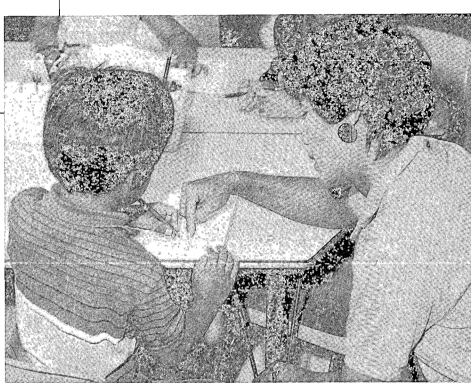

Classroom Connections Between Reading and Writing

Blackburn (1984), a first grade teacher experienced in the writing process approach, outlines five ways in which writing and reading can be connected to one another at the classroom level. In the discussion below, we emphasize how each connection strengthens children's concepts about reading, leading them to become more actively involved in directing their own learning to read.

According to Blackburn, the importance of *invention* is that it allows children to take charge of their own learning right from the start. In the reading of books, as in writing, children are permitted to approximate the performance of mature readers, as advocated in Chapter 6. For example, they can begin by paraphrasing the story lines in books and later start to attend more closely to the words and letters in the text itself. Allowing this type of approximation is consistent with the idea that reading is the process of constructing meaning from text, and the children can begin to construct meaning from text with whatever reading and language skills they have. They can write their own stories even though they are not yet able to spell many words or construct grammatically correct sentences.

Choice is valuable in helping children develop their own tastes in reading. Having a choice gives children the opportunity to reflect on what is important to them. Blackburn found her students often selected books on familiar topics. This made it easier for them to make predictions and to use context clues to identify words. Having a choice about what to write motivates children to put their thoughts down on paper and seek to express them in a coherent fashion.

Discussion occurs during writing conferences (described in more detail below) and around books. Children in classrooms with a writing process approach come to see themselves as authors and so tend to take a more critical and questioning attitude toward the writing of the adult authors whose works they read. They seem to feel that they are in a more direct *social interaction* with the author. They also seem more aware of the importance of the reader's purpose and reactions when reading a particular text. Reading, like writing, becomes an active process. Here, for example, are questions Blackburn's students asked of Chrissy, a child who had just read aloud to the group a story from a basal reader (*P, I,* and *E* are the students' initials).

> *P:* Why did you want to read this story?
> *I:* Do you think the author should have added more information?
> *E:* Do you think this book is easy or hard?
> *P:* How did you learn to read this?
> *P:* Do you think you could write a better story than this?
> *I:* I wonder who the author is.
> *P:* What do you think you'll work on next?
> *E:* Do you think it's going to be hard?   (p. 372)

Notice that the children's last two questions highlight the idea that writing is an ongoing process.

Revision, according to Blackburn, requires lingering over a text and being able to see it from different perspectives. In writing, writers learn to rethink what they have written, while in reading they learn to look for different interpretations of the text. The principle of revision is reinforced for students through the discussion of text, books and one's own writing, with classmates and teacher.

Publication involves the public demonstration of the child's ability, whether in reading or writing. Blackburn (1984) writes:

> The individual who writes a book or learns to read one sits in the author's chair and reads the book to the class. Each child is known for the books he or she has published and for the books he or she is able to read. The achievement gives the child status, but this status isn't conferred by the teacher through ranking and judging the child's performance and ability. It comes from the class as a whole in

appreciation of what the author/reader has added to the community's resources. What is first an individual achievement, quickly becomes the accomplishment of all as they go on to master the new books they are introduced to. (pp. 372–373)

▌ INSTRUCTIONAL ACTIVITIES

Writing Folders

The purpose of using writing folders (Newman, 1983, developed by Graves) is to show students that writing is an ongoing process of developing and expressing one's own ideas. This approach can be used with students of any age.

Give each student a file folder with his or her own name on it. Students keep all of the writing they are working on in their folders. Have students put the date on each piece of writing and keep pages for each piece clipped together. Often, they will have more than one piece in progress at the same time. Having all this material in one place gives students an awareness of the writing process and of their own development as writers.

When using this approach, *topic choice* is essential. That is, students should always be allowed to decide what they want to write about. In the inside front cover of their folders, students can keep a list of topics they might write about at some future time.

Teachers most often use folders simply as a means to keep a complete record of all of the writing an individual child has done. In Newman's approach, however, use of writing folders is meant to provide privacy, to encourage students to take risks when they write and to concentrate on the message of each piece, rather than the conventions of writing. For this reason, Newman recommends that the teacher ask students' permission before reading the material in their folders.

Writing Conferences

Writing conferences give students the opportunity to gain insight into their own writing. The conference centers on a particular piece the student has written. It gives the writer the opportunity to learn about the effectiveness of his or her writing and to answer questions about the topic chosen or process used to write about it. The writer may meet with the teacher or with another student. In many classrooms the writer often meets in conferences with other students before meeting with the teacher.

Russell (1983), drawing upon the work of Calkins (1979), had sixth graders in her class refer to the following list of basic questions when conducting a writing conference with one of their classmates. The questions can be applied to any topic and give the child conducting the conference ideas to be discussed with the writer. A much shorter and less elaborate list may be used in a class with younger children.

1. What is your favorite part?
2. What problems are you having?
3. Which part are you having trouble with?
4. How do you feel?
5. Does your writing end abruptly? Does it need a closing?
6. Do you show feelings or events with specific examples or do you only tell about them?
7. Does your lead sentence "grab" your audience?
8. Do your paragraphs seem to be in the right order?
9. Is each paragraph on one topic?
10. Can you leave out parts that repeat or that fail to give details about your subject?
11. Can you combine some sentences?
12. Can you use precise verbs such as "sprinted" instead of "ran quickly" in places?
13. What do you plan to do next with this piece of writing?   (p. 335)

Because students will be at different stages in their writing, Russell and others have found it impractical to have a set time when everyone in the class must take part in writing conferences. Instead, allow students to decide when they need a conference about a particular piece of writing, and with whom they would like to have the conference. You and your students may need to try a number of different arrangements before arriving at the best way to manage writing conferences. Russell and her students worked out the following set of procedures. Procedures will vary from class to class, but this is an example of a workable system and should give you an idea of the kinds of issues which may need to be resolved.

1. Three conference centers were designated. The students asked permission to conference. The rest of the students in the room were to be quiet and writing.
2. Students were to take their basic list of questions with them to a conference center so they could refer to them if necessary.
3. The writers were to read their drafts orally to their conferencing partners.
4. There was to be no proofreading or correction of mechanical errors at these sessions.
5. Students were to have a minimum of one conference session for each writing assignment.
6. Writers were to have the option of conferencing only with me.   (p. 336)

Publishing Children's Writing

Graves (1983b) stresses that "[m]oving toward a more durable product that will be shared with other audiences leads children to fuss more over the exactness of their writing" (p. 845). Publishing children's writing in little books shows them that their work is valued and is good enough to be shared with others. Publishing emphasizes the idea that writing is a form of communication requiring a consideration of one's audience. Thus, it reinforces the concept of authorship, including the responsibilities authors have to their readers.

Children do not need to publish every piece they write, and they should be led to understand that authors often publish only a small number of the pieces they have written. Let the children select the pieces they want to publish. With younger children, these may be typed, one sentence to a page, using a primary typewriter. Include a title page with the author's name. Put the pages in a durable and attractive cover of some kind, using oaktag, wallpaper samples, etc., and staple or sew the book together. Allow the author to illustrate each page. Be sure the title is also printed on the front cover of the book.

Place the books the children have published in the library corner, to give them the same status as tradebooks. Treat the publishing of books as a special occasion by announcing the authors and titles of new books to the class.

The Author's Chair

The "author's chair" is a chair where individual children can sit and read aloud to the other students. The child sitting in the author's chair reads aloud to the class one of his or her own drafts or published books, a classmate's published book, or a tradebook. At times the teacher may also read a book to the class.

After the book has been read, the first response made by the audience is to *receive* or express acceptance of the piece. As Hansen (1983) describes it, the children will clap for the author and then make comments about the parts of the book they liked best. Then the audience addresses questions to the author.

If a tradebook has been read, and the author therefore is not present, the group speculates about the author's possible responses. When dealing with tradebooks, the children know that they, as readers, can agree or disagree with the decisions made by professional authors. A great deal of learning takes place in these sessions:

> These children learn that sometimes authors leave out too much information and may have to explain their texts. But the questioners learn much more than just the answers to their queries. They have gathered to respond to another author's work, and they continue to learn it's their responsibility as readers to ask questions. (p. 973)

Besides setting up an author's chair, you can choose a child to be "author of the week" (Graves & Hansen, 1983). Put a photograph of the child on the bulletin board along with a list of the titles of the student's published books. Put the books in pockets and encourage the other children to post comments about them. From among these published books, have the author choose his or her favorite, and make copies for the other children to read. Give the author of the week several opportunities to sit in the author's chair and read aloud to the class, particularly his or her own published books.

His classmates respond with interest to the story being read by this boy, seated in the Author's Chair.

Having an author's chair in the classroom gives teachers the chance to observe the development of their students' concept of authorship. Using the author's chair as one of their focal points, Graves and Hansen (1983) studied first grade children's learning to read and write, especially development of their concept of authorship. They observed children going through three phases in understanding this concept. In the *replication phase*, the children began with a vague notion that authors somehow "write books." They had little or no understanding of what an author actually did when writing a book. In the *transition phase*, the children began to see themselves as authors. Once they had gone through the different parts of the writing process themselves, including publishing a book, the concept of authorship became real to them. In the *option-awareness phase*, the children recognized that authors made many decisions while writing. For example, they could decide in their own writing to describe what actually happened or to add a fictitious event to make a story better. Teachers could observe to see if their own students go through similar phases.

Many of the experiences that students have with the writing process approach will serve to strengthen their reading comprehension ability. First, students are encouraged to value their own background knowledge and experiences, information which can be important in reading comprehension. Second, students become aware that texts are written by authors, human beings like themselves, whose work should be critically evaluated. Third, when students are comfortable with writing and can write with some ease, they are better able to write down their thoughts about the books, stories, articles, and other texts they read. As we pointed out in our discussion of ETR lessons, having students write about their reading is a good means of encouraging them to think more deeply about what they have read. In Chapters 3 and 4 we will discuss the kinds of writing about reading you may want your students to do.

▌ SUMMARY

We started this chapter by describing the functions the reader must accomplish to achieve comprehension. We brought out the complexity of the process of reading comprehension by comparing it to the process of writing. Both were shown to be acts of composing, demanding the individual's active, thoughtful involvement.

In the first key concept we focused on the role of background knowledge in reading. We demonstrated how comprehension requires much more than just being familiar with all the words in a passage. Readers also must make use of knowledge of the topic, and of knowledge of different text structures. We presented a three-part framework for comprehension lessons which included a prereading phase to teach students to access relevant background knowledge. This framework, called the experience-text-relationship (ETR) approach, is based on guided discussion of texts. Through a sample series of lessons, we showed how a teacher might guide students to understand a story, both through discussion and writing activities.

In the second key concept we explained how teachers might mediate or involve students with text ideas. We presented an example showing how a teacher used responsive questioning to draw ideas from students, rather than telling them the answers. We related mediating to Vygotsky's idea of the gradual release of responsibility. We also described approaches teachers might use to encourage students' active participation in discussions.

In the third key concept we looked at the importance of strategies and metacognition in reading for meaning. We discussed how teachers might give students information about reading comprehension strategies, both through explanations and modeling. To help students become strategic readers, we recommended three approaches teachers might follow: modeling of comprehension monitoring, training in question-answer relationships (QARs), and reciprocal teaching.

In the fourth key concept we showed how teachers could strengthen students' comprehension ability by following a process approach to the teaching of writing. At the classroom level, important connections between reading and writing can be made for students. In the writing process approach, students have the opportunity to learn about the five subprocesses of writing, to make choices about topics, and to use critical judgment in evaluating their own writing and the writing of others. These experiences carry over to reading and encourage students to take charge of their own growth in reading, as well as in writing.

▌ BIBLIOGRAPHY
References

Anderson, R. C., & Pearson, P. D. (1984). A schema-theoretic view of basic processes in reading comprehension. In P. D. Pearson (Ed.), *Handbook of reading research.* New York: Longman.

Au, K. H. (1979). Using the experience-text-relationship method with minority children. *The Reading Teacher, 32* (6), 677–679.

Au, K. H., & Kawakami, A. J. (1984). Vygotskian perspectives on discussion processes in small group reading lessons. In P. L. Peterson, L. C. Wilkinson, & M. Hallinan (Eds.), *The social context of instruction: Group organization and group processes.* New York: Academic Press.

Au, K. H., & Kawakami, A. J. (1986). Influence of the social organization of instruction on children's text comprehension ability: A Vygotskian perspective. In T. E. Raphael (Ed.), *Contexts of school-based literacy.* New York: Random House.

Au, K. H., & Mason, J. M. (1981). Social organizational factors in learning to read: The balance of rights hypothesis. *Reading Research Quarterly, 17* (1), 115–152.

Baker, L., & Brown, A. (1984). Cognitive skills and reading. In P. D. Pearson (Ed.), *Handbook of reading research.* New York: Longman.

Blackburn, E. (1984). Common ground: Developing relationships between reading and writing. *Language Arts, 61* (4), 367–375.

Bransford, J. D., & Johnson, M. K. (1973). Considerations of some problems of comprehension. In W. C. Chase (Ed.), *Visual information processing.* New York: Academic Press.

Brown, A. L., & Smiley, S. S. (1977). Rating the importance of structural units of prose passages: A problem of metacognitive development. *Child Development, 48,* 1–8.

Calkins, L. M. (1979). Children learn the writer's craft. *Language Arts, 57,* 207–213.

Clay, M. M. (1975). *What did I write?* London: Heinemann.

Collins, A., & Smith, E. (1980). *Teaching the process of reading comprehension* (Tech. Rep. No. 182). Urbana, IL: University of Illinois, Center for the Study of Reading.

Cunningham, P. M., Moore, S. A., Cunningham, J. W., & Moore, D. W. (1983). *Reading in elementary classrooms: Strategies and observations.* New York: Longman.

Danner, F. W. (1976). Children's understanding of intersentence organization in the recall of short descriptive passages. *Journal of Educational Psychology, 68,* 174–183.

Duffy, G. G., & Roehler, L. R. (1987). Teaching reading skills as strategies. *The Reading Teacher, 40* (4), 414–418.

Duffy, G. G., Roehler, L. R., & Hermann, B. A. (1988). Modeling mental processes helps poor readers become strategic readers. *The Reading Teacher, 41* (8), 762–767.

Fitzgerald, J. (1983). Helping readers gain self-control over reading comprehension. *The Reading Teacher, 37* (3), 249–253.

Forrest, D. L., & Waller, T. G. (1979, March). *Cognitive and metacognitive aspects of reading.* Paper presented at the meeting of the Society for Research in Child Development, San Francisco.

Freire, P. (1985). Reading the world and reading the word: An interview with Paulo Freire. *Language Arts, 62* (1), 15–21.

Graves, D. H. (1981). Patterns of child control of the writing process. In R. D. Walshe, *Donald Graves in Australia—"Children want to write . . ."* Exeter, NH: Heinemann.

Graves, D. (1983a). *Writing: Teachers and children at work.* Exeter, NH: Heinemann.

Graves, D. (1983b). Teacher intervention in children's writing: A response to Myra Barrs. *Language Arts, 60* (7), 841–846.

Graves, D., & Hansen, J. (1983). The author's chair. *Language Arts, 60* (2), 176–183.

Hansen, J. (1983). Authors respond to authors. *Language Arts, 60* (8), 176–183.

Hayes, D. A., & Tierney, R. J. (1982). Developing readers' knowledge through analogy. *Reading Research Quarterly, 17,* 256–280.

Humes, A. (1983). Research on the composing process. *Review of Educational Research, 53* (2), 201–216.

Marr, M., & Gromley, K. (1982). Children's recall of familiar and unfamiliar text. *Reading Research Quarterly, 18,* 89–104.

Mehan, H. (1979). *Learning lessons.* Cambridge, MA: Harvard University Press.

Myers, M., & Paris, S. (1978). Children's metacognitive knowledge about reading. *Journal of Educational Psychology, 70,* 680–690.

Newman, J. M. (1983). *Whole language activities.* Monographs on learning and teaching. Publication #1. Halifax, Nova Scotia: Department of Education, Dalhousie University.

Palincsar, A. S. (1984). The quest for meaning from expository text: A teacher-guided journey. In G. G. Duffy, L. R. Roehler, & J. M. Mason (Eds.), *Comprehension instruction: Perspectives and suggestions.* New York: Longman.

Palincsar, A. S., & Brown, A. L. (1984). Reciprocal teaching of comprehension-fostering and comprehension-monitoring activities. *Cognition and Instruction, 2,* 117–175.

Pearson, P. D., & Johnson, D. D. (1978). *Teaching reading comprehension.* New York: Holt, Rinehart & Winston.

Raphael, T. E. (1982). Question-answering strategies for children. *Reading Teacher, 36* (2), 186–190.

Raphael, T. E. (1986). Teaching Question Answer Relationships, revisited. *Reading Teacher, 39* (6), 516–522.

Russell, C. (1983). Putting research into action: Conferencing with young writers. *Language Arts, 60* (3), 333–340.

Roehler, L. R., & Duffy, G. G. (in press). Teacher's instructional actions. In P. D. Pearson (Ed.), *Handbook of reading research,* Volume 2. New York: Longman.

Scheu, J. A., Tanner, D. K., & Au, K. H. (1989). Integrating seatwork with the basal lesson. In P. Winograd, K. Wixson, & M. Lipson (Eds.), *Improving basal reading instruction.* New York: Teachers College Press.

Shultz, J., Erickson, F., & Florio, S. (1982). Where's the floor? Aspects of the cultural organization of social relationships at home and at school. In P. Gilmore & A. Glatthorn (Eds.), *Children in and out of school.* Washington, DC: Center for Applied Linguistics.

Stein, B. S., & Bransford, J. D. (1979). Constraints on effective elaboration: Effects of precision and subject generation. *Journal of Verbal Learning and Verbal Behavior, 18,* 769–777.

Tierney, R. J., & Pearson, P. D. (1983). Toward a composing model of reading. *Language Arts, 60,* 568–580.

Wagoner, S. A. (1983). Comprehension monitoring: What it is and what we know about it. *Reading Research Quarterly, 18* (3), 328–346.

Winograd, P., & Paris, S. G. (1988). A cognitive and motivational agenda for reading instruction. *Educational Leadership, 46* (4), 30–36.

Children's Books Cited

Bennett, R. (1978). The secret hiding place. In W. Durr, J. LePere, B. Niehaus, & B. York (Eds.), *Sunburst.* Boston: Houghton Mifflin.

Greydanus, R. (1980). *My secret hiding place.* Mahwah, NJ: Troll Associates.

Miles, M. (1971). Annie and the old one. In W. Durr, J. LePere, & R. H. Brown, *Passports.* Boston: Houghton Mifflin.

Taylor, P. (1978). Mrs. White's hat. In L. G. Botko, J. K. Heryla, V. K. Klassen, & J. Manning (Eds.), *Dragon wings: Basics in reading.* Glenview, IL: Scott, Foresman.

Further Readings

Duffy, G. G., & Roehler, L. R. (1987). Improving reading instruction through the use of responsive elaboration. *The Reading Teacher, 40* (6), 514–520.

Hansen, J. (1987). *When writers read.* Portsmouth, NH: Heinemann.

Holmes, B. C., & Roser, N. L. (1987). Five ways to assess readers' prior knowledge. *The Reading Teacher, 40* (7), 646–649.

Pearson, P. D., & Dole, J. A. (1987). Explicit comprehension instruction: A review of research and a new conceptualization of instruction. *Elementary School Journal, 88* (2), 151–165.

Shanahan, T. (1988). The reading-writing relationship: Seven instructional principles. *The Reading Teacher, 41* (7), 636–647.

Wixson, K. K., & Peters, C. W. (1989). Teaching the basal selection. In P. N. Winograd, K. K. Wixson, & M. Y. Lipson (Eds.), *Improving basal reading instruction.* New York: Teachers College Press, pp. 21–61.

Developing Children's Appreciation of Literature and Comprehension of Stories

From an interview with Mike, who had read *The High King* by Lloyd Alexander:

> *Interviewer:* If you could be one of the characters from *The High King*, which would it be?
> *Mike:* Either Gwydion or Taran. They seemed the most noble. It seemed like they shared the same ideas I have.
> *(Mike described the friendship between Gwydion and Taran. "Close friends," he said, "go all out to help each other. They are loving, understanding, and selfless.")*
> *Interviewer:* Is it important to you in the books you read that there be some sort of good or noble idea?
> *Mike:* Um-hmm. If you go to battle just because you feel like killing someone, that's just stupid.
> *Interviewer:* What major point do you think Lloyd Alexander was trying to get across in this book?
> *Mike:* I don't know. The point he got across to me was to care more about a million people, or three people, than one person—yourself.
> (Cramer, 1984, p. 257)

■ OVERVIEW

We begin this chapter by discussing the concept of response to literature, and the value of having children experience literature. We describe genres of literature and literary elements which teachers can help students understand. We emphasize the importance of using literature to encourage students' voluntary reading. Next we turn to specific, systematic approaches teachers can use to build students' ability to comprehend stories. Then we look at how writing can be used as a means of encouraging students to think more deeply

73

about the novels and stories they read. Finally, we show how thematic units may be used to allow students to explore particular themes at length. Building on a theme in earlier chapters, we show how social interaction, in the form of discussion with teachers and peers, can lead students toward a greater understanding and appreciation of literature.

Chapter 3 is organized around the following key concepts:

Key Concept 1: The teacher should help children learn to appreciate books and stories by encouraging them to respond to literature.

Key Concept 2: The teacher should have a purpose for having students read a particular story, and should follow systematic procedures for planning and conducting story comprehension lessons.

Key Concept 3: The teacher should give children opportunities to use writing to clarify thoughts about stories and literature.

Key Concept 4: The teacher should involve students with several books or stories related to a theme.

▌ PERSPECTIVE
Motivating Children to Read on Their Own

There is a big difference between *being able* to read and *wanting* to read or *enjoying* reading. In this chapter we will look not only at ways of helping children develop the ability to comprehend fiction, but also at ways of helping them become motivated to read on their own.

Children who enjoy reading are those who have learned to become personally involved with text. Kindergarten children enjoy reading along with the teacher the words spoken by the Three Billy-Goats Gruff, lowering their voices when speaking the part of the biggest billy goat. They empathize with Ira, a little boy who is teased by his sister for wanting to take his teddy bear along when he goes to spend the night at Reggie's house. Older children laugh aloud at the antics of Pippi Longstocking and are moved by Wilbur the pig and his spider friend in *Charlotte's Web*. A child who is teased for being small or keeping to himself may be comforted by the story of *Crow Boy*.

This special interaction between the reader and the text might be thought to create what Dillon (1984, p. 227) calls "a unique aesthetic experience of knowing and feeling" and a form of "new life." To Rosenblatt (1978), this interaction results in the creation of a "poem." As Rosenblatt uses the term, a poem is the reader's response to and interpretation of the text:

The poem, then, must be thought of as an event in time. It is not an object or an ideal entity. It happens during a coming-together, a compenetration, of a reader and a text. The reader brings to the text his past experience and present personality. Under the magnetism of the ordered symbols of the text, he marshals his resources and crystallizes out from the stuff of memory, thought, and feeling a new order, a new experience, which he sees as the poem. This becomes part of the ongoing stream of his life experience, to be reflected on from any angle important to him as a human being. (Rosenblatt, 1978, p. 12)

To give children the opportunity to enjoy these experiences, and to help them acquire the habit of reading, teachers want to make sure that children become involved with good literature. Sutherland and Arbuthnot (1986) suggest that children's literature "consists of books that are not only read and enjoyed, but also that have been written for children and that meet high literary and artistic standards" (p. 5).

Response to Literature

As you saw in the interview with Mike, used to open this chapter, students can have wonderful experiences and gain valuable insights through works of literature. Encouraging students to respond to literature is an important part of reading and language arts instruction. Students learn to respond to literature by having their ideas and feelings accepted and shaped by other readers, including more experienced ones, such as their teachers. Perhaps one of the greatest gifts a teacher can give students is the opportunity to respond to literature.

In previous chapters, you learned that reading involves a dynamic interaction among the reader, text, and the social context in which reading takes place. Similarly, Purves (1985) argues that response to literature may be understood in terms of the relationships among the writer, the text, and the reader. Both the writer and the reader draw upon background knowledge, including knowledge of literature and knowledge of the world.

> . . . the writer does not simply put words down at random and depart from the scene. We can say that the writer inhabits a world and, in the writing, expresses the experience of it. The world is not simply a world of external reality; it is also a world of artifacts called literature, and the writer is aware of tradition and convention. Out of this awareness, and from the expressive and poetic impulse, comes the poem. The reader approaches the poem, aware that it is such an expression and aware, too, that the poem is part of a larger poetic body. Some readers have more experience of that poetic body than others. All readers have experiences of the world and of aspects of that which the poem is treating. (pp. 62–63)

The term *poem*, as it is used in this paragraph, may be extended to include all works of literature.

Purves believes that a particular work of literature may have a meaning shared by many readers. However, it will also have a special significance, or personal meaning, which will be different for each reader. In other words, a large number of readers may share a response to a work of literature, and at the same time no two responses will be exactly alike. The exercise should help you see how this can be the case. The practical implication is that it is

Exercise

(1) Read the poem.

THE SHARKS

Well, then, the last day the sharks appeared.
Dark fins appear, innocent
as if in fair warning. The sea becomes
sinister, are they everywhere?
I tell you, they break six feet of water.
Isn't it the same sea, and won't we
play in it any more?
I liked it clear and not
too calm, enough waves
to fly in on. For the first time
I dared to swim out of my depth.
It was sundown when they came, the time
when a sheen of copper stills the sea,
not dark enough for moonlight, clear enough
to see them easily. Dark
the sharp lift of the fins.

—Denise Levertov

(2) Jot down your reactions to the poem. For example, what emotions did you feel? What do you think the poem is about? What is its overall message or lesson?

(3) Meet with a partner or small group to compare your reactions to the poem. What shared meaning or responses did you have in common? What unique meaning or significance did the poem have for individuals?

You were probably able to detect some meaning likely to be shared by many readers. We hope you were also able to learn about some interpretations of the poem by other readers, that you would never have thought of yourself! The purpose of this exercise was to make you aware of both these dimensions of response, shared and personal, that you and your students will experience through literature.

important for teachers to consider both the personal significance a work may have for each student, as well as the common, shared meaning the work is likely to have for many readers.

Purves also sees social context as an important factor in response to literature. He suggests that response to literature is influenced by the audience to which the response is directed. For example, the comments you might make about a poem could be quite different, depending on whether you are speaking to a fellow student or to your English instructor. As a teacher, you will want to remember that you are an important member of the audience for your students, and that you should try to respect and accept their responses.

What form will students' responses to literature take? Sutherland and Arbuthnot (1986) answer the question in this way:

> Response can take many forms. It can be overt and immediate. Then again, it may not be distinguishable at once and, perhaps, not ever. Many responses to literature do not surface until long after the book has been put down. Even then, the response may be a composite of responses to many literary works which have influenced the reader. A composite literary response can emerge, for instance, when we try to deal with a minor misfortune by stating our belief in humanity's ability to succeed through perseverance, an idea we may have encountered in many works of literature, popular as well as classic. A response may surface in an unexpected way, as when children respond to a cartoon character with giggles because the character reminded them of Henry Huggins. More clearly defined is the response of children saying, simply, that the story character has the same problems that they themselves have.   (pp. 503–504)

We see then that response to literature may have many dimensions and take many forms.

Drawing upon the work of Purves and Rippere (1968) and Squire (1964), Sutherland and Arbuthnot suggest the following framework for thinking about response to literature:

The emotional reaction.   Readers may become so engrossed in reading a story that they almost feel they are right there with the characters. Readers may see relationships between the character's problem and their own personal experience. An emotional response usually stems from this kind of intense involvement with literature. The involvement which begins with an emotional response may then serve as the foundation for responding to the work in other ways.

The interpretive reaction.   Readers may notice and make interpretations based on the author's use of metaphor, symbols, and other literary devices. Or interpretive response may involve making inferences about characters' motives or the setting. Readers may also think of the reasons the author had for writing the story, or the message the author intended to convey.

The critical reaction.   Critical responses are those in which readers make judgments about the literary quality of the story or react to elements such as the plot, characterization, mood, style, or the author's point of view. Identifying the genre of a work is another type of critical reaction.

The evaluative reaction.   One kind of evaluative response has to do with the emotional appeal of the story, another with the merit of the work compared to others of the same genre. Still another kind of evaluative response involves the overall lesson communicated through the work, and whether the reader finds the lesson acceptable or unacceptable in ethical terms.

In the sample lessons described later in this chapter, you will see examples of all of these responses. You will also see that it is possible for students to respond to literature through a variety of activities. Although we will be emphasizing written response, children may also respond by retelling the story and through drama and art.

Key Concept 1

The teacher should help children learn to appreciate books and stories by encouraging them to respond to literature.

▌ GENRES OF CHILDREN'S LITERATURE

Students' responses to any work of literature are likely to be richer if they can see it in relation to other works, similar and different, as well as to their own life experiences. For this reason, it is helpful from kindergarten on for children to have many experiences with different types of literature. When you are thinking of the books you will use with your students, you may want to remember that there are a number of different forms or genres of children's literature. By helping your students to become familiar with different genres of literature, you may help to increase both their literary understanding and appreciation.

According to Sutherland and Arbuthnot, children's literature may be divided into nine major genres:

1. picture books
2. folktales
3. fables, myths, and epics
4. modern fantasy
5. poetry
6. modern fiction
7. historical fiction
8. biography
9. informational books

Drawing upon the work of these authors, we briefly describe the important characteristics of each genre. Instructional guidelines are presented for the genres many elementary teachers introduce to children.

Picture Books

Picture books play an important part in the classroom reading program in the primary grades, particularly in kindergarten. A key here is the quality of the illustrations and whether they can attract and hold children's attention. With picture books that tell a story, you might help children attend to the emotional responses of the characters and their problems. Sutherland and Arbuthnot point out that picture books of lasting value play up two themes: love or reassurance and achievement.

The Caldecott Medal is awarded each year to the illustrator of the most outstanding picture book. Caldecott award books young children especially enjoy include *Time of Wonder* by Robert McCloskey, *The Snowy Day* by Ezra Jack Keats, *Sam, Bangs, and Moonshine* by Evaline Ness, and *Sylvester and the Magic Pebble* by William Steig.

With Mother Goose, ABC, counting, and concept books you can point out the games that are played with language or illustrations. Read the books aloud to kindergarten and first grade students and then place them in the classroom library area. Encourage the children to read the books on their own or with other children. Many of these books will become classroom favorites, to be read aloud to the children several times.

Folktales

Children are today the main audience for folktales, which are part of a heritage based in oral tradition. According to Sutherland and Arbuthnot, qualities of folktales children find appealing are that they are filled with action, convey a clear sense of right and wrong, often include rhyme and repetition, and end in a satisfying way.

Because most of these tales were meant to be told, rather than read silently, they lend themselves well to reading aloud, storytelling, puppetry, and creative dramatics. In any event, call the children's attention to interesting language (e.g., "And I'll huff and I'll puff and I'll blow your house down"), the recurring pattern in each episode (e.g., as in *Goldilocks and the Three Bears* or *The Three Little Pigs*), and what Sutherland and Arbuthnot term "the old verities that kindness and goodness will triumph over evil if they are backed by wisdom, wit, and courage" (p. 54). Excellent collections of the folktales of many different groups are now available, and you may wish to introduce your students to folktales from African, North American Indian, and Asian groups, as well as to American tall tales and traditional European tales.

Fables, Myths, and Epics

Fables, myths, and epics, like tales, have their source in folklore and are also important parts of the child's literary heritage. They are more moral in nature. Fables, such as those by Aesop, present straightforward, simple lessons.

Myths often provided explanations for troubling or little understood aspects of the human condition, such as disease or the changing of the seasons. *Children of Odin* (Colum, 1962) is an example of a collection of myths written for children. Epics such as the *Iliad* and the *Odyssey* are usually cycles of tales describing the challenges faced by legendary heroes.

Both myths and epics can be highly complex and symbolic, but older children may find the stories both fascinating and inspiring. Very young children will usually only be interested in a simple version of the plot of these stories, but older children may be referred to versions which, while written in clear language, preserve interesting detail.

Modern Fantasy

According to Sutherland and Arbuthnot, fantasy "is the art form many modern writers have chosen to . . . lay out for children the realities of life—not in a physical or social sense, but in a psychological sense" (p. 226). Modern fantasy encompasses everything from Beatrix Potter's story of Peter Rabbit, to the elegant and elaborate novels of Lewis Carroll, J. R. R. Tolkien, Ursula Le Guin, and Madeleine L'Engle. These books, which present imaginary worlds and events which could not really happen, can appeal to children for the same reasons as folk tales, fables, myths, and epics. When reading such books, children experience a sense of adventure and escape and can come to understand different ways of approaching life's problems.

Books you feel the class as a whole will find appealing may be read aloud to the children, one chapter each day. A brief discussion, including reactions and predictions, may follow each day's reading. When the novel has been completed, interested children may be encouraged to read other works by the same author.

Basal readers contain much modern fantasy, often beginning with animal stories in the early grades and moving to excerpts from novels in the later ones. In the key concept after this one, we cover ways of improving children's comprehension of these and other stories.

Poetry

Poetry plays on emotions, triggers insight, and develops an appreciation for the beauty and power of language. Sutherland and Arbuthnot suggest that children enjoy the "singing quality" of poetry, its story elements, humor, and appeal to the senses. They provide an excellent listing of poets whose work is often enjoyed by children, ranging from Edward Lear to Myra Cohn Livingston. Here are the guidelines they suggest for the use of poetry:

Do read poetry aloud often.
Do provide a variety of poems in records, books, and tapes.
Do make several anthologies available to children.

Do select contemporary poetry as well as older material.
Do help children avoid sing-song reading aloud.
Do choose poems with comprehensive subject matter.
Do encourage the writing of poetry.
Do choose poems that have action or humor.
Do try choral readings.   (p. 227)

Help children understand how the words create feelings and images to convey the author's message. Older children can begin to look closely at figurative language.

Modern Fiction

This realistic form of fiction, according to Sutherland and Arbuthnot, introduces children to the lives of families past and present, to worlds similar to or very different from their own. While some modern fiction, such as mysteries, is written largely to entertain, other books explore deeper themes, such as being different or alone, and touch on controversial topics. An example of the former is *Encyclopedia Brown Saves the Day* by Donald Sobol (1970), while an example of the latter is *Julie of the Wolves* by Jean George (1972). In considering which of the vast array of books of this genre to introduce to the class or recommend to individual children, Sutherland and Arbuthnot propose these guidelines:

> If these books center on children's basic needs; if they give them increased insight into their own personal problems and social relationships; if they show that people are more alike than different, more akin to each other than alien; if they convince young readers that they can do something about their lives—have fun and adventures and get things done without any magic other than their own earnest efforts—then they are worthwhile books.   (p. 333)

Basal readers include many selections about children in real-life situations. These, too, offer opportunities to promote story comprehension.

Historical Fiction

Historical fiction for children introduces characters, often children themselves, in an authentic setting of the past. For example, the story of *Sarah, Plain and Tall,* a woman from Maine who comes to live on a prairie farm, is told through the eyes of Anna, a young girl. According to Sutherland and Arbuthnot, such writing should show life in an accurate and honest way because children generally do not have the background knowledge to evaluate the material critically. Otherwise, much the same criteria can be used for selecting historical fiction as with other stories, and similar teaching methods can be applied.

The authors point out that in true historical fiction, the picture painted of the historical period is an integral part of helping the reader to understand the events in the story. This is likely to make the facts much more interesting to children. Because of this possibility, historical fiction can serve as a bridge to informational text, particularly in social studies. Point out to the children that there are ideas to be remembered as well as appreciated. Encourage them to seek out other books on the same historical period to verify information or to learn more. Help children to identify the important historical events in the story (for example, the situation of slaves in the period before the Civil War, in *A Gathering of Days: A New England Girl's Journal, 1830–32*), to trace the story line, and to separate important ideas in the text from incidental details simply used to add a bit of color.

Biography

A good biography, or account of someone's life, will be historically accurate and treat its subject as an individual, not merely as the ideal or representative of a group. *Carry On, Mr. Bowditch* (Latham, 1955) is an example of an excellent biography written for children. Sutherland and Arbuthnot recommend that biography and historical fiction be used to reinforce one another, because both give children a sense of what it was like to "be there" in another time and place.

Teachers might have students read about different people from the same era and then contrast their views and experiences. For example, for the Revolutionary War period, students could read biographies of an American patriot and a British loyalist.

Informational Books

Informational books for children cover a huge number of topics, and books can be found to match the natural curiosity of every child to learn more about something. Examples of science books for children are *Benny's Animals* (Selsam, 1966) and *Evolution Goes On Every Day* (Patent, 1977). This genre is discussed further in Chapter 4.

▌ INSTRUCTIONAL ACTIVITIES
Literature Activities and Library Centers

Morrow and Weinstein (1986) developed a program with two components: (1) literature activities to be used as part of the regular reading program, and (2) the creation of inviting library centers. Their purpose was to see how these components affected second graders' voluntary reading and attitudes toward reading. As a result of the program, children's voluntary reading of literature increased substantially, and this increased rate of reading continued even after the special literature activities had been discontinued. The program had equal benefits for both good and poor readers. Although tested with second

Besides commercially published tradebooks, the library area in this third grade classroom contains books written by individual students and class books, such as the one this girl is reading.

graders, the ideas used in the program are readily adapted for other grade levels (refer also to Chapter 6).

Teachers in the program spend about 20 minutes a day on literature activities. Some activities are carried out on a daily basis. These include:

- reading or telling stories to children
- discussing stories that had been read
- encouraging children to read whenever they had spare time
- encouraging children to check books out of the library center to take home
- reminding children to keep track of books read on index cards located in the library center

About three times a week, teachers carry out certain other activities. The activities teachers choose from include:

- having the principal, custodian, secretary, or a parent read to the class
- having children write to authors
- arranging for children to read and tell stories to classes at lower grade levels
- showing movies or filmstrips of books
- using literature in content area lessons
- having children make their own books

- using a creative storytelling approach, such as puppet shows or prop stories

In addition to these literature activities, an area in each classroom is set up to serve as a library center. The area chosen is in a quiet part of the room and partitioned off. It is easily seen and reached and can hold at least five children at a time. Each library area has shelves for displaying books so their covers are visible. Libraries are stocked with 90 paperback books, children's magazines, a felt board and felt-board stories, a roll movie, books accompanied by audiotapes, and materials children can use to make their own books. There is a bulletin board urging the children to read and to record the books read on index cards. Pillows are added to make the area inviting.

Morrow and Weinstein found that it was necessary to have a wide variety of materials, including props and pillows, to entice the children to the library center. But the extra materials did not prove distracting once the children got there. Book reading was found to account for 70 percent of the activity in the library centers.

You might want to use some of the ideas for literature activities and library corners tested by Morrow and Weinstein. Whether you decide to follow their program rather closely, or to branch out on your own, it is important to remember that the two components, literature activities and library centers, work together. Students' appreciation of literature and voluntary reading are fostered when teachers promote social interaction around books. Once students start being interested in literature and reading, then it is helpful for books to be readily accessible and for the physical environment for reading to be inviting.

Sharing Books

Plan times for the children to share books. The important idea here is to let children see how reading can be a social experience, as well as one experienced alone. For example, set up occasions for discussions of favorite books. Children could take turns signing up to talk about a book they've just read and answer other children's questions about it.

Use this and other means to encourage children to recommend good books to other children. This creates a "community of readers" with classmates in a network to offer one another suggestions about what to read next (Hickman, 1984).

Books can also serve as a basis for oral interpretation, creative drama, art projects prepared by small groups, or games such as charades. For example, Cleary (1978) suggests the following five-day program for the sharing of plays:

Day 1: Students divide into small groups, select a play, and read it in its entirety.

Day 2: Within each group, students determine who will take each role and then rehearse by reading the parts aloud.

These first graders take turns reading aloud from a favorite story-book. Sharing reading in this way can be enjoy-able and motivating for many children.

Day 3: Students rehearse the play, adding sound effects.

Day 4: Students tape record the plays, which may then be listened to by other students who read the same play.

Day 5: Groups may listen to their own tape recording or to those of other groups.

Manna (1984) suggests a number of different activities for working with plays. For example, students can summarize and discuss an act or scene after they have read it aloud. They can also focus on key scenes as a way of understanding the characters' motives, or draw a diagram of the stage as a stimulus for discussing characters' relationships and placement. Manna also presents a list of plays suitable for use with students in different grades.

Cleary (1978) also recommends the sharing of reading with another class of older or younger children. You could assign partners and have each read to the other. Cleary conducted a high school remedial reading program called the "super sport reading program." She had high school athletes who were poor readers practice reading easy books aloud in her reading resource room, then visit an elementary school to read and discuss the books with poor readers in the fourth and fifth grades. Each boy visited the other school four times, three times to read and the fourth to share poetry and help the younger children to write poetry.

Another procedure is to send books home for students to share with family members. Younger children can take home books to read with their parents or older siblings, while older children might be encouraged to read to younger brothers and sisters.

Reading Aloud to Children

Read to the whole class every day so they will see that literature can be a source of pleasure. For young children, you could read well known fairy tales so they can understand how such stories are often constructed—from "once upon a time" to "and they lived happily ever after." Read them books with fanciful language so they hear how games are played with words. Read older children chapters from novels that will draw them out of a narrow world view. Let children know that you enjoy books and like to read.

Library Corners and Book Floods

Create an inviting area in the classroom with pillows and a rug or perhaps a comfortable sofa. Flood this library corner with five to ten new books a week (Elley & Mangubhai, 1983). These books may come from the school library, or the teacher may want to borrow additional books from the public library. Books may be tied to a literature unit, such as that described in Key Concept #4, or to social studies, science, or other topics the class is studying. Read aloud all or just a small part of most of the books to the children, creating interest in books children might not have thought to pick up on their own. Encourage the children to seek out books of interest during free time or time allocated for recreational reading. Children then have the opportunity to read for enjoyment and practice, with no book reports required.

Sustained Silent Reading

Sustained silent reading (SSR), also referred to as uninterrupted sustained silent reading (USSR), is an activity giving students class time to read on their own. Its purpose is to encourage reading for pleasure, outside of the classroom as well, and to give students the chance to practice and apply reading skills. We recommend that sustained silent reading occur every day. It should be remembered, however, that SSR will be much more effective if it is accompanied by literature activities, book sharing, and other approaches which promote social interaction around books (Manning & Manning, 1984).

Levine (1984) suggests that the teacher follow these rules for sustained silent reading:

1. Have each student select his or her own book. Make sure there are plenty of books of different kinds available.
2. Have the students read silently for a set period of time. Begin with a short

time, such as ten minutes, and then gradually extend the period, perhaps with older students to as much as forty minutes.
3. Spend the time reading yourself, and allow no interruptions. Set an example for the children by being a good role model, rather than using the time to grade papers or plan lessons.
4. Make sure the entire class is reading silently together.
5. Do not require reports or record-keeping, ask questions, or do anything which might discourage the reluctant reader.

Teachers working with kindergarten and first grade children, or with reluctant readers, may wish to use "booktime" (Hong, 1981) as a way of preparing the children for sustained silent reading. Hong offers the following suggestions, based on her experiences with a group of first graders: Include only five to seven children in the teacher-supervised booktime reading group. Have booktime occur at the same time every day, so that it becomes part of the children's routine. Begin with a period of five minutes or so and work up to a period of ten to fifteen minutes. Encourage each child to choose a different book, but allow pairs of children to read the same book together, if this arrangement seems likely to be more motivating. Let the children share ideas by speaking quietly to one another. At other times during the day, be sure to read aloud to the children, and to place the books read in an area where they are readily accessible.

Making the Most of Visits to the Library

Prepare the children for visits to the school or community library so they will know how to use the time to find books they will enjoy reading. Discuss with the class as a whole, or with individuals, topics or types of books they might find interesting. With reluctant readers, you might begin by tying the reading of library books to their other interests, in computers, popular music, dancing, television shows, car racing, and so on.

▌ THINKING ABOUT THE ELEMENTS IN STORIES

Children's understanding and enjoyment of literature may be enhanced if they become familiar with the different elements within stories. We present below two somewhat different ways of looking at story elements, as well as ideas for helping children learn about them.

Story Structure

What exactly is a story? While it is possible to come up with many different definitions, Stein and Policastro (1984) suggest that we think of good stories as those which involve some kind of *conflict* or problem and draw some kind of emotional *response.* In addition, many simple stories have the following *structure* or *grammar* (Stein & Nezworski, 1977):

> *Setting*—The main character is introduced and the time and place of the story may be described.
> *Initiating event*—Something happens which leads the character to think about trying to achieve some goal.
> *Internal response*—The character has thoughts or feelings about the situation.
> *Attempt*—The character takes action to reach his or her goal.
> *Consequence*—There is some outcome, successful or not, because of the character's action.
> *Reaction*—The character has thoughts or feelings about the course of action or goal.

In exploring further the basic idea that reading is the process of constructing meaning from text, we see that children learn gradually to comprehend more complicated stories as they move through the grades. Over this time they develop an increasingly refined concept of what a story is (e.g., Applebee, 1978) and an awareness of story structure (e.g., Stein & Glenn, 1979), as outlined above. In general, older children, in the fifth grade and above, seem better able to recall and retell stories which do not have a standard structure or do not present events in chronological order (Stein & Nezworski, 1977). This is because they already have considerable knowledge of story structure which they can use to help them understand and remember stories. They are also better able to remember the characters' internal responses and reactions than younger children, who tend to focus on the consequence alone (Stein & Glenn, 1979).

In short, story comprehension, like text comprehension in general, develops over time and can be improved through instruction.

Teaching About Story Structure

Gordon and Braun (1983a) developed procedures to teach children about story structure. The purpose of this program was to improve children's ability to comprehend stories, as well as to write stories on their own, and it was used successfully with fifth graders (Gordon & Braun, 1983b).

Figure 3.1 shows a simplified diagram for classroom use. This is an "ideal" story structure, one containing all elements in a straightforward order. Many actual stories will not contain all of these elements, and parts within each episode may occur in a different order from that shown. Folk tales, fairy tales, and fables, especially those in which a pattern of events is repeated, will lend themselves well to lessons on story structure.

Gordon and Braun (1983a) suggest the following steps:

1. Begin with an "ideal" story such as "The Owl and the Raven" to provide an overview of structure and to introduce story grammar terminology.

Figure 3.1
Schematic Representation
of Story Structure

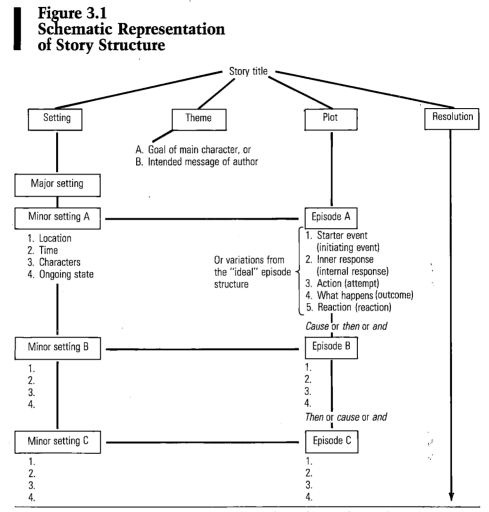

Source: From "Using story schema as an aid to reading and writing" by Christine Gordon and Carl Braun, *The Reading Teacher,* November 1983. Copyright © 1983 International Reading Association, Inc. Reprinted with permission of Christine Gordon and the International Reading Association.

Use a diagram of the story and fill in story information under each category as content is elicited from the children. . . . Give the children copies of the diagram minus the story information. They then write the paraphrased story content on their own copies.

2. Set reading purposes by posing schema-related questions prior to having children read a story segment. Elicit responses to the question after the reading.

3. Use well organized stories initially and the inductive teaching approach. Have children first identify the major setting in each of three different stories, then the starter event of the first episode in each of three differ-

ent stories, and so on, before trying to identify all story components in one section. Thus the structure element is held constant while story content is varied.

4. When children can associate story content with specific text structure categories on the diagrammed stories, begin asking the story-specific questions. Continue to expect paraphrased story content as answers.

5. Gradually introduce less well organized narratives, so children will learn that not all stories are "ideal" in structure.

6. To help children handle structure variability, use the macrocloze technique on transparencies and individual structure sheets for less well organized stories. In macrocloze, some categories already contain story content; others are left blank for the children to complete.

7. Guide children to start asking their own schema-related or story-specific questions before reading. Have them read to find answers for their own oral or written questions. Knowledge of story grammar will serve as a framework on which to develop the prereading questions. (pp. 119–121)

Gordon and Braun suggest that knowledge of story structure can also be of benefit when children write. The teacher might begin by guiding the group in composing a brief story with one or two episodes. Then students might work together in a small group to compose a story, without the teacher's help. The teacher can have the students identify the components in their group story, and students may revise the story to add missing components. Finally, students can be encouraged to apply their knowledge of story structure when composing their own individual stories.

Literary Criticism

A second view of story elements is that which a literary critic might take. This view suggests concepts and terms children can be taught to enhance their understanding and appreciation of stories. Cullinan (1981) recommends, however, that the teacher keep to the following guidelines:

> The literary concepts that a structuralist approach emphasizes can and should be taught to children, but only when they are ready to learn them—when they have a need to know and an experiential base upon which to anchor the concepts. Labels without concepts are detrimental to children's growth in the study of literature and often obscure the areas of study that need to be emphasized. Teachers aware of literary concepts *and* the levels of children's development can provide information and support when it is appropriate. (p. 497)

The following list of major literary elements, proposed by Lukens (1990), should give you an idea of the concepts and terms to be introduced to your students, particularly those in the upper grades. A realistic approach is to teach children about a particular element only when it is especially important in the story they are reading. But over time, whether you are using books or basal reader stories, all of these elements can be touched upon.

1. *Character:* The person or, as is often the case with children's stories, the personified animal or object involved in the action of the story. You can teach children to learn about characters by reading about their actions, speech, and appearance, or the comments of other characters or the narrator. Children can also be introduced to the idea of *character development*, that the character may change over the course of the story.
2. *Plot:* The order of events in a story, showing the actions of the characters, and usually involving some kind of *conflict*. Children can be taught to look for a *sequence* of events and to identify the problem the characters face. You can also point out that the author may choose to present events in *chronological order* or with *flashbacks*.
3. *Setting:* The time and place of the story, usually described in some detail. Children can be taught to identify both. You can help them distinguish between stories in which the setting is merely a *backdrop* or relatively unimportant to the plot, or much more *integral* or important.
4. *Theme:* The idea that helps tie all other story elements together, that gives the story some overall meaning. Often, the theme is a truth about the human condition which the author wishes to convey. You can teach children to look for the theme of the story and point out to them that we often remember the theme after other details have been forgotten. Perhaps using the terms in parentheses, you can also teach them that themes may be *explicit* (obvious) or *implicit* (hidden or only suggested). There can also be *primary* (important or major) themes and *secondary* (less important or minor) themes. Teachers should be aware, too, that certain stories written for children, such as some adventure or humorous works, do not necessarily have a theme.
5. *Point of view:* The perspective taken in the telling of the story. Teach children to recognize different points of view and how they can give a particular slant to the information presented. Sometimes one of the characters tells the story; this is the *first-person* point of view. At other times, the story is told from an *omniscient* or all-seeing point of view, which allows the writer to present the thoughts and feelings of several characters. There is also the *objective* point of view, where the writer concentrates simply on describing events, leaving interpretation to the reader.
6. *Style:* The author's use of words, how language is used to create an effect. As Lukens (1990) puts it, style is "*how* an author says something, as opposed to *what* he or she says" (p. 139). You can point out to your students examples of figurative language, hyperbole and understatement, puns and word play, and words and phrases with interesting or appealing sounds. With this approach your goal is to give them an appreciation for beautiful or effective use of language, and literary terms do not necessarily have to be used.
7. *Tone:* Use of style to convey the author's feeling about the subject of his or her writing. Teach children that tone has to do with the author's atti-

tude toward the story and its readers and may reveal aspects of his or her personality. Help your students learn to recognize different kinds of tone, whether the story is light-hearted and humorous, gentle and warm, or grand and heroic.

In this key concept you became familiar with different genres of children's literature, and you learned about story and literary elements you may wish to teach your students. We also emphasized the connection between children's appreciating literature and wanting to read on their own. Now we will shift the focus somewhat, by turning to a detailed discussion of instructional frameworks for developing students' ability to comprehend stories.

Key Concept 2

The teacher should have a purpose for having students read a particular story, and should follow systematic procedures for planning and conducting story comprehension lessons.

FRAMEWORKS FOR STORY COMPREHENSION LESSONS

These frameworks include prereading, guided reading, and postreading phases and can be used to organize a series of lessons based on the same story text. Besides giving children a thorough understanding of the story being read, they have the potential to improve children's overall ability to comprehend stories.

Inferential Comprehension Strategy

The purpose of this strategy is to improve children's ability to make inferences about text. Hansen (1981) initially tested this lesson framework with second graders, and later adapted it for use with poor readers in the fourth grade (Hansen & Hubbard, 1984; Hansen & Pearson, 1983). Basal reader stories were used, but other texts could easily be substituted. In this procedure, four lessons are needed for each story.

Planning. Preview the story and select three important ideas, or ideas that it might be difficult for the children to understand. Write two questions for each idea: (1) about aspects of the children's experience related to the idea, and (2) about a story-specific prediction.

Hansen (1981) gives this example of a pair of questions:

For example, in one story the isolated idea was that when people are embarrassed they break eye contact. In the story, Dick looked at his feet when a barber expressed displeasure about Dick's dog. The previous experience question was, "What do you do when you feel embarrassed?" [The prediction question was] "In our story, Dick feels embarrassed when the barber asks him if Stanley is his dog. What do you think he will do?" (p. 667)

Day 1: Introduce new vocabulary words. The inferential comprehension strategy does not require any one way of doing this. For ideas, you may wish to refer to Chapter 5 or to the basal series teacher's guide.

Day 2: Using each of your three pairs of questions, discuss with the children background knowledge they might use to draw inferences about the story and have them come up with predictions. For each question asked, have the children write their individual response. Allow the children time to discuss and exchange ideas before having them write. Encourage a diversity of responses rather than pressing the children to reach agreement.

Day 3: Have the children read the story, following a normal guided reading procedure. That is, have the children read a portion of the story, then stop for discussion, read again, stop for discussion, and so on until the story is finished. At this point in her study, Hansen gave the children a worksheet with ten open-ended questions. You might use such a worksheet for seatwork to be completed on Days 3 and 4.

Day 4: Provide the children with instruction in word recognition. Again, no specific procedures are required as part of the inferential comprehension strategy, so you may wish to refer to Chapter 7 or the teacher's guide.

The inferential comprehension strategy, like the experience-text-relationship method, builds on children's background knowledge and encourages prediction. It differs from this other lesson framework, however, in focusing specifically on children's ability to make inferences and to write out their responses.

Central Story Content Lessons

Beck, Omanson, and McKeown (1982) developed and tested a reading lesson framework for use with basal reader stories, to highlight central story content for children and reduce potential comprehension problems. This framework recognizes the critical role of background knowledge and the importance of focusing children's attention on important, rather than unimportant, story information. The method used to identify important story information was based on use of a story map (Beck & McKeown, 1981; Omanson, 1982). Use of this lesson framework improved third graders' ability to recall information and answer questions about the story.

The four lesson components redesigned by Beck et al. are:

1. pre-story preparation
2. pre-SRU (silent reading unit) preparation
3. illustrations accompanying the text
4. post-SRU questions

We present below recommendations which are adaptations of the procedures used by Beck et al.:

1. *Pre-story preparation.* When planning the lesson, identify the key concepts in the story. Design questions or activities to familiarize children with these concepts or, if they already know them, to call their attention to their importance. One of the stories used in the study by Beck et al. was entitled "The Raccoon and Mrs. McGinnis." Mrs. McGinnis' wish came true because of a series of coincidences. Thus, the concept of coincidence was targeted.

2. *Pre-SRU preparation.* This has to do with activities to prepare children for the story segment about to be read. Design these activities (usually, questions or explanations) to serve two purposes: first, to call children's attention to important events in the story segment to be read next; and second, to activate concepts covered in the pre-story preparation.

3. *Illustrations.* The important point about illustrations is that they should aid story comprehension. They can do this if they reinforce central story content, but not if they deal with minor details or conflict with the text. Examine the illustrations carefully and plan to call children's attention only to those which accurately depict central story content.

4. *Post-SRU questions.* These are intended to help the children "envision" the main events in the story. Design questions to target the main events and avoid asking questions on details irrelevant to the main events. Work out questions which cover events in the order of their occurrence in the story.

Figure 3.2 shows a sample story map and the post-SRU questions which grow logically from it. The story, "A Big Lunch for Father" (Marshall, 1983), is representative of those appearing in preprimers, reading textbooks often used with children in kindergarten and first grade. At the top of the figure are summary statements of the central theme, or the important idea a teacher might decide to develop, and the problem.

The story map helps the teacher to see appropriate pre-SRU questions for "A Big Lunch for Father." The theme has to do with surprises and the problem is that the children have to take their father his lunch. It would be logical, then, for the teacher to begin a lesson on this story by developing the concepts of running errands and of being surprised. Questions about running errands might include the following:

Do you ever run errands to help your mother and father?
What kinds of errands do you do?
Have you ever had trouble while running an errand?
What happened?

Questions about surprises might include:

Have you ever been surprised?
What happened to surprise you?

Figure 3.2
Story Map and Questions for
"A Big Lunch for Father"

Central theme: The children set out to surprise Father, but they are the ones who get surprised instead, first because the picnic basket is empty, and second because Father gives them a "big lunch" of fish.

Problem: Amy and Sam have to take Father his lunch.

Questions: What did Mother ask Amy and Sam to do?
Who were the children going to surprise?

Episode #1: Amy and Sam stop for a swim and a frog takes some of the lunch.

Questions: What did Amy and Sam want to do?
What happened while they were swimming?

Episode #2: They stop to look at some pigs and a rooster takes some of the lunch.

Questions: What did they stop to look at?
What happened to the lunch?

Episode #3: They stop to take a nap and a fox takes some of the lunch.

Questions: What did Amy and Sam do next?
What happened while they were napping?

Episode #4: They find father, who is sitting on the pier fishing. Sam says, "Surprise, Father!" and the children hand him the picnic basket. But when Father looks inside it, he finds there is nothing there.

Questions: Where did Amy and Sam find Father?
What was he doing?
What did Sam say when he saw Father?
What problem did Father discover?
How did Amy and Sam feel then?

Resolution: Father has caught some fish which he suggests they eat for lunch instead.

Questions: What happened at the end of the story?
What did they eat instead?

Questions to get at the central theme:
Who was supposed to be surprised?
Who got surprised instead?
What two things happened to surprise the children?

Exercise

The purpose of this exercise is to familiarize you with the use of story maps for planning lessons.

(1) Select a story which might be taught to a group of elementary school students. The story may be from a tradebook or from a basal reader.

(2) Begin by reading the story carefully. Identify the central theme or important idea you would like the students to grasp. Write this information in a box at the top of a sheet of paper, as shown in Figure 3.2. If you aren't certain about the central theme or important idea you want to develop, go on to Step 3.

(3) Identify one or more concepts to be brought out in the prereading or pre-SRU phase of the lesson, and write these below the central theme box. For examples, see the prereading questions developed for "A Big Lunch for Father."

(4) Make a map for the story along the lines of that shown in Figure 3.2. If this particular type of mapping doesn't fit your story, refer to the discussion of the story structure approach under Key Concept #1 for other ideas about mapping. Or develop your own variety of map. Remember that the main reason for mapping is to understand how the story is structured, not to force the story into a certain form of map.

If you have not yet written out the central theme or important idea, do so now.

(5) Develop at least one question for each item in your story map, as shown in Figure 3.2. Be sure to develop a set of questions to bring out the central theme.

(6) If you have the opportunity, use the story map and questions developed in this exercise as the basis for teaching a reading lesson to a group of students. Compare this lesson to others you have taught, when you did not use story mapping to aid in your planning. Did story mapping help you to teach story comprehension more effectively? If so, why do you think it helped?

Have you ever tried to surprise someone else?
Were you successful?

Episodes in the story and the resolution of the problem are shown in the other boxes in Figure 3.2. Questions appropriate for each part of the story are listed below the relevant boxes. The set of questions at the bottom of the figure is designed to allow the teacher to reinforce the children's understanding of the central theme.

Unlike the inferential comprehension strategy, the central story content approach does not emphasize the making of predictions. It is similar, however, in building on children's background knowledge. Perhaps the outstanding feature of this approach is that it directs children's attention to important story information and so is likely to lead to their understanding the theme of the story.

You may have noticed that central story content lessons are much like experience-text-relationship (ETR) lessons. Pre-SRU questions are those which would generally occur during the experience phase of ETR lessons. Most post-SRU questions, those about particular episodes in the story, would occur during the text phase of ETR lessons. Finally, questions to reinforce children's understanding of the central theme would usually occur during the relationship phase of ETR lessons.

▌ INSTRUCTIONAL ACTIVITIES
Using Seatwork to Improve Students' Comprehension Ability

In addition to receiving teacher-led lessons to develop their comprehension ability, students will also benefit from independent practice activities. In other words, the teacher first teaches students about some aspect of comprehension. Then the teacher gives students a seatwork assignment to be completed independently. This assignment is designed to have students apply on their own the strategies, concepts, and other new information just gained from the lesson.

In Chapter 2 we described a series of experience-text-relationship lessons based on a story entitled "Little Hippo." In that series of lessons we showed you how the teacher ended each lesson by explaining their seatwork assignment to the students. The teacher made certain that students understood how the assignment was related to the lesson they had just received. The next day, the teacher often began the lesson by referring back to the seatwork assignment and having students share their work.

In the following section, we describe three formats for independent seatwork assignments (Scheu, Tanner, & Au, 1986). These formats were tested with children in a second grade classroom, but they may be adapted for use with younger and older students. However, it is important for you to remember that worksheets like these, even when carefully designed, need to be *directly related to the lessons* you are giving your students. Independent assignments and lessons should be closely tied together as part of an instructional cycle.

The example below is based on a basal story entitled "What Mary Jo Shared" (Udry, 1976). The story is about Mary Jo's worries about not knowing what to bring for her class' daily sharing time. One day she decides to share her new umbrella, but she finds that many other children have umbrellas, too. Another day she decides to share her grasshopper, only to notice that someone else has five grasshoppers! The problem grows larger and larger in Mary Jo's mind. Finally, she comes up with the solution of taking her father to school for sharing time.

In the following section we discuss how the teacher planned her lessons, integrating independent seatwork activities with instruction, and present the sample worksheet formats. They were designed to provide practice with (1) vocabulary development, (2) main idea, and (3) sequencing.

Vocabulary Development

Planning. The teacher used two criteria to select vocabulary words: how important the words were to the story and whether they were likely to cause the students difficulty. These were usually words the children knew in spoken but not printed form. She focused on the words during the small group lesson and also included them in the worksheet she prepared for the students.

Example. On the first day the teacher planned to have the children read the first four pages of the story. From these pages she selected the vocabulary words *share, before, listen, owned, shook, afraid, hardly,* and *many.* During the lesson she checked to see if students knew the words. Words they did not know were discussed in the context of the story. The general format the teacher used for the students' worksheet is shown in Figure 3.3. In Figure 3.4 you see how the teacher added information to the worksheet from the story "What Mary Jo Shared," so that the worksheet could be assigned to the students for independent practice.

On another day, the teacher touched upon the skill of classification during the lesson, when she had the students discuss things that would be good or not good for sharing time. Students practiced and reviewed both central vocabulary and classification skills in a worksheet using the format shown in Figure 3.5. At the top of the first column, the teacher wrote "Things Good to Share," and at the top of the second column, "Things Not Good to Share." The students chose the words for each column from a word bank containing the following items: schoolbag, elephant, breakfast, grasshopper, cornfield, moon, kitten, umbrella, mountain, letter, window, and frog. Some of these words were from "What Mary Jo Shared," and others were from stories read earlier.

Main Idea

Planning. When first thinking about the lessons for the story, the teacher identified an overarching theme to be used to focus the discussion. After the children were starting to grasp the theme, the teacher reinforced their understanding in their worksheets.

Example. The teacher selected "facing fears" as a suitable theme for "What Mary Jo Shared." She decided not to have the students do an entire worksheet only on the main idea. Instead, she embedded work with the main idea in worksheets on vocabulary and sequencing. In the vocabulary work-

∎ Figure 3.3
Vocabulary Worksheet

Name _____   _____

Vocabulary   _____

```
┌─────────────────────────────────────────────────────────────────────────┐
│                              *Word Bank*                                  │
│                                                                           │
└─────────────────────────────────────────────────────────────────────────┘
```

Directions: Fill in the blanks using words from the <u>Word</u> <u>Bank</u>.

_____

_____

_____

_____

_____

_____

_____

_____

_____

_____

Directions: Think about the above story as you answer these questions.

_____

_____

_____

_____

_____

_____

_____

Source: Figures 3.3, 3.4, 3.5, and 3.6 from "Designing seatwork to improve students' reading comprehension ability" by Judith Scheu, Diane Tanner, Kathryn Hu-pei Au, *The Reading Teacher,* vol. 40, no. 1, October 1986. Copyright © 1986 International Reading Association, Inc. Reprinted by permission.

▍ **Figure 3.4**
Vocabulary Worksheet for
"What Mary Jo Shared"

Name _____ Cloverleaf – p. 180 - 183

Vocabulary "What Mary Jo Shared"

afraid	before	*Word Bank*	shared	shook
many	listen		owned	hardly

Directions: Fill in the blanks using words from the <u>Word Bank</u>.

Mary Jo never _____ anything at school.
She was afraid to stand _____ the
other children and tell about anything. She
didn't think they would _____ to her. Mary Jo
really did want to share, but she was _____
to try. One morning it was raining. Mary Jo
could _____ wait for school. She was going to
share the first umbrella she had ever _____.
At school she saw _____ other umbrellas. When
Miss Willet asked her to share, she _____ her head.

Directions: Think about the above story as you answer these questions.

1. What problem does Mary Jo have at school everyday?
   _____

   _____

2. Why is Mary Jo afraid to share?
   _____

3. How do you think Mary Jo will solve her problem?
   _____

   _____

█ **Figure 3.5**
Classification Worksheet

Name _____   _____

Classification   _____

Directions: Group words from the BANK under each title below.

_____

_____	_____
_____	_____
_____	_____
_____	_____
_____	_____
_____	_____
_____	_____

Think about the story as you answer these questions:

_____

_____

_____

_____

_____

_____

_____

sheet she inserted the question: "What problem does Mary Jo have at school every day?" (as shown in Figure 3.4, question 1). In the sequencing worksheet she prepared for the last day's work with the story, she placed the question: "In what important way was Mary Jo like Henry?" (a character in another story who also had fears).

Sequencing

Planning. When preparing her lesson, the teacher determined whether a certain sequence of events brought out the theme of the story. If such a sequence could be found, the teacher had students identify these events during lessons and review them in seatwork assignments. When students were completing these particular worksheets, they were practicing sequencing and at the same time learning about the story's theme.

Many stories have the elements of problems, events, and resolution. After students have learned about these elements, they can apply this knowledge as they complete the reading of a given story. The final worksheet they complete can provide for a review, in terms of story elements, and for interpretation of the theme.

Example. In "What Mary Jo Shared" the teacher guided the students to see the steps Mary Jo took to solve her problem. She related these events to the theme of "facing fears." Students then reviewed the sequence of events independently, in a sequencing worksheet, as shown in Figure 3.6. Under the directions at the top, the teacher inserted the following sentences:

Mary Jo was happy about sharing her father.
Mary Jo took her grasshopper to school.
Mary Jo had a bad dream about sharing.
Mary Jo was afraid to share.
Mary Jo took her umbrella to school.

Benefits of integrated seatwork. What benefits can you expect from using this approach of linking reading lessons with carefully designed seatwork assignments? Scheu et al. found that students benefited in the following ways:

We discovered that as the teacher introduced and discussed the worksheets at the end of the reading lesson, the students began showing an awareness of the connections. After a time, they were able to differentiate between their own worksheets and those prepared for other reading groups by looking for the name of their basal story in the corner of the page.

These second graders were also able to identify purposes of the worksheets other than "getting it done." For example, when practicing a sequencing activity, they could explain that "This is how our story went." When asked "Where did your teacher get the words for this worksheet?" they could answer, "They're from our story." When asked why the teacher had chosen those particular words, they replied, "So we can learn the hard words."

Students were also observed to show a greater awareness of the theme of the story, both in teacher-led lessons and in completing worksheets. They started to realize that all stories had certain elements in common. As one student remarked, "It seems like there are problems in all our stories." (pp. 24–25)

Earlier in this chapter we discussed procedures for helping students learn about story structure. Cudd and Roberts (1987) developed an approach based on story frames, which cover the same elements as story structure training. Their approach is similar in design and intent to the approach developed by Scheu et al., in integrating independent practice assignments and instruction. In the approach developed by Cudd and Roberts, primary grade students are provided with instruction on the elements in stories. As students become familiar with story elements, the teacher has them work with story frames. A

▌Figure 3.6
Sequencing Worksheet

Name _____   _____

Sequencing   _____

Directions: Read these sentences.

_____

_____

_____

_____

_____

Directions: Write the sentences as they happened in the story.

1. _____

2. _____

3. _____

4. _____

5. _____

Directions: Think about the sentences as you answer these questions.

_____

_____

_____

_____

_____

story frame provides students with sentence starters. To complete the sentences correctly, students have to think about the main events and important ideas in the story.

A basic frame, which does not require students to know the sequence of events, is shown in Figure 3.7. A frame which would be somewhat more difficult for students to complete, because it requires an understanding of the sequence of events, is shown in Figure 3.8. Refer to the article by Cudd and Roberts (1987) for designs for four other story frames. One of the advantages of the story frame approach, and of the approach developed by Scheu et al., is that both give primary grade students a start in writing about their reading.

▮ **Figure 3.7**
Basic Frame with No Sequence
of Events

Title ___The New Pet___

The problem in this story was ___Chen wanted a___

___puppy.___

This was a problem because ___his appartment was too___

___small for a dog.___

The problem was finally solved when ___his mother got___

___him a kitten.___

In the end, ___Chen played with the kitten.___

Source: Examples 1 and 2 from "Using story frames to develop reading comprehension in a 1st grade classroom" by Evelyn T. Cudd and Leslie L. Roberts, *The Reading Teacher*, October 1987. Copyright © 1987 International Reading Association, Inc. Reprinted with permission of Evelyn T. Cudd and the International Reading Association.

▮ **Figure 3.8**
Basic Story Frame

Title ___The Best Birthday___

In this story the problem starts when ___Maria gets sick and___
___she can't have a birthday party.___

After that, ___her friends want to make her___
___feel better.___

Next, ___they go get a clown and ask___
___him to help.___

Then, ___the clown goes to Maria's___
___house.___

The problem is finally solved when ___the clown makes___
___Maria laugh.___

The story ends ___when Maria says this is___
___the best birthday ever.___

Key Concept 3

The teacher should give children opportunities to use writing to clarify thoughts about stories and literature.

USING WRITING TO CLARIFY THOUGHTS ABOUT A NOVEL

In Chapter 2 we described the process approach to writing and some of its benefits. One of the benefits we did not discuss then is that, when students have become comfortable with expressing their thoughts in writing, they can use writing to express their thoughts and feelings about novels. Writing is one way that students can respond to literature. Writing is especially useful when students are exploring the complexities of a novel, because writing often encourages deeper thinking about the text.

We recommend that teachers working with students in the second grade and above center their reading instruction on full-length novels, at least part of the time. The approach we will be describing for teaching reading with novels (based on Au & Scheu, 1988) is appropriate for students in the third grade and above and may be adapted for use with second graders. The value of having students read entire novels, rather than shorter selections or excerpts, comes in the rich literary understandings they develop, as you will see in the example, centered on *Sadako and the Thousand Paper Cranes.* This novel by Eleanor Coerr is the story of a young girl who develops leukemia after being exposed to radiation from the atomic bomb dropped on the city of Hiroshima during World War II.

Two components of the approach will be emphasized here:

1. Teacher-led small group lessons;
2. Work with learning guides.

You are already quite familiar with procedures for conducting small group reading comprehension discussions, such as responsive questioning, and you will see in the sample lessons how the teacher made use of these procedures.

Learning guides are teacher-created worksheets kept together in folders for individual students. In the observations presented below, you will see that the writing students do in their learning guides prepares them to contribute ideas during small group discussions. It is the combination of writing assignments and discussions that helps build students' understanding of the novel.

In addition to thinking about how writing assignments and discussions work together, there are two other points you will want to consider as you read the observations below. First, you will want to notice the types of writing assignments the students were given. You will see that three of the assignments were quite structured, while others were open-ended. The structured assignments permitted the teacher to focus on instruction of specific comprehension strategies: identifying the important ideas and supporting details, using visual displays to organize information, and comparing and contrasting the first and second parts of a chapter.

Open-ended assignments, on the other hand, permitted students to explore their own envisionments of the novel, including their feelings and uncertainties. For example, students wrote diary entries, pretending that they were Sadako.

There seems to be a place for both types of writing. However, more capable readers and writers may not need as much work with structured assignments.

Second, you will want to notice how the students' understanding of and involvement with the novel steadily increased. At the beginning they did not grasp the difference between an important idea and a supporting detail and did not seem very committed to their reading and writing. However, as time went on, they developed a better grasp of important ideas and supporting details. Furthermore, their writing became lengthier and more interesting, and some even began urging others to do a better job!

To convey the flavor of this instructional approach, four days in the experiences of a group of fourth graders will be described. The observations were made in B. J. Moffett's classroom, and the students were in the third of four reading groups.

Observations are given by date so you can judge the amount of time that passed in between. For each of the four days we tell you about the independent writing assignments the students did and show how students' writing was made a part of the teacher-guided lesson.

Observations of January 11th: Important ideas and supporting details

On this day, as on all others, the teacher began the group's lesson by having the students share the work they had done. Their learning guide page is shown in Figure 3.9. Students were supposed to write about the two important ideas in Chapter 3, with a supporting detail for each.

From the perspective of an adult reader, it was fairly obvious that the two major ideas in Chapter 3 were:

1. Sadako was chosen for her school's relay team, which was to compete during the race at the Peace Day gathering.
2. Sadako became dizzy during the race, the first sign that she was ill.

Only one of the students, Albert, was able to identify both important ideas and provide supporting details. He wrote:

> *Main idea:* She got picked for the race.
> *Details:* She felt happy. She was excited.
> *Main idea:* She was dizzy.
> *Details:* She did not tell no one.
>   It started [during] the race.

▌ Figure 3.9
▌ Worksheet for Chapter 3

REVIEW

Chapter 2 was about _____

_____

IMPORTANT IDEA & DETAILS

Two main things happen in Chapter 3. Tell what each is and details about them.

1. Important idea: _____

_____

    Details: _____

_____

_____

2. Important idea: _____

_____

    Details: _____

_____

_____

Draw a picture to go with each.

1)	2)

▌ **Figure 3.10**
▌ **Visual Display for Chapter 3**

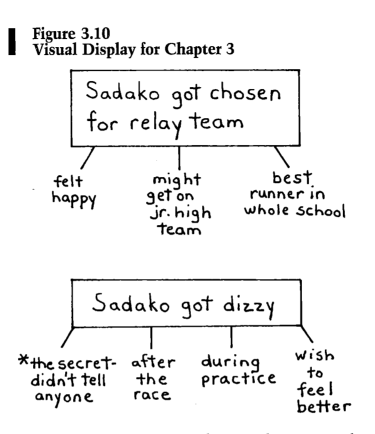

The other students' answers either mixed important ideas with supporting details, or used the same item more than once.

During the lesson the teacher soon discovered that the students did not understand the difference between an important idea and a supporting detail, or about the relationship between the two. At this point, she began a visual display (see Figure 3.10) to show the students that much of the information in Chapter 3 could be organized around the two important ideas. First, she drew two rectangles, one for each of the important ideas. Albert suggested what should go in the first rectangle: "She got picked."

"Chosen for the relay race," the teacher said, rewording his answer. Through questioning she elicited supporting details, as shown in the figure. She followed a similar process for the second important idea and its supporting details.

You probably noticed how the teacher used the first part of the lesson to assess how much students knew, and then used modeling to show them how to organize their thoughts.

Observations of January 22nd: Putting story information in a visual display

Along with teaching the students about important ideas and supporting details, the teacher had them try to organize information by making their own visual displays. The directions on their learning guide page indicated that they should draw a visual display of the problem in the story and the main events. Although the students had seen the teacher model this procedure on many occasions, they had not had much practice making visual displays on their own.

When the students met for their reading lesson, the teacher discovered that three of the four had been able to write down the problem, that Sadako had leukemia. These students created visual displays with information at three levels. For example, the display Pete drew is shown in Figure 3.11.

The teacher started drawing a visual display to organize the ideas the students were presenting. The students agreed that the problem "Sadako has leukemia" should go in the center. Edward voluntarily shared much of the information from the chapter. The teacher asked, "What do we call what Edward is sharing?" "Details," the students answered. The teacher suggested that they slow down and think about the details from the chapter. She said she would add these details to the visual display.

Details concerning how Sadako developed leukemia and the nature of the disease elicited further discussion. "Why didn't she die right away?" the teacher asked. Albert knew that it took a while for the disease to progress.

"What will happen to Sadako now that she's in the hospital?" the teacher asked. The students replied that she would have tests and x-rays, and the teacher added this information to the visual display. "What about her running?" the teacher asked. "She might not be able to run any more," Linda answered. Later the teacher asked, "What does she know about people who go in the hospital?" "They never come out," Edward responded.

An interesting feature of this lesson was that the teacher retaught the concepts of important idea and supporting detail, but from a slightly different perspective. By now, the students had a much better grasp of the concepts and were better able to apply their knowledge to tasks based on the novel.

The students' next assignment was to write a diary entry, pretending that they were Sadako. Several of the students showed they not only understood the events in the story, but also how Sadako was feeling. Here is what Pete wrote:

> Dear Diary,
>
> When I ran to the school yard I fell and a teacher helped me up and I said I was ok in a weak voice. Then she told me to go home. And I had to go to the hospital. I [went] to the Red Cross hospital. They said I had leukemia but that's impossible.

Observations of February 5th: Comparing the first and second parts of the chapter

By the time the students reached the last chapters of *Sadako*, they had become engrossed in the story. Most were motivated to do a better job with their writing, in terms of both the quality and quantity of ideas.

On this day, the students were to complete a compare/contrast page in their learning guides. The task was to write in one column about how Sadako

▌ **Figure 3.11**
▌ **Visual Dispay for Chapter 4**

MAIN IDEA, NOTING DETAILS

Title of the Story: _____

DIRECTIONS: 1. Draw a visual display of the problem in the story and the main events.
              2. Put the problem in a box and put events and solutions in circles coming from the box.
              3. Other details and information can be written on lines coming from the circles.

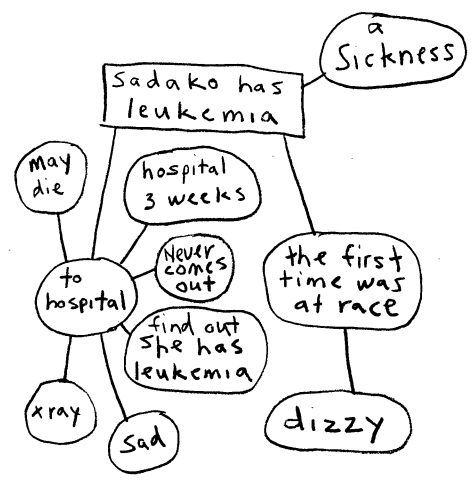

felt during the first part of the chapter, and in another column about how she felt during the second part of the chapter. For example, for the second part of the story Linda had written:

- she felt sad [because] she had the dizzy spells
- and she has to go back to the hospital
- [felt] the pain

- did not eat enough
- Sadako does not get to run or race any more
- her swollen gums hurt so much that she could not chew
- Sadako called [herself] a turtle
- kind of feels happy [because] she gets a kimono

Linda even went over to Edward's desk to look at his worksheet and to inform him that he needed to write more! At this point, then, the students were concerned not only about their own writing, but about the writing of others in their group.

When the teacher started the group's reading lesson, she began another visual display which she said she would organize in the same way as the learning guide page. As the discussion progressed, the teacher added information to the visual display.

Later in the discussion the teacher asked, "Is there anything else to show how she's feeling in the second part?" Linda shared that Sadako felt happy because she had been given a kimono. The teacher added this information to the visual display and asked why this made Sadako happy. The students answered that Sadako hadn't had a kimono before the race and had had to wear her mother's kimono.

The teacher then used responsive questioning to lead the students to understand that Sadako might feel a sense of guilt about the kimono. Although she was pleased to have it, she knew her parents had had to spend money, which had been difficult for them to obtain. Albert said that Sadako felt both happy and sad, and showed where that information was given in the text.

Near the end of the discussion, the teacher asked if Sadako could still make cranes. "She can barely make them," a student replied. The group discussed Sadako's thoughts, that one of her friends had died and she would be next.

"What makes her think that she still has hope?" the teacher asked. "The cranes," responded the students. "The cranes become a symbol," the teacher explained, writing the word *symbol* on the board. The students knew a flag was a kind of symbol, and the teacher helped them understand that a symbol stands for something. "Cranes are a symbol of what?" she asked. "Hope," said Albert.

Observations of February 8th: Open-ended writing

The students had finished reading the last chapter of *Sadako* and the teacher began the day's discussion by asking for a brief review of the previous chapter. Linda summarized the main points. Sadako had felt so good that she was able to go home. Then she felt bad and had to go back to the hospital.

As the discussion proceeded, one student mentioned how difficult it had become for Sadako to fold the cranes. To help the students understand the significance of this idea, the teacher asked, "How much strength do you think it takes to fold an origami crane?" The students compared the folding of a crane to the folding of a paper airplane. This comparison helped them recognize that Sadako had very little strength left. They knew this was evidence of how serious her illness had become.

The students had worked on a learning guide page asking them to write about the chapter. Albert shared his writing with the group:

> Sadako [was] thinking [what it would] be like dying. She was trying to fold another crane but she was too weak. The doctor made her go to sleep. She woke up. Everybody was there. Sadako slept again and never woke up.

Edward was disturbed by the information that Sadako's family had been with her as she died. He didn't think he would want to be present when anyone was dying. The teacher helped the students understand that often people want to be there because "it's their last chance to say goodbye." Linda related this to her experience when her grandfather had died. She shared how she and her family had felt at the time.

The teacher incorporated Linda's ideas as she focused the students' attention on the feelings of Sadako and her family. Edward read a section of the text describing their feelings. As the students discussed this section they came to understand that Sadako was not just thinking of herself, but also of her parents.

Albert suggested that Sadako's mother might have leukemia also. The teacher clarified the point that Sadako's mother had not been affected, although at one time she thought she might be. In order to help the students recognize the onset of the disease as a consequence of war, the teacher asked, "What does this tell you about the causes of radiation and the atom bomb?" One student replied that radiation "can go anywhere," implying that bombs do not discriminate among the people they affect.

The teacher asked, "What about Sadako and her family? Did they have anything to do with the war?" When students agreed they did not, the teacher asked, "What does that tell you about war?" One student showed a clear understanding of the author's message when he responded that "innocent people" are often the ones affected.

The students engaged in a lively discussion about conflict between countries and how such conflicts might be dealt with. They concluded that countries' leaders should talk together so that bombing could be avoided, because as Albert stated, "Radiation could kill everyone." Edward suggested that their reading group "talk with the Russian men and tell them about Sadako." Linda said, "We should send these books [Sadako] to the government and tell them to read it."

For their last learning guide assignment, the students were asked to complete a final page in Sadako's diary. The teacher said, "Pretend you're Sadako and you have the strength to write one more time. Write your feelings."

The group went to their desks and quickly became engaged in their writing task. Albert's piece revealed his own concerns, as well as his empathy for Sadako:

> This is the last thing I will do [because] in one second I will die. What would it be like dying? Would it be sore? Would I feel nothing? Or would it be like a shock?

As you can see, much of the value of this approach lies in the commitment students develop when they read a novel with a powerful message. Not all students are enthusiastic readers to begin with. When they start reading a novel, they may be rather indifferent. However, before long they are drawn into the novel. They are then able to grasp subtle and sophisticated ideas, and to draw relationships between the characters' experiences and events in their own lives. Their knowledge of reading concepts, such as important ideas and supporting details, also increases. Finally, they have the chance to share their thoughts and feelings about literature with their classmates and teacher.

In this approach it is important to take some time to think about the novels you will be asking your students to read, because study of a particular novel may continue for three weeks, a month, or even longer. Teachers use various selection criteria. For example, they look for novels with themes of relevance to students' lives, having character development and an interesting plot. They check to see if novels offer opportunities to develop students' vocabulary and appreciation for fine use of language. In many cases the novels teachers select are not like the books students choose to read on their own, but are much more challenging.

Other novels teachers have successfully used with this approach include:

Island of the Blue Dolphins by Scott O'Dell
Mrs. Frisby and the Rats of NIMH by Robert O'Brien
Pippi Longstocking by Astrid Lindgren
A Taste of Blackberries by Doris Buchanan Smith

∎ INSTRUCTIONAL ACTIVITIES
Open-Ended Writing Activities

Buckley (1986) suggests a number of writing activities students can work on with a partner before, during, or after the reading of a story. These activities allow students to integrate reading and writing while sharing their thoughts about literature with peers. Here are some possibilities for open-ended writing in response to reading, based on Buckley's ideas:

- Tell students the title of the story or novel they will be reading. Have partners make predictions about the text. Have them predict who the characters might be, what the story will be about, and when and where it takes place.
- Have partners meet to discuss and write a sequel to the story. They will continue the plot with new events and problems, even adding new characters if they wish.
- Discuss with students how the story was written from a certain point of view (e.g., it might have been told by one of the characters). Have partners discuss and write part of the story from another point of view.

Have them think of changes that might occur, due to the change in perspective.

- Have partners imagine that the story took place in another setting (e.g., in the city rather than the country, or in the present rather than in the past). Have them discuss and then write about how these changes would affect the characters and events.
- Have partners discuss and write a description of one of the characters, including her appearance, behavior, beliefs, and motives.
- Have partners discuss and write a letter to the main character. Ask them to include their opinions of what the character did, and any questions they want to ask the character. Students may exchange letters and write replies, answering as they think the character would.
- Have partners discuss and write a critique of the story, telling what they found exciting and interesting, and what they found boring. Have them include quotations or otherwise identify the part of the text that supports their opinions. Have students compare the story to another story, telling which they preferred and why.
- Have partners rewrite the story, or a scene from the story, in the form of a play. Be sure students understand how they may use a narrator to give the audience needed information. If students are interested, give them the opportunity to read or act out their play for the class.
- Have partners discuss and write about the similarities and differences between two characters in the story. Or have them compare a character in one story with a character from another story.

Although Buckley designed these activities to be used during the reading of basal reader stories, they can also be used when students are reading novels. Remember to give students adequate preparation for writing activities. For example, if students are engaging in a certain kind of writing activity for the first time, have them begin the assignment under your supervision. Remember also to tie writing activities to your reading lessons. For example, if you have spent time discussing the characters with students, it would be appropriate to have them write about the characters.

Finally, give students the chance to share their writing with classmates and with you. Students will usually put much more thought and effort into their writing if they know it will have an audience. And, as you saw in the sample lessons based on "What Mary Jo Shared" and *Sadako and the Thousand Paper Cranes*, having students share their writing is an excellent means of stimulating discussion about stories and novels.

Key Concept 4

The teacher should involve students with several books or stories related to a theme.

CREATING A LITERARY ENVIRONMENT THROUGH THEMATIC UNITS

Up to now, we have mainly discussed ways of involving students with individual works of literature. Yet students can gain even more if they have the opportunity to read several works of literature related to the same theme, and experience individual works as part of a unit of study. Many different themes might be pursued. The theme for some units might deal with an aspect of human experience, such as facing challenges. Other units might center on a particular children's author, such as Yoshiko Uchida, or on a particular genre, such as folktales. A unit with the theme of outer space might combine fiction and nonfiction reading. These are only a few examples, and you can probably think of many others.

There are several reasons why students might gain more from reading selections organized by thematic units than from reading unrelated selections. Reading related works gives them the opportunity to develop a deeper knowledge of particular topics and genres. By the second, third, or later works, students have considerable background knowledge of the theme and can com-

Students in this fourth grade class made models of their own cupboards, after reading the novel, *The Indian in the Cupboard.* Art activities are an excellent means of encouraging students to respond to literature.

pare and contrast one work with another. Also, voluntary reading is promoted over time, if students have had enough exposure to particular topics, genres, and authors to develop their own tastes in reading.

Thematic units need not be as elaborate as the focus units described below, and teachers certainly do not need to present all literature within thematic units. However, the focus unit approach does provide a framework for organizing the reading of several related books and a wide variety of activities.

Focus Units in Literature

Moss (1984) developed an instructional model based on the focus unit. The focus unit is an instructional sequence centered on literature and used to build students' comprehension ability and interest in literature.

In the focus unit approach, the teacher begins by setting goals and objectives. The overall goal is always to help students view literature as an important part of their lives, but each individual unit is also designed to accomplish more specific purposes, depending on the students' needs and interests. Next, the teacher chooses a focus or theme for the unit, such as survival tales, and identifies the books to be included in the unit. Books are chosen both for group story sessions and for students' independent reading.

For example, Moss developed a unit for grades one and two with a focus on friendship. In part, she chose this theme because it might provide children with insights into their own social relationships. In addition to the general goals of developing critical reading and writing skills, the unit included the specific objectives of improving students' story comprehension skills in terms of understanding the plot, logical relationships between story events, and characters' motives.

The focus unit approach has the following key elements:

1. story sessions
2. comparing stories and developing concepts
3. independent reading
4. creative writing
5. creative expression

Each of these elements will be explained more fully, with examples from the focus unit on friendship.

The story session. Perhaps the key element in each focus unit are the story sessions, which become part of the classroom routine. In a story session, the teacher reads aloud one or more selections and then leads the group in a discussion.

For example, the teacher opened the focus unit on friendship by reading aloud *Amos and Boris* by William Steig. This story tells of the friendship between a mouse and a whale who learn to appreciate one another's special qualities. Here is what happened during the story session:

After reading the story aloud, the teacher provided opportunities for spontaneous comments and then introduced questions about the narrative structure. For example, the questions, "What were the problems in the story?" and "How were they solved?" were used to focus attention on the plot. In response, one child explained, "First Amos [the mouse] was about to drown and Boris [the whale] saved him, and then Boris got stranded on land and Amos helped get him back to the water. They each had a problem and the other solved it!" . . . Questions about the characters in this story were intended to draw attention to the special relationship which developed between the tiny mouse and the enormous whale:

> How did these characters differ?
> How did they learn about each other?
> How do you think they felt about each other?
> How did they "show" their feelings?
> What did they enjoy doing together?

These questions encouraged discussion about building friendships and provided practice in the use of vocabulary associated with social skills and friendship interactions. (pp. 150–151)

The second group story session centered on *The Checker Players* by Arnold Venable, while the third was based on *Two Good Friends* by Judy Delton. Both books are about friendships between characters with very different personalities.

Comparing stories and developing concepts. Because stories are introduced in a well planned order, it becomes natural during later story sessions for the teacher and students to draw upon ideas discussed in earlier sessions. The cumulative nature of discussions is an important feature of the focus unit approach. All earlier stories and discussions form the context for developing concepts, making predictions, and drawing conclusions during the reading of each new work. Eventually, all of the selections read can be discussed in relationship to one another.

In the friendship focus unit other books used for reading included *Frog and Toad Are Friends* by Arnold Lobel, *Harlequin and the Gift of Many Colors* by Remy Charlip, *Here Comes the Strikeout* by Leonard Kessler, and *What's the Matter with Carruthers?* by James Marshall. Experiences with all of these books led children to see that compassion and sensitivity were important aspects of friendship. Here is Moss' description of what happened near the end of the focus unit:

> By the time the last book, *Timothy's Flower* by Jean Van Leeuwen, was read aloud, the children were ready to think about all the stories in the collection as a cohesive group bound by common themes. They identified these themes in the last group discussion:
>
> "Sometimes friends are really different like Duck and Bear . . . and that witch and the little bird . . ."
>
> "And Amos and Boris! And Spider Jane made friends with a fly! Spiders usually eat flies!"

"I liked Tawny and Dingo. Those two [a sheep dog and a lamb] were really different, but they were such great friends!"

"Sometimes the friends are more alike. In *Turtle and Snail* and *Fast Friends* . . . they're both about a turtle and a snail who start out being friends because of their shells."

"And Timothy gets to be friends with that lady because they both like flowers."

"And all those friends liked to do things together and they helped each other."

"And they liked to give presents to each other."

"And sometimes they got mad but they stayed friends and they tried to understand the other one." (pp. 154–55)

The children's comments suggest that they had achieved the goal of developing a better understanding of the nature of friendship.

Independent reading.   In each focus unit students also have the opportunity for independent reading of thematically related books. The books for independent reading should be selected so that there will be some suitable for every student in the class, given different interests and degrees of reading proficiency. There is a period of silent reading every day, and during the group story sessions, children are encouraged to speak about the books they have read independently. Students' personal reading experiences add another dimension to discussions, and if they have especially enjoyed a certain book, their classmates are likely to want to read it, too.

Among the books recommended for independent reading in the friendship focus unit are *The Tale of Tawny and Dingo* by William Armstrong, *Snowy and Woody* by Roger Duvoisin, *Evan's Corner* by Elizabeth S. Hill, *A Bargain for Frances* by Russell Hoban, and *Spider Jane* by Jane Yolen.

Creative writing.   In the focus unit approach, experiences with literature serve as a stimulus for creative writing. Students become acquainted with new words and ideas, with new genres, and with story elements. They learn about authors' styles and techniques. First through discussion, and then through writing, children have the chance to respond to different literary selections.

In the friendship focus unit, children engaged in a variety of group and independent projects growing from their reading experiences. For example, during the discussion of *Amos and Boris*, the teacher pointed out to the children that the whale and mouse could not stay together because they needed to live in different environments. The teacher asked the group, "Do any of you have a friend who lives far away?" The children discussed how difficult it was to be separated from a friend and how it might be possible to keep up a friendship over a long distance. This discussion led to a writing project in which children wrote letters to penpals, friends who lived far away, or children in other classrooms.

Later, the children were asked to think of a common theme for *Amos and Boris*, *The Checker Players*, and *Two Good Friends*. After they came up with some points they all agreed upon, the teacher wrote their ideas down on a large chart. Using the chart as a starting point, the children composed their own stories about friendships between two individuals very different from one another.

Creative expression.   Creative expression in focus units may involve art, drama, dance, and music. These activities give children other ways to respond to literature, as well as other ways to explore themes and concepts. Some activities are designed for the whole class and reinforce specific concepts developed in group story sessions. Children may choose other activities depending on their own interests.

In the friendship focus unit, other projects related to the reading of *Amos and Boris* included presenting the story or a favorite part of it in drama, art, music, or dance. Moss describes how one group of children decided to work together. Some acted as musicians and made sounds of the ocean. Others danced as if they were waves around the two children acting as Amos and Boris. Still others painted a mural of a seascape.

You have probably noticed that the focus unit approach could incorporate many of the literature activities and instructional strategies you have learned about in this chapter. For example, themes may be based on any of the genres of children's literature. Story sessions could be designed to teach children about story structure, or they could be used to bring out central story content. Writing activities might include those described in this chapter. Finally, independent reading within focus units might be supported through classroom libraries, sustained silent reading, and book sharing.

∎ SUMMARY

We began this chapter by discussing response to literature. We emphasized that teachers should consider both the shared meaning a literary work is likely to have for many readers, and the personal significance it may have for an individual reader. The practical implication here was that teachers should respect and accept their students' varying responses to literature.

In the first key concept we discussed how teachers could encourage students to respond to literature. We suggested that teachers give their students experiences with a variety of literary genres, including folktales, poetry, modern fiction, and biography. We showed how literature activities used in combination with well designed library corners could encourage voluntary reading. We recommended that students be taught about story structure and about literary elements.

Two general approaches for conducting story comprehension lessons were discussed in the second key concept: the inferential comprehension strategy and central story content lessons. We pointed out that students should have the opportunity to practice and apply reading comprehension strategies independently. For this reason, we recommended that teacher-directed lessons and students' independent assignments be tied together in the same instructional cycle. We gave some examples of assignments that could be used to build comprehension ability, for example, having students write about the sequence of events.

The message in the third key concept was that writing could be used to help students clarify their thoughts about literature. We showed how writing could be woven into the teaching of reading with a novel. In our example, the teacher often began lessons by having students share their writing. We suggested that students' writing served as a means of getting them to think more deeply about the novel, laying the foundation for rich group discussions. We also presented some ideas for having students work with partners to discuss and write about stories and novels.

In the fourth key concept we explored the idea of the thematic unit or focus unit. In these units teachers present students with the opportunity to read stories with others, to read stories on their own, and to discuss all of the reading they have done. Students also have the chance to respond to literature through creative writing and expression. The advantage of the thematic unit is that it allows students to explore a theme in depth, and to see relationships among several works of literature. An overall theme in this chapter was that understanding and appreciation of literature are fostered when students have the opportunity to share their thoughts and feelings about their reading with the teacher and with one another.

▌ BIBLIOGRAPHY

References

Applebee, A. N. (1978). *The child's concept of story: Ages two to seventeen.* Chicago: University of Chicago Press.

Au, K. H., & Scheu, J. A. (1988, May). Writing to clarify thoughts about literature. Paper presented at the Annual Meeting of the International Reading Association, Toronto.

Beck, I. L., & McKeown, M. G. (1981). Developing questions that promote comprehension: The story map. *Language Arts, 58* (8), 913–918.

Beck, I. L., Omanson, R. C., & McKeown, M. G. (1982). An instructional redesign of reading lessons: Effects on comprehension. *Reading Research Quarterly, 17* (4), 462–481.

Buckley, M. H. (1986). When teachers decide to integrate the language arts. *Language Arts, 63* (4), 369–377.

Cleary, D. (1978). *Thinking Thursdays: Language arts in the reading lab.* Newark, DE: International Reading Association.

Cramer, B. B (1984). Bequest of wings: Three readers and special books. *Language Arts, 61* (3), 253–260.

Cudd, E. T., & Roberts, L. L. (1987). Using story frames to develop reading comprehension in a 1st grade classroom. *The Reading Teacher, 41* (1) 74–79.

Cullinan, B. E. (1981). *Literature and the child*. New York: Harcourt Brace Jovanovich.

Dillon, D. (1984). Editor's note. *Language Arts, 61* (3), 227.

Elley, W., & Mangubhai, F. (1983). The impact of reading on second language learning. *Reading Research Quarterly, 19*, 53–67.

Gordon, C., & Braun, C. (1983a). Using story schema as an aid to reading and writing. *The Reading Teacher, 37*, 116–121.

Gordon, C., & Braun, C. (1983b). Teaching story schema: Metatextual aid to reading and writing. Paper presented at the Annual Meeting of the American Educational Research Association, Montreal.

Hansen, J. (1981). An inferential comprehension strategy for use with primary grade children. *The Reading Teacher, 34*, 665–669.

Hansen, J., & Hubbard, R. (1984). Poor readers can draw inferences. *The Reading Teacher, 37* (7), 586–589.

Hansen, J., & Pearson, P. D. (1983). An instructional study: Improving the inferential comprehension of fourth-grade good and poor readers. *Journal of Educational Psychology, 75* (6), 821–829.

Hickman, J. (1984). Research currents: Researching children's response to literature. *Language Arts, 61* (3), 278–284.

Hong, L. K. (1981). Modifying SSR for beginning readers. *The Reading Teacher, 34* (8), 888–891.

Levertov, Denise (1956). Sharks. In Donald M. Allen (Ed.) (1964), *The new American poetry* (p. 66). New York: Grove Press.

Levine, S. G. (1984). USSR—A necessary component in teaching reading. *Journal of Reading, 27* (5), 394–400.

Lukens, R. J. (1990). *A critical handbook of children's literature* (4th ed.). Glenview, IL: Scott, Foresman.

Manna, A. L. (1984). Making language come alive through reading plays. *The Reading Teacher, 37* (8), 712–717.

Manning, G. L., & Manning, M. (1984). What models of recreational reading make a difference? *Reading World, 23* (4), 375–380.

Morrow, L. M., & Weinstein, C. S. (1986). Encouraging voluntary reading: The impact of a literature program on children's use of library centers. *Reading Research Quarterly, 21* (3), 330–346.

Moss, J. F. (1984). *Focus units in literature: A handbook for elementary school teachers*. Urbana, IL: National Council of Teachers of English.

Omanson, R. C. (1982). An analysis of narratives: Identifying central, supportive, and distracting content. *Discourse Processes, 5*, 119–224.

Purves, A. C. (1985). That sunny dome: Those caves of ice. In C. R. Cooper (Ed.), *Researching response to literature and the teaching of literature: Points of departure* (pp. 54–69). Norwood, NJ: Ablex.

Purves, A. C., with Rippere, V. (1968). *Elements of writing about a literary work: A study of response to literature*. Urbana, IL: National Council of Teachers of English.

Rosenblatt, L. (1978). *The reader, the text, the poem: The transactional theory of the literary work*. Carbondale, IL: Southern Illinois University Press.

Scheu, J., Tanner, D., & Au, K. H. (1986). Designing independent practice activities to improve comprehension. *The Reading Teacher, 40* (1), 18–25.

Squire, J. (1964). *The responses of adolescents while reading four short stories*. Urbana, IL: National Council of Teachers of English.

Stein, N., & Glenn, C. (1979). An analysis of story comprehension in elementary school children. In R. Freedle (Ed.), *New directions in discourse processing* (Vol. 2 in Advances in discourse processes). Norwood, NJ: Ablex.

Stein, N., & Nezworski, T. (1977). *The effects of organization and instructional set on story memory* (Tech. Rep. No. 68.). Urbana, IL: University of Illinois, Center for the Study of Reading.

Stein, N. L., & Policastro, M. (1984). The concept of a story: A comparison between children's and teachers' viewpoints. In H. Mandl, N. L. Stein, & T. Trabasso (Eds.), *Learning and comprehension of text.* Hillsdale, NJ: Erlbaum.

Sutherland, Z., & Arbuthnot, M. H. (1986). *Children and books* (7th ed.). Glenview, IL: Scott, Foresman.

Children's Books Cited

Armstrong, W. (1979). *The tale of Tawny and Dingo.* Harper & Row.

Blos, J. W. (1979). *A gathering of days: A New England girl's journal, 1830–32.* Scribner's.

Charlip, R. (1973). *Harlequin and the gift of many colors.* Parents' Magazine Press.

Coerr, E. (1977). *Sadako and the thousand paper cranes.* Dell.

Colum, P. (1962). *Children of Odin,* ill. by E. Sandoz. Houghton Mifflin.

Delton, J. (1974). *Two good friends.* Crown.

Duvoisin, R. (1979). *Snowy and Woody.* Random House.

George J. (1972). *Julie of the wolves,* ill. by J. Schoenherr. Harper & Row.

Hill, E. S. (1967). *Evan's corner.* Holt, Rinehart and Winston.

Hoban, R. (1970). *A bargain for Frances.* Harper & Row.

Keats, E. J. (1963). *The snowy day.* Viking.

Kessler, L. (1965). *Here comes the strikeout.* Harper & Row.

Latham, J. (1955). *Carry on, Mr. Bowditch,* ill. by J. O. Cosgrove. Houghton Mifflin.

Lindgren, A. (1950). *Pippi Longstocking,* tr. by F. Lamborn, ill. by L. S. Glanzman. Viking.

Lobel, A. (1970). *Frog and Toad are friends.* Harper & Row.

MacLachlan, P. (1985). *Sarah, plain and tall.* Harper & Row.

Marshall, J. (1972). *What's the matter with Carruthers?* Houghton Mifflin.

Marshall, J. (1983). A big lunch for father. In W. K. Durr, J. M. Le Pere, J. J. Pikulski, & M. L. Alsin, *Boats.* Houghton Mifflin Reading Program.

McCloskey, R. (1958). *Time of wonder.* Viking.

Ness, E. (1967). *Sam, Bangs & Moonshine.* Holt, Rinehart & Winston.

O'Brien, R. C. (1971). *Mrs. Frisby and the rats of NIMH,* ill. by Z. Bernstein. Atheneum.

O'Dell, S. (1961). *Island of the blue dolphins.* Houghton Mifflin.

Patent, D. (1977). *Evolution goes on every day,* ill. by M. Kalmenoff. Holiday House.

Selsam, M. (1966). *Benny's animals, and how he put them in order,* ill. by A. Lobel. Harper & Row.

Smith, D. B. (1973). *A taste of blackberries,* ill. by C. Robinson. T. Crowell.

Sobol, D. (1970). *Encyclopedia Brown saves the day,* ill. by L. Shortall. Nelson.

Steig, W. (1971). *Amos and Boris.* Farrar, Straus and Giroux.

Steig, W. (1969). *Sylvester and the magic pebble.*Windmill/Simon & Schuster.

Udry, J. M. (1976). What Mary Jo shared. In W. K. Durr, J. M. Le Pere, M. L. Alsin, R. P. Bunyan, & S. Shaw, *Cloverleaf.* Houghton Mifflin Reading Program.

Van Leeuwen, J. (1967). *Timothy's flower.* Random House.

Venable, A. (1973). *The checker players.* Lippincott.

Waber, B. (1972). *Ira sleeps over.* Houghton Mifflin.

White, E.B. (1952). *Charlotte's web*, ill. by G. Williams. Harper & Row.

Yashima, T. (1955). *Crow boy.* Viking.

Yolen, J. (1978). *Spider Jane.* Coward, McCann and Geoghegan.

Further Readings

Cullinan, B. E. (Ed.) (1987). *Children's literature in the reading program.* Newark, DE: International Reading Association.

Galda, L. (1988). Readers, texts and contexts: A response-based view of literature in the classroom. *The New Advocate, 1* (2), 92–102.

King, M. L., & McKenzie, M. G. (1988). Research currents: Literary discourse from the child's perspective. *Language Arts, 65* (3), 304–314.

Morrow, L. M. (1989). Creating a bridge to children's literature. In P. N. Winograd, K. K. Wixson, & M. Y. Lipson (Eds.), *Improving basal reading instruction* (pp. 210–230). New York: Teachers College Press.

Tunnell, M. O., & Jacobs, J. S. (1989). Using "real" books: Research findings on literature based reading instruction. *The Reading Teacher, 42* (7), 470–477.

Watson, D. J., & Davis, S. C. (1988). Readers and texts in a fifth-grade classroom. In B. F. Nelms (Ed.), *Literature in the classroom: Readers, texts, and contexts* (pp. 59–67). Urbana, IL: National Council of Teachers of English.

Chapter 4

Developing Study Skills and Teaching Comprehension of Expository Text

Here are four readers' recollections of books that triggered new interests:

In the eighth grade, I thought I had found my life's work when we started to study electricity. I even remember trying to read some engineering books, and especially one on armature winding. I read the biography of Thomas Edison and dug into everything I could find on electricity. That was the first year I asked for books for Christmas.

By my last two years my reading tastes had changed to mysteries and war. Strangely enough the war novels were usually documentary. I would spend hours following the blow by blow account of the fall of the Remagen Bridge. I mapped out troop movements of the Battle of the Bulge and of Rommel's Africa corps. Here for once a major impact had been made upon me by literature. Largely through my reading, I decided to major in history in college.

I think Madame Curie became my idol as a result of her biography. At the time I was very interested in science and thought I would one day become a doctor. Her biography was an appealing example. *Arrowsmith* was also about a scientist and therefore another of my favorites. (Hope I have the title right.)

A very definite influence on my reading at this time was a growing interest in science. In the 10th grade I decided medicine was my field and I would become a great woman doctor. Of course, I read Elizabeth Blackwell over and over. Another favorite was *Microbe Hunters*. One of my other favorites was *Madame Curie*, a book I still enjoy. My burning desire to become a doctor faded during my junior year when my progress was blocked by a monster known as Chemistry, but my interest in scientific books remains with me, perhaps because I married a doctor. (Carlsen & Sherrill, 1988, pp. 80–81)

▌ OVERVIEW

We turn in this chapter to students' comprehension of nonfiction or expository text. Much of the reading students do in school is of expository text, rather than narratives. For example, students generally read expository text when they study social studies, science, and other content areas. We start by presenting a social studies unit to illustrate how students might use both reading and writing to study a particular topic.

In the first key concept we describe frameworks teachers can use to conduct reading lessons based on expository text. Like other lesson frameworks we have discussed, these begin by building on children's background knowledge.

In the second key concept we acquaint you with some of the different structures authors often use to organize expository text. Then we present two approaches you can follow to help students learn about these structures and apply this knowledge to gain a better understanding of their reading material.

In the third key concept we discuss the whole idea of studying. We explain that different strategies will be needed to meet the different purposes people have for reading expository text. We describe several approaches you can use to improve students' study ability, for example by teaching them to identify the main idea and to summarize. We also give examples of study guides.

In the fourth key concept we cover research projects and report writing. We present an approach teachers can use to guide students toward success in this area, through the integration of reading and writing activities.

Chapter 4 is organized around the following key concepts:

Key Concept 1: The teacher should follow systematic procedures for planning and conducting content area reading lessons.

Key Concept 2: The teacher should help students to learn about and apply knowledge of the different structures often found in expository text.

Key Concept 3: The teacher should help children develop strategies for studying expository text.

Key Concept 4: The teacher should involve students in research projects integrating reading and writing.

▌ PERSPECTIVE

Expository or Informational Text

The terms *expository* or *informational* are often used to describe text written for the purpose of conveying factual information, explaining ideas, or presenting an argument. Content area text is still another term you may see applied to this type of text, because in school settings, text of this sort is usually associated with social studies, science, and other content area subjects. Expository text may be contrasted with narrative text or stories, which usually contain elements such as characters, a setting, and a plot, and are often written to reveal an aspect of human nature or to entertain. Expository text generally differs from narrative text both in purpose and structure.

Children's reading of expository texts can cover a wide range of types and topics. In addition to textbooks, there are many informational books intended for children, including numerous award-winning books on natural and physical science topics. Other expository material written for children includes newspapers and magazines, discussed in Chapter 12.

As we might expect, students generally find expository text more difficult to comprehend than narrative. For example, the fourth graders studied by Alvermann and Boothby (1982) could distinguish between these two types of text and judged the expository selection to be more difficult. Students often have more trouble comprehending exposition for a number of different reasons. For one thing, during the primary grades they generally do not have much experience reading expository text. For another, their teachers do not usually teach them the strategies needed for understanding expository text. Finally, children may not have sufficient background knowledge of the topic of the selection, or of the structure of the text. In this chapter, we will be discussing these factors in more detail and suggesting instructional solutions.

Building on Process Approaches to Reading and Writing

Recent research suggests that the most effective approaches for developing students' ability to comprehend and study expository text are consistent with those described in earlier chapters of this textbook. For example, Nelms (1987) discusses the value of looking at reading and writing as composing processes when teaching social studies. To illustrate the kind of content area instruction he recommends, he provides the following description of activities in the classroom of Ms. B., a middle grades teacher. Ms. B. decided to teach a unit on Argentina. Experienced teachers like Ms. B. generally make decisions about what to teach on the basis of curriculum guides, current events, or students' own interests. Notice how Ms. B. begins the unit of study by assessing what the students already know about the topic and by letting them formulate the questions they want to pursue. Next, she organizes their questions into a study guide and lets them pursue the answers by reading several different sources of information.

> Ms. B. begins the unit by writing in large letters on the chalkboard, ARGENTINA. She then asks students to brainstorm for 10 minutes on what that word means to them. Someone records their suggestions on the board in single words or brief phrases, accepting misinformation as well as accurate information. Ms. B. then asks students to write briefly, perhaps 5–10 minutes, on "What I Know and What I Would Like to Know about Argentina." They divide into groups of three and read their papers aloud, noting and underlining sentences or brief passages that they like because they provide good information, raise good questions, or are especially

clear, interesting, or even humorous. Students who know very little about Argentina are encouraged to write what they would like to know or what they can imagine from what they heard in the brainstorming session. The occasional students who already know quite a lot may be encouraged to write about how they learned about Argentina, for example, from a relative who lives there, from a movie they saw recently, or from a pen pal or church project. If there is time, each group shares a writing with the class or good passages from several writings. The first lesson ends with Ms. B. asking the students to formulate three questions each that they would like to have answered about Argentina. Students draw from their personal interests or imagination and from their imagined role as young social scientists.

Ms. B. then constructs a study guide or tentative unit plan, using these questions. She uses some students' work verbatim, combines and modifies others, expands or limits others, and, if necessary, contributes some of her own. The next day students receive the guide and again are divided into groups. Each group receives the text of a different resource: articles from *World Book* encyclopedia or *Compton's Illustrated* encyclopedia, an article from *National Geographic*, an introduction to a biography of Eva Peron that gives some background on the country, a *Time* or *Newsweek* story written during the Falkland Islands crisis, one or more chapters from trade books on Latin America, a picture book that they might consider reading to a younger brother or sister. Each student is asked to read the material (or scan as appropriate), applying a formula she calls W-D-Q: W requires them to list key *words*, especially those with which they are unfamiliar or of which they are uncertain of the meaning; D requires them to record *data*, especially answers to study questions or other interesting or relevant details; Q requires them to initiate further *questions* or rephrase and refine questions already raised. Students then compare notes within groups and each group prepares to report its findings to the class. This process may be repeated several times, inasmuch as time permits, until students are reasonably satisfied that they have met their goals. At some point, the students as a group may read and do a critical review of the textbook, view films or filmstrips, and hear guest lecturers or conduct interviews. Students use multiple texts on the same topic. Inevitably, these will represent different perspectives or emphases, involve some reinforcement and overlap, and present some contradictions in fact or interpretation. Learning will be less tidy but richer.   (p. 580)

As you go on to read the rest of Nelms' description, notice how Ms. B. links language arts, art, music, and even math experiences with the unit on Argentina. Every so often, she checks on the students' progress by having them write about what they have learned and what they would like to learn next. In their writings, students are also allowed to share their feelings about their work, positive and negative. Finally, the students produce a class book.

In addition, during language arts period, Ms. B. introduces the language(s) of Argentina, focuses on a poem written by an Argentine poet or excerpts from a novel that is set in Argentina, or encourages students to write stories, poems, or fictional diaries with Argentine characters and settings. Whenever feasible, Ms. B. has persuaded the art teacher to show some art works from Argentina or introduce native Argentine crafts or artists. In music, students hear and learn some

Argentine songs. The librarian has been persuaded to display Argentine materials for a month and to prepare annotated lists of books and other materials for students and their parents. Even in math, some word problems have been written (or are written by students) to reflect Argentine situations (e.g., average rainfall per month, rate of inflation, percentage of urban/rural population, cost of living index).

Periodically through the unit, usually at the end of a period, students are again asked to do a timed writing on "What I Know and What I Need to Know about Argentina" or "What I Have Learned and Need to Learn" or even "What I Understand and What I Don't Understand about Argentina." Again, they share these with one another. In these writings they are also to express their personal responses—surprise, confusion, excitement, sympathy, disapproval, convictions, questions. As a culminating project, the class produces a book on Argentina for their parents, each student contributing a chapter on one element of their study with suggestions and revisions derived from conferences with the student's writing group and Ms. B. As a group, they write a preface, stating their most important conclusions or generalizations about Argentina. To reinforce the notion that learning is open-ended (an ongoing process), the book includes a list of suggested readings and a list of interesting but as yet unanswered questions. Everyone contributes to the book, each according to his or her own interest and ability and with varying degrees of assistance from Ms. B. as requested. Ms. B., however, has set common tasks and, whenever necessary, has inserted questions and/or objectives from the required curriculum guide. Whenever possible, she has let these concerns grow from students' own comments and questions. When she inserts her own, it is to supplement students' interests, not to displace student initiative. Most of Ms. B.'s overt contributions, however, are comments on processes: locating information, evaluating sources, drawing conclusions. During all the activities she conducts brief conferences with students.   (pp. 580–581)

You saw in this description how a teacher might use the approaches we advocated in earlier chapters. For example, Ms. B. encouraged the students to develop their own questions and to think actively and critically about their reading. She allowed students to work together and to share ideas with one another, as well as with her. She emphasized strategies for learning, as seen in her use of the technique she called W-D-Q and in her comments on the processes students were using, such as for locating information. There is the sense in this description that Ms. B.'s classroom is a community of learners using reading and writing to explore an interesting subject.

Nelms points out five ways that writing may promote active learning of content area information. First, writing can be used to inventory knowledge. As we saw in Ms. B.'s classroom, an inventory should be taken at the beginning of a unit, to guide the teacher's planning. Ms. B. also used writing to gauge students' progress as they moved through the unit.

A second use of writing is to initiate learning. Students may be asked to come up with questions, as Ms. B. did. They may also use writing to state hypotheses, to set goals for further study, and in general, to focus their research. Third, writing can be used to consolidate learning. In addition to note taking, students may use writing to restate important points or summarize

Even second grade students can write research reports, when the teacher structures the activity carefully. An important part of the process comes in sharing their writing and receiving feedback from classmates and the teacher.

what they learned from a chapter or lecture. They also use writing to reflect upon what they have learned in a journal, or to organize information in a research report.

Fourth, according to Nelms, writing may be used to personalize learning. In this case students make connections between the information learned and their own experiences. For example, a student might write a story imagining what his life would be like if he lived in Argentina. A final use of writing in study of a content area is to clarify thinking. Nelms points out that regular writing improves students' understanding of new concepts, or at the very least helps them to identify what they are finding confusing.

Importance of Expository Comprehension

Teaching students to read and write on the basis of expository text can be exciting and interesting, as shown in Nelms' description of Ms. B.'s classroom. The methods used by Ms. B., as well as others to be described in this chapter, will be an important part of your teaching repertoire. This is because improving students' ability to comprehend expository text is at once one of the most important, and also most difficult, goals you will need to accomplish as an elementary school teacher.

By the time students are attending secondary school, the majority of the texts they are expected to deal with will be expository in nature, rather than narrative. Certainly, most reading in the workplace involves reading for specific information (e.g., Guthrie, 1984). This suggests that learning to comprehend and study expository text is at least as important as learning to comprehend and appreciate stories and literature. However, because the reading program in many classrooms centers on use of basal readers, which consist primarily of stories, teachers probably pay less attention than they should to helping children learn to comprehend expository text.

Teachers working with students in the fourth, fifth, and sixth grades generally are very aware of how important it is for their students to be able to read and comprehend expository text. In the conventional view, these are the grade levels when "reading to learn" begins to be emphasized over "learning to read." Typically, though, upper grade teachers find that many of their students have a great deal of difficulty reading and studying content area material. Part of the reason may be that the students have not had much previous experience with texts of this type.

Our view is that even kindergarten children can be given some experience with expository text; this would generally involve reading such material aloud to the children. Certainly, opportunities to work with expository text should be provided to first, second, and third grade students. By the time students are in the fourth grade and above, perhaps half or more of the reading instruction they receive should involve expository text.

Key Concept 1

The teacher should follow systematic procedures for planning and conducting content area reading lessons.

▌ THE CONCURRENT PRESENTATION APPROACH

Because elementary students often have difficulty dealing both with the content and structure of expository text, teachers need to follow clearly organized plans for conducting content area lessons. The general approach to content area reading instruction we recommend involves *concurrent presentation of content and skills* (Moore & Readence, 1983; a similar approach is recommended by Gaskins, 1981). This approach is aimed at giving students knowledge of the topic as well as at giving them the necessary comprehension and study strategies, a point to be discussed further in Key Concept #3.

Moore and Readence note that there are three effective procedures for providing concurrent content and strategy instruction. These are *simulating, debriefing,* and *fading.* These procedures are all consistent with the idea of the gradual release of responsibility to students.

Simulating is defined by Herber (1978) as a method of preparing students for a real experience by first taking them through a series of activities contrived to simulate that experience. Working with the specially contrived activities gives students the opportunity to practice the strategy they later will be encouraged to apply independently. According to Moore and Readence, simulating can involve first giving students rules for learning from text. After teaching the rules, the teacher has the students practice them with sample materials selected especially for that purpose. Then the students are asked to apply the rules in work with content area textbooks and other materials they normally use. Such a procedure might be used with the sequence for main idea comprehension developed by Baumann (1984; presented on pages 152–153).

Debriefing involves the teacher's asking students questions about their use of a particular strategy. The purpose of debriefing is to have students introspect, to reflect upon the procedure itself and their thoughts while using it. Teacher questions during a lesson might include the following:

> How did you realize that some information was missing? How did you know some information was incorrect? How did you decide what seems to be the most important information? How did you decide what information supported the most important ideas? Might this be a useful means to help you read and learn from other text reading assignments? (Moore & Readence, 1983, p. 400)

Fading is a process where the teacher at first provides a great deal of guidance when students are executing the strategy, and then gradually reduces the amount of guidance as students become better able to use the strategy on their own. This is the process seen in the reciprocal teaching procedure developed by Palincsar (1984; described on pages 59–61). At first the teacher must model the asking of questions. Later students are able to ask questions partly on their own, with some help from the teacher. Finally, they are able to ask questions with little or no teacher help.

In every content area reading lesson, plan to use one of these procedures. All have the advantage of actively engaging students in the lesson and making them aware of the purposes of instruction and of the steps involved in learning. A second advantage is that all are designed to move students toward independence in learning to comprehend and study expository text.

FRAMEWORKS FOR EXPOSITORY COMPREHENSION LESSONS

We next present three frameworks for expository comprehension lessons: the concept-text-application approach (CTA; Wong & Au, 1985), the directed reading-thinking approach (DRTA; Stauffer, 1969), and K-W-L (Ogle, 1986). All start with taking an inventory of students' background knowledge about the topic, and all are methods of actively involving students in thinking about expository text.

CTA is an appropriate choice if you are working with children who are likely to need considerable guidance while reading and extra help with concepts central to an understanding of the text. It is a good overarching framework the teacher can use when trying to give students a general understanding of how to approach content area texts. DRTA can be used at all grade levels to develop students' ability to make and test predictions while reading. Used together, CTA lessons and DRTA lessons can provide students with a solid foundation for comprehending expository texts. After students have this foundation, the teacher may want to move on to K-W-L. K-W-L differs from the other two frameworks in providing a way of transferring responsibility for comprehension from the teacher over to the students. As discussed in Chapter 2, this transfer, through a gradual release of responsibility, should be built into all areas of reading and writing instruction.

Concept-Text-Application Approach

The concept-text-application (CTA) approach developed by Wong and Au (1985) is a framework for organizing lessons to improve comprehension of expository text and can be used with students from the second grade on up. It takes students through prereading, guided reading, and postreading phases of instruction. The CTA approach incorporates many of the basic ideas developed by Herber (1978) and by Estes and Vaughan (1978); refer to these textbooks for a detailed treatment of content area reading issues, especially for upper elementary grade students.

The CTA method is based on the idea that effective reading instruction starts by building on children's background knowledge. The approach is based on guided discussion and is best used with small groups. At least two 20 to 25 minute lessons are required to complete the reading of most expository selections, whether in a basal reader, content area textbook, or children's magazine.

The CTA method is designed to complement the ETR method for teaching comprehension of stories, as described in Chapter 2. It too incorporates three different phases. The concept assessment/development or *C* phase is a prereading discussion during which the teacher tries to find out what the students already know about the topic of the text. Unfamiliar concepts and vocabulary necessary for understanding the text may be introduced during this phase. During the text or *T* phase, purposes for reading are set and there is guided reading and discussion of the text. Finally, during the application or *A* phase, the students are encouraged to put to use the new information learned.

Planning. First, preview the text and identify the main idea or central theme you wish to focus on. If necessary, do some background reading on the topic. Second, reread the text and work out the visual structure to be developed with the children during the lesson. For example, Figure 4.1 shows the visual structure used by a teacher to plan a second grade lesson based on "The Monster of Loch Ness" (Shogren, 1978). When making up the structure, you may also wish to note vocabulary to be covered. Then plan the application or follow-up activity. In the example, the teacher decided to have the children conduct a survey of their classmates.

▌ **Figure 4.1**
▌ **Do You Believe in Monsters?**

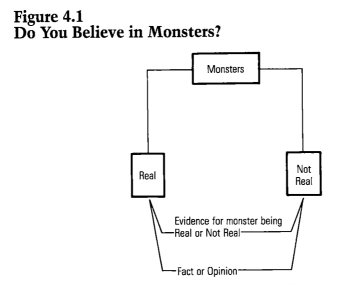

Does echo sounder help provide evidence
that monster is real or not real?

Source: (Figures 4.1 and 4.2): Figures 1 and 2 from "The Concept-Text-Application Approach: Helping Elementary Students Comprehend Text" by JoAnn Wong and Kathryn Hu-pei Au, March 1985, *The Reading Teacher.* Reprinted by permission of the authors and the International Reading Association.

Concept assessment/development.   Try to capture the children's interest at the very start of the lesson. In our example, the teacher generated a lot of discussion by asking the children if they believed in monsters. Then move on to more focused questions to identify key concepts and vocabulary unfamiliar to the children. For example, in this lesson the children had to be taught that *loch* was the Scottish word for lake.

Text.   After assessing background knowledge and developing important concepts and vocabulary, move into guided reading of the text. Work with the children to set a purpose (usually, a question to be answered) for the reading of each segment. Have them read the segment and then discuss the information covered. Continue alternating periods of silent reading and discussion until the text has been completed.

After the first segment is discussed, lay out the framework for the visual structure. During each discussion period, continue to add to it. Figure 4.2 shows the visual structure completed in this manner for the lessons on the Loch Ness monster. The items in the structure were those mentioned by the children, and the lines were drawn after the children decided whether each item supported the view that the monster was "real" or "not real." The teacher used this visual structure to bring out the central theme, whether the monster was real.

When working with primary grade students, you may wish to teach

▌ **Figure 4.2**
Completed Visual Structure on the
Loch Ness Monster

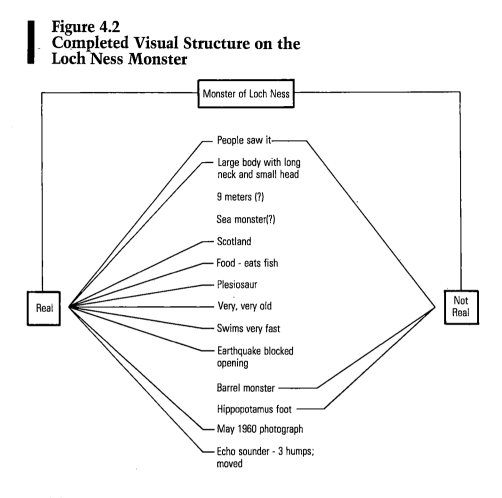

useful vocabulary not present in the text. For example, over the course of the sample lessons, the teacher introduced the terms *evidence, fact,* and *opinion,* all words not in the text. For additional ideas for teaching vocabulary, refer to Chapter 5.

Watch during the *T* phase for signs that you should help the children build up background knowledge and fit new text information with what has already been understood. For instance, in the sample series of lessons, the teacher found that the children did not understand how an echo sounder worked. She had to explain this to them because the text provided little information on this point. Then she led them to see how an echo sounder might be used to locate the monster.

Application. Immediately after the entire text has been read, have the children try to summarize and synthesize the information. During this process, encourage them to refer to the visual structure. After the review, have the children engage in evaluative and divergent thinking. In this case, the children began on their own to debate the issue of whether the monster was real.

Finally, have the children engage in one or more follow-up activities. These may be very simple, taking perhaps only a half hour of class time, or more elaborate, stretching across several weeks. Possibilities include writing group or individual reports incorporating information from tradebooks and the encyclopedia, making a display or mural, or sharing information learned orally with the rest of the class. In our example, the children polled their classmates to see how many thought the Loch Ness monster was real. They then made a bar graph to display the results.

CTA lessons can easily be used as a springboard for SEARCH projects, described below. In this case, children highly interested in the topic continue to work on it.

Directed Reading-Thinking Activity (DRTA)

Stauffer's (1969) Directed Reading-Thinking Activity encourages active involvement with text by having students generate hypotheses about text and then check on the accuracy of their predictions. The DRTA can be used with virtually any kind of reading material, selections in content area textbooks as well as in basal readers. As Spiegel (1981) points out, it is especially useful when students already have the necessary vocabulary and background knowledge. In practice, there are many variations to the basic DRTA concept. Here is the one we prefer:

Step 1: Tell the children the title of the selection or show them an illustration. On the basis of this information, have them make predictions about the story. If an informational text is being used, an alternative is to have them tell what they already know about the topic. Write predictions and other ideas on the board.

Step 2: Pointing out to the children that they will be reading to see if the text verifies the information on the board, have them read a portion of the text silently.

Step 3: Reopen the discussion by having the children go down the list of predictions and ideas on the board, telling which were verified. Point out to the children that there are several possibilities. The idea could be:

1. Verified by the text (in which case, you can have a child read the relevant sentence aloud);
2. Disproved by the text (again, a child might read the relevant sentence aloud);
3. Only partially verified or disproved, with more information being required to make a definite decision about whether the idea is right or wrong;
4. Shown to be only partially right or wrong, but definitely requiring revision on the basis of text information;
5. Not mentioned.

Items in the list are rewritten, marked as true, crossed off if false, and so on. New hypotheses may also be added. Thus, the list should become a running record of important text information.

Step 4: Alternate periods of silent reading and discussion until the whole text has been read. Older children who have participated in this procedure before may be asked to copy the original list from the board and directed to read and then revise the list on their own, for seatwork. In all cases, emphasize the quality of the reasoning students are doing, rather than just the correctness of their initial hypotheses. Point out how the process of mentally generating and revising hypotheses is something that should always be done while reading.

K–W–L

This approach developed by Ogle (1986) is based on the idea that teachers should begin expository comprehension lessons by honoring what students already know about the topic, and by helping them decide what else they would like to learn about it. The letters *K*, *W*, and *L* stand for the three basic steps in the procedure: assessing what I Know, determining what I Want to Know, and recalling what I Learned through reading. Each student uses a worksheet, shown in Figure 4.3, to record ideas as the lessons progress.

Step K—What I know. You will be working with students' prior knowledge at two levels. Start by having the students brainstorm, to come up with ideas they already have about the topic. On the chart paper, the chalkboard, or an overhead projector, record the ideas the students share. Be sure to center brainstorming on a concept specific enough to link directly to the information students will encounter in their reading.

Ogle illustrates the need for specificity in the following way. If the students are going to be reading about sea turtles, the teacher should ask a question such as, "What do you know about sea turtles?" not, "What do you know about animals that live in the sea?" or, "Have you ever been to the beach?" These last two questions will lead to an overly general discussion which it may be difficult for the teacher to steer around to the specific subject of sea turtles. The idea is to activate students' prior knowledge of sea turtles or whatever the specific topic of the text happens to be, because this is the knowledge that will help students comprehend the text.

Ask more general questions only if students seem to know little about the specific topic. For example, if they do not have information about sea turtles, you might ask, "What do you know about turtles?" Then you can ask them if the information volunteered might be true of sea turtles, too.

When students volunteer ideas, help them to become aware of areas of uncertainty and areas they would like to know more about. Ogle suggests asking questions such as "Where did you learn that?" and "How could you prove that?" Questions like these prompt students to think about their own

Figure 4.3
K-W-L Strategy Sheet

1. K—What we know	W—What we want to find out	L—What we learned and still need to learn

2. Categories of information we expect to use

A.   E.
B.   F.
C.   G.
D.

sources of information and whether their ideas are sound or speculative. Your questions may also encourage other students to provide information supporting a different interpretation. These points of disagreement help to establish purposes for later reading. In the second part of brainstorming, you will involve students in thinking about the general categories of information they are likely to find in the text. Begin by telling students that they should now think about the kinds of information they will probably be reading in the article. Have them look at the list of ideas generated during the discussion, and ask if any of the ideas go together in a general category.

In the beginning, you may need to model this step. For example, with the topic of sea turtles, Ogle suggests that the teacher might say, "I see three different pieces of information about how turtles look. Description or looks is certainly one category of information I would expect this article to include" (p. 566). The teacher would then write this category ("how sea turtles look") under the Categories of Information heading, modeling what students will do later on their own worksheets. The teacher would continue by asking students if they can refer to the list and think of another category on their own. They will then be able to come up with other categories, such as "what sea turtles eat" and "dangers to sea turtles." You might want to have students read several articles on similar topics, for example, various kinds of sea animals, so that they learn about categories and develop deeper knowledge in a certain area.

Step W—What do I want to learn? As you take students through the two levels of brainstorming, you will find that they are coming up with questions. As described above, students may present conflicting ideas, or they may think of categories that they do not yet know anything about (e.g., "parts of the world where sea turtles live"). You will want to highlight for students areas of conflict or uncertainty, and areas where nothing is yet known. These areas and questions provide purposes for reading which grow out of students' own interests.

Most of Step W is conducted as a group activity. However, just before you have students begin to read, ask them to write down on their own individual worksheets the questions they most want to pursue. This gives each student a chance to set personal purposes for reading.

If the article is long or has a structure students might find confusing, you may want to preview it with them before they start reading. This gives you a chance to alert them to the match or mismatch between the questions they generated and the actual content of the article. For example, categories of interest to some students may not be covered. Depending on the article and on students' reading ability, you may have them read the article as a whole or break the article into segments for guided reading and discussion.

Step L—What I learned. After students have finished reading the article, ask them to write down what they learned from it. Have them refer back to their questions to decide if the article provided the relevant information. If it did not, you might suggest that they do other reading to find the answers. Ogle recommends this step as a means of letting students know that their own personal interests are important, even if they were not addressed by the author of the article.

Example of interaction in a K-W-L lesson.   Ogle provides the following transcript excerpt, taken from a lesson given to fourth graders, based on a children's magazine article entitled "The Black Widow." The teacher used this article as part of a unit on animals.

Teacher: Today we're going to read another article about animals. This one is about a special kind of spider—the Black Widow. Before we begin the article, let's think about what we already know about Black Widows. Or if you aren't familiar with this kind of spider, think about some things you know about spiders in general, and we can then see if those are also true for the Black Widow. [Teacher writes *Black Widow spider* on the board and waits while students think about their knowledge of spiders. Next, she elicits ideas from children and writes their contributions on the board.]

Tony: Spiders have six legs.

Susan: They eat other insects.

Eddie: I think they're big and dangerous spiders.

Teacher: Can you add more about what you mean when you say they're big and dangerous?

Eddie: They, they, I think they eat other spiders. I think people are afraid of them, too.

Steph: They spin nests or webs to catch other insects in.

Tom: My cousin got stung by one once and almost died.

Teacher: You mean they are dangerous to people?

Tom: Yah, my cousin had to go to the hospital.

Teacher: Does anyone else know more about the Black Widow? Tammy?

Tammy: I don't think they live around here. I've never heard of anyone being stung by one.

Teacher: Where do Black Widows live? Does anyone know? [She waits.] What else do we know about spiders?

John: I think I saw a TV show about them once. They have a special mark on their back. I think it's a blue triangle or circle, or something like that. If people look, they can tell if the spider's a Black Widow or not.

Teacher: Does anyone else recall anything more about how they look? [She waits.] Look at what we've already said about these spiders. Can you think of other information we should add?

John: I think they kill babies or men spiders. I'm not sure which.

Teacher: Do you remember where you learned that?

John: I think I read an article once.

Teacher: OK, let's add that to our list. Remember, everything on the list we aren't sure of we can doublecheck when we read.

Teacher: Anything more you think you know about these spiders? [She waits.] OK, before we read this article let's think awhile about the kinds or categories of information that are likely to be included. Look at the list of things we already know or have questions about. Which of the categories of information have we already mentioned?

Peter: We mentioned how they look.

Teacher: Yes, we said they're big and have six legs. And someone said they think Black Widows have a colored mark on them. Good, description is one of the main categories of information we want to learn about when we read about animals or insects. What other categories of information have we mentioned that should be included?

Anna: Where they live; but we aren't sure.

Teacher: Good, we should find out where they live. What other kinds of information should we expect to learn from the article? Think about what kinds of information we've learned from other articles about animals.

Diane: We want to know what kind of homes they make.

Raul: What do they eat?

Andy: How they protect themselves.

Cara: How do they have babies? How many do they have?

Teacher: Good thinking. Are there other categories of information we expect to learn about? [She waits.] We've thought about what we already know and what kinds of information we're likely to learn from an article on Black Widow spiders. Now what are some of the questions we want to have answered? I know we had some things we weren't sure about, like where the spiders live. What are some of the things you'd like to find out when we read?

Cara: I want to know how many baby spiders get born.

Rico: Do Black Widows really hurt people? I never heard of that, and my dad knows a lot about spiders.

Andy: Why are they called Black Widows? What's a widow?

Teacher: Good question! Does anyone know what a widow is? Why would this spider be called a "Black Widow"?

[After eliciting questions from several students, the teacher asks each child to write their own questions on their worksheet.]

What are the questions you're most interested in having answered? Write them down now. As you read, look for the answers and jot them down on your worksheet as you go, or other information you don't want to forget. [The students read the article.]

Teacher: How did you like this article? What did you learn?

Raul: The Black Widow eats her husband and sometimes her babies. Yuck! I don't think I like that kind of spider!

Steph: They can live here—it says they live in all parts of the United States.

Andy: They can be recognized by an hourglass that is red or yellow on their abdomen.

Teacher: What is another word for *abdomen?* [She waits.] Sara, please look up the word *abdomen.* Let's find out where the hourglass shape is located. While Sara is looking that word up, let's check what we learned against the questions we wanted answered. Are there some questions that didn't get answered? What more do we want to know?

(Ogle, 1986, pp. 567–569)

The discussion continued in this vein, with the teacher helping the students to integrate their new knowledge about Black Widow spiders with their prior knowledge about spiders and other animals. Ogle emphasizes that the teacher's goal is to see that students retain control over exploration of the topic. In K-W-L the teacher tries to extend students' inquiry beyond the limits of a single article. The students' questions, not the content of a particular text, are the force driving the activity.

> ### Key Concept 2
>
> The teacher should help students to learn about and apply knowledge of the different structures often found in expository text.

∎ EXPOSITORY TEXT STRUCTURES

The term *structure* refers to the organization of ideas in text, including the location of more or less important information and the means used to connect ideas to one another. As you learned in Chapter 3, many simple stories follow a similar structure or grammar. In contrast, expository selections written for elementary school students do not follow any one structure. The research indicates that students will frequently encounter four or five different structures when reading expository materials, and that several different structures are likely to appear in the same selection (e.g., Schallert & Tierney,

1981). This greater variety of structures is probably one reason students find it more difficult to understand expository texts than to understand narratives.

Here are five different structures your students are likely to meet when reading expository text (categories based on Piccolo, 1987; see also Meyer & Freedle, 1984; Richgels, McGee, Lomax, & Sheard, 1987).

1. *Descriptive paragraph.* This addresses a specific topic and discusses its attributes.

> *Example:* Notice the lines of a globe that run across from left to right. They are called lines of latitude, and they form circles that run in the same direction as the equator. The smallest circles are near the north and south poles and the largest are near the equator. These lines measure how far north or south of the equator places are. [The text continues to define other terms.]

2. *Sequence paragraph.* The topic sentence is supported by details which need to be presented in a certain order to make sense. Signal words include *before* and *after*.

> *Example:* The first Europeans to come to America settled along the Atlantic coast. They knew very little about the territory beyond the coast. But soon after the American Revolution, more people crossed the ocean. Families needed places to live and grow crops. Sometimes several families formed a small settlement, usually near a river or stream. As spaces for farming were taken, the frontier kept moving westward. After a while, wilderness turned into settlements and settlements into towns.

3. *Cause/effect paragraph.* The topic sentence describes a certain situation, supported by the details which follow. Signal words and phrases are *so, so that, because of, as a result of, since,* and *in order to,* and *instead.*

> *Example:* In Europe during the fifteenth century, many small kingdoms joined into larger nations. These large nations began to fight with each other and they needed money for their soldiers. In order to get the money, they turned to trading. One of these new nations, Spain, was interested in trading with China and India. But the only route people knew about was around Africa. In 1492, Spain sent out a small fleet of three ships to find a new route to the East. They sailed across the Atlantic Ocean. Instead of finding China, the three ships discovered America.

4. *Comparison/contrast paragraph.* Subjects are compared and/or contrasted, and supporting details point to differences and similarities. Signal words and phrases are *different from, same as, alike, similar to, resembles, compared to, unlike, but,* and *only.*

> *Example:* Unlike a globe, a flat map allows you to see the whole world at one time. You can make maps of small parts of the world. For example, you could make a map of our state or city. These can't be shown on a globe. But a flat map distorts the real surface. Only a globe can show the rounded surface of our planet.

5. *Problem/solution paragraph.* A problem is stated and supporting details set out the problem, causes of the problem, and solutions. Signal words and phrases are *a problem is, a solution is,* and *the problem is solved by.*

Example: Many people in the northern states wanted to end slavery, but in the South they wanted to keep it. Northerners wanted Congress to pass a law ending slavery in all states, in the new states just being formed and in the South. [The text continues by describing how people worked to put an end to slavery.]

Research suggests that by the sixth grade, many students are starting to become aware of the different structures of expository text (Richgels, McGee, Lomax, & Sheard, 1987). Students in the fourth grade and above may be good candidates for lessons that teach them about text structure. For example, Armbruster, Anderson, and Ostertag (1987) found that fifth graders taught to recognize the problem/solution text structure could use this knowledge to comprehend social studies material.

Teaching About Expository Text Structure

Piccolo (1987) recommends procedures for teaching students about expository text structures, adapted from McGee and Richgels (1985). Graphic organizers are used to help students visualize the structures and to organize their own writing. Piccolo suggests that teachers begin by teaching students about the sequence structure, because it is most like the narratives with which children are already acquainted. After the sequence structure, you might move on to the cause/effect, descriptive, problem/solution, and comparison/contrast structures, in that order.

Piccolo suggests that you gather or compose at least three model paragraphs for each structure you plan to teach. Make sure the paragraphs conform to the graphic organizer for that structure, as shown in Figures 4.4 through 4.6. Each graphic organizer consists of boxes and lines intended to make the nature of that structure clear to students.

Figure 4.4
Questions Students Can Use to Help Identify Text Structures or Write Original Paragraphs

Descriptive
Do you want to tell the reader what something is?

Sequence
Do you want to tell someone how to do something or make something?

Cause/effect
Do you want to give reasons why something happens or exists?

Problem/solution
Do you want to state some sort of problem related to your subject and offer some solutions?

Comparison/contrast
Do you want to show the similarities or differences between a certain topic and the topic you are writing about?

Source: (Figures 4.4, 4.5, 4.6) Excerpts from pp. 841–845 and figures 1, 2, and 4 from "Expository text structure: Teaching and learning strategies" by Jo Anne Piccolo, *The Reading Teacher,* May 1987. Copyright © 1987 International Reading Association, Inc. Reprinted with permission of Jo Anne Piccolo and the International Reading Association.

▍ **Figure 4.5**
Sample Graphic Organizer and the
Corresponding Sequential Paragraph

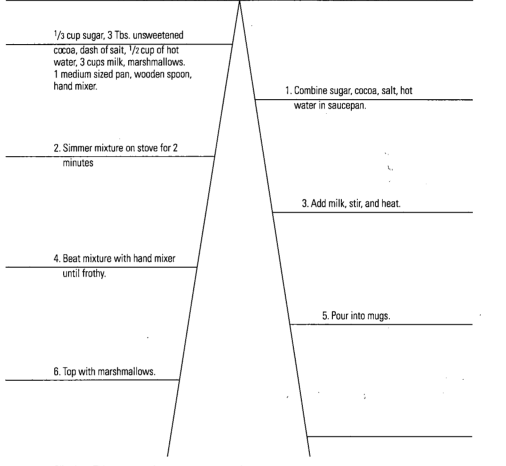

Sequence

Topic sentence: To make hot cocoa for a cold winter's day, you need the following ingredients:

$^1/_3$ cup sugar, 3 Tbs. unsweetened cocoa, dash of salt, $^1/_2$ cup of hot water, 3 cups milk, marshmallows. 1 medium sized pan, wooden spoon, hand mixer.

1. Combine sugar, cocoa, salt, hot water in saucepan.

2. Simmer mixture on stove for 2 minutes

3. Add milk, stir, and heat.

4. Beat mixture with hand mixer until frothy.

5. Pour into mugs.

6. Top with marshmallows.

Clincher: This tasty treat is sure to warm you up!

How to Make Hot Cocoa
To make hot cocoa for a cold winter's day, you need the following ingredients: $^1/_3$ cup of sugar, 3 tablespoons of unsweetened cocoa, a dash of salt, $^1/_2$ cup of hot water, 3 cups of milk, and some miniature marshmallows. You will also need a medium sized saucepan, a wooden spoon, a hand mixer, and mugs. First, combine the sugar, the cocoa, a dash of salt and the hot water in the saucepan. After you do this, put the mixture on the stove and simmer for 2 minutes. Next, add the milk, stir, and heat. Finally, beat this mixture with a hand mixer until frothy. You are now ready to pour the hot cocoa into mugs and top with the marshmallows. This tasty treat is sure to warm you up!

Figure 4.6
Model Organizer for Descriptive
Paragraph

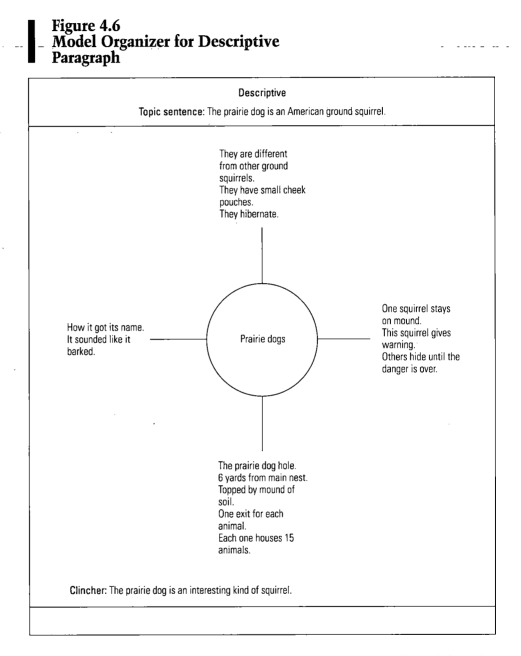

Descriptive

Topic sentence: The prairie dog is an American ground squirrel.

They are different from other ground squirrels.
They have small cheek pouches.
They hibernate.

How it got its name.
It sounded like it barked.

Prairie dogs

One squirrel stays on mound.
This squirrel gives warning.
Others hide until the danger is over.

The prairie dog hole.
6 yards from main nest.
Topped by mound of soil.
One exit for each animal.
Each one houses 15 animals.

Clincher: The prairie dog is an interesting kind of squirrel.

In teaching students about each text structure, you will (1) define the structure, (2) use model paragraphs and the graphic organizer to show students the key feature of the structure, (3) model the writing of a paragraph following the graphic organizer, (4) create a graphic organizer with different information and model the writing of another paragraph, and (5) read an expository text to discover the structures used.

Lesson 1

Step 1: Explain to the class that expository text structure is a name given to the organization of paragraphs that give the reader specific information about a topic. Just as a story contains characters, setting, episodes of the plot, and a goal, expository paragraphs contain a topic sentence with supporting details. And, just as there are different types of stories like fairy tales, tall tales, myths, there are different types of paragraph structures.

Step 2: Introduce the label and define it. Explain that each text structure answers a specific question (Figure 4.4). After this, show the class the graphic organizer for the paragraph on the overhead projector (Figure 4.5). Explain that the graphic organizer is used to show the pattern of a paragraph.

Step 3: Distribute copies of the paragraph that corresponds to the graphic organizer. Read the paragraph together. Then ask the class to try to locate the signal words or phrases in the paragraph that clue the reader to the organization of that structure. Make a list of these words on a chart that gives the name of the structure and its definition along with a picture of the graphic organizer.

Step 4: Explain that topic sentences clue the reader that a particular structure is being used by the author. Sequential paragraphs, for example, have topic sentences that may include the word "steps," or phrases like "In order to make . . . you must follow these directions."

Step 5: Using another example of a paragraph with that same pattern, give the class a copy of the graphic organizer. The graphic organizer will include the topic sentence. Then, on the overhead, model the writing of a paragraph that follows the graphic organizer. Do this as a class. Make sure that the students use the appropriate signal words or phrases in the paragraph.

Lesson 2

Step 1: Instruct the students to choose a topic about which they want to write. For example, when using the sequential structure, this topic can be how to make something.

Step 2: Have each student make a jot list which contains all the details that are to be included in the paragraph. A sequential jot list, for example, may contain all the needed materials and the steps involved in the process.

Step 3: Give each student a copy of the graphic organizer and instruct them to organize a paragraph on the organizer. If they need practice in writing topic sentences, it should be done at this point through modeling.

Step 4: When the organizer has been completed, have the students compose original paragraphs.

Lesson 3

Step 1: From the class collection of paragraphs, choose good examples and poor examples and share them. With the good ones, point out the strength of the topic sentence and the use of appropriate signal words. With the poor samples, have the students participate in the revision process by making suggestions for changes.

Step 2: Following the group activity, hand the papers back so the students can revise and correct their own paragraphs.

Lesson 4

The purpose of this lesson is to show the students how to extract information from a paragraph and put it into simple terms using the graphic organizer to guide them. Using another model, copy the paragraph for each student and make a transparency of a blank organizer. As a class, read the paragraph and fill in the organizer. This activity also prepares them for using graphic organizers for notetaking.

Lesson 5

When the students are familiar with the text structures, the signal words, the graphic organizer, and the corresponding text structure question, give them practice in locating and naming patterns used by authors in content area texts, encyclopedias, or other reference books. This activity will show the students that textbook authors use these structures to organize information. Additionally, it builds a foundation for notetaking. (Piccolo, 1987, pp. 841–844)

Piccolo provides further suggestions to help students to apply what they have learned about expository text structures, to improve their understanding of content area materials. For example, when you provide students with a study guide (as discussed later in this chapter), you can use the labels for the questions you include. For example, if students are going to read about nutrition in their science textbook, some of your questions might be labelled as follows:

Description: What are carbohydrates?
Cause/Effect: What happens when people do not eat enough carbohydrates?
Comparison/Contrast: How are carbohydrates different from proteins?

Piccolo also suggests that you show students how to use the headings in content area textbooks, encyclopedias, and other sources to make predictions about the kind of question likely to be answered in that section. You might put the questions in Figure 4.4 on a chart for students' reference.

Finally, when students are studying new material, they can take notes while reading, using the graphic organizers. Headings and subheadings can serve as the basis for topic sentences. They can also review their notes when studying for a test.

If you are interested in helping students learn to apply knowledge of expository text structures to writing as well as to reading, you may be interested in a program entitled Cognitive Strategies Instruction in Writing (CSIW; refer to Englert & Raphael, in press, and Englert, Raphael, Anderson, Anthony, Fear, & Gregg, 1988). CSIW is consistent with a process approach to writing and teaches students to plan, organize, draft, edit, and revise pieces for several different expository text structures. Students have the benefit of teacher as well as peer modeling of the strategies, and extensive opportunity to discuss their ideas.

> **Key Concept 3**
>
> The teacher should help children develop strategies for studying expository text.

▌ IMPORTANT ASPECTS OF STUDYING

Anderson and Armbruster (1982) define studying as reading with the requirement of having to perform some mental task or procedure, referred to as the *criterion task*. The criterion task might be taking a test, writing a report, or carrying out an experiment. Obviously, each type of criterion task places somewhat different demands on the student. This perspective helps us understand that we need to show students how certain study strategies can be useful in helping them meet the demands of different criterion tasks.

In order to study effectively, Anderson and Armbruster point out, students need knowledge of the criterion task. The more they know about what they have to learn and do, the better they are likely to perform. For example, if we have a list of the topics to be covered on a test, we will study those topics and ignore information on others. If we know that the test will require us to write essays, we might construct outlines for questions likely to be asked. On the other hand if we were going to take a multiple-choice test, we might just make a list of important facts.

The practical implication of this finding is that you should make sure your students have adequate knowledge of the criterion task. Tell them exactly what information you want them to learn. Also tell them how their learning will be evaluated.

According to Anderson and Armbruster, effective studying requires students to learn how to focus attention on the critical information and to think of a way to organize it, so that it can later be used. That is, students must be able to locate text segments that contain the important ideas and figure out how to remember them.

What makes information important also depends on the reader's purpose. For example, suppose that the reader is searching a newspaper article about activities at the state legislature in order to learn about the status of a certain bill. In this case the reader scans the article for the relevant paragraphs and then reads those very closely, ignoring information in the rest of the article. On the other hand, suppose that the reader is interested in gaining an overview of the major bills being considered by the legislature. In this case the

Exercise

Quickly look over the article below. Then go to the questions below and try to decide how you might reread the article differently, given each of the situations described.

BALLOONS NOT FOR ALL ARTERIES

After a surge in the popularity of balloon angioplasty, the American Heart Association and the American College of Cardiology have issued guidelines for use of the procedure, in which a tiny balloon is threaded through an artery and inflated to clear blockage. More than 200,000 such procedures are expected to be performed next year, says Dr. Thomas J. Ryan, chief cardiologist at Boston University Medical School.

An expert panel, headed by Dr. Ryan, suggests that the procedure is most successful in men under 65 who have a single, small, soft plaque easily reached with a catheter. Patients at increased risk are those over 65, women, and persons with prior bypass surgery or a history of high blood pressure, diabetes or damage in more than one artery.

A successful angioplasty will widen the artery channel by more than 20 percent, reduce blockage to less than 50 percent of the artery's diameter, and not cause heart attack during the procedure (which occurs in four to five percent of cases) or complications requiring immediate bypass surgery (3.5 percent of cases).

The hospital should have a backup team of bypass surgeons available, the panel urged, and physicians doing balloon angioplasty should be required to take a formal course. Learning the technique by observation or attending "how-to" seminars is not enough, the panel says.

—Lawrence K. Altman, M.D., in *The New York Times*

(1) How would you approach this article if you were supposed to write a one-paragraph summary for a biology class?

(2) How would you approach this article if you were a physician wanting to contact an expert on the balloon angioplasty procedure?

(3) How would you approach this article if someone you knew well had a heart problem?

(4) Can you think of other situations which might lead someone to approach the reading of this article in a particular way?

The purpose of this exercise has been to show that readers may take many different approaches to the reading of informational text. What influences the way we read an article or other selection is the purpose we have for reading.

When working with students, teachers will want to be sure they have in mind definite purposes for reading informational text. These purposes will vary from occasion to occasion, and so meeting these purposes will call for the use of different reading and study strategies.

reader skims the whole article, looking for the key pieces of legislation but making no effort to remember detailed information on any particular bill. Thus, the information important in the first case is no longer important, because the reader has a different purpose.

Students can be taught to look for signals in the text which may mark information important for different purposes. Identifying and knowing how to use these signals is a part of studying effectively. Among these signals are titles, headings, main idea statements, and key words. The study strategies listed below all involve use of these signals in one way or another.

Effective Focusing Techniques

Reading and study skills that can help students locate and focus on important information include the following:

Skimming and scanning. In skimming, students move quickly through the text, getting a sense of its content and structure. Skimming is similar to previewing, described earlier, where students are taught to use such signals as chapter titles. In scanning, students have a set purpose for reading and search quickly through the text to locate relevant information. In this case, key words might be an important signal.

Using references and test guides. After students know the topic to be studied, they often need to locate the information in textbooks, tradebooks, dictionaries, encyclopedias, newspapers, and magazines. To identify these sources, they should be able to use the card catalogue to find materials in a library. Once the source is located, students should be able to use other aids (such as a table of contents, index, headings, and guide words) to pinpoint the information sought. Some elementary students may learn to carry out computer searches.

Using visual aids. Students survey illustrations and photographs, graphs and other figures, tables, and maps. Students should be able to "read" or derive meaning from these visual aids, just as they do from text.

Effective Study Techniques

Anderson and Armbruster (1982) reviewed research on the following common studying techniques: underlining, note-taking, summarizing, student questioning, outlining, and representing text in diagrams. We present below a brief definition of each technique:

Underlining. Students draw a line under important text information, using such signals as topic sentences. *Highlighting* information with a marker is like underlining. According to Anderson and Armbruster, this tech-

While the teacher meets with half of the class, other fourth graders study independently. These students have been introduced to note-taking and also to the use of visual structures to organize ideas.

nique can be effective because students have to make decisions about what to underline, and so presumably separate important from unimportant information. Check their choices of underlined material occasionally to determine if they are actually picking out important information, and watch for students who may have a tendency to "over-underline."

Note-taking. Students seek such signals as key words or phrases in the text, and jot them down or generate phrases on their own. This technique can be effective because it encourages students to reflect on the material when deciding what to write down. If students take notes on information important to the criterion task, this can be a good way of focusing attention properly. Look over their notes occasionally to see that they are learning to take down the information needed to accomplish the criterion task.

Summarizing. Students arrive at a condensed version of important text information, using such signals as summary statements (e.g., sentences beginning with phrases such as "in conclusion"). The summary may be stated verbally or written out. The key to effective use of summarizing is to make sure that the students actually reorder and reword text information, and that this kind of deeper processing of main ideas is required in the criterion task. For example, summarizing may not help with recall of details. More information about summarizing is presented in the next key concept in this chapter.

Student questioning. Students state or write down their own questions about the text. Students can be taught to generate certain kinds of questions, such as those about the main idea, and to look for different signals of importance, depending on the criterion task. This technique can be effective because it causes students to think about and work actively with the text.

Outlining. Students organize text information under major and minor headings, as described later in the hierarchical summary procedure, making use of such signals as subheadings. According to Anderson and Armbruster, most students need to be given careful instruction before they are able to outline text on their own. A problem may arise if students become preoccupied with the outline format itself and proceed to fill in information without really thinking very much about it. Instead, students should learn to use the outline format as a means for organizing and thinking more deeply about text information. Outlining can be very time-consuming. Thus, depending on the criterion task, it may not be the most efficient studying technique.

Representing text in diagrams. Students develop a diagram containing pieces of text information and showing the relationships among the various pieces. Concepts, vocabulary, main ideas, fact, and details can all be included. The diagram is often called a *structured overview* (Herber, 1978), a map, or a web. These diagrams are forms of *visual structures* or *visual displays*, but their purpose is only to show features of the text. They do not include what students already know about the subject, as in semantic mapping, discussed in Chapter 5. As with outlining, mapping must be carefully taught to students and can take a lot of time.

▌ INSTRUCTIONAL GUIDELINES

In Key Concept #1 we introduced the idea of the concurrent presentation of content and skills. In keeping with this idea, we recommend that instruction in study skills be embedded in content area instruction. That is, teach children to use a certain study technique as it fits with the criterion task in a content area unit. For example, suppose that your students have just completed a social studies unit on Japan. You plan to have them write a short essay comparing their own lives to the life of a student their age in Japan. Summarizing the text, bringing out the key information to be covered in the essay, might be appropriate here. To take another example, suppose that your students are working on a unit about the history of their region of the United States. You think it important for them to remember some of the causes of the events described later in the text. Outlining might be appropriate here.

Be careful in selecting a study skill to see that this kind of match exists. Do not have the children use a more complex strategy, such as summarizing or outlining, if no good purpose is served. For example, suppose that you are teaching a science unit about electricity. You want the students to learn certain concepts and terms, and you will be giving them a short-answer, fill-in-the-blank test. In this case, having the students underline and take a few notes may be sufficient.

The idea here is to give students a sense of the kinds of study skills they can use to meet different criterion tasks. Having them use an overly elaborate strategy for a simple criterion task will not give them this sense. Rather, try to give students the message that different study skills should be used to meet different goals.

▌ INSTRUCTIONAL ACTIVITIES

Main Idea Comprehension

Being able to comprehend the main idea of a passage can be a skill useful across a whole range of criterion tasks. Often, understanding the main idea gives students a way of remembering and organizing information being studied. Baumann (1984) devised a program effective in teaching sixth graders to comprehend main ideas. The students received eight 30-minute lessons as described below. Distinctive features of this program included teaching students to identify supporting details along with main ideas, and not separately; giving them heuristics to foster concepts about main ideas (e.g., visualizing the main idea on an umbrella with supporting details beneath); and having them compose main idea statements instead of simply recognizing them.

In Lesson 1, students were taught to identify a main idea when it was explicitly stated in a paragraph (i.e., each paragraph had a clear topic sentence). They were also shown how to pick out details which supported the main idea.

In Lesson 2, students were introduced to the idea that the topic sentence can be implicit, as well as explicit. They were taught how to identify the "dominant relationship" described by the "subordinate topics" or details in a paragraph. Lesson 3 provided students with a review of the information presented in the first two lessons.

Lessons 4 and 5 moved students from working with paragraphs to working with passages. Students were taught in Lesson 4 to look for explicit statements of the passage theme, and in Lesson 5 for implicit themes. They were told when dealing with passages to think of a "detail" as the main idea of a particular paragraph. Thus, these two lessons built directly upon the foundation laid in the first lessons.

Lessons 6 and 7 focused on the generating of main idea outlines, first for passages with explicit main ideas and then for passages with implicit main ideas. Finally, in Lesson 8, the students reviewed and practiced all of the main idea skills previously introduced.

Instruction in each lesson followed a sequence of five steps. The instructor began by informing students of the purpose of the lesson and of the value of the particular main idea skill to be targeted. In the second step a sample text illustrating use of the skill was presented. The third step was direct instruction of the skill; the fourth, application activities; and the fifth, independent practice.

Writing a Summary

When students write a summary of text information, they begin by analyzing the text and then restate the ideas in their own words. In this way, summarizing promotes their active involvement with both the structure and content of expository text. Summarizing is one of the abilities that differentiates good from poor readers, and learning to summarize can improve poor readers' comprehension (Brown & Day, 1983).

Summarizing is an activity which teachers may introduce as early as first grade, although systematic instruction (as described below) should probably occur in the fourth through sixth grades. Because even college students have difficulty with summarization, teachers should not expect elementary students to master this writing technique. Rather, the purposes of giving the children some direct instruction in writing a summary are to give them experience with the task, some knowledge of the procedures followed in producing an adequate summary, and a sense of the features which differentiate a good from a poor summary.

The following suggestions for helping elementary students learn to write summaries take them through the steps and rules recommended by Hare and Borchardt (1984), as shown in Figure 4.7. As you can see, the process is quite complex. For this reason, teachers may wish to introduce summarization to only some of the students in the class. Or they may find it easier to teach summarization to small groups of students, rather than the whole class at once.

On the first day, discuss with the students why it can be useful to write a summary of text information. Help them to understand that, by analyzing the text and rewriting the important information, they will be better able to learn and remember it. If the children have prepared reports before, point out that summaries are often incorporated into reports.

Introduce the students to the four rules for writing a summary, as shown in Figure 4.7. Discuss each of the rules with them, so they have a general idea of the procedures involved. Using a familiar passage from a content area textbook, lead the group in constructing a rough draft of a summary, following the four rules. Write the summary on the board, using the children's suggestions for wording.

On the second day, have the children work with you to improve the summary. Follow the suggestions for polishing presented at the bottom of Figure 4.7. When the summary is completed, allow the children to ask questions and make comments about the process of writing a summary. Help them to understand that writing a summary is a very demanding task.

Figure 4.7
Four General Steps to Help With the
Four + Specific Rules for Writing
a Summary

1. *Make sure you understand the text.* Ask yourself, "What was this text about?" "What did the writer say?" Try to say the general theme to yourself.

2. *Look back.* Reread the text to make sure you got the theme right. Also read to make sure that you really understand what the important parts of the text are. Star important parts.

Now Use the Four Rules for Writing a Summary

3. *Rethink.* Reread a paragraph of the text. Try to say the theme of that paragraph to yourself. Is the theme a topic sentence? Have you underlined it? Or is the topic sentence missing: If it is missing, have you written one in the margin?

4. *Check and double-check.* Did you leave in any lists? Make sure you don't list things out in your summary. Did you repeat yourself? Make sure you didn't. Did you skip anything? Is all the important information in the summary?

Four Rules for Writing a Summary

1. *Collapse lists.* If you see a list of things, try to think of a word or phrase name for the whole list. For example, if you saw a list like eyes, ears, neck, arms, and legs, you could say "body parts." Or, if you saw a list like ice skating, skiing, or sledding, you could say "winter sports."

2. *Use topic sentences.* Often authors write a sentence that summarizes a whole paragraph. It is called a topic sentence. If the author gives you one, you can use it in your summary. Unfortunately, not all paragraphs contain topic sentences. That means you may have to make up one for yourself. If you don't see a topic sentence, make up one of your own.

3. *Get rid of unnecessary detail.* Some text information can be repeated in a passage. In other words, the same thing can be said in a number of different ways, all in one passage. Other text information can be unimportant, or trivial. Since summaries are meant to be short, get rid of repetitive or trivial information.

4. *Collapse paragraphs.* Paragraphs are often related to one another. Some paragraphs explain one or more other paragraphs. Some paragraphs just expand on the information presented in other paragraphs. Some paragraphs are more necessary than other paragraphs. Decide which paragraphs should be kept or gotten rid of, and which might be joined together.

A Final Suggestion

+. *Polish the summary.* When a lot of information is reduced from an original passage, the resulting concentrated information often sounds very unnatural. Fix this problem and create a more natural-sounding summary. Adjustments may include but are not limited to: paraphrasing, the insertion of connecting words like "and" or "because," and the insertion of introductory or closing statements. Paraphrasing is especially useful here, for two reasons: one, because it improves your ability to remember the material, and two, it avoids using the author's words, otherwise known as plagiarism.

Source: From "Four general steps to help with the four specific rules for writing a summary" by Victoria C. Hare and Kathleen M. Borchardt, *Reading Research Quarterly,* vol. 20, no. 1. p. 66. Reprinted by permission of Victoria C. Hare and the International Reading Association.

Later group discussion lessons to practice preparing summaries may be timed to coincide with the children's completion of different sections in social studies or science textbooks. Teachers continue to lead the children in summarizing passages already read and understood, following the four rules.

If the children show signs of understanding the overall process, teachers may wish to have them begin to work on summarizing a passage which has not already been studied. At this stage the children are introduced to the four steps at the top of Figure 4.7. The summary continues to be written through a process of group discussion.

After the children have had several teacher-led group experiences with unfamiliar passages, they may be ready to try writing summaries on their own, either individually or by working with partners. The children can discuss the strengths and weaknesses of their summaries and talk about parts of the process they are finding difficult. Again, the goal is to give students experience with summarization, not to have them produce perfect summaries, so the discussion should emphasize the process of writing a summary, and not only the qualities of the summaries they have prepared.

Hierarchical Summary Procedure

Taylor (1982) designed this procedure to improve students' ability to deal with the structure and organization of expository text. It should enable fifth and sixth graders to learn and remember information and to write better expository compositions. Taylor reports that most students can master this procedure after eight one-hour lessons. The five steps in the hierarchical summary procedure (previewing, reading, summarizing in an outline, studying, and oral retelling) are described below. Taylor emphasizes the importance of having students write the idea *in their own words* rather than allowing them simply to copy from the text.

Previewing. To begin, students preview a three to five page segment from a content textbook that has headings and subheadings. With the aid of the teacher, students generate a skeleton outline for the segment by writing a Roman numeral for every major section in the reading selection, as designated by a heading. Then they write a capital letter for every subsection, as designated by a subheading. Finally, they leave five or six lines between capital letters where they will list important supporting details from each subsection. By the time students prepare their third hierarchical summary they should be able to generate skeleton outlines on their own.

Reading and outlining. After making skeleton outlines, students read the material subsection by subsection, writing a summary of each subsection as they go. With the teacher's guidance, they generate a main idea statement in their own words for an entire subsection, then they list two to four important supporting details for the main idea they just generated. As a class, they discuss the supporting details they wrote down. Then students repeat the process with the next subsection.

Before students go on to the new section of the text, they generate a topic sentence in their own words for the section they just finished reading. They write this topic sentence by the appropriate Roman numeral on their papers. In the left margin they write key phrases for any subsections which seem to go together. They draw lines between the key phrases and corresponding subsections. Finally, students discuss their topic sentences and key phrases with the teacher. An example of a hierarchical summary is presented in Figure 4.8.

After doing three hierarchical summaries, students should be able to complete them on their own after beginning them with the teacher. By their

∎ **Figure 4.8**
Hierarchical Summary for Social
Studies Text Selection Containing
One Heading and Six Subheadings

I. *Johnson developed many programs to fight injustice and poverty.* *

A. *Lyndon Johnson became President of the U.S. after Kennedy was assassinated.*†
hard worker, tried to carry out some of Kennedy's programs.‡

Civil
Rights§

B. *Johnson fought for a civil-rights law.*†
purpose: to protect Blacks from discrimination in hotels and restaurants; Blacks had
not been allowed in some hotels or restaurants in the South.‡

C. *Johnson persuaded Congress to pass a law ensuring all people the right to vote.*†
protected Black people's right to vote, literacy test now illegal.‡

D. *Johnson started a "war on poverty."*†
job training, education for poor people, plans for a "Great Society."‡

Great
Society
Programs§

E. *Johnson persuaded Congress to develop a Medicare program.*†
for people at least 65 years old, hospital bills paid, doctor's bills paid in part.‡

F. *Johnson persuaded Congress to pass a law giving money to schools.*†
purpose: to improve education of children from poor families; one billion dollars in
aid to schools.‡

* topic sentence for entire selection as designated by a heading
† main ideas for subsections as designated by subheadings
‡ supporting details for main ideas
§ key phrases connecting subsections

Source: "A summarizing strategy to improve middle grade students' reading and writing skills" by Barbara M. Taylor, *The Reading Teacher*, November 1982. Copyright © 1982 International Reading Association, Inc. Reprinted with permission of Barbara Taylor and the International Reading Association.

sixth hierarchical summary, students should be able to write them independently and compare them to a model prepared by the teacher.

Studying and retelling orally. After reading the textbook material and writing their hierarchical summaries, students study the material. They review the information in the summaries, distinguishing among topic sentences for sections, key phrases connecting subsections, main ideas of subsections, and important details in support of these main ideas.

Finally, students retell orally what they have learned. They tell a partner everything they can remember about the material, thinking of information they wrote on their hierarchical summaries. The partner looks at the summary as the student retells, reminding the students of unrecalled information (Taylor, 1982, pp. 202–204).

According to Taylor, the ideas described above can also be adapted to texts without headings. In this case, have the children first read part of the text. Then have them try to come up with their own main idea statements. Have them list details to support each main idea. Finally, help them compose a topic sentence for the text.

Study Guides

The study guide is perhaps the most widely used technique for helping students comprehend informational text (Wood, 1988). A study guide may be based on a chapter in a content area textbook or on another expository selection. Study guides include questions for students to answer, as well as other activities designed to call students' attention to certain concepts and facts. Because students generally complete study guides on their own or while working with peers, they have the opportunity to learn to apply comprehension strategies more or less independently. Students in the fourth grade and above will generally benefit from working with study guides, and some types of guides may be appropriate for use with younger students.

According to Wood (1988), the use of study guides is based on the idea that skillful teacher questioning can help students construct meaning from text.

> Study guides use questions and other tasks to activate students' prior knowledge, to have them mentally and graphically translate the written content, and to encourage them to draw inferences while they are reading. In this way students are not merely adopting an alternative set of teacher or text oriented propositions, but rather they are interacting personally and socially (aided by their peers) with the printed material. Through this dynamic interaction, students engage in deep processing of text as they seek to reconstruct the author's message and make sense of what they read. (p. 913)

As you probably inferred from reading this quotation, study guides are based on the same theories of reading and instruction already introduced in this textbook.

We will present two types of study guides described by Wood (1988). The first, the point of view reading guide, appears to be particularly useful when students are first being introduced to guides for studying expository text. This is because the point of view reading guide allows students to make use of personal experiences and of understandings they have probably developed while reading narratives. The second, the interactive reading guide, has the advantage of allowing teachers to use study guides to foster cooperative learning.

Point of view reading guide. The point of view reading guide encourages students to think actively about informational text by having them adopt a number of different perspectives. Questions in the point of view reading guide are presented in an interview format. As Wood states, "Instead of just reading about a particular character, students actually become that individual" (p. 913). This approach makes history, science, and other subjects real to students.

For example, Figure 4.9 shows a guide designed to help students learn about the War of 1812. While working through the guide, students must take

■ Figure 4.9
■ Point of View Reading Guide

Chapter 11: The War of 1812

You are about to be interviewed as if you were a person living in the United States in the early 1800s. Describe your reactions to each of the events discussed next.

Planting the Seeds of War (p. 285)

1. As a merchant in a coastal town, tell why your business is doing poorly.

The War Debate (p. 285–7)

2. Explain why you decided to become a war hawk. Who was your leader?
3. Tell why many of your fellow townspeople lowered their flags at half mast. What else did they do?
4. What was the reaction of Great Britain to you and your people at that time?
5. In your opinion, is America ready to fight? Explain why you feel this way.

Perry's Victory (p. 287)

6. In what ways were your predictions either correct or incorrect about Americans' readiness to fight this war?
7. Tell about your experiences under Captain Perry's command.

Death of Tecumseh (p. 288)

8. Mr. Harrison, describe what really happened near the Thames River in Canada.
9. What was Richard Johnson's role in that battle?
10. Now, what are your future plans?

Death of the Creek Confederacy (p. 288)

11. Explain how your people, the Cherokees, actually helped the United States.
12. Tell about your leader.

British Invasion (p. 288–90)

13. As a British soldier, what happened when you got to Washington, D.C.?
14. You headed to Fort McHenry after D.C.; what was the outcome?
15. General Jackson, it's your turn. Tell about your army and how you defeated the British in New Orleans.

The Treaty of Ghent (p. 290)

16. We will end our interview with some final observations from the merchant questioned earlier. We will give you some names and people. Tell how they fare now that the war is over: the British, the Indians, the United States, Harrison, Jackson.

Source: (Figures 4.9, 4.10) Excerpts from pp. 913–915 and figures 1 and 3 from "Guiding students through informational text" by Karen D. Wood, *The Reading Teacher,* May 1988, pp. 912–919. Copyright © 1988 International Reading Association, Inc. Reprinted with permission of Karen D. Wood and the International Reading Association.

the perspective of individuals in several different roles, whose experiences during the war would have been quite different. Among others, students consider the situations of the merchant whose business is doing poorly, of the war hawk, of the soldier under Captain Perry's command, and of the Cherokees.

Wood suggests that the teacher first model and guide students through this activity. Students can be asked to write their responses in the first person, adding details from their own experiences to information presented in the text. Students are likely to do better thinking if they put themselves into their writing. Otherwise, students might be tempted simply to copy their answers from the text.

Wood uses the following examples to illustrate the advantages of having students write in the first person. Suppose that students were asked to answer the interview question: "In your opinion, were the Americans ready to fight?

Explain why you feel this way." Here is the kind of answer likely to be composed by a student writing in the first person:

> No, we weren't ready to fight. Some of us, the war hawks, wanted war. Others didn't. Some New Yorkers at the Battle of Niagara stood by as their friends got killed. We lacked unity. We didn't even have muskets and other equipment. Some of us had to use our own guns or borrow some.

On the other hand, here is the kind of answer likely to be given when a student does not adopt a particular perspective but instead copies the answer from the text.

> No. Because at the battle of Niagara, a group of New York soldiers, refusing to leave New York, stood and watched their outnumbered comrades, across the river, being killed.

In the first answer, the student is actively involved with the information and has elaborated and made inferences. In the second answer, the student is merely parroting the text.

The example of the point of view reading guide presented in Figure 4.9 shows its use in social studies. Wood recommends that it be used in science as well. For example, students could think about life in the ocean from the perspective of a shark or other sea creature.

Interactive reading guide. Throughout this textbook we will be emphasizing the benefits of having students work with other students, as well as on their own or with their teachers. With the interactive reading guide, students can work together to comprehend and learn from expository text. Wood describes the approach in the following way:

> . . . with the interactive reading guide, the teacher directs the strategy in orchestral manner, sometimes requiring responses from individuals, pairs, or small groups. Additionally, instead of merely answering literal level or fill in the blank questions, students may be asked to predict, develop associations, read to a partner, reorganize information according to the text's structure, or recall in any order what was read. (p. 915)

An example of an interactive reading guide is shown in Figure 4.10.

The teacher has the class as a whole discuss what was learned from each activity as it is completed, even if students have been working in pairs or small groups. Because the text is being read in segments, the discussion process is essentially like guided reading. Thus, the teacher has the time to straighten out misunderstandings and to highlight key concepts.

Wood suggests that the teacher will probably want to have the whole class work through the guide together, although at times more able students may be allowed to move ahead. The teacher will want to see that students understand when each activity should be completed and to check on students or groups who may need extra help.

∎ **Figure 4.10**
Interactive Reading Guide

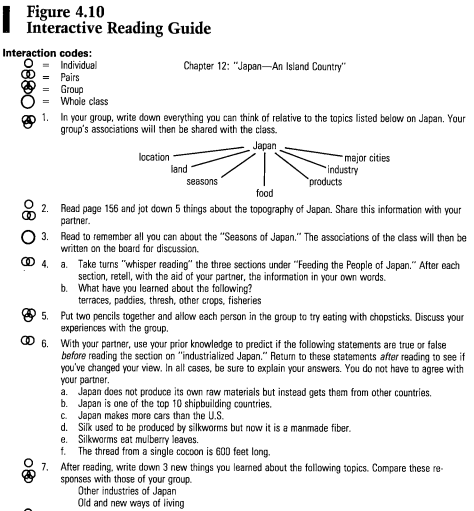

Interaction codes:
○ = Individual
⊕ = Pairs
⊛ = Group
◯ = Whole class

Chapter 12: "Japan—An Island Country"

⊛ 1. In your group, write down everything you can think of relative to the topics listed below on Japan. Your group's associations will then be shared with the class.

location — Japan — major cities
land industry
seasons products
food

○ 2. Read page 156 and jot down 5 things about the topography of Japan. Share this information with your partner.
⊕

◯ 3. Read to remember all you can about the "Seasons of Japan." The associations of the class will then be written on the board for discussion.

⊕ 4. a. Take turns "whisper reading" the three sections under "Feeding the People of Japan." After each section, retell, with the aid of your partner, the information in your own words.
   b. What have you learned about the following?
      terraces, paddies, thresh, other crops, fisheries

⊛ 5. Put two pencils together and allow each person in the group to try eating with chopsticks. Discuss your experiences with the group.

⊕ 6. With your partner, use your prior knowledge to predict if the following statements are true or false *before* reading the section on "industrialized Japan." Return to these statements *after* reading to see if you've changed your view. In all cases, be sure to explain your answers. You do not have to agree with your partner.
   a. Japan does not produce its own raw materials but instead gets them from other countries.
   b. Japan is one of the top 10 shipbuilding countries.
   c. Japan makes more cars than the U.S.
   d. Silk used to be produced by silkworms but now it is a manmade fiber.
   e. Silkworms eat mulberry leaves.
   f. The thread from a single cocoon is 600 feet long.

○ 7. After reading, write down 3 new things you learned about the following topics. Compare these re-
⊛   sponses with those of your group.
      Other industries of Japan
      Old and new ways of living

○ 8. Read the section on "Cities of Japan." Each group member is to choose a city; show its location on the
⊛   map in the textbook, and report on some facts about it.

○ 9. Return to the major topics introduced in the first activity. Skim over your chapter reading guide re-
◯   sponses with these topics in mind. Next, be ready to contribute, along with the class, anything you have learned about these topics.

It is probably wise to make the arrangements for partners and small groups before a particular interactive study guide is introduced. Wood suggests that teachers consider using Fader's Buddy System (1976). This system groups students of different ability levels together, to be responsible for one another's learning. However, groups are formed so that ability differences are not so great that it is difficult for students to work together on an activity.

Completing work with an interactive reading guide may be fairly time-consuming, because of the many opportunities for discussion and student response. However, students will gain a deeper understanding of the material and the completed guide can serve as the basis for further study and review.

Guidelines for using study guides. Wood provides a number of practical suggestions for the successful use of study guides:

Include a review of content—Frequent review of information learned improves long term understanding and retention (Good & Grouws, 1979). As can be seen in each example, the culminating activity involves a mental and then written review of the major concepts, events, or people. Students are asked to associate and recall all they can, retrieving information while it is still readily accessible.

Be creative in designing the guides—The more creative the guide is in appearance and in content, the more likely students will want to engage in the reading assignments. A guide on the cardiovascular system for a health class, for example, may follow the shape of a heart with questions or activities marking significant locations. Likewise, guide questions and activities should stimulate creative thinking and engage as many of the senses as possible (see Figure 4.10, Number 5).

Group and pair students—The interactive reading guide described here is designed specifically to capitalize on the many advantages of cooperative learning. Yet all reading guides should have some element of student-to-student and student-to-teacher interaction. . . .

Skim guide and text before beginning—Skimming the guide and the text before beginning should become automatic to students after the initial explication and modeling sessions. This survey step helps to solidify their purpose for reading and allows them to "see where they are going before they get there."

Explicate and model—Ample research attests to the value of modeling and demonstrating skills and strategies before assigning independent practice (Berliner & Rosenshine, 1977; Duffy, 1981). It is essential that the purpose of the reading guides be thoroughly explained and students "walked and talked through" the assignment. In this way, they can begin to understand metacognitively why such guides can help them learn.

Circulate and monitor—The most effective teachers continually circulate and monitor class assignments (Evertson et al., 1984; Kounin, 1970). Such an involvement in the lesson allows the teacher to assist individuals or groups and to determine who may need further encouragement.

Follow with a discussion—Reading guides need teacher direction and are most valuable when students are not sent off to work alone or are not required to merely turn in their assignment when finished. Follow up discussions of guide responses are essential with each lesson to increase interest, learning, and later recall.

Use reading guides judiciously—Reading guides should not be designed for every chapter or selection. As with any strategy, their novelty would soon wear off and their utility diminish. Use of guides should be limited to portions of the text which may be difficult reading for students or which are particularly suitable for such modification.

Avoid assigning grades—Reading guides are adjunct aids developed to assist students with the reading of informational material. Therefore, they should not be graded in the competitive sense. Since the finished guides are often the result of group effort, group members should be given either a "complete" or an "incomplete," if graded at all.

Encourage strategic reading—Strategic readers read purposefully and with direction and they know what to do when something fails to make sense. In short, they know what strategies to use and when to use them (Paris, Lipson, & Wixson, 1983). Reading guides are a means of making students aware of the range of strategies necessary for successful comprehension. Yet it is essential to explain how these strategies generalize to other contexts within and outside the classroom environment and how they can still be employed independently when no reading guide is available.

Since teachers cannot provide one-on-one assistance to their students, reading guides have been called "tutors in print form" (Wood & Mateja, 1983). They help guide students through the reading of informational text by using questions or statements to reduce the amount of print students must deal with at a given time. When used as suggested, reading guides provide a vehicle to channel peer interaction, thereby using the most valuable teaching resource available in the classroom—the students themselves (pp. 917–919).

> **Key Concept 4**
>
> The teacher should involve students in research projects integrating reading and writing.

∎ REPORT WRITING

At the beginning of this chapter, we presented Nelms' (1987) description of the teaching of a unit on Argentina, as a way of illustrating how reading and writing can be integrated in the study of a particular topic. Nelms showed how Ms. B. actively involved students with the topic in a number of different ways, including having them interview people, read in a variety of books and magazines, and share information in a class book. As we also mentioned in Key Concept #2, students will learn more when they must become involved with reading and writing in ways which require them to think actively about the material. When students are reading for specific purposes, especially those they set for themselves, they generally make more of an effort to read carefully and accurately.

Students' efforts are likely to be even greater if they know that they must understand the information well enough to put it down in writing. Berkowitz (1988) found that sixth graders who constructed their own maps to organize ideas in expository text were able to recall more than students who studied maps prepared by the experimenter. Thus, having students draw upon expository text in their writing is a powerful way of fostering their reading comprehension. It seems logical, then, that teachers will want to have students write research reports, perhaps based on their reading of a number of different books and articles. Of course, the ability to write a report is valuable in and of itself.

While report writing is a task with which we are all familiar, it is also one which students at the college level, not to mention the elementary level, often find daunting. As Beach (1983) writes:

> While the informational report has been a staple of the elementary school classroom for many years, the headaches associated with this task (for both teachers and students) have become almost as traditional as the assignment itself. (p. 213)

Fortunately, given what is now known about heightening children's interest in reading and writing and about the writing process, we have some exciting new approaches to report writing.

A Process Approach to Report Writing

Beach (1983) describes an approach to report writing consistent with a process approach to writing and with the idea that students should take control of their own reading and writing activities. Beach's approach highlights the critical points in the process where students are likely to need the teacher's help and spells out steps the teacher can take. Among these steps are activities intended to keep students from being overwhelmed by their material, to make it easier for students to find pertinent facts, to deal early on with issues involved in organizing a report, and to "enable students to devote their time and energies to communicating instead of regurgitating" (p. 214).

The approach is based on the premise that students will learn more when they are personally involved in their writing tasks. Specifically, they should be writing about a topic they find interesting and addressing their writing to an audience they think important, in this case, their classmates. While Beach tested this approach with poor readers in the third and fourth grade, it is a sound way to introduce all students to report writing.

Here is an overview of Beach's approach. The teacher opens the unit with an activity to stimulate interest in the subject. Students engage in discussion and then choose a specific topic they wish to explore further. Next the teacher takes students through focusing activities. Students generate questions about their topics, then revise their questions with the help of peers. Further focusing takes place as students organize their reports, search for facts, and take notes. Then they write their reports, following a process approach to writing.

When you read the more detailed description of Beach's approach presented below, you will notice possible ties to other instructional approaches described earlier in this chapter. For example, experience with K–W–L lessons will prepare students to generate a list of questions. Lessons to familiarize students with expository text structures will prepare them to read articles on their topic with greater understanding. Lessons on study skills such as notetaking will also prove beneficial. In brief, having students engage in report writing, following Beach's approach, gives students the opportunity to apply and see the benefit of many of the strategies and skills you have taught them.

Activities to Stimulate Interest

In the sample unit described by Beach, the teacher began by reading *The Desert Is Theirs* (Baylor, 1975) aloud to the class. The students then discussed the book. To pique students' curiosity, the teacher asked questions including, "Why is the desert theirs and not ours?" and "How would you have to feel and act to make the desert yours?" Beach describes how the students became interested in several different topics including scorpions and certain birds who live among cactus needles.

Next, the teacher helped the students generate a list of all the topics, related to the desert, that they would like to know more about. Students used this list to select the topics they would be researching. In this case the teacher had all of the students write about desert animals, so that the whole group would share in the experience of learning to write reports about topics in the same overall category. Beach notes that students can use the list to decide on their own topics, once they have become more skilled at report writing.

Before each student chose an animal to write about, the teacher led the group in a discussion about the form their reports would take. Beach refers to this step as the process of establishing a genre plan. The idea here is to give students a clear picture of the types of information they will be gathering and of the way their reports will look at the end. The discussion covered how students might start their reports, the facts they might include, and the order in which facts might be presented. The group also discussed how long their reports should be and how the reports could be made interesting to read. Beach suggests that the teacher provide the students with models of finished reports. For example, the teacher might write a sample report on the chalkboard or show students actual reports written by other students.

To maintain students' interest, Beach suggests that throughout the unit, teachers periodically introduce artifacts, books, posters, and other materials.

Students may be helped to decide on their topics or they may pick up new information that motivates them to continue their investigations.

Activities to Focus Students on the Report

After students have chosen their topics, the teacher focuses their attention on the purpose of the report, their audience, and the genre plan. Students were asked to write down all the questions they had about the animal they had chosen. Then they read their questions aloud, and the teacher listed all of the different types of questions for the group to see. The teacher then had the students discuss and revise the list, in view of the audience and function of the report. The idea was to arrive at a list consisting of the questions likely to be of interest to a typical third or fourth grader. In the sample unit, the list included: "Is it dangerous?" "What does it look like?" "Where does it live?" and "Does it fight other animals?"

Beach views the step of having students generate the list of questions as central to the success of their report writing. He feels that having a set list of questions removes the kind of uncertainty that leads students to copy long passages verbatim from their sources. Instead, the realization that they are searching for the answers to specific questions makes it easier for students to take down just the few words needed. The list guides students' search for information and helps them to distinguish between relevant and irrelevant information. Also, the list serves to remind students of the interests of their audience.

After the teacher and students had agreed upon the list of questions, the next step was to put the questions into a logical order. If students' reports are going to be longer than a single paragraph, Beach recommends that the group discuss what will go into each paragraph in the report. To get students started, the teacher might ask students what they would want to know first about the topic, or what the most important facts might be. Gradually through discussion, the group will work out an order for the questions, clustering them into different paragraphs if necessary. In the sample unit, the students decided that the first paragraph should deal with the animal's appearance. It would include questions such as the following:

> What is the animal's name?
> How big is the animal?
> What color is the animal?
> Is it covered with fur, skin, feathers, and so forth?
> Does it have special parts such as claws, fangs, and so forth?
> What makes it look different from other animals?
> Are there reasons why the animal looks this way that might be interesting to tell
>   about? (p. 216)

The group decided that other paragraphs would cover the animal's habitat and what it ate.

With the organization of their reports in mind, the students began gathering information from several sources. At this point the teacher might teach the students to scan the encyclopedia and other references for the sections that contain the information they are seeking. Students can also be taught to jot down just the few words to answer their questions.

Report Writing Activities

Beach recommends that the teacher continue to assist students at this stage, by referring back to model reports presented earlier. In the sample unit the students were shown how notes were taken for a model report, how the notes were put into sentences, and how the sentences in turn were put into paragraphs. By modeling this procedure, the teacher showed the students how they would arrive at a first draft of their reports. After modeling the procedure, the teacher used another set of notes to gives students guided practice in preparing a first draft. A student was chosen to read the first draft while others listened and suggested improvements. Students did not begin writing their own first drafts until after they had had both modeling and guided practice. Beach writes:

> Perhaps the most important aspect of this modeling process is that it shows students that the composition of a report depends heavily on the writer switching roles from writer to reader and back in order to judge the effectiveness of what has been written. To emphasize this point, students were encouraged not only to read to themselves what they had written but to work in teams where one child listened as the author read the report aloud; then the two listed suggestions for improvements. This approach to the revision process focuses attention on writing as communication . . . (p. 217).

After the students had produced and revised their first drafts, the teacher had the students take turns reading their reports. Beach recommends that teachers have students follow a procedure developed by Crowhurst (1979), in which students direct their comments toward helping the author to improve his piece. Beach presents this example of a student's draft for which others were able to offer suggestions for improvement.

It lives in the southwestern U.S. A tarantula is a hairy spider . . . (p. 217).

The author reversed the order of these two sentences in his second draft.

Students' reports can be published or made public in a variety of ways. In the sample unit, the teacher posted the reports on a bulletin board in a school corridor. In Nelms' example, presented earlier in this chapter, students' reports were compiled in a class book. Students might also publish their reports as individual booklets.

The following example shows how a third grader's writing was improved through Beach's approach. The student composed the piece below when asked to write about Easter eggs:

As part of a social studies unit, students in this third grade class created models of traditional Hawaiian villages and wrote brief reports on large file cards. In preparing their reports, students followed a process approach to writing.

The easter eggs are different corlers. There are red purle black blue green. We corler the easter eggs because it is a nice corlers. And after they are corler you hide them.

During the sample unit, the student wrote the following first draft of a report on the kangaroo rat:

Kangaroo Rat

It is a rat. It can hop five feet. It is tan and white. And it is on foot long. And it lives in the desert. It has a black tail. It has a burrow. It walks in the night.

Here is the student's final draft:

The Kangaroo Rat

It is a rat. But it is called a kangaroo rat because it hops on its two back feet like a kangaroo. It can hop five feet high. It is tan on top and white on the bottom. It is on foot long. It has a black tail. It lives in a burrow. It only comes out at night. It lives in the desert.

As you can see, there is a dramatic difference between the student's first and final drafts.

Other Recommendations

Beach thinks that students should be taken through the report writing process at least four times a year. The sample unit shows how students might be introduced to report writing. On students' second, third, and later times through the cycle, the teacher should be able to reduce the amount of assistance given. Beach emphasizes that it is essential to repeat the process if students are to gain independence in report writing. The types of topics or the form of the reports should be varied from time to time to broaden students' report writing ability. Ideally, Beach suggests, students would participate in variations of this same approach during their fourth, fifth, and sixth grade years.

Beach feels that two features of the approach contribute to its effectiveness:

First, accepting children's concerns about a topic instead of imposing adult issues as report topics enables the teacher to utilize students' curiosity and motivation to aid in achieving the goal. And second, organizing ahead of time reduces the task to a size that is manageable for elementary school students.

It is also important to note that many of the students enjoyed the unit because they felt they were learning how to do an important academic task, rather than being assigned the task and then allowed to sink or swim. Students' comments to me both during and at the conclusion of the unit indicated not only that they enjoyed the activities we had engaged in but that they felt better prepared to meet the reporting tasks they will face in the future. (p. 220)

❚ SUMMARY

In this chapter we looked at the development of students' comprehension of expository text and of study skills. This area of instruction may be particularly challenging for teachers, because students generally find it easier to deal with narratives than with expository or informational text. It is important to create many opportunities for students to work with informational text. Thus, in the perspective section, we presented a sample social studies unit, to show how reading and writing ability could be developed during content area instruction.

In the first key concept we discussed three frameworks for teaching comprehension of expository text: K-W-L, the content-text-application approach (CTA), and the directed reading-thinking activity (DRTA). All are designed to have students think critically about expository text, for example, by raising questions, applying what they have learned, or making predictions.

The second key concept dealt with the different structures often found in expository text: description, sequence, comparison/contrast, and problem/solution. Research suggests that knowledge of these structures can improve students' comprehension of exposition. Two instructional approaches were recommended for familiarizing students with text structures, both incorporating writing as well as reading.

The focus in the third key concept was on studying, and here we emphasized the need for teachers to help students consider their purpose in studying, and to select the strategy which might best meet their purposes. Three strategies were emphasized: identifying the main idea, summarizing, and outlining (hierarchical summary procedure). We also discussed the use of study guides as a means of helping students learn to explore the ideas in expository text on their own and with peers.

In the fourth key concept we looked at the value of teaching students to write research reports, not only because report writing is of value in and of itself, but also because it can enhance reading comprehension. In this key concept, as in the rest of this chapter, we pointed out the effectiveness of teaching students to generate questions and to set purposes for reading expository text. Students will better learn to comprehend and to study if they participate in setting their own goals and directions for reading. Also, their active involvement with exposition is increased when students not only read but write about text ideas.

∎ BIBLIOGRAPHY
References

Altman, L. K. (1988). Balloons not for all arteries. In "News of Medicine," *Reader's Digest*, December, p. 69.

Alvermann, D. E., & Boothby, P. R. (1982). Text differences: Children's perceptions at the transition stage in reading. *The Reading Teacher, 36* (3), 298–302.

Anderson, T. H., & Armbruster, B. B. (1982). Reader and text—Studying strategies. In W. Otto & S. White (Eds.), *Reading expository material*. New York: Academic Press.

Armbruster, B. B., Anderson, T. H., & Ostertag, J. (1987). Does text structure/summarization instruction facilitate learning from expository text? *Reading Research Quarterly, 22* (3), 331–346.

Baumann, J. F. (1984). The effectiveness of a direct instruction paradigm for teaching main idea comprehension. *Reading Research Quarterly, 20* (1), 93–115.

Beach, J. D. (1983). Teaching students to write informational reports. *Elementary School Journal, 84* (2), 213–220.

Berkowitz, S. J. (1986). Effects of instruction in text organization on sixth-grade students' memory for expository reading. *Reading Research Quarterly, 21* (2), 161–178.

Berliner, D. C., & Rosenshine, B. V. (1977). The acquisition of knowledge in the classroom. In R. C. Anderson, R. J. Spiro, & W. E. Montague (Eds.), *Schooling and the acquisition of knowledge*. Hillsdale, NJ: Erlbaum.

Brown, A. L., & Day, J. D. (1983). Macrorules for summarizing texts: The development of expertise. *Journal of Verbal Learning and Verbal Behavior, 22*, 1–14.

Carlsen, G. R., & Sherrill, A. (1988). *Voices of readers: How we come to love books*. Urbana, IL: National Council of Teachers of English.

Crowhurst, M. (1979). The writing workshop: An experiment in peer response to writing. *Language Arts, 56*, 757–762.

Duffy, G. G. (1981). Teacher effectiveness research: Implications for the reading profession. In M. L. Kamil (Ed.), *Directions in reading: Research and instruction,* Thirtieth Yearbook of the National Reading Conference. Washington, DC: National Reading Conference.

Englert, C. S., & Raphael, T. E. (in press). Developing successful writers through cognitive strategy instruction. In J. E. Brophy (Ed.), *Advances in research on teaching.* Greenwich, CT: JAI Press.

Englert, C. S., Raphael, T. E., Anderson, L. J., Anthony, H. M., Fear, K. L., & Gregg, S. L. (1988). A case for writing intervention: Strategies for writing informational text. *Learning Disabilities Focus, 3* (2), 98–113.

Estes, T., & Vaughan, J. L. (1978). *Reading and learning in the content classroom.* Boston: Allyn & Bacon.

Evertson, C. M., Emmer, E. T., Clements, B. S., Sanford, J. P., & Worsham, M. E. (1984). *Classroom management for elementary teachers.* Englewood Cliffs, NJ: Prentice-Hall.

Fader, D. (1976). *The new hooked on books.* New York: Berkley Publishing.

Gaskins, I. W. (1981). Reading for learning: Going beyond basals in the elementary school. *The Reading Teacher, 35* (3), 323–328.

Good, T., & Grouws, D. (1979). The Missouri Mathematics Effectiveness Project: An experimental study in fourth grade classrooms. *Journal of Educational Psychology, 71,* 355–362.

Guthrie, J. T. (1984). Literacy for science and technology. *Journal of Reading, 27* (5), 478–480.

Hare, V. C., & Borchardt, K. M. (1984). Direct instruction of summarization skills. *Reading Research Quarterly, 20* (1), 62–78.

Herber, H. L. (1978). *Teaching reading in content areas.* (2nd ed.). Englewood Cliffs, NJ: Prentice-Hall.

Kounin, J. (1970). *Discipline and group management in classrooms.* New York: Holt, Rinehart and Winston.

McGee, L. M., & Richgels, D. J. (1984). Teaching expository text structure to elementary students. *The Reading Teacher, 38* (8), 739–748.

Meyer, B. J. F., & Freedle, R. O. (1984). Effects of discourse type on recall. *American Educational Research Journal, 21* (1), 121–143.

Moore, D. W., & Readence, J. E. (1983). Approaches to content area reading instruction. *Journal of Reading, 26* (5), 397–402.

Nelms, B. F. (1987). Response and responsibility: Reading, writing, and social studies. *Elementary School Journal, 87* (5), 571–589.

Ogle, D. M. (1986). K-W-L: A teaching model that develops active reading of expository text. *The Reading Teacher, 39* (6), 564–570.

Palincsar, A. S. (1984). The quest for meaning from expository text: A teacher-guided journey. In G. G. Duffy, L. R. Roehler, & J. M. Mason (Eds.), *Comprehension instruction: Perspectives and suggestions.* New York: Longman.

Paris, S., Lipson, M., & Wixson, K. (1983). Becoming a strategic reader. *Contemporary Educational Psychology, 8,* 293–316.

Piccolo, J. (1987). Expository text structure: Teaching and learning strategies. *The Reading Teacher, 40* (9), 838–847.

Richgels, D. J., McGee, L. M., Lomax, R. G., & Sheard, C. (1987). Awareness of four text structures: Effects on recall of expository text. *Reading Research Quarterly, 22* (2), 177–196.

Schallert, D. L., & Tierney, R. J. (1981). The nature of high school textbooks and learners: Overview and update. Paper presented at the annual meeting of the National Reading Conference, Dallas.

Spiegel, D. L. (1981). *Reading for pleasure: Guidelines.* Newark, DE: International Reading Association.

Stauffer, R. G. (1969). *Reading as a thinking process.* New York: Harper & Row.

Taylor, B. (1982). A summarizing strategy to improve middle grade students' reading and writing skills. *The Reading Teacher, 36,* 202–205.

Wong, J. W., & Au, K. H. (1985). The concept-text-application approach: Helping elementary students comprehend expository text. *The Reading Teacher, 38* (7), 612–618.

Wood, K. D. (1988). Guiding students through informational text. *The Reading Teacher, 41* (9), 912–920.

Wood, K. D., & Mateja, J. A. (1983). Adapting secondary level strategies for use in elementary classrooms. *The Reading Teacher, 36,* 492–496.

Children's Books Cited

Baylor, B. (1975). *The desert is theirs,* ill. by P. Parnall. New York: Scribner's.

Shogren, M. (1978). The monster of Loch Ness. In R. B. Ruddell, M. Shogren, & A. L. Ryle, *Moon magic.* Boston: Allyn & Bacon.

Further Readings

Hennings, D. G. (1982). A writing approach to reading comprehension—Schema theory in action. *Language Arts, 59* (1), 8–17.

Hess, M. L. (1989). All about hawks or Oliver's disaster: From facts to narrative. *Language Arts, 66* (3), 304–308.

Manolakes, G. (1988). Comprehension: A personal experience in content area reading. *The Reading Teacher, 42* (3), 200–202.

Nessel, D. (1988). Channeling knowledge for reading expository text. *Journal of Reading, 32* (3), 231–235.

Smith, P. L., & Tompkins, G. E. (1988). Structured notetaking: A new strategy for content area readers. *Journal of Reading, 32* (1), 46–53.

Zarnowski, M. (1988). Learning about fictionalized biographies: A reading and writing approach. *The Reading Teacher, 42* (2), 136–142.

Chapter 5

Teaching Vocabulary and Word Meanings

Words have often been called slippery customers, and many scholars have been distressed by their tendency to shift their meanings and slide out from under any simple definition. A goal of some clear thinkers has been to use words in more precise ways. But though this is an excellent and necessary step for technical jargon, it is a self-defeating program when applied to ordinary words. It is not only that words are shifters; the objects to which they must be applied shift with even greater rapidity.
(Labov, 1973, p. 341)

▋ OVERVIEW

Having presented views of comprehension processes in the last three chapters, we now move to the building blocks of reading. In this chapter we focus on learning new words, those which are not in students' oral vocabulary. These are words whose meanings are known partially or not at all. We discuss the role that word meanings play in text reading and the importance of context for teaching word meanings. We point out that having a good vocabulary helps students read with understanding and that doing a lot of reading can itself be a way of increasing vocabulary.

Because being able to read words fluently and with understanding is dependent on a strong oral vocabulary, we stress learning about words as part of oral language and concept development. We recommend that word meaning instruction be related to students' background knowledge and the topics in which the words are used. Throughout the chapter we maintain two themes: One is that word learning should be a lifelong pursuit because of the large number of dimensions by which words can be understood and learned. The other is that students should be taught varying strategies, which they can use to learn new word meanings on their own, in the context where the words appear.

Our discussion in Chapter 5 is organized around the following key concepts:

Key Concept 1: Teachers should help children understand the meanings of words.

Key Concept 2: Students need to understand how new words are connected to the topic and context in which they appear.

Key Concept 3: Students need to expand their knowledge of word meanings by analyzing words into familiar roots and affixes.

Key Concept 4: Teachers need to help children learn words by connecting words to conceptual structures.

▋ PERSPECTIVE
Words and Their Meanings

A dilemma will confront you as you set about to help children learn meanings of words. You want your students to understand the words that they read, and use the knowledge to aid their comprehension. You might think that any kind of vocabulary instruction would benefit children's word knowledge and their comprehension. However, the research shows that vocabulary instruction usually affects only word knowledge; it generally fails to improve students' comprehension (Nagy, 1988; Stahl & Fairbanks, 1986).

These findings do not mean that word meanings cannot be taught or that vocabulary instruction ought to be abandoned. How then can you teach children about meanings of words so that they will remember the words and use the knowledge of the words to aid their text comprehension? The answer to this question is complex, and takes most of the chapter to answer.

You need to know more about the nature of words themselves, for as the opening quote states, words are "slippery customers." Take the word, *give.* Anderson (in press) pointed out how its meaning, "to confer ownership of something without receiving a return" (from Webster's Third International Dictionary, 1964), works fine with the sentence, *John gave Mary a present.* When Mary took the present, ownership was conferred, and John did not expect anything in return. But how about:

John gave Mary a kiss.
John gave Mary a shot of penicillin.
John gave Mary a lecture.
John gave Mary a warm greeting.

Most of the objects that were "given" are not tangible objects, so the definition has to be stretched. While there is no core meaning of "granting or conferring ownership" among these sentences, a common thread does exist. Anderson (in press) suggests:

> the relationship among the senses of *give* is better characterized as one of "family resemblance," to use Wittgenstein's (1968) famous metaphor. In a human family there is a greater or lesser degree of resemblance among the members. The nature of the resemblance shifts from member to member, without there necessarily being any one clear respect in which all are alike (manuscript p. 7).

The same exercise can be carried out with many other words. Try coupling the verb, *eat*, with different nouns, including *man, baby, dog,* and *waves.* You should notice that the sense of "eating" changes with each noun, though with a family resemblance among the meanings.

The reason we emphasize this point is that you need to be aware that words have context-sensitive meanings. Neither teaching dictionary definitions nor having students write out definitions of words is sufficient to enable students to connect these contexts to word meanings and text comprehension. Hence, the most obvious type of instruction, word definitions, is unlikely to help students understand the words in ways that they can use to achieve a better understanding of the texts they are reading.

Since you will not want to require children to memorize definitions in dictionaries because dictionary definitions are overly general statements about word meanings, what will you do? You can teach word meanings in

Exercise

You probably take for granted that your vocabulary consists of words for which you have varying degrees of personal and public meaning. That is, you know most words when you read them in context, you have personal references or connections to many of the words, and you are able to use most of them appropriately in spoken and written context. But do you have acceptable dictionary definitions stored? To answer this question, think about whether you understand the following words (we expect you will instantly say yes for most of them), but then try defining them. It's not so easy.

bounty
desolate
dispute
essential
gnarl
harbinger

An important characteristic of proficient readers is an ability to understand words in context. Such word understanding ability does not require readers to be able to recite the definitions of the words.

context of the text in which they appear. If word meanings are taught within the framework of their underlying concepts, then children can better understand the words and relate their meanings to the story themes and story details. Remembering this point will help you develop alternatives to teaching words.

Key Concept 1

Teachers should help children understand the meanings of words.

Even though words are "slippery customers," you can help students broaden their understanding of words within the texts in which they appear. A first step is for you to have a deeper understanding of the nature of words and how the words could be taught. A second step is to try out and then expand on our instructional examples.

▌ NATURE OF WORD KNOWLEDGE

Although we seldom think about *how* we know words, there are several important ways in which we understand words (Menyuk, 1988). One way is that all words are either classified as *function* words or as *content* words, that is, their role in sentences, or syntactic form. Take the sentence, "Jane played in the park." The noun (Jane), verb (played) and object (park) are content words and the preposition (in) and article (the) are function words. Content words carry the burden of meaning and function words contribute to the grammatical sense of a sentence. As expert readers, we know this distinction implicitly but do not think about it unless confronted by a new word. Then we might apply this knowledge in order to unravel part of the text meaning. But that is not all we know.

Words in our language represent universal experiences associated with *objects, events,* and their *attributes,* or characteristics. All languages have words for the objects we use (such as foods, clothing, transportation), for the events in which we participate (such as verbs of motion, location, state, or affect), and for attributions about objects and events (such as descriptions of size, shape, color, texture, function, and relationship). When we learn new words, we more or less automatically *denote* or classify words as objects, events, or attributes of particular kinds. Beyond that we know particular denotative information about the words.

In addition to form class and denotative knowledge of words, we learn when and where to use words. That is, we acquire knowledge about *connota-*

tive meanings, which are rules or sets of distinctions for deciding whether an object, event, or attribute is a member of a category. Menyuk's (1988) following examples aptly describe this notion:

> For example, for polite communication the learner must acquire the distinctions between such terms as "stingy" and "thrifty," "fat" and "heavy," "cheap" and "inexpensive" that on the surface appear to be synonymous. The first term in each of these pairs connotes a negative aspect of the attribute categorized. Children learn that the same word can be interpreted in different ways depending on context. In the example ["His *dog* always fetched the evening paper for him." "It's a *dog*-eat-*dog* world."], the meaning of the word "dog" in one sentence represented or denoted an object category, but in the other the word connoted a category of persons with particular characteristics. Metaphors, similes, and idioms—so-called figurative language—are also forms of connotative meaning. For example, the idiom "break the ice" suggests, in general, to make interaction possible. A simile such as "She's as beautiful as a sunrise" suggests, in general, that her beauty is similar to that of a wonder of nature. A metaphor such as "The falling snowflakes were twirling ballerinas" suggests, in general, that the falling snowflakes were spinning in the manner in which ballerinas spin. (p. 136)

Words are also related to other words. Menyuk describes three types of relationships: categorical, parallel, and connecting relationships. One kind of a categorical relationship is a hierarchy—think of taxonomies. We know, for example that the word *animal* is the superordinate or category title for *bird*, and that *robin* is a member of that group. Another categorical relationship is that words fit particular topics, such as the topic of royalty (*king, queen, princess, prince, castle, knights*). Words can be also grouped by function (*strolling, trudging, roaming, strutting*), or by word families, that is, sets of words that contain the same root word (e.g., the *act* family includes *acting, actor, actress, react, reaction, activity*).

Parallel relationships are those of antonymy in which words are opposite in meaning (e.g., *day/night, big/little*), synonymy in which words are similar in meaning (e.g., *woman/lady, big/large*), and homonymy in which words have the same pronunciation but unrelated meanings (e.g., *main/mane, pear/pair*). These concepts are frequently taught to children in the early and middle school years.

Connecting relationships are those which link ideas within and across sentences. The connections vary in their sophistication and difficulty for students to understand and use. The terms *and* and *then*, for example, are probably learned before terms that mark other connections such as *so, because, although, before, after, until, unless, if . . . then, while,* and so on.

To summarize, we can say that the competent language user acquires at least five types of knowledge about word meanings:

1. Denotative meanings, beginning with basic form class (function, content; part of speech), universal experiences (objects, events, attributes), as well as particular conceptual characteristics.

2. Connotative meanings, that is, rules or distinctions for deciding the applicability of particular words to other contexts (e.g., using adjectives such as *sweet* or *hard* to refer to people, not just to objects), and figurative language, principally idiom, simile, and metaphor.
3. Categorical relations (e.g., hierarchies, topics, functions, word families).
4. Parallel relationships (homonyms, synonyms, and antonyms).
5. Relational terms that connect ideas in sentences, including terms marking cause (e.g., *because*), time (e.g., *when, while*), and disjunction (e.g., *but, although*).

▍ INSTRUCTIONAL GUIDELINES

Children enter kindergarten and first grade having had widely different experiences of using language and learning about concepts, and so differ greatly in their knowledge about word meanings and their underlying concepts. Before and during the first two or three years of school, children learn primarily about denotative meanings of words. Children in the middle grades and adolescence continue learning about the denotative nature of words and acquire more sophisticated concepts about the other four aspects of language.

Word meaning development at all ages is closely tied to concept development and learning about new ideas. For young children, however, it is especially important that oral language experiences provide a central role in vocabulary development. Younger children learn from direct experiences and from listening to stories, so you should provide a wide range of field trip and book reading experiences, interspersed with discussion of students' experiences with and opportunity to use new words in context.

For older children, you can provide experiences for them to hear, read, and write new words. You ought also arrange for experiences that extend their knowledge of word connotations and conceptual relationships among words. Opportunities to analyze the ways that authors use language and to analyze and categorize words appearing in different text contexts are likely to be effective approaches.

Young children and those who enter school with limited home language experiences can be expected to have difficulty dealing with words as objects in and of themselves. Thus, the learning of new vocabulary can better be accomplished by engaging children in activities and having them talk about their experiences. At these times new words can easily and naturally be introduced, used, and learned. For example, while the children are shaping objects out of clay, a teacher can extend their vocabulary by introducing terms such as *mold, twist, pound, pinch, fasten,* and *smooth.*

Obviously, when they first enter school, children are able to speak many more words than they are able to read. That is, their oral vocabulary will be much larger than their reading vocabulary, their store of sight words. As time goes on, though, there is a gradual shift, with reading vocabulary becoming equal in size to oral vocabulary and then usually becoming much larger. Most mature readers can read many more words than they hear or use in everyday conversation, even on topics where many technical terms or unusual words could be applied. Thus, the relationship between oral vocabulary and reading vocabulary changes over time. At first, words are spoken and then read. Later, words may be read and then spoken.

Because kindergarten and first-grade children are far from making this shift, we want to emphasize the development of new concepts and oral vocabulary. For example, we can model the proper use of a new term, read stories with interesting words, and encourage children to express their ideas in a more complete and accurate form. But while we may show children the printed form of newly learned words, we do not expect those words to be added immediately to their reading vocabulary.

∎ INSTRUCTIONAL ACTIVITIES

Meanings of Unfamiliar Words

Jenkins, Matlock, and Slocum (1989) found that students could be taught a general strategy for deriving the meanings of unfamiliar words. The approach was as follows:

Substitute a word or expression for the unknown word.
Check the context for clues that support your idea.
Ask if substitution fits all context clues.
Need a new idea?
Revise your idea to fit the context.   (p. 221)

During the lessons, the teacher showed students a sentence containing an unfamiliar word, read the sentence aloud, and solicited possible meanings for the unknown word, advising students to use the five-step procedure. A second sentence using the same unfamiliar word was then shown and students were asked to revise their idea if necessary and figure out a meaning that fit both sentences. Here are two sentences that the authors used:

In a tense situation an *unflappable* person will make decisions no matter what the reporters ask her.
She remained totally *unflappable* despite the angry crowd.

Field Trips and Other Opportunities for Direct Experience

Almost all kindergarten and first-grade programs include opportunities for children to go on field trips, whether to visit the supermarket, the zoo, the fire station, or to see a play. Older children could visit an art or science museum or see an historical landmark. Use these opportunities to develop the children's language and increase their vocabularies.

Step 1: Before going on the field trip, have the children discuss what they expect to see. Make a list of their predictions, and during the discussion, expand their use of language. Also use this pretrip discussion to introduce concepts to the children. For example, if the class is going to the supermarket, talk about the different types of food they are likely to see (dairy products, produce such as fruits and vegetables, meats). On a piece of chart paper, print the familiar as well as new words used in discussion. A similar procedure can be used for older children. For example, if they are going to an art museum, discuss and list names of artists whose work they will see. Different periods in the history of art and the techniques used to produce the works might also be discussed.

Step 2: During the field trip chat with the children about what they are seeing and whether their predictions are being confirmed. Have parents or other adults accompanying the group converse with the children in this same manner. Encourage the children to ask questions about what they are seeing. Point out how the concepts discussed earlier relate to what they are seeing. ("See, all the dairy products are together in this part of the store.") Older children can be allowed to move around independently after a preliminary orientation. They may be asked to use the new vocabulary in a variety of ways, such as when jotting down notes about different works of art.

Step 3: After the field trip, have the children talk about what they saw. Encourage them to use precise terms and point out the words used on the chart, or, if new words come up, add them to the list. The discussion can lead to a language experience chart, drawing, or, for older children, a written report showing appropriate use of the new terms.

Step 4: At later times, try to remember to use the new vocabulary when speaking to the children and encourage them to use the new words when appropriate occasions arise. ("We're having both milk and ice cream with our lunch today. Do you think there's anything similar about them, something that we learned from our trip to the supermarket?") For older children, new terms could be used when continuing studies in related areas. For example, if the students had learned the term *portrait*, they could be asked to discuss what they had learned about colonial times from having seen portraits painted at that time.

In-class activities, such as baking cookies, setting up an aquarium, or carrying out science experiments, can also be used as opportunities for increasing oral vocabulary. Begin with an introductory discussion in which you expand or modify children's responses by filling in more accurate terms. Then encourage children to use the new vocabulary while the activity is going on. Have older children use new vocabulary in their writing to describe what happened and what they learned. Throughout, remember to use new vocabulary yourself when speaking to the children and to encourage them to continue using the new terms.

Developing Vocabulary Knowledge Through Oral Language Lessons

Herman (1988) suggests a way to develop students' general language skills, including vocabulary knowledge in kindergarten where community helpers are studied as part of the curriculum. In this work, one goal was to help students understand firefighters' contribution to the community by exploring their job responsibilities and equipment used to carry out their job. Another goal was for students to express such knowledge by using appropriate "firefighter" words. A field trip to a fire station and books and pictures would link new knowledge with prior knowledge, would actively involve students, and would teach vocabulary in meaningful context.

A few key concepts were chosen for conceptual focus of the unit: firefighters' work, firefighters' equipment, and firefighters' feelings. The teacher selected words that were likely to be encountered by young children such as *rescue, alarm, helmet, hatchet, engine, "being ready,"* and *brave.*

The teacher chose a picture of a firefighter at work from her file. She taped it to the chalkboard and asked the students, "What do you see in this

A direct experience provides an ideal opportunity for vocabulary building. Speaking with a fireman and seeing a fire engine close up give these students the chance to learn and use new vocabulary in a meaningful context.

picture?" Students responded with words like *truck, hose,* and *boots.* The teacher recorded their responses and extended their vocabulary when appropriate. For example, one student said the firefighter was wearing a hat. The teacher asked if anyone knew the special name for a firefighter's hat. Because no one knew, she provided the word *helmet.* She connected the written word to the picture by drawing a line to the item. Although the teacher focused the discussion on firefighters' equipment, students also shared what they knew about firefighters' work (p. 7).

The introductory activity helps students learn new words (e.g., *helmet*), elaborate their understanding of other words (e.g., *engine*), and begin developing a network of firefighter words. It also enables the teacher to assess students' prior knowledge, and guide planning for future lessons.

The field trip is preceded by discussion in which children predict what they might see at the fire station. The teacher praises students' use of new terms and lists their predictions on the board, referring to the labeled chart or story when appropriate. She extends the discussion by asking what children would like to ask the firefighters and how they think firefighters feel. These questions are also recorded on the board. The discussion helps students understand that when they think about what they will see beforehand, the trip is more interesting and they will learn more.

While at the fire station, correct use of terms is modeled, students learn how firefighter words are related (e.g., the fire *engine pumps* water through the *hose* to put out the fire), and new words and ideas that the firefighters mention are pointed out. Students are encouraged to use correct terms and ask questions, especially about firefighters' feelings.

After the trip, the teacher guides students in writing a group thank-you letter after thinking about one thing they learned or something they saw that was really interesting. The teacher records their responses in letter form on chart paper and praises correct use of new terms and insights gained on the trip.

Developing Vocabulary Knowledge Through Reading a Novel

Herman (1988) also suggests how a fourth grade teacher might use the novel *Harriet and The Crocodiles* for vocabulary development. The book contains a compelling story line and many new words—but not an overwhelming number. The lesson fits within an overall goal to enhance students' ability to comprehend and enjoy good literature.

The first step is to map out important elements of the story line to guide comprehension instruction and to select words for vocabulary instruction. Particular attention is paid in each chapter to words that are critical to understanding the text and to words that are likely to be met again by students.

A second step is to divide each set of words into three categories for instruction: (1) words to be taught directly by the teacher, (2) words to be learned by looking them up in the dictionary, and (3) words to be learned by using story context. Teacher-taught words require concept development in order to understand them (e.g., *frenzy*). Dictionary words can be learned by students on their own because they are concrete (e.g., *cardigan*) or represent familiar concepts (e.g., *snout*). Context words can be understood partially or completely by thoughtfully considering the surrounding text.

To initiate the instruction of the first set of words, the teacher writes a known phrase on the chalkboard: *great emotion.* She invites students to add words or phrases that this initial phrase triggers. The teacher might add *wild excitement,* and students might contribute *crazy, out-of-control,* and *hysterics.* The teacher can now draw an arrow down and write *frenzy* under the list:

great emotion
wild excitement
crazy
out of control
hysterics
↓
frenzy

The teacher can help students understand how *frenzy* is related to the other phrases, invite them to think of a word that means the opposite of *frenzy,* and have them contribute personal examples related to *frenzy* (e.g., after winning a championship game) and use the term while relating examples. The teacher might end by asking students to predict what in the story might cause a frenzy.

Vocabulary Development During the Reading Aloud of Storybooks

New words can be introduced by reading stories aloud to students because they can listen to your expression of new words in meaningful contexts (Elley, 1989). The steps to be followed are similar in principle to those used for other vocabulary lessons. They are readily adapted for use with older children, when you might read chapters of a novel aloud instead of storybooks. This general plan was drawn from work by Mason, Peterman, and Kerr (1989).

Model. Before reading, encourage discussion of the story that is to be read to students. Information about title, author, setting and characters, and type of text is useful to set the stage for listening. During the prereading discussion, model the words you suspect are new for some students by using them in context or by demonstration. Some teachers actually bring in examples of the new objects that are described in the story. Others highlight their importance by writing them on the board as they speak.

Guided practice. During the reading, if you think a word is new for some students, stop and ask them to tell what the words mean, or offer interpretations of their meanings in context. Do this quickly, however, and not too often, so that the ideas in the story are not lost. Some teachers elaborated by relating new words to picture or text information or to other known words. You might also elaborate by pointing out how the word fits within that particular context or to other words or how connecting words tie certain story ideas together.

Supported independence. To elicit students' use of new language in the story, encourage them to comment and ask questions as the text is read aloud. After the whole story or chapter is read, ask students to discuss the story using some of the new words they heard that are listed on the board. Add any other new words by rereading phrases or sentences that contain them and ask students to explain the meanings.

Independent practice. From the compiled list of new words on the board, encourage students to use their favorites in storytelling or creative writing activities.

Figurative Language

Some instruction for older students' word understanding might focus on figurative language. You might involve students in analysis and use of figurative language after listening to and interpreting a poem. Here is an example taken from *Carousels*, (1986, p. 366):

> Here is an interesting use of figurative language in today's poem. Listen to it. It is called *Night Comes*, by B. S. deRegniers:
>
> > Night comes leaking
> > Out of the sky.
> > Stars come peeking.
> > Moon comes sneaking,
> > Silvery sly.
> > Who is shaking,
> > Shivery quaking?
> > Who is afraid of the night?
> > Not I.

The teacher might ask students to interpret the poem, writing their comments on the board about how the words were used metaphorically. Then see if they can think of other figurative language words that could have a similar impact but portray a different message (such as crashing and blasting or dipping and tipping). A next step would be for students to extend figurative language to a poem of their own construction, "Let's take the basic poem structure and substitute other figurative language words for *leaking, peeking, sneaking, shivery-shaking, quaking.* Try to hold onto most of the rest of the words as you come up with your own theme to express with the figurative language words." Students could be given copies of the poem with blank lines where the figurative language words appear in the poem and work within the basic form, or they could construct new figurative language poems.

Alternatively, although this approach might be difficult for students, the teacher could direct students to replace the content words rather than the metaphorical terms. You might say, "Let's see what else we can write about using these figurative language words. What topic could you represent metaphorically with words like *leaking, peeking,* and so on? (How about vehicles on a dark city street?) Now make up a new poem in which you put the words into a new context." Students could be given copies of the poem with blanks where the words, *night, sky, stars, moon, afraid* appear and again they could work alone or in groups together to construct new poems. The poems could be read to classmates or written out for newsletters that are sent home.

Thinking Trees

The earlier instructional suggestions presented ways of denoting word meanings and using figurative language. Our final example suggests a way to help students categorize words into hierarchical relationships.

An interesting way to set up a hierarchical structure for students to learn appears in Nagy (1988), drawn from Kirby and Kuykendall (1985). Students help to set up the hierarchy and in the process generate vocabulary items, see relationships among words, and explain meanings of words to each other. The example is taken from the theme of "inventing."

To teach students using this sort of lesson, feature the learning goal, in which students are to understand and gain practice in structuring words as hierarchical relationships. The topic of inventing a new transportation system in this example supports the word learning goal.

Take the questions listed in Figure 5.1 (pp. 186–187) one by one and have students generate answers. Their answers will vary from those on the figure. This is appropriate since the goal is to extend the experiences of your students. Your questions are likely to include the following:

What kind of transportations are there?

What kinds of problems are associated with cars? (or take another example that your students have given) . . . Can you think of other problems? Now, take the three most serious problems and think of solutions for each.

Now, go back to the first step. Can you invent a type of transportation that might solve your three serious problems? (Have students work in small groups to try to solve and write about the problems.)

Key Concept 2

Students need to understand how new words are connected to the topic and context in which they appear.

THE ROLE OF CONTEXT IN LEARNING NEW WORDS

New words can be learned when they appear in contexts that are meaningful. The context can be the room in which a conversation takes place or the story in which a paragraph appears. Context-supported written information appears in surrounding words, phrases, and sentences, and through the overriding topic.

Words which are taught to students in a meaningful context, either a spoken or written context, are likely to be learned more readily than words taught apart from such contexts (Jenkins & Dixon, 1983). The context makes it easier for students to connect the new words to their existing knowledge about that larger context. Associating new vocabulary with concepts that are already known is a powerful way to learn.

Exercise

Write down what you think the word "symptoms" means. Now look at the exercise on page 188 and write what the word means in that context. Compare your two definitions. How and why are they different?

The advantage of context learning, however, does not mean that students will be able to rely completely on context cues to figure out new words, for text context should not be the only source of support. Many times text context is too weak to help readers understand much about the words. According to Nagy and Herman (1987), children can learn about one in twenty words from one exposure to a text. Under what circumstances might context be helpful and when might it not be helpful? You will have a fairly good idea from looking at the next set of sentences. Try to define the following words based on the sentence contexts:

The *portmanteau* was used on every trip.
Among certain vegetables, *noctuid* can be destructive.
The judge *approbated* the papers.
Hadal regions contain strange, sightless creatures.

You probably figured out that the words were content words, not functional, and you knew whether they described objects, events, or attributes. And perhaps the context provided some help, though you probably wished for a paragraph instead of one sentence. For example, what do you use on trips— a suitcase, coat, or umbrella? What might be destructive to vegetables— perhaps insects or bacteria? You might combine background knowledge about the topic or the word family with the context and then come closer to an accurate meaning. Now, if you go to the dictionary, you could extend your

▌ Figure 5.1
▌ A Thinking Tree Activity

ON YOUR OWN

Let's say that you are interested in inventing something to improve transportation. "Transportation" is a huge subject, and you could end up just spinning your wheels. One way to organize your thinking is to take a large idea like transportation and subdivide it into small units. For example, what kinds of transportation are there?

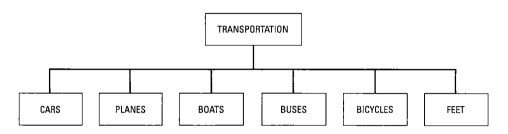

Can you think of other kinds of transportation?
Now what kinds of problems are associated with cars? Can you think of other problems?

Now we're going to subdivide each problem associated with cars. Think about what kinds of solutions or inventions already exist to solve these problems. Make each problem the heading for a list. We've started the lists for you.

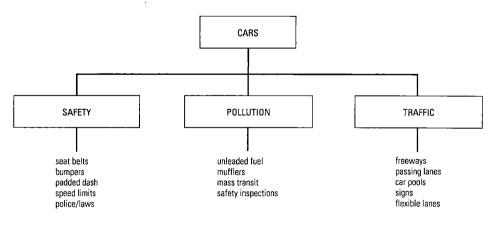

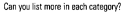

Can you list more in each category?

▌ Figure 5.1
▌ (continued)

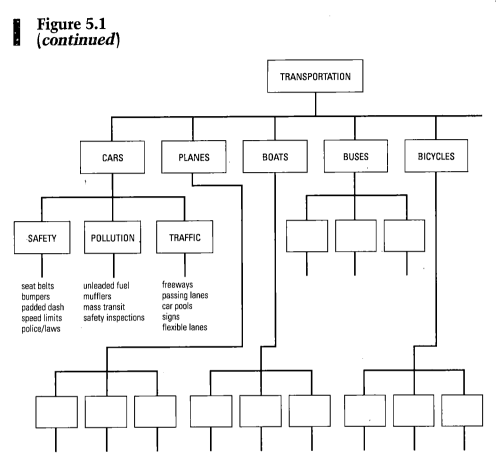

Can you think of anything not yet invented that might help solve the problems of safety, pollution, and traffic? Make a list.

Source: From *Teaching Vocabulary to Improve Reading Comprehension* by William E. Nagy. Reprinted by permission of the National Council of Teachers of English.

understanding a little further, but you are still likely to feel uneasy about adding some of these words to your writing or speaking vocabulary unless you were already familiar with the concepts and topics within which these words are typically used. That is, you need to understand the connotations for use. More experience with the words within the general topic is usually needed to pick up connotative nuances of the words.

Thus, when reading words that are in new conceptual domains, you cannot expect a single context example to be a sufficient source for complete word understanding. On the one hand, even one exposure often gives you some new knowledge about the words. In fact, each experience of reading or hearing new words in context will add a bit to your store of knowledge about meanings. This may help to explain why students who are avid readers have larger vocabularies, a point discussed in the next section.

(1) Read through the passage below and try to get a general idea of what it is about.

In seasonal allergy ("hay fever"), the specific source of the patient's trouble can often be identified by careful history-taking. Skin testing and *in vitro* immunologic tests can often be utilized to provide definitive evidence; these measures are appropriate only when an allergen such as dog dander must be identified to assist in environmental treatment or when immunotherapy is being considered. . . . In patients with year-round allergic symptoms, differentiation from nonallergic rhinitis may be more difficult. Indirect evidence for an allergic etiology for nasal symptoms includes other manifestations of atopy . . . and a history of typical allergic rhinitis in one or both parents. (Barker, Burton, & Zieve, 1982, pp. 175–176)

(2) On a sheet of paper, write down what you think the passage is about.

(3) By referring back to the passage, see if you can figure out at least partial answers to the following questions. Jot down these answers:

(a) What is a seasonal allergy?

(b) What is an *in vitro* immunologic test? Why would such a test be given?

(c) What is an allergen? Give an example of an allergen.

(d) What is nonallergic rhinitis?

Most of us would find the sample passage very difficult to understand. Yet we are still able to provide at least partial answers to several of the questions. Here is the reasoning that might be used in trying to answer the questions. As you read further, think about the reasoning that you did.

(a) Although many readers have not seen the words *seasonal* and *allergy* together before, they do know what each individual word means. It helps that the layman's term "hay fever" is given.

(b) Many readers have some sense of what a skin test would be and guess that an *in vitro* immunologic test may involve injections or something else besides just a scratch on the skin. They infer that such a test would be given to provide evidence that the person has a seasonal allergy.

(c) The word *allergen* resembles allergy, so many readers think it is probably the substance that causes the illness. Readers might not be certain of what dog dander is, but they know that it is an example of an allergen.

(d) Many readers know that *rhinitis* is probably a kind of medical problem, although they may still be uncertain about exactly what it is. They can guess that there must be at least two types of rhinitis, nonallergic and allergic, and that the first type is *not* related to seasonal allergies.

The purpose of this exercise was to give you a sense of the kinds of reasoning proficient readers use to figure out the meaning of unfamiliar words contained in the texts they read. Readers use the context provided by the passage as a whole and by surrounding words. They look for words and phrases they already understand, such as *hay fever*, and relate these to terms they are uncertain of. They use background knowledge. They analyze individual words (*allergen, nonallergic*). All of these are strategies we want children to learn to use too.

Fostering Wide Reading

Nagy, Herman, and Anderson (1985) demonstrated that, on average, children infer the meanings of about 3000 words a year, though there are tremendous variations in this average. Since a few hundred words are learned from school instruction, the remaining must be learned from encountering new words in texts that are read in school and at home, from television, and from talk with family, community members, the teacher, and classmates.

The biggest differences in children's rate of vocabulary learning are thought to be due to variations in out-of-school reading. Children vary greatly in the amount of reading they do, and these differences are closely connected to their reading achievement. In a study of fifth-graders, Fielding, Wilson, and Anderson (1986) found that 10 percent of the children did no out-of-school reading. The middle 50 percent read for an average of only four minutes per day. Only 10 percent of the children, the better readers, read for more than 25 minutes per day. If you were to get most of your students to spend up to 25 minutes a day at home reading, then Nagy and Herman (1987) estimate that they would learn somewhere between 750 and 1500 new words a year from out-of-school reading. This goal is well worth reaching for.

The implications of this research are clear. If we want to help children increase their vocabularies for the purpose of becoming competent, school-successful readers, we should try to motivate them to read for information and for pleasure outside the classroom. Most children could benefit from doing much more voluntary reading than they now do (for ways of motivating voluntary reading, see Chapter 12).

The need to encourage voluntary reading is further underscored by studies suggesting that reading comprehension probably cannot be directly improved simply by teaching children new words and their meanings. One of the few successful attempts required twenty minutes of class time for each word learned (Beck, Perfetti, & McKeown, 1982).

The sheer volume of words students apparently must learn is another reason for not relying on direct training alone. School books read by many students in grades one through twelve contain about 90,000 distinct words, according to Nagy and Anderson (1984). There is no way this number of words can be taught directly. The largest number ever reported taught was 1800 in one year, but it was on a specialized topic (Draper & Moeller, 1971).

In the past, many educators assumed that most word meanings were learned through instruction and so concluded that children should be taught the meanings of most new words before reading. Teachers are still advised in some basal programs to teach the meaning of all new vocabulary words before they begin having children read a selection. The logic behind this idea, the "preteaching of vocabulary," is that this knowledge will greatly improve children's ability to comprehend the text.

While preteaching vocabulary can be helpful to comprehension in some instances, such preteaching has to be done selectively. Particularly if the

On the board, this fourth-grade teacher displays cards with new vocabulary from the novels her students are reading. Students' interest in learning new words carries over from guided discussion lessons to their voluntary reading.

meanings of new words are taught out of context, preteaching is likely to have little or no effect on comprehension.

There is also a very good reason *not* to preteach all new vocabulary. Following this procedure may deny children the opportunity to practice working out meanings of new words on their own, from the context of the passage.

Classroom vocabulary instruction should be aimed at teaching children strategies for learning new words in sets, with all the words being related to the same topic. The key is to build on the children's background knowledge of the topic, merging the learning of new word meanings with what they already know. The way to do this is to have the children engage in *active processing* of the new words. We concentrate on showing how they can understand and remember the new words by making connections to their background knowledge, and how the new words can be useful in expressing ideas more accurately.

▮ INSTRUCTIONAL ACTIVITIES

Teaching New Words Around a Topic

The following approach is adapted from those developed by Draper and Moeller (1971) and Palincsar (1984). It works particularly well with texts on content area topics such as science and social studies. Technical terms in these texts are usually repeated regularly (Cohen & Steinberg, 1983), so the children have the opportunity to encounter them more than once. They are likely, then, to see how the text will be easier to read and the topic better understood if the terms are added to their vocabulary. The approach described below can easily be used with children from the third grade on up.

Step 1: Give a brief introduction to the topic, perhaps doing no more than naming it, if the children are likely to be quite familiar with it. Elicit from the children what they already know about the topic and have them predict the information to be presented in the first segment of text to be read.

For example, take the case of a sixth grade teacher presenting a lesson on the circulatory system. The lesson is centered around the second section in a health textbook chapter entitled "Your Body Systems at Work." The third page of this section of the chapter is shown in Figure 5.2.

The teacher began the lesson by asking the children what they knew about the circulatory system. The children did not know what the term *circulatory* meant, but when she told them it had to do with blood and the heart, they came up with many ideas, e.g., the heart pumps blood through the body, blood travels through blood vessels, people can have a condition known as high blood pressure. The teacher wrote these ideas on the chalkboard and told the children they would be reading to find out if these statements were true, and also to learn other things about the circulatory system.

Step 2: Have the children read the text segment silently. As they read, have them write on a separate sheet of paper the words with meanings they do not know or are unsure of. Use text segments of just a paragraph or two for younger children or if the text is on a difficult topic. Older children can be assigned longer segments to read on their own.

In the lesson on the circulatory system, the teacher had the children read the set of five pages silently. While reading, the children wrote down such terms as *hemoglobin, antibodies,* and *platelets.* The teacher walked around the room and noted the terms that seemed to be puzzling them.

▌ **Figure 5.2**
▌ **Your Body Systems at Work**

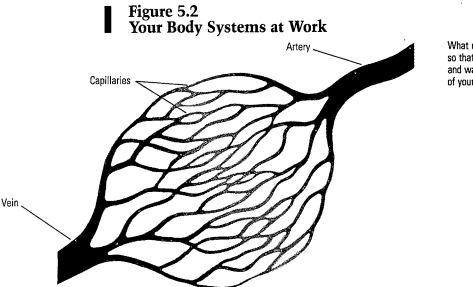

Artery

Capillaries

Vein

What connects arteries to veins so that food substances, oxygen, and wastes can pass in and out of your blood?

Step 3: Ask the children to give an oral summary of the text segment read. Work with the group to construct an accurate and concise summary from the different responses given. You may wish to write notes and then the final summary itself on the board.

In our sample lesson, the text was organized into seven shorter parts, signaled by subheadings. Each part covered a topic such as red blood cells, white blood cells, and the heart. The teacher had the children summarize the text orally as a group. That is, she first had them state in a few sentences what the entire section had been about. Then she had them give the important facts under each subheading.

Step 4: As the summary is being developed, problem words may also be written on the board. If convenient, group these words by subheadings. Although all words may be discussed, most of the time should be devoted to those related to the main idea (if any) of the text. Have children talk about the likely meaning of the words, and then have them return to the text to look at the sentence and paragraph contexts of some of the problem words. Help children work out the meanings from context.

In the sample lesson, the children were asked while summarizing to note any problem words they had come across in that particular part of the text. Under the subheading of red blood cells, several of the children said they were uncertain about the term *hemoglobin*. The teacher felt it was important for the children to understand this term so she had the children reread and then discuss the relevant section of the text.

Step 5: Clarify through discussion the context-supported definition of problem words or have the children consult a dictionary to find the appropriate definition. You might have them write the word and its definition in a diary of new words on that topic.

Step 6: Keep the special terms listed on the board or put them on a piece of chart paper to be displayed and referred to over the period of time the topic is being studied. Encourage the children to use the terms during discussion and in writing reports. When these terms reappear later, be sure the children notice them. If children do not spot them, call the terms to their attention. For example, in a later health lesson, the children read about diseases of the circulatory system, where they were called upon to apply their understanding of terms such as *artery*.

Concept of Definition Procedure

Rationale. Since one of our goals is to help students become independent in learning new words while reading, it may be important to make sure they have a good *concept of definition,* as Schwartz and Raphael (1985) suggest. These investigators point out that, when encountering a word they don't understand, skilled readers have the ability to work out a definition by using context and combining new information with existing background knowledge. Giving students the ability to do the same could contribute to their becoming much better readers.

How can teachers help children develop a concept of definition? According to Schwartz and Raphael, children often first need help in learning about the type of information needed to define a word. Second, they need to know how the information should be organized.

The approach proposed by Schwartz and Raphael centers on the use of simple word maps, adapted from those described by Pearson and Johnson (1978). To construct an adequate word map, students need to bring together three pieces of information:

1. The class of which the concept is a part: What is it?
2. The properties that distinguish the concept from others in the same class: What is it like?
3. Examples of the concept: What are some examples?

The structure of a word map is shown in Figure 5.3 (from Schwartz & Raphael). Presented in Figure 5.4 is a completed word map for the concept of *sandwich*. In the concept of definition procedure developed by Schwartz and Raphael, students teach themselves new word meanings by understanding three categories of information that comprise a definition. Students can learn the strategy in a sequence of four lessons, as described below (adapted from Schwartz & Raphael, 1985). The procedure was tested with fourth and fifth graders and can easily be used with students in any of the upper elementary grades.

First day: preparation. Before teaching the lesson, choose three or more concepts the children already know to use as examples in a categorization task showing the components of a definition. For each concept, prepare a list

▎ Figure 5.3
▎ Structure of a Word Map

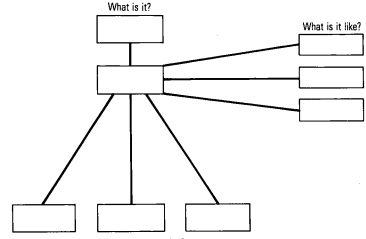

What is it?

What is it like?

What are some examples?

Figure 5.4
Completed Word Map for *Sandwich*

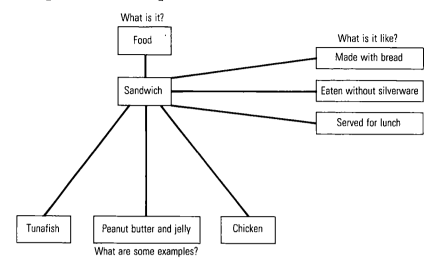

of information including the concept class, at least three properties, and at least three examples. Sample lists of two concepts, *soup* and *clown*, are shown below.

SOUP	CLOWN
chicken noodle	wears a lot of makeup
served with sandwiches	Bozo
tastes good	a person
is a liquid	works in a circus
cream of mushroom	does funny things
eat it with a spoon	wears bright colored clothes
served before the main dish at dinner	likes children
vegetable noodle	rodeo clown
made from milk sometimes	Oopsy
served in a bowl	has a large fake red nose

Conducting the lesson. Begin by giving children explicit information about the purpose of the procedure and what they will be doing. Discuss with them how knowing the meanings of words helps with understanding material being read. Explain to them that the procedure they will be learning will enable them to judge whether they know the meaning of a particular word.

Introduce the children to the structure of a word map (see Figure 5.4). Draw this structure on the chalkboard, putting the labels *What Is It?* above, *Examples* below, and *What Is It Like?* to one side. This gives you a place to list the information for class, examples, and properties. Tell the children that this is a kind of picture which shows three things we generally know when we have a really good understanding of a word. Tell them that they will be learning what these three things are by completing word maps for a number of words they already know.

Have the children work from the lists prepared earlier. Ask them to place the information from the list for each word into the three categories in the word map. Here, for example, is an exchange between a teacher and students which occurred when the children were trying to categorize the information for the word *computer:*

T: To answer the question, "What is it?" you need a very general word. This is a word that would answer the question, "What is it?" for many different words. Look on your list under the word *computer.* Can you find a very general word that answers the question, "What is it?" It could answer the question for lawn mower, or dishwasher, or pencil sharpener, as well as computer.

S: Machine.

T: That certainly is very general, and it does answer the question, "What is it?" Now we'll talk about the question, "What is it like?" The answer to this question gives details about the word being studied. For example, the details for computer are descriptions of what computers are like. These descriptions tell things about computers and how they are different from other machines like lawn mowers, pencil sharpeners, or dishwashers. Can you find any?

S: Has a keyboard.

S: Can play games on it.

S: Has a screen to read from.

T: Yes, those are properties of computer; they answer the question, "What is it like?" To answer the last question, "What are some examples?" check the list again. Do you see any examples of computers?

S: Apple IIc.

S: IBM PC.

S: It isn't on the list, but there is the TRS-80 computer.

T: Excellent. You used information from the list, and also from your own experiences.   (Schwartz & Raphael, 1985, pp. 201–202)

After you have worked through a number of examples with the children, have them try to map and write definitions for some words on their own. They can begin by using words from the lists already prepared. Have them map a word of their own choice using background knowledge to complete the map. Then have them write a definition for the word they just mapped. Here is an example of a definition a student might have written after mapping the word *clown:*

A clown is a person who entertains you. He wears a lot of makeup and does funny things. He usually works in a circus. Some examples are Bozo and Oopsy and a rodeo clown.

Second day: preparation.   Look for a number of passages where information about the target word is presented in the surrounding context. Try to locate passages which give "complete contexts," that is, those providing the class three properties and three examples. Content area textbooks may be a good source of passages, although you may have to modify them to make them more complete. An example of a complete context is shown below:

CROPS

Have you ever been to a farm? Have you ever seen a farmer work with his crops? Crops come from seeds planted by the farmer early in the spring. The farmer takes care of his seeds all spring and summer long. Early in the fall, crops are harvested and taken to market. At the market they are sold to people like you and me. Farmers can plant different kinds of crops. Some plant potatoes. Some plant onions. Some plant corn and tomatoes. Fresh crops sure taste good!

Conducting the lesson.   Let the children know that the purpose of the lesson is to teach them to locate in passages the information needed for a definition. Work through several sample passages with the children. Tell them what the target word is and ask them to mark the information to be put in the word map. Have them transfer the information to the map, then generate either oral or written definitions.

Once the children understand the approach, emphasize that it is not necessary to have exactly three properties or three examples. Let them know that some words have less than three properties or three examples and that more ideas important to an understanding of the word can often be included.

Third day: preparation.   This time look for a number of passages when the context is less complete. These "partial context" passages will not give all of the information students need to complete a map and arrive at a definition for the target word. An example of a passage providing only partial context is shown below:

ENVIRONMENT

You hear a lot these days about our environment, but what exactly is it? We hear a lot of talk about a clean environment. Many parts of our environment need cleaning. The better our environment, the happier we can be.

Conducting the lesson.   Begin by letting the students know that passages will not always provide all the information they need to define a word adequately. Have them work through a passage as in the second lesson and identify the additional information needed. At this point the students may realize on their own that the missing information may be found in dictionaries and encyclopedias or in other books. If not, lead them to this conclusion. Encourage the children to use other references to complete their maps and definitions for the target words. Also, if they are not applying their own background knowledge, remind them to do so.

Fourth day: preparation. Again select a number of passages with only partial context. For each target word, make up an incomplete definition, e.g., one which lacks one of the three kinds of information or presents fewer than three properties or examples. A sample is shown below:

ASTRONAUT

The space shuttle is in space again, this time with five astronauts on board. What an exciting job to have! I'll bet people like John Glenn and Sally Ride really enjoy their work.

Definition: Astronauts enjoy their work. Examples of astronauts are Sally Ride and John Glenn.

_____ This is a complete definition.
_____ This is not a complete definition. Things to add are:

Conducting the lesson. Tell the students that the purpose of this lesson is to have them try to write down word definitions, incorporating all three kinds of information, but without necessarily mapping it first. Ask the children to think about the parts of the map and to try to put the information together in their minds.

Present the partial context passages and incomplete definitions and ask the students to see if the definitions are complete. Tell them that they should write in the missing information for definitions they find to be incomplete. Discuss with the students the kinds of thinking they are using to decide what is missing from the definitions and where they might find the information needed.

Key Concept 3

Students need to expand their knowledge of word meanings by analyzing words into familiar roots and affixes.

WORD ANALYSIS AS PART OF VOCABULARY DEVELOPMENT

Teaching students to identify the meaning-bearing parts of words, or *morphemes*, is likely to be an important strategy for expanding vocabularies. Word roots, prefixes, suffixes, and inflected suffixes are morphemes. The word *transportation*, for example, contains the root, *port*, the prefix, *trans-*, and the suffix, *-ation. Ability* has a less obvious root, *able*, plus the suffix, *-ity.* The words *reflexes* and *smaller* have the inflections *-es* and *-er.* Students who can analyze words in these ways have strategies that they can use as they are reading which could enable them to identify and understand a vastly larger number of words.

Structural analysis, or analysis of words into morphemes, has for many years been an important part of most vocabulary instruction because before the end of third grade, students are confronted with an onslaught of affixed words. Even first-grade books contain many inflections, particularly -s, -ed, and -ing. Students must be able to read these words. However, research has not consistently supported the effectiveness of structural analysis instruction (Johnson & Baumann, 1984). Instruction must be carried out carefully so as not to mislead students (one student told us that *earl* meant "something to hear with"). Word analysis needs to be taught in context and in conjunction with text-meaning cues. Students may then recognize words and derive meanings of unfamiliar words without misconstruing the analysis process.

We recommend the following general principles: Begin with concepts that are most meaningful to students and that are exemplified by words appearing in the materials they are reading. Provide representative examples of the concept being taught and develop clear instructional steps. Teach the word analysis strategies with words that are in sentence or story contexts.

▌ INSTRUCTIONAL ACTIVITIES

We describe two kinds of strategies that you can teach to move students toward independence in vocabulary learning: applying knowledge of familiar roots and understanding the role of affixes in words. Notice in these examples how students are taught to analyze the structure of words placed in sentences rather than in isolation. As with earlier activities, these involve instruction in which you lead students to use reasoning and problem-solving to achieve word understanding.

Applying Knowledge of Familiar Roots and Affixes

Students need to determine whether a new word is *related in meaning* to any words they already know. From a knowledge of affixes, root words, and how compound words are formed, children can have some idea of a word's meaning. They can check their initial hypotheses about it by considering the context provided by the surrounding sentence or passage.

We estimate from the findings of Nagy and Anderson (1984) that, for each root word, children who employ this strategy can probably work out the meanings of about seven new words. This includes about four words formed with regular or irregular inflections, and about three words formed with affixes or as compounds. As you can see, a child who could learn seven new words for each root word known has a great advantage in dealing with school reading material.

In teaching this strategy, begin by familiarizing students with the concept of the *word family*. Word families consist of words that are closely related in meaning, as we see in the following pairs:

senselessly	senseless
washcloth	wash
elfin	elf
litigant	litigate
gunner	gun
everyday	every
theorist	theory

As mature readers we are able to distinguish word pairs like those above from others which are visually but not meaningfully related. These words would not be taught as part of the same word family. For example:

inlay	lay
hookworm	hook
fender	fend
apartment	apart
prefix	fix
misgiving	give

In other words, a word family includes words whose meanings could be predicted or derived from knowledge of the root word.

For instructional purposes, think of a word family as all those words derived from the same root and related in meaning. For example, the word family of *drive* would include the forms *driver, driver's, driving, drives, drove, driven, drivable, driverless,* and *drivenness*. It would also include the compound words *overdrive, drivein,* and *driveway*. Thus, in this word family, there are at least 15 meaningfully related words.

You will want students to make connections between root words they already know and the obvious related words formed with affixes and through compounding. You certainly would lead them to the insight of relatedness, perhaps by having them carry out dictionary searches using root words that are well known to them and that you know are productive (you will find good examples by scanning their dictionary for words that contain many suffixes and are productive compound words). To keep the activity meaningful, students would need opportunities to use their new words in creative writing activities.

As with other types of word identification strategies, most instruction in morphemic analysis should take place around the children's reading of connected text. The point here is not merely for the children to be able to identify words but for them to discover their meanings. For this purpose, children should be given the opportunity to use the context provided by the phrase, sentence, or passage in which the word to be analyzed is found, since these contexts often provide many valuable clues to meaning. There is little point in teaching morphemic analysis on words taken out of context, because this just makes the task artificial and more difficult.

Word Reductions and Expansions

This activity is adapted from one successfully tried out with second graders by Condry (1979). The steps below can be used to give children a sense of how root words are built upon to form other words.

Step 1: Begin with a set of root words or words containing inflections and affixes the children already know by sight. Place the words in sentences. For example, you could have children find the root word in the context of sentences such as these:

Bill is the *owner* of this bicycle.

Tammy and Terry have an *argument* every day.

Or you could have children add affixes to the root word to complete sentences such as these:

Bill used to own this bicycle. He was its _____.

Tammy and Terry always argue. They have an _____every day.

Step 2: Have the children discuss how the new words and their meanings are different from the originals.

Step 3: Discuss with them how the "taking apart" strategy they used when trying to identify and work out the meanings of unfamiliar words is related to the "putting together" strategy they used to make up the longer words.

Other suggestions. Condry found that it was easier for children to find the root word than to find the affix or inflection, and easier to learn suffixes and inflections than prefixes. This suggests that children probably should first be taught to pick out root words. They can later be taught to spot word endings (suffixes and inflections), and then to identify prefixes.

Introducing Common Prefixes and Suffixes

You can provide systematic instruction regarding affixes from about the second grade on, although Hanson (1966) found that first graders were also able to benefit from instruction on the most common patterns (-s, -ed, -ing). Over several years of reading instruction, students can be taught about inflected and other suffixes and prefixes using the words that they have learned to read. Below are the more common forms taken from analyses by White, Sowell, and Yanagihara (1989):

Inflected suffixes

-s, -es
-ed
-ing

Common suffixes

-ly	-ness
-er, -or	-ity, -ty
-ion, -tion	-ment
-ible, -able	-ic
-al, -ial	-ous, -eous, -ious
-y	

Common prefixes

un-	over- (meaning *too much*)
re-	mis-
in-, im-, ir-, il- (meaning *not*)	sub-
dis-	pre-
en-, em-	inter-
non-	fore-
in-, im- (meaning *in* or *into*)	de-

White et al. (1989) point out three complications you need to be aware of when teaching prefixes: inconsistent meanings (*un-*, *re-*, *in-*, and *dis-* contain at least two distinct meanings), false analysis (attempting to separate words that are not prefixed words such as *uncle, reason, invent*), and an overly literal interpretation (e.g., interpreting *indelicate* to mean *not fragile*).

Lessons on prefixes. Because students are frequently confused about what prefixes are, White et al. (1989) recommend a set of six lessons, beginning with a lesson that explicitly defines and teaches the concept of a prefix through example and nonexample. Lesson 1 teaches: (1) A prefix is a group of letters that go in front of a word. (2) It changes the meaning of a word. (3) When you peel it off, a word must be left (p. 305). Instances and noninstances of prefixed words are also generated during this lesson. Lessons 2 and 3 teach the negative meanings of *un-*, *dis-*, *in-*, *im-*, *ir-*, and *non-*; Lesson 4 presents two meanings of the prefix, *re-*; Lesson 5 has alternative meanings of the prefixes taught in the second and third lessons; Lesson 6 presents three less common prefixes, such as *en-*, *em-*, *over-*, and *mis-*.

White et al. (1989) suggest that Lessons 2–6 have the following form:

Show students sentences containing the targeted prefixed words, some with familiar roots and some with unfamiliar roots. The words may contain suffixes as well.

Imagine this sentence is displayed for students: "John didn't come home when he was told; he disobeyed his father."

The teacher would ask, "What word looks as if it has a prefix?" and "When you peel off *dis-*, is there a word left?"

The rest of the dialogue might go something like this: "What does *obey* mean? Did John obey his father? So what does *dis-* mean here? And *disobeyed* means what? Does that make sense? Remember, when you try to figure out words with a prefix, you should always check to see that the meaning makes sense." (p. 305)

Lessons on inflected suffixes and other suffixes. Although inflected suffixes will probably be taught as part of word identification in context, a point which is covered in Chapter 7, it may be appropriate to present at least two general notions to students in the middle elementary grades: (1) Words containing suffixes can be dismantled to identify root words and their meanings, and (2) Some spelling changes in the root words often occur when adding suffixes. Again, the work of White, Sowell, and Yanagihara (1989) has useful instructional suggestions. The initial lesson teaches the concept of a suffix in a way similar to the teaching of prefixes. The next few lessons should be examples of inflections and two or three of the other suffixes. Have students identify the suffixed word, remove it, and identify the root word. Begin by using examples in which there is no spelling change from the base word. Later lessons should illustrate the three major kinds of spelling change: (1) consonant doubling (*thinner, swimming, begged, funny*), (2) *y* to *i* (*worried, flies, busily, reliable, loneliness*), and (3) deleted silent e (*baking, saved, rider, believable, refusal, breezy*) (p. 306).

Strategic Analysis of Words

Herman and Weaver (1988) developed a successful word analysis technique for intermediate grade students. Students are taught a two-part strategy and are given a visual prompt for the strategy (Figure 5.5). Then, based on the information derived from the strategy, students come up with "best guesses" about the unknown words which are descriptions, not definitions. The two-part strategy is:

- Look into words—recall familiar word features, roots, and affixes and students' own past experiences with the words.
- Look around the words—flow of events and mood in that part of the text and at nearby sentences and phrases for other meaning clues.

An advantage to techniques of this sort is that students learn to use an analytic tool while keeping text content information in mind. We think this instructional example offers a valuable approach for teaching students how to study words. Your vocabulary instruction should integrate word analysis with students' background knowledge and with text information. Analytic techniques are not valuable learning tools on their own, but when placed in conjunction with reader knowledge and text context, they can be quite valuable. This principle is further explicated in the next key concept.

Figure 5.5
Visual Prompts for Context Strategy
Instruction

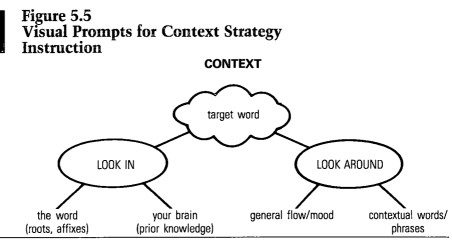

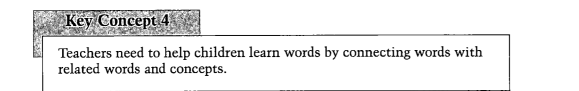

Source: "Visual Prompts for Context Strategy Instruction" from *Contextual Strategies for Learning Word Meanings: Middle Grade Students Look In and Look Around,* P. Herman and R. Weaver. Paper presented at the National Reading Conference, 1988. Reprinted by permission.

Key Concept 4

Teachers need to help children learn words by connecting words with related words and concepts.

GROUPING WORDS INTO CONCEPTUAL MAPS

Effective vocabulary instruction can be difficult because words are labels for concepts, and to learn word meanings necessarily involves concept development. We have known for a long time of the close relationship between vocabulary, or knowledge of meanings, and reading comprehension (e.g., Davis, 1944). Children who do well on vocabulary tests typically have high reading comprehension test scores. Those with low vocabulary test scores usually are poor comprehenders. A plausible explanation of the relationship between vocabulary and reading comprehension is stated in the *knowledge hypothesis* (Anderson & Freebody, 1983; Mezynski, 1983). According to this hypothesis, a word in a reader's vocabulary indicates personal knowledge, not only of that word but of the reader's underlying concepts as well. Children who obtain high scores on vocabulary and comprehension tests have had wide, culturally literate experiences. They have learned many words as part of those experiences. This sum of knowledge is represented or indexed by vocabulary and is what enables better comprehension. Consider, for example, how your understanding of a story about an *aunt* and *uncle* would be hampered if you lacked knowledge of kinship systems.

All readers find that texts which contain many new words are more difficult to read, but if the concepts that underlie the text are familiar, readers can link the words conceptually and still comprehend them. For example, readers who know something about the field of electronics will understand such terms as *ultrasonics, electrostatic transducer,* and *capacitor.* In contrast to others who know little or nothing about electronics, these readers could even understand an article that added new terms about how to build an ultrasonic ranging system by mapping new terms with the familiar ones. Thus, the knowledge hypothesis fits with previous discussions in this textbook of the importance of background knowledge for text comprehension.

While the knowledge hypothesis helps account for the way vocabulary contributes to reading ability, it is also important to realize that reading itself can improve vocabulary (Ingham, 1981; Nagy, Herman, & Anderson, 1985). Competent readers have the ability to pick up new words and their meanings from text. That is, they have learned how to learn the meanings of new words through reading. The exercise you did earlier on page 188 will help you understand this idea.

As you can see, the relationship between vocabulary and reading comprehension works in both directions. Knowledge of word meanings contributes to one's ability to understand text. However, being able to read well also enables one to learn the meaning of new words.

The practical implication is that children should have the opportunity to learn the meanings of words directly, through voluntary reading and from instruction. The instruction involves teaching them to work out meanings of words while they read from conceptual maps.

A mapping technique is effective for vocabulary development for the following reasons:

> First of all, it activates appropriate background knowledge, getting students to think about experiences in their own lives that relate to the theme. This may seem unnecessary, but it has been found that students often do not spontaneously bring the knowledge they possess to bear when reading or when learning new words. Second, the procedure allows the teacher to identify and assess the specific background knowledge of the students in that class. The teacher can then make sure that new concepts and words are related to experiences that are meaningful to those particular students. Third, it provides a rich basis for further writing, as well as reading.   (Nagy, 1988, p. 11)

The overall mapping approach for vocabulary development can have the following steps, according to Nagy (1988), as part of a prereading lesson activity:

1. Select one or more texts that contain a theme students are familiar with, such as an aspect of exploration, transportation systems, inventions, or feelings. In preparation, note words in the selection that are related to the theme. The words will include, but should not be limited to, difficult or new words.

2. Put a word or phrase on the board and ask students to say or write down any words they can think of that are related to this theme.
3. Have students make a composite list on the board in which words are grouped into categories. Help students label the categories.
4. Lead a discussion about how new words relate to familiar words and concepts as part of sharing of personal experiences and using the concepts that elaborate on the theme.

There are limitations to this approach because of the nature of most stories—most new story words cannot be clustered into a single map. If you think in terms of story *themes*, however, you can feature words that are most important for understanding the text. Some words will not be taught, and some will not be understood in the reading, but that is not usually a problem. Not all words need to be understood in order for students to comprehend a passage.

▌ INSTRUCTIONAL ACTIVITIES
Vocabulary Building in Grade One

Mapping was recommended in the comprehension chapters and is also appropriate for vocabulary building. In this example, first graders have read an expository text about sea otters and will organize the information using the new words and concepts in order to write and illustrate their own reports for a science folder on wildlife. The example (see Figures 5.6 and 5.7) and instructional procedure was developed by Heimlich and Pittelman (1986):

Day 1
1. Place a picture of sea otters on the chalkboard. Then print the words *Sea Otters* below the picture and draw a circle around the words.
2. Ask the students to think about sea otters and to share as many words as they can that relate to the topic.
3. Discuss and record on the map information and words that the students suggest. Write this information on the chalkboard in clusters (categories) using white chalk.
4. As necessary, add and define key vocabulary words important to story comprehension (words that had been suggested in the lesson). Write these words on the map with blue chalk.
5. Discuss each of the clusters or categories of words and determine appropriate labels or headings. Add these to the map.
6. Have the students read the story by following the procedure suggested in the teacher's manual.
7. After the students have finished reading the story, ask them to suggest new information that can be added to the map. Write this information on the map using green chalk (see Figure 5.6).

Figure 5.6
Initial Classroom Map
for *Sea Otters*

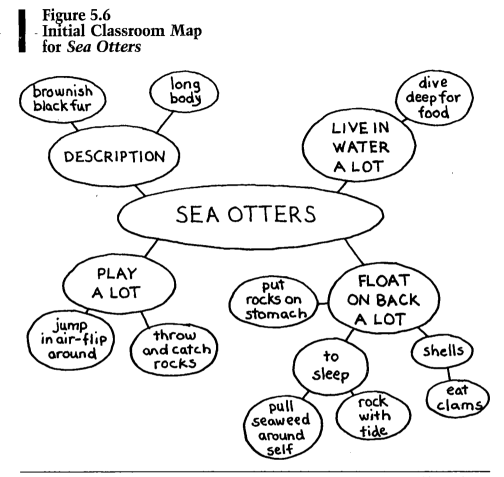

Source (Figures 5.6, 5.7): Figures 4 and 5 and p. 16 from "Semantic Mapping: Classroom Applications" by Joan E. Heimlich and Susan D. Pittelman, an IRA Service Bulletin, 1986. Copyright © 1986 International Reading Association, Inc. Reprinted with permission of Joan Heimlich and the International Reading Association.

Day 2
1. Review the information about sea otters on the semantic map. Ask the students what else they would like to know about sea otters.
2. Give the students resource books to read for additional information about sea otters. Have the students write down important information they learn from reading these books.
3. Have the students use their notes during a discussion period in which they share the information about sea otters gained through their independent reading. Add new information to the map using red chalk.

Figure 5.7
Completed Classroom Map
for *Sea Otters*

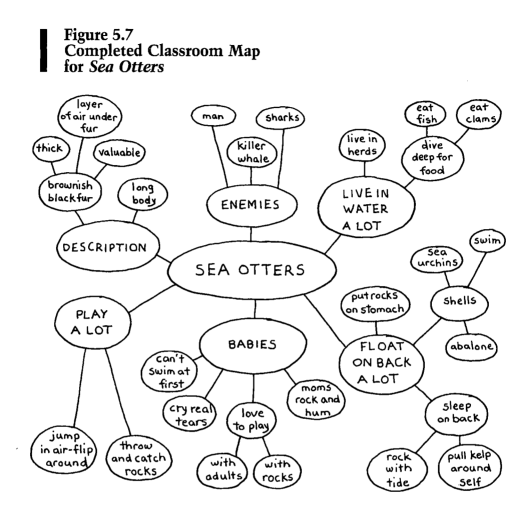

Day 3
1. Briefly review the categories on the semantic map.
2. Tell the students that you are going to show them a filmstrip about sea otters and they should look for information to add to the categories on the semantic map.
3. Show the filmstrip.
4. Discuss the information from the filmstrip. Add this new information to the map using yellow chalk (see Figure 5.7).
5. Direct each student to select three to five facts about sea otters from the map. Have students use these facts to write complete sentences. These will form their reports about the sea otter.

6. Have the students illustrate their reports.
7. Let each student read his or her completed report and share the accompanying illustration with the entire class. Place these reports in the students' wildlife folders.

Semantic Categories

A vocabulary learning program based on introducing words by semantic categories (meaningfully related collections) is described by Beck, McCaslin, and McKeown (1980; see also Beck & McKeown, 1983). The purpose of this program is to teach vocabulary well enough to enhance comprehension. It emphasizes the development of "word consciousness," with the aim of making students more aware of words in general. Grouping the words into meaningful sets helps students learn and remember word meanings and make connotative distinctions.

The program was designed to give children an in-depth knowledge of word meanings through a carefully planned sequence of activities. It was successfully used with fourth graders who were presented with groups of eight to ten words, as listed in Figure 5.8 (Beck et al., 1980). The *people* category, for example, included such words as *accomplice, virtuoso, rival,* and *philanthro-*

∎ **Figure 5.8**
Words Selected for Vocabulary
Instruction by Cycle

Cycle	Semantic Category	Words Taught
1	People	accomplice, virtuoso, rival, philanthropist, novice, hermit, tyrant, miser
2	What You Can Do With Your Arms	beckon, embrace, knead, flex, hurl, seize, nudge, filch, thrust
3	Eating	obese, glutton, devour, appetite, fast, wholesome, nutrition, famished, edible
4	Eyes	gape, spectator, binoculars, squint, focus, scrutinize, glimpse, inspector
5	Moods	cautious, jovial, glum, placid, indignant, enthusiastic, diligent, envious, impatient
6	How We Move Our Legs	stalk, galumph, vault, trudge, patrol, meander, strut, lurch, dash
7	Speaking	wail, chorus, proclaim, mention, banter, commend, berate, urge, retort
8	What People Can Be Like	frank, gregarious, independent, ambitious, impish, obstinate, vain, generous, stern
9	Ears	eavesdrop, rustle, audible, din, volume, melodious, serenade, shrill, commotion
10	More People	acquaintance, journalist, introvert, scholar, prophet, merchant, scapegoat, ancestors, extrovert
11	Working Together or Apart	feud, ally, foe, conspire, diplomat, compromise, pact, harmony
12	The Usual and the Unusual	typical, monotonous, obvious, habitual, unique, exotic, extraordinary, peculiar

Source: Table from *The Rationale and Design of a Program to Teach Vocabulary to Fourth Grade Students* by Beck, McCaslin, and McKeown. Reprinted by permission of Isabel L. Beck.

This fourth grader gives himself a point on the Word Wizard chart for having used a new vocabulary word appropriately. Beck and her colleagues developed this activity to promote students' interest in vocabulary.

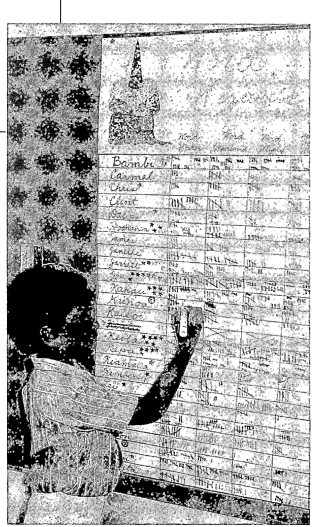

pist. Words were grouped in this way to allow the children to build relationships among them.

The children received a five-day cycle of instruction on each set of words. Each day's lesson lasted about thirty minutes. The first couple of lessons were designed to be fairly easy, while the later lessons were more demanding. Each cycle covered a range of tasks, including defining, sentence generation, oral production, and games calling for rapid responding. The point of presenting students with a variety of tasks was to help them develop a rich understanding of the words and the ability to use them flexibly (for further details refer to Beck, McCaslin, & McKeown, 1980).

When introducing semantically related words, here are three activities you can try (adapted from Beck & McKeown, 1983):

Pantomime. If the set of words can be acted out, read the children a story containing the words and have them pantomime the action associated with each word. For example, one of the sets of words used centered on the theme "how we move our legs." It included words such as *galumph, trudge,* and *meander.* The teacher read a story that used these words, and when each was mentioned, the children acted out that movement.

Concept learning. This activity requires students to identify the critical features which differentiate a word from others with somewhat similar meanings. It also allows students to see ways in which some words are related in meaning. To do this, present the students with two possible uses of the target word. Have them select the one showing the correct use of the target word and then give reasons for their choice. Beck and McKeown (1983, p. 624) give the example of this pair of choices for the target word *beckon:* "a friend motioning you to come into her house to see her new puppy" or "a friend telling you over the telephone about her new puppy." The first choice, but not the second, gives the concept that to beckon someone you must be able to see the person and use a physical gesture to signal that person to come closer to you.

Context generating. Have the children imagine and then describe a situation involving each word in the category. For example, with the *people* category, you could have them tell what the person might do (e.g., an *accomplice* might drive a getaway car, while a *hermit* might be walking alone, and a *novice* would be in a driver education car). With the *ears* or *eyes* categories, you might have the children talk about and then perform an action for the target word. For example, they can act out what people do when they *gape, squint,* and *scrutinize.*

▌ SUMMARY

We opened this chapter by explaining that word meaning instruction is quite difficult because word meanings are "slippery." What words mean slides around depending on the particular context in which they appear. Another reason that instruction is difficult is that we don't store definitions in our heads, so we can't simply teach students to learn words by defining them. The third reason is that words are closely connected to the concepts that they represent, and so they usually should not be taught separately from those concepts, and they cannot be easily learned unless students already have a partial understanding about the concepts.

Our four key concepts attempt to resolve these instructional problems with four solutions. First, we recommend that you enhance students' word meaning development by presenting new words, offer opportunities to use new words in speech and in writing, and teach underlying concepts that draw on the new words, using both oral and written language contexts. Secondly, we suggest that you teach new word meanings in context and in combination with conceptual definitions. In the third key concept, we recommend that you help students analyze words into their morphemic structures, and in the fourth we advise you to construct big picture perspectives with conceptual maps. All four require students to relate words to text context or to the underlying concepts. As a group, the key concepts help to build students' repertoire of strategies for independent word learning, enhance their knowledge of words, and improve their understanding of the texts they read.

Finally, we remind you of the importance of encouraging out-of-school reading because research suggests that the meanings of most words are not learned through direct instruction, but are acquired in large part through voluntary reading. While this finding does not mean that you should abandon the practice of teaching vocabulary, it does suggest that you should help students develop effective strategies for understanding and learning new words in context. Thus, our four solutions carry the underlying goal of helping students learn new word meanings on their own through listening to, noticing, and using new words in oral and written context.

▌ BIBLIOGRAPHY
References

Anderson, R. C. (in press). Inferences about word meaning. In A. Graesser & G. Bower (Eds.), *Psychology of learning and motivation.* New York: Academic Press.

Barker, L. R., Burton, J. R., & Zieve, P. D. (1982). *Principles of ambulatory medicine.* Baltimore: Williams & Wilkins.

Beck, I. L., McCaslin, E. S., & McKeown, M. G. (1980). *The rationale and design of a program to teach vocabulary to fourth-grade students.* Pittsburgh: Learning Research and Development Center, University of Pittsburgh.

Beck, I. L., & McKeown, M. G. (1983). Learning words well—A program to enhance vocabulary and comprehension. *The Reading Teacher, 36* (7), 622–625.

Beck, I. L., Perfetti, C., & McKeown, M. G. (1982). The effects of long-term vocabulary instruction on lexical access and reading comprehension. *Reading Research Quarterly, 74,* 506–621.

Cohen, S. A., & Steinberg, J. E. (1983). Effects of three types of vocabulary on readability of intermediate grade science textbooks: An application of Finn's transfer feature theory. *Reading Research Quarterly, 19* (1), 86–101.

Condry, S. (1979). A developmental study of processes of word derivation in elementary school children and their relation to reading. Unpublished doctoral dissertation. Ithaca, NY: Cornell University.

Davis, F. (1944). Fundamental factors of comprehension in reading. *Psychometrika, 9,* 186–197.

Draper, A. G., & Moeller, G. H. (1971). We think with words (therefore, to improve thinking, teach vocabulary). *Phi Delta Kappan, 52,* 482–484.

Elley, W. (1989). Vocabulary acquisition from listening to stories. *Reading Research Quarterly, 24,* 174–187.

Fielding, L., Wilson, P., & Anderson, R. C. (1986). A new focus on free reading: The role of tradebooks in reading instruction. In T. E. Raphael (Ed.), *Contexts of school-based literacy.* New York: Random House.

Freebody, P., & Anderson, R. (1983). Effects on text comprehension of differing proportions and locations of difficult vocabulary. *Journal of Reading Behavior, 15,* 19–40.

Hanson, I. (1966). First grade children work with variant word endings. *The Reading Teacher, 19,* 505–507.

Heimlich, J., & Pittelman, S. (1986). *Semantic mapping: Classroom applications.* Newark, DE: International Reading Association.

Herman, P. (1988). Vocabulary knowledge. In C. Carroll (Ed.), *Literacy resource notebook.* Honolulu, HI: Kamehameha Schools.

Herman, P., & Weaver, R. (1988). *Contextual strategies for learning word meanings: Middle grade students look in and look around.* Paper presentation at the National Reading Conference, Tucson, AZ.

Ingham, J. (1981). *Books and reading development.* Portsmouth, NH: Heinemann.

Jenkins, J. R., & Dixon, R. (1983). Vocabulary learning. *Contemporary Psychology, 8,* 237–260.

Jenkins, J. R., Matlock, B., & Slocum, T. (1989). Two approaches to vocabulary instruction: The teaching of individual word meanings and practice in deriving word meaning from context. *Reading Research Quarterly, 24,* 215–235.

Johnson, D., & Baumann, J. (1984). Word identification. In P. D. Pearson et al. (Eds.), *Handbook of reading research.* New York: Longman.

Kirby, D., & Kuykendall, C. (1985). *Thinking through language, Book one.* Urbana, IL. National Council of Teachers of English.

Labov, W. (1973). *The boundaries of words and their meanings.* In C. J. Bailey & R. Shuy (Eds.), *New ways of analyzing variation in English.* Washington, DC: Georgetown University Press.

Mason, J., Peterman, C., & Kerr, B. (1989). Reading to kindergarten children. In D. Strickland & L. Morrow (Eds.), *Emerging literacy: Young children learn to read and write.* Newark, DE: International Reading Association Publications.

Menyuk, P. (1988). *Language development: Knowledge and use.* Glenview, IL: Scott, Foresman and Company.

Mezynski, K. (1983). Issues concerning the acquisition of knowledge: Effects of vocabulary training on reading comprehension. *Review of Educational Research, 53,* 253–279.

Nagy, W. (1988). *Teaching vocabulary to improve reading comprehension.* Urbana, IL: National Council of Teachers of English.

Nagy, W. E., & Anderson, R. C. (1984). How many words are there in printed school English? *Reading Research Quarterly, 19,* 304–330.

Nagy, W., & Herman, P. (1987). Breadth and depth of vocabulary knowledge: Implications for acquisition and instruction. In M. McKeown & M. Curtis (Eds.), *The nature of vocabulary acquisition.* Hillsdale, NJ: Erlbaum.

Nagy, W. E., Herman, P., & Anderson, R. C. (1985). Learning words from context. *Reading Research Quarterly, 20,* 233–253.

Palincsar, A. W. (1984). The quest for meaning from expository text: A teacher-guided journey. In G. G. Duffy, L. R. Roehler, & J. Mason (Eds.), *Comprehension instruction: Perspectives and suggestions.* New York: Longman.

Schwartz, R. M., & Raphael, T. E. (1985). Concept of definition: A key to improving students' vocabulary. *The Reading Teacher, 39* (2), 198–205.

Stahl, S., & Fairbanks, M. (1986). The effects of vocabulary instruction: A model-based meta-analysis. *Review of Educational Research, 56,* 72–110.

White, T., Sowell, J., & Yanagihara, A. (1989). Teaching elementary students to use word-part clues. *The Reading Teacher, 43,* 302–308.

Children's Books Cited

Carousels, Level F (1986, p. 366). Boston: Houghton Mifflin.

Waddell, M. (1984). *Harriet and the crocodiles.* New York: Simon & Schuster.

Further Readings

Anderson, R., & Nagy, W. (in press). Word meanings. In P. D. Pearson et al. (Eds.), *Handbook of Reading Research* (2nd ed.). New York: Longman.

Deighton, L. (1959). *Vocabulary development in the classroom.* New York: Teachers College, Columbia University.

Mason, J. M., Kniseley, E., & Kendall, J. (1981). Effects of polysemous words on sentence comprehension. *Reading Research Quarterly, 15,* 49–65.

McKeown, M., Beck, I., Omanson, R., & Perfetti, C. (1983). The effects of long-term vocabulary instruction on reading comprehension: A replication. *Journal of Reading Behavior, 15,* 3–18.

McKeown, M., & Curtis, M. (Eds.) (1987). *The nature of vocabulary acquisition.* Hillsdale, NJ: Erlbaum.

Pearson, P. D., & Johnson, D. D. (1978). *Teaching reading vocabulary.* New York: Holt, Rinehart & Winston.

Pilon, A. B. (1984). Reading to learn about the nature of language. In A. Harris & E. Sipay (Eds.), *Readings on reading instruction.* New York: Longman.

Wixson, K. (1986). Vocabulary instruction and children's comprehension of basal stories. *Reading Research Quarterly, 21,* 317–329.

Wood, K. D., & Robinson, N. (1983). Vocabulary, language, and prediction: A prereading strategy. *The Reading Teacher, 36* (4), 392–395.

Introducing Reading and Writing in Kindergarten

The first time I asked Wally if he wanted to write a story he looked surprised. "You didn't teach me how to write yet," he said.

"You just tell *me* the story, Wally. I'll write the words."

"What should I tell about?"

"You like dinosaurs. You could tell about dinosaurs." He dictated this story.

The dinosaur smashed down the city and the people got mad and put him in jail. "Is that the end?" I asked. "Did he get out?"

He promised he would be good so they let him go home and his mother was waiting.

We acted out the story immediately for one reason—I felt sorry for Wally. He had been on the time-out chair twice that day, and his sadness stayed with me. I wanted to do something nice for him, and I was sure it would please him if we acted out his story.

It made Wally very happy, and a flurry of story writing began that continued and grew all year. The boys dictated as many stories as the girls, and we acted out each story the day it was written if we could.

Before, we had never acted out these stories. We had dramatized every other kind of printed word—fairy tales, storybooks, poems, songs—but it had always seemed enough just to write the children's words. Obviously it was not; the words did not sufficiently represent the action, which needed to be shared. For this alone, the children would give up play time, as it was a true extension of play. (Paley, 1981, pp. 11–12)

▌ OVERVIEW

This chapter describes the early development of reading and writing, *emerging* or *emergent literacy,* and the importance of a wide range of experiences for learning, understanding, and making functional use of literacy. Because most children enter school with some knowledge about reading and writing but not about how to read or write independently, it is important to plan informal, child-directed literacy activities. Hence, the perspective section presents guidelines for fostering literacy development. The kindergarten teacher's aim should be to establish an environment for learning that builds upon children's existing strengths and experiences.

The first key concept suggests that the learning materials should have a range of functions for kindergarten children. The second suggests how teachers can understand what kindergarten children know about literacy and the third describes appropriate instructional techniques. The fourth explains how to sequence the instruction and the last one recommends ways to organize the classroom so that instruction is situated in a meaningful context. Throughout, we emphasize the importance of responsive teaching and teacher-guided literacy experiences which allow learning to occur within familiar and meaningful contexts and to proceed at a pace that stretches but does not overwhelm children.

Chapter 6 is organized around the following key concepts:

Key Concept 1: Kindergarten literacy materials should be selected to serve varying functions so that children understand why to read and write.

Key Concept 2: Kindergarten children's emerging knowledge about literacy should be monitored so that lessons can be adjusted to fit children's level of competency.

Key Concept 3: Kindergarten literacy lessons and activities should be based on scaffolding principles so that children understand how to carry out reading and writing activities.

Key Concept 4: Kindergarten reading and writing lessons and activities should be carefully sequenced, beginning with familiar information, building on children's background knowledge and language, and culminating in independent action.

Key Concept 5: Kindergarten reading and writing activities should be situated in meaningful contexts so that children begin to direct their own learning and treat reading and writing as problem-solving ventures.

∎ PERSPECTIVE
The Emergence of Reading and Writing

Literacy, one of children's most significant cognitive achievements, begins long before children read words or identify letters (Mason and Allen, 1986; Teale, 1987). Its roots are in early communications with parents who begin telling stories to their infants and even reading to them. They discuss story concepts with their toddlers, helping them relate story events to personal experiences, and extending their story understanding in terms of character development, event sequences, and problem-solutions (Snow & Ninio, 1986;

Wells, 1986). They talk to them about language in more formal ways, such as by asking what words mean (definitions) and how they fit with other words and concepts (classification) (Watson & Olson, 1987). These kinds of experiences help children comprehend and appreciate written stories and lead them toward reflective thinking about language (Egan, 1987; Olson, 1984).

Parents encourage preschool children to play with alphabet books, magnetic letters, and letter blocks and toys. They praise their use of paper and writing utensils to draw and scribble. Incidentally, they point out printed words in context, answer children's questions about print, and reread favorite storybooks that children insist on rehearing for the nth time (Durkin, 1966; Mason, 1980). Finally, without realizing its importance, they model literacy processes, and thereby demonstrate why people read and write (Taylor, 1983).

If all parents provided literacy introductions of this sort, kindergarten teachers' jobs would not be difficult. Children would enter kindergarten understanding many basic concepts about reading and writing (Mason, 1984). Written story knowledge would be quite well developed, and children would not find it difficult to follow stories that are read to them and participate in the discussions. They would be able to retell stories accurately without leaving out important elements, answer questions about story ideas, and use text and picture information effectively to recite or read familiar stories.

Letter and print concepts would also be partly understood (Mason, Stewart, & Dunning, 1986). Children would have begun to separate spoken language into word units. They would distinguish words that rhyme and perhaps even hear letter-name sounds in words. They would know that letters have names and be able to recognize, name, and perhaps write a few letters. They would know that spoken words, with their own name being a primary example, could be written down and preserved in one or another form.

But not all parents provide their children with a literacy background likely to support success in school. (Mason & Kerr, 1988). Many do not because it was not part of their upbringing. Some speak a different language at home. Others do not because they believe that reading instruction is the teacher's responsibility. Still others cannot purchase books and writing materials or have lives too chaotic or too time-pressed to arrange literacy-sharing activities with their children.

In these circumstances kindergarten teachers will need to introduce children to literacy activities that other children have experienced at home. Figure 6.1 presents the 1986 recommendations prepared by the Early Childhood Literacy Development Committee of the International Reading Association which appeared in the journal, *The Reading Teacher* (pp. 820–821).

Key Concept 1

Kindergarten literacy materials should be selected to serve varying functions so that children understand why to read and write.

▐ CONNECTING LITERACY TO FUNCTIONAL USES

According to Heath (1983), literacy serves *instrumental, social interactional, recreational,* and *critical/educational* uses. These four functions can be used to guide the selection of materials and activities. We report next how each can be embedded in kindergarten reading and writing materials and activities.

Kindergarten children use literacy *instrumentally* to solve everyday problems. They might notice pedestrian signs for crossing streets, identify food package labels by the words in context, or pick out clothes or toys by label. They might operate appliances or other things by using letter and word information, for example: *H* and *C* for hot and cold water faucets; *In* and *Out* for doors; *Off/On, Volume,* and *Channel* number for the TV; *Start* and *Cancel* for the microwave; and *Power, Enter, Shift, Escape,* and so on for computer use. They might name and identify things by their printed names. Some will learn street, school, store, classmate, and family names. Labeled objects and

▐ Figure 6.1
▐ Recommendations on Literacy
▐ Development

1. Build instruction on what the child already knows about oral language, reading, and writing. Focus on meaningful experiences and meaningful language rather than merely on isolated skill development.
2. Respect the language the child brings to school, and use it as a base for language and literacy activities.
3. Ensure feelings of success for all children, helping them see themselves as people who can enjoy exploring oral and written language.
4. Provide reading experiences as an integrated part of the broader communication process, which includes speaking, listening, and writing, as well as other communication systems such as art, math, and music.
5. Encourage children's first attempts at writing without concern for the proper formation of letters or correct conventional spelling.
6. Encourage risk-taking in first attempts at reading and writing and accept what appear to be errors as part of children's natural patterns of growth and development.
7. Use materials for instruction that are familiar, such as well-known stories, because they provide the child with a sense of control and confidence.
8. Present a model for students to emulate. In the classroom, teachers should use language appropriately, listen and respond to children's talk, and engage in their own reading and writing.

9. Take time regularly to read to children from a wide variety of poetry; fiction and non-fiction.
10. Provide time regularly for children's independent reading and writing.
11. Foster children's affective and cognitive development by providing opportunities to communicate what they know, think and feel.
12. Use evaluative procedures that are developmentally and culturally appropriate for the children being assessed. The selection of evaluative measures should be based on the objectives of the instructional program and should consider each child's total development and its effect on reading performance.
13. Make parents aware of the reasons for a total language program at school and provide them with ideas for activities to carry out at home.
14. Alert parents to the limitations of formal assessments and standardized tests of pre-first graders' reading and writing skills.
15. Encourage children to be active participants in the learning process rather than passive recipients of knowledge, by using activities that allow for experimentation with talking, listening, writing, and reading.

Source: "Joint statement on literacy development and pre-first grade," *The Reading Teacher,* April 1986, pp. 820–821. Copyright © 1986 International Reading Association, Inc. Reprinted with permission of the International Reading Association.

learning centers in the classroom, objects and price tags in stores, and menu items in restaurants might also be noticed. In a prekindergarten class we observed, by January most of the children were able to read their names at roll call and to find their name tags at the snack tables, and were beginning to recognize each others' names.

Young children make *social interactional* use of literacy by sending and receiving greeting cards and letters. They might notice and react to advertisements, newspapers, magazines, and bulletins. They might construct notes to others or themselves, use the calendar and telephone book, and read written rules and notices about classroom helpers, schedules, and obligations. Some will dictate stories and reports and make up written messages to others. Bissex (1980) told about her four-year-old son who got her attention by writing the message, R U DF (Are you deaf?).

Children make *recreational* use of literacy through their play with literacy materials. This has been noted in their attempts to read and write, drawing, dramatic play, and listening to stories. Recreational use takes place with the help of adults through story listening, story dictation, and depicting stories through art or dramatization. Children are likely also to look at and try to read books that have been read to them. One prekindergarten teacher set up an office in the dramatic play center and children pretended to read, type, write, staple and fold paper, mail letters, use the phone book, make phone calls, and take notes. Because they had made a visit to the office and interviewed the secretary, they knew about a number of office tasks, and were even putting papers in and out of a mock duplicating machine.

Adults and older siblings (usually older sisters) direct young children to make *critical/educational use* of literacy. They teach children concepts about print, how to form and recognize letters and words, and how to remember stories, talk about ones they have heard, and construct their own. They have children respond to ABC books and other letter materials, draw and write, listen to and reread books, and memorize and recite rhymes and songs.

Literacy Materials for Kindergarten

A classroom library. Children's books serve recreational, social interactional, and educational uses by depicting our culture, its history, and what is important. Because they serve these functions in ways that are accessible to young children, children's books are your most important resource. If you teach kindergarten, you should become a connoisseur of children's literature, keeping track of new trade books that are published in the book review section of the *New York Times* on Sunday and a children's literature journal such as *The New Advocate.* Also, once yearly, *The Reading Teacher* publishes lists of children's favorite books. Through these sources, develop your own library of books to read to children and for a classroom library so that children can sample and borrow books for home use.

As we reported in Chapter 3, Morrow and Weinstein (1986) found that children will use classroom libraries that are attractive and up-to-date and contain many appropriate books. For comfort, the area should be carpeted and contain pillows for a few children and should be partially partitioned from the rest of the room, but inviting and accessible. We found, for example, that children did not use a well-stocked book center because it was in an out-of-the-way loft. Books that the teacher has just read and new ones that extend story reading and project topics should be prominently displayed. Additional useful features might include props for dramatization such as puppets, stuffed animals, flannel boards, and story records with accompanying books for listening opportunities.

Alphabet books.   Instructional ABC books, blocks, and games have been created for generations to introduce children to print. We recommend that you begin collecting your favorites for your class. Keep in mind that ABC books vary in usefulness and sophistication. The most appropriate ones for kindergarten children display upper- and lowercase letters in a manuscript-print type font and contain pictured words that are familiar to children. If you decide to teach letters by having them remember one key word for each letter, you will need books that contain one memorable example for each letter.

Several ABC books can take children a long way toward understanding some literacy concepts. With repeated opportunities to read ABC books with an adult, kindergarten children could begin to distinguish and locate upper- and lowercase letters, name letters, connect letter names with objects beginning with the letter, and perhaps even hear beginning sounds in words.

Predictable, caption, big, and little books.   Although classic children's literature forms the heart of early recreational reading experiences, other kinds of books can serve instructional and recreational functions. *Many predictable* books, which contain language and pictures that make reading and remembering the text easier, have become available in recent years. You can find published guides to predictable books (see for example, Bridge, 1986). *Caption* books are labeled pictures. *Big* books are enlarged versions of uncomplicated stories. *Little* books are very simple six-to-ten-page books that present familiar concepts with pictured phrases or short sentences.

Books of this nature are featured in a number of new programs for young children. The Reading Recovery Program (Clay, 1985) which was devised to offer the lowest-achieving first grade New Zealand children an opportunity to catch up in reading has materials that some kindergarten teachers in this country have begun to use. The program starts children with soft-cover caption and predictable books that are in color and depict fanciful or realistic-event stories. A Little Books program (McCormick and Mason, 1989), was developed to give Head Start and kindergarten children who are at risk for reading failure a meaningful understanding of how to read. These books, produced as line drawings so they can be reproduced at low cost, are introduced to children in school and then given to them for reading at home.

Kindergarten children participate in the shared reading of a Big Book. Big Books with predictable language and enlarged text help teachers develop children's reading ability in a meaningful and enjoyable way.

Books of this type, because of their simple structure, are also effective in leading children into book writing. For example, one book, called *Eggs* (McCormick & Mason, 1989), features counting and has the following text and illustrations:

One baby chick, peep. (one chick, 4 little eggs, 1 big egg)
Two baby chicks, peep. (2 chicks, 3 little eggs, 1 big egg)
Three baby chicks, peep. (3 chicks, 2 little eggs, 1 big egg)
Four baby chicks, peep. (4 chicks, 1 little egg, 1 big egg)
Five baby chicks, peep. (5 chicks, 1 big egg)
One big baby duck, quack. (5 chicks, 1 duck)

One child who learned to read this book then rewrote it, replacing *chicks, peep* with "birds, cheep" and the last page to say, "One big baby dinosaur, ROAR." He created a book that was better than the original!

Burris and Lantz (1983) recommend that predictable books be constructed by teachers or teachers and children working together. Examples include a book called, *I can smell.* On each page place a scratch-and-smell sticker, a picture of the object and the sentence, "I can smell a _____." Another might be a book called, *Where are we?* using photographs of children involved in school or neighborhood activities. On each page, place a single photograph along with a descriptive sentence. A simpler book could be called, *Who are we?* Under the photograph of each child might be the sentence, "I am _____." Other books that might be created could be about topics such as *Our School, Pets, Zoo Animals, Buildings in Our City, What We Can See (hear, taste, or feel), Tools We Use, Vehicles We Like to Ride in, Our Neighborhood.* Children could help by selecting items to be pictured and labeled and making a picture and copying or dictating text for each page.

Other printed materials. Directives, names, labels, and advertisements are examples of other print materials to use in kindergarten, particularly for instrumental or social interactional functions. Try to take the social perspective and eye-view of a five-year-old to locate good samples for your classroom. Certainly, you will want environmental printed words located in and around the neighborhood of your school. Magazines, newspapers, greeting cards, package labels and containers, and advertising materials are just a beginning. In all likelihood, you can enlist the help of your students to collect and draw examples each year. Then, use them as part of selected classroom projects.

For example, you might use small replicas of traffic, highway, and local business signs for a unit on your community, travel, or city and country comparisons. You might want examples of labeled clothing, newspapers, food containers, or a telephone book. Examples of greeting cards might be used for a unit on communication or as a source of ideas for constructing cards to send to others.

A classroom writing center. Writing can be used for any of the four functions, and most children can begin to use a writing center from the beginning of the year. The center should have various types of paper, crayons, pencils, and markers. It may also include materials for book construction: folded paper and stapler or hole punch and yarn. Pictures from old books, catalogs, food ads, etc., could also be made available. Daily opportunities should be provided for using the writing center, with children rotated through in small groups. If possible, an adult should be available to assist, and children should be encouraged to work together and help each other. Writing should be broadly defined to include drawing, labeling pictures, listing or copying letters and words, invented spellings, and constructing reports and stories (see Figure 6.2 for a child's labeled drawing).

Recently, computers have been added to some kindergarten classrooms. The software programs make all the difference, due to differences in ease of use, educational value, and novelty. Since new programs come on the market every month, if you are going to use computers with students, you will need to appraise the software. Look for: (a) menu-driven programs which rely on a small number of words or symbols and few steps so that children can operate

▌ **Figure 6.2**
Example of a Labeled Drawing Using
Invented Spelling

them independently and move quickly into the activity; (b) activities involving content, skills, and strategies that children understand or are doing as part of the regular program: and (c) activities in which children work in pairs or groups so that communication, problem-solving, story writing, reporting, or documentation are central to the activity. Avoid programs that simply replace worksheets with out-of-context, repetitive letter and word practice.

▌ INSTRUCTIONAL ACTIVITIES

Adults read and write for varying reasons, and their accompanying strategies vary as well. Children, at first, are not aware that adults use different strategies to read, write, and remember information. Nonetheless, they need to learn how to keep track of, or *monitor*, their thinking and reading and writing actions (Mason, 1985). When a text they are listening to does not make sense, for example, they need to ask questions. When they begin to read simple texts, they need to know that the task will be easier if they look at the picture or remember the predictable language context or look at the initial letters for possible clues. When they begin writing, they need to know that they can draw to fill in what they can't write or find and copy words or invent spellings by writing the letters they hear. We present ways to foster strategic approaches when introducing beginning reading and writing concepts.

Repeated Reading and Retelling

One way children could be helped to begin using strategies is to have them retell and reread stories. Children will use listening comprehension strategies if they can listen to, talk about, or pretend to read the same book again and again. Sulzby (1985) found that children's retellings sounded more and more like the book they had heard. In three repeated pretend-readings of a picture storybook, Pappas and Brown (1987) found that the child continued to work on the important story elements. Similarly, Lartz and Mason (1988) had a child retell a story over an eight-week period. The child gradually improved her retellings by asking questions, studying the pictures and story and making up dialogue between the pictured characters and depicting reasons for their actions. Eventually, she began to study and figure out some of the printed words. Because book rereading benefits children's development of story understanding and is an activity that children enjoy, we recommend that you balance reading of new books with rereading of favorite books to your kindergarten children.

Letters and Sounds

You can introduce strategies for recognizing and printing letters by using the upper- and lowercase letters in children's names. Give children many opportunities to print letters and hear the sounds with familiar words. Take their dictated stories and put their favorite words on the wall. Have them sign their name on their work and label their pictures, using whatever letter information they know.

To begin teaching children how to hear and remember consonant sounds, make them aware that most letter names suggest their principal sounds (e.g., the letter *t* is "tee," you hear its sound when you say its name, and it goes with words like *tall, terrible, tiny*). One approach is to focus on one or two new letters for about a week. Another approach is to teach letters informally in the context of stories children are writing about or reading. A third approach uses key words. With any of these approaches, letters easy to hear and say are good starters, letters such as *b, t, s, m.* Take care when you teach the sound of *c* because its name often misleads children into assuming that the sound is /s/ instead of /k/. Expect *w, h, y,* and *x* to be difficult because the names of these letters do not lend clues about their sounds.

If you focus on one letter each week, you can play games with letters and their sounds to help them make more extended use of letter-sounds. For example, have children think of many different words that begin with the letter. Write these words on the blackboard and review them during the week. You might end the week with a story children have dictated that features the letter. Alternatively, have them search magazines and catalogs and copy or cut out labeled pictures of objects that begin with the letter. Then, children can select their best picture examples of objects that begin with each letter for a class book, poster, or bulletin board display.

If you introduce letters and their sounds using stories, you might find or make up a story that features one or two letters and read it to children several times. Ask children to find and use words beginning with the featured consonants. Then give children pages with each letter written clearly in upper- and lowercase and with ample space for them to draw one or more pictures describing words in their story that contain featured letters.

If you use a key word approach, direct them to one or two key words that begin with each letter (common objects, such as ball or bike for *B*, cake or cat for *C*, dog or desk for *D*, fish or finger for *F*). Have them draw pictures of the objects that stand for the letter. If they are able, have them label or copy the key words under their pictures. Then you can say, "You know that *cat* begins with the /k/ sound so how might this new word begin?" You could also show children labeled pictures and other words that have the same initial letter and sound to match the key word and its letter.

Strategies for Writing

Reading and writing are closely related and at times inseparable, especially in the experiences of young children. When we speak here of writing we refer to the process of putting one's thoughts on paper, not to tracing letters or copying. Kindergarten experiences with writing can further literacy development by helping children to see more clearly some of the uses of print, such as recording important information, communicating with others, and organizing ideas. As a creative activity, writing helps children to arrange their thoughts and to express their ideas more formally and precisely. Furthermore, children become more familiar with the properties of written language when they translate their own oral language into print. Finally, writing provides insights into letter sounds, spelling patterns, and words.

When children begin to draw, scribble, use invented spellings, or use conventional spellings to write, you might encourage them to label pictures and construct their own books. You might arrange written conversations between children, and respond in writing to their written ideas and questions. Children should keep writing folders and when a piece is finished, they can share their writing with the class. For example, with "Author's Chair Time," children meet as a group and a child-author sits in the chair, reads the story to the class, and helps lead a discussion about it afterward. With "Publication," children rewrite the piece, illustrate it, tape or staple it together, put on a hard cover, and place it in the library corner for everyone to read.

To encourage writing, Graves (1981) sets up conferences in which children are asked about the ideas that they have written or pictured. After a conference they can go back and expand, revise, and correct their ideas. The writing process and the topic are controlled by the child writer.

Structured writing activities may foster growth in children's understanding of writing. Here are some activities that can provide stimulation that can be accomplished through drawing or writing words. Notice that the suggestions lead to different writing situations and purposes.

Responding to storybook reading
Responding to feltboard stories
Responding to storybook dramatization
Responding to a photograph or picture
Responding to a field trip or a group activity
Writing and responding to letters from the teacher
Pen pal writing with children
Constructing signs and labels for block play
Constructing shopping lists for housekeeping
Making lists of items for sale in a play store
Writing invitations for special events
Writing notes for remembering to do or complete something

Here is how one teacher stimulated a child to become interested in writing a story (Beardsley & Marecek-Zeman, 1987):

Aaron: I don't want to do this. I don't have any pictures and stories. (He glances beseechingly at the teacher.) Can I be finished now?

Teacher: Aaron, I thought you might want to put this on your paper. (She shows him a Polaroid picture of Aaron, Andrew, and Jamie seated in a structure they had made on the playground with large hollow blocks.) Do you recognize anything in this picture?

Aaron: (His face brightens) Yeh! That's the Wind Vader! Jamie, Andrew, and me designed it! We were all awesome in there. See the laser gun? We can make one tomorrow and put in a computer like a tank.

Teacher: Neat, Aaron. Now you can tell me the words you want to be in a story about the Wind Vader. (She poises her pen over the paper, ready to write.)

Aaron: (Taking the pen from her hand.) I can write the words, you can help me with the sounds.

Teacher: What story do you want to say about the Wind Vader?

Aaron: I want to say: We built the Wind Vader. Andrew was driving. We all built a giant space ship. (The teacher says each word carefully, helping Aaron to "hear" the significant sounds of the words he wants to write. He writes: I BLT WND VADR ANDREW WES DRIVG WE GINT SPASP.)

Teacher: Aaron, you make me want to dance.

Aaron: (Looking puzzled) Why?

Teacher: Because you make me feel so excited and happy when you tell such a special story about the Wind Vader that you and your friends built together. That makes me feel like dancing.

Aaron: (Smiling) Yeh! Can we make a copy of this so I can take this home to show my mom and leave one at school?
Teacher: Yes, Aaron. That sounds like a good idea. (p. 163)

Reading and writing in kindergarten were once thought impossible tasks. But, with rules and regulations about how to read and write stripped away, children can begin to read and draw or write to express their ideas and spell what they hear. Time can be found in the school day for exploration and thoughtful reaction to story events, with children learning that reading and writing are important and serve many purposes. Arrangements can be made for children to share their reading with the teacher and each other and to discuss and collaborate on their writing, making reading and writing activities cooperative and socially interactive ventures. These approaches will help children develop effective strategies and will help them understand why they should bother learning to read and write.

Key Concept 2

Kindergarten children's emerging knowledge about literacy should be monitored so that lessons can be adjusted to fit children's level of competency.

▮ ASSESSMENT OF EMERGENT LITERACY

If teachers have an effective system for observing and monitoring young children's rapidly changing literacy knowledge, they can help children learn about how to read and use their language to communicate, report, write, and invent interesting stories. Although children do not have a similar grounding in literacy when they enter kindergarten, observation and interviews with them will determine what support to provide, how to stage effective learning activities, and how to evaluate the success of the activities. In the next four sections we suggest ways to monitor and keep track of children's emerging literacy development.

We place the information here rather than in the assessment chapter because more specific information is needed about how to evaluate kindergarten children's progress. Most of the tasks we describe can be carried out in small groups. To record children's responses, list each task and devise a checklist indicating whether or not the children were successful. In addition, you could take notes on their relative success, the extent to which they needed help to succeed, how interested they were in a task, and how willing they were to keep trying.

Concepts and Functions of Literacy

You can check children's understanding of emergent literacy concepts with tasks that involve handling and reading books (Clay, 1985; Lomax & McGee, 1987; Mason & Stewart, 1989). Watch how children pick up and look at books—where they start, which way they go, and what they look at. For example, you could hand books to children and ask them to show you the front and where to begin and end reading. Determine whether they know reading directionality concepts by having them point to where to begin and where to go next, where the top and bottom of the page is, the first page, the first word, the next line, and the last word on. the page. If you ask how many words there are, notice whether they count letters or words. If they know about upper and lowercase letters, words, and sentences, see if they can find a "big" letter like the lowercase examples you show them, and point to words, letters, and sentences. You might even ask them to tell you why certain punctuation marks are used.

You can assess children's early strategies for reading books. Although few kindergarten children use letter and letter-sound cues either alone or in conjunction with picture and sentence information to identify words, many are likely to understand the value of picture information, especially if they have learned to recite stories by hearing them over and over. One way to check whether children are beginning to use any of these strategies is to show them a book that contains pictures and a few words on each page. Read the title and the first page or two. Then hand the book over and ask them to try to read it. Note their reading attempts, errors, self-corrections, comments, and questions with respect to problem-solving strategies they use to pretend read or to read part of the text. You may be surprised to find some kindergarten children making good use of picture information to guess at words or remembering and trying out phrases that are repeated. Some may even figure out a few written phrases and make good guesses about others.

Most kindergarten children know that print is used in different ways. To determine whether they realize its varying functions, show them a range of printed materials and ask them to describe what might be printed there and how it might be used. Materials could include printed objects such as a page of a telephone book, newspaper, grocery ad, recipe, directions for putting something together, board game, newspaper advertisement, junk mail, food wrappers, dollar bill, cash register receipt, grocery list, business or personal letters and greeting cards, a menu from a popular local restaurant, food discount coupons, TV guide, report card, workbook page, preprimer, children's picture books, alphabet books, children's magazines, and a catalog. You can also ask children to read product logo words in context. Young children who see food labels in and around their house begin to recognize these and other words in their pictured context, words such as MILK, McDONALD's, COKE, EXIT, HOT, COLD, BREAD, PEPSI, and M&M's.

Children who have had opportunities to read words in context may know that the words they say must match the number of printed words under the picture. They might also expect that printed word labels describe the picture. A few have figured out that the initial letter of a printed label has a sound that matches the pictured object. One way to check how far children have progressed is to show them one- and two-word labeled pictures and ask them what the word(s) under the picture might say (Peterman & Mason, 1984). Some labels could be obvious (e.g., *ball* under a picture of a baseball) and some could be somewhat difficult (e.g., *rag dolls* under a picture of some rag dolls) or quite difficult (e.g., *door* under a picture of a house with an oversized door). Another way to evaluate whether children connect or match spoken words with written words is to ask children to point to the words in a short passage as you read it aloud or read it after watching you read it (Morris, 1981). You could use the first sentence in a nursery rhyme or a familiar story. "Little Miss Muffet," for example, contains some two-syllable words that could pose a challenge for children who do not yet realize that some words have more than one syllable.

Knowledge of Letters and Words

Letter knowledge begins with an ability to distinguish letters from numbers and to recite the alphabet. Pointing to named letters and then naming and writing upper- and lowercase letters come later. Ask children to recite the alphabet (or sing the alphabet song) and point to letters that you name. If they can do these tasks, check them on whether they can point to and name upper-case and then lowercase letters.

Entering kindergarten children are not likely to recognize words out of context, but later in the school year, you can determine whether they are beginning to recognize words they see frequently in school, such as their own and each others' names, color words, names of learning centers, and words that you have taught them. Be sure to test the words in the context in which they have been used or learned. We do not think that knowing words out of context is important in kindergarten.

Writing

Writing presents another view of children's thinking and understanding about print. To determine whether they have begun to understand the writing process, you can ask them to write their name and as many other words as they know. Some children will even be able to write out some words or parts of a sentence that you dictate. When you ask children to write or spell without imposing rules about how to write, observe what they put down, and then ask them what they wrote. More advanced children could be given a writing topic such as writing what they remember about a storybook they have just heard that you read to everyone. Some will look for the title of the book and copy it. A few will simply make scribbles that look like letters. Others will write their name and other words they know. Still others may draw a picture of an

If you are in contact with any preschool or kindergarten children now, spend about 20 minutes with one child. Bring in paper, a writing tool, some labeled pictures, and an easy storybook. Your goal is to find out what they know about reading in order to plan an appropriate lesson. Can they print or recognize their name? Do they know what STOP says if the word is drawn in the sign? If you were to hand them labeled pictures (e.g., advertisements of cereal, toothpaste, soaps, or soft drinks), would they be able to tell you what the large print said? If you hand them a book, can they turn it right-side up, find the first page, show you where to begin reading, and tell you what it might be about? If they heard you read the first part of the story, could they retell the important events, remember main characters, or explain meanings of some of the story words? What would they do if you wrote down part of what they said and then asked them to point to the words as you read it back? Judge what concepts children have from tasks such as these. Then, think of one school task that would be appropriate for an independent activity, one that would make a reasonable instructional activity, and one that would be too difficult or too easy. Explain why.

incident from the story and label it or attempt to write words and phrases about the story.

When children write for different purposes and on different topics, you will better understand what principles children understand about written language (Stewart & Mason, 1989; Sulzby, 1989). Children's scribbles can look like written text. So, look for scribbles that are letterlike, or sets of letters that are separated into wordlike units (some children use dots to represent spaces between words). Also, notice whether they write in a left-to-right and top-to-bottom direction. Children's talk about their writing should be meaningful. So, whether they scribble or draw a picture, ask what they have made and note the extent to which the talk makes sense and tells a connected story. If they label their picture, note whether the label is meaningfully connected to the picture.

When children write or try to write words, their attempts will show progressively more sophisticated spelling strategies. The letters they choose may be prephonemic, that is, have no connection to word sounds (e.g., CIIICI for *pat*). They might be early phonemic (e.g., C or K for *cat*) or contain transitional letters or invented spellings (e.g., KT or KIT for *kite*). Finally, they might include some conventional spellings. More information about these principles is found in books by Bissex (1980), Clay (1975), Ferreiro and Teberosky (1982), Mason (1989), or Temple, Nathan, Burris, and Temple (1987).

Oral and Written Language Comprehension

When children are read to at home, they notice the way books are written and how written language sounds. Since these experiences give them ideas for identifying and making sense of book concepts and strategies for remembering book information, you need to know how effectively children can convey these ideas. Ask children to dictate a story to you. Or ask for retellings of stories that you have read to them. You might ask who was in the story, what happened first and next, what events were important, or how characters solved the problem. Or you could have them draw pictures about particular aspects of the story or school events that they experienced and then tell about what they drew. For all of these tasks you will determine whether they can construct a coherent account of story events.

You can ask them about their understanding of words as well. See if they can name and tell about pictures of objects and describe what things go together (e.g., categories of food, clothing, animals), and how they can be used. Finally, to determine if they can describe routine events sensibly and in an orderly way, ask about what they do at home and on the way to school. Ask about everyday events such as bedtime, getting up, eating a meal, and going shopping.

Obviously, you will not gather all of this information on every kindergarten child in your class, but what you can do is have everyone do a few of the tasks at the beginning of the year. As you become acquainted with the children, use some of the other tasks to help you better understand individuals who are not participating in group activities or have puzzling behaviors. Children's attempts to do the tasks and answer your questions will provide new insights into their understandings of literacy.

Key Concept 3

Kindergarten literacy lessons and activities should be based on scaffolding principles so that children understand how to carry out reading and writing activities.

SUPPORTING LITERACY ACQUISITION IN THE CLASSROOM

Although children who learn to read early are usually read to at home, it is not merely a matter of time spent on reading. Lancy (1988) showed that the quality of interaction is important. Mothers whose kindergarten children were beginning to learn to read carried out joint activities. They linked the story to children's experience preceding the reading, they asked comprehension questions during the reading, and they discussed the book after the reading. When the child tried to guess at words using a number of clues (picture, initial letter, context), the mothers often supplied unknown words if the child hesitated. These mothers established an effective scaffold for book reading activities, one that supported children's initial attempts to read and understand written texts.

Morrow (1986) also demonstrated the importance of scaffolding. Student teachers helped some children to retell the stories they had heard by guiding them to tell who the story was about, when and where it happened, what was the problem, how a solution was attempted, and how the problem was solved. They had other children draw pictures about the stories. Children whose retellings were guided had higher listening comprehension scores on those stories and could more completely recall other stories.

Before considering how you might establish appropriate instructional scaffolds for kindergarten children's reading and writing, think about all the things you do automatically when you read a book. For example, you turn the book to the right side, find the first page, begin to move your eyes in the proper direction, use the table of contents and illustrations properly, and predict text content from title, author, heading, initial sentences, and skimming of the text. When you write, you plan before you write, drawing on your background knowledge, focusing on your topic and purpose for writing, and thinking about your reader. Children need to see you model these processes. They need to see you look over a text, point out the direction in which to read, think aloud about predicting a text, watch you plan how to write, say a word slowly as you write, and go back over a text to reread and edit. Modeling these processes provides the first part of the scaffold that children need to understand how to read and write.

Children will acquire many literacy skills and strategies first by watching you model reading and writing processes and then by having you supervise and coach them as they try out the same activities. Through the dual procedures of modeling and coaching, children will learn, for example, to describe important aspects of a story, see how written messages are made meaningful, and try out activities that involve reading and writing. Modeling and coaching are techniques that are commonly used by experts (e.g., master craftsmen, medical practitioners, research professors) to train students to carry out new activities successfully. Collins, Brown, & Newman (in press), who suggest that modeling and coaching are two essential aspects of scaffolding, describe them as follows:

> Modeling involves showing how the expert does the task, while explaining why it is done that way. In reading modeling might consist of reading aloud in one voice, while verbalizing all your thought processes (e.g., guesses about what a word means, what the author intends, what you think will happen next, and so on) in another voice.
>
> Coaching consists of observing students while they carry out a task, trying to diagnose the difficulties they are having, and taking some corrective action (e.g., giving hints, selecting particular tasks, showing them why not to do something). In reading, coaching might consist of having students give summaries, with the teacher helping to formulate and then revise them.   (manuscript p. 12)

Modeling the Act of Reading

On some occasions when you read to young children, model the act of reading. You could name parts of the book, point out the direction your eyes move to read, and describe your thoughts as you prepare to read. Modeling will work best if you have a Big Book, so that everyone can see the print and pictures clearly. You might say, "First, I'll look at the title of the book" (point to the title); "Now, I'll find the beginning of the story"; "Here's the first word"; "This is the way I read" (run your finger from left to right under a line of print): "Now I'll read the next page" (turn the page or let the child know that you've read the left page and will now read the one on the right); "This is the end." On other occasions, especially when there are several words or more than one line to a page, you can put your finger under each word as you read aloud. Kindergarten children are likely to mimic these actions as they look at books and will better understand terms that you use (e.g., *letter, word, title, beginning*).

Combs (1987) found that modeling book reading led to significant improvements in kindergarten children's recall of stories. Teachers modeled thinking aloud about important aspects of the story, demonstrated what to look at and the direction for reading, and reread portions of the text to show how readers confirm or make changes in their understanding of a story.

While reading a storybook aloud to her class, the teacher models behaviors such as page turning and reading the text from left to right.

Coaching the Act of Reading

Paley (1981), who taped and transcribed children's activities, listened to her tapes and observed the children in order to understand how to help them learn. One effective coaching approach was to have children discuss and act out stories that they had dictated and that she had read to them. Often, their discussions continued for several days. As children asked questions, she hinted or demonstrated other solutions, arranged for them to experiment, and discussed their findings and interpretations. Dramatizing and discussing stories, as we quoted in the chapter introduction, played a key role in helping children gather meaning from stories.

▋ INSTRUCTIONAL ACTIVITIES

Shared Book Experience: Modeling into Coaching

Holdaway (1979) describes an approach for introducing and helping children learn about and begin to read familiar stories, rhymes, and songs. The ideas were then adapted by Brown, Cromer, and Weinberg (1986) for children in rural South Carolina kindergartens. They found the children were much better prepared for first grade after four months of shared book experiences. Children listened to and read stories with their teacher. They also dramatized stories, retold stories with puppets, drew murals to illustrate a story, engaged in science projects, made up songs that drew on story incidents, and used story-related manipulatives or story pictures for counting and classifying. Shared book experiences led to higher year-end test scores and greater involvement in school literacy activities.

Holdaway's program was based on a model the author calls the Pre-School Bedtime Story Learning Cycle. It began as a 30 minute per day class experience, but by the end of two months was lasting 60 minutes. Teachers selected 20 books every two weeks that were either already favorites or were likely to become favorites after the children had heard them.

They enlarged three or four of the books they judged would be popular (Big Books). After trying out the stories, they also decided to write some songs and poems in enlarged print so that the children could look at the print as they joined in singing or reciting.

Each day one or two new books were modeled, one being a Big Book, and previous popular books were reread. As old stories were reread, children joined reading the predictable parts. Each lesson finished with a new story that the teacher read aloud. This process was repeated throughout the first month of the program, with one or two new stories and a new poem or song presented every day. More popular stories were enlarged for further study.

By the third week, when children could imitate the process of reading, teachers began to coach them so that they would predict words and story ideas. Teachers began talking about printed words and how to go about working with print. For children who began to show interest in phonetic principles, an alphabet book was introduced. Throughout the program, opportunities for developmental activities were related to each story and explored in the playhouse, block corner, and painting corner. The storybooks were placed in the library corner and made available for children to borrow. Teachers found that children were exploring books independently and in groups, often with one child taking the role of teacher, imitating what had been modeled for them.

Modeling Reading with Little Books

Helping children understand the act of reading by learning to read a set of Little Books has been used successfully with preschool children who might otherwise fail in school (McCormick & Mason, 1989). The steps involve modeling the reading act, sharing book reading with children, discussion time, independent reading, and story-extension activities. Work in progress by Mason and colleagues shows that children can engage in shared reading of a new book each week. Preschool and kindergarten teachers introduce the book on Mondays, review it and other books informally during the week, and encourage children to read the books to one another during free choice time. On Fridays, teachers lead children in a related reading, writing, or dramatic play activity and give copies of the book for children to keep at home.

In the example that follows, kindergarten teachers introduced and discussed the book, *Time for Bed*, with whole class groups (Mason, Peterman, & Kerr, 1989). Notice in the excerpts that follow how teachers modeled and coached as they introduced the book and helped children take over the reading.

One teacher began, saying, "This book you'll notice is not as long as the others, is it?"

Child: Huh-uh.
Teacher: And the words—are they the same as the other books that we had?
Child: No.
Teacher: What does this kind of tell you? . . . That you could probably read once you learn the words. I would like to read it first and I'd like you to look at the pictures and maybe someone will know the words.

Another teacher engaged children in reading immediately, saying, "Maybe we can try to figure out what it says together."

Child: Time
Teacher: Time—
Child: to get up.
Child: for
Teacher: for—
Child: Bed.
Teacher: *Time for Bed* is the name of this story. Raise your hand if you can tell me what the picture on the cover shows.

A third teacher had children predict the book title and content after covering the title with a piece of paper. She called on children for possible titles and then asked what the story might be about and why. Her first comment was, "This is a front cover to the story. Now look at that front cover. Who thinks they could think of—name a title of the story."

A fourth teacher focused on a key idea from the story, with the following introduction, "The story that I'm going to read to you today is a very short story, and in it, there's a sequence . . . The thing that happens first, you put first, the thing that happens next you put next. All right, Katy, if you were going to get ready for supper, what is one of the things you would have to do first?"

Some teachers then called on children to describe their experiences with the story topic. One said, "I'd like you to close your eyes for a minute and think about when you go to bed. What is your time for bed? When you're finished thinking about your time for bed, open your eyes and we'd like to hear a little bit about your time for bed." She called on most of the children one by one, who described their bedtime events, and then said, "Let's find out whether this boy or girl did the same things that you did in your time for bed."

This Little Book contained a picture and short sentence on each of five pages: *Brush your teeth. Read a story. Get a hug. Climb in bed. Nighty night, sleep tight.* As one might expect with such a simple text, teachers seldom elaborated on or asked text comprehension questions. Some did coach children to look at words and use the initial letter to confirm a word. Here is one example:

Teacher: How did you know that this one was not "Read a book"? How did you know that it wasn't "book"?

Child: It starts with an "s."

Teacher: Oh, good.

Child: And then a "t" and then an "o."

Teacher: Okay!

Child: And then an "r" and then a "y." It wasn't b-o-o-k.

Teacher: So you knew even though the picture gave you a hint of a book that it was going to be "story."

After reading the book, teachers briefly reviewed the text with children so that they could take over the reading, writing, or story action. Here are three ways they got the children started:

- I'll read a line and you read a line.
- Let's see if we can all read it together. [Read it] one more time, and I would like you to pretend to do the things that it says.
- We're going to take this book back to the table and I have a brand new, never before been used, set of letters. They're very special . . . We're going to make the word "bed." We're going to make some other words that are a lot like "bed," words that you sang about.

Writing Using Children's Language

The term *language experience approach* or *LEA* (Allen, 1976) is used in a number of slightly different ways. We describe below a modeling/coaching approach that helps children to express ideas orally, in their own words. The phrases and sentences they generate become the "text" that encourages reading. The language experience approach is a powerful way to help children see that thoughts expressed orally can be written down and given a permanent form for all to see. This helps children develop a sense of "authorship" of the text (Ringler & Weber, 1984).

LEA can be used with the whole class, with smaller groups of children, and with individuals. In each case, the same three basic steps are followed (adapted from Hall, 1976, and Ringler & Weber, 1984).

Step 1: Oral language, or having the children express their thoughts. Your first task is to stimulate a lively discussion focused on a particular topic. Therefore, you want to make sure the children have something interesting and exciting to talk about. If the children are helping you set up an aquarium or a cage for a rabbit, observing tadpoles grow and change or a caterpillar spin a cocoon, these and similar experiences are sure to generate a lot of talk. Making sandwiches, baking cookies, carving pumpkins, and other high interest activities with a definite sequence of steps offer excellent prospects. Field trips, school programs, and other special events, such as a classroom visit by a friendly policeman, can also stimulate an animated exchange of ideas. It's best to start with direct experiences like these, but later pictures and storybooks can also be used.

Ask the children open-ended questions, and try not to ask any more questions than necessary to keep the conversation flowing but also well-focused. Encourage the children to explain exactly what they mean. However, don't correct them if they speak in dialect forms or use words imprecisely. Instead, paraphrase and extend their responses in Standard English and supply more precise vocabulary. Create a warm, accepting environment for the free communication of ideas, and try to draw shy children into the discussion.

Step 2: Writing or recording the children's ideas. When you feel that the children have developed a sense of the important aspects of the experience, you are ready to begin writing down their ideas. Many teachers write with a black felt marking pen on chart paper tacked to the wall. Write down what the children say without correcting them, unless you feel the message will be ambiguous or unclear. If so, try to have the children rephrase the idea on their own. By taking care in these matters, you ensure that the language and ideas written down remain the children's own.

As you write, model the writing process by saying each word, and sometimes even say each of the letters. After a time, you can make remarks about the conventions of writing, such as that each sentence is started with a capital letter, and ended with a period.

Language experience charts should be short and memorable, often no more than six or seven sentences. After the chart has been composed, discuss with the children what an appropriate title might be, and write the title at the top. If you are working with a small group of children, you can write their names into the story or at the bottom of the chart. Here is an example of some statements that a small group of kindergarten children might have dictated after discussing pets. In this case, the teacher began each statement by naming the child. At another time, she might have left out "_____ said" and ended with the statement, "This was written by Jane, Paul, Marianne, and Vera."

Our Pets

Jane said, "I like my fuzzy wuzzy kitten."
Paul said, "I'm going to get a big dog soon."
Marianne said, "My mother says I can have a puppy."
Vera said, "We can't have pets in our building."

Step 3: Reading and working with the chart. When the chart has been completed, have the children read it together (with help from you if necessary) and then perhaps call on individuals to read the whole story (if it is very short) or the sentence each composed. Sentences can be read in order and then out of order, as you point to the words for the children. Observe whether or not the children show great interest in the text. Only those charts which hold their attention should be used for follow-up activities.

If ideas in the chart represent a sequence, the sentences can be written on long strips of tagboard, and the children can practice reading the sentences and putting them in order. You could ask the children if they want to add any words from the chart to their word boxes. Post the charts around the room and encourage the children to practice reading them and referring to them if they want to know how to spell a word. Finally, when too many charts start to accumulate, let each child have a turn to take a chart home.

Sharing Children's Writing

Drawing on work by Graves and Hansen (1983), Au (1988) recommends the following five steps for having children share what they have written with classmates. Modeling and coaching are an integral part of the teaching.

1. Have the whole class seated on the carpet.
2. Call one child to the front of the group, to sit in the Author's Chair.
3. Because at first children may be hesitant about reading their writing or talking about their drawings, the teacher may need to model what an author says by indicating important or interesting aspects of the child's piece or by asking the child questions. This introduction will help children talk about their drawings and describe what they have written to the class.
4. Elicit comments and questions from the class and encourage the author

to respond. Coach them to ask good questions and comments. One way is to say, "What do you like about this child's picture?"
5. Applaud each child after the piece has been shared with the class.

Modeling and coaching are basic techniques that make instructional scaffolding possible. Instead of telling children what to do, say, or learn, teachers can model, demonstrate, and help children as they try. We recommend that you first use the techniques with topics that you enjoy teaching to children. Although you may feel awkward or uneasy at first about modeling your thought processes, observing children's reactions, and allowing them to take the lead in making comments and asking questions, we believe you will soon discover that the techniques provide a better balance in classroom lessons. You will also find that your children better understand the topics and how to carry out learning tasks.

> ### Key Concept 4
>
> Kindergarten reading and writing lessons and activities should be carefully sequenced, beginning with familiar information, building on children's background knowledge and language, and culminating in independent action.

▌ PLANNING EMERGENT LITERACY LESSONS OVER TIME

This key concept describes ways for you to frame modeling and coaching techniques over time. As we also described in Chapter 2, regarding reciprocal teaching, what you teach and how you teach a particular topic will change as the children become more skilled. What you want is to achieve a gradual release of responsibility for the topic or skill, leading away from you being in charge toward children being in charge. To accomplish that, you will modify your participation with children, becoming more of an observer than an instructional leader, while children gradually take over a task. Modeling and coaching techniques, which are often used sequentially or in coordination, are embedded in the process. You could, for example, model how to read a caption book, coach children to read it with you, and then watch them as they read it without help. For some books, this can be done within a single lesson, though more often it will be done over a week's period.

Rogoff (1986) espouses the notion of *guided participation* to describe this sequence of instruction. She means that an active role is played by children as well as adults while children are learning. Over time, children become more involved with the task and more self-directed. Simultaneously, teachers gradually decrease their feedback and assistance to the children regarding performance. Rogoff expresses the process this way:

"In the instructional process of guided participation, the adult leads the child through the process of solving the problem, and the child participates at a comfortable but slightly challenging level. The child is actively involved in the joint solution of the problem" (p. 31).

Five characteristics of guided participation, according to Rogoff, ought to be kept in mind when planning your instruction:

- *Provide a bridge* between concepts that are familiar to children and those to be learned. Initially, the teacher translates the new task into familiar terms and draws connections between the new and the familiar.
- *Provide structure for learning.* The structure of the task is carefully planned to help the child organize and remember important information and be able to see steps in a task or the connections among ideas.
- *Transfer task and learning responsibilities.* Children need to view new examples or tasks and connect them to what they know and can solve similarly. This requires teacher sensitivity to children's competence in a particular task and their willingness to take charge of the learning activity.
- Make sure that *active participation is part of the instructional sequence.* At early stages, children imitate the teacher; gradually they carry out the task with and then without support. Teachers begin by modeling, then add coaching, and eventually are observing as the children operate independently.
- *Allow instruction some times to be explicit and other times to be tacit.* On some occasions teachers will direct children to say or carry out a task in an exact way. On other occasions they will provide hints about crucial features of the task or suggest choice points in moving from one step to the next.

These guidelines should make it easier to plan a guided participation approach. When you organize your kindergarten instruction, check that it takes advantage of these characteristics.

▌ INSTRUCTIONAL ACTIVITIES
Reading—Listening to Complex Narratives

Listening comprehension can be taught in the context of well-crafted children's stories. Choose stories that you are confident children will enjoy and understand. Easy stories use a series of parallel events and repeated language. *Goldilocks and the Three Bears* is a good example. Harder stories contain more surprising or more complicated plots. *Strega Nona,* by Tomie dePaola, is an example of a harder story.

We recommend a guided participation approach when reading well-crafted children's stories. Children will be better able to organize and identify important text information, they will more completely comprehend the stories they are listening to, and eventually they will be more able to understand stories without your help.

Taking our example from Mason, Peterman, and Kerr (1989), we show next how expert teachers introduced the narrative, *Strega Nona*, and how they questioned children to prepare them for organizing ways to listen and understand the story. They all used *Active Participation*. Other guided participation features that they employed are noted in brackets. One teacher began by noting, "The same man, Tomie, drew the pictures, and he retold an old tale." She continued with the following questions:

Teacher: What is it to retell an old tale [*Structure*]—you think—Alex?
Child: It means—to read it all over.
Teacher: To retell is to read it over again or tell it over again. So he's retelling. He is telling it over again [*Bridge*]. What is a tale, Matthew?
Child: A tale is some old story that is not true. It won't never, never happen.
Teacher: Oh, a tale is a story that will never, never happen.

This teacher also had children predict the content from the cover, saying, "By looking at the cover, who do you think or what do you think this book is going to be about [*Structure*]?"

Child: A little woman.
Teacher: A woman. Uh-huh. What do you think, Matthew?
Child: And a bunny and a peacock.
Teacher: Okay, so it looks like a woman has a bunny and a peacock and . . . [*Bridge*].
Child: A bird.
Teacher: And a bird. Uh-huh. Justin?
Child: A tree.
Teacher: And a tree outside. Do you think this might be her house [*Bridge*]?
Child: Yes.
Teacher: So she lives in this house, and this might be her yard [*Bridge*]. Is there anything else that gives you any clues to what the story might be about [*Structure*]? Matthew?
Child: She has a hat on her head.
Teacher: What is the clue that tells you that she lived longer ago rather than now [*Structure*]? (Children look at the cover picture.)
Child: 'Cause she's old.
Teacher: She looks old. Do we not have any old people now [*Structure*]?
Child: Yeah.
Teacher: We do. When we went to the nursing home we saw old people. So we do have old people [*Bridge*]. What do you think, Justin? Why do you think this happened long ago [*Structure*]?

Child: Her dresses go all the way down to her feet.
Teacher: Her dress goes all the way down. Did we see the people at the nursing home with dresses all the way down to their feet [*Structure*]?
Child: No.
Teacher: So. But a long time ago, they did wear dresses that were long, didn't they [*Bridge*]?

Teachers also gave children a purpose for reading. One said, "I want you to think about what happens to the boy in the story and what special kind of person this lady is, what she can do that no one else can do. I want you to listen to the story [*Structure*]."

During the reading, teachers modeled how to think about and interpret the text. Here are some examples of modeling in which teachers gave *Explicit* information about words and text ideas. Information in quotes are text sections that teachers were reading. Their text interpretations follow:

> ". . . a pot that could cook all by itself." You didn't have to put anything into it.
> ". . . He didn't see Strega Nona blow three kisses to the pasta pot." She's going in (points to picture) and then she went back to the pasta pot and blew three kisses.
> ". . . he was thinking, 'my chance has come.'" This wiggly line shows us what he was thinking in his head. And there's a picture of the pasta pot there.
> "String him up, the men of the town shouted." That isn't very nice, is it?

Teachers also coached children to think about story concepts by answering their questions. In these six examples, teachers coached children to construct their own bridges from what they knew to the ideas in the text and to set up meaningful structures for understanding the text.

Example 1
Teacher: What's a potion?
Child: It's kind of like a thing you drink or other—something like that.
Teacher: Sort of a special medicine.
Child: And when—and when you drink it you might turn into a frog.

Example 2
Teacher: Who is Big Anthony?
Child: The one that has to do all those—all that work.
Child: He's a slave.
Teacher: Well, I wouldn't say he's a slave. He's a helper. There's a difference between a slave and a helper.
Teacher: What do you think he was thinking?
Child: I'll steal the pot.
Child: I'll make the pot work.
Teacher: He'll make the pot work? Okay, let's see what happens.

Example 3
Teacher: How do you think the people feel toward Big Anthony? . . . Aaron?
Child: Afraid, 'cause they think it's—I don't know.
Teacher: Well, go on. That's a pretty good start. You want to help him out, Dennis?
Child: I think he's gonna fall under the pasta and he's gonna suffercate.
Child: Well, I think they're mad. Probably mad.
Child: Yeah.
Teacher: Why, Eli?
Child: 'Cause—cause they thought he knew—he would be able to take control of it.
Child: He knew what he was doing (inaudible) I think.

Example 4
Teacher: How do you think she's going to feel (about the spilled pasta)?
Child: Angry.
Teacher: At who?
Child: Big Anthony.
Teacher: Why do you think she'll be angry with him?
Child: Because he touched the pot.
Teacher: Let's see.

Example 5
Teacher: Why is all of this happening to Big Anthony now?
Child: 'Cause he made the pot boil.
Teacher: That's right. Why (did the pot keep boiling)?
Child: Because he didn't blow the three kisses.
Teacher: Right.

Example 6
Teacher: Why is she going to make him eat it (the pasta)?
Child: He made the mess.
Teacher: He made the mess. But why do you think she wants him to eat it? Eli?
Child: For the punishment.

After the reading, teachers usually began by recognizing comments from children about the story. Then they asked how the story ended and by asking questions that reviewed the critical story ideas, they provided a base for *Transfer* of story structures. Among the questions were the following:

What do the people think about Strega Nona? She's supposed to be able to do what?
Why did she need a helper?
So when she went away, what did Big Anthony do?
Was he able to stop the pot from boiling? . . . Why?
So what happened?

Do you think that Big Anthony should have been punished?
Why do you think it was a good punishment?

Learning About Concepts Through Book-Reading

By reading to kindergarten children, teachers can introduce informational topics. Again, a guided participation approach will be effective because concepts can be modeled and explored in simple contexts and children can learn about them gradually. Early lessons will involve more teacher modeling and coaching, but as children repeat the activity with several topics, they can gradually take a greater role in asking questions, summarizing, and relating information from one book to another.

You should choose topics that are from current social studies or science activities, making sure the topics are meaningful and interesting so that children can connect them to personal experiences. Suppose, for example, you wanted to prepare a demonstration or a class experience around the topic, *shadows*. Again, from lesson transcripts collected by Mason, Peterman, and Kerr (1989), we describe ways to introduce, read, and follow up on a topic.

The three examples of book introductions show how teachers help children make *Bridges* between the new book and earlier experiences and *Structure* the new information. The teachers used modeling and coaching techniques so that the children would verbalize the concepts and make connections between familiar and new information. Again, in these transcripts, guided participation features are noted in brackets.

Example 1
Teacher: The story that I'm going to read today is called *Sh—adows*, shadows. Christopher, we read a shadow book last week, didn't we [*Bridge*]?
Child: Uh-huh.
Teacher: Would you go get that one out of the Book Nook—the shadow book that we read last week? (The teacher continues by naming the authors and leading the children to compare the pictures, which were photographs in the new book and drawings in the old.)

Example 2
Teacher: What I want to hear about is what you saw (on the playground). What I asked you to look for. Something—What did you see [*Bridge*]? Ben?
Child: When I was running on the sidewalk, I saw my shadow.
Teacher: And what was it doing?
Child: It was moving with me.
Teacher: Did you try to catch it?
Child: Yes.
Teacher: Cedric?

Child: When I was—when I just come out and Nick was running, I was running, too. I said, "Nick, do you see your shadow?" And I didn't know the shadow was there so I had to look down and then I saw my shadow.

Teacher: Why do you think you could see your shadow so well today [*Structure*]? Emily?

Child: The sun.

Teacher: Because the sun is very bright. What do you need in order to have a shadow? What do you have to have? Katy?

Child: Like a person.

Teacher: You have to have an object, don't you? It could be a person or a building. And what else do you have to have? Brian?

Child: Lots of sun.

Teacher: And lots of sun. And what makes the shadow, then, when you have the sun and an object—how do you get a shadow? (The teacher tries to elicit the idea that a surface is needed, but children don't say that and she does not tell them.)

Example 3

Teacher: I brought this [desk lamp] for a very special reason. You're going to have to watch very carefully. I'm not going to turn the lights on when I read this and you're going to have to just watch. You see my head on the chalkboard? My head's not on the chalkboard (Teacher holds up a desk lamp so that it casts a shadow of her face on the board.) [*Structure*].

Child: Yes it is.

Teacher: Where? My shadow.

Child: Your shadow! Your shadow!

Child: Hey! Now, it's over here.

Child: Light makes shadows.

Teacher: Why does light make shadows [*Structure*]?

Child: Because it does.

Child: Because they're bright and the sunlight goes right through you.

Teacher: There are a lot of things that are bright—gold's bright [*Bridge*].

Child: Because you're just blocking the light and it can't get through and it makes a shadow because it's all the way around.

Teacher: Oh-ho! I've got my same light—I've got my same hand. Why is my hand not up there now [*Structure*]? (Teacher has turned the lamp sideways.)

Child: Because you're putting it down.

Teacher: Oh, so the direction has something to do with it [*Structure*].

Child: You have to have it on a wall or something.

Teacher: It has to be on a wall. It couldn't be on a skirt? (She moves the lamp so a shadow forms on her lap.)

Child: [Inaudible.]

Teacher: Oh, so I don't have to have a wall? I could have a skirt? What do I have to have? I have to have some sort of surface, don't I [*Structure*]?

During the reading of the text, teachers continued to structure text concepts by modeling how to elaborate on the text and coached children to express the important ideas. Here are two examples:

Example 1
Teacher: (After reading, "What makes a shadow," the teacher brings out a flashlight.) Now let's see if I can make a shadow.
Child: I got lights like that—a flashlight.
Teacher: So, if I have a light, an object—that's my hand—and a surface is the wall, I have a shadow [*Structure*].
Child: The farther away it is, the bigger it gets.
Child: Wow!
Teacher: So when I move my hand, the shadow changes, doesn't it [*Structure*]?

Example 2
Teacher: Now, sometimes, if I were to have two lights, how many shadows do you think we would have [*Structure*]?
Child: Two.
Child: One.
Teacher: Well, let's see if we would. Here's one light. Now, if I turn another one on—
Child: Two!
Teacher: It does make two, doesn't it?

After teachers read the book about shadows, they continued to structure children's thinking by suggesting follow-up activities for later that day or another day. Some directed children to look for shadows or to play shadow tag games outdoors. One teacher said, "Can you think of something you're going to look for on the way home from school?"

Child: Shadows.
Teacher: And when we go on the playground tomorrow, we can look for some more—
Child: Shadows.

Morning Message

The morning message is an activity described by Kawakami-Arakaki, Oshiro, and Farran (1989) which allows children to observe and participate in the writing process, and over the course of the school year develop increasing independence in understanding and reading written information. Au (1988) outlines procedures that kindergarten teachers have used to construct their own daily messages. The examples are from ongoing work by J. Stewart:

1. Demonstrate the process of writing. Pause before writing and tell children you are thinking about what to write. Slowly write the mes-

After writing the morning message on the board, the teacher guides the class in reading the message aloud. Often, as in this example, part of the message refers to a recent classroom event.

sage, one that is relevant and interesting to all children. Stewart observed one teacher who wrote, "Good morning. Today we are going to have fun. We are going to see a puppet show." Then she encouraged children to figure out the text. You can guide and support reading by placing a hand under each word and pause to give children time to identify words. At first, read the message while writing it. Later, as you repeat words and phrases and as they realize that it will be a current, meaningful message, they will learn to figure it out. If children need help to identify words, point out significant letter and word features and context clues. Then, reread it with the children so that everyone hears fluent, smooth reading.

2. Have children paraphrase or discuss the meaning of the message. You might ask one or two questions with the message used as an example:

What does *having fun* mean?
What have you done that is fun?
What is a puppet show?
Has anyone ever played with a puppet?
What makes the dolls puppets?
How can you make a puppet?

3. Ask individual children to circle letter and word features of the message that they noticed. At first, point out important features such as identical words or letters, rhyming words or words beginning with the same letter, conventions of print, punctuation, and capitalization. Then let children choose and point out the features they have observed. To prompt them, you could ask:

Who can find the words, *Good morning?*
Who can find the word *fun?*
What letter does *fun* begin with? . . . and what sound do we have at the beginning of the word?
Do you know any other words that begin with the sound that you hear in the beginning of the word *fun?*

4. Provide skill instruction based on features of print which the children have begun to notice on their own and encourage children to apply these learned concepts to other reading and writing that they do. Some teachers in Stewart's classes had children draw pictures and dictate, label, or write about their picture. Sometimes, teachers wrote a message about a story that children would listen to later. Some used words that were signs in the room, and soon children were reading classroom signs and labels, including the calendar and the weekly schedule.

5. As the year progresses, you can write a message on the board before the children come into class. You will find children trying to read the message. It is also possible to write longer messages with more complex content so that children can learn to identify more complex written concepts.

These instructional examples demonstrate, for reading, listening, and writing, how guided participation is a gradual process of helping children become more skilled. As you monitor and modify the task and your participation with children, you will see how children can take on larger responsibilities for learning. If you set up learning tasks as problems that children are able to solve, provide bridges between familiar and unfamiliar concepts, establish learning routines and structures, arrange for opportunities to try out skills with new materials, make sure that everyone is actively involved, and keep your instruction flexible, you will successfully guide children to learn new concepts and skills.

Key Concept 5

Kindergarten reading and writing activities should be situated in meaningful contexts so that children begin to direct their own learning and treat reading and writing as problem-solving ventures.

▮ ESTABLISHING MEANINGFUL LITERACY ACTIVITIES

In Chapter 1 we pointed out that reading is a social process which can be thought to involve different contexts (Smith, Carey, & Harste, 1982). The *situational context,* or the setting for a reading event, needs to be realistic. Learning tasks should be kept as complete as possible and connected to their social and functional context (see Figure 6.3 for a child's "report"). Taylor (1983) argues for this holistic instructional perspective because young children need opportunities to experience diffuse, moment-to-moment uses of print. She advocates "carefully planned, public and cooperative literate learning environments for prekindergarten and kindergarten children [where] . . . children can learn the functions of print before they are introduced to the abstract literate activities of first-grade classrooms" (p. 94).

Haussler (1985) also suggests that literacy develops when children have opportunities to use print materials for personal functions, when teachers stimulate the processes of reading and writing that have already begun at

▮ Figure 6.3
Example of Functional Writing

home, and when teachers observe children for clues about how to better organize the classrooms and expand on children's developing literacy.

In the next section, we offer examples of instructional activities that are situated in their learning context, are meaningful to children, and have functional value.

▌ INSTRUCTIONAL ACTIVITIES

Reading Children's Names

Begin the school year by teaching children to recognize their own names. It's a good idea to check with parents about how the child is to be addressed (some go by a nickname, some by a middle name because their first name is the same as that of a relative, and so on). Print children's names on cards and put these above storage places or at their desks or table spaces. Have another set of cards to hold up, to see if the children are learning to recognize their names. Use the cards often, for example, by showing them one at a time for children to line up for recess or get ready for a snack. The cards can also be used for listing special helpers and for signing up to use a learning center. Before the semester is over, many children will recognize not only their own names but also those of their classmates.

Connecting Language with Words in School

Signs and labels provide a bridge between functional use of things and the written word. Many items and places in the classroom can be labeled. Labels can be put on shelves showing the location for art and writing materials, and on chairs and other furniture that children use.

To develop familiarity with signs and their functions in the school, take children in groups of about five for walks through the school building. Stop in front of a sign and ask the children the following questions:

- What does that sign say? Usually someone will know and say it. If not, ask what they think its purpose is and then help them to figure out the words, as is suggested below. An EXIT sign is ideal for beginning this activity because it is common, uncomplicated, and likely to be prominently located.
- Can you read that word or those words? Put your hand under the word you want them to name and move your hand from left to right. Then give each child an opportunity to read.
- Why is that word there? What does it mean? Elicit answers about its use or function.
- Are there any other signs like this around here? Encourage children to explain why there is only one PRINCIPAL's OFFICE but several EXIT signs. See if anyone can lead the group to another EXIT sign.

Proceed with the following activities:

- Copy sign words onto tagboard. Say the words and then name each letter as you form it to help the children remember the word. At first use the same letter case as that in the real sign, but later transcribe the words in lowercase.
- Put copies of the signs at a word-learning table for review by the children. When a child forgets what one of the words says, a quick trip down the hall will usually be enough to spur recall. Later, children can print the words themselves or copy them to label their drawings. Keep track of the signs noticed by the children and add them to the collection. Eventually, there will be enough for a classroom book called "Signs in My School."

Connecting Language with Printed Words Outside of School

A similar approach can be developed for signs and labels near the school. You or a parent could photograph neighborhood signs on restaurants, public buildings, the park, the school, and the street. Be sure the photograph includes part of the setting such as the building on which the sign is placed. Alternatively, take the class on a sign walk in the neighborhood. You might find words such as STOP, NO PARKING, TOW AWAY ZONE, and the name of the street and school. When children see a sign or label, have them discuss what the message might say and why. Then read the message to the children and photograph it. As children reread the message, tape record their response. When the pictured signs are developed as slides or enlarged as prints, you can show the signs along with children's taped responses. Children might also read along with the tape as they view the pictured words. Later, prints can be made of the signs and collected into a book for children to read.

Personal Sets of Words

Some kindergarten children want to tell you words they would like to learn. You can print each word at the bottom of a card, allowing a space for children to draw a picture that helps to depict the word. You might also print the word alone on the reverse side of the card. Children draw a picture for each word and place it in their *personal word box* or folder. Children can look at their words, sort them (for example, putting all words starting with *B* together, looking for all the words containing an *E*), or refer to them when they are writing and want to know how a word is spelled.

Listening—Stretching Children's Understanding of Action Words

Take advantage of kindergarten children's delight in dance and body movement to teach them new words for expressing ways that they can move, an idea suggested to us by a teacher, Sarah Wheeler.

- Make sure there is a clear, unobstructed area for moving freely and safely.
- Begin with body movements that children are familiar with such as hopping, skipping, marching, body twists in place, arm circles, knee bends, or toe touches.
- Tell children to vary their movements. Here are some suggestions: Think of a favorite animal and demonstrate how it moves; think of a flower, bush, or tree and show how it moves; move as a light breeze, a cold wind, rain, or snow; make the movement slower . . . faster; or make it using less space . . . without moving feet or arms.
- Have children sit down together in a circle and talk about the different movements they created. Ask them to describe what they were doing and think of different words to describe the movements. How did it feel to move? What were they thinking? Have them describe one of the movements they made and an interesting movement they saw someone else make.
- Write down phrases that children use to describe what they did and observed. Whenever possible, offer new or more accurate action words for the more general words they are likely to use. Here are some suggested words to replace go, *walk, run, turn,* and *jump* (or make up your own list): *wiggle, squirm, stretch, bend, twist, turn, flop, fall, shake, swing, sway, rock, spring, bounce, bob, spin, whirl, revolve, curl, rise, lunge, tumble, totter, lurch, lean, sag, slouch, droop, pounce, creep, roll, gallop, leap, prance, strut, limp, hobble, scurry, trudge, tramp, stalk, plod, sprint, scramble, slink, hustle.*
- End the lesson by rereading or having children find the written phrases that describe what they did and then draw a picture about and label one of their actions.

Writing

Martinez and Teale (1989) show how kindergarten children can spend part of each day writing. To ensure that children feel comfortable about writing in ways they understand, you will want to carefully structure its introduction. Write a message on the board and show examples of how children their age write with scribbles, drawings, random letters, and invented spellings. Include your conventionally spelled version and explain that this is how these writings would appear in a book. This will help children realize that writing is a form of shared communication.

Make writing a daily activity, sometimes with individually chosen topics and sometimes with topics that you assign. Connect prewriting experiences with creative dramatics activities, feltboard stories, and hands-on experiences so as to foster greater motivation and a deeper understanding of written information.

Make your writing topics functional and your tasks and story writing situations like those in the real world. Milz (1985) suggests writing to establish ownership and identity by labeling possessions, papers, pictures, and books. Coat hooks and cubbies can be marked in children's names, and books can be signed out by the children. Written communication can be built by using mailboxes for each child and the teacher, and personal notes can be sent to classmates, to pen pals in other classes, and to the teacher.

Writing needs to be supported by an adult at the writing center as often as possible. The adult can discuss a topic with children before writing, encourage children to write the words and organize the ideas for the writing piece, and be an appreciative audience after it is completed. By reading a piece to the adult who can then rewrite the child's scribbles or unreadable text, the child is helped to remember the text and the adult has a record of the child's oral and written language development.

Crowell, Kawakami, and Wong (1986) arrange for children to write after the daily Morning Message. As they write and help each other, the teacher confers with individual children to guide their efforts. She might help them apply the writing conventions that had been modeled during the Morning Message or support other attempts to create meaningful texts. She also encourages them to discuss topic choices with classmates and help one another as they write.

For example, the teacher noticed that one child, Kimo, wanted help in writing *park* for the sentence, "I went to the park." He had written:

I   W   to   the

One child said, "Park, park, puh, puh, puh." Another added, "It's a P. Write P." Kimo wrote B, so a third child wrote a P in the corner of his paper, saying, "That's a P." Then Kimo wrote a P, completing his message. The teacher praised the effort and was pleased to see Kimo could use a strategy for continuing to write successfully without the teacher's help.

APPLYING THE KEY CONCEPTS TO A CLASSROOM SITUATION

We will now try to give you a picture of children engaged in a kindergarten reading program consistent with our key concepts. Imagine the following: It is early January in an urban classroom with children from more than a half dozen different ethnic backgrounds. The classroom is divided into six different activity areas, and four or five children are in each. Two of these areas, for painting and blocks, are near the entrance to the room because children involved in those activities won't be bothered by the bustle of people entering or leaving.

In the opposite corner of the room is an area where pairs of children are lying on a thick rug, propping themselves up with pillows, looking at picture books and quietly reading other easy books. The teacher had read one of the books the day before, and the pair of children lucky enough to get their hands on it are most animated.

This kindergarten classroom is set up to allow children to participate in many different activities, including painting, drawing, writing, reading books, and teacher-led lessons. From her small-group teaching area, the teacher can monitor all of the activity centers.

In the other corner of the room is a group of children with headsets, all listening to a tape and following along in copies of the same little book. Several children point with their fingers at the words, and one is periodically being nudged by his neighbor so he will know when to turn the page.

Most of the children are sitting at two separate tables near the center of the room. They are hard at work, using crayons or large pencils to draw and to write. Each child is doing something different, and two do not have a single letter printed, but all are trying to express ideas they see as important. The teacher is sitting with one child who is being asked to read what he had printed with the picture he drew. She is printing his message on a separate strip of paper as he "reads" what he wrote. She will staple this to the bottom of his paper and hang it with several other labeled pictures. He understands that his message is being printed again so that she can read it, and is not made to feel that his spelling is wrong. The teacher knows that he will gradually learn standard notation and spelling.

The children in this class will have a chance either this day or the next to go to each of the activity areas. They spend about 20 minutes in each area, except at the writing tables, where they may stay longer. As we leave, the teacher is calling the group to the front of the room, where she will be reading them a new story. The children begin to clean up and put their things away. While the teacher waits for all to assemble, she holds up and praises the children's drawings and writing, calling the groups' attention to interesting details and reading aloud the phrases and sentences composed.

How did the school year begin in this orderly, productive classroom, and how did it change toward the end of the year? Here are some of the deliberate steps that the teacher took to reach the situation described above by the middle of the year.

Since some children in the class had not had nursery school or day care experience, the teacher began by establishing a few clear procedures, such as showing the children where they should keep their belongings, and discussing a few rules for conduct, such as the importance of sharing materials. She established a simple schedule and routine that she knew they could learn to follow, beginning the school day with a whole class discussion or show-and-tell time, followed by a time when they could choose from among play, art, or academic activities. The morning was then rounded out with snack time, story reading, and music.

She carefully introduced the children to all materials, such as blocks and puzzles, books and letter games, clay and paint, so that they would be prepared to work on their own. Finally, she observed them carefully while they played or worked in order to learn which children needed help in learning to interact properly with other children, which needed more guidance or supervision in working independently, and which showed no interest in books and other academic activities. By giving help when needed and encouragement to try new activities, she prepared the children over a period of weeks to work and learn in a group setting and got to know the personality and special abilities of each of them.

By the end of the school year, all the children had received an introduction to the many functions of reading and writing, and most had developed considerable knowledge of the forms of literacy, as well. They enjoyed learning, were able to work independently, at least for periods of up to half an hour, and were prepared for more formal, first grade instruction.

Differences between the scene in this classroom in January and at the end of the year were not immediately obvious. The children were still working at separate learning centers, although more time was now spent in small group lessons with the teacher. These were predictable book reading, language experience, and listening comprehension lessons, with both storybooks and informational books, with some time being spent in work on letter sounds, reading or reciting easy-to-read and favorite stories, and writing.

The major difference was in the type of help the teacher was giving the children and in the type of learning they were doing. More children were working together, reading and writing, and the teacher's interactions with them were now largely about academic matters, rather than about routines or how to carry out and complete work tasks and projects. Transitions took less time as the children now anticipated the switch to another activity (e.g., they began to pick up materials even before the teacher signaled that it was time for them all to gather to hear a new story). In general, there was a more grown-up, I-know-what-I'm-doing attitude among the children. This self-confidence, combined with a broad background of reading and writing experiences, gave them an excellent start toward the acquisition of literacy.

▌ SUMMARY

We began by looking at the nature of young children's early experiences with reading. Although these vary from child to child, many enter kindergarten already knowing quite a bit about reading and writing. All children, however, need an opportunity to build upon home literacy experiences. For children who come to school with a meager foundation, we reminded you how important your role will be to develop children's understanding of literacy.

In the first key concept we discussed the importance of connecting literacy with instrumental, social interactional, recreational, and educational functions. In the second key concept we suggested ways to observe and keep track of children's emergent literacy progress. In the third, we focused on modeling and coaching as two appropriate methods of acquainting young children with written language. Among the activities recommended were shared book reading and rereading, writing using children's oral language, and sharing by children of their written pieces.

In the fourth key concept we stressed the idea that early reading instruction is framed in social interactions and that those interactions must change over time in order to lead children toward independence. All children come to school with strengths in oral language and with knowledge of the world, although they will differ in their understandings of written stories. This key concept highlighted how to bring literacy into the classroom with book reading and writing and change the focus or approach as children become more skilled. Finally, in the fifth key concept we pointed out ways of involving children in meaningful literacy activities, situated in functional and context-supported tasks.

Throughout this chapter, we emphasized that kindergarten teachers should arrange that students learn to use literacy materials for different functions, that they apply varying methods and sequences for the instruction, and that children's study of words, letters, sounds, and print concepts should be meaningful, useful, and interesting.

▌ BIBLIOGRAPHY

References

Au, K. (1988). Concepts of print (Ch 6). In J. Carroll (Ed.), *Literacy resource notebook.* Honolulu, HI: Kamehameha Schools.

Allen R. V. (1976. *Language experience in communication.* Boston: Houghton Mifflin.

Beardsley, L., & Marecek-Zeman, M. (1987). Making connections: Facilitating literacy in young children. *Childhood Education, 63,* 159–166.

Bissex, G. L. (1980). *GNYS AT WRK: A child learns to write and read.* Cambridge, MA: Harvard University Press.

Bridge, C. (1986). Predictable books for beginning readers and writers. In M. Sampson (Ed.), *The pursuit of literacy: Early reading and writing.* Dubuque, IA: Kendall/ Hunt.

Brown, M., Cromer, P., & Weinberg, S. (1986). Shared book experiences in kindergarten: Helping children come to literacy. *Early Childhood Research Quarterly, 1*, 397–406.

Burris, N., & Lantz, K. (1983). Caption books in the classroom. *The Reading Teacher, 36*, 872–875.

Clay, M. (1975). *What did I write?* Portsmouth, NH: Heinemann.

Clay, M. (1985). *Early detection of reading difficulties* (3rd ed.). Portsmouth, NH: Heinemann.

Collins, A., Brown, J. S., & Newman, S. E. (in press). Cognitive apprenticeship: Teaching the craft of reading, writing, and mathematics. In L. B. Resnick (Ed.), *Knowing, learning, and instruction: Essays in honor of Robert Glaser.* Hillsdale, N.J. Erlbaum.

Combs, M. (1987). Modeling the reading process with enlarged texts. *The Reading Teacher, 40*, 422–426.

Crowell, D., Kawakami, A., & Wong, J. (1986). Emerging literacy: Experiences in a kindergarten classroom. *The Reading Teacher, 40*, 144–149.

Durkin, D. (1966). *Children who read early.* New York: Teachers College Press.

Early Childhood and Literacy Development Committee of the International Reading Association (1986). Joint statement on literacy development and pre-first grade. *The Reading Teacher, 39*, 819–821.

Egan, K. (1987). Literacy and the oral foundations of education. *Harvard Educational Review, 57*, 445–472.

Ferreiro, E., & Teberosky, A. (1982). *Literacy before schooling.* Portsmouth, NH: Heinemann.

Graves, D. (1981). Patterns of child control of the writing process. In R. Walshe (Ed.), *Donald Graves in Australia.* Rosebery NSW: Primary English Teaching Association.

Graves, D., & Hansen, J. (1983). The author's chair. *Language Arts, 60*, 176–183.

Hall, M. A. (1976). *Teaching reading as a language experience.* Columbus, Ohio: Charles E. Merrill.

Heath, S. B. (1983). *Ways with words: Language, life and work in communities and classrooms.* New York: Cambridge University Press.

Holdaway, D. (1979). *The foundations of literacy.* New York: Ashton Scholastic.

Kawakami-Arakaki, A., Oshiro, M., & Farran, D. (1989). Research to practice: Integrating reading and writing in a kindergarten curriculum. In J. Mason (Ed.), *Reading and writing connections.* Boston: Allyn & Bacon.

Lancy, D. F. (1988). *Parents' strategies for reading to and with their children.* Paper presented at the American Educational Research Association annual meeting. New Orleans, LA.

Lartz, M., & Mason, J. (1988). Jamie: One child's journey from oral to written language. *Early Childhood Research Quarterly, 3*, 193–208.

Lomax, R. G., & McGee, L. M. (1987). Young children's concepts about print and reading: Toward a model of word reading acquisition. *Reading Research Quarterly, 22*, 237–256.

Martinez, M., & Teale, W. (1989). The ins and outs of a kindergarten writing program. *The Reading Teacher, 40*, 444–451.

Mason, J. (1980). When *do* children begin to read? *Reading Research Quarterly, 15*, 203–227.

Mason, J. (1984). Early reading from a developmental perspective. In D. Pearson (Ed.), *Handbook of reading research*. New York: Longman.

Mason, J. (1985). Cognitive monitoring and early reading: A proposed model. In D. Forrest, G. MacKinnon, & T. Waller (Eds.), *Meta-cognition, cognition, and human performance*. New York: Academic Press.

Mason, J. (1989). (Ed.) *Reading and writing connections*. Boston: Allyn & Bacon.

Mason, J., & Allen, J. (1986). A review of emergent literacy with implications for research and practice in reading. In E. Rothkopf (Ed.), *Review of Research in Education*, Volume 13. Washington, DC: American Educational Research Association.

Mason, J., & Kerr, B. (1988). *Literacy transfer from parents to children in the preschool years*. Paper for the Conference on the Intergenerational Transfer of Cognitive Skills, San Diego, CA: Applied Behavioral & Cognitive Sciences, Inc.

Mason, J., Peterman, C., & Kerr, B. (1989). How teachers read to kindergarten children. In D. Strickland & L. Morrow (Eds.), *Emerging literacy: Young children learn to read and write*. Newark, DE: International Reading Association.

Mason, J. M., Peterman, C., Powell, B., & Kerr, B. M. (1988). *Reading and writing attempts after reading to kindergarten children*. Technical Report No. 419. Urbana, IL: Center for the Study of Reading.

Mason, J., & Stewart, J. (1989). Emergent literacy assessment for instructional use in kindergarten. In L. Morrow and J. Smith (Eds.), *The role of assessment in early literacy instruction*. Englewood Cliffs, NJ: Prentice-Hall.

Mason, J., Stewart, J., & Dunning, D. (1986). Measuring early reading: A window into kindergarten children's understudy. In T. Raphael, with R. Reynolds (Eds.), *Contexts of school-based literacy*. New York: Random House.

McCormick, C., & Mason, J. (1989). Fostering reading for Head Start children with little books. In J. Allen & J. Mason (Eds.), *Risk makers, risk takers, risk breakers: Reducing the risks for young learners: literacy practices and policies*. Portsmouth, NH: Heinemann.

Morris, D. (1981). Concept of word: A developmental phenomenon in the beginning reading and writing process. *Language Arts, 58*, 659–668.

Morrow, L. (1986). *The effect of one-to-one story readings on children's questions and responses*. Paper presented at the Annual meeting of the National Reading Conference, Austin, Texas.

Morrow, L., & Weinstein, C. (1986). Encouraging voluntary reading: The impact of a recreational reading program on children's use of library centers. *Reading Research Quarterly, 21*, 330–346.

Olson, D. (1984). "See! Jumping!" Some oral language antecedents of literacy. In H. Goelman, A. Oberg, & F. Smith (Eds.), *Awakening to literacy*. Portsmouth, NH: Heinemann.

Paley, V. (1981). *Wally's stories*. Cambridge, MA: Harvard University Press.

Pappas, C., & Brown, E. (1987). Learning how to read by reading: Learning how to extend the functional potential of language. *Research in the Teaching of English, 21*, 160–184.

Peterman, C., & Mason, J. (1984). *Kindergarten children's perceptions of the form of print in labeled pictures and stories*. Paper presented at the annual meeting of the National Reading Conference, St. Petersburg, FL.

Ringler, L. H., & Weber, C. K. (1984). *A language-thinking approach to reading: Diagnosis and teaching*. San Diego, CA: Harcourt Brace Jovanovich.

Rogoff, B. (1986). Adult assistance of children's learning. In T. Raphael (Ed.), *The contexts of school-based literacy.* New York: Random House.

Smith, S. L., Carey, R. F., & Harste, J. C. (1982). The contexts of reading. In A. Berger & H. A. Robinson (Eds.), *Secondary school reading: What research reveals for classroom practice.* Urbana, IL: National Conference on Research in English and ERIC Clearinghouse on Reading and Communication Skills.

Snow, C., & Ninío, A. (1986). The contribution of reading books with children to their linguistic and cognitive development. In W. Teale & E. Sulzby (Eds.), *Emergent literacy: Writing and reading.* Norwood, NJ: Ablex.

Stewart, J. (1986). A study of kindergarten children's awareness of how they are learning to read: Home and school perspectives. Unpublished doctoral dissertation, University of Illinois.

Stewart, J., & Mason, J. (1989). Preschool children's reading and writing awareness. In J. Mason (Ed.), *Reading and writing connections.* Boston: Allyn & Bacon.

Sulzby, E. (1985). Children's emergent reading of favorite storybooks: A developmental study. *Reading Research Quarterly, 20,* 458–581.

Sulzby, E. (1989). Forms of writing and rereading from writing: A preliminary report. In J. Mason (Ed.), *Reading and writing connections.* Boston: Allyn & Bacon.

Taylor, D. (1983). *Family literacy: Young children learning to read and write.* Portsmouth, NH: Heinemann.

Teale, W. (1987). Emergent literacy: Reading and writing development in early childhood. In J. Readance & R. Baldwin (Eds.), *Research in literacy: Merging perspectives: Thirty-sixth yearbook of the National Reading Conference* (pp. 45–74). Rochester, NY: National Reading Conference.

Temple, C., Nathan, R., Burris, N., & Temple, F. (1987). *The beginnings of writing* (2nd ed.) Boston: Allyn & Bacon.

Watson, R., & Olson, D. (1987). From meaning to definition: A literate bias on the structure of word meaning. In R. Horowitz & S. J. Samuels (Eds.), *Comprehending oral and written language* (pp. 329–353). New York: Academic Press.

Wells, G. (1986). *The meaning makers.* Portsmouth, NH: Heinemann.

Children's Books Cited

DePaola, T. (1982). *Strega Nona.* San Diego, CA: Harcourt Brace Jovanovich.

Goor, R., & N. (1981). *Shadows: Here, there, and everywhere.* New York: Thomas Crowell.

McCormick, C., & Mason, J. (1989). *Little books.* Glenview, IL: Scott, Foresman.

Further Readings

Clay, M. (1979). *Reading: The patterning of complex behavior.* Portsmouth, NH: Heinemann.

Dyson, A. H. (1984). Emerging literacy in school contexts: Toward defining the gap between school curriculum and child mind. *Written Communication, 1,* 5–53.

Gambrell, L., & Sokolski, C. (1983). Picture potency: Use Caldecott Award books to develop children's language. *The Reading Teacher, 36,* 868–871.

Graves, D. & Stuart, V. (1985). *Write from the start: Tapping your child's natural writing ability.* New York: Dutton.

Harste, J. C., Woodward, V. A., & Burke, C. L. (1984). *Language stories and literacy lessons.* Portsmouth, NH: Heinemann.

Holdaway, D. (1986). The structure of natural learning as a basis for literacy instruction. In M. Sampson (Ed.), *The pursuit of literacy: Early reading and writing.* Dubuque, IA: Kendall/Hunt.

Snow, C. (1983). Literacy and language: Relationships during the preschool years. *Harvard Educational Review, 53,* 165–189.

Teale, W., & Sulzby, E. (1986). Emergent literacy as a perspective for examining how young children become writers and readers. In W. Teale & E. Sulzby (Eds.), *Emergent literacy: Writing and reading.* Norwood, NJ: Ablex.

Yaden, D., & Templeton, S. (1986). *Metalinguistic awareness and beginning literacy: Conceptualizing what it means to read and write.* Portsmouth, NH: Heinemann.

Chapter 7

Teaching Word Identification Skills

Suppose a teacher has placed an attractive picture on the wall and has asked her children for a story which she will record under it. They offer the text "Mother is cooking" which the teacher alters slightly to introduce some features she wishes to teach. She writes.

> Mother said,
> "I am baking."

If she says, "Now look at our story," 30 percent of the new entrant group will attend to the picture.

If she says, "Look at the words and find some you know," between 50 and 90 percent will be searching for letters. If she says, "Can you see Mother?" most will agree that they can, but some see her in the picture, some can locate "M," and others will locate the word "Mother."

Perhaps the children read in unison "Mother is . . ." and the teacher tries to sort this out. Pointing to *said*, she asks, "Does this say *is?*" Half agree it does because it has "s" in it. "*What letter does it start with?*" Now the teacher is really in trouble. She assumes that children *know* that a word is built out of letters but 50 percent of children still confuse the verbal labels "word" and "letter" after six months of instruction. She also assumes that the children know that the left-hand letter following a space is the "start" of a word. Often they do not. She says, "Look at the first letter. It says s-s-s-s," and her pupils make s-noises. But Johnny who knows only "Mother" and "I" scans the text haphazardly for something relevant, sights the *comma* and makes s-noises!

(Clay 1979, p. 120).

▮ OVERVIEW

In this chapter we present ways to help children develop strategies for identification of words, first in context with known words and later with relatively unknown words. We begin by looking at how skilled readers proceed through text and what beginning readers need to know, continuing with descriptions of the relationships between word identification and reading comprehension. We explain how beginning readers can learn to identify words within the context of meaningful and supportive texts. Then, after describing two principal characteristics of written words that enable more effective word identification lessons, we explain ways to assist students in using strategies in combination with one another. Teaching students how to look for evidence that they are identifying words correctly as they monitor their comprehension of a text is the essence of an integrated approach to reading.

Chapter 7 is organized around the following key concepts:

Key Concept 1: Printed words are best recognized if they are taught in meaningful contexts and represent ideas that children hear, read, and write about.

Key Concept 2: Word identification involves an understanding of letter sound and letter cluster relationships.

Key Concept 3: Word identification involves an understanding of concepts about syllables and other letter groups.

Key Concept 4: Word identification is a problem-solving process, requiring a combination of strategies, to achieve fluent and rapid reading.

▌ PERSPECTIVE
Process of Word Identification

Reading is the process of constructing meaning from text. It takes place through an interaction among many subprocesses, including word recognition and analysis, accessing word meanings, parsing sentences syntactically, and constructing a meaningful representation of a text (Perfetti, 1985). In order for the reader to focus on the meaning, words need to be identified *automatically*, so rapidly that little time need be devoted to their recognition. Instructionally, the goal is to help children to identify words effortlessly.

Word identification stands between perception of letters and larger chunks of text. Word identification, then, is not an end in itself, but is an intermediate step toward text comprehension.

Words, as you learned in Chapter 5 on vocabulary, map into meaning bearing language units. When skilled readers read, the eyes are moving purposefully in search of that meaning. How they carry out that search has been known since Huey (1908) observed their eye movements. He found that the eyes move in saccades or jumps across the page. The eye makes brief fixations or stops onto one or two words at a time to identify that part of a text upon which the eye is focused. According to McConkie (1984), even though it seems that our eyes are almost always moving when we read, in reality they are moving only about 10 percent of the time. We do not pick up information during saccades but only when a fixation is made. We also unconsciously plan where the next fixation will be before our eyes begin their next jump. These and other findings make it clear that skilled reading is a carefully controlled process involving well organized and efficient movements of the eyes to predetermined locations in the text.

An important component of the controlled process of reading, which is closely connected to the reading purpose, is sensing the text as a whole. In addition, attention must be paid to individual words, which leads to word identification, direction of the next eye movements, and information that furthers an understanding of the text (McConkie & Zola, 1987).

The average skilled reader reads simple texts at a rapid rate—about 300 words per minute, or about 200 milliseconds per word. The word identification process takes about one-third of that time. The remaining time is presumably devoted to comprehension processing. What goes on, then, during that 60 millisecond period that the eye is focused on word identification?

The current model of word identification for skilled readers involves a duel mechanism (Rayner & Pollatsek, 1989). One mechanism, which we will call the *direct access system*, allows word pronunciations and their meanings to be recognized directly and automatically. Most common words—words that appear frequently in texts such as pronouns, articles, and frequently read nouns and verbs, are recognized in this way. In the sentence you just read, for example, automatic recognition probably occurred for the words, *most, that, in, such, as, and, are,* and *this.* Although you knew the remaining words in that sentence, they are not nearly so high in frequency so you probably recognized them by the second mechanism, a *pattern-based system.* Although slower, this mechanism provides a way of recognizing less common words and words never before seen using an ongoing construction of plausible pronunciations.

With the second mechanism, words are recognized through letter cluster pattern recognition, analogies to known words, and rules. Thus, you might recognize *sap* and *cap* because of the *-ap* pattern. You might pronounce *vate* and *rate* based on the long vowel/silent *e* pattern. Pronunciation of *bight* and *might* could be through recognition of the *-ight* cluster. Thus, you would not make the unsophisticated guess that *bight* is pronounced "big-hit" because you know that *-ight* operates as a cluster and has a predictable sound pattern. You can make these judgments without conscious thought about the process because of your extensive knowledge of common words, rules, and letter cluster patterns.

In summary, then, we can say that two systems are required for identifying words. A direct access system allows high frequency words to be "looked up" and identified instantaneously after the eye fixates on them. A slower, pattern-based system enables readers to recognize most other words using knowledge of similarly formed words and rules for analyzing the words into letter sounds and letter clusters. The direct route enables rapid recognition of the most frequently appearing words, and the pattern-based mechanism enables identification of less common words.

Development of Word Identification Skills and Strategies

When children begin reading, they have neither a large store of sight words nor an understanding of letter pattern regularity. They must then be dependent on context rather than letter information. Typical four-year old children recognize few words out of context except perhaps their first name and common sign and label words such as STOP or MILK or M&M's. Even these words are usually recognized imperfectly, as Masonheimer, Drum, & Ehri (1984) showed by substituting XEPSI for PEPSI without children noticing (children still called it "Pepsi"). Gough, Juel, and Griffith (1986) even found children at this age paying more attention to a thumb print on a card containing a word they were learning than on the letters!

Although children at this early stage of reading make little use of letter information, unique letter cues are often noticed and used to remember words (e.g., *monkey* might be remembered because there seems to be a tail at the end or *look* because of two eyes in the middle). They will know some words on food packages and in sentences in which they were learned but not elsewhere. By the end of first grade, however, most children have acquired skills for recognizing many high frequency words directly, and are acquiring an understanding of the second pattern-based mechanism by using spelling-to-sound regularities. As a result, the two word identification mechanisms increase in use and the need for pictures and surrounding text context to recognize words begins to decline in importance (Simon & Leu, 1987). How do these changes occur?

As we described in the last chapter, before children become aware that language can be observed and analyzed into words and letter patterns, they scribble and explore books, they listen to stories and dictate their own, and they pretend to read and write. They see letters and some words repeatedly in the same contexts. While looking at an alphabet book with parents, they might see the word *apple* accompanied by the letter A and a picture of an apple. Parents might help them recognize and print their first name. At breakfast there may be Special K cereal with an oversized K on the box. On outings, they might visit a McDonald's restaurant and see the sign with the golden arches. Early experiences with environmental print in conjunction with letter recognition and letter naming apparently provide a groundwork for word identification (Ehri, 1987). We often hear a young child saying, for example, that she knows a particular word because it begins like her name or we see a child use letters from his name to try to write other words. This is the foundation for word identification: words are meaningful and can be recognized in context, and letters have names and are connected to words that begin with the same sound. From this foundation, children can move toward analyzing of words into sounds.

It is generally agreed that phonemic awareness is necessary for understanding spelling-to-sound correspondences of English words (Ehri, 1987). *Phonemes* are the word sounds that can be heard. Most letters are represented by one phoneme (but not *x*—listen to its sound in *box*). Here are examples of words that contain three phonemes: *c-a-n, m-i-ne, b-a-ll, b-l-ow, th-a-t, th-r-ee.* Children must be able to hear phonemes within words in order to be good readers, because hearing phonemes enables them to learn how to separate words into sounds and connect the sounds with particular letters.

Phonemic awareness is seldom taught, though when it was taught, children's word reading improved (Bradley & Bryant, 1981; Lundberg, Frost, & Petersen, 1988). More typically, the roots of phonemic awareness are in home literacy experiences. Alphabet books and rhymes help children hear beginning and ending phonemes. In fact, Maclean, Bryant, and Bradley, (1987) determined that English children's knowledge of nursery rhymes at age three was strongly related to phonological awareness and early reading performance.

Early on, children are not aware of phonemes within words. They are more likely to hear syllable junctures (e.g., *ba-by, el-e-phant*). Then they become aware that most one-syllable words have two parts, an *onset* and a *rime* (Trieman, 1985). The onset is the initial (consonantal) portion of the syllable (e.g., *m* in *mask*, *gr* in *grab*, or *spr* in *spring*), or is missing (e.g., *and*). The rime includes the vowel nucleus and ending consonants (e.g., *ask* in *mask*, *ab* in *grab*, *ing* in *spring*). Trieman found that young children analyze spoken words into onsets and rimes before they identify phonemes.

After children hear syllables and onset/rime segments, they begin to distinguish phonemes. The easiest and first recognized are usually initial consonants; next, final consonants; and then sounds in the middle. At this time children might play word-sound games. Bissex (1980), for example, reported her son's discovery that he could remove the *l* from *please* and have the word *peas.* Children spontaneously notice and try to write rhyming words and words that begin with the same sound. In these ways, they start to understand English letter-sound regularity and common spelling-to-sound patterns. They begin to recognize words in print by sounding out at least the first letter. Eventually, they figure out new words based on their knowledge of letter patterns in known words, and they pronounce and spell many words on their own.

Ehri and Wilce (1987) proposed that knowledge about how to match letters to sounds progresses in a developmental fashion, beginning with knowledge of letter names. Children first use letter names to spell parts of words, often one prominent letter for each syllable, spelling *cat* as *k*, *you* as *U*, and *are* as *R*. Next, children learn to segment words into phonemes, and are able to identify many or most phonemes in words, though not necessarily correctly. During this time *cat* might be spelled phonetically (*kt* or *kat*). Finally, children move into the morphemic stage, "when the principle of one letter for every sound loses its grip and spellers begin to utilize word based spelling regularities to generate spellings" (p. 62). At this point children can understand and deal in a flexible manner with letter cluster patterns (e.g., *-ite, -ight, -eam, -ed, -ing*). They also begin to recognize some words by analogy to words with similar patterns. Goswami (1986) found that even beginning readers could figure out words by analogy. They recognized a new word, *peak*, for example, by recalling the pronunciation of a word they had been taught, *beak*. They even used a word that was the title of the story to decode by analogy other new words in the story.

As children build their stores of known printed words and recognize predictable letter patterns, recurring letter sequences are also noticed. So, words containing commonly occurring rimes (e.g., *met, ride, bait, dear*) become easier to learn and remember than words with uncommon rimes (e.g., *noise, aisle, suit, friend, choir*). Such letter-sequence knowledge begins to be used for word identification in about second grade (Adams, in press), and by fourth grade, is extended to recognition of syllable boundaries in multisyllable words. For example, children can correctly predict that *har-dball* is not appropriate because *-dball* cannot be a syllable in English.

In brief, by the end of first grade, many children are utilizing both word identification mechanisms to read less complex words fluently, and some use the second mechanism to identify longer and more complex words. Thus, most children recognize 50 percent or more of high frequency words immediately and make good use of written English letter clusters and similar words to figure out or decode many other words by rule or analogy. By the end of third or fourth grade, then, only uncommon, multisyllable words are difficult to identify (Adams, Huggins, Starr, Rollins, Zuckerman, Stevens, & Nickerson, 1980), but as children read widely and meaningfully, even these words become accessible.

Implications for Instruction

Children need to see, hear, and attempt to read words in a wide variety of contexts so they can learn to apply different word recognition strategies. They need opportunities to figure out words, partly by analyzing sounds in words and partly by checking their sense in context. Attending to meaning and sentence structure cues as well as letter cues will enable them to connect word identification with text comprehension and to use strategies commensurate with the whole reading act.

Nevertheless, text understanding, not word identification, is the primary reading goal. Thus, you want to ensure a balance between word identification activities and comprehension (Resnick, 1979) and provide opportunities to integrate word study with text reading (Clay, 1979). While there are occasions when one or the other is emphasized for a teaching point, we advise that to the greatest possible extent words be taught in context, and word analysis be kept within the framework of meaningful texts. Integration of one with the other, or a balance between the two, is more likely to lead to successful reading.

As you study these key concepts, keep in mind as well that instruction in word identification need not be singularly focused on reading. Opportunity to write is also valuable. Writing allows children to construct and then read their own words. Writing, in a sense, reverses the conceptual process because it requires children to take apart the words that they hear, while reading involves putting together the letters into sound clusters. Writing also allows children to construct hypotheses about the sounds that they hear as they try to spell words. Thus, writing can play an important instructional role in word identification. Children can be led to apply and expand on strategies they derive from both reading and writing activities.

Key Concept 1

Printed words are best recognized if they are taught in meaningful contexts and represent ideas that children hear, read, and write about.

▋ ESTABLISHING A SET OF KNOWN READING VOCABULARY WORDS

Reading involves the integration of all parts of a text: sounds, syllables, words, morphemes, phrases, sentences, paragraphs and story units. In order to keep this complex act as simple as possible, build your instruction on what children know, their oral language. Words you want learned and remembered, such as classroom words, words in stories, and words to exemplify concepts you teach, should be meaningful and familiar.

Without being instructed to do so, beginning readers often collect their own stock of *sight words* (Byrne, in press). Sight words are words that children have memorized as wholes, with little or no attention to their letter sounds. Decoding skills typically come later, when children have a set of sight words, a beginning awareness of rhyming patterns, and can connect a few sounds to letters, such as connecting initial sounds of some words with their letters.

Having children learn perhaps fifty or so words by sight lays the foundation for letter sound analysis and decoding by analogy. Words that are well learned can serve as anchors for figuring out new words (Clay, 1985: Gaskins,

Downer, & Gaskins, 1986). For example, if children know the word *me* well, they will recognize it in and out of context, they will write it effortlessly, and they will more easily learn similar words such as *she, he, we* and *my.* Starting with known words enables children to establish stronger connections among the printed words they are learning and between oral and written language.

To make efficient use of your instructional time, teach productive sight words—words from children's readers that are the most frequently occurring in written language. Beginning readers will then be able to experience more successful reading and will feel more confident when reading. We have listed in Figure 7.1 the 200 most frequently appearing words in children's reading materials. The first 100 make up about 50 percent of the words appearing in a typical school reading text. The most common word, *the,* occurs about 75 times in every 1000 words of text; the 100th word, *know,* occurs about 1.13 times; the 200th word, *want,* occurs about .53 times; by contrast, the 1000th word, *pass,* occurs about 0.01 times. The first 200 or so words are those that children will read over and over again, so helping children learn to read them

Figure 7.1
200 Most Frequently Occurring Words

1. the	31. but	61. into	91. long	121. also	151. great	181. sound
2. of	32. what	62. has	92. little	122. around	152. tell	182. below
3. and	33. all	63. more	93. very	123. another	153. men	183. saw
4. a	34. were	64. her	94. after	124. came	154. say	184. something
5. to	35. when	65. two	95. words	125. come	155. small	185. thought
6. in	36. we	66. like	96. called	126. work	156. every	186. both
7. is	37. there	67. him	97. just	127. three	157. found	187. few
8. you	38. can	68. see	98. where	128. word	158. still	188. those
9. that	39. an	69. time	99. most	129. must	159. between	189. always
10. it	40. your	70. could	100. know	130. because	160. name	190. looked
11. he	41. which	71. no	101. get	131. does	161. should	191. show
12. for	42. their	72. make	102. through	132. part	162. Mr.	192. large
13. was	43. said	73. than	103. back	133. even	163. home	193. often
14. on	44. if	74. first	104. much	134. place	164. big	194. together
15. are	45. do	75. been	105. before	135. well	165. give	195. asked
16. as	46. will	76. its	106. go	136. such	166. air	196. house
17. with	47. each	77. who	107. good	137. here	167. line	197. don't
18. his	48. about	78. now	108. new	138. take	168. set	198. world
19. they	49. how	79. people	109. write	139. why	169. own	199. going
20. at	50. up	80. my	110. our	140. things	170. under	200. want
21. be	51. out	81. made	111. used	141. help	171. read	
22. this	52. them	82. over	112. me	142. put	172. last	
23. from	53. then	83. did	113. man	143. years	173. never	
24. I	54. she	84. down	114. too	144. different	174. us	
25. have	55. many	85. only	115. any	145. away	175. left	
26. or	56. some	86. way	116. day	146. again	176. end	
27. by	57. so	87. find	117. same	147. off	177. along	
28. one	58. these	88. use	118. right	148. went	178. while	
29. had	59. would	89. may	119. look	149. old	179. might	
30. not	60. other	90. water	120. think	150. number	180. next	

accurately in stories and to write them independently will boost proficiency in the first word identification mechanism and enable concentration on words they haven't seen in print before.

There are alternative high frequency lists that you might also want to study. One is composed of words from children's written and oral language vocabularies (Dolch, 1941). Another is a core of 227 book words based on the most frequently cited storybooks (400 books) for beginning readers (Eads, 1985). These lists contain many of the same words, though the emphasis on oral vocabulary and storybook words extends the set of important words.

How might you decide which sight words to teach beginners? Above all else, words should be meaningful and useful to children. Meaningful words are those in children's oral vocabulary. Useful words are those occurring frequently in children's texts. What other criteria ought to be considered? Three others are part of speech, decodability, and word length. Keep in mind, however, that words can be simultaneously classified on all of these dimensions. You will want to use your best judgment in deciding which words to promote for sight recognition.

Part of speech is important because content words, especially nouns that represent concrete objects and verbs that represent actions, are generally more memorable and easier to learn than are function words, that is, prepositions, adjectives, and adverbs. Content words are more understandable and easier for children to visualize. Nonetheless, function words cannot be ignored. They are the "glue" words that hold content words in the text together and when presented in context, they can also be learned.

Decodability, or regularity of letter-sound patterns, is important because words which contain consonants whose sounds can be clearly heard (e.g., *bad, pit, gate, bike*) and which represent more common letter clusters (e.g., *bed/red, ten/men, bell/sell*) are easier to learn than words which contain irregular letter patterns (e.g., *the, are, one, said*).

Word length may also make a difference because short, one-syllable words appear more frequently in texts and are often easier to learn than longer, multiple syllable words. Moreover, they are generally emphasized in preprimers

Exercise

Reread the paragraph about word length, checking words that are among the 100 highest frequency words. How many did you check? What words are left? Are most of them content words? Now do the same exercise with a first-grade text from a basal reading series. What do you notice now? How many words in this text are among the 100 highest frequency words and how many are not? What can you say about the words that you did not check? What implications might you draw about teaching the first-grade text?

and primers. However, many short words are function words and contain irregular letter-sound patterns, so word length needs to be considered in conjunction with other criteria.

Recognizing Words in Meaningful, Pictured Contexts

If children are reading easy, predictable books, they can figure out many words by studying the illustrations and remembering the sentence frames. A well-illustrated book can be particularly useful for identification of content words (e.g., one sentence on each page, clarified by the picture). Sentence frames can be predictable (e.g., "Once upon a time . . "), and sentence frames can be repeated (e.g., "Brown bear, brown bear, what do you see?"). When, in addition, the text is at the right level of difficulty for children and the words are in their oral vocabulary, there will be little need for individual word identification preparation before reading. However, children will still need a good book introduction and appropriate support during the reading. With that combination, even entering first grade children will be able to read several stories a week. Furthermore, texts can be in a more natural form and story ideas can be fun for children to read and reread.

Choosing the right books, introducing them successfully, and providing the right amount of support during the reading will not at first be easy. Here are some suggestions to make your word identification instruction better connected to text comprehension and your teaching task more effective. Many of the ideas come from techniques developed by New Zealand teachers and described by Clay (1985) for use in the Reading Recovery Program.

Keep word identification in context. Use stories that contain plentiful, helpful illustrations. The New Zealand program has children begin with very easy books. Book difficulty is based on whether phrases or sentences are repeated, whether story lines and words can be predicted from pictures, how long the text is, and how many unfamiliar words the text contains. Stories at the easiest levels are very short, with a well-known word or short phrase on a page which is easily predicted from the illustrations or with the same phrases repeated on each page. For example, one story features a character holding one new object on each page, with the name of the object printed at the bottom. The last page shows the character dropping the objects with the text reading, "An accident." Midway through the program are longer stories of 10 to 15 pages, two or three lines and clarifying pictures on each page, and phrase repetition. For example, one story shows a grumpy husband who growls or shouts at people until the wife gives him a kiss, after which he smiles at everyone. Later stories contain several sentences on each page, less useful pictures, and only a few repeated phrases. A number of the stories are rewritten favorites, including *The Three Little Pigs, The Little Red Hen,* and *The Gingerbread Man.*

Labeled picture books provide a particularly effective opportunity to teach children multiple word recognition strategies.

Read and reread words in stories. If stories are brief, children can read a new story and one or more favorite old ones every day. The previous day's new story can be read without help in order to determine whether the text is at the right level of difficulty. During and after story reading, word concepts can be taught based on problems children had reading particular words.

Connect words to the whole text. Story introductions ought to draw children's attention to the important ideas. Walk children through the text using the illustrations, point out some of the text phrases, and identify a few new words. For example, you might name the story title, discuss the cover illustration, leaf through the book to suggest clues that children will need as they try to read, and help children identify one or two new and important words. Keep in mind to tailor each introduction so that books are at the right level of challenge. Initially you might read the entire story with the children. Later, you might describe only a page or two.

Develop self-monitoring strategies. During the reading, especially at the beginning of the school year, teach children to keep track of the words by pointing with their finger as they read. Help children just enough for them to be successful while engaging in problem solving about what words say and mean. Modify the instructional approach based on what each text offers (e.g., good picture cues, text repetition), what strategies children seem ready to learn (e.g., can they begin to use more than one cue source?), and what strategies they are beginning to use independently (e.g., do they study picture cues; do they decode the first letters of new words; do they reread and try to self-correct?). One goal is for children to figure out new words, notice letter pattern relationships among words, and correct their own errors without neglecting meaning. A second goal is for children to acquire flexible word identification strategies. These include *picture cues* (Do you see something there that might help?), *earlier occurrences of a word* (Where have you seen that word before?), *story information* (What do you think it ought to say?), *repeated phrases* (What did the story say on the page you just read?), and *letter information* (What word do you know that starts that way?).

Teaching word identification in context can be difficult but is well worth the effort. If you have chosen appropriate books and find time for rereading, and if your story introductions are effective, so that children monitor and correct their own reading errors, you will have prepared them in the best possible way to identify a large number of words they know orally but have not read before. If they have received well-orchestrated support during the reading, children will make few errors, they will keep track of the meaning, and they will learn to use various strategies to figure out the new words.

Establishing a Writing Environment

Another effective and meaningful way to help children learn high frequency words is to accompany reading with writing opportunities (Clay, 1983; Dobson, 1989). Writing activities can be carried out in classrooms where children have dissimilar abilities so long as children can proceed at their own level of competency. By hearing and saying letters as they write, children realize how to connect the sounds they hear with words they are writing. Second, writing helps children to pay attention to their own oral language, which is difficult to analyze while they are speaking. Third, since their written words are visible, children can think about what words they want to write next as well as to edit words they have just written.

Another advantage to writing is that it can take place in quick transition periods or as a part of longer lessons. For example, children can write down words they know well as an initiation to a lesson. They can construct one line reactions to stories they read or hear. They can also take turns at constructing words at a chalkboard or on a magnetic board during free choice time. As part of a lesson, children might write a new ending or a new version of a story that

The writing of this kindergarten child shows his use of invented spelling. Encouraging children to write letters for the sounds they hear in words is an excellent means of helping them develop knowledge of spelling-to-sound correspondence.

they finished reading in the reading group. If they can't write letters or words yet, drawing will do as a beginning step, extended by talking about the piece to the teacher or classmates. If they are beginning to write but cannot spell, invented spellings are accepted.

Writing has the additional advantage of allowing you to view children's emerging analysis of words and thus to determine the next teaching steps. It is obvious when one child is asked to make the word *top* out of magnetic letters and the letters CPATPOM are displayed that there is no sense yet of letter-sound coordination. Another child who constructs TP, however, is hearing two letter sounds and so can be encouraged to hear consonant sounds in other words. Because invented spellings provide such useful information, we recommend that you not require correct spellings. When children can use the sounds they hear in words, an analytic perspective about words is promoted. Research suggests that children will become satisfactory spellers when using invented spelling (Ehri, 1989). Moreover, when compared to children who are encouraged to spell conventionally in creative writing, those using invented spelling write longer creative writing pieces, use a larger number of different words, and can read more words (Clarke, 1988).

Allowing invented spellings does not preclude modeling correct word spellings or having children carry out word fluency practice. Clay (1985), for example, recommends that children practice words that they use frequently in their writing—words such as *I, is, me, to, in, of, see, up, a, and, like, look, we, come, the.* Thus, you can encourage children to write most words the way they hear them and arrange for them to learn conventional spellings of words that are particularly useful.

▍ INSTRUCTIONAL ACTIVITIES

The following instructional ideas follow from the three principles suggested above, namely, teach word identification in meaningful contexts, arrange for reading, and incorporate writing into the reading program.

Contrasting High Frequency Words

When the opportunity arises to teach high frequency words, present the "bricks" along with the "mortar." That is, begin by showing the high frequency words in meaningful phrases or sentences made up of concrete nouns, adjectives, and action verbs. Something of the meaning of high frequency words can be given to the children by contrasting them. For example, one morning a first grade teacher wrote the following "morning message" to her class:

> Linda brought her pets to school today.
>
> One is a boy rabbit and his name is Timmy.
>
> The other is a girl rabbit and her name is Tammy.

After the children had figured out her message, the teacher wrote:

> His name is Timmy.
>
> Her name is Tammy.

She asked the children to read both sentences, and some referred back to the message to read them correctly. She then discussed with the children differences between words in the two sentences (*his* and *her*; *Timmy* and *Tammy*).

This example shows how you can make up your own exercises to teach high frequency words such as *is* and *her* in a meaningful context, and have children notice differences in the spelling of words.

Using Predictable Materials

In the following activity, developed by Bridge, Winograd, and Haley (1983), books with highly predictable or structured language were used to help children learn sight words. Lessons with these materials were found to be more effective than those conducted with a preprimer from a basal reader series.

You might start with the patterned books used in the Bridge et al. study: *Brown Bear, Brown Bear, What Do You See?*, *Fire, Fire, Said Mrs. McGuire*, *The Haunted House*, and *Up the Down Escalator*, all by Bill Martin; and *Jimmy Has Lost His Cap, Where Can It Be?* and *The Elephant's Wish* by Bruno Munari.

Bridge et al. list the following steps for using each patterned book. You will need to prepare in advance a large chart with the text of the book, sentence strips, and individual word cards. If the children are working with a basal reader, you can select words which appear in both the structured language books and the basal. The same basic steps listed below can also be used with a language experience chart.

Step 1: Read the book aloud to the group. Then read it again, this time encouraging the children to try to predict what comes next. Let the children take turns reading the book in a chorus.

Step 2: Read the story from the chart with the children. Give children the sentence strips, which they try to place under the corresponding lines on the chart. Then give them the individual word cards, also to be placed under the matching words in the chart.

Step 3: Have the children read aloud in a chorus the whole story from the chart. Place the individual word cards in random order at the bottom of the chart. Have the children match the word cards to the words on the chart.

Repeated Reading

Children can learn words in context by reading the same passage over several times. Dowhower (1987) found two successful approaches:

1. Children read independently and receive word identification help on request. They reread and rehearse each passage orally or silently to themselves until they reach a reading rate of 100 words per minute.
2. Children listen first to a passage on tape and when they can read simulta-

neously with it, they rehearse the passage without the tape. They reread and rehearse each passage orally or silently to themselves until they reach a reading rate of 100 words per minute.

These techniques helped second-graders who had below average reading rates improve their reading rate, word reading accuracy, and comprehension. They allowed "students to learn gradually to operate at a phrasal level, much as a singer learns a new song—practicing the word grouping until the phrasing and rhythm sound right to the ear" (p. 404).

Writing and Reading

A number of suggestions for integrating writing into primary grade reading programs are found in Hansen, Newkirk, and Graves (1985). We report two of their suggestions next. The first is about how to establish a writing process classroom in first grade. The second is about extending writing across the curriculum.

In the second week of school, first grade teacher Carol Avery has children write their first class book, *Our Fun in the Sun*. They compose or dictate individual pages about summer experiences which the teacher types in conventional spellings, pastes up with their drawings, and fastens the pages into book form. Seeing their own words in print makes children aware from the beginning of school about how their language can be put into written form and what to compose in journals. Later, they learn to write based on ideas from trade book stories that the teacher reads daily to children, and from social studies, science topics, and poetry.

Another teacher, Kathy Matthews, extends writing across the curriculum by developing an accepting environment, asking questions, and providing a wide range of writing experiences. To develop an accepting environment, she encourages children to "gently challenge each other, read and voice their own hypotheses, and . . . read and write about the phenomena on their own" (p. 64). To foster word identification within this environment, she encourages children to help one another identify and spell words. She asks open-ended questions to encourage thinking, explaining, justifying, and speculating. She asks word identification questions such as, "How do you know that word? How might you find out? Is there another way?" Matthews also surrounds children with opportunities to write. This makes it possible for them to try writing many different words within a range of text contexts. Here are her suggestions:

- Journals and booklets for personal narratives.
- Daily news for the class newspaper.
- Responses to books they read or heard in the listening area.
- Records of personal experiences with a classroom activity.
- Descriptions about how to carry out an activity.
- Records of observations and discoveries.

- "End-of-day books" of children's significant events, feelings, reactions, descriptions of classroom jobs they enjoy, menus for snacks, and notes to the teacher.

▌ UNDERSTANDING LETTER-SOUND PATTERNS IN WORDS

The achievement of literacy is more difficult for English-speaking children than for many other language speakers because the correspondence between letters and sounds in English is not particularly regular. Venezky (1970) points out that while single letter-to-sound correspondences are not dependable, there is regularity between vowel consonant clusters and their sounds. For example, the *i* sound is not dependable by itself but it is when clustered with particular consonants such as *-ight, -ill, -ir, -in*. One reason that English spelling patterns are complex is that standardization of English spelling in the 1700s was less than ideal, according to Yule (1986), and many foreign words have been imported into our language.

Unfortunately, many of our most common words hold minor or unique sound patterns (e.g., notice the irregular sounds for the vowels in these words: *put, girl, come, they, was, says*). As a result of this irregularity, many words that first graders are expected to read cannot be sounded out. They need to be learned one by one as sight words. Thus, while a letter-sound analysis will be useful for many words, it cannot be the only word identification strategy that children use.

This point helps to put phonics in proper perspective. In general, have children use letter analysis only on words already in their oral vocabulary. Then, when teaching words in context, be sure that children learn irregular words as sight words and regular words in terms of generalizable letter-sound patterns. When observing children's reading attempts, keep track of their rapidly changing understanding of words and letter sounds so that you can adapt your instruction accordingly.

Guidelines for Teaching Phonics to Beginning Readers

Major consonant patterns are the most common sounds for each consonant (e.g., *b*ag, *c*at, *d*og, *f*an, *g*ot, *h*at). Each consonant has one major sound, though some consonant sounds change because of the vowel that follows (e.g., *c*at,

Exercise

(1) Here are some pseudowords that you can pronounce without difficulty because you have many examples of similar words stored in your memory: PAND, PLENT, TUNCH, KINE, SHAINT, PLOAT. Write down some rhyming words that you are reminded of when you try to pronounce them.

(2) Now, here are some pseudowords whose vowel sound you might not be sure about: SPOVE, SLIND, CREAT, GOOT, GOUR, SHERE. You are likely to think of words that contain quite different pronunciations. The first one, SPOVE, for example, might remind you of *love* or of *rove*. Why are the others troublesome? Write down some examples, and you will probably discover that, unlike the first set of pseudowords, you will think of rhyming words whose vowel sounds differ.

(3) Now that you realize that you can use real words with similar appearing letter patterns to pronounce new words, we will ask you to take one further step. Write down words you think of that rhyme with and contain the same ending letters in the following sets of words:

1. COT   COLD   OFF
2. HAT   CAR   WATCH
3. TRUCK   FUR   PUT
4. PIN   FILL   HIGH

The differences you found in each column of words point out the usefulness of rhyming for some but not all patterns. Notice that only the words in the first column have short vowel sounds. The others are affected by surrounding consonants. Can you figure out some more general principles about how consonants affect vowel sounds?

Perhaps you can now see why children should not be taught rules per se. Having children learn overly general rules will be wrong too often and less satisfactory than learning about sets of words that contain generalizable spelling and sound patterns. You will want to be sure that you teach and help children generalize to useful patterns, that is, to the patterns that contain many examples. So, before you use rhyming in your teaching, do this little exercise—try to generate rhymes to the example word you are considering so you will see whether the pattern will help children make generalizations.

city, *gum*, *gem*), or because of their location in the word (e.g., *bomb*, *yellow*, *penny*). Nevertheless, because consonants have quite regular sounds and are readily distinguished in words, children usually notice these sounds in words first and find them easiest to learn. In fact, many children will know the major sounds of most of the consonants when they enter first grade.

Arrange for beginning readers to read most words in the context of stories, in their own written pieces, or in texts that you write while they watch. Expect them to separate sentences into words (though you'll have to introduce the notion that some words have more than one part or syllable) and words

Earlier, the kindergarten children in this group dictated a story about sea turtles. In this lesson, the teacher is using words from the children's story to build knowledge of initial consonants.

into onset (or initial letter) and rime (the remaining part of the word). Begin with easier consonants, particularly those whose name signals the principal sound (which is true for all consonants except *c, g, h, w,* and *y*). Examples of the principal and minor patterns for consonant sounds in initial and final positions are in Figure 7.2. To prepare children for later instruction in decoding by analogy, help them notice likenesses between the first letter of words they know well and new words that begin with the same letter and sound. For example, when they can read and write *me,* remind them that knowing that word will help them identify other words beginning with m.

Children can be taught to notice and hear letter-sound relationships in initial word positions if you draw their attention to the first letter with questions (examples from Clay, 1985): "What do you expect to see at the beginning of xxx?" or "Do you know a word that starts with those letters?" In the same way you can later ask questions about word endings.

When two or more consonants make one sound, they are called *digraphs;* when each letter can be separately heard, they are called *blends.* Examples of both of these patterns are in Figure 7.3. The more common consonant digraphs, *th, sh* and *wh* can be presented along with the initial consonants when children are learning words that are seen again and again (study Figure 7.1 for examples). Many words that are in children's oral vocabulary can be

❚ Figure 7.2
Consonant-Sound Patterns

Major and Minor Examples	Major Patterns in Initial and Final Positions	Minor Pattern Examples
b	bat cab	climb
c	cat	city cellar cello muscle
d	dot pad	handkerchief helped
f	fan cuff	of
g	gate big	gem gnat sign garage
h	hat	honest
j	jaw	Juanita
k	kite	knight
l	lamp	would colonel
m	man ham	
n	nest pen	
p	pot cap	corps pneumonia
q	queen	
r	run tar	
s	sat pass	boys sugar aisle
t	ten pet	depot
v	valentine	
w	war row	answer
x	xylophone box	
y	yellow penny	
z	zebra buzz	

▌ **Figure 7.3**
▌ **Examples of Two-Letter Blends**
▌ **and Digraphs**

Blends	bl	cl	fl	gl	pl	sl	br	cr	dr	fr	gr	pr	tr	st	sk

Digraphs	ch	sh	ph	th	wh	gh	ck

figured out using the illustration or text context and the initial letter sound. For example, if children know the word *the,* you can lead them to figure out *then* and *them, this* and *that,* and perhaps even *they.* If you think they will not be able to understand, give them a hint in the form of a question so there is still some thinking left for them to do. Clay (1985) suggests: Would xxx make sense? Would xxx fit there? Do you think it looks like xxx?

Guidelines for Teaching More Advanced Beginning Readers

When you believe that your students can analyze more than the first consonants in a word without losing the meaning, they may be ready to consider *rimes,* that is, the vowel and ending consonant patterns (e.g., the *at* rime generates words such as *cat, sat, rat, fat*). These patterns are also called *phonograms.* There are three types of phonograms to keep in mind as you teach: consonant, vowel, consonant clusters (CVC); consonant, vowel (CV) or consonant, vowel, consonant, silent *e* (CVCe); and consonant, vowel, vowel, consonant (CVVC). Examples of each are found in Figure 7.4. Use these examples to help children read new phonograms. So, you might choose *cat* as an example or key word for three letter words ending in *-at,* and later extend it to four and five letter words (e.g., *flat, sprat,* or *brat*) and to two syllable words containing the *-at* syllable (e.g., *battle, matter*). Usually, you will have children study examples of CVC patterns first because they are the easiest to learn. CVCe patterns also begin appearing in the first reading books and so can be presented in first grade. However, CVVC patterns, as a group, should be presented later because each vowel pattern has a different sound, making them much harder to learn.

The reason for focused instruction on these three types of patterns is that the vowel sounds can more often be predicted within each of these syllable environments. A single vowel supported on either side by a consonant typically has a short sound (e.g., *pat*). When there is no second consonant or when the second consonant is followed by a silent *e,* the vowel typically has a long sound (e.g., *be, pane*). When there are two vowels together, other letter sounds are evident (e.g., *pain, peak, point, peek*). Examples of the most common sounds for each are presented in Figure 7.4 (Major Patterns).

Figure 7.4
Vowel-Sound Clusters

	Major Patterns (Presented as Phonograms)	Consonant-influenced Patterns	Minor Patterns (Examples)
Consonant-Vowel-Consonant (CVC) Clusters:			
a	bad, dad, glad cat, sat, fat back, sack, tack bag, rag, tag can, ran, man cap, map, tap ash, cash, mash last, fast, mast band, strand, land	star, far, car, call, tall, wall bank, sank, thank bang, hang, sang	what was wand war
e	bed, led, red set, met, get less, mess, chess pen, hen, ten send, bend, end nest, best, rest neck, deck, peck bent, sent, tent	her fern	
i	bin, pin, tin chip, tip, lip bit, fit, hit dip, rip, skip dish, fish, wish sick, pick, tick ink, think, mink	sir hill, mill, bill mind, kind, rind fight, tight, light child, mild	pint sign
o	hop, chop, drop pot, got, hot clock, dock, rock	for roll, toll, troll most, post, ghost cold, hold, told song, long, gong	clothes off won worn
u	mug, bug, rug sun, fun, run duck, truck, luck junk, sunk, trunk	fur hurt dull, hull, skull	pull truth
Consonant-Vowel-Consonant-Silent E (CV and CVCe) Clusters:			
a/e	ate, gate, skate gave, cave, save cake, bake, lake plane, cane, mane same, lame, tame	care, bare, dare tale, pale, sale	have are dance
e/e	he, me, we these	here were there	fence
i/e	fine, mine, nine bike, like, hike hide, wide, slide	tire, fire, hire pile, smile, file	give since

(continued)

▌ Figure 7.4
▌ Vowel-Sound Clusters (*continued*)

	Major Patterns (Presented as Phonograms)	Consonant-influenced Patterns	Minor Patterns (Examples)
o/e	go woke, choke, joke bone, tone, phone	core, bore, tore pole, hole, sole	love once come lose
u/e	use, muse, fuse	sure, pure, cure	
	blue, true, sue	nurse, purse	

Consonant-Vowel-Vowel-Consonant (CVVC) Clusters:

	Major Patterns (Presented as Phonograms)	Consonant-influenced Patterns	Minor Patterns (Examples)
ai, ay	say, day, hay train, brain, pain	air, hair, chair jail, hail, mail	said plaid
au, aw	law, saw, thaw draw, claw, paw	haul, maul crawl, bawl	laugh
ea	tea, sea, pea peach, teach, each leave, weave, heave	dear, fear, sear earn, learn bear, tear, pear deal, peal, heal	great break
	bread, dead, head		
ee	bee, tree, see peep, deep, keep feet, beet, meet	cheer, sneer, seer heel, eel, feel	been
ei, ey	they, hey, grey vein, rein weigh, neigh	their, heir veil	key weird seize
eu, ew	new, grew, few		sew
ie	die, lie, pie		
	chief, grief, thief	tier, pier field	friend
oa	boat, coat, oat boast, toast, roast	boar, roar, soar goal, coal	broad
oi, oy	boy, toy, joy join, coin, loin	choir boil, toil, soil	
oo	too, coo, moo room, loom, boom goose, moose, loose	door pool	brooch book flood
	book, look, took		
ou, ow	cow, now, sow found, sound, mound mouse, house	flour howl	
	blow, crow, flow dough, though	course	group could
ui	fruit, suit	build	suite

However, as we reminded you in the last exercise, there are no steadfast rules. When the second consonant is an *r* or *l*, for example, the vowel sound is modified (e.g., *part, pall, pare, peer, pair, pour*), the letter *w* changes the *a* and *o* vowel sounds in words like *word* and *wash*, and the cluster *-ght* in words like *light* affects the preceding *i*. Other examples of consonant-influenced patterns are presented in the third column of Figure 7.4.

Be assured that we do not advise you to memorize and teach all of these patterns to children formally. Nevertheless, you as the teacher need to understand vowel cluster pattern regularities in order to decide how and when to help children learn reliable patterns and figure out new words. If you understand which patterns are regular, then you can take advantage of incidental opportunities to teach a strategy or help a child decode an unknown word in context. Figure 7.4 also presents many common word examples of each pattern so you can use some of these examples to extend the point we made about distinguishing unique words from generalizable phonograms.

▌ INSTRUCTIONAL GUIDELINES

Your goal in teaching phonics is for children to acquire word identification strategies befitting the second processing mechanism by analyzing words into phonemes and generalizing from clustered letter-sound patterns. For this to be possible, children will need to understand language regularities, use the strategies they know flexibly, and use them in varying contexts. Keep the following guidelines in mind:

1. Teach children useful and easily distinguished phonetic principles. For example, to teach the most common sound for each consonant, remind children of cues from alphabet letter names. If children learn to distinguish these sounds in different positions in the word and in different combinations (e.g., *b* as /b/ in *ball, rub, rubber, brown,* and *blue*), you will have taught children the main concept about the letter. You would not need to teach consonant blends (e.g., *br, bl*) or minor patterns (e.g., the silent *b* as in *lamb*) except incidentally, as they appear in stories, and only if children are confused.
2. Because there are variations to most regular letter-sound patterns, teach children to check whether words they have decoded make sense in the sentence and story context. If not, they need to persevere and try another strategy.
3. Exemplify phonetic principles with good examples in texts. You might use poems or stories that feature words beginning with a consonant you are teaching or rhymes that repeat ending patterns. You could also write your own texts using words in Figure 7.4.

∎ INSTRUCTIONAL ACTIVITIES

Teaching Children to Apply Knowledge of Similar Words

This activity derives from the following recommendation by Tovey (1980):

> Instruction which requires children to deal constantly with abstract or technical language related to phonics does not warrant the time and effort often expended. This time might better be spent reading. Then, when word recognition problems are encountered, children could be shown or helped to discover known words containing the same sound-symbol relationship(s) as the unknown word. For example, if the unrecognized word were *knight,* the child could be shown *know, knee* and *knife* and *light, might,* and *right* in order to discover the relationship(s) in question. This eliminates talk about silent letters and long vowels. (pp. 436–437)

As implied above, the best phonics lessons are often those which occur when children are facing an immediate problem in word identification, that is, when they are reading a selection in a basal reader, a storybook, or other connected text. This is a *teachable moment,* a unique opportunity for student learning, when you can use the procedure outlined by Tovey. You can do this if you have prepared children to analyze words into familiar patterns. Here are stages to move the children toward independence in using this strategy:

Stage 1: Write on the board words the children already know that begin with the same letter and sound as the unknown word. Then write words with the same ending. (At a very early stage, you will want to introduce children to the concept that words with the same ending often *rhyme* with one another.) Encourage them to use a problem-solving strategy to read the words.

Stage 2: When the children have had a number of Stage 1 experiences, have them suggest words they know beginning with the same letter or letters as the unknown word, and write these on the board. Then, have them suggest words they know with the same ending. Again, encourage them to put the sounds together.

Stage 3: Finally, when children encounter unknown words that fit a major pattern, encourage them to use the strategy of comparison with words with similar beginning and ending letters or a similar letter cluster.

Teaching Phonics with Phonograms

Ringler and Weber (1984) present a general teaching plan for phonics based on the use of phonograms, rhyming words spelled with the same ending. They give the following rationale:

> Rhyming words are ideal for teaching phonic analysis because they incorporate letter clusters or phonograms familiar to the learner. A goal of this instruction is

to focus learners' attention on the written features of words they already know auditorily. (p. 134)

Examples of phonograms are listed in Figure 7.4 according to the type of cluster (e.g., *bad, dad, glad, sad, mad, tad, lad, fad*). We recommend that you use the following steps to introduce some of the major patterns as phonograms, beginning with CVC clusters.

Planning.   Select the specific phonogram for instruction based on diagnostic information (for example, teach a phonogram the children encountered while reading and were not yet familiar with). Choose the words you will use. For example, if the phonogram is *-op*, you might choose *hop* and *drop* from Figure 7.4, adding others likely to be familiar to the children, such as *stop*, *mop, top, pop*, and *cop*.

Introduction.   To call children's attention to the phonogram, have them listen to a poem or play a word or rhyming game. For example, you might make up silly phrases such as "Pop, the cop, stops the hopper." Or have children try to think of phrases including rhyming words, such as *the fat cat* or *the cat on the mat.*

Learning the letter-sound relationship.   Pronounce a series of words (e.g., *pep, pop, pot*). Have the children respond when they hear a word with the phonogram being taught. Then write the words on the board and have the children underline or circle the letter-sound pattern in each word. Help the children to notice that all the words containing the phonogram have a common ending but different initial letters and beginning sounds.

Substitution.   Have the children substitute different initial letters/ sounds to form other words with the targeted phonogram (e.g., *pop→top, drop, stop*). Begin with words known by sight or familiar in meaning and move on to having the children try to identify new words independently.

Application.   Find or prepare texts of various lengths (sentences, paragraphs, poems, stories) containing the targeted phonogram. Have the children first do some oral reading so you can see if the word identification strategy is being applied in context. Follow up with practice in more natural silent reading activities.

Decoding by Analogy

Gaskins et al. (1986 ,1987) developed a decoding by analogy strategy which is referred to as "Model and teach by compare/contrast." The approach is appropriate when children are confronted with new words in their reading books. One way, modeling the strategy, is useful when the teacher does not expect children to be able to make an analogy to a known pattern. The other way, used when they know the pattern, is to remind children of the decoding by analogy strategy and let them work out the solution.

1. Model a word using compare/contrast to decode a one syllable word when there is a good chance students do not know a word with the spelling pattern in the new word.

    Sentence: I need to go *back* to work now. (Teacher reads the sentence saying "blank" for the underlined word. Then she says, "The spelling pattern in the new word is a-c-k. I know a word with that spelling pattern—sack. If s-a-c-k is sack, then b-a-c-k must be back.")

2. Teach the new word by compare/contrast if a word with that vowel pattern has been taught earlier in the program.

    Sentence: The *band* will play at the fair. Teacher asks: "What is the spelling pattern in the underlined word?" (Children respond with a-n-d.) "Can you think of a word we have already learned that has that vowel pattern?" (Children think of or find the key word *and* from among the words posted on the wall.) "If a-n-d is and, what is b-a-n-d?" (Children say the word *band*.)

Key Concept 3

Word identification involves an understanding of concepts about syllables and other letter groups.

▌ UNDERSTANDING SYLLABLES AND OTHER COMPLEX WORD PATTERNS

As you learned in the introduction, good readers are able to identify words using the processing mechanism in which letter cluster patterns are analyzed. From Chapter 5 you learned that good readers analyze words structurally into *morphemic* units. For example, the word *insights* can be divided into three smaller units: *in-, -sight,* and *-s.* The *-sight* part of the word is the root, or base word. The *in-* part is a *prefix* which changes the meaning of the root, and the *-s* part is an *inflection* which assigns a plural but does not otherwise change the root meaning. Other common inflections signal possession (child's), person or tense (hunts, hunted, or hunting), or comparison (higher or highest). Children need to carry out this kind of analysis in order to identify complex words.

Structural analysis is the process that readers use to read *multisyllabic* words, compound words (words made up of two roots, such as *gingerbread* or *rainbow*), and *contractions,* such as *I'm* and *can't.*

Skilled readers can identify complex multisyllable words and figure out new words by relying on letter cluster analysis and separating roots from affixes. When verified or used in combination with context, skilled readers can pronounce and sense the meanings of most words they see in texts. Take, for example, the pseudoword, *prespander.* You are likely to notice the prefix and suffix (*pre-, -er*) and focus on the middle segment, working by analogy from *and* to *hand* or *span* to *spand.* At the heart of the process is a number of approaches that readers use to separate words into recognizable and pronounceable chunks. Your instructional goal, then, is to help children break multisyllable words into recognizable chunks that they can interpret meaningfully.

Cunningham (1975–1976) suggests that good readers go through the following processes:

- Good readers search through their memory of similar words and compare the unknown to the known. To see if part of the word looks like a known word, readers might, for example, find root words,such as *close,* in *enclosure, form* or *conform* in *conformation,* and *pack* or *package* in *prepackage.* They might see the similarity of *barber* to *barbet,* or *pounce* to *pronounce.* They would try to pronounce the whole word after picking out familiar parts and listen to see if they recognize the word if it fits the context.
- They segment unfamiliar words into chunks of the largest manageable unit. Sometimes they look for and block off prefixes or suffixes and concentrate on the word root, as we suggested with the pseudoword, *prespander.*
- They compare the chunks to known words, phonograms, or familiar letter clusters, looking for recognizable patterns. For example, they might recognize CVC or VC phonograms, separate these as the first syllable, and try out a short vowel sound, as in *cab-bage, ap-ple, pic-ture, blan-ket, car-pet, mir-ror, el-bow, fin-ger, can-dy, bab-ble, bad-lands.* Alternatively, they might notice a CV, V, or CVV cluster as the first syllable, trying out other vowel sounds, as in *ba-by, na-ture, bou-quet, boo-ty, bi-son, o-ver, ma-ple, fau-cet, la-tex, bea-con.*
- Longer words in readers' oral or listening vocabulary may be segmented by recognizing CVC, CV, or VC clusters and verified from surrounding context, as *pop-u-late, doc-u-men-tary, pres-i-den-tial, es-ca-late, syl-la-ble, un-der-stand.*
- If the word is not known in other ways, readers form and use their own rules or strategies for analyzing unknown words and comparing or contrasting known parts with the unknown. For example, you probably have never seen *tenemental, tompion, preconize,* or *desiderative* before, but you might piece together the pronunciation using parts that you know (e.g., *pre-con-ize*). If you then could see the word in context, you might find support for your conjecture (e.g., "The historian preconizes the reign of Louis Fourteenth as the happiest period in French history.")

Exercise

To understand how readers use a word and word-part comparison process for identifying words, cover up the right column below and try to pronounce the unfamiliar words listed on the left. Then look at the correct pronunciation on the right. You will probably notice that most of your pronunciations depended on identifying familiar word chunks and one-syllable patterns.

diffuseporous	/dif-ūs-pōr-əs/
peripatetic	/per-ə-pə-tet-ik/
spalpeen	/spal-pēn/
teratogenesis	/ter-ə-tə-jən-ə-səs/
utriculus	/yu-trik-yə-ləs/
bladdernose	/blad-ər-nōz/
barbet	/bār-bət/

▌ INSTRUCTIONAL ACTIVITIES

Word Reductions and Expansions

This activity is adapted from one successfully tried out with second graders by Condry (1979), as well as another developed by Floriani (1979) for use with remedial readers. The steps below can be used to give any group of children a sense of how root words are built upon to form other words.

Step 1: Begin with a set of root words or words containing inflections and affixes the children already know by sight. Place the words in sentences. For example, you could have children find the root word in the context of sentences such as these:

Bill is the *owner* of this bicycle.

Tammy and Terry have an *argument* every day.

Or you could have children add affixes to the root word to complete sentences such as these:

Bill used to own this bicycle. He was its _____.

Tammy and Terry always argue. They have an _____ every day.

Step 2: Have the children discuss how the new words and their meanings are different from the originals.

Step 3: Discuss with them how the "taking apart" strategy they use when trying to identify and work out the meanings of unfamiliar words is related to the "putting together" strategy they used to make up the longer words.

Other suggestions. Condry found that it was easier for children to find the root word than to find the affix or inflection, and easier to learn suffixes and inflections than prefixes. This suggests that children probably should first be taught to pick out the root word. They can later be taught to spot word endings (suffixes and inflections), and then to identify prefixes.

Floriani (p. 156) recommends teaching according to the order shown below. In following this approach, the teacher begins with inflections but then introduces a mixture of prefixes and suffixes.

Level 1: s, ed, d, ing
Level 2: y, ies, ly, es, er
Level 3: un, re, est, en, ful
Level 4: ex, pre, be, dis, in, ion,
         tion, sion, cian, ous, ness,
         ture, ment, ish, less

Teaching Contractions

Contractions appear quite early in children's beginning readers, especially in stories that attempt to model oral language. One contraction, *don't,* even appears among the 200 most frequently occurring words. Contractions can be confusing to many children because they look strange and cannot be decoded in the usual manner. Strategies for teaching children to handle them may need to be developed once children begin seeing them in their reading materials. At first, you can simply tell them the word, pronouncing the whole contraction as you run your finger under it. Later you can help them understand the concept.

Here is an approach you might use when you think children are ready to understand the principle of contraction. They should know several contractions by sight and words such as *I, you, we, they, have, do, not.* Then, when a new contraction appears in a story, choose one they know best and use it as a model and example. Show them the well-known contraction and its uncontracted form. Have children read both forms in text context. Then, help children use this example to figure out other contractions. You might have them think of others and construct uncontracted forms. You might also have them write sentences that feature contractions.

Teaching Inflections

Inflections are suffixes that change word tense, gender number, and so on. Such changes appear early in children's texts, with endings such as *s, ed, ing, er, ly.* When these inflections appear frequently in children's reading materials, attention should be called to them so that children will acquire general strategies for recognizing and decoding them. The *-s* and *-es* inflections can be understood in reading contexts. The *-ing* inflection ought to be presented with a good example, a verb children know well, and referred to when children are confronted with new -*ing* inflections.

The *ed* ending sound is more complex, as it contains three different sound patterns: a separate syllable (*wanted, nested*), a /d/ sound (*showed, called*), and a /t/ sound (*looked, worked*). Although these probably do not need to be separately taught, keep in mind that children might be temporarily confused by the differences.

We recommend that you teach an inflection when it is needed for reading. Exemplify the construct with well-known words that are in children's oral vocabulary. Model reading the word with and without the inflection. Arrange for children to hear and see the word read and written in and out of context, with and without the inflection. Have children construct inflected words from known words, put them into context orally, and then write them into sentences. Here is an example approach for teaching the inflection *ing:*

1. Write the known word, *go*, on the board. Make an *ing* strip and say the word without and then with the ending: *go, going.*
2. Have children say the word without and then with the ending.
3. Write four or five other words children know in a column on the board. The list might include some of these words: *look, work, say, walk, find, do, read, sing.*
4. Have children say a word and then place the *ing* strip next to the word and say the inflected word. Do this with each word.
5. Say a sentence with *go* and then with *going.* Write the sentence with the inflected word on the board.
6. Have children think of sentences for each of the other words. Write on the board one good example for each inflected word.
7. Give children more examples of known verbs that can be inflected without doubling the final consonant or deleting a final letter. Review the additional words by having children read them quickly.
8. Provide children independent or cooperative work time to copy or construct their own sentences.

Later lessons can focus on verbs in which the final consonant is doubled (e.g., *setting, running, hopping*) and the final *e* is dropped (e.g., *using, coming, taking, naming*).

Multisyllabic Words

Introducing multisyllable words.   Teaching multisyllable words begins when children read their first book and point to words as they read. When they come across a multisyllabic word they will probably point to the next word for the second syllable. The mistake gives you a teaching opportunity. Have children practice clapping to words so they will learn that some words have more than one clap. In all likelihood, no further explanation of multisyllable words will be needed in first grade.

Analysis of multisyllable words. Shefelbine (1987) proposes that rules for dividing words are not important for children to learn. Instead, children need to be able to pronounce syllable units and identify frequently occurring syllables rapidly. Second, they need varying strategies to identify possible syllables in a flexible manner so as to separate large words into familiar syllables, affixes, and roots. Third, they need to relate unknown written words to words they have in their speaking or listening vocabulary.

We would add that word analysis tasks should be studied in text contexts as often as possible. Roth and Beck (1987) found that isolated word practice, even though it leads to substantial increases in children's word recognition and decoding skills, does not necessarily improve reading comprehension. To that end, we recommend that picture books, narratives, folktales, and informational books be included in the curriculum so that children will have opportunities to read new and long words in many different contexts and on topics of their choice.

> Word identification is a problem-solving process, requiring a combination of strategies, to achieve fluent and rapid reading.

▌ UNDERSTANDING HOW TO SELECT APPROPRIATE WORD IDENTIFICATION STRATEGIES

Efficient word identification depends on use of a combination of strategies (Cunningham, 1975–1976), and, as Clay (1985) describes, on cross-checking between one cue system and another—letters, letter groups, syntax, and text meaning. Children must be taught to rely on several strategies to identify words and then to check their solution by cross-checking. In this section we discuss how a teacher can help children coordinate and use several strategies effectively as they read. The goal is for children to monitor their reading so they can use varying strategies appropriately and in ways that allow them to focus on text meaning.

Many words that occur frequently in texts will be identified by sight, through writing practice, and from repeated readings. Other words will be identified through the study of words and patterns and by analogy to known words. Both mechanisms are aided appreciably when reading and writing take place in meaningful contexts. When picture information, syntax, and text meaning are used to support word identification, reading can take place in a more integrated fashion. Thus, children need to know how to use more than one cue system:

Exercise

There are various ways in which printed language can provide cues. Decode the following sentence keeping in mind how you solved it. What were the cues you used?

Lxttxxx xxx nxx xxx xxly clxxx xxed xxx rxxxxxg xxrds.

The adult reader is helped by knowing:
- the letter symbols
- the sounds of English
- the frequently used function words of English and their patterns of occurrence
- the pronounceable sequences of English words
- the sentence patterns of English

(Clay, 1979, p. 260)

- Context and meaning: use of pictures and gist of the text.
- Letters and sounds in words: initial and final letters in words, regular letter-sound patterns, and recognizing words by analogy to known words.
- Word parts: contractions, inflections (e.g., *-s*, *-ed*), affixes (e.g., *un-*, *con-*, *-tion*), and syllables.
- Syntactic structures: written sentence patterns.

Monitoring Reading

Beginning readers' eye movements are not as well organized as are skilled readers'. Children make an incredible number of retracings of the print as they read, primarily because the task is so complex for them. Words are easily forgotten, and a word painfully figured out on one page might be misread on the next. Later in the year, although they recognize words accurately, many children read in a choppy fashion rather than smoothly and effectively. In subsequent years, they may read fluently but have difficulty remembering important ideas or understanding the text as a whole. Monitoring of reading is a complex process, begun early, and continually adapted as new reading skills are acquired.

Before children try to identify words as they read, as we described in Chapter 6, they are likely not to know how to keep track of the print, and some will not even know where to begin or in which direction to proceed. They need to monitor their reading by pointing to the print, using their finger to help them coordinate their speech with their eye movements. If they can't do this, you can model the approach as you read to them or with them and ask them to "Read with your finger just like me."

Because beginning readers recognize few words, they are overly dependent upon context. This is not a problem if you encourage children to figure out new words in their stories by looking at the pictures, noticing words or phrases that are repeated, and predicting what is likely to be written. When they say something that does not make sense, you can repeat what they said and ask if it makes sense, or you can direct them to look at the picture and think again about the text. When they stop and try to self-correct, praise them for noticing a problem, not just when the effort was successful. When they ignore the print entirely and make up text, direct them to the initial letters of the words they skipped or misread and have them try again. In these ways, you begin guiding them to use a combination of effective word recognition strategies.

When beginning readers attend to word information as they read and make a mistake, they might ignore the error, invent text, or skip over the words. You want them to self-monitor their reading and stop to check the problem, reread, and attempt to self-correct. They might notice that the number of words they have said does not match the number on the page, that what they say does not make sense, or that what they say does not look like the print. To figure out a solution to the problem, they could reread from the beginning of the sentence, look at the picture for more information, study the word, or think about the context. You may need to intercede, and through questions, help them to recover text meaning or accuracy. Clay (1985) suggests that you could say, "You said . . . Does that sound right?" or "Can you say it that way? if you want to emphasize syntactic pattern cues. If you want them to focus on the text meaning you might say, "You said . . . Does that make sense?" And, if you want them to use letter cues, you could say, "Does it look right?"

If children are trying to correct their errors but are using only one cue source (e.g., they are only looking at the letters), then you should help them learn to consider more than one way to figure out a hard word. You can praise the child for studying one cue but ask for another way. Clay suggests, "You almost got that page right. There was something wrong with this line. See if you can find what was wrong. . . . How did you know? . . . Is there any other way we could know? . . . Yes. That was good. You found two ways to check on that tricky new word" (p. 73).

Older and more skilled readers will make fewer word errors. Those who are self-monitoring will stop and figure out the problem if the text does not make sense, possibly by searching earlier sections, rereading what the author stated as the goal of the section, reading ahead for gist, or possibly deciding that the author wrote something poorly or incorrectly. Children who do not monitor their comprehension will need to be coached, as we suggested in the comprehension chapters.

In all of these examples, there is no one solution. Children must learn a number of ways to monitor their reading and to use fix-up strategies when there is a problem. Children need to show flexibility in their reading of words and phrases, and to be aware of how letters and words operate within their larger context. Children will want to know letter-sound analysis, syllabication and letter clusters, little words in big words, and decoding by analogy, and be able to use syntactic structure, phrasing, semantic content, and illustrations. You can find out what strategies beginning readers use by noticing omissions, insertions, and changes in a text while they read aloud. Older children's strategy use cannot be viewed directly because they make few word recognition errors, though you could have them discuss what they did and how they figured out the hard parts of the text and made sense of it.

Using Teachable Moments

Many of our instructional examples have used *teachable moments* to help children identify words. By teachable moments we mean giving an impromptu lesson when children encounter a problem. You can remind them of similar known words, help them break a word into known letter groups, or show them how to search for cues to solve their problem. At other times, you will not want to break the flow of comprehension activity to work on word

(1) Arrange for a child who is a below average reader to read aloud the first 50 or so words from a story. Ideally, the story should be difficult enough so the child makes a few errors, that is, about four or five errors in a 50 word text. Make a copy of the text so that you can mark down all errors, rereadings, and self-corrections. Do not correct errors unless the child asks for help or is hopelessly confused. When the child has finished reading, go back to one of the errors that was corrected and ask, "How did you figure that out?" Then, find one part that was not corrected and ask, "Try that again." Write down the child's responses to both. If the child made no errors, locate places where the child reread or hesitated and ask what thinking was involved at that point.

(2) Afterward, mark all the errors and self-corrections that seem to be tied to these three sources: *Meaningful* (M) (The text was kept meaningful, even though the words didn't match those on the page); *Sentence form* (S) (A word was chosen that fit the sentence up to the point of the error); and *Word substitution* (W) (A word was substituted that was like some of the letters or sounds in the word, such as "cat" for the word *cold*). You can double code because many errors and self-corrections involve more than one cue system. Now consider what you've marked and the child's answers to your two questions. Do you see the child using more than one source of information for cues or does one source predominate? Was the child self-monitoring while reading? What can you say about the child's reading skill at this time?

identification, and you will just tell the students what the word is. In these instances you may want to jot down the unfamiliar word and where it first occurred in the text. Then, after the passage has been read, give a short lesson to show students what they could have done to identify it on their own, illustrating use of combined strategies.

Here is an example from a lesson with a first grade child: The child had stumbled several times on the words *would* and *could,* and the teacher had corrected her mistakes. However, because these were words that the child would read often, the teacher decided to teach her to distinguish the similarly patterned words. So, she stopped the lesson and had the child write on the board the word she had just read, *would.* The teacher said, "Take away one letter and replace it with another to make *could.*" The child thought about it, and carried out the correct replacement. Then the teacher said, "Now, can you take away one letter and put in two letters to make *should?*" After a longer thinking time, the child was able to make the substitution. The child rewrote and read the words correctly. Next, she constructed the three words from magnetic letters. Finally, they went back to text reading. On another day, the teacher checked the child's recognition of the words in context and found that she had retained the words.

❚ INSTRUCTIONAL GUIDELINES

We suggest the following guidelines so that most of your word identification instruction will be situated within meaningful reading and writing contexts and be flexibly organized to change as children become more proficient:

1. Support word learning by using words that are in children's oral vocabulary and are clearly represented by picture and text context. Highlight the process of using context information when teaching the words. Point out the words as they are read so that children will look at the print.
2. Although at first children will not be able to identify words on the page, they will as you model word pointing and then have them point to the words as they read. When they make errors, ask questions that lead them to use pictures and other context information.
3. Provide children with many stories to read, beginning with caption books (pictures labeled with words or phrases) and predictable books (phrases are repeated frequently or can be predicted from accompanying pictures). In the story introduction, read and point to a few words in the story, letting children figure out the remaining ones by using repeated words and phrases and picture information.
4. Lead children into dialogue stories and other more complex texts so that they can use picture, syntax, and semantic information to figure out the words. When children read more complex stories, direct their attention

to story ideas and accompanying illustrations which will be helpful in figuring out new and difficult words.

5. Make sure children have opportunities to read and reread stories until they can render them confidently and with expression. Arrange also for daily writing to extend story reading so that children can use story words in their own writing.

6. Teach word analysis from the words that children are reading and writing and use their own well-learned words to exemplify word patterns that you want to teach. First you will help them to understand word and syllable distinctions and then to notice initial letters and phonograms and to use known parts of words to figure out new words by analogy. Work toward recognition of multisyllable words by showing them inflections and how to use syllables, root words, and affixes they recognize to break apart and read longer words.

7. Arrange for word fluency practice by having children practice writing common words that appear in their written stories. Children might write these words several times, in different places, and with magnetic letters in order to obtain diversified practice.

∎ INSTRUCTIONAL ACTIVITIES

A Strategy-Based Approach to Reading and Word Identification

Clay (1979) surveyed teachers to determine how they used books for reading instruction. She found that they usually had children read, analyze the text, and reread during group reading lessons. That is, after children were helped to read a story aloud, the teacher asked questions about the story. Word study followed and the text was reread in that lesson and on subsequent days. The teachers listed the following examples of strategies they taught and helped children to integrate. Many of their suggestions may help you to place word identification instruction within the broader context of story reading lessons:

I teach understanding related to the story.

I use a small blackboard and give special examples as errors arise.

I encourage children to find and correct errors.

I group initial words in a list:

shaving
shouted
shop

I invite discovery of a new word by analogy:

went
sent
lent
bent

I use words again the next day or next week.

I observe closely what children are saying and doing.
I try new tactics, a new approach.
I work with a particular word, emphasizing it. (p. 175)

∎ SUMMARY

The teaching of word identification is an important part of the beginning reading program, because the ability to identify words rapidly and to read with comprehension are closely linked. But being able to read words quickly does not automatically make one a good reader, able to read with understanding. Thus, instruction in word identification should aim to have children take on word recognition as a problem-solving process, and should be balanced with comprehension instruction.

In the first key concept we discussed the first method that children can use to identify words, which is simply to know them by sight. It is important to begin with common and meaningful words and recognize the words in books and through writing activities. In the second key concept we provided guidelines and activities for teaching children to use knowledge of letter-sound relationships. We introduced the concepts of major patterns, minor patterns, and consonant-influenced vowel patterns. These concepts help us see which letter-sound relationships to emphasize in instruction. In the third key concept we looked at how children could be taught to use the patterning of syllables to identify multisyllable words.

Finally, we discussed under the fourth key concept how no one strategy is sufficient in and of itself to identify all words. Thus, we emphasized the importance of leading children toward independence in word identification through a combination of strategies as they monitor their text reading and understanding. We concluded by recommending a strategy-based approach so students will be able to recognize words in an efficient manner. Throughout this chapter we emphasized the importance of providing instruction in word identification, not as an end in itself, but within the broader framework of reading for meaning.

∎ BIBLIOGRAPHY

References

Adams, M. (in press). *Phonics and beginning reading.* Cambridge, MA: MIT Press.

Adams, M. Huggins, A., Starr, B., Rollins, A., Zuckerman, L., Stevens, K., & Nickerson, R. (1980). *A prototype test of decoding skills.* Bethesda, MD: National Institute of Child Health and Human Development.

Bissex, G. (1980). *GNYS AT WRK: A child learns to write and read.* Cambridge, MA: Harvard University Press.

Bradley, L. & Bryant, P. (1981). Categorizing sounds and learning to read—a causal connection. *Nature, 301,* 419–421.

Byrne, B. (in press). Studies in the unbiased acquisition procedure for reading: Rationale, hypotheses, and data. In P. B. Gough (Ed.), *Reading acquisition.* Hillsdale, NJ: Erlbaum.

Clarke, L. (1988). Invented versus traditional spelling in first graders' writings: Effects on learning to spell and read. *Research in the Teaching of English, 22,* 281–309.

Clay. M. (1979). *Reading: The patterning of complex behavior.* Portsmouth, NH: Heinemann.

Clay, M. (1983). Getting a theory of writing. In B. Kroll & G. Wells (Eds.), *Explorations in the development of writing.* New York: Wiley.

Clay, M. (1985). *The early detection of reading difficulties* (2nd ed.). Portsmouth, NH: Heinemann.

Condry, S. (1979). *A developmental study of processes of word derivation in elementary school children and their relation to reading.* Unpublished doctoral dissertation. Ithaca, NY: Cornell University.

Cunningham, P. (1975–76). Investigating a synthesized theory of mediated word recognition. *Reading Research Quarterly, 11,* 127–143.

Dobson, L. (1989). Connections in learning to write and read: A study of children's development through kindergarten and first grade. In J. Mason (Ed.), *Reading and writing connections.* Boston: Allyn & Bacon.

Dolch, E. (1941). *Teaching primary reading.* Champaign. IL: Garrard.

Dowhower, S., (1987). Effects of repeated reading on second grade transitional readers' fluency and comprehension. *Reading Research Quarterly, 22,* 389–406.

Eads, M. (1985). Bookwords: Using a beginning word list of high frequency words from children's literature K-3. *The Reading Teacher, 38,* 418–423.

Ehri, L. (1987). Learning to read and spell words. *Journal of Reading Behavior, 19,* 5–31.

Ehri, L., & Wilce, L. (1987). Do cipher readers read and spell better than cue readers? *Journal of Educational Psychology, 79,* 3–13.

Floriani, B. D. (1979). Word expansions for multiplying sight vocabulary. *The Reading Teacher, 33,* 155–157.

Gaskins, I., Downer, M., & Gaskins, R. (1986). *Introduction to the Benchmark School word identification/vocabulary development program.* Media, PA: Benchmark Press.

Gaskins, I., Downer, M., Anderson. R., Cunningham, P., Gaskins, R., & Schommer, M. (1987). A metacognitive approach to phonics: using what you know to decode what you don't know. *Remedial and Special Education, 9,* 36–41.

Goswami, U. (1986). Children's use of analogy in learning to read: A developmental study. *Journal of Experimental Child Psychology, 42,* 73–83.

Gough, P., Juel, C., & Griffith, P. (1986). *Reading, spelling, and the orthographic-cipher.* Paper presented at the Conference on early reading. Center for Cognitive Science, University of Texas at Austin.

Hansen, J., Newkirk, T., & Graves, D. (1985). *Breaking ground: Teachers relate reading and writing in the elementary school.* Portsmouth, NH: Heinemann.

Huey, E. B. (1908). *The psychology and pedagogy of reading.* New York: Macmillan.

Lundberg, I., Frost, J., & Petersen, O. (1988). Effects of an extensive program of stimulating phonological awareness in preschool children. *Reading Research Quarterly, 13,* 263–284.

Maclean, M., Bryant, P., & Bradley, L. (1987). Rhymes, nursery rhymes and reading in early childhood. *Merrill Palmer Quarterly.*

Masonheimer, P., Drum. P., & Ehri. L. (1984). Does environmental print identification led children into word reading? *Journal of Reading Behavior, 16,* 257–271.

McConkie, G. (1984). The reader's perceptual processes. In G. G. Duffy, L. R. Roehler, & J. M. Mason (Eds.), *Comprehension instruction: Perspectives and suggestions.* New York: Longman.

McConkie, G., & Zola, D. (1987). Visual attention during eye fixations while reading. In M. Coltheart (Ed.), *Attentions and performance XII: The psychology of reading.* Hillsdale, NJ: Erlbaum.

Perfetti, C. (1985). *Reading ability.* New York: Oxford University Press.

Rayner, K., & Pollatsek. A. (1989). *The psychology of reading.* Englewood Cliffs, NJ: Prentice-Hall.

Resnick, L. B. (1979). Theories and prescriptions for early reading instruction. In L. B. Resnick & P. A. Weaver (Eds.), *Theory and practice of early reading* (Vol. 2). Hillsdale, NJ: Erlbaum Associates.

Ringler, L., & Weber C. (1984). *A language-thinking approach to reading.* New York: Harcourt Brace Jovanovich.

Roth, S., & Beck, I. (1987). Theoretical and instructional implication of the assessment of two microcomputer word recognition programs. *Reading Research Quarterly, 22,* 197–218.

Shefelbine, J. (1987). *Syllabication reading strategies: A model for assessment and instruction.* Paper presentation at the National Reading Conference.

Simon, H., & Leu, D. (1987). The use of contextual and graphic information in word recognition by second-, fourth-, and sixth-grade readers. *Journal of Reading Behavior, 19,* 33–47.

Tovey, D. R. (1980). Children's grasp of phonics terms vs. sound-symbol relationships. *The Reading Teacher, 33* (4), 431–437.

Trieman, R. (1985). Onsets and rimes as units of spoken syllables: Evidence from children. *Journal of Experimental Psychology, 39,* 161–181.

Venezky, R. (1970). *The structure of English orthography.* The Hague: Mouton

Yule, V. (1986). The design of spelling to match needs and abilities. *Harvard Educational Review, 56,* 278–297.

Children's Books Cited

Martin, B. (1967). *Brown bear, Brown bear, what do you see?* New York: Holt, Rinehart and Winston.

Martin, B. (1970). *Fire, fire, said Mrs. McGuire.* New York: Holt, Rinehart and Winston.

Martin, B. (1970). *The haunted house.* New York: Holt, Rinehart and Winston.

Martin, B. (1970). *Up the down escalator.* New York: Holt, Rinehart and Winston.

Munari, B. (1980). *Jimmy has lost his cap, where can it be?* New York: Philomel.

Munari, B. (1980). *The elephant's wish.* New York: Philomel.

Further Readings

Adams, M. J., & Huggins, A. W. F. (1985). The growth of children's sight vocabulary: A quick test with educational and theoretical implications. *Reading Research Quarterly, 20,* 262–281.

Barron, R. W. (1981). Reading skill and reading strategies. In A. M. Lesgold & C. A. Perfetti (Eds.), *Interactive processes in reading* (pp. 299–327). Hillsdale, NJ: Lawrence Erlbaum Associates.

Calfee, R., & Piontkowski, D. (1981). The reading diary: Acquisition of decoding. *Reading Research Quarterly, 16*, 346–373.

Ehri, L. C., & Wilce, L. S. (1987). Does learning to spell help beginners learn to read words? *Reading Research Quarterly, 12* (1), 47–65.

Ferroli, L., & Shanahan, T. (1987). Kindergarten spelling: Explaining its relationship to first-grade reading. In J. E. Readance & R. S. Baldwin (Eds.), *Research in literacy: Merging perspectives* (pp. 93–99). Thirty-sixth yearbook of the National Reading Conference. Rochester, NY: National Reading Conference.

Juel, C. (1986). Support for the theory of phonemic awareness as a predictor of literacy acquisition. In J. A. Niles & R. V. Lalik (Eds.), *Solving problems in literacy: Learners, teachers, and researchers* (pp. 239–243). Thirty-fifth yearbook of the National Reading Conference. Rochester, NY: National Reading Conference.

Teaching Reading to Students with Special Needs

Intelligence is a mystery. We hear it said that people never develop more than a very small part of their latent intellectual capacity. Probably not; but *why* not? Most of us have our engines running at about ten percent of their power. Why no more? And how do some people manage to keep revved up to twenty percent or thirty percent of full power—or even more?

What turns the power off, or keeps it from ever being turned on?

During these past four years at the Colorado Rocky Mountain School my nose has been rubbed in the problem. When I started, I thought that some people were just born smarter than others and that not much could be done about it. This seems to be the official line of most of the psychologists. It isn't hard to believe, if all your contacts with students are in the classroom or the psychological testing room. But if you live at a small school, seeing students in class, in dorms, in their private lives, at their recreations, sports, and manual work, you can't escape the conclusion that some people are much smarter part of the time than they are at other times. Why? Why should a boy or girl, who under some circumstances is witty, observant, imaginative, analytical, in a word, *intelligent*, come into the classroom and, as if by magic, turn into a complete dolt?

(Holt, 1964, p. 5)

■ OVERVIEW

In this chapter we discuss the teaching of reading to children with special needs. For many classroom teachers, there is no topic of greater practical concern. We begin with a discussion of how the basic approach to be used with students with special needs should be much like the approach used with all other students. That is, reading instruction should still be seen as developing children's ability to construct meaning from text, by building upon existing background knowledge and skills. We discuss the fact that reading failure generally seems to be due to poor instruction, rather than to children's backgrounds and abilities.

Teachers often find that students' special needs fall into just a few broad areas. The first area concerns the needs of poor readers, those who are in the bottom third or fourth of the class in reading ability. We provide guidelines suggesting how instruction for poor readers should be handled, and describe activities for building their comprehension and word identification ability.

A second type of special need is that associated with cultural differences. We point out that teachers need to be aware of differences in students' communication styles and background knowledge.

Language differences represent a third type of special need, for students who speak English as a second language or who speak a nonstandard dialect of English. The situation here is complicated, because cultural differences are an issue with these students as well. Recommended instructional activities center on literature and storybook reading and on writing, as well as on techniques to increase knowledge of English, and of Standard English in particular.

The fourth type of special need highlighted in this chapter is that shown by gifted readers. Here the recommended approaches center on independent inquiry projects and the reading of thought-provoking books.

Chapter 8 is organized around the following key concepts:

Key Concept 1: Teachers should know how to provide sound classroom reading instruction to children who are poor readers.

Key Concept 2: Teachers should know how to respond to cultural differences which can influence children's learning to read.

Key Concept 3: Teachers should know how to respond to differences in language which can influence children's learning to read.

Key Concept 4: Teachers should know how to provide sound classroom reading instruction to gifted readers.

∎ PERSPECTIVE
Meeting Special Needs

The main idea you should take from this chapter is that the reading instruction given to students with special needs should be much like the reading instruction given to all other students. This is an idea you may find surprising. For many years, educators spent time trying to place students with special needs into categories, such as learning disabled, bilingual, and so on. Today we know that this process of labeling is not at all precise (e.g., Shepard, Smith, & Vojir, 1983) or useful, and that our time is better spent on good teaching.

Researchers have discovered that almost all children can make good progress in learning to read if they receive high quality instruction, of the kind described in the other chapters in this textbook, on comprehension, word identification, vocabulary, and other topics (e.g., Wong-Kam & Au, 1988). In fact, the most likely cause of reading problems is not children's ability, but poor instruction (Allington, 1983).

What works with poor readers? Here are some findings. You will notice that they include many of the same recommendations that we have made for students in general.

Wong-Kam and Au (1988) suggest the following three principles for working with poor readers in the upper elementary grades:

1. Bring all students in the class together as a community of readers and writers, so that poor readers can be accepted by other students.
2. Integrate reading and writing instruction, through the use of learning guides and other kinds of meaning-oriented approaches, so that poor readers can always see the larger purposes of literacy.
3. Provide explicit skill and strategy instruction and opportunities for application, so that poor readers can become more and more independent in word identification.

Similarly, Gaskins (1988) recommends that poor readers:

1. spend the maximum amount of time engaged in reading books and stories at a comfortable reading level;
2. receive direct instruction regarding important skills and strategies;
3. participate in a writing program which emphasizes the process of writing and provides opportunities for meaningful reading and heightened self-esteem. (p. 754)

As you can see, following these and other similar suggestions might be essential for poor readers, but at the same time, they are valuable suggestions for other students, too.

As a classroom teacher, you will want to think about the reading experiences you are giving the poor readers in your class. Do they have as much opportunity to develop comprehension ability as the other students? As much opportunity to write? As much opportunity to engage in recreational reading? Remind yourself that poor readers may gain even greater benefit from these activities than other students.

Coordinating Instructional Resources

In order to meet the needs of poor readers, classroom teachers often have to learn to coordinate their work with that of resource teachers and others.

In some schools, children with special needs remain in their homerooms all day. Sometimes the resource teacher, or an aide, enters the classroom to tutor the children or help them complete seatwork assignments. In many schools, however, the children are taken from the classroom and given read-

ing or language instruction by a resource teacher. This type of pull-out procedure, in which children are removed from their regular classrooms, is often
used in the federally funded Chapter 1 program for poor readers in low-income
communities; bilingual or second-language programs; and programs for the
gifted and talented.

The danger in many of these situations is that the classroom teacher may
no longer be responsible for providing reading instruction to children with
special needs. The teacher loses touch with the children's needs in learning to
read and fails to provide continued classroom support for reading.

For children who are experiencing difficulty with learning to read, the ab-
sence of classroom support may be quite damaging. Allington's (1983) findings, discussed in detail later in this chapter, point to the importance of setting aside adequate time to teach special students to read. For many children
with reading difficulties, the time provided in resource room instruction is
inadequate in and of itself. They continue to need the classroom teacher's
help. For this reason, it seems best for the classroom teacher to view outside
reading instruction as supporting or supplementing classroom reading instruction, rather than replacing it entirely. Also, outside instruction seems to
be more effective if it is coordinated with classroom reading activities rather
than being completely separate or different (e.g., Johnston, Allington, &
Afflerbach, 1985).

There are important reasons for classroom teachers to be actively involved in the reading instruction of special students. First, keeping in touch
with all students' progress in learning to read helps in the planning of more
effective whole-class lessons. Especially as students get older, most lessons
involve some kind of reading. If teachers are familiar with the reading progress of special students, they will know how to structure such lessons to per-
mit them to participate. This will be important if special students are to have
valuable in-class reading opportunities, for example when reading instruction
is being integrated with science and social studies lessons. Second, by taking
the time to teach reading to all students, even those who receive outside instruction, teachers make it less likely that some students will feel neglected
or inferior.

Curriculum Scope

Often, whether children with reading problems are taken from the classroom
or given reading instruction by their homeroom teacher, the tendency is to
give them lessons which focus solely on word identification. Reading programs which emphasize word identification or phonics to the exclusion of
comprehension and vocabulary building are sometimes presented as a remedy
for children's reading problems. Such programs are frequently represented as
being particularly effective with children from disadvantaged backgrounds or

with children who learn more slowly. They cannot, however, be considered complete and balanced developmental reading programs.

As discussed in more detail in Key Concept #1, phonics-only instruction is not generally beneficial and may actually slow learning to read, instead of speeding it. The danger in programs which consist entirely of phonics activities, such as the learning of sound-symbol relationships, is that they give children with reading problems a misleading picture of what reading is all about. The children never have the opportunity to develop the concept that reading is the process of constructing meaning from text. The more they are deprived of experiences with constructing meaning from text, for example, as in the reading of storybooks, the less likely it is that they will ever become competent readers. A sound reading program for students with special needs will always include many comprehension activities in addition to those in word identification.

In fact, a sound reading program for students with special needs should go beyond just these basics. Research by Singer, McNeil, and Furse (1984) suggests that a broad curriculum, one which goes beyond the acquisition of basic reading skills, is likely to be beneficial for all students, including low achievers. A narrow curriculum is one that stresses only basic skills, while a broad curriculum covers the basics plus the content areas and fine arts.

Thus, reading instruction for students with special needs should be broad in scope, bringing out the many different functions of literacy, including its importance in learning information in the content areas, such as social studies and science. Such instruction should emphasize comprehension while also including opportunities for the development of writing, vocabulary, and word identification abilities. The idea is to provide special-needs children with a complete and balanced program of reading instruction, one that touches upon the different functions of literacy and the different facets of reading ability.

Classroom Climate

Often, students with special needs may develop feelings of inferiority and of not being valued as members of the class. This may occur because they are taken from the classroom for reading instruction and thus marked as being different. Or, if they remain in the classroom, they may not have many opportunities to succeed at reading and writing and to be recognized for their achievements. Teachers may need to work at helping students with special needs gain a feeling of belonging to the class and of being successful readers (refer to Chapter 11 for further discussion of this point).

This goal can be accomplished if teachers organize the classroom as a literate community, where readers and writers are constantly sharing their work, communicating with and learning from one another (e.g., Holdaway, 1979).

We have highlighted the sharing of literature, information learned through reading expository text, and one's own writing as being particularly effective ways of developing the classroom as a literate community (refer to Chapters 2, 3 and 4). Students with special needs should be drawn into this community and encouraged to participate along with all of the other students. Teachers can play a key role in establishing the values of the classroom community which make it possible for special students to be accepted.

The sense of community in the classroom is best encouraged through reading and writing activities which promote cooperation, and not just competition. The students can also be led to discuss ways of helping one another and the value in applauding one another's efforts. All students, but especially those with special needs, benefit in such a classroom environment.

In summary, teachers need to be aware of several of the typical weaknesses in the reading instruction provided to students with special needs, especially those who are experiencing difficulties in learning to read. They should be sure to provide these students with adequate classroom time for learning to read, coordinating reading instruction with that provided by resource teachers. They should be sure that the reading instruction given to students with special needs is well balanced, with activities in comprehension as well as word identification, in the content areas as well as basic skills, and in writing and recreational reading. Finally, they should be sure to create a classroom climate which promotes a sense of community, so that all students have the chance to be recognized as successful readers.

Key Concept 1

Teachers should know how to provide sound classroom reading instruction to children who are poor readers.

▌ WHY DO SOME CHILDREN BECOME POOR READERS?

In teaching reading, many classroom teachers experience the greatest difficulty in working effectively with children in the "low group," those in the bottom third or quarter of the class. We will refer to these students as *poor readers*. These students appear to be making very slow or, in some cases, inconsistent progress in learning to read. Some may also appear to be more inattentive or restless than the good readers in the class.

Children will, of course, enter school differing in many ways, including aptitude for learning to read and previous experiences with literacy. The research suggests, however, that *many students' slowness in learning to read is highly related to the quality of the instruction they receive.* In general, it seems that poor readers never have the opportunity to learn to read well because they consistently receive lessons of poor quality. Thus, our point of view is that teachers should work to provide high quality instruction to poor readers.

Allington (1983) summarizes evidence to support the view that *"good and poor readers differ in their reading ability as much because of differences in instruction as variations in individual learning styles or aptitudes"* (p. 548; italics in the original). His review indicates five areas in which the instruction given to poor readers differs from that given to good readers.

1. *Allocation of instructional time.* Teachers seem to allocate about the same amount of time for teaching reading to good and poor readers. However, Allington argues that this treatment is in fact unequal, because poor readers need *more* instructional time to overcome their reading deficits.

2. *Engaged instructional time.* During reading lessons, poor readers show more off-task behavior or less engagement with the reading task than good readers. According to Allington, the problem is *not* that poor readers are naturally inattentive or hyperactive. Rather, he suggests that much off-task behavior results because the type of instruction given to poor readers allows them to be distracted by signals from a number of different sources. This is related to the fact that poor readers engage in oral reading more often than good readers.

3. *General instructional emphases.* While the lessons given to good readers tend to focus on meaningful discussions of the text, those for poor readers are generally organized around letters and words and oral reading. Poor readers appear to receive more instruction on word identification and less on comprehension. Thus, poor readers seem to have less chance than good readers to gain an understanding of reading as the process of constructing meaning from text.

4. *Quality and mode of assigned reading.* In first-grade classes, Allington found that good readers did more reading every day than poor readers (about three times as many words). Furthermore, good readers do about 70 percent of their reading silently, while poor readers do most of their reading orally. This is a dangerous trend because, in general, the amount of time spent in silent reading seems to be positively related to reading achievement. Also, good readers tend to be questioned and evaluated on their understanding of the text, while poor readers are assessed on the word-for-word accuracy of their oral reading.

5. *Teacher interruption behavior.* Teachers tend to correct and interrupt poor readers much more frequently than good readers. These practices are damaging to poor readers, Allington suggests, because they prevent them from engaging in self-monitoring and self-correction when reading. As dis-

cussed at many points in earlier chapters, both self-monitoring and self-correction are important components of reading comprehension, but poor readers apparently have little opportunity to practice them.

▌ INSTRUCTIONAL GUIDELINES

On the basis of this review, Allingon arrives at the following recommendations for working with poor readers (adapted from Allington, 1983, pp. 554–556):

1. *Assess the teaching behaviors you use when giving lessons to poor readers.* Before changing anything, become aware of what you are already doing. Tape record a number of the lessons you give to your slowest learners, review the tapes, count such features as the number of interruptions, and identify behaviors to be changed. Try to make the needed changes and then tape record lessons to make comparisons. Over time, see if you can detect any changes in the students' behavior. A good way to measure your success is by the number of low-group students you are able to move into materials typically used with students who are reading at grade level.

2. *Give poor readers a second daily reading lesson.* Try to give slow learners the extra instructional time they need to overcome their disadvantage. Remember, however, that these lessons must be of high quality. Not just time, but what happens during reading lessons, is the critical factor.

3. *Be sure poor readers spend a substantial amount of time in silent reading.* If you add a second reading lesson, Allington suggests that you allow only silent reading during this time. In any event, anticipate the students' having difficulty with silent reading at first, since few of them will have had much previous experience with it. Be sure to set purposes for silent reading and remind the children to use strategies such as skipping over unknown words and then coming back to them later. Try not to offer too much help. In the beginning, use a highly structured lesson framework, such as the DRTA, and break the story into relatively short segments for silent reading. Begin with texts the students should find quite easy.

4. *Every day, give students the opportunity to read easy material for the purpose of increasing their reading fluency.* Poor readers often have developed the habit of labored, word-by-word reading. Thus, you want to give them the feeling of moving smoothly through the text often experienced by good readers. This is a matter both of selecting easier-to-read texts and of giving poor readers the chance to develop reading habits more like those of good readers. To develop a sense of fluency, a suitable procedure is the method of repeated readings, described below.

5. *Teach students to monitor their own reading performance.* Emphasize to poor readers the importance of "making sense" when reading, and be sure to give them the chance to correct their interpretations of the text.

Through tape recordings or other means, check to be certain that you are not encouraging them to become dependent on *your* monitoring. Do not jump in immediately and correct a student's error during discussion or oral reading, but give students the chance to correct themselves. For example, ask for an explanation of the answer or have the student reread. Set purposes for reading and have students check to see if their reading has met these purposes. For other suggestions to build students' self-monitoring of their own word identification, refer to Chapter 7.

6. *Have poor readers spend more time in recreational reading, or in reading for information, and less time with worksheet and workbook assignments.* The reading required by worksheet and workbook assignments is unlike the reading of text and tradebooks (e.g., Osborn, 1984). Especially for poor readers, valuable time is wasted if students are doing these peripheral assignments rather than actually reading for meaning. Use easy texts for independent reading and hold students responsible for discussing their reading or for writing a brief report. If a teacher's aide is available, he or she can be asked to listen to students' retellings or summaries and to discuss their reading with them.

▌ HANDICAPPED STUDENTS

Among the poor readers in the classroom may be a number of handicapped students. Included in this broad term are students who are learning disabled, mentally retarded, visually or hearing impaired, speech impaired, physically handicapped, or emotionally disturbed. Some may be multiply handicapped. Under the provisions of Public Law 94-142, referred to as the Education of the Handicapped Act, handicapped students are to be given individualized instruction and *mainstreamed*, or educated as much as possible in regular classroom environments.

As it concerns the classroom reading program, the first implication of this law is that teachers should participate in developing the individualized education plan (IEP) drawn up for each handicapped student in the classroom. The IEP should present in writing the educational program, including provisions for reading instruction the school is providing to meet the student's special needs. The IEP is usually developed by the special education teacher and/or other school personnel with expertise in special education, and the classroom teacher, with the cooperation of the child's parents.

The second implication of the law, because it emphasizes mainstreaming, is that teachers need to know how they can help the handicapped student learn to read in the regular classroom. Handicapped children who are poor readers should probably be provided with instruction consistent with the guidelines above and including activities such as those listed below. This means that their overall program of reading instruction will emphasize com-

A handicapped student who is mainstreamed feels accepted as part of the class. This helps the student become a full participant in the classroom community of readers and writers.

prehension, with special provisions for developing their awareness of thinking and reasoning processes, for increasing their reading fluency, and for encouraging independent silent reading.

▌ INSTRUCTIONAL ACTIVITIES

Be sure to give poor readers a full range of instruction, just as you do good readers. Include comprehension activities described in Chapters 2 through 4, vocabulary activities in Chapter 5, and word identification activities in Chapter 7. Comprehension activities mentioned earlier, found to be particularly effective with poor readers, are the inferential comprehension strategy (see Chapter 3) and reciprocal teaching (see Chapter 2).

We will be describing four different instructional activities for use with poor readers. We recommend that you start with the first and then move on to the other three, depending on the needs of your students. The first recommended activity is retelling. Retelling is a good place to start because it promotes poor readers' active involvement with the text as a whole. If students can retell passages with accuracy, they may not need instruction in the second approach, think-alouds. With think-alouds, the teacher is able to show poor readers what good readers do, when they encounter problems while reading a text.

The third activity, oral reading for meaning, encourages students to correct their own errors in identifying words by thinking of whether the word they have suggested makes sense in terms of the passage, as well as the pattern of letters in the word. The fourth activity, repeated reading, is appropriate for students who need practice in order to coordinate word identification skills and to read more fluently.

Retelling to Enhance Reading Comprehension

Retelling seems to be effective at promoting text comprehension because it requires the reader to provide a personal version of the text. To come up with this personal version, the reader must think about the text in a holistic manner, considering both its organization and important points. Good readers are quite accustomed to thinking about text in this way, but poor readers are not. This is why retelling can be particularly effective strategy for use with poor readers (e.g., Kapinus, Gambrell, & Koskinen, 1988).

We will be describing procedures teachers can use with somewhat older students, but all of these procedures can readily be adapted for use with children in kindergarten and first grade. These children can be asked to do retellings after they have heard books or passages read aloud (Morrow, 1985).

Koskinen, Gambrell, Kapinus, and Heathington (1988) give the following recommendations for retelling:

Begin by giving the students reasons for engaging in retelling. Tell them how retelling activities will help them to become better readers. For example, you might explain how retelling can give them practice in being good reporters and also help them see if they have understood their reading.

Model retelling for students. Read a short text to them and then retell it yourself, highlighting important points. Koskinen et al. recommend using a brief passage of perhaps 50 to 100 words, which you can retell in two or three sentences. Here is an example showing how a teacher might model retelling:

Teacher: I'm going to read you a short passage about the harmless hog-nosed snake, and then I'm going to retell the story to you. When I retell it, I'm going to try to include all the important ideas. As I read the passage, I want you to listen for the important ideas.

Animal Actor

The hog-nosed snake is harmless even though it pretends to be dangerous. When it opens its mouth it hisses loudly. It pretends it is going to bite. But then, if its enemy isn't frightened, the hog-nosed snake rolls over and acts dead. It lies very still. Most animals don't care to eat dead snakes, so the enemy usually goes away. The hog-nosed snake doesn't know that it is acting. That is just one of the ways the hog-nosed snake stays alive.

Teacher: Now I'll retell the passage to you without looking at my story. Listen to see if I include all the important ideas.

The hog-nosed snake hisses and pretends it is going to bite when an enemy approaches. If the enemy isn't frightened, the snake rolls over and pretends to be dead. The hog-nosed snake pretends to be dangerous and pretends to be dead in order to protect itself from enemies.

Teacher: Did I include all the important ideas?

At this point the teacher would accept contributions from the students. For example, a student might want to add that hog-nosed snakes don't realize they are acting; they are just trying to stay alive.

Teacher: We can become good reporters if we practice. Retelling passages is a good way to help remember and understand what you read.

(Koskinen et al., pp. 893–894; in the original, the word *story* is used instead of *passage,* and the word *storyteller* instead of *reporter.*)

After modeling retelling, give students the chance to practice on their own. Have students read or listen to a passage. Tell them to think of the important ideas and events, so they will be able to retell the story to someone else. Let students retell the passage as a group. Provide cues, as necessary. For example, you might remind them to say something about the main characters, the setting, or important events. When the group has grasped the idea of retelling, pair students up. Have the students read a short text and retell it to their partners.

Be sure students know how to respond positively to one another's retellings. You might tell them that their purpose as listeners is to be able to say one thing that they liked about their partner's retelling. Model the kinds of positive comments students might make, such as "You remembered to tell about all the important points in the passage," or "Your story had a beginning, middle, and end." By making sure students understand their role as listeners, you help them to pay attention and to be actively involved. And if they want to receive compliments, they will also put more effort into their own retellings.

Let students practice reading and retelling passages during their independent assignment time. Given regular practice opportunities, students will show significant improvement.

When they have become proficient at retelling with a partner, encourage students to retell stories silently, in their heads. Explain that this silent retelling will help them understand and remember what they read.

When introducing students to retelling, use short passages that pairs of students can read and retell in 10 or 15 minutes. Choose materials at students' independent or instructional levels. Materials may include basal reader stories, language experience stories, or library books. Begin with narratives and later move to expository passages.

Think-Alouds

Davey (1983) suggests that teachers model for poor readers the techniques good readers use to overcome comprehension problems. The purpose of this procedure is to make poor readers aware of the different strategies they can use when they experience difficulty with a particular text. The teacher thinks aloud, verbalizing thoughts while reading orally. It is important for the teacher to remember what the thinking people do while reading is not something anyone can actually observe. That is, just observing a reader scanning a page and then turning it gives no indication of all the activity going on in the reader's mind. The use of think-alouds is a way around this problem, because the teacher provides poor readers with a window into the mind of a good reader. Like the confirmation strategy, this activity is also consistent with the theme of helping children to acquire particular comprehension strategies and to become aware of the thought processes used while reading.

First, select a passage to read aloud that contains points of difficulty, contradictions, ambiguities, or unknown words. (You may want to develop your own materials for this step—short, with obvious problems.) As you read the passage aloud, students follow along silently, listening to how you think through these trouble spots. Here are some examples of points to make during think-alouds:

1. *Make predictions.* (Show how to develop hypotheses.)

   From this title, I predict that this section will tell how fishermen used to catch whales.
   In this next part, I think we'll find out why the men flew into the hurricane.
   I think this is a description of a computer game.

2. *Describe the picture you're forming in your head from the information.* (Show how to develop images during reading.)

   I have a picture of this scene in my mind. The car is on a dark, probably narrow, road; there are no other cars around.

3. *Share an analogy.* (Show how to link prior knowledge with new information in the text.) We call this the "like a" step.

   This is like a time we drove to Boston and had a flat tire. We were worried and we had to walk three miles for help.

4. *Verbalize a confusing point.* (Show how you monitor your ongoing comprehension.)

   This just doesn't make sense.
   This is different from what I had expected.

5. *Demonstrate fix-up strategies.* (Show how you correct your lagging comprehension.)

Figure 8.1
Self-Evaluation of Think-Alouds

While I was reading how did I do? (Put an X in the appropriate column.)

	Not very much	A little bit	Much of the time	All of the time
Made predictions				
Formed pictures				
Used "like-a"				
Found problems				
Used fix-ups				

Source: Excerpts and figure from "Think aloud: Modeling the cognitive processes of reading comprehension" by Beth Davey, *Journal of Reading,* October 1983, pp. 45–46. Copyright © 1983 International Reading Association, Inc. Reprinted with permission of Beth Davey and the International Reading Association.

I'd better reread.

Maybe I'll read ahead to see if it gets clearer.

This is a new word to me—I'd better check context to figure it out.

When you have completed your oral reading, encourage students to add their thoughts to yours.

After several modeling experiences, students can work with partners to practice think-alouds, taking turns in reading orally and sharing thoughts. The listening partner may add thoughts after the oral sharing has been completed. Again, carefully developed materials should be used initially (short, with obvious problems). Move then to school materials of various types and lengths. Finally, encourage readers to practice thinking through materials silently. This is the final step toward using the strategies independently. We used checklists of various types (see an example in Figure 8.1) to stimulate student involvement and verify that readers were using this procedure (Davey, 1983, pp. 45–46).

Oral Reading for Meaning

The purpose of this procedure, developed by Taylor and Nosbush (1983), is to improve poor readers' ability to identify words in context. Specifically, the student is encouraged to correct his or her own errors and to consider whether miscues make sense in the context of the passage. The four steps in the procedure involve having the student read orally, praising the student for self-correcting, instructing the student to make sure words make sense in the context, and providing direct instruction in word identification skills. Word identification instruction is based on the kind of errors just made.

The procedure requires the classroom teacher or a tutor to spend a brief time working with individual students. It proved effective with poor readers in the third grade,and can probably be used with students from the second grade on up.

Step One: To conduct oral reading for meaning, work with a student on a one-to-one basis for 10 to 15 minutes. The student reads 100–300 words aloud from material on his/her instructional level. Record any miscues the student makes, but, to avoid interruption, provide as little feedback as possible while the student is reading. Encourage the student to do the best she/he can without teacher assistance.

Step Two: After the student has finished reading aloud, praise the student for something she/he has done well during the oral reading. If possible, focus this praise on any self-corrections the student made, particularly on miscues which interfered with meaning. Encourage the student to engage in more self-correcting in the future when she/he comes across miscues that don't make sense.

Step Three: Discuss one or two miscues that the student didn't self-correct. They should be ones that didn't make sense but that occurred in sentences with good context clues. For example, if a student read, "The shepherd came and stood before the *thorn* where the king sat" (for "The shepherd came and stood before the throne where the king sat"), "thorn" would be a good miscue to discuss because it doesn't make sense for a king to sit on a thorn. On the other hand, if a student read, "He had *barely* read the words" (for "He had scarcely read the words"), "barely" would not be a good miscue to discuss because the error hasn't interfered with meaning.

To discuss an uncorrected, semantically inappropriate miscue, read the sentence in which the miscue occurred just as the student read it. Then ask the student if there seems to be a word in the sentence which doesn't make sense, giving guidance if necessary. Then help the student decode the troublesome word, stressing the use of context and phonics. For example, you might say, "What word beginning with *thr* would make sense here? Where would a king sit?" Also, continually remind the student that, in the future, after decoding a word like "thorn" that doesn't seem to make sense, she/he should stop and correct the error. It is through repetitive reminders to self-correct that eventual improvements in the student's self-correcting behavior will be seen.

Step Four: Finally, provide the student with on-the-spot instruction in a word identification skill that the student has had difficulty with during oral reading. You may decide to skip this step if you do not have an additional five minutes or so to spend with an individual student on a particular day.

On days when you are able to carry out this last step, however, select just one area which seems particularly troublesome. Perhaps you noticed the student had a problem with a word identification skill that had also caused problems for that student on a previous occasion. If a student has read "know" for "now," you may choose to provide five minutes of instruction on words with two different sounds for *ow*. Or, if the student has read "through" for "thought," you might provide instruction on this frequently confused pair of basic sight words. Perhaps the student has made several errors involving the endings of words, for example, endings have been frequently omitted or inserted. You might work for a few minutes on these words, stressing the need to pay more attention to word endings when decoding.

As an alternative to focusing on a problem, you might choose to reinforce a word identification skill that was recently taught. For example, if the students recently studied common sounds for *ea*, you and the student might locate and discuss words containing *ea* in the material just read aloud (Taylor & Nosbush, pp. 235–236).

To be effective, the oral reading for meaning procedure should be used with individual students on a regular basis, probably two or more times per week. You may wish to work with two or three poor readers at first, and concentrate on their instruction for a four to six week period. Then, select a second set of poor readers to receive the procedure for a second four to six week period. Monitor the progress of the students in the first group and provide maintenance lessons as needed.

When using the approach of oral reading for meaning, you will want to remember that your goal is to help poor readers search for and use cues from two or more systems at the same time. As we pointed out when discussing word identification in Chapter 7, it is important for students to be able to coordinate the use of various word identification skills.

Clay (1979) discusses this idea in terms of the square shown in Figure 8.2. This figure presents the four different types of cues children can use to identify words, and shows how each type of cue can be used as a cross-check against another. According to Clay, children need to learn to search for cues in the meaning of the passage or story, in the sequence of words, and in the sequence of letters. When children are unsure about words, they should be reminded to search for cues and to cross-check one source of cues against another.

As shown also in the figure, Clay suggests teachers use the following questions to encourage children to search for cues:

- Cues in sentence structure (syntax):
  Say "You said . . . Does that sound right?"
- Cues from the meaning (semantics):
  Say, "You said . . . Does that make sense?"
- Cues from the letters (graphic cues):
  Say, "Does that look right?"
- Or more generally:
  Say, "What's wrong?"
  (Clay, 1979, p. 73)

Figure 8.2
Four Types of Cues Used in
Word Identification

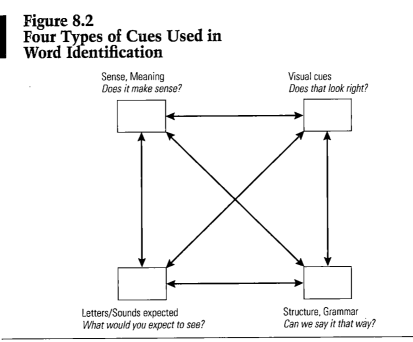

Sense, Meaning
Does it make sense?

Visual cues
Does that look right?

Letters/Sounds expected
What would you expect to see?

Structure, Grammar
Can we say it that way?

Source: From *The Early Detection of Reading Difficulties* by Marie M. Clay. Copyright © 1979 by Marie M. Clay. Reprinted by permission of Heinemann Educational Books Limited.

Clay uses the following example to show how a teacher might foster searching behavior.

T: You almost got that page right. There was something wrong with this line. See if you can find what was wrong.

Ch: (Child silently rereads checking)
I said Lizard but it's Lizard's.

T: How did you know?

Ch: 'Cause it's got an "s."

T: Is there any other way we could know? (Search further)

Ch: It's funny to say "Lizard dinner"! It has to be Lizard's dinner like Pete's dinner, doesn't it?

T: (Reinforcing the searching)
Yes. That was good. You found two ways to check on that tricky new word. (p. 74)

Oral reading for meaning, described above, will work most effectively if you are aware of trying to develop students' ability to use the various cue systems as cross-checks for one another. The goal, in Clay's words, is for the student's reading to work as a self-improving system.

With poor readers, we are not only concerned about accurate word identification. All too often, we see students who can read quite accurately, but are reading in a painfully slow and plodding way. Another step, then, is to be concerned with developing poor readers' ability to read fluently, or smoothly and automatically.

Repeated Readings

The purpose of the method of repeated readings described by Samuels (1979) is to improve the reading fluency of poor readers. In this method students read a short, meaningful passage several times until they can read it fluently. They then move on to a new passage. This procedure allows poor readers to experience ease in reading and improves their word identification ability. The method can be used with students at all grade levels.

According to Samuels, fluency has two components: speed and accuracy. He advises teachers to have students read with greater speed rather than with complete accuracy. This prevents poor readers from being overly hesitant or fearful when reading. Each time students reread the text, they find it easier and easier to recognize the words. Because little attention is then required for word identification, more attention can be paid to comprehension. Thus, Samuels argues, repeated readings should also lead to improved comprehension of the passage.

Here are some suggestions Samuels makes for using the method of repeated readings:

1. Match the amount of material to be read to the student's reading skill. With very poor readers, begin with passages as short as just 50 words, and increase the length of passages gradually. (In our experience, we find it important for students beginning to work with the method of repeated readings to be motivated to participate in the activity and not to become discouraged. Therefore, teachers should look for short passages on topics of interest to the students.)
2. If working with very poor readers, first read the passage with or to them, and then have them practice it. You could also make a tape recording of the passage and have them read along with the recording until they are able to read the passage on their own.
3. Have somewhat more capable students select the books or other materials they wish to read. Break longer texts into segments of about 200 words for the students to work with. This enables the students to experience much more success.
4. Time the students' reading, or have them time themselves. Have each student keep a graph showing improvement in reading times.
5. To build comprehension, ask students a different comprehension question after each rereading of the text. We think another possibility would be to have students report on anything new or interesting noticed during the rereading.
6. Enlist the help of other students, aides, or parents. Have them listen to the students read and time their readings. They can also keep records of

word recognition errors. You can then work with other students, knowing the poor readers have others to help with their practice.

Lauritzen (1982) suggests two modifications to the method of repeated readings to make it easier for classroom teachers to use. These modifications may be especially useful if you are working with younger children.

1. *Choose selections with rhyme, rhythm, and sequence, following oral literature patterns.* Lauritzen recommends folktales such as *Henny Penny, Old Mother Hubbard, The Gingerbread Boy, The Three Little Pigs, The Turnip,* and *The Old Woman and Her Pig.* Poetry and song lyrics are also good choices.

2. *Have the students read in a group rather than individually.* First, read the selection aloud. Then have students follow along by looking at the words. Have them work from copies of the book or from a chart, or print the words on the chalkboard. Then have the children echo your reading, saying each line, sentence, or paragraph (choose the length of the segment according to the structure of the text). Finally, have the group read the entire selection in unison.

Let the children read the text as many times as they wish, working individually, in pairs, or in small groups. Have them listen to a tape if you have made one. Let them continue to read in unison for two days or more. When the children can read the text fluently, let them read it to other students, parents, or the principal.

To develop word identification skills, break the text into segments by putting verses, sentences, or words on cards or strips of oaktag. Have the students put the cards or strips together in the proper order in a pocketchart or on a table top.

Key Concept 2

Teachers should know how to respond to cultural differences which can influence children's learning to read.

▮ CULTURAL DIFFERENCES

The ability to communicate with students is obviously critical to effective teaching. Differences in culture, we believe, often cause problems in learning to read because teachers find that they are unable to communicate well with culturally different students. For example, in Chapter 1 we described the difficulties some teachers encountered during reading lessons with children of Polynesian-Hawaiian ancestry (Au & Mason, 1983). However, no difficulties were experienced by other teachers, who used a style of interaction resembling talk story, a common speech event in the homes of Hawaiian children. These teachers were successful because they used an interactional style compatible with the children's culture.

While we often think of the term *culture* as applying to physical objects, such as clothing and foods, it also applies to behaviors and values. According to Goodenough (1971), culture includes the standards we follow in our own behavior, as well as the standards we use to judge the behavior of others. Of particular significance in classrooms is the part of culture that involves rules for behavior in face-to-face communication. These are important in all kinds of teacher-led lessons, whether large group, small group, or individual.

Each culture has its own rules for what constitutes proper and respectful behavior. These rules reflect the deeply held values and beliefs of members of that culture. These rules and values make up what Philips (1983) terms *invisible culture*. They are invisible because neither the members of the culture nor the members of other cultures are usually aware of them. We can, however, learn about invisible culture if we make a conscious effort to do so.

The practical implication of this view of culture is that teachers should be aware of the rules for face-to-face communication likely to be followed by the culturally different students in their classes. They should also be aware of the cultural values reflected in those rules. Without this awareness, miscommunication and misunderstanding are likely to result, during reading lessons and at other times. Teachers may misunderstand and misjudge students, and in turn find themselves being misunderstood. Thus, if you are working with culturally different students, a primary goal will be to bridge the gap between the style of communication and values of the home and the school.

Examples of Cultural Differences in Communication Styles

To make this general idea more concrete, we discuss below three studies showing how differences in invisible culture may affect teachers' ability to communicate with culturally different children. In reading about these studies, keep in mind that there are often great differences among the students of any particular ethnic background, due to such factors as family income, parents' educational level, and family values and beliefs. The findings below, then, should be seen as *examples* of the types of cultural differences in communication style found to be important with particular groups of children in particular settings. They cannot automatically be applied to all children from those ethnic groups.

Questioning at home and at school. Reading lessons often center on question-answer exchanges between teacher and students, as discussed in Chapter 2. Culturally different children, however, may not be familiar with classroom question answering routines (e.g., Boggs, 1972). This can make it difficult for them to learn during ordinary reading lessons.

Evidence for this idea comes from a study by Heath (1982). She compared the use of questions in three settings: Trackton, a working-class black community; the classrooms of the children from this community; and the homes of their teachers. In the classrooms and teachers' homes, Heath found that teachers often asked questions for the purpose of "training" children. The children were expected to give answers already known by the adult. When the child was looking at a book, such questions would include: "What's that?" "Where's the puppy?"

In Trackton, on the other hand, children were not generally asked questions for which the adult already knew the answer. Instead, they were asked open-ended questions with answers unknown to the adult. For example, in the passage below, the grandmother's first question has to do with what her grandson is planning to do next with the crayons. Another type of question often asked of Trackton children called for them to make comparisons, stating how one thing was like another. As shown in the passage, the grandmother's second question called the boy's attention to the fact that one of the crayons was the same color as his pants. Heath writes:

> At early ages, Trackton children recognized situations, scenes, personalities, and items which were similar. However, they never volunteered, nor were they asked by adults, to name the attributes which were similar and added up to one thing's being like another. A grandmother playing with her grandson age 2;4 asked him as he fingered crayons in a box: "Whatcha gonna do with those, huh?" "Ain't dat [color] like your pants?" She then volunteered to me: "We don't talk to our chil'un like you folks do; we don't ask 'em 'bout colors, names, 'n things." (p. 117)

When they first entered school, then, Trackton children were unprepared to answer teachers' questions, which often had to do with such information as telling the colors or names of objects. With Heath's help, the teachers tried to adjust their teaching materials and questioning strategies, to incorporate familiar scenes and questions more like those asked of the children by Trackton adults. They started by using pictures of the community and countryside and, rather than asking known-answer questions, asked questions such as the following:

> What's happening here?
> Have you ever been here?
> Tell me what you did when you were there.   (p. 124)

Questions like this drew many more responses from Trackton children.

The teachers also helped Trackton children develop the skills needed to answer typical classroom questions about situations or objects and their attributes. To do this, they taped certain lessons, and then added to them questions of the type unfamiliar to Trackton children. Children in the class who were able to answer this kind of question taped answers to them. All of the children were then able to listen to the tapes at the learning centers. By listening to the tapes, Trackton students were able to hear the kind of questions teachers typically asked and the kinds of answers teachers expected to hear. As time went on, the teachers invited Trackton students to assist them in preparing the questions and answers to be taped. In this way the children were gradually able to learn classroom question-answer routines. The teachers also held discussions with the children about different types of questions and the kinds of answers called for.

If you think it appropriate to follow a plan like that described above, you might want to go one step further and make a direct connection to the kinds of questions asked in reading lessons and assignments. For this purpose, teach the children about question-answer relationships, following the program developed by Raphael (1982) and described in detail in Chapter 2. Have the taped questions and answers reflect all three types of question-answer relationships.

Other examples of cultural differences in communication style. As the work of Heath suggests, when teachers and children are unable to collaborate or "hook up" in a way that allows teaching to take place, students' learning to read is bound to suffer. Teachers who are able to work effectively with culturally different students seem to be those who use a communication style consistent with the values of the students' culture.

For example, research by Cazden, Carrasco, Maldonado-Guzman, and Erickson (1980) points to the importance of *cariño*, or a caring relationship, as seen in the interactions of a first-grade teacher with her Mexican-American students. Speaking in Spanish, the teacher communicated a sense of caring by using terms of endearment in addressing the children, reinforcing norms of politeness and respect, and in showing her knowledge regarding their families.

Another example is provided by the work of Erickson and Mohatt (1982). Building on earlier work by Philips (1972), these researchers found that it was important for teachers of Odawa Indian students to avoid exercising direct social control. According to their findings, teachers were likely to have more difficulty providing effective lessons if they ordered students around, singled them out before the class, and waited for all the students to do the same thing at the same time. In contrast, teachers were likely to have less difficulty if they gave orders in a less direct way (saying, for example, "It's time for people to stop running around" instead of "Sam, stop running around"), questioned children individually or in small groups, and allowed the students to shift from one activity to another in a gradual fashion. According to Erickson and Mohatt, this second style of interaction is effective because it is consistent with the high value the Odawa attach to respecting individual autonomy. In this view, one person should not openly order another person around or otherwise openly try to control his or her behavior.

Differences in Background Knowledge

Teachers should also be aware that differences in background or cultural knowledge may lead to different interpretations of the same text. For example, Reynolds, Taylor, Steffenson, Shirey, and Anderson (1982) had a group of black and a group of white eighth-graders read the same letter. The letter could be interpreted either as describing "sounding," a ritual form of verbal insult likely to be familiar to black students, or as describing a physical fight. Black students applied their knowledge of sounding in interpreting the text, while white students, who did not have this same kind of cultural knowledge, thought the text was about a fight. Differences in culture thus led to differences in students' understanding of the text.

With texts used to teach reading, as with any other texts, readers are expected to "fill in the gaps" in text from their own background knowledge. If the background knowledge of culturally different students differs from that of their teachers, the students may use sound logic, yet arrive at interpretations teachers think incorrect. For example, with the text described above, teachers might not recognize that students are applying knowledge of sounding. Thus, teachers should be careful not to reject answers which, on the surface, seem to be wrong. Rather, they should try to find out how the child arrived at the answer. By focusing on the process of thinking, rather than simply on whether the answer was right or wrong, teachers will be able either to offer the child other useful background knowledge or a sounder line of reasoning.

Guidelines for Dealing with Cultural Differences

Teachers can and should be optimistic about their ability to work with culturally different students. This is because we know that teachers are able to adjust their interactional styles in order to communicate more effectively with their students (e.g., Erickson & Mohatt, 1982). Furthermore, students often can learn to communicate more effectively with their teachers. Following the guidelines below will get you and your students off to a good start.

1. *Be aware of cultural differences as a source of children's problems in learning to read.* Read to find out more about the differences which may be affecting your ability to work effectively with some children (see, for example, Cazden, John, & Hymes, 1972; Trueba, Guthrie, & Au, 1981; and Chu-Chang, 1983). Consult with other teachers and school staff or with parents and members of the community about possible sources of difficulty.

2. *Try to adjust your own style to help bridge the communication gap.* This is often difficult to accomplish on your own. If possible, have someone observe or videotape you so you can become more aware of exactly how you are interacting with your students.

3. *Help the children understand conventional school styles of speaking and answering questions.* You might wish to try the procedure developed by Heath or other means to make the children aware of typical school expectations for speaking and turntaking. Even if you can teach effectively by bridging the communication gap, you will still need to prepare your students to deal with the ways of the school. Their future academic success usually depends on their making this adjustment. This does not mean asking the children to give up the communication style and values of their own culture. Rather, it is a matter of helping them understand that a different communication style may be appropriate in certain kinds of situations.

4. *Build upon the children's strengths, by looking for areas of knowledge and interest they already possess.* All children have background knowledge and interests which can and should serve as the starting points for reading instruction. If you are working with students whose background is different from your own, the students' knowledge and interests may not be immediately obvious to you. During lessons or when children are working on assignments, watch for signs of interest. Try a range of topics and activities to spark enthusiasm, and repeat those that seem successful. For some children, times other than formal classroom lessons, for example, informal chats at recess or lunch, may offer you a better opportunity for learning about their interests.

▌ INSTRUCTIONAL ACTIVITIES

Experience-Text-Relationship Method

While it can be used with all children, the experience-text-relationship (ETR) method, described in Chapter 2, can be an especially effective way of organizing text comprehension lessons given to culturally different children. This is because the opening experience phase of discussion gives the teacher a chance to see what the children already know about the topic of the text. Starting from the children's background knowledge, the teacher can then make meaningful connections to text ideas. This method thus offers a good way of building upon the children's strengths.

Shared Book Experience

While the shared book experience (Holdaway, 1979; refer also to Chapter 6) is an excellent approach for any group of beginning readers, it was originally developed in classrooms with students who were from several different cultural backgrounds, and is an especially sound approach for culturally different children. At the heart of the shared book experience is the reading together of stories, some in "big books." The "big books" are versions of storybooks enlarged so that the text can be seen clearly when lessons are given to the whole class. When reading, the teacher tries to capture the children's interest and attention, just as a parent would when reading a child a bedtime story. The children are encouraged to "chime in" and then to discuss the story. The books are placed where the children may easily get hold of them, and children are encouraged to try to read them on their own. Favorite books are reread for the whole class, sometimes by the children themselves. Later, the teacher may introduce word identification activities with these same books. For a complete description, refer to Holdaway (1979, especially Chapter 4; see also Slaughter, 1983). Figure 8.3 outlines the objectives and activities in the three stages of work with each new storybook or other literary experience, such as a poem or song.

Figure 8.3
Three Stages in the Course of a
New Literary Experience

A. Discovery

Introduction of the new experience in the listening situation with maximum participation in predictable, repetitive structures, and in the problem solving strategies of decoding.

Objectives

To provide an enjoyable story experience to all of the children. *(This objective should not be sacrificed to any other purpose.)*
To induce a desire to return to the book on subsequent days.
To encourage participation by inducing children to chime in
  on repetitive sections,
  suggest an obvious word,
  predict possible outcomes,
  engage in suitable expressive activities.
To provide a clear and spoken model for the book language.
To induce sound strategies of word solving by encouraging and discussing suggestions, at an appropriate skills level and without unduly interrupting the story. Remember that the thrill of problem-solving is a natural and proper part of the enjoyment of a story.

B. Exploration

Rereadings—usually on request—for familiarization and teaching where applicable. Increasing unison participation is natural to this re-experience.

Objectives

To establish firm oral models for the language of the book.
To deepen understanding and response.
To provide opportunities for all children to gain oral practice of the language of the story by unison, group and individual participation.
To help children become aware of the special structures of the story so that these may be used in reconstructing and decoding in later independent readings, or be used as patterns for personal expression.
To teach relevant reading skills in relation to the text, especially sight vocabulary, structural analysis and the use of letter-sound relationships in strategies of decoding.
To provide further expressive activities based on the language of the book both to personalize response and to provide purposeful practice of the language models.
To provide additional, enjoyable listening experience for slower children who require more repetition than others to develop strong memory models. Listening post activity is most useful for this purpose.

C. Independent Experience and Expression

Independent retrieval of the experience in reading or reading-like ways by individuals or small groups. Creative exploration and expression of meanings from the experience, involving all the expressive arts.

Objectives

To provide opportunities for independent reading by individuals or very small-groups (Sometimes one child will act as teacher in guiding others through the book).
To give a sense of individual achievement and competence.
To encourage the development of self-monitoring and self-correction, using the familiar language models.
To encourage expressive activities using the interests and the language arising from the book so that children will identify more fully with the story and internalize the language as a permanent part of their competence.

However, the total programme is concerned with a great wealth of literary experience happening together, and within this richness different children seek out their own preoccupations, determining for themselves where their own 'working face' in language learning will be from day to day. To give some order and security to this diversity of experience, the daily input session tends to have a predictable structure something like the following:

1. **Tune-in** Verse, song, and chant—favourite and new. Enlarged print and charts are always central.

2. **Favourite stories** Rereading of stories, usually by request but sometimes planned. Unison participation. Learning reading-skills in context. Dramatic and other relaxing counterparts. Exploring syntax—substitution, simplification, extension, transformation, innovating on verse and story structure.

(continued)

▮ **Figure 8.3**
Three Stages (*continued*)

3. **Language activities** Alphabet study and games. Learning other cultural sequences. Exploring language—riddles, puzzles, vocabulary games; exploring writing—approximations towards spelling.

4. **New story** Introducing new story for the day either in normal or enlarged form. Word-solving strategies induced within the unfolding context of a new language experience. Modelling how print is unlocked.

5. **Independent reading** Enjoying old favourites—individual or group. Pointing encouraged—pointers available. Much playing at being teacher—children teach each other.

6. **Expression** Related arts activity either individual or group. Painting, group murals, construction, mask-making for drama. Group drama, puppetry, mime. Writing—innovating on literary structure (teacher as scribe).

   (Note: 5. and 6. interchangeable in order.)

Source: From *The Foundations of Literacy* by Don Holdaway. Copyright © 1979 by Don Holdaway. Reprinted by permission of Ashton Scholastic.

Using Literature to Develop Children's Understanding of Different Cultures

The guided reading of literature to develop positive attitudes about oneself and others can contribute to a sense of community in classrooms with students from different cultural backgrounds. Through books, perhaps read aloud by the teacher or recommended as independent reading, students can gain an appreciation of other cultures and of individual differences. They may also come to a better understanding of their own problems and the problems of others (Bohning, 1981). Among the books you read to your students, be sure to include some to help your students feel pride in their own cultures as well as respect for the cultures of others. For listings of suitable books see Rollock (1974), Aoki (1981), and Gilliland (1982), or check the book selection aids listed in Sutherland and Arbuthnot (1986).

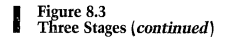
Key Concept 3

Teachers should know how to respond to differences in language which can influence children's learning to read.

▮ DIFFERENCES IN LANGUAGE

In this section, we first discuss the teaching of reading to students who speak English as a second language, and second, the teaching of reading to students who speak a dialect. In both cases, we focus on teaching the students to read texts written in Standard English. Biliteracy, or the ability to read and write in two languages, is a highly desirable educational outcome (for a discussion, see Goodman, Goodman, & Flores, 1979; Hudelson, 1987) but a topic beyond the scope of this textbook.

It is important to remember that cultural and language differences are usually operating together. That is, children who speak a language other than English or a dialect of English often come from nonmainstream cultural backgrounds, as well. Thus, in classroom settings, teachers will generally need to be thinking simultaneously of the information covered under Key Concepts #2 and #3 in this chapter.

Students Who Speak English as a Second Language

Students who speak English as a second language (referred to as ESL students) have in common the fact that the first language they learned to speak was not English. Other than that, they are a tremendously diverse group. When teaching reading to ESL students, then, you will want to have some knowledge about the children's family background, cultural background, and native language, as well as their proficiency in English.

The arrangements for providing English reading instruction to ESL students differ from school to school. In some schools students are taken from their regular classrooms to receive instruction in a class designed for ESL students. In others they remain in their homerooms but may receive tutoring or small group lessons from a bilingual aide. In still others no special services may be available for them.

The approaches used to teach reading to ESL students vary greatly. In some cases the children may be taught in a manner which emphasizes the learning of English exclusively. In others one of a number of approaches to *bilingual education* may be followed. Bilingual education involves programs specially designed for ESL students or students who can use two languages. However, bilingual education approaches reflect differences in the value attached to the students' first language. In transitional bilingual education, use of the native language is encouraged primarily as a means of helping the children make the transition to English language instruction. In maintenance approaches students are given the opportunity to develop skill in both English and the native language. English may be emphasized, the two languages may be given equal instructional time, or the children's first language may be emphasized.

Teachers working with ESL students should realize that bilingual education is often a controversial topic. Thus, it is important to be aware of the views the community and school system have about bilingual education. Different views naturally lead to different educational goals and practices. For example, in some communities, parents may have the goal of biliteracy. In others, parents may be most concerned that the schools assist their children to speak and read only in English.

Obviously, one major difference between a classroom reading program for children who speak English as a second language, and one for children whose first or only language is English, must be in the attention given to language development in English. In other words, the teacher will want to help ESL

Displaying words written in both Spanish and English is one way of showing students that their Spanish-language skills are valued in the classroom.

students develop the knowledge of English needed to support the understanding of texts written in English.

In terms of their knowledge of English, ESL students include (1) those who speak some English but are more proficient in a language other than English, and (2) those who are monolingual speakers of another language. These students are also referred to as LEP (limited English proficiency) students.

All of these children, even monolingual speakers of another language, should be encouraged to work with print and books during the time that they are acquiring further knowledge of English. With ESL students, as with others, the reading of books can itself be an effective means of learning about language, as demonstrated in research by Elley and Mangubhai (1983). Elley (1981) argues that an early exposure to books and reading is likely to be beneficial to ESL students. He recommends that high-interest books be used to encourage students to read to satisfy their own curiosity, rather than satisfying the teacher.

Remember also that ESL students come to school with a knowledge of their own language and its uses in communicating with others. They also bring with them a vast amount of knowledge of the world. The effective teacher recognizes that the students have these strengths. In teaching ESL students to read in English, then, the teacher should help them make use of this prior knowledge to learn to speak and read English.

There continues to be considerable debate about whether ESL students will progress best if first taught to read in the native language (for a detailed discussion of these issues, see Hudelson & Barrera, 1985; Barrera, 1983, 1984). Current research suggests that it is *not* necessary to delay teaching children to read in the second language until after they have learned to read in the first.

Barrera (1983) points out that children can and do learn to read successfully in two languages, the native and non-native, and that some bilingual children may even move themselves into reading through the non-native language first. She has observed these to be common occurrences in classrooms where the reading program is oriented to comprehension rather than to phonics. This is the case because young ESL students in comprehension-emphasis programs approach reading as a meaning-making process in both languages. That is, they do not see reading in Spanish (or other native languages) as one thing and reading in English as another. Rather, in trying to construct meaning from text, they pay less attention to the particular language code, Spanish or English, than to the overall message of the text.

Barrera suggests that the problems supposedly presented by the child's having to deal with two languages at once may lie primarily in the way the teaching of reading to ESL students has typically been conceptualized in the past, largely as phonics training. This limited view of the issues probably does not lead to the most effective reading instruction for young ESL students, either in the native language or in English. However, if the reading program focuses mainly on comprehension, the children can be taught to read simultaneously in both the native and non-native languages, or in the non-native language first.

Knowledge of this point may be a comfort to teachers who find their options limited by practical realities. Often, teachers may find they have little choice: ESL students may have to be taught to read first in English, and reading instruction will probably have to begin well before the students have a great deal of knowledge of English. These situations may come about because there is a shortage of qualified teachers and suitable instructional materials. Matters are further complicated, particularly in urban classrooms, if the ESL students come from many different language backgrounds.

In any event, even when students receive reading and language instruction from well-qualified ESL teachers, classroom teachers still should monitor students' progress in learning to read and make sure that they receive adequate classroom opportunities to develop English reading and writing skills. Diaz, Moll, and Mehan (1986) emphasize the importance of giving Spanish-dominant students the opportunity to apply Spanish speaking and reading skills in learning to read texts written in English. For example, although reading an English text, the children could be allowed to discuss the ideas in Spanish. They recommend that English reading lessons focus on comprehension, whether ideas are discussed in English or in Spanish. If the children speak in English, they suggest that the teacher concentrate on the ideas the children are expressing and not spend much time correcting their grammar and pronunciation.

In general, then, we suggest that the reading instruction provided for ESL students be much like that for students who speak English as a first language, in the sense that it should be oriented largely to the teaching of comprehension, or the constructing of meaning from text. If comprehension-oriented reading instruction can be provided, ESL students can learn to read simultaneously in both the native language and in English. If the children are being taught to read first in the native language, the teacher should try to allow them to use native language reading and speaking skills to promote learning to read in English. To further students' knowledge of English and appreciation for literature, the teacher's reading aloud of good books should be an integral part of the reading and language program.

Guidelines for Improving Students' English Proficiency

The most important general guideline teachers should follow is to focus on children's *ideas* rather than the exact form used to express them. The teacher's goal is to try to understand the messages the children are seeking to communicate, however limited their proficiency in English, and to respond positively to these messages. Correcting children's grammar or drilling them on proper pronunciation does little to develop language (for discussion of this point, see Gonzales, 1980) and might discourage them from continuing to speak up. Try to follow the guidelines below when working with ESL students (adapted from Gonzales, 1981, pp. 178–180):

1. *Create a comfortable atmosphere for ESL students to try speaking English, and encourage them to begin speaking when they feel ready to do so.* According to Gonzales, ESL students may go through a "silent period" when they are in fact learning English but not yet ready to speak it. Remind yourself to be patient and supportive while the children are starting to learn English, and do not expect instant proficiency.

2. *Accept the children's accents.* Do not drill them on standard pronunciations or isolated sounds. Making sure that ESL students have many opportunities to speak and listen to native speakers of English will lead naturally to improvement in this area.

3. *Make your meaning as clear as you can and check for understanding.* Gonzales recommends using gestures and other nonverbal means to show children what you want them to do. Model the steps in completing assignments. Use alternate wordings. Perhaps have other children explain directions to the class in their own words. Then ask the children if they have understood, and be prepared to offer more help if necessary. Ask questions requiring answers with several words. This will ensure that you do not just get back rote answers and so have a better chance of uncovering the misunderstandings an ESL student may have.

4. *Speak warmly in a normal and natural tone of voice to ESL students.* It is not necessary to speak more slowly or loudly.

(1) Arrange to observe the same teacher providing instruction to two different groups of students, one a group of high achievers and the other a group of low achievers.

(2) While observing, write down as much as you can about what the teacher and children say and do during the lesson. Try to record information enabling you to answer the following questions:

What were the children supposed to learn during this lesson (i.e., what was the teacher's purpose for teaching the lesson)?

What questions or tasks did the teacher pose for the children?

How interested and involved were the children?

What materials were used?

(3) Analyze your observation notes for similarities and differences in the answers you obtained to the four questions above. In what ways were the lessons similar? In what ways did they differ? What do you think accounts for the differences? In your opinion, was instruction equally beneficial for both groups?

Keep your observations in mind while reading about the research findings described below. Compare these findings to the patterns you discovered. This research highlights the fact that teachers are often unaware of how differences in the lessons given to good and poor readers may be handicapping poor readers even more. Even with the best of intentions, we may make serious errors in our approach to improving the reading ability of some children.

5. *If you can, explain the purpose of the lesson in the students' native language.* Giving ESL students a preview of what to expect will make it easier for them to follow directions and explanations given in English.

▌ INSTRUCTIONAL ACTIVITIES

Storybook Reading

Hough, Nurss, and Enright (1986) recommend storybook reading as a natural approach for promoting ESL students' English language development and literacy. You have already learned a great deal about storybook reading in earlier chapters, so the following recommendations deal with specific approaches to storybook reading that may be particularly beneficial for ESL students.

Read books to ESL students frequently, perhaps twice a day. Try to do the reading in small groups of five to seven children. ESL students may feel more comfortable in a small group and so may be more willing to speak up. Involve children in a discussion of the book. Ask a variety of questions to get students involved.

Use verbal cues, such as exaggerating intonation or changing your voice to signal that different characters are speaking. Use nonverbal cues, such as pointing to the illustrations or gesturing to indicate characters' actions. These cues may make it a bit easier for ESL students to follow the story.

Select predictable books, those with a pattern, refrain, or predictable sequence of events. Encourage the students to chime in or to anticipate the words you are about to read. For suggestions of predictable books, refer to Rhodes (1981) and Tompkins and Webeler (1983). Also, many predictable books are included in the Story Box program developed by the Wright Group.

Read favorite stories over again on several occasions. ESL students will gain confidence as they find themselves able to recite the text when you come to familiar phrases. They will become familiar with English language patterns, vocabulary, and the sequence of events in the stories. All of this knowledge will help them to understand and appreciate new books. It is also helpful to allow children to listen to tapes or records as they follow along in the book.

Hough et al. also recommend using follow-up activities which encourage children to retell the story and use its language patterns. For example, children could act out events in the story. Or they could retell the story in their own words, by commenting on the pictures on each page of the book.

Book Floods

Elley and Mangubhai (1983) found that "book floods" improved ESL students' reading achievement. Approximately 50 new books were introduced to each class of ESL students (ages 9 to 11) at four or five week intervals. Children benefited from the book floods whether they learned through the shared book experience or silent reading method. In the silent reading method, the books were displayed and the teachers regularly read some of them aloud, with 20 to 30 minutes per day allotted for sustained silent reading.

Elley and Mangubhai offer the following conclusions and practical suggestions. First, allow the children to have access to a variety of books. Elley and Mangubhai feel that books should be selected for interesting content rather than for controlled vocabulary or sentence length. Second, they recommend having a large number of books, perhaps 150, available to the children. Included among these should be a number of popular western children's stories, such as versions of the Three Pigs, Cinderella, and Red Riding Hood, which they found many children to enjoy. Books from the Ladybird series were also popular.

Writing

ESL students' knowledge of English reading and writing is strengthened when teachers involve them in a process approach to writing (e.g., Hudelson, 1987; Edelsky, 1986). The process writing activities described in Chapter 2, such as the use of writing folders, are appropriate for second language learners as well as students whose first language is English. When involved in a process approach to writing, ESL students can learn about the functions of literacy (Hudelson, 1987), revision, and spelling (Seda & Abramson, 1988).

The use of dialogue journals may be of special benefit to ESL students (Hudelson, 1987), but it is also a useful approach with other students as well.

Staton (1980) describes the use of dialogue journals in a sixth-grade classroom. With modifications, the procedures can be used with second-graders and perhaps even with younger children. The purpose of the journals was to allow the teacher to give students individual attention, to motivate students to write about experiences important to them, and to help them improve their writing. Mrs. Reed, the teacher in this class, found dialogue journals to be an excellent way of getting to know her students and of building positive relationships with them. Staton writes:

> From a language perspective, the openness of the journal as a forum for personal problems as well as academic ones captures the natural function of language as intentional communication about what matters most to the person. An attitude of trust and interest in everything the writer says characterizes Leslee Reed's attitude toward her students and what they write in their journals. "I learn something new every day about each one of them. They are fascinating to get to know." It is no wonder that their willingness to express their own ideas, feelings, and experiences in written language improves and creates in them a confidence about writing in general that too few people their age or any age enjoy. (p. 518)

Here are some guidelines for the use of dialogue journals based on the experiences of Reed and Staton:

1. Make sure each student has a notebook or binder to serve as a private journal. Let the students know that they will be writing to you, and that you will be writing back to them. Tell them that no one else will see the journals, except with their permission.
2. Let the students choose whatever they want to write about. Have them write on a regular schedule. In Reed's classroom the students wrote in their journals every day; once a week would seem to be the minimum. Have some minimum amount of writing the students must do each time. In Reed's classroom this was three sentences. Make some specific arrangements about when journal writing will take place. In Reed's classroom this was after the students had finished all their other assignments. Journal writing might also be done as homework.
3. Let the students know that the journals can be used to raise questions they might feel uncomfortable asking in class. For example, Reed encouraged students to ask her questions about lessons. These questions gave her valuable feedback about her own teaching. In their journals students also sought advice about personal problems, such as a conflict with a bully on the playground.

4. Make sure you have the time to write back to students, so they receive responses to their writing right away. Do not correct students' writing, but provide models for correct spelling and grammar in your responses. Respond to student's ideas and messages, rather than to the forms used in their writing.

Language Experience

Using the language experience approach helps young ESL students, who cannot yet read in any language, to get started in reading. Refer to Chapter 6 for a discussion of LEA. With ESL students as with all other children, the reading aloud of books should always be used along with LEA. This ensures that the students will be exposed to a wide variety of written, and not only oral, language patterns.

Hudelson and Barrera (1985) recommend using a variation of the language experience approach with ESL students who are just beginning to speak English, for the purposes of involving them in lessons. In this procedure, the teacher writes cloze sentences on the board for the children to complete. For example, suppose that the teacher has brought a grocery sack containing different kinds of vegetables. The children could be asked to complete sentences such as:

_____ said, "I like to eat _____."

_____ said, "I don't like to eat _____."

_____ said, "The biggest vegetable is _____."

_____ said, "The smallest vegetable is _____."

After the blanks have been filled in, the children could reread all the sentences.

Students Who Speak a Dialect of English

In the view of linguists, *all* speakers of English are speakers of a dialect (Barnitz, 1980). What we commonly refer to as Standard English or as "good" or "proper" English is itself a dialect or version of the English language. The difference between this particular dialect and all others is that it has the greatest prestige, being widely used by television broadcasters, business leaders, government officials, and others in influential positions.

While there are differences between written and oral versions of English, spoken Standard English is generally considered to be closer to the commonly published forms of English, in terms of grammar and vocabulary. Thus, children who speak a nonstandard dialect of English have often been thought to be at a disadvantage in learning to read. There is, however, little evidence to support the view that speaking a dialect actively interferes with learning to read (e.g., Hart, Guthrie, & Winfield, 1980; Au, Tharp, Crowell, Jordan, Speidel, & Calkins, 1984). In particular, its effect on comprehension (spoken or written) is minimal (Alexander, 1979). Nor is there evidence to support the view that drilling children on Standard English grammar and pronunciation improves learning to read.

In teaching reading to dialect-speaking students, current research suggests that the source of the problem is probably in cultural differences in communication styles and teachers' attitudes toward children's language, rather than just the children's speaking of a nonstandard dialect (e.g., Au et al., 1984). Thus, teachers working with children who enter school as speakers of a nonstandard dialect should be aware of cultural differences, as discussed earlier, and seek to develop a positive attitude about the children's language and abilities. They should have some understanding of nonstandard dialects in general as well as of their students' particular dialects.

Alexander (1979) makes the following points in discussing black dialect (also referred to as Black English or Vernacular Black English), and these points apply as well to other dialects. First, most dialect speakers are actually bidialectal. That is, they speak the dialect in informal situations or when addressing other speakers of the same dialect, but can easily switch to Standard English in formal situations or when addressing those who do not speak the dialect. Second, there are many different versions of Black English or black dialect. Dialects vary by region as well as by social class, younger speakers may use different vocabulary from older speakers, and so on. All dialects, like Standard English or any other version of a language, follow definite rules and are complete, effective language systems.

Teachers should be aware that dialect speakers' use of speech features different from those of Standard English is *not* a sign of inferior language or thinking ability. Rather, it is simply a sign that the children are expressing themselves in an alternate, more familiar language code. For example, Barnitz (1980) gives the following examples of frequently cited syntactic differences between black dialect and Standard English:

> *"Be" verb:* To show ongoing action or states of being, VBE speakers may say "I *be* pretty [every day]." However, to show a particular instance instead of habitual aspect, the speaker may delete the *be* verb: "My friend pretty [today, wearing makeup]."
>
> *Past tense:* The past tense marker is often deleted. "The man walk yesterday." This process often results from the consonant cluster simplification rule.
>
> *Existential it:* The speaker may say "It['s] a man in our yard" instead of "There [is] a man in the yard." (p. 781)

But while teachers must show respect and appreciation for the children's own language, they should still be aware of making sure that the children are becoming more and more familiar with Standard English. Having knowledge of Standard English will make it easier for the students to learn to read texts written in Standard English, which will make up the vast majority of the material they encounter.

Guidelines for developing dialect speakers' knowledge of Standard English. The most important general guideline is the same as that stated for working with ESL students: focus on the child's ideas rather than the exact form used to express them. Other recommendations are as follows:

1. *Create an accepting atmosphere for the use of language, one where students will feel comfortable using the dialect but also have the opportunity to learn Standard English.* This is accomplished by allowing students to express their ideas in the dialect. You will, however, respond in Standard English, modeling the use of Standard English pronunciation, vocabulary, and syntax for the students. You will not need to correct the students. Rather, the way to encourage learning is to continue to engage them in discussion of the topic, so they will have the opportunity to use the Standard English forms you modeled.

2. *Accept the children's accents.* As with ESL students, correcting pro-

Dialect speakers, in common with all other students, benefit from having easy access to books and the opportunity to share reading with others.

nunciation or providing drill on isolated sounds is ineffective. Variations in pronunciation generally do not affect dialect speakers' ability to make themselves understood. Allow students to use dialect pronunciations or substitutions when reading orally. Do not correct their reading unless it is apparent that the meaning of the text has been changed.

3. *With older students, discuss in a sensitive manner how Standard English may be appropriate in some situations, and the dialect in others.* Help them to understand the advantages of being able to use Standard English at certain times. Encourage them to practice using Standard English forms during reading lessons, for example, but do not correct them when they use the dialect instead.

Recommended sequence of instruction for beginning readers. The recommended sequence of beginning reading instruction for young dialect speakers is like that recommended in Chapter 6 for most other kindergarten and first-grade students, and in this chapter for young ESL students. In other words, begin by reading aloud to the children, both high quality children's literature and predictable books. Allow the children plenty of opportunity to express their responses to literature orally, in writing, and through art. Give the children the opportunity to write every day, following a process approach.

▌INSTRUCTIONAL ACTIVITIES

The following variation of the language experience approach may be beneficial in increasing children's knowledge of Standard English (adapted from Gillet & Gentry, 1983, pp. 361–363).

Extending the Language Experience Approach

Step 1: Begin the lesson following the usual method for having the children dictate a story. In other words, introduce a stimulus for discussion, and take down the children's story without changing the language used. See Figure 8.4 for a story dictated by first-grade children in Jamaica and then transformed following the procedures outlined by Gillet and Gentry.

Step 2: Introduce a Standard English version. Gillet and Gentry recommend that the teacher rewrite the children's original story in Standard English. This story is then printed on chart paper in the same manner. Alternately, if the children are already somewhat familiar with Standard English, the teacher could work with the group to arrive at a Standard English version. Introduce this version as "another story" about the same topic and have the children read it aloud, in the usual way.

Step 3: Have the children revise their sentences. Reintroduce the original story and have the children review it. Then have each child revise and

Figure 8.4
Sentence Transformations from
"Funny Fruits"

They	were	in	a	bag.
(Cookies)	were	in	a	box.
Cookies	were	in	a	jar.
(Words) and (pictures)	were	in	the	books.
Shoes and socks	were	(under)	the	big bed.
A dog and a cat	were	inside	the	red barn.
The fruit	felt	squishy	and	round.
The (apple)	felt	hard	and	bumpy.
The (puppy)	felt	soft, warm	and	wiggly.
The (new) baseball	felt	(very) hard.		
The ripe mango	(tasted)	sweet	and	delicious.
The old shoes	(looked)	dirty	and	worn out.

Source: From "Funny Fruits" and "Bridges between nonstandard and standard English with extensions of dictated stories" by Jean W. Gillet and J. R. Gentry, *The Reading Teacher,* January 1983. Copyright © 1983 International Reading Association, Inc. Reprinted with permission of Jean Gillet and the International Reading Association.

expand upon his original statements. Encourage the children to make each sentence longer and more detailed and interesting, using phrases such as, "Can you think of another way to say that?" and "What would you like to add?" Do not use wordings (such as "How can you make this sentence correct?") which suggest that the earlier sentence was inferior. While you may wish to make a few corrections at this point, do so sensitively and do not expect the children's new story to be entirely in Standard English. Have the children practice reading the new story.

Step 4: Have the children practice sentence transformations. Use sentences from any of the three versions of the story to show the children how sentences can be produced by substituting different words. Write the original sentences on the chalkboard or on chart paper. Put a copy of the sentence below, leaving a blank to indicate where the new words can be substituted. Have the children suggest words to fill the blank.

Sample story obtained in Step 1

Funny Fruits

Mandy said, "They was in a bag—a lunch bag."
Kareem said, "They was some kind of fruits."
Tonya said, "Teacher say feel it."
Jerome said, "They was real squishy."

Version developed for Step 2

The Mystery Bag

Mandy, Kareem, Tonya, and Jerome learned about some funny fruit. First, we looked at a lunch bag. Second, we each put one hand into the bag. We each felt the funny fruit. Then, we talked about the fruit. We tried to guess what the fruit was. Last, we wrote a story about the funny, squishy fruit.

Version developed during Step 3

Funny Fruits

Mandy said, "First, we looked at the lunch bag."
Kareem said, "There were some fruits in the bag."
Tonya said, "Our teacher said to put in your hand and feel around but don't tell what it is.
Jerome said, "The fruit felt squishy and sort of round."

Sentence transformations from Step 4 (see Figure 8.4)

Activities for Older Students

Among others, Alexander (1979) recommends the following classroom activities which are in keeping with guidelines presented earlier. All may, of course, be adapted for use with children who speak any nonstandard dialect.

Have your students read some of the poems of black literature which offer opportunities for performance-response, perhaps the poetry of Gwendolyn Brooks and Langston Hughes.
Discuss the major dialect areas in the United States.
Discuss reasons for the different dialects and why we should respect dialectal differences.
Read passages in other English dialects to your students to help them appreciate the variability of English and the legitimacy of their own dialect.
Discuss and role-play different situations in which vernacular Black English dialect and Standard English dialect would be used.
Teach the grammatical constructions of Standard English dialect. Provide time for practice of grammatical constructions.   (pp. 575–576)

If you are following a process approach to the teaching of writing, you will be able to teach students about Standard English grammar when it is time for them to edit their pieces. You may also want to give the class mini-lessons on features of Standard English grammar that might be useful in their writing. In general, relating grammar lessons to students' writing will be more effective than teaching grammar for its own sake and having students complete textbook grammar exercises.

Baugh (1987) recommends building students' knowledge of Standard English by having them work with the lyrics of popular songs. He points out that most black musicians, including Michael Jackson and Stevie Wonder, use Standard English in their songs. Students may be asked to write out the lyrics, discuss the meaning of particular terms or phrases, and compose some lines of their own. These activities may help to change dialect speakers' perceptions that school literacy is often boring and unrelated to their own lives and interests.

Key Concept 4

Teachers should know how to provide sound classroom reading instruction to gifted readers.

▌ GIFTED READERS

The term *gifted* is generally applied to students who have an exceptionally high level of achievement or ability in a particular field. However, a student who shows special talent in one area is not necessarily equally gifted in all other fields of endeavor. For example, one child may have exceptional musical talent while another may excel in science. These two students are both gifted, but not in the same way.

It makes sense, then, not to treat all gifted students identically, but to address their needs according to areas of special talent and interest. Thus, because this textbook is about reading instruction, we will be concerned here with ways teachers can meet the needs of children who have exceptional ability in reading and working with text information. We will refer to these students as *gifted readers*.

Wallen (1974) describes gifted readers as those who are so advanced that they have little to gain from the reading materials and activities normally given to others of their age and grade. To the classroom teacher, it will be evident that these students can easily handle classroom reading and writing assignments, as well as reading assessment tasks appropriate for their grade. Their standardized reading test scores will generally be at stanine 9 or perhaps 8.

Often, gifted readers are able to comprehend both the details and larger ideas in text much more readily than other students in the class. They generally appear to have a much broader base of knowledge and vocabulary, across a range of topics, than their peers. They are fluent readers and generally experience no problems at all with word identification.

But while gifted readers may show a similar pattern of reading ability and achievement, they may be very different in terms of such factors as study habits, especially the ability to work independently; the topics they find to be interesting; and personality, whether outgoing or shy, confident or less secure. Teachers will want to consider these other factors when developing classroom programs for gifted readers. For example, some gifted readers may enjoy working alone and being given the opportunity to study independently.

Others may benefit from receiving more teacher guidance and may prefer to engage in group activities.

In what ways might the reading activities of gifted readers be somewhat different from those for the rest of the class? Renzulli (1988) suggests that activities for the gifted might emphasize higher level thinking skills, less structured teaching strategies, and controversial issues. Activities with these features give gifted readers the chance to learn about and explore the basic concepts and inquiry methods of different disciplines, such as history, biology, psychology, and so on.

▮ INSTRUCTIONAL GUIDELINES

1. *Provide gifted readers with systematic and challenging instruction in comprehension.* Such lessons should encourage gifted readers to think deeply and not superficially about text ideas, so that they learn to make good use of their special talents. For lesson ideas, refer to the Instructional Activities section under this key concept.

2. *Have gifted readers spend more time in recreational reading, or in reading for information, and less time with worksheet and workbook assignments.* Often, gifted readers do not need the type of practice provided by worksheets and workbooks. During time that other students might be spending with these activities, gifted readers can be allowed to read independently, following their own interests or a plan worked out with the teacher. You may wish to use an individualized reading approach as described in Chapter 11.

3. *Be sure to give gifted readers a balance between opportunities for independent discovery and participation in reading activities involving other students.* Gifted readers, even when able to work independently for relatively long periods of time, should also be given ample time to interact with other children. They can be valuable contributors to the classroom community and so should be given the chance to discuss their ideas with others. Gifted readers may be placed in reading groups in some cases, or given other, somewhat less structured ways of sharing their ideas with other students. For example, a gifted reader who especially enjoys reading independently might be encouraged to discuss favorite books with other children.

4. *Be sure to give gifted readers the opportunity to work actively and creatively with the ideas gained through reading.* Gifted readers, along with other children in the class, can benefit from being given time to write every day. Part of their writing may be reflections on what they have read, stories in the style of a favorite author, or a report to be shared with the class. Other expressive activities might include dramatizations and art projects. Gifted readers might also conduct science experiments or interview experts to develop more fully ideas gained through reading. In short, reading can be used as a springboard to further the students' own literary or content area interests.

▌ INSTRUCTIONAL ACTIVITIES

The following instructional activities are designed to challenge gifted readers by encouraging independence and the use of higher level thinking. All allow teachers to work in a systematic, but not restrictive, way with these students.

Inquiry Reading

In the inquiry reading approach recommended by Cassidy (1981), the gifted reader conducts independent research on topics of interest. The student selects the topic, carries out the research, and then presents the findings to others. This cycle takes about four weeks and occupies time otherwise spent in basal reader instruction. The approach can be used by classroom teachers working with gifted readers in the third through sixth grades. Here are the steps in the instructional sequence:

First week

1. *Defining the term "inquiry."* Have the students discuss the meaning of inquiry, looking the word up in a dictionary if necessary.
2. *Presenting the requirements.* State the requirements for conducting the inquiry: that the students will each choose a question to investigate, that the inquiry will take up about four weeks, and that the end product will involve communicating the results.
3. *Discussing areas of interest.* Hold a brainstorming session and help each student to arrive at a list of interesting topics.
4. *Formulating questions.* Tell the students to develop three questions for possible investigation. Help each student to settle on one of these questions, neither too narrow nor too broad, to be the subject of the inquiry.
5. *Discussing references and resources.* Hold another brainstorming session to help the children come up with a list of references, such as the encyclopedia, books, or magazines. Also have them identify someone they can consult about the topic. This may be a parent or a professional in the field.
6. *Reviewing interview procedures.* Help the students draw up plans to conduct an interview of their chosen expert. Have the students write or phone the person for an appointment and then make up a list of interview questions.
7. *Identifying a sharing activity.* Early on, have the children decide how they will be sharing their findings. This procedure helps add direction and focus to their inquiry efforts.
8. *Developing a contract.* Help the students to set deadlines for completing each step in the inquiry.

Second and third weeks

1. *Reviewing methods for taking notes.*
2. *Locating references in the school or public library or at home.* If the

students are unfamiliar with the process, assist them (or enlist the help of the librarian) in finding useful sources of information. The students then proceed to gather facts and ideas, writing the information on file cards or sheets of paper.

3. *Keeping a folder.* Have the students collect their notes in a folder. Staple a card with the student's question to the outside of the folder. Remind students to check back to be sure that their notes are all addressed to this question.
4. *Sharing problems and successes.* Conduct one or two sessions for the purpose of having the children share with one another the progress being made in their inquiries. Allow the students to offer suggestions to one another.
5. *Holding individual conferences.* Meet with each student individually to review his or her contract and make any adjustments needed.
6. *Constructing projects.* By the third week, students are usually spending most of their time putting their projects together.

Fourth week

1. *Completing projects.* Help students finish up, perhaps also suggesting adjustments to their original plans.
2. *Holding a dress rehearsal.* Have members of the group act as the audience for one another. Let the children suggest ways that other students' projects might be improved. Help the children adjust their presentations so the entire session, encompassing the sharing of all of the children in the group, will last no longer than 90 minutes. The presentations may take different forms. For example, a child may give a talk, speaking from an outline and notes, or read just part of a written report aloud and let the other members of the class know that the full report will be placed in the class library.
3. *Presenting to an outside audience.* The outside audience may consist of other students in the class, parents, or another homeroom.
4. *Evaluating the inquiry.* Meet with each student to go over the contract and finished project. Discuss what went well as well as areas that might have been handled differently.

Instruction to Improve Purpose-Setting and Question-Asking

Gifted readers often benefit from activities giving them the opportunity to learn to set their own purposes and to raise their own questions for reading. In keeping with this idea, Bates (1984) recommends that gifted readers be given instruction with the DRTA (see Chapter 4). They may also make up their own study guides (see the reading guides activities in Chapter 4), instead of working from a study guide prepared by the teacher.

In these activities the teacher will generally wish to guide, rather than totally direct, the students' reading efforts. At the same time, the teacher has the chance during these lessons to monitor the development of the children's reading comprehension abilities. It is important to do so to ensure, for example, that gifted readers learn to read carefully as well as quickly, and that they learn to base conclusions on text information and not just background knowledge.

Great Books Approach

Trevise (1984) recommends that teachers have gifted readers from the second grade on up work with the Junior Great Books Reading and Discussion Program developed by the Great Books Foundation. While reading the recommended "classics" students could meet for group discussions. Students in the discussion groups need not all be in the same grade. Discussion should focus on the universal themes in the books, as well as on the author, particular content, and style of writing. If teachers ask many open-ended questions and make the discussions challenging and interesting, the approach can have many advantages. These include encouraging gifted readers to read more widely, by reading books besides basal readers and textbooks; to read more critically, by having to analyze the texts read; and to read more creatively, by being asked to share individual responses to what they have read.

Heinl (1988) recommends having gifted readers write about the books, not just discuss them. Students might summarize chapters or the book as a whole, identify an overall message in the book and provide evidence supporting their interpretation, or write a critique.

Vocabulary Development Through Literature

Howell (1987) describes a number of vocabulary activities, some based on the reading of children's literature. These activities may be used with all students in the class, but gifted readers may find them especially enjoyable.

Figurative language/idioms. Have students read a book using many idioms, such as one from Peggy Parish's Amelia Bedelia series. For example, in one book Amelia is told to dust the furniture, so she sprinkles it with dusting powder! Discuss with students the difference between what Amelia was supposed to do and what she actually did. Then read to students about the other tasks facing Amelia, and have them guess what she did instead.

Palindromes. Familiarize students with the concept of a palindrome, a word or phrase with letters in the same order, whether it is read backwards or forwards (e.g., *Otto*). Then invite students to solve some palindrome riddles, such as those presented in *Too Hot to Hoot* (Terban, 1985). Encourage students to make up some palindrome riddles of their own.

Etymology. Build students' interest in words by introducing them to books about the history of words. Present students with a "word for the day" and challenge them to learn its meaning and history.

▌ **Figure 8.5**
Children's Books for Delightful
Vocabulary Study

Basil, Cynthia. *How Ships Play Cards: A Beginning Book of Homonyms.* New York, N.Y.: Morrow, 1980.
Burchfield, R. W., ed. *A Supplement to the Oxford University Dictionary.* Oxford, England: Oxford University Press, 1976.
Gwynne, Fred. *A Chocolate Moose for Dinner.* New York, N.Y.: Windmill/Dutton, 1976.
Gwynne, Fred. *The King Who Rained.* New York, N.Y.: Windmill, 1970.
Hoban, Tana. *Push-Pull Empty-Full.* New York, N.Y.: Macmillan, 1972.
Hunt, Bernice K. *The Whatchamacallit Book.* New York, N.Y.: G. P. Putnam's Sons, 1976.
Lobel, Arnold. *Frog and Toad Are Friends.* New York, N.Y.: Harper and Row, 1970.
Maestro, Guilio. *What's a Frank Frank? Tasty Homograph Riddles.* New York, N.Y.: Clarion, 1984.
Merriam, Eve. *A Gaggle of Geese.* New York, N.Y.: Knopf, 1960.
Moscovitch, Rosalie. *What's In a Word? A Dictionary of Daffy Definitions.* Boston, Mass.: Houghton Mifflin, 1985.
O'Dell, Scott. *Island of the Blue Dolphins.* Boston, Mass.: Houghton Mifflin, 1960.
Oxford English Dictionary. Oxford, England: Oxford University Press, 1933.
Parish, Peggy. *Amelia Bedelia.* New York, N.Y.: Harper and Row, 1963.
Sperling, Susan K. *Murfles and Wink-A-Peeps: Funny Old Words for Kids.* New York, N.Y.: Clarkson N. Potter, 1985.
Spier, Peter. *Fast-Slow, High-Low: A Book of Opposites.* Garden City, N.Y.: Doubleday, 1972.
Steig, William. *The Amazing Bone.* New York, N.Y.: Farrar, Straus and Giroux, 1976.
Steig, William. *Sylvester and the Magic Pebble.* New York, N.Y.: Simon and Schuster, 1969.
Terban, Marvin. *Eight Ate: A Feast of Homonym Riddles.* New York, N.Y.: Clarion, 1982.
Terban, Marvin. *In a Pickle and Other Funny Idioms.* New York, N.Y.: Clarion, 1983.
Terban, Marvin. *Too Hot to Hoot: Funny Palindrome Riddles.* New York, N.Y.: Clarion, 1985.
Viorst, Judith. *Alexander and the Terrible, Horrible, No Good, Very Bad Day.* New York, N.Y.: Atheneum, 1972.

Source: "Language, literature, and vocabulary development for gifted students" by Helen Howell, *The Reading Teacher*, February 1987, p. 504. Copyright © 1987 International Reading Association, Inc. Reprinted with permission of Helen Howell and the International Reading Association.

Introduce students to the idea that the meaning of certain words has changed over time. Let students examine some of these changes, for example, by tracing the history of modern slang terms. Also, familiarize them with the fact that some once common words are no longer in use, such as those presented in *Murfles and Wink-A-Peeps* (Sperling, 1985).

Involve students in imaginative and humorous games of word play. For example, students could be asked to think of a "daffy definition," such as those provided by Moscovitch in *What's In a Word? A Dictionary of Daffy Definitions* (1985). Here is an example of a daffy definition:

Miasma: What's making it difficult for me to breathe.   (p. 32)

Books for vocabulary study recommended by Howell are listed in Figure 8.5.

▌ SUMMARY

Throughout this chapter we emphasized the importance of providing meaningful, high-quality instruction to students with special needs. In the perspective we made the point that students with special needs should receive instruction much like that provided to all other students. We wrote of the importance of providing these students with integrated instruction in reading and writing. We also emphasized the importance of coordinating the instructional resources available for students with special needs, and of how the classroom teacher should be the main person responsible for their reading instruction.

In the first key concept we discussed the effective instruction of poor readers. The main reason poor readers continue to progress slowly in learning to read seems to be that they often receive faulty instruction. To correct this problem, we recommended approaches for improving students' comprehension as well as word identification ability.

In the second key concept we looked at how differences in culture and communication styles can influence children's learning to read. We recommended that teachers see their goal as bridging the gap between the culture of the home and the culture of the school. Literature-based activities, including the shared book experience, seem to be effective in improving the learning to read of students from different cultural backgrounds.

We addressed the issue of language differences in the third key concept. We examined the teaching of reading to students who speak a language other than English, and the teaching of reading to dialect speakers. In both cases we highlighted the need for teachers to attend to students' ideas rather than to their grammar or pronunciation. Recommended instructional activities included the reading and discussion of storybooks, writing in dialogue journals, and variations on the language experience approach.

Finally, in the fourth key concept, we covered instructional activities teachers can use with gifted readers. We recommended inquiry reading, reading and writing about great books, and vocabulary activities.

In this chapter we described activities which might be particularly beneficial for students with certain kinds of special needs. However, you will probably have noticed that almost all of these activities can just as well be used with other students, too. The main idea in this chapter was that, while effective instruction for students with special needs might be different in certain specific ways, its essential features are those we have described in other chapters. In this sense, sound reading instruction for one is sound reading instruction for all.

▌ BIBLIOGRAPHY
References

Alexander, C. F. (1979). Black English dialect and the classroom teacher. *The Reading Teacher, 33* (5), 571–577.

Allington, R. L. (1983). The reading instruction provided readers of differing abilities. *Elementary School Journal, 83* (5), 548–559.

Aoki, E. M. (1981). "Are you Chinese? Are you Japanese? Or are you just a mixed-up kid?" Using Asian American children's literature. *The Reading Teacher, 34* (4), 381–385.

Au, K. H., & Mason, J. M. (1983). Cultural congruence in classroom participation structures: Achieving a balance of rights. *Discourse Processes, 6* (2), 145–167.

Au, K. H., Tharp, R. G., Crowell, D. C., Jordan, C., Speidel, G. E., and Calkins, R. (1984). KEEP: The role of research in the development of a successful reading program. In

J. Osborn, P. Wilson, & R. C. Anderson (Eds.), *Reading education: Foundations for a literate America.* Boston: D. C. Heath.

Barnitz, J. G. (1980). Black English and other dialects: Sociolinguistic implications for reading instruction. *The Reading Teacher, 33* (7), 779–786.

Barrera, R. B. (1983). Bilingual reading in the primary grades: Some questions about questionable views and practices. In T. H. Escobedo (Ed.), *Early childhood bilingual education: A Hispanic perspective.* New York: Teachers College Press.

Barrera, R. B. (1984). The teaching of reading to language-minority students: Some basic guidelines. In F. W. Parkay, S. O'Bryan, & M. Hennessy (Eds.), *Quest for quality: Improving basic skills instruction in the 1980s.* Lanham, MD: University Press of America.

Bates, G. W. (1984). Developing reading strategies for the gifted: A research-based approach. *Journal of Reading, 27* (7), 590–593.

Baugh, J. (1987). Research currents: The situational dimension of linguistic power in social context. *Language Arts, 64* (2), 234–240.

Boggs, S. T. (1972). The meaning of questions and narratives to Hawaiian children. In C. Cazden, V. John, & D. Hymes (Eds.), *Functions of language in the classroom.* New York: Teachers College Press.

Bohning, G. (1981). Bibliotherapy: Fitting the resources together. *Elementary School Journal, 82* (2), 166–170.

Cassidy, J. (1981). Inquiry reading for the gifted. *The Reading Teacher, 35* (1), 17–21.

Cazden, C. B., Carrasco, R., Maldonado-Guzman, A. A., & Erickson, F. (1980). The contribution of ethnographic research to bicultural bilingual education. In J. Alatis (Ed.), *Current issues in bilingual education.* Georgetown University Round Table on Language and Linguistics. Washington, DC: Georgetown University Press.

Cazden, C., John, V., & Hymes, D. (Eds.) (1972). *Functions of language in the classroom.* New York: Teachers College Press.

Chu-Chang, M. (Ed.) (1983). Comparative research in bilingual education: *Asian-Pacific-American perspectives.* New York: Teachers College Press.

Clay, M. M. (1979). *The early detection of reading difficulties* (3rd ed.). Auckland, New Zealand: Heinemann.

Davey, B. (1983). Think aloud—Modeling the cognitive processes of reading comprehension. *Journal of Reading, 27* (1), 44–47.

Diaz, S., Moll, L. C., & Mehan, H. (1986). Sociocultural resources in instruction: A context-specific approach. In *Beyond Language: Social and cultural factors in schooling language minority children.* Los Angeles: Evaluation, Dissemination and Assessment Center, California State University.

Edelsky, C. (1986). *Writing in a bilingual program: Habia una vez.* Norwood, NJ: Ablex.

Elley, W. B. (1981). The role of reading in bilingual contexts. In J. T. Guthrie (Ed.), *Comprehension and teaching: Research reviews.* Newark, DE: International Reading Association.

Elley, W., & Mangubhai, F. (1983). The impact of reading on second language learning. *Reading Research Quarterly, 19,* 53–67.

Erickson, F., & Mohatt, G. (1982). Cultural organization of participation structures in two classrooms of Indian students. In G. B. Spindler (Ed.), *Doing the ethnography of schooling: Educational anthropology in action.* New York: Holt, Rinehart & Winston.

Gaskins, R. W. (1988). The missing ingredients: Time on task, direct instruction, and writing. *The Reading Teacher, 41* (8), 750–755.

Gillet, J. W., & Gentry, J. R. (1983). Bridges between nonstandard and standard English with extensions of dictated stories. *The Reading Teacher, 36* (4), 360–364.

Gilliland, H. (1982). The new view of Native Americans in children's literature. *The Reading Teacher, 35* (8), 912–916.

Gonzales, P. C. (1980). What's wrong with the basal reader approach to language development? *The Reading Teacher, 33* (6), 668–673.

Gonzales, P. C. (1981). How to begin language instruction for non-English speaking students. *Language Arts, 53* (2), 175–180.

Goodenough, W. (1971). *Culture, language, and society:* Addison-Wesley module. Reading, MA: Addison-Wesley.

Goodman, K., Goodman, Y., & Flores, B. (1979). *Reading in the bilingual classroom: Literacy and biliteracy.* Rosslyn, VA: National Clearinghouse for Bilingual Education.

Hart, J. T., Guthrie, J. T., & Winfield, L. (1980). Black English phonology and learning to read. *Journal of Educational Psychology, 72,* 636–646.

Heath, S. B. (1982). What no bedtime story means: Narrative skills at home and school. *Language in Society, 11* (2), 49–76.

Heinl, A. M. (1988, December). The effects of the Junior Great Books Program on literal and inferential comprehension. Paper presented at the Annual Meeting of the National Reading Conference. Tucson.

Holdaway, D. (1979). *The foundations of literacy.* Sydney, Australia: Ashton Scholastic (distributed in the United States by Heinemann).

Holt, J. (1964). *Why children fail.* New York: Dell.

Hough, R. A., Nurss, J. R., & Enright, D. S. (1986). Story reading with limited English speaking children in the regular classroom. *The Reading Teacher, 39* (6), 510–514.

Howell, H. (1987). Language, literature, and vocabulary development for gifted students. *The Reading Teacher, 40* (6), 500–504.

Hudelson, S. (1987). The role of native language literacy in the education of language minority children. *Language Arts, 64* (8), 827–841.

Hudelson, S., & Barrera, R. (1985). Bilingual/second language learners and reading. In L. Searfoss & J. Readence (Eds.), *Helping children learn to read.* Englewood Cliffs, NJ: Prentice-Hall.

Johnston, P., Allington, R., & Afflerbach, P. (1985). The congruence of classroom and remedial reading instruction. *Elementary School Journal, 85* (4), 465–477.

Kapinus, B. A., Gambrell, L. B., & Koskinen, P. S. (1988). The effects of practice in retelling upon the readers. Thirty-sixth yearbook of the National Reading Conference. Rochester, NY: National Reading Conference.

Koskinen, P. S., Gambrell, L. B., Kapinus, B. A., & Heathington, B. S. (1988). Retelling: A strategy for enhancing students' reading comprehension. *The Reading Teacher, 41* (9), 892–896.

Lauritzen, C. (1982). A modification of repeated readings for group instruction. *The Reading Teacher, 36* (4), 456–458.

Morrow, L. M. (1985). Retelling stories: A strategy for improving young children's comprehension, concept of story structure, and oral language complexity. *Elementary School Journal, 85* (5), 647–661.

Osborn, J. (1984). The purposes, uses, and contents of workbooks and some guidelines for publishers. In R. C. Anderson, J. Osborn, & R. J. Tierney (Eds.), *Learning to read in American schools: Basal readers and content texts.* Hillsdale, NJ: Lawrence Erlbaum Associates.

Philips, S. (1972). Participant structures and communicative competence: Warm Springs children in community and classroom. In C. Cazden, V. John, & D. Hymes (Eds.), *Functions of language in the classroom*. New York: Teachers College Press.

Raphael, T. E. (1982). Question-answering strategies for children. *The Reading Teacher, 36* (2), 186–190.

Renzulli, J. S. (1988). The multiple menu model for developing differentiated curriculum for the gifted and talented. *Gifted Child Quarterly, 32* (3), 298–309.

Reynolds, R. E., Taylor, M. A., Steffenson, M. S., Shirey, L. L., & Anderson, R. C. (1982). Cultural schemata and reading comprehension. *Reading Research Quarterly, 17,* 353–366.

Rhodes, L. K. (1981). I can read! Predictable books as resources for reading and writing instruction. *The Reading Teacher, 34* (5), 511–518.

Rollock, B. (1974). *The black experience in children's books.* (Rev. ed.) New York: New York Public Library.

Samuels, S. J. (1979). The method of repeated readings. *The Reading Teacher, 32,* 403–408.

Seda, I., & Abramson, S. (1988). English literacy development of young, linguistically different learners. University Park, PA: Pennsylvania State University, Division of Curriculum and Instruction, unpublished manuscript.

Shepard, L. A., Smith, M. L., & Vojir, C. P. (1983). Characteristics of pupils identified as learning disabled. *American Educational Research Journal, 20* (3), 309–331.

Singer, H., McNeil, J. D., & Furse, L. L. (1984). Relationship between curriculum scope and reading achievement in elementary school. *The Reading Teacher, 37* (7), 608–612.

Slaughter, J. P. (1983). Big books for little kids: Another fad or a new approach for teaching beginning reading? *The Reading Teacher, 36* (8), 758–762.

Staton, J. (1980). Writing and counseling: Using a dialogue journal. *Language Arts, 57* (5), 514–518.

Sutherland, Z., & Arbuthnot, M. H. (1986). *Children and books* (7th ed.). Glenview, IL: Scott, Foresman.

Taylor, B. M., & Nosbush, L. (1983). Oral reading for meaning: A technique for improving word identification skills. *The Reading Teacher, 37* (3), 234–237.

Tompkins, G. E., & Webeler, M. (1983). What will happen next? Using predictable books with young children. *The Reading Teacher, 36* (6), 498–502.

Trevise, R. (1984). Teaching reading to the gifted. In A. Harris & E. Sipay (Eds.), *Readings on reading instruction*. New York: Longman.

Trueba, H. T., Guthrie, G. P., & Au, K. H. (Eds.) (1981). *Culture and the bilingual classroom: Studies in classroom ethnography*. Rowley, MA: Newbury House.

Wallen, C. J. (1974). Fostering reading growth for gifted and creative readers at the primary level. In M. Labuda (Ed.), *Creative reading for gifted learners: A design for excellence*. Newark, DE: International Reading Association.

Wong-Kam, J., & Au, K. H. (1988). Improving a fourth grader's reading and writing: Three principles. *The Reading Teacher, 41* (8), 768–772.

Children's Books and Programs Cited

Junior Great Books Reading and Discussion Program for Students from Second Grade Through Senior High School. Great Books Foundation, 307 N. Michigan Ave., Chicago, IL 60601.

Moscovitch, R. (1985). *What's in a word! A dictionary of daffy definitions.* Boston: Houghton Mifflin.

Sperling, S. K. (1985). *Murfles and wink-a-peeps: Funny old words for kids.* New York: Clarkson N. Potter.

Story Box. San Diego: The Wright Group.

Terban, M. (1985). *Too hot to hoot: Funny palindrome riddles.* New York: Clarion Books.

Further Readings

Barnitz, J. (1985). *Reading development of nonnative speakers of English.* Orlando, FL: Harcourt Brace Jovanovich.

Cunningham, P. M. (1988). When all else fails . . . *The Reading Teacher, 41* (8), 800–805.

Moll, L. C. (1988). Some key issues in teaching Latino students. *Language Arts, 65* (5), 465–472.

Shumaker, M. P., & Shumaker, R. C. (1986). 3,000 paper cranes: Children's literature for remedial readers. *The Reading Teacher, 41* (6), 544–549.

Topping, K. (1989). Peer tutoring and paired reading: Combining two powerful techniques. *The Reading Teacher, 42* (7), 488–494.

Walters, K., & Gunderson, L. (1985). Effects of parent volunteers reading first language (Ll) books to ESL students. *The Reading Teacher, 39* (1), 66–69.

Assessment in the Classroom

At a time when Americans are placing greater emphasis upon educational assessment and accountability, it is ironic that the nation's reading educators and teachers find themselves on the horns of a dilemma created, at least in part, by their
very ability to evaluate how well children are learning to read. The tools which
are intended to help the teacher in the classroom have paradoxically become the
chains which frustrate individual initiative and innovation and limit professional
prerogative. At the root of this problem is a notion of perceived accountability
which manifests itself in many, often contradictory, ways. On the one hand, for
example, there is the widespread belief among the public, local, and state school
boards, and many professional educators that educational accountability can be
truly and accurately fixed on the basis of test results. For many teachers, on the
other hand, such a belief has not contributed to their sense of professional competence and well-being; to the contrary, this belief has eroded significantly their perceptions of their prerogatives as professional educators and their ability to make
or influence important decisions about educating the nation's children.
(Pearson & Valencia, 1987, p. 3)

▌ OVERVIEW

Assessment instruments are intended to improve instruction, and to that end,
teachers evaluate students daily with questions and written tests and tasks.
Students' comments, responses, and accomplishments are then used to judge
how to modify and improve instruction. Formal, standardized tests are also
used to rank or compare students' knowledge, skill, and achievement against
others in the same grade. How valuable these tests are depends on the confidence with which teachers can use the scores as a basis for determining
whether the material in the curriculum has been learned, and whether students are ready to progress to the next unit or pass into the next grade. Decisions of this magnitude need to be made confidently. The quality of the assessment instruments as well as how they were administered and whether
students were adequately prepared for them are obviously important. However, as you will learn in this chapter, standardized tests are heavily criticized, and other kinds of assessment instruments are being developed for use
in classrooms.

Building on the need for change in classroom assessment, in the perspective section we describe new ways of thinking about assessment. Then, in the key concepts, we distinguish three assessment goals and offer a way to integrate them. The three assessment goals are drawn from ongoing work by Vavrus and Calfee (1988). One goal is for assessment results to guide teachers' planning and to help them improve their instruction in the classroom. A second is to help teachers monitor students' progress, and a third is to provide appropriate information about individual students who may need special instruction or services.

The first key concept describes *initial assessment* goals. The goals include measures of skills and background knowledge of students which the teacher can use to construct a coherent plan for instruction. The second key concept presents *ongoing assessment* goals. Goals of monitoring literacy growth are comparisons of past goals and plans with students' current progress. Goals that maintain a record are accomplished with critical pieces of evidence tracing students' progress. The third key concept explains *focused assessment*, or ways to understand how to teach students who present significant problems or challenges to the teacher. Finally, in the fourth key concept we present an *integrated plan* that you can use to weave the three goals into your instruction.

Chapter 9 is organized around the following key concepts:

Key Concept 1: Classroom assessment at the beginning of the school year can measure students' initial knowledge and skill for planning.

Key Concept 2: Classroom assessment during the school year utilizes portfolios for monitoring and recording students' progress.

Key Concept 3: Classroom assessment can take the form of focused assessment of individual children.

Key Concept 4: Assessment should be integrated into the curriculum.

∎ PERSPECTIVE

Changes in Assessment Procedures and Goals

One criticism of assessment instruments is that the skills and concepts that are instructionally important, which could lead to suggestions about how or what to teach, are seldom measured. Another criticism is lack of authenticity. The test situation or test procedure may keep the skills and concepts from being accurately measured. A third criticism is that assessment instruments may not be sufficiently wide-ranging, missing important aspects of ability and achievement. They should measure learning and understanding over time in a number of different learning contexts, and with a number of different types of questions.

Assessment instruments that you are probably most familiar with are administered to large groups of students and, to reduce costs, are machine-scored, with multiple choice responses. These procedures, however, reduce the possibility of understanding *why* children choose particular responses. Test formats in which children construct answers could offer a better opportunity of understanding why errors are made and determining what children have learned. Examples of students' work, interviews with students about how they solve problems, and observations of students as they work are just a few alternative ways to monitor and evaluate students' progress.

Items in most published assessment instruments are made reliable by differentiating students in terms of an overall ranking, or a percentile score, but this process ignores differences in students' rank that are due to culture, language spoken in the home, the region of the country where a student was raised, family background, the quality of the high school, and the quality of the classroom instruction. The result is an unfair or incomplete picture of a student's ability.

Items are determined to be valid through grouping into general concepts of word attack, vocabulary, and comprehension, but scores on these general topics aren't particularly useful for teachers. As a result, reading assessment instruments may not inform teachers about what their students need to learn or have already mastered.

We recommend that you augment once-a-year "snapshots" of student achievement with ongoing assessments and frequent documentation of student progress. You can assess your students in collaboration with them, and you can use the information to construct plans for lessons and learning goals. You can construct a variety of assessment instruments and strategies, formal as well as informal. You can also use multiple sources of information and a variety of learning contexts. Many dimensions of students' knowledge and skills will then be measured and the process of learning, not merely performance under a test situation, can be evaluated. As a result of these changes, your assessments can be more closely linked to your curricular goals and can be more easily explained to students and their parents.

Valencia, Pearson, and McGinley (in press) describe the new assessment movement as one that is more contextualized, that is, more closely connected to classroom learning. They suggest the following five attributes of these changes:

- *Assessment is continuous.* Learning is a continuous, dynamic process. Not only does learning take place over time, but the learner and task change with every new situation (manuscript p. 3).
- *Assessment is broadly based.* Multiple measures are preferable to single indices but in the typical American press for efficiency, we are prone to look for single indices of the effectiveness of any enterprise. However, we need multiple measures of any behavior or trait. The more measures we have, the more we can trust any given conclusion about the performance of a student or a group (manuscript p. 4).
- *Assessment should be collaborative.* There are many constituencies who have a stake in school assessment—students, teachers, parents,

administrators, school board members, the community and the larger society. Each of these audiences may require somewhat different information and each needs to be involved in helping to shape the assessment agenda. . . . But the essence of the collaborative criterion lies in collaboration with students. When we work *with* students in developing assessments, we communicate our support of their learning process (manuscript p. 4).

- *Assessment must be grounded in knowledge.* Those who accept the responsibility of being "assessors" must be knowledgeable about the content or processes they are assessing. In the case of literacy, they should be familiar with both basic and instructional processes in reading, writing, and language (manuscript p. 4).

- *Assessment must be authentic.* This is the requirement of functional learning and ecological validity. Just as instruction should focus on learning to achieve genuine literacy purposes, so too should assessment be anchored in tasks that have genuine purposes. . . . Assessment tasks should be similar to the learning tasks; students should not be faced with totally new tasks when they are tested on a strategy or a body of knowledge that they have been dealing with for some time (manuscript p. 4).

You can see that this new view of assessment is different in a number of ways. When you think of assessment as continuous and broadly based, when you build collaboration into your plans, and when you seek more information about measuring students' progress, you will have a more useful evaluation system. You will have the opportunity to play a more active role in assessment, and by achieving a deeper understanding of your students, you will discover new ways to plan, evaluate, and improve your own instruction.

Key Concept 1

Classroom assessment at the beginning of the school year can measure students' initial knowledge and skill for planning.

▌ AN EXPANDED VIEW OF ABILITY

You can draw radically different views of students' ability depending on what questions you ask and in what contexts you observe children working. Yet, most formal tests evaluate children in only one context and draw upon only two aspects of ability: verbal or linguistic abilities, and logical or mathematical abilities. Although these two aspects of ability predict how well students are likely to do in school, they are not adequate measures of their success after school. But what about other abilities? Gardner (1988) studied the concept of multiple intelligence and isolated the following seven mental faculties or intelligences:

> Linguistic intelligence, as exemplified in the work of a poet; logical-mathematical analysis—and here you might look at a scientist or mathematician; musical analysis; spatial understanding; bodily kinesthetic thinking—the dancer, athlete, surgeon; and two forms of personal understanding—interpersonal knowledge of other persons, such as a teacher or a salesman might use; and intrapersonal knowledge, which means knowing one's own strengths and needs and using that knowledge to act in the world. (p. 5)

Drawing on Gardner's work, you might assess students at the beginning of every school year by gathering information about several dimensions of ability. You might give a formal assessment, or you could study standardized tests that were given to your students in a previous year. You can talk to students and their parents in order to learn about students' interests, their outside school activities, and their other strengths. For example, do they have musical, athletic, or analytic skills? Do they have friends, do they show leadership characteristics, and are they able to communicate their personal needs to others?

You will also want to know the extent to which students' home and community environment supports schooling. Is English spoken at home? Have parents established a routine, such as reading to children in the early years and allowing them to read at bedtime or at another regular time? Do students read outside school and if so, what and how often? Given the importance of voluntary reading (a topic discussed in Chapter 12), you will want to know its extent as soon as possible. You might inquire about the availability of literacy materials, including library books, in the home and community and also about parents' understanding of the important role they need to play in monitoring their children's homework, encouraging out-of-school reading, and supervising television viewing.

Guidelines for Assessment

Searly and Stevenson (1987) proposed a set of eight guidelines which they used as a basis for assessment. They organized each in terms of indicators of students' development over 12 years of schooling. Their guidelines are as follows:

1. Students have the ability and desire to read, listen, and view for enjoyment and information.
2. Students can and will read and compose literature to extend and clarify their own experiences.
3. Students can and will paraphrase, predict, and question ideas encountered in written and spoken language.

4. Students are aware of the literary tradition, its purpose, its complexity, its relationship to culture, and its value.
5. Students apply knowledge of written and spoken language in a variety of language situations.
6. Students use language to discuss language when constructing their own messages and when analyzing the messages of others.
7. Students express thoughts, feelings, and experience in written and spoken language.
8. Students organize and evaluate new experiences and ideas in written and spoken language.

Consider these guidelines as you plan your instruction for the year and as you informally talk to students about their reading and writing interests and activities. The guidelines will help you to think of reading and writing more broadly, and to evaluate your students on several dimensions and in multiple ways.

EXAMPLES OF BEGINNING-OF-THE-YEAR ASSESSMENT

Informal Assessment

Functions of literacy. How do your students use literacy in their daily lives? There are a number of questions that you could ask informally or give as a short written questionnaire. Here are some suggested topics which you might compare with other activities (e.g., sports, music, art, TV viewing, and playing with friends):

- Book sharing with friends
- Use of school and community libraries
- Opportunity to select and purchase books
- Membership in book clubs
- Subscription to children's magazines
- Size of home library of books they can read
- Amount of reading at home and whether it is a regular activity
- Favorite book, author, or reading topic
- Diary keeping
- Use of writing for certain purposes
- Amount, purpose, and type of out-of-school reading
- Interest in particular topics or literature
- Educational television viewing

Background knowledge of topics. Before establishing the major topics for the school year, it is wise to determine how much information students already know about the topics. What background knowledge do they already have? What topics does the whole class know next to nothing about? On which topics do students vary a great deal in their knowledge? Answers to all of these questions will help you plan your instruction.

Holmes and Roser (1987) suggest five ways to assess the amount and quality of students' prior knowledge about a topic. The authors compared the five ways in terms of quantity of information, effectiveness, and efficiency. We use their questions about the topic of snakes to exemplify the techniques.

- *Free recall.* ("Imagine that in this story is written everything there is to know about snakes. What do you think it would say? . . . Are you sure that is everything?") The teacher writes down or students record their own recalls. This procedure is effective but is not efficient because each student has to be tested separately unless students can write out their own recalls. Also, a complete picture is not obtained, especially among younger students, because students tend to recall more information for early parts of a story than for later parts.
- *Word association.* ("Today we are going to play a word game about snakes. I'll say a word and you tell me everything you can think of about that word as it relates to snakes. For example, if the topic were cats and I said 'paws' you might say: four of them, have claws, have pads on the bottom, walk on them.") With this approach the teacher constructs subtopics that can be keyed by words or phrases and records students' responses or has students do the recording. This is relatively effective and efficient and generally yields good information.
- *Structured questions.* (On the topic of snakes shedding their skin, questions could be developed such as, "Does a snake keep the same skin its whole life?" Additional questions could be asked to probe more specific aspects of the subtopic, such as, "What happens to it? How does it get the skin off? How often does the skin come off?") This approach takes time to develop good questions, but once the questions have been constructed, the approach yields useful information.
- *Recognition.* The teacher develops questions based on subtopics, and uses a modified multiple choice format so that students can select from possible answers, circling all sentence endings which are true as a way of assessing recognition of correct information ("Cold-blooded means: having cold blood, having a constant body temperature, changing temperature with one's surroundings, never being too hot.") This technique is very time-consuming for the teacher to develop good questions and responses but once done takes little time for students to answer and for the teacher to correct.
- *Unstructured discussion.* (Students might be encouraged to describe experiences of seeing or touching a snake and then telling about any books, movies, or other experiences about the topic.) This approach appears not to be helpful because students have difficulty staying on the topic.

Metacognition. Students ought to be asked how they learn and what strategies they use to read, study, remember information, and complete assignments. If you want to know about your class in general, your questions could be carried out through group discussion. If you want to know about particular students' strategies, then individual interviews or written questionnaire responses will be needed. Here are some possible ways to ask questions about metacognition:

Stewart (1986) studied kindergarten and first grade children's metacognition with two questions: "How are you learning to read at home?" and "How are you learning to read at school?" The appropriateness and complexity of response indicates whether students understand and can think about their own learning.

Stupey and Knight (1988) asked three questions of three- to ten-year-old children. Their questions were: "What is reading?" "What is reading for?" and "What do people do when they read?" Responses were evaluated in terms of four levels of ability to represent their reading skills. The four levels are: a single idea, relating one idea to another, relating one set of ideas to another set, and describing abstract relationships. They found that older children gave higher-level answers. You could also use these questions in your class to evaluate individual differences in reading awareness.

In unpublished work, Mason and colleagues held a discussion with students at the end of kindergarten, first grade, and second grade. They asked them to talk about what next year's students would need to do to learn to read or to become better readers. After a five-minute discussion, students were given paper on which to draw or write the three ideas that they thought were the most important for next year's class. Those children who drew or used invented spellings were asked to tell what they had drawn or written so that their ideas could be recorded. Even in kindergarten, most children could describe important ideas. This approach can be done at the beginning of first and subsequent grades with the question, "What do you think your class needs to learn this year to be good readers?" Variations in response will provide helpful information about students' awareness of the process of learning to read.

Paratore and Indrisano (1987) assess children's awareness of making the transition from learning to read to reading to learn (about fourth grade). Their interview questions, which include the following, can be asked in a written form for older students:

How do you choose something to read?
How do you get ready to read?
When you come to a word you can't read, what do you do?
If the text you are reading does not make sense, what do you do?
When you have a question you can't answer, what do you do?
What do you do to help remember what you've read?

How do you check your reading?
If a young child asked you how to read, what would you tell him/her
to do?

Formal Assessment

Norm-referenced, standardized tests are intended to show whether students
have learned what others in the same grade typically have learned. That is,
they assess students' performance in relation to the performance of a large,
representative group of students. The scores represent overall achievement
rather than a particular ability. In some schools the tests are given every year,
while in others they are used for gatekeeping or sorting purposes, typically in
the first, fourth, and seventh grades. Scores are likely to be in every child's
cumulative folder to mark progress through school.

Typically, norm-referenced reading tests contain subtests of decoding,
comprehension, and vocabulary to measure the *relative success* of the student in these areas. You can examine and compare reading achievement of
your students with students the test makers have determined are typical. You
can use them at the beginning of the school year to learn which students are
below the norms for that grade and are likely to need a more concentrated
reading program, and which are above and will benefit from an accelerated
program. You may also use the test scores to group students for reading. However, you cannot use them for diagnosis of individual students.

How Norm-Referenced Tests Are Scored and Reported.   All items on the
test are scored as either right or wrong. The total number that a student gets
right is called a raw score. By itself, the raw score means little. Instead, interpretation is based on one of several kinds of "derived scores." The derived
score indicates how a child's performance compares with the performance of
the norm group. Typically, comparisons are made in terms of percentile ranks,
stanines, and grade equivalents. Baumann and Stevenson (1982) present a complete description of each. Here is a brief explanation:

A *percentile rank* describes the likely rank of a student's score in terms of
the percent of the total. A rank of 1 percent is given to students who score the
lowest, while a rank of 50 percent is given to students in the middle. To calcu-
late a child's percentile rank within your class:

1. Determine the number of children who got lower scores;
2. Divide by the total number of children in the group;
3. Multiply by 100.

To determine children's percentile ranks in comparison to national norms,
refer to the tables provided by the test maker. Merely read across the table
from the raw score to the normed percentile equivalent.

Another derived score on a norm-referenced test is the *stanine*. A stanine is a number from one through nine, where one represents the poorest performance, five is average, and nine is the best. Stanines are derived from a normal, bell-shaped curve of scores that clusters many scores in the middle region and very few at the extreme. While each stanine includes a range of percentile ranks, more ranks are represented by the middle stanines than by the extreme stanines. Stanines and percentiles are related as follows:

Stanine	Percentile
9	96–99
8	89–95
7	77–88
6	60–76
5	40–59
4	23–39
3	11–22
2	4–10
1	0– 3

Stanines are useful because they show each child's score in terms of deviations from the normed average, or the population mean. Read from the test maker's table the conversion of a raw score to a stanine. You can interpret a stanine of 4, 5, or 6 as representing a fairly typical score, a stanine of 3 as borderline, and a stanine of 2 as a low score. A stanine of 7 represents an above average score and 8 is a high score. A score in stanine 1 is exceptionally low, while a score in stanine 9 is exceptionally high.

A *grade equivalent score* compares the performance of a child to the average performance of groups of children in the different grades. The number expresses level of reading achievement in grades and tenths of grades. For example, a score of 3.9 is supposed to mean the score that would be earned by the average third grader at the end of the school year.

We do not recommend relying on grade equivalent scores because they do not have adequate statistical properties either for making comparisons among children or decisions about instruction. For example, a third grader who obtains a grade equivalent score of 6.5 on a reading test is not necessarily reading at the sixth grade level. Likewise, a third grader who tests at grade 1.5 may not need a first grade book. A small change in the raw score of either of these children can mean an alarming advance or decline in the supposed grade level.

Instead of using grade equivalent scores to evaluate children and your instruction, learn to use stanines or percentiles. To do this, study the raw and derived scores of your average students. Get a sense of whether the middle-of-the-roaders are indeed performing at the 40–60th percentile, at a stanine of 4 to 6. Having established a sense of the middle group, look at the groups at either end. If a child seems misplaced, go back to the cumulative record and study earlier test information to see if there has been a change in relative performance. That is, do not assume that one test score yields a complete picture or a final judgment of a child's performance.

While a particular test score is not useful instructionally, the stanines or percentiles from several tests or subtests from one test can be placed together to study a child's performance in various dimensions of reading. If a child does very well on a particular test relative to his or her own average on the other tests, this may indicate a special strength. Similarly, a score much lower than the child's average may suggest an area of weakness. However, remember that all tests contain a margin of error. Don't make too much of small fluctuations from one test to another. Test makers always list the margin of error. (This is called the standard error.) Or you could use the rule of thumb that a difference of two stanines might be important while one less than that might just show a temporary fluctuation.

Approaching Test-Taking

Children do not necessarily know how to take tests. That is, test scores may be depressed because students lack test-taking skills, and their scores will not be accurate indicators of their reading ability. It may be helpful, then, to teach students how to take a test and give them opportunities to practice the test format. Stewart and Green (1983) describe several ways to prepare children for test-taking:

1. Teach children how to take tests well before the formal testing date. Explain to them why tests are given, why there are special rules for test-taking, and how tests are made and scored.
2. Find practice materials that match the format of the test. Explain to children how to answer the type of question in order to make the best use of their time. Younger children need practice in how to mark correct items. If they use a separate answer sheet, they need advice about how to keep track of the items on the score sheet. Older children taking a reading comprehension cloze test should know to scan a whole paragraph before trying to fill in most of the items. On a multiple-choice comprehension test, they should read the questions before reading the text and look for the answers in the text. If they can't find the answer they should read the alternatives and use a process of elimination to make a best-guess response.
3. During test-practice sessions, set up a test-taking atmosphere. Separate children's desks, establish quiet, have them all turn the test over at the same time, and make them aware of the time limitations.
4. At first, give additional time to children who cannot complete the task within the specified limit. Gradually decrease the allotted time.
5. Children need to develop a serious attitude toward test-taking. You may need to give advice to individuals about their performance. For example, discuss with slow test-takers how they can move through items in the

Test-taking time re-
quires the full con-
centration of the teacher
as well as of the stu-
dents. Here the teacher
checks to make sure a
student has completed
all of the items.

test more efficiently. Convince children who go too fast and miss many items that they need to work more carefully. Help anxious children realize that they really do know much of the information and will do better when they relax. Impress upon all the children that they should try to be accurate and to complete as many items as possible.

Key Concept 2

Classroom assessment during the school year utilizes portfolios for monitoring and recording students' progress.

▌ DEVELOPING ONGOING MEASURES
▌ OF STUDENT PROGRESS

There are a large range of possible ways to assess students during the school year. Shanahan (1987) points out, for example, that you will need new assessments of reading comprehension when you require students to read longer passages, when you want answers that are based on constructive notions of comprehension, and when you need students to describe or demonstrate their ability to use reading strategies. You will also need different assessment instruments for word identification. Regarding word identification, Clay (1985) recommends that oral rereading of new texts be used to determine the extent to which students are using more than one strategy and text cue system.

Unfortunately, assessment approaches of this nature are not coordinated, and, without a general overview of students' ability and progress, you could easily miss important characteristics. Valencia, Pearson, and McGinley (in press) suggest that teachers develop a repertoire of assessment characteristics so that they can construct *portfolios of students' work*. Portfolios are simply folders in which you and your students place a range of examples of formal and informal test results and accomplishments which you can use to plan and evaluate your teaching and students' progress.

What you might collect and use to prepare assessment instruments can be thought of in terms balancing five characteristics. The authors recommend that each characteristic be placed on a continuum, that is, spread out on a scale. Figure 9.1 shows a summary of the five characteristics.

Wide variations exist in the *structure* of assessment instruments. An instrument is more or less structured depending on the extent to which there are directions for taking the test, predetermined questions, correct responses, and whether there are time limits and norms. Standardized tests are structured. A semi-structured assessment could be samples that students choose of their best writing which the teacher evaluates using a holistic scoring system. An unplanned question/answer interaction with students after a text was read could be a spontaneous assessment by recording the quality of their questions or responses.

Independent of structure is the issue of who *controls* the assessment, the teacher, the student, or both together. At one end of the scale, students evaluate themselves, and at the other, teachers control the assessment, though occasionally teachers and students negotiate or work out an assessment in a collaborative fashion.

Assessment can be recorded through several *modes*. The most durable, as well as the most common, are paper-and-pencil written test responses. They are easy to collect and they provide clear evidence of student skill and knowledge. Interviews and observations, however, can be equally important. An

Figure 9.1
Characteristics of Assessment

Assessment Characteristic	Level of Teacher Control		
	High	Medium	Low
Structure	structured	semi-structured	spontaneous
Locus of control	teacher	collaborative	student
Mode	written samples	interviews	observations
Focus	detailed information	holistic	general
Intrusiveness	intrusive		unintrusive

interview can be one initiated by the teacher or student, and it can be structured or spontaneous, written out or tape recorded as an oral interview. Observations also vary in locus of control and the extent of structure. At a spontaneous level, a teacher might keep a notepad and jot down notes about students during work time or at other occasions. Structured observations are also possible to use, such as ones in which particular behaviors are looked for and checked off or counted.

The *focus* of an assessment instrument describes its detail. A narrowly defined construct could be the number of punctuation or spelling errors in a writing piece. At a middle level of the continuum are holistic scoring systems, such as those used to evaluate a written report in which the organization and relatedness of the piece might be judged. At the other end the focus of the assessment might be simply on how well a set of responses, a speech, a written story, or some other product serves the function for which it was intended.

Assessment instruments vary also in their *intrusiveness*. Those most intrusive are usually more structured, with more durable samples of work. Measures that are not intrusive are likely to be spontaneous interactions that use shared control or collaboration, and they are often based on unplanned observations. Less intrusive measures allow teachers to collect information about students in their own working environment as well as in recess, before or after school, and during unstructured periods.

The authors give examples, in scenario form, to show how a teacher can think of assessment using these five characteristics. We have adapted two of their examples for you.

1. A fifth-grade teacher wants to help students improve their self-monitoring of comprehension, especially when they read long pieces of literature. As they read a chapter, he has them record and mark trouble spots with "Post-its." After the group discusses the chapter, he holds individual conferences. He listens to a student summarize the chapter, and if there were comprehension problems, they review the notes on the Post-its, discussing the trouble spots and strategies for coping with the difficulties. The teacher jots down some notes about the session, perhaps adding the student's notes for a record in the portfolio. The assessment is rated as semi-structured and collaborative. The mode is a written sample; the focus is holistic; and the approach is somewhat intrusive.

2. A middle school teacher studied the students' science book and selected a topic to be covered in one month that she thought would be ideal for teaching report-writing. Students were required to select a subtopic of personal interest that was related to the topic, state a hypothesis, gather information from three sources, and develop a report that would be shared with classmates and turned in to the teacher. Earlier, students had learned to use different resources to gather their information and to select and narrow their topics of study. During the month she worked with students individually and in groups on synthesizing information for the reports. Students with common topics also formed groups for sharing and providing feedback

to one another about their reports. The final reports were presented to the class orally and handed in to the teacher for grading.

The second example shows that several kinds of assessment were carried out during the month. The teacher used a checklist to observe the strategies students were using for getting started and revising their reports. This was a semi-structured, teacher-controlled, holistic, unintrusive observation system. During the month the teacher had students make notes twice weekly in their learning logs about new learning, and their experiences, insights, and problems as they worked. The logs were shared with the teacher when students wanted feedback. The assessment samples were spontaneous, unintrusive, holistic, and controlled by the students. The final report, a written sample, was evaluated in two ways: with structured measures controlled by the teacher which contained detailed and holistic measures; and with a student-controlled, structured, self-evaluation questionnaire.

These examples indicate how you can keep the five characteristics in mind, blend formal with informal assessment, include students in the evaluation procedure, and provide them with opportunities to demonstrate varying talents and strengths. You can develop assessment instruments both to evaluate students' progress and to adapt and improve your instruction.

▌ ONGOING OR DURING-THE-YEAR ASSESSMENT

Reading Assessment

You can extend your understanding of students' thinking by assessing the process of learning, not merely final performance. According to Wood (1988), a dynamic assessment approach, based on work by Feurestein, Rand, and Hoffman (1979), is most appropriate. To evaluate the process of learning, you should assess students while teaching them, encourage interaction with students as part of the assessment, and look for broader demonstration of capabilities. Relying on the terminology we presented from Valencia, Pearson, and McGinley (in press), you will turn to semi-structured and spontaneous instruments, collaborate with students, make extensive use of interviews and observation, and focus on holistic and functional measures.

Wood (1988) recommends that you extend one-to-one assessment by evaluating the students during their reading group lesson. In Figure 9.2 she gives an overview of how well students comprehend a story and what the teacher might do to help them. This kind of record could be repeated at regular intervals, copied, and placed in each student's portfolio.

Criterion-Referenced Tests

Criterion-referenced tests are narrowly focused on particular skills and topics. They are intended to measure the extent to which students have mastered that information. This is done by comparing the number of items answered

■ Figure 9.2
■ Group Comprehension Matrix

Story *The Mandarin and the Magician*   Date *October 14th*

Genre: Narrative (realistic, fantasy)   Grade *4th*
        Poetry
        Plays
        Exposition

* New student—Oct. 1st

	Kelly	Ryan*	Tonya	Marti	Jason	David	Teresa
Makes predictions about story	S	+	—	S	—	+	—
Participates in the discussion	S	+	S	S	—	+	S
Answers questions on all levels	—	+	S	S	S	+	S
Determines word meanings through context	—	+	—	—	—	S	—
Reads smoothly and fluently	+	+	+	S	—	+	S
Can retell selection using own words	S	+	+	S	S	S	—
Comprehends after silent reading	N	N	N	N	N	N.	N
Can read "between the lines"	—	S	S	—	—	S	—
Possesses broad background knowledge	S	S	—	—	—	S	—

Comments: *The students had much difficulty comprehending the story until I provided much more background informa-tion. Their predictions were not as accurate and abundant as usual—largely due to their lack of knowledge of Chinese dynasties. Jason remains very quiet unless asked specific questions. He is much more responsive one-to-one. While his recall is good, his oral reading is very choppy. Teresa is always willing to volunteer any answers although her recall is on the literal level. Ryan may need to move up another level—will test individually.*

Often	+		Words to review:
Sometimes	S		*dynasty*
Seldom	—		*Mandarin*
Not observed	N		*queue*

Source: Figures 9.2 and 9.6 from "Techniques for assessing students' potential for learning" by Karen Wood, *The Reading Teacher,* January 1988, pp. 443 and 444. Copyright © 1988 International Reading Association, Inc. Reprinted with permission of Karen D. Wood and the International Reading Association.

correctly with some absolute standard, usually the curriculum published with the test.

Criterion-referenced tests typically measure what children are taught from particular programs and curriculum packages. They appear, for example, as end-of-level tests in basal reading programs. They are intended to check children's competence on the particular skills taught during the school year and to estimate whether students are ready to proceed to the next reading unit or reading level. There are also criterion-referenced reading testing programs that can be purchased for more general use. An example of a page from a more general comprehension test appears in Figure 9.3. However, tests such as this do not necessarily measure what the students were taught, since teachers do not necessarily teach all the tested concepts.

Figure 9.3
Example of a Criterion-Referenced
Test Page

Reading Comprehension | 28

Andy is just two years old. He likes to go to the store with his father. Andy likes to sit in the shopping cart. He can see bright cans, fruit, and cookies.
Sometimes Andy takes cans out of the cart. He drops them on the floor. Then Andy laughs. But his father does not laugh. Guess who has to pick up the cans?

5. Where does Andy go with his father?

   O To the park
   O Up to his room
   O To the sandbox
   O To the store

6. Where does Andy sit?

   O With his father
   O In the cart
   O On the floor
   O On a chair

7. Who drops things?

   O Andy's father
   O The cart
   O Andy
   O Cookies

8. This story is about

   O cookies.
   O shopping.
   O carts.
   O Andy's father.

Criterion-referenced tests are developed by defining first a set of concepts or skills that form the backbone of the subject being taught. Reading is organized into skills that are listed in the *scope and sequence* chart of published reading programs (this is discussed in Chapter 10). The general construct for the approach is found in Bloom's taxonomy (1956). It is assumed that children should understand and master certain skills and that the skills are ordered from easy to difficult. For example, Bloom's taxonomy describes *recognition* of information as an easier skill than *analysis* or *synthesis* of information. It is also assumed that once the skills are mastered, children can use them both with the materials they used for learning and with new materials. For example, if children learned to recognize the sequence of events in the *Three Billy-Goats Gruff* story, they would also recognize the sequence of events in other stories. Based on these assumptions, a set of test questions is developed to measure children's mastery of the skills.

Administering commercial criterion-referenced tests.   If you want to use a criterion-referenced test you should administer it directly after teaching the instructional unit. You may give it individually or to groups. In either case, seat children so they can work independently, and give them enough time to complete all items. If children get tired, testing may be stopped at the end of a subtest and continued another day.

If test directions are in the children's test booklet, you can give them a copy of the test and, after they have read the directions, let them proceed at their own pace until the test is completed. If children ask for clarification about a test item, you may help them understand the questions, but do not give the answer, and then note that aid was given to the child. With teacher-administered tests, the directions are read to the children by the teacher. If children do not understand the directions, you may reinterpret them. Again, children are allowed to work at their own pace because these tests usually measure knowledge of the topic or skill rather than speed of response.

How criterion-referenced tests are scored and reported.   Scoring is done by marking answers as right or wrong, though if an unclear answer is given, you may question the child and give partial credit. Interpretation depends on the approach used by the test maker. Typically, tests in basal readers use a score of 80 percent or above as a passing score. A score of 80 percent or higher indicates that the children have mastered most of the information and are ready for the next unit in the textbook. A low score could mean that the children did not understand the lesson and need to have the lesson retaught. However, it simply could mean that they needed more practice examples, or that they understood the lesson but not the test-taking procedure. Discussing the task with the children should help you determine whether to give instruction, practice on the skills, or coaching on the procedure.

Finding out that children did not learn the material means that you need to study the instructional situation. Was the failure the result of poor classroom instruction? Perhaps children needed a more complete explanation or more guided practice. Were the children not ready for the instruction in the first place? Perhaps you needed to present background information or a clearer introduction to the unit. Use the assessment results to evaluate your teaching as well as students' progress. Then, place students' scores and your reactions in their portfolios.

Student Record-Keeping

Cumulative records of particular skills can be kept by the students themselves, a suggestion made as long ago as 1926 by Nila Banton Smith. Here is her approach for testing and keeping track of reading comprehension accuracy and reading rate:

> In giving the tests (at regular, two-week intervals), the teacher selects some portion of a story in a reader and explains to the children why they are to read it. She should take care to have the selections for all the tests of as nearly the same degree of difficulty as is possible. At a given signal the pupils open their books and read silently for a specified time, at the end of which they are given a signal to stop. They close their books, number their papers from one to ten, and write "yes" or "no" in response to the questions which the teacher asks on the content of their reading. . . . In taking a speed test, the pupil finds the designated place, puts his finger in his reader at this place, and then closes the book. At a given signal each one opens his book and reads for one minute silently, when the teacher gives the signal to stop by saying "Mark." He then places a dot after the last word read and counts the total number of words covered during the entire minute. (pp. 95–96)

Smith suggests that graphs be constructed for comprehension accuracy and for reading speed. For comprehension accuracy, list the scores from 0 to 10 on the left margin, placing 0 at the bottom of the graph, as shown in Figure 9.4. The child's name would be on the top and the testing dates along the top or bottom margin. After the test is scored, children fill in the square marking the score they received or make a bar graph by filling in the squares from 0 to the score they received. A reading speed graph lists words per minute on the left margin, beginning at the bottom with 40 and, counting by 20's, going to 240. The top and bottom margins would be identical to the reading accuracy graph. Graphing could be done in the same way or as a series of dots connecting one score to the text (see Figure 9.5).

While there are better ways of testing comprehension than the yes-no test suggested by Smith, we think the general approach for keeping track of children's progress is sound. You would be testing children on what they are learning, frequent records would be kept, even young children would be able to do the record-keeping, and you would have an easy way for children to monitor their own progress. These records would be kept by children but eventually added to their portfolios.

Figure 9.4
Cumulative Record of Comprehension
Accuracy

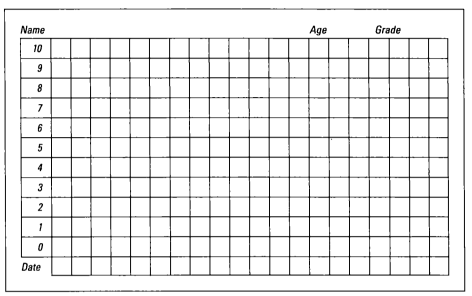

Figure 9.5
Cumulative Record of Reading Speed

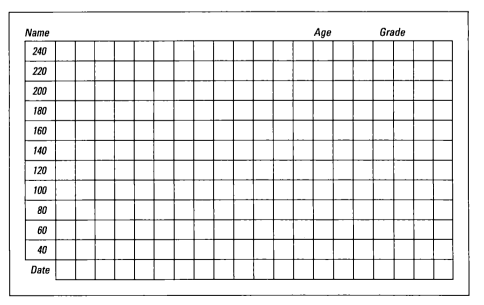

Constructing a Criterion-Referenced Comprehension Test

Johnston and Pearson (1982) recommend that you construct criterion-referenced tests to measure reading comprehension because your own tests can be more closely matched to your instruction. There are three steps to the test construction.

Decide how to measure comprehension. The first step is to decide *what* you want to measure. Here are four possibilities:

1. Measure children's *prior knowledge of the subject* before you teach it. For example, before having children read an expository selection, you can have them try writing out answers to a set of questions about the text. After they have read the selection, have them write the answers again and compare their two sets of answers.
2. Measure children's *ability to comprehend different text structures.* Find two texts about the same topic that are written in quite different ways. For example, you could find differently organized selections about the desert in two social studies textbooks. One might be written as a narrative and the other as a descriptive passage. Construct questions that focus on the information found in both texts. Have students read one, discuss answers to the questions, then read the other and discuss the answers again as a way to measure their ability to find information in different kinds of texts.
3. Measure children's *reasoning and critical thinking* as they read. You might have children explain information from the text, have them evaluate text information, or ask them to justify their answers. For example, you could have children explain or justify how they determined the most important idea in a paragraph. You would learn whether they can go beyond selecting answers, such as explaining how they chose important information.
4. Measure children's *ability to read text information quickly and remember it accurately.* For example, you could have children read a text and answer questions in a fixed period of time. You would evaluate separately their reading speed and accuracy in order to help them realize that both are important and may be practiced by using different reading strategies.

Decide how to set up test items. The second step to constructing a comprehension test is to decide *how* to ask your questions. Refer back to the suggestions we made earlier, since the same question-structuring principles apply.

Trying out the test. The third step is to *choose materials and try out* the test. Suppose you want to measure children's ability to reason and think as they read. One appropriate testing approach is to use teacher-structured short answer questions. You might ask children to complete the statement, "This paragraph is mainly about _____," followed by a request for a justification of their answer which requires detailed information from written samples. Materials for this test may be drawn from familiar content area textbook material that children are using or have completed. Alternatively, the same questions could be used in classroom discussions, and you could observe their willingness to participate and the clarity and appropriateness of their oral responses. Now you may refer back to Figure 9.1 (p. 363) to construct some other approaches.

Key Concept 3

Classroom assessment can take the form of focused assessment of individual children.

DEVELOPING FINELY TUNED MEASURES OF INDIVIDUAL STUDENTS

There is not sufficient time in your school day to make a detailed assessment of each student. However, there will be a few students in your class about whom you are puzzled. They are not responding to your instruction or do not seem to be making adequate progress. You will want further information about such students. As Chall and Curtis (1987) note, there needs to be determination of, first, "the levels and strengths and weaknesses of reading and related language and cognitive abilities, and second, determination of the most effective instructional procedures for overcoming the difficulty" (p. 785).

They recommend that students' strengths and needs be assessed in eight areas: word recognition, word analysis, spelling, oral reading, reading rate, word meaning, comprehension, and written composition. Then, in trial lessons, teachers try out different methods of instruction and materials. Teachers rely on the test results and trial lessons to design a remedial plan for teaching throughout the semester. The plan is detailed in four ways: the components to teach, teaching activities, materials, and levels of difficulty of materials.

This approach can be adapted for classroom teachers by constructing profiles of students' ability. Chall and Curtis (1987) suggest that, along with the most recent achievement test and the level of the basal reader, the teacher add three reading components:

(a) Accuracy and rate of word recognition and analysis (from oral reading of connected text, spelling, etc.)

(b) Vocabulary, background knowledge, schemata; estimated from the kind of reading students do, the way they define words, their free associations to words and ideas, their ability to use context, etc.

(c) Comprehension: estimated from classwork—recall of what is read, identifying important ideas, facility with comprehension tasks in workbooks, comprehension of textbooks in social studies and science, results on cloze tasks (p. 787).

These three components can be developed for individual assessment of students by using more or less structured instruments that vary in locus of control, mode, focus, and intrusiveness.

Examples of Individual Assessment

Reading comprehension. Wood (1988) offers a way to organize important comprehension information on an individual profile card (Figure 9.6). Her approach is a structured observation with holistic scoring that is controlled by the teacher but is not intrusive. Wood makes a point of allowing the child to be evaluated after both oral and silent reading, with varying text genres and levels of text difficulty, different recall procedures, and varying degrees of collaboration. These allow the teacher to determine how a student works and learns best by systematically varying the more important reading comprehension variables.

For poor readers and younger students, Wood's profile can be extended to include assessment of word identification. Again, the instrument would involve structured observations and holistic scoring. The assessment. compo-

Figure 9.6
Individual Comprehension Profile

Name   _Eric Matthews_   Date   _September 3_   Grade   _3_

	Reading type		Genre					Recall mode			Degree of guidance			Overall compr.	Comments
	Oral	Silent	Poetry	Plays	Realistic fiction	Fantasy	Nonfiction	Free recall	Probed recall	Infer, predict	Background knowl.	Preteaching vocab.	Assist during rdg.	1 = none 2 = some 3 = most 4 = all	
Level 2_2 p. 41	✓				✓			✓	✓		–	–	–	3	_A little choppy at first, then very fluent with accurate recall_
Level 2_2 p. 76	✓			✓				✓	✓	✓	–	–	–	4	_Very fluent reading and retelling_
Level 2_2 p. 168		✓					✓	✓	✓	✓	–	–	–	4	_Needs no assistance—has control over word recognition and comprehension_
Level 3_1 p. 101	✓				✓			✓	✓		–	–	–	2	_Some fluency problems & sketchy recall (e.g., misread "trail" for "trial," "beautiful" for "body")_
Level 3_1 p. 96	✓					✓		✓	✓	✓	✓	✓		3	_With help, recall is improved; can predict and infer (e.g., Why do you think . . .)_
Level 3_1 p. 66		✓					✓	✓	✓		✓	✓	✓	4	_Had difficulty recognizing "ambulance"–"emergency." Defined "Red Cross" & "swerved." This helped!_
Level 3_1 p. 119		✓					✓	✓	✓	✓	✓	✓		4	_Tried with and without guidance. Comprehension is improved with help._

Overall assessment: _Eric's comprehension while reading silently seems better than while reading orally. Can retell in own words at level 3, but gives more detail when probed or prompted. With assistance, seems to benefit from instruction in this material._

Appropriate placement level 3_1

nents are drawn from those devised by Clay (1985), some of which were presented in Chapter 7. Word identification accuracy, reading fluency, and self-monitoring are added to the profile.

Word identification accuracy uses the rule of thumb of three levels of reading: (3) easy (95–100% of words accurately read or self-corrected); (2) instructional (90–94% of words accurately read or self-corrected); and (1) hard (less than 90% of words accurately read or self-corrected). Reading fluency can also be gauged with three levels: (3) expressive and smooth; (2) some expression and some hesitation or rereading that is choppy; (1) word-by-word reading, voice, or finger pointing. Self-monitoring of word identification can be assessed with three levels: (3) rereads and self-corrects half or more of errors using picture, printed word, and text cues; (2) rereads or self-corrects occasionally or fewer than one in four errors and uses only one or two cue sources; (1) seldom rereads or self-corrects and uses only picture or printed word cues or appeals for help. The revised profile card requires oral reading, as shown in Figure 9.7.

Informal Reading Inventories

An informal reading inventory (IRI) has for many years been a popular approach for measuring children's reading ability (Betts, 1960). It may provide information about children's word reading, their reading fluency, how they try to correct their errors, and what they comprehend. An IRI can give you a more holistic or integrated account of reading problems and help you judge reading progress. You can use IRI results to decide on the appropriate reading group placement of children who join the class part way into the school year. Some teachers use IRI's to help select appropriate independent reading materials for children. They are an invaluable instrument for understanding individual children's reading problems.

Setting up an IRI. Choose sections of texts of at least 100 words long that begin a chapter, story, or text section. The materials need to vary in difficulty from below, at, and above the average reading level for the grade you teach. Make two copies of each page. Next, construct five to ten post-reading comprehension questions for each selection. Be sure the questions assess a range of information. Betts (1960) recommends questions on:

Recall of facts
Association of an appropriate meaning with a term
Identifying a sequence of events
Drawing conclusions
Applying information

Another approach is to ask the child, "What do you remember about this selection? . . . What else do you remember? . . . Anything else?"

Arrange a 20 to 30 minute time limit for administering the inventory to each child, perhaps using an aide to give it or to monitor the class while you

Figure 9.7
Revised Individual Reading Profile

Name _____   Date _____   Grade _____

Text Level	Genre					Word Identification			Recall Mode			Degree of Guidance				Comments
	Poetry	Plays	Realistic fiction	Fantasy	Nonfiction	Accuracy	Fluency	Self-monitor	Free recall	Probed recall	Infer/predict	Bkg. knowledge	Pret. Vocabulary	Assist read	Overall comp.	

Overall assessment:

give it. Hand the child the text, beginning with the easiest selection, and allow the child to scan or read it silently before reading aloud. When the child reads aloud, use your copy of the selection to mark reading miscues. Here are some types of errors and the way you can mark them:

Omission—circle words that are left out.
Substitution—add substituted words above the misread words.
Insertion—mark a caret for the extra words.
Repetition—place a wavy line beneath repeated words.
Unknown word—place a circled *p* over words that the examiner must pronounce for the child.

Figure 9.8 shows a sample passage with the child's oral reading errors marked and scored.

Scoring and interpretation of an IRI. To score word reading errors, count the number of mistakes that the child made, ignoring repetitions. Then count the number of words in the text. To score comprehension from questions that were asked, count the number of questions answered correctly. To score free

▌ **Figure 9.8**
▌ **Example of Oral Reading Miscues**
▌ **and Scoring**

<u>Text</u> ℗	<u>Error</u>	<u>Score</u>
A cat sat in his boat.	(unknown word)	1/6
The wind blew _∧ it the boat.	(insertion)	1/5
The boat tipped over.	(repetition)	0/4
The cat fell (in the water.)	(omission)	1/6
The cat was mad wet.	(substitution)	1/4

Total words   25   Total errors   4/25

Total correct   21/25

Percent correct   84%

recalls, make up a 0–10 point scale to indicate how complete the retelling was. You could, for example, give two points each for description of story beginning, story characters, problem, attempted solution, and ending.

The next step is to transform each score into a percentage of the total. The accuracy percentile is the number of words read correctly divided by the total number in the text. The comprehension percentile is the number of correct responses divided by the total possible score (usually 10). Then you may interpret the scores. You can use the percentage of words read accurately and the percentage of information remembered to determine whether a text is at the appropriate level of difficulty for reading.

A text is thought to be at the right level for instruction if a child reads 85 to 95 percent of the words correctly and answers at least 80 percent of the questions. It is thought to be appropriate for independent reading if the child can read 95 percent or more of the words correctly. Scores below 80–85 percent are thought to be at the frustration level, indicating that the passage is far too difficult for the child.

Judging the pattern of word recognition errors is another way to use IRI results. You could look at the pattern of omissions, substitutions, and insertions and the types of words misread to judge how a child is trying to read, or refer to Chapter 6, Clay (1985), or Silvaroli (1973) for more detailed suggestions. You could also apply IRI constructs in unstructured situations, such as observations of students reading to one another.

Key Concept 4

Assessment should be integrated into the curriculum.

▌ INTEGRATING ASSESSMENT WITH INSTRUCTION

The *teaching-learning cycle* is a sequence of steps that allows you to use assessment information to improve reading instruction. It is not the only set of procedures you could use to integrate assessment with instruction, but it is a straightforward and practical one. It synthesizes ideas from the detailed instructional approaches we have recommended in the earlier chapters of this book with the suggestions made in this chapter for using formal and informal tests, observations, and interviews.

Step 1: Assessing Students' Needs Before Teaching an Instructional Unit

Effective teachers want to have some idea of what their students already know and can do based on goals from the strands (sets of related skills) listed in the scope and sequence chart of the commercial reading program or in the district's curriculum. You can compare those goals with information about students' knowledge and interests that are in their portfolios. The purpose is to find out which goals or objectives individual students already seem to have met, and which they appear ready to learn next.

You may also need to measure their specific knowledge of the planned set of lessons. While you won't have the time and resources to conduct extensive testing, there are some straightforward and reasonable possibilities. Refer back to the suggestions made in the first key concept of this chapter about measuring background knowledge (p. 354). If you are using a basal series, there may be criterion-referenced tests matched to the strands in its scope and sequence chart, and these tests may be administered to the whole class at once or to smaller groups of children. This pretest assessment gives an idea about how much children know about the topic and helps you decide whether it needs to be taught, and if so, how much work it will be to teach it.

Your skill as an *observer*, rather than as an interpreter of test scores, is most valuable in establishing a system of useful, ongoing assessment within the classroom. Listen carefully to students' responses during the instruction of a reading lesson to determine their level of understanding. For further information about their capabilities, carefully examine their first completed assignments. At times you may want to interact with students while they are completing seatwork assignments, to get an idea of the problem-solving strategies they're using or need to learn. In other words, every contact with the students, in person or through their work, can provide you with information about their needs in learning to read.

You won't want to omit this initial step, even if you are just doing some kind of informal checking. Obviously, an effective classroom reading program cannot be developed on the basis of sheer guesswork. This step allows you to gather information about your students in order to make informed rather than haphazard instructional decisions.

To illustrate the idea of assessing needs before teaching, let's suppose that you were working with a fifth grade class. You were particularly concerned

Assessment is fully integrated with instruction in this classroom setting. By carefully observing this child while she reads and writes, the teacher is able to monitor progress and make informed instructional decisions.

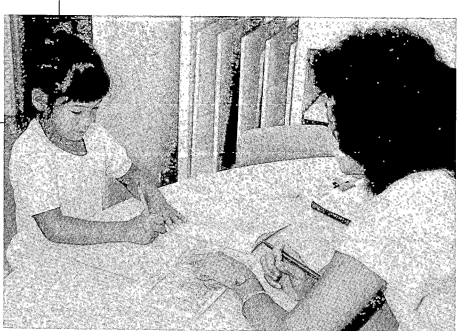

about the long-term development of their reading comprehension abilities, and your major goals were mostly in that area. You suspected that your middle and low ability reading groups needed to work on learning to summarize what they had read. You checked this by noticing their reluctance to respond and tendency to give vague or poorly worded story summaries during small group, teacher-led discussions. When looking at their first completed seatwork on that topic, you also noted that they were unable to locate or write down the main idea on their own.

Step 2: Setting Immediate Goals for Instruction

Next, set immediate goals for instruction, or specific objectives for student learning. On the basis of your assessment, formal or informal, which you have in your portfolios, you determine where the students are along the strands you have decided to emphasize. Once students are "placed" on the strands, you have some idea of the immediate goals to help them reach. The reason for being as accurate as possible in setting realistic immediate goals for students' learning is to use your time and theirs to the best advantage.

Seek to meet these goals through a combination of activities. Instruction may be through teacher-led activities (see Step 3 below), through assignments pursued by small groups of students working with indirect teacher supervision, or through independent seatwork assignments (these last two are part of Step 4).

In our example, suppose you had set as an immediate goal for your middle group to develop an understanding of how to summarize paragraphs from expository prose passages, using already covered chapters from the social studies textbook. Because the concept of summarizing is such a difficult one, you would not use unfamiliar materials. Also, you would not ask them to summarize whole passages because you wanted them to understand the approach first with short pieces of text. You intended to teach them how to summarize by modeling the approach yourself and then giving them opportunities to "be the teacher" and try out the approach, getting corrective feedback from you and then from other students in the group. For independent practice seatwork, you decided to have them write summaries from paragraphs in easy, second grade expository texts.

Step 3: Providing Instruction to Meet Goals

In Step 3 the focus is primarily on giving teacher-directed lessons which are "on target" or at the students' *instructional* level. This is the level of difficulty at which students are challenged but at the same time, with the teacher's assistance, are able to acquire new skills and knowledge. Because students within a class of 25 or more will generally have very different needs in learning to read, you may regroup them for particular reading topics. These groups should be more similar in instructional level, and so Step 3 lessons are often given to eight to ten students, rather than to the class as a whole.

In our example, you began by having a general discussion of what a summary is, why it might be important to construct one, and how you are going to help them do it, following the ideas regarding lesson scaffolding in Chapter 4 of this textbook. You gave them the first paragraph in the social studies text, asked them to read it to themselves, and then modeled how you would summarize the paragraph. You invited students to comment on your summary. Next, you called on a student to "be the teacher," having everyone read the next paragraph and then seeing if the student teacher could come up with a summary. You carried this basic plan on in several lessons or until the students were able to use the same kind of thinking without corrective feedback from you. Then you made notes for some students' portfolios about their reactions to the lessons or their movement toward independence.

Step 4: Providing Opportunities for Student Practice and Discovery

In Step 4 the focus is on lessons and assignments which are easier or "below target." Having introduced the new process or information in Step 3, students are to practice and apply the concept or skill in a slightly different way. Opportunities for discovery would involve assignments requiring them to use their skills and background knowledge to gain new understandings on their own. These lessons and assignments are said to be at the students' *independent* rather than instructional level. More often than not, Step 4 involves seatwork or other assignments the children are to complete largely on their own, with little or no assistance from the teacher. Some samples of students' work are added to the portfolios, perhaps the best examples picked by students themselves.

Neither in Step 3 nor Step 4 does the teacher give lessons or assignments at the students' *frustration* level, or so far "above target" as to be of practically no benefit at all. In preparation for meeting future goals, it's sometimes wise in Step 3 to introduce students to skills and knowledge they aren't yet able to master or grasp completely. But a lot of time can be wasted if students are faced with teacher-directed lessons on material much too difficult for them or left to struggle on their own with frustration level seatwork assignments.

In our example, you followed your plan of having the children work with short, easy text materials. When they could summarize them, you had them try to summarize more difficult and longer materials. You expected that they should eventually be able to write down the main ideas of text from current lessons.

Step 5: Checking on Student Progress

Check often to see if the children are progressing in a satisfactory way toward meeting both the narrowly defined goals and the broader goals of learning to read. Observe them when working on seatwork assignments or participating in group lessons, look at writing samples, and, if available, administer criterion-referenced tests. This process, much like that described in Step 1, now determines if the students are ready to move ahead to face new goals. Again, in practice, your observations and judgment are generally the deciding factors. But test results can provide converging evidence about what the children have learned. Both kinds of evidence may be included in portfolios.

In our example, you found on the first day that the children had to struggle quite a bit. Their responses during the lessons improved, but several members of the group did not seem to be able to construct a summary without considerable help from others. The seatwork assignments were similarly of an uneven quality and the criterion-referenced comprehension test showed only small gains.

Going Ahead: Setting New Goals

If your check shows that students have met the immediate learning goal, new goals are set for their instruction. The students are not ready to enter a new teaching-learning cycle, focused on another goal or set of goals. Thus, having completed Step 1, the assessment step, you can pick up with Step 2 and move on through the rest of the cycle.

In our example, you might have decided after five days that you would spend more time on this immediate goal. This was because of its importance and because most of the children seemed almost, but not quite, able to apply the concept at this basic level. If all went well, you would then have moved on to another goal, perhaps targeting vocabulary development related to science lessons. The children had begun the study of growing plants, so it looked like a good time to relate the important concepts to the new terms. The concept of summarizing texts could now be introduced with a different factual selection, thus allowing for some review as well as new learning.

Continuing to Target the Same Goals: Providing Further Instruction and Opportunities for Practice and Discovery

What you teach isn't the same as what students learn. If the goal hasn't yet been met, as shown by the evidence gathered in Step 5, provide more instruction. This means going back through Steps 3 and 4 within the same teaching-learning cycle. Several different methods are often available for teaching particular types of reading skills so that a variety of means can be employed to reach the same end. Simple repetition may also be used selectively.

In our example, you decided to work for three more days on summarizing social studies paragraphs and to continue with seatwork assignments along similar lines. In addition, you decided to have the children include in their book reports a summary of the central theme of the books they had chosen for independent reading. Children in the group were invited to share their book reports at the end of several lessons, and you pointed out how the concept of summarization could be applied to these books, as well. At the end of the three days, you repeated the criterion-referenced test using new examples. You found that the children did very well on the criterion test (85% or better) and made a moderate improvement on the other test. You and the children were now ready to move on to another comprehension topic.

∎ SUMMARY

In this chapter we provided you with a perspective about assessing instruction and children's performance. In the first section we described how views about assessment have changed. The first key concept provided an explanation of how to use assessment instruments to plan your instruction for the school year. The second suggested ways to set up assessment portfolios to monitor and record student progress during the year. The point here was to extend your knowledge about testing and assessment to those approaches that could be used during classroom lessons. The third provided information about coordinating assessment data with individual instruction. In the last key concept we explained how you might integrate information from observations and tests into classroom instruction by following the teaching-learning cycle and applying an understanding of various forms of formal and informal assessment.

∎ BIBLIOGRAPHY

References

Baumann, J. F., & Stevenson, J. A. (1982). Using standardized reading achievement test scores. *The Reading Teacher, 35,* 648–654.

Betts, E. (1960). *Handbook on corrective reading for the American Adventure Series.* New York: Row, Peterson & Company.

Bloom, B. (1956). *Taxonomy of educational objectives.* New York: David McKay Company.

Chall, J., & Curtis, M. (1987). What clinical diagnosis tells us about children's reading. *The Reading Teacher, 40,* 784–788.

Clay, M. (1985). *The early detection of reading difficulties.* Portsmouth, NH: Heinemann.

Feurestein, R., Rand, Y., & Hoffman, M. (1979). *The dynamic assessment of retarded performance.* Baltimore, MD: University Park Press.

Gardner, H. (1988). Alternatives to standardized testing: An interview with Howard Gardner. *The Harvard Educational Letter, 4,* 5–6.

Holmes, B., & Roser, N. (1987). Five ways to assess readers' prior knowledge. *The Reading Teacher, 40,* 646–649.

Johnston, P., & Pearson, P. D. (1982). Assessment: Responses to exposition. In A. Berger & H. A. Robinson (Eds.), *Secondary school reading: What research reveals for classroom practice.* Urbana, IL: ERIC Clearinghouse on Reading and Communication Skills and the National Conference on Research in English.

Paratore, J., & Indrisano, R. (1987). Intervention assessment of reading comprehension. *The Reading Teacher, 40,* 778–783.

Pearson, P. D., & Valencia, S. (1987). Assessment, accountability, and professional prerogative. In J. Readence & R. Baldwin (Eds.), *Research in literacy: Merging perspectives.* Rochester, NY: National Reading Conference.

Searly, D., & Stevenson, M. (1987). An alternative assessment program in language arts. *Language Arts, 64,* 278–284.

Shanahan, T. (1987). A survey of student literacy experiences in a large-scale state assessment. In J. Readence & R. Baldwin (Eds.), *Research in literacy: Merging perspectives.* Rochester, NY: National Reading Conference.

Silvaroli, N. (1973). *Classroom reading inventory* (2nd ed.). Dubuque, IA: Wm. C. Brown.

Smith, N. (1926). *One hundred ways of teaching silent reading for all grades.* Chicago: World Book.

Stewart, J. (1986). *A study of kindergarten children's awareness of how they are learning to read: Home and school perspectives.* Unpublished doctoral dissertation, University of Illinois.

Stewart, O., & Green, D. (1983). Test-taking skills for standardized tests of reading. *The Reading Teacher, 36,* 634–639.

Stupey, D., & Knight, C. (1988). *Concepts about reading from a developmental perspective.* Presentation at the Annual Meeting of the National Reading Conference, Tucson, Arizona.

Valencia, S., Pearson, P. D., & McGinley, W. (in press). Assessing reading and writing in the middle school classroom. In G. Duffy (Ed.), *Reading in the middle school* (2nd ed.). Newark, DE: International Reading Association.

Vavrus, L., & Calfee, R. (1988). *A research strategy for assessing teachers of elementary literacy: The promise of performance portfolios.* Presentation at the Annual Meeting of the National Reading Conference, Tucson, Arizona.

Wood, K. (1988). Techniques for assessing students' potential for learning. *The Reading Teacher, 41*, 440–447.

Further Readings

Bailey, J., Brazee, P. E., Chiavaroli, S., Herbeck, J., Lechner, T., Lewis, D., McKittrick, A., Redwine, L., Reid, K., Robinson, B., & Spear, H. (1988). Problem-solving our way to alternative evaluation procedures. *Language Arts, 65* (4), 364–373.

Bruton, B. (1977). *An ounce of prevention plus a pound of cure: Tests and techniques for aiding individual readers.* Santa Monica, CA: Goodyear.

Burns, P. C., & Roe, B. D. (1980). *Informal reading assessment: Preprimer to twelfth grade.* Chicago: Rand McNally.

Crowell, D. C., Au, K. H., & Blake, K. M. (1983). Comprehension questions: Differences among standardized tests. *Journal of Reading, 26*(4), 314–319.

Educational Leadership (1989, Spring). [This issue of the journal is dedicated to assessment.]

Hood, J. (1978). Is miscue analysis practical for teachers? *The Reading Teacher, 32*, 260–266.

Kubiszyn, T., & Borich, G. (1990). *Educational testing and measurement: Classroom application and practice* (3rd ed.). Glenview, IL: Scott, Foresman.

Readence, J. E., & Moore, D. W. (1983). Why questions? A historical perspective on standardized reading achievement tests. *Journal of Reading, 26*(4), 306–313.

Scruggs, T. E., White, K. R., & Bennion, K. (1986). Teaching test-taking skills to elementary grade students: A meta-analysis. *Elementary School Journal, 87* (1), 70–82.

Shuy, R. W. (1981). What the teacher knows is more important than text or test. *Language Arts, 58*, 919–929.

Wixson, K. L. (1979). Miscue analysis: A critical review. *Journal of Reading Behavior, 11*, 163–175.

Yarborough, B. H., & Johnson, R. A. (1980). How meaningful are marks in promoting growth in reading? *The Reading Teacher, 33*(6), 644–651.

Chapter 10

Instructional Approaches and Materials

Some may argue that many teachers are not prepared for the freedom to use their subjectivity during reading instruction—that, at least, we must set alternatives between which teachers may choose. This strikes me as logic akin to Mary McCarthy's observation that Americans find the poverty of others romantic. Would reading researchers, policymakers, or administrators sit still while others choose the objectives, methods, materials, and intended outcomes of their work? I think not. Why, then, do the majority of these groups condone the rationalization of reading programs? What should be done, it seems to me, is to provide teachers with information, and *allow them* (not require, prescribe, or legislate) the opportunity to formulate the available choices, to argue over them, and then to choose for themselves. Perhaps it is unwise to underestimate teachers' capabilities outside their alienated circumstances of rationalized present practice, even if it elevates the importance of the positions of reading researchers, policymakers, or administrators to do so.
(Shannon, 1987, p. 327)

■ OVERVIEW

This chapter presents information about the professional tools that teachers use for reading instruction. What are they and how are they used? A first response might be to say, "Books. Reading is taught by having students read books." Such an answer, however, is only part of the answer.

Most students read stories of one sort or another in their daily lessons. These are usually stories in an anthology, a set of texts that are part of commercial reading curriculum packages—basal reading programs. More than 95 percent of teachers rely on basal reading programs (Dole, Rogers, & Osborn, 1987) and use the materials during 75 to 90 percent of a reading lesson time (Fisher et al., 1978). In addition to text reading, there is discussion of vocabulary, the text topic, and the contents of the text. A skill lesson and directions for independent work fill the remaining lesson time.

For each grade, a basal reading program is composed of a designated anthology of stories, poems, and expository texts. Typically, three sets of materials accompany each anthology: (1) a teacher's guide of lesson-by-lesson suggestions for presenting the text, teaching the associated skills, and providing the follow-up activities; (2) worksheets, bound into workbooks, for individual practice of reading skills; and (3) end-of-unit assessment tasks. Increasingly, however, other materials and programs have been developed and added to reading instruction, such as classroom computers, listening and writing centers, and teacher-selected sets of reading books. We have described many of the changes in earlier chapters, particularly the comprehension chapters. Here we describe how all of these ideas can be organized into lessons.

In the perspective section of this chapter we explain *why* there are different instructional methods and materials and *how* they differ, a result of changes in social conditions and in theories about the reading process. The first key concept describes materials: basal reading programs and tradebooks. The next two key concepts suggest alternative ways to organize a reading program in order that reading and writing activity and book reading play a more prominent role in reading lessons. The last key concept offers advice about planning and evaluating reading materials and programs.

Thus, views about teaching reading are described, with suggestions for ways to adapt and evaluate them in order to strengthen instruction. Our goal is for you to know how to analyze and select appropriate instructional materials as well as to construct your own lesson packages and achieve greater reading gains for your students.

Chapter 10 is organized around the following key concepts:

Key Concept 1: Basal reading programs are intended to provide a complete instructional package for teaching all levels of reading.

Key Concept 2: An individualized reading approach features a diverse selection of books to foster reading.

Key Concept 3: An integrated language arts approach can foster the development of reading and writing.

Key Concept 4: Teachers should establish instructional goals and guidelines for evaluating reading materials.

▌ PERSPECTIVE
Changes in Teaching Reading

You will have a better understanding of reading instruction in the United States if you see the connection between contrasting approaches to reading instruction and the changing needs and attitudes of the society. Smith (1965), and more recently, Venezky (1987) have pointed out historical connections.

ABC texts. In colonial times reading education was bound to religious concepts. Young children were taught letters and words with religious verses and moral messages. Older children read or memorized selections from the Bible. For most adults reading meant the exact recollection of information and so instruction was directed to this purpose. The earliest reading materials were actually religious tracts, prefaced by alphabetic instruction that children were required to memorize. Here are three examples from the New England Primer:

> *F* Foolishness is bound up in the heart of a child, but the rod of correction shall drive it far from him.
>
> *G* Grieve not the Holy Spirit.
>
> *H* Holiness becomes God's House forever.

From the Primer, children were taught to read the Bible. Often this took place by memorizing and reciting passages.

Oral reading. As our country was being settled and wars for independence were fought, other reading purposes arose. Children's reading began to focus on patriotism and political freedom as well as moral values. Since there was little printed material available for children or adults, oratory was emphasized for transmitting news and ideas. Children were trained to become eloquent and expressive oral readers. The text was to provide a useful message, but was simplified for beginning readers. Reading selections contained a full lesson plan, preceded by rules for reading and followed by separate sections on pronunciation, comprehension, and spelling. Here is an example of a selection from the popular reader, the *McGuffey's Eclectic Primer* (1881). The two-page text also listed nine new story words, gave a pronunciation key for four letters and included a picture of a cat and children at the seashore. It is reproduced in Figure 10.1.

Basic readers. At the turn of the century social conditions for reading changed in many ways. Abundant reading materials such as newspapers, periodicals, and books were published. Rapid transportation facilities brought them to rural as well as urban areas of the country. Compulsory education laws made it necessary for all children to attend school and learn to read. Philosophers were beginning to propose that instruction be centered on interpretation of text meaning rather than on its exact recall. Moreover, with the decrease in the length of the working day and increase in mechanical devices for household care, reading was becoming a leisure time activity. Smith (1926) described these accompanying social changes:

> The goal of reading instruction is no longer solely that of teaching the child to read the Bible, nor is it that of training him to read orally with such expression and eloquence that he will sway his audience. There is now no particular need for

Figure 10.1
A Nineteenth-Century Reader

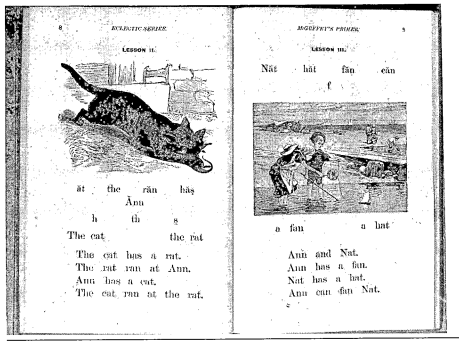

Source: From *McGuffey's Eclectic Primer,* American Book Company, 1909.

oratory. The chief emphasis is placed upon training the child to get the *complete thought* from the page and to get it as *quickly and accurately* as possible. (emphasis by Smith, p. 9)

ABC and syllable recitation methods were gradually replaced by whole word instruction, and silent reading and text comprehension became the new emphasis. Children were to be taught fluent silent reading, and to learn to comprehend and interpret printed information. More care was taken that first-read texts be understandable to young children. These changes were reflected in a heavily used primer developed by Bryce and Spaulding in 1916. The first lesson, for example, had children memorize a set of phrases that rhymed. The teacher was to introduce it by telling children a story that made the little text meaningful. The text is reproduced in Figure 10.2.

Individualized reading.   During the first quarter of the century with the advent of standardized testing, an alternative instructional approach was developed that emphasized wide reading according to children's interests. Smith (1965) suggested that it came about when educators realized there were

▌ **Figure 10.2**
▌ **An Early Twentieth-Century Reader**

Source: From *Aldine Readers: Primer* by Catherine T. Bryce and Frank E. Spaulding, Newson & Company, 1916.

large individual differences among children in reading. Called *individualized reading* or a *book-centered approach*, it favored the replacement of reading textbooks and group instruction techniques with independent reading of books that fit children's interests and reading ability, and with individual conferences.

One late nineteenth-century proponent of individualized reading was Charles Eliot, then the president of Harvard University. According to Smith (1965), Eliot collected all the elementary school reading materials being used to teach reading at that time and had two adults read them. Although 37 percent of all school time was devoted to the study of reading and the English language, he found that two adults could read in only 46 hours everything that elementary school children were supposed to spend six years reading. Eliot (1898) argued that children should be reading far more books.

Individualized reading has never won wide acceptance. Even though it can be effective, it is cumbersome to use because teachers must provide a set of books for every child and develop lessons and practice materials on their own.

Linguistic programs. Another method of teaching reading arose from analyses of the letter-to-sound patterns of English. According to Venezky

(1987), letter-sound analyses were first written about in the 1700s, demonstrating the "deficiency, redundancy, and irregularities in the orthography of the English language" (Webster, 1783, cited by Venezky, 1987, p. 254). Decoding was taught by memorizing syllables from tables (e.g., *ba, be, ab, eb, bla, ble, bad, bed*). This approach was reintroduced in the 1960s by Bloomfield and Barnhart (1961) who demonstrated that texts could feature words with regular letter-sound patterns (such as the phonograms presented in Chapter 7). These words could be taught in sets and presented in contrived stories. The following example is from the first reading lesson by Bloomfield and Barnhart (p. 60). It is designed to teach the *an* pattern which is then practiced with nine new words. There are no pictures to go with this 42-word text:

> Dan ran. Nan ran.
> Van ran. A man ran.
> Nan can fan Dan.
> Can Dan fan Nan?
> Dan can fan Nan.
> Nan, fan Dan.
> Dan, fan Nan.
> Dan ran a van.
> Dan ran a tan van.
> A man ran a tan van.

Basal reading programs.   Today, reading is taught with materials that are published by about 150 independent publishers, about five of whom serve most of the school market. The materials are called *basals*, or *basal readers*, and they come as part of reading, integrated reading, language arts, and literature programs. The term derives from that used at the turn of the century, basic books. Basal reading companies produce materials used by about 90 to 95 percent of all American school children several times a week, if not daily (Flood & Lapp, 1986).

Basal programs are intended to provide a complete set of graded materials for teaching, practicing, and testing reading. Texts in children's reading books or readers have until recently been graded by difficulty according to *readability formulas*. The formulas are based on sentence length and either the number of syllables in words or the number of uncommon words. Texts with short sentences and one syllable or common words are considered to be easier to read than texts with a larger proportion of long sentences and many multisyllable words. Because formulaic changes in natural texts often warp authors' intended meanings, fewer texts are currently being altered to match the grade-level formula. Vocabularies are less confined and sentences vary more in length. Although more interesting stories are appearing in the readers, different, strategy-based reading techniques must now be taught.

Forecasting Change in Reading Practices

At the present time reading instructional principles are on the edge of another change, this coming about in part because greater use is made of scientific reading materials, including those related to computers, and in part because of reductions in the need for low-skill jobs. The present requirement for literacy goes beyond fluent silent reading or an ability to decipher or interpret printed information. There is now a need for critical and analytic thinking, as discussed in Chapter 1.

Higher levels of literacy involve the ability to express one's ideas effectively, the ability to identify propaganda and use reasoning and disciplined thought, and the ability to evaluate, not merely remember, information read. This means that teachers will be asked to go beyond teaching children to read fluently and comprehend text information. They will need to teach them to be reflective thinkers, capable of analyzing and judging information, and able to express themselves in written as well as oral form, aspects of reading presented in Chapters 2, 3, and 4.

Teachers are themselves beginning to change. A greater number of primary grade teachers are using materials that enable writing and shared book reading. Literature-based programs throughout the elementary school, process writing, and well-crafted expository texts for students to learn from, not merely to practice reading, are also being requested.

We interpret this shift in literacy to indicate the importance of text analysis and of looking upon reading as an active, problem-solving activity. Reading instruction will need to involve widespread reading and writing, advanced reading comprehension skills, and an understanding of how to use the computer for reading, writing, and information storage.

> **Key Concept 1**
>
> Basal reading programs are intended to provide a complete instructional package for teaching all levels of reading.

CHARACTERISTICS OF BASAL READING PROGRAMS

A basal reading program is a sequentially arranged series of reading textbooks, workbooks, teacher's guides, scope and sequence charts, tests, and supplementary practice materials. When using these materials, you should remember that reading instruction is meant to focus on the children's reader, the textbook containing stories and other selections. The texts are selected for their high interest and appropriateness at each grade level, and for their usefulness in teaching skills. Practice materials are selected to support the texts and skill lessons. Children are assumed to achieve reading fluency and to develop effective comprehension strategies from the readings and practice materials. Evaluation is typically carried out by asking children comprehension questions, listening to them read, and giving end-of-section tests.

As a package, basal reading programs offer an organized and complete set of up-to-date materials and practices (McCallum, 1988). However, Durkin (1987) argues that the quality of commercial materials is not sufficiently high. Shannon (1987) found that many teachers accepted too readily the lesson guidelines found in the basal programs, and then depreciated their role as thoughtful instructors. Thus, an overreliance on prepared lessons or an insufficiently critical attitude toward them could lead to inflexible and inappropriate instruction. Barr and Sadow (1989) point out that teachers need to become better judges about which reading materials and instructional suggestions to assign or omit and how to ask good questions and evaluate students' responses during story reading lessons.

Reading Skills

The skill lessons, presented in the teacher's guide, explain how to teach a skill and provide follow-up practice. The skills covered in these lessons are applied to increasingly difficult texts as children move up the grades. The teacher is expected to select from the lessons only those skills that children need to study, to integrate the text reading with instruction in those skills, and to provide guided and independent practice using the skills. The skills are listed at the beginning of the lessons and also in the scope and sequence chart in the teacher's guide. The skills are grouped under headings such as:

Decoding and word recognition
Vocabulary
Comprehension
Reference and study skills
Language and literature skills

Decoding is taught from word identification and word analysis lessons located in the teacher's guide and with practice materials found in the student workbook. The 1989 Scott, Foresman basal program, for example, includes phonics, word family, and structural analysis skills.

Vocabulary is usually taught by definition, reading words in context, and structural analysis. New vocabulary words are repeated several times in the stories, giving children practice reading them in skill lessons, and in some workbook exercises.

Comprehension is taught through story questioning and coordinated skill lessons. Among the skills taught are understanding the main idea, drawing conclusions, predicting outcomes, recognizing cause-effect relationships, and

Becoming Familiar with the Teacher's Guide

Choose the teacher's edition of a recently published basal program, if possible, one that you have used or will use for teaching, and go through as many of the steps below as possible.

Locate the scope and sequence chart and determine how skills are differentiated on the chart (e.g., instruct, review, expose). Highlight the ones requiring *instruction* for the grade level you have chosen. Choose one skill that you highlighted and find the set of lessons where it is first taught. Now complete the following activities:

(1) Judge whether the skill is related to the text students are to read and provides examples of guided and independent practice.

(2) Outline how you would teach the set of lessons that go with the text— which activities you would select, and how you would order them.

(3) Explain how you might extend or modify lesson activities for exceptionally high- or low-achieving students.

(4) Describe how you would teach the new words. Consider how important they are for text comprehension as well as the likelihood they could be accurately read and interpreted in the text context.

(5) Describe how you would maintain a focus on text reading and teach skills through or with the text rather than separate from it.

(6) Compare your analyses with other students in the class who chose different skills or grade levels.

understanding an author's purpose. Workbook exercises are available to reinforce the lessons.

Reference and study skills are taught through lessons appearing in the guide and in short texts in the children's reader. These skills include locating and evaluating information. Practice exercises appear occasionally in the workbook.

Literary and language skills are taught in lessons from the guide, which are often related to story activities. The skills include analysis of types of literature, elements of stories, writing devices, grammatical relations, and word forms.

∎ INSTRUCTIONAL ACTIVITIES

To give you an idea about how lessons are organized in basal readers, we have chosen three examples from third grade Scott, Foresman programs. The first is a story from a 1983 reader, the second is realistic fiction from a 1989 reader, and the third is an informational article from the same 1989 reader.

A Third Grade Story

One example is Lesson 6 from a grade three Scott, Foresman (1983) reader. It contains a one-page expository selection about how to make a hand puppet, a skill lesson on ordering text information, and a story, "Somebody Stole Second," by Louise M. Foley. Children are asked to pronounce and then define seven new words. The teacher is then to tell children what the story will be about and to remember the order of story events as they read. Several questions are provided for checking comprehension. Shown in Figure 10.3 is the first page of the eight-page story. The story begins with a clever play on words and continues as an amusing mystery story. It is not a difficult text for average students.

To use a lesson like this effectively, be sure to read over the guide lessons and the story carefully, making notes about their purpose and approach. Be sure you know how to relate the skill lessons to the text so that you can bring out the connections when you teach. You must also decide whether the skill lesson, the vocabulary words, and the text content and structure all should be taught. They should challenge and not bore or discourage children. Here are the factors you would consider in making these decisions:

▌Figure 10.3
▌Lesson from a Basal Reading Selection

Source: From *Somebody Stole Second* by Louise Munroe Foley. Copyright © 1972 by Louise Munroe Foley. Reprinted by permission of Delacorte Press, a division of *Bantam, Doubleday, Dell Publishing Group, Inc.*

1. Since the comprehension skill lesson is about ordering information, ask yourself whether your students have any idea about how to order a set of events as they read. Will this activity be totally new or is it something that could be done with guided practice? If new, you might have students refer to the text to make puppets and plan on taking most of the group's reading period for the activity. On the other hand, if it is familiar, the children may just apply the skill under your guidance, while reading the story, and omit the puppet text and lesson on ordering information.

2. If the new story words are difficult for children to pronounce, list them on the board for children to practice pronouncing. If the meanings of the words are not known, you can have them read the story sentences in which they appear and try to figure out the meanings from context or by relating them to words they know. This might be done after the children read the story. Refer to Chapter 7 for further suggestions.

3. Consider what your instructional purpose will be. If the story is to be read purely for fun, you can introduce the topic and let children read it independently. If it is to be read for reading fluency practice, you might have them read aloud as a group, read after you read, or read with partners. If the story is going to be studied for the purpose of improving comprehension skills, you need to consider how to set up a lesson. You could follow the suggestion in the guide on ordering information, or you could highlight the problem in the story. The children might read the first page, discuss the problem, and then predict what the characters might do. On subsequent pages the children could predict and then focus on the setting and characters. After reading, they could describe events in the correct order or fill out a diagram on the blackboard of the ordered information. Refer to Chapter 3 for other suggestions.

Third Grade Realistic Fiction

A second example is taken from Unit 4 of a Scott, Foresman (1989) Level 3/1 reader. This unit contains an eleven-page story, *Peter's Brownstone House* by Hila Colman, and five recommended independent reading books. A comprehension skill lesson is on recognizing comparative relationships that is extended with a workbook practice page. A word study and vocabulary skill lesson that reviews syllabication has two syllabication workbook practice pages, presents activities for introducing 20 new words, and offers one workbook word practice page. There are suggested guided reading discussion questions and drama and writing activities to carry out during and following story reading. There are also two follow-up workbook activities and additional activities for limited English proficient students. The unit is intended to be covered in one week and has a clearly organized structure. Even so, you need to ask how to teach such a unit effectively.

Study the text beforehand that students are to read, for the text should be at the heart of your week of lessons. Ask yourself questions about your students' background knowledge for understanding the text. Be alert for un-

Figure 10.4
Third Grade Realistic Fiction

A city such as New York has many old homes among the new, tall buildings. In this story, Peter likes living in an old house. Read to find out what Peter learns about his old house. As you read, notice comparisons the characters make.

Peter's Brownstone House
by Hila Colman

Once, a long time ago, a beautiful house was built in New York City. It had a wide stoop and an iron railing with a gate in front.

Inside, the rooms were large, with high ceilings. Almost every one had a fireplace. Many of them had glittering lamps that were lighted with hundreds of tiny candles. The stairway, with its smooth, dark wood, was wide and graceful.

The people who built the house wanted it to last for many, many years. The house did last for many years, although it was slowly surrounded by tall buildings.

Even then people still lived in it: a boy named Peter and his great-grandfather, whom he called Grandpa.

Peter, however, hated the old house. He wanted to live in the tall, new apartment building across the way. His best friend John lived there. Then Peter could ride up and down in the elevator. He could say good morning to the jolly doorman.

But Grandpa loved his old, old house. He hated new apartment buildings. "Nothing is the way it used to be," he grumbled.

Unit 4   81

82   Unit 4

Source: From *Peter's Brownstone House* by Hila Colman. Copyright © 1963 by Hila Colman. Reprinted by permission of Morrow Jr. Books (A Division of William Morrow & Company).

familiar text concepts, difficult or unusual text structures, misleading illustrations, complex or unclear sentences, and unknown words. With respect to words, decide whether the new words listed for teaching are in students' oral but not their written vocabularies (i.e., they would be understood only if read by others in context), neither (they are completely unfamiliar), or both (they are meaningful and readable words in context). The first two pages of the story are shown in Figure 10.4.

Notice that the setting and story characters are presented clearly and a possible story problem is suggested in the last two paragraphs on the second page. You could imagine a plausible continuation of the story. As it happens, an unexpected event causes Peter to change his mind so that he appreciates the house and wants to continue living there. All of the words in the story are likely to be in average students' *oral* vocabulary, although several multisyllable words could be hard for some to identify. Most of the sentences are not complex and have straightforward meanings. The text concepts about living in an old house in a big city would not have been experienced but could be imagined by students.

Now look over the skill lessons and workbook pages and decide which to teach and in what order. We recommend that you use the ETR approach (Chapter 3), and teach the vocabulary and comprehension skill lessons as needed either before or after students read the text. If you think that students will not be able to figure out many of the words, you could preteach words needed for understanding the text. Otherwise, we favor a brief vocabulary introduction so that students begin to read on the first day of the week's work with the unit. They could use *semantic* and *syntactic* cues to figure out the new words as they read. We also favor independent reading and project writing activities suggested in the unit that build on the text and are used after text reading and the skill lesson, probably on the last two days. At that time you can work with individuals or small groups who need additional support or help to read, reread, and use effective reading and writing strategies with the text.

Third Grade Informational Article

A third example is from Unit 13 of *City Spaces* (Scott, Foresman, 1989). The unit contains an eleven-page text and recommends two others for independent reading. A comprehension skill of distinguishing fact from opinion statements has a two-page text for students to read and react to, a writing activity, and one workbook practice page. The vocabulary skill lesson is on synonyms and antonyms and has two workbook practice pages. Sixteen new words can be introduced in sentence context and by definition, or partially through mapping, riddles, and a workbook page. Following the guided reading are comprehension discussion and workbook questions, a mapping activity, and a study skill workbook page graph that continues a part of the text theme.

The text, *Old, Older, Oldest,* by Leonore Klein, is written as though the author is communicating directly with the reader by asking questions at the beginning and end of the text. It begins with:

Who is old?
Are you old?
Or are you young?

The second page ends with:

What is really old? Is sixty-five old? Is eight old?
It's hard to say.

The next several pages offer evidence that age is relative to the species. For example, the last lines on some of the pages are:

An adult Mayfly is old when it is *three days* old!
Mice don't live to be older than *four* years.
How old is old for a furry, gray squirrel? *Eight* years is old!
The fact of the matter is, a hippopotamus is an old
   hippopotamus when he is *forty* years old.

The last two pages describe five generations of people and what they can do, concluding with:

Some young people feel old already.
Some old people feel young.

How old are you?
Do you feel old? Do you feel young?
How old would you like to be?

This text has an unfamiliar structure because it is an argument in which the conclusion comes at the beginning with, "What is really old? . . . It's hard to say." This is followed by examples that provide evidence for the conclusion, that age in years cannot be used to determine what is really old. The last two pages narrow the concept further, pointing out that age could still be a subjective decision. The text has many content words that could be hard to read because they are seldom seen in children's texts (e.g., *mayfly, hippopotamus, swan, parrot, tortoise, pearl mussel, aquarium*). Moreover, the text contains a bar graph, and the last two pages are packed with information. Thus, a rich introduction is required in order for students to understand the concepts in this text.

To decide on an order of the lessons, consider the usefulness of each segment for text comprehension. We think that the text would benefit from a vocabulary skill instruction before reading, but recommend that a comprehension skill lesson be developed around the line of argument in the text. Follow-up comprehension might also involve the suggested text mapping, discussion, and writing activities.

Applying Suggestions from Other Chapters

The three lesson examples describe how you might analyze basal reading lessons for your instruction. We recommend that at first you select from among the listed activities and skill lessons, and order them based on their usefulness for text reading and your instructional priorities. When this instruction is running smoothly, we recommend that you explore ideas from earlier chapters in this textbook and from reading journals and other sources. Use the texts, but modify the skill lessons and practice activities so that your instruction better matches students' needs and interests and your underlying instructional philosophy. Eventually, as we describe in the next two sections, you might choose text materials as well. Particularly important is to engage students in learning that is situated in real reading and writing tasks that foster independence in word identification, vocabulary development, text comprehension, and critical analysis.

Key Concept 2

An individualized reading approach features a diverse selection of books to foster reading.

▌ CHARACTERISTICS OF INDIVIDUALIZED READING

In an individualized reading approach, children choose their own reading materials so their reading is directly related to their interests and knowledge. Since reading choices are made individually, teachers have conferences with children to discuss each text and give help with word recognition, word meanings, and comprehension. Teachers evaluate children's reading by giving them questions to answer and by listening to them read aloud. They also keep track of the number of books that children read, topics they are interested in, and their progress toward reading more complex materials.

According to West (1964), the individualized method of reading allows for:

> . . . individual differences while at the same time recognizing interest and purpose as prime factors in the learning process. It is designed to allow the child to develop his own unique direction and pace rather than to fit him into a prescribed mode of development supposed typical or normal for his age group. It makes provision for reading activities which develop the needed reading skills in functional settings, capitalizes upon opportunities for the development of skills in other areas of the curriculum and throughout the school day, and recognizes the interrelationship of all the language arts—speaking, listening, reading, and writing—which are based on a wide variety of interesting experiences closely related to the real activities and interests in the child's life that provide entries into learning situations. (p. 37)

Individualized reading can be recommended because it helps children enjoy reading and fosters more reading. Another advantage cited by Stott (1982) and Yamada (1983) is that children have the opportunity to read long selections. Stott had children read novels while Yamada had them read historical fiction. Individualized reading can be criticized because it does not provide step-by-step skill instruction and evaluation. However, research in the 1950s and 1960s summarized by West (1964) suggests that well-planned individualized reading programs do not hamper children's progress in learning to read.

General Guidelines for Organizing an Individualized Reading Program

Because research supports the value of an instructional emphasis on comprehension, silent reading, and the reading of good literature, we believe individualized reading should have a definite place in classroom reading programs. However, use of an individualized reading approach, or even the supplementing of a basal program with tradebooks, does require the teacher to do more advance preparation. The individualized approach cannot be carried out merely by providing children with an assortment of books to read. Thus, West (1964) recommends attention to these basic elements:

1. Choosing book materials.
2. Organizing the classroom.
3. Monitoring reading activity.

This student reads a book of her own choice as part of an individualized reading program. Guidance is provided through conferences with the teacher.

4. Evaluating reading growth.
5. Providing reading strategy instruction.

Choosing book materials. You need to know where or how to find appropriate books for children to read and you must decide what guidelines to follow for helping children to choose topics and books.

Arbuthnot (1957) offered the following good advice for identifying well-written stories and informational materials. Of stories, she said, "In general children like stories with an *adequate theme,* strong enough to generate and support a *lively plot.* They appreciate *memorable characters* and *distinctive style"* (p. 16). Of informational texts, she wrote:

> The best we can do here is to set up criteria for judging these books on the basis of *scrupulous accuracy* (unless our text is accurate our reading is worse than useless; accuracy is the most important criterion for judging any informational book), *convenient presentation* (we want the material presented in such a way that we can find what we are looking for quickly and comfortably; this is equally true of children), *clarity* (information for any age level should be written directly and sensibly, with obvious respect for the reader's intelligence), *adequate treatment* (it is essential that enough significant facts be given for a realistic and balanced picture), and *style* (a lively, well-written text is an invaluable bait to learning). [p. 545, emphasis added]

In your classroom library, you should plan to have at least fifty different books at a time. Bring in new books regularly from the library. Some multiple copies are necessary for books that you will want several children to read and discuss together, or that you know are going to be very popular. To build up a diverse collection of books, magazines, and children's reference materials at the lowest possible cost, check possible resources in your community (for example, children's books may be purchased from library, school, and garage sales). There are probably books in the back cupboards of your school building, and extra or older books in your school district's resource materials center. Have your children join school book clubs and purchase and exchange paperback books. Then encourage children to lend their books to one another and your classroom library.

One way to locate good books is to look at journals, including *Language Arts*, *The New Advocate*, *The Horn Book*, and *The Reading Teacher*, which regularly publish topically organized lists of children's books. Some examples of anthologies of special purpose tradebooks published in *The Reading Teacher* are included in the list of further readings at the end of this chapter. These lists appear regularly, so be sure to consult new issues of journals yourself. Once a year *The Reading Teacher* also publishes a list of the new books children reported they liked the best. The 1989 listing appears in October (1989) with 112 titles.

Another way to identify good books is from the list published yearly by the American Booksellers Association Children's Book Council. The year's best-selling tradebooks are organized under the headings *Very First Books*, *Picture Books*, *Fairy Tales*, *Beginning-to-Read Books*, *Fiction for Readers 8–12*, *Informational Books for Readers Under 8*, and *Informational Books for Readers 8 and Older*. Copies of the list can be obtained through your local librarian or bookseller. Librarians also have a list of good books in *The Elementary School Library Collection: A Guide to Books and Other Media* (1988).

Finally, high quality stories, poems, and informational texts can be found in anthologies of children's literature. An anthology by Sutherland and Livingston (1984) provides examples of poetry, folktales and myths, realistic and historical fiction, biography, and informational articles. It also contains articles on how to present and explain good literature to children.

Organizing the classroom. Most classrooms, because they use basal reading programs, are organized into three ability groups. Individualized reading requires a different approach. For example, Burrows (1952) developed this weekly pattern:

At the beginning of each reading period the class discusses who needs new materials, who needs to go to the library, and who needs the teacher's help. It takes five to ten minutes to get everyone reading.

Monday: The teacher invites children who are reading books difficult for them to sit near her for help. This procedure encourages children of different reading abilities to sit and read together.

The teacher has individual conferences with two or three children while the others in the class read silently by themselves. Conferences are set up at the teacher's request or by the children's signing up on a list.

Tuesday: The Monday program is continued with more individual conferencing.

Wednesday: The period is devoted to group discussion about favorite books, dramatization, reading aloud, or sharing of illustrations. Individual conferences may be needed to help some children plan or prepare their presentations.

Thursday: Conferences are held with six or seven children while the rest read independently or work on written assignments.

Friday: Children bring their reading records up to date. The teacher checks their records and holds conferences with several individuals. Most of the children do some independent reading and some get books ready for weekend reading at home.

Monitoring reading activity.   Regularly scheduled conferences are an integral part of individualized reading. The teacher begins with questions that lead the child to describe what was learned from the text. Questions could lead the child to describe characters, their problems, and attempted resolutions. Questions could also focus on the sequence of events central to the plot and their relationship to the characters' goals and problems. A child might be asked to summarize the main ideas or discuss important factual information. Any problems the child has had in interpreting the text or reading particular words ought to be discussed. Finally, oral reading fluency can be checked by asking the child to read a favorite section as well as a section that the teacher chooses.

Evaluating growth.   The teacher makes checklists and brief notes to describe the quality and accuracy of children's comprehension and their oral reading fluency. These help the teacher keep track of reading problems and over time show where improvements have been made. The children keep chronological records of the books they have read. For each completed reading, a child should list the date the book was completed, book title, author, publisher, and number of pages. Children could also list each book they have read on a separate card and give a 2-3 sentence commentary such as what interested them the most or what they learned from their reading. Commentaries can be kept with the book to help other children decide whether they want to read it.

Providing skill instruction.   One problem with individualized reading is that no provision is made for systematic skill instruction. Most children will need to be taught more effective ways to read and learn from their reading. To get an idea of the areas of instruction you might need to teach, refer to a basal scope and sequence chart for your grade or rely on suggestions from Chapters 2-7. You probably will want to set aside one or two hours a week for group instruction lessons.

▌ INSTRUCTIONAL ACTIVITIES

Picture books and storybooks available in libraries and bookstores generally are not written for the purpose of teaching children to read. While they certainly can be used for instruction, teachers may wish to be aware of both the strengths and weaknesses which may be found in tradebooks for beginning readers.

Using Tradebooks with Beginning Readers

In comparison to basal reader selections, tradebooks usually have longer texts and harder words. Yet Gourley (1984) found that children do not necessarily make more errors as they try to read tradebooks. She also found that tradebooks often contain devices to support young children's reading. These devices include rhyming and the repetition of phrases.

Another possible problem with tradebooks is that their plots are often more complicated than those of basal selections. Thus, children may miss the main point of a story. One solution, recommended by Galda (1982), is to have children act out the stories. Since dramatic play does not come easily to some children, you may need to help them learn how to participate. Galda had children imagine themselves as the character and asked questions such as, "What are you going to do now, Wolf?" Sometimes she modeled participation by acting out one of the characters herself. She relied on six criteria for the dramatic play (from Smilansky, 1971). These were applied following the reading of favorite familiar stories such as "The Three Bears" or "The Three Billy-Goats Gruff." You can use these guidelines when you want children to have a better understanding of a story.

1. Imitate or role-play the actions and words from the story;
2. Substitute make-believe objects for real objects;
3. Use make-believe actions and situations;
4. Have the play last about ten minutes;
5. Be sure the children interact within the framework of the storyline as they act out their parts;
6. Encourage verbal communication in expressing the ideas from the story.

Using Tradebooks to Foster Report Writing

Moss (1982), a language arts teacher, suggests ways to lead children from reading stories to writing their own texts. She demonstrates the approach with a reading instructional unit for fourth-graders around the contrast between traditional folktales and contemporary tales. To begin, the class reads and listens to a variety of traditional folktales and fairy tales from different countries. Then a series of discussions get children to identify the common patterns and themes. Moss suggests that children work independently or with a partner and then as a group to discuss the distinctive features of folktales. This phase of the unit is likely to go on for several days before an adequate list is compiled.

In the next phase, children read and listen to several modern fairy tales. She recommends stories by J. Williams (for example, *The Practical Princess and Other Liberating Fairy Tales*, 1978) because they are amusing spoofs on folktales. Children answer questions such as the following:

How is this story similar to traditional fairy tales?
How is this story different from the traditional fairy tale?
What techniques did the author use to create humor or surprise?
How are the characters similar to or different from those in traditional fairy tales?
What message is today's author trying to convey, different from that of the traditional fairy tale?

When the children are adept at reading, interpreting, and comparing folktales, you can have them create their own modern fairy tales. First, they need to review the characteristics of the classic and modern tales. Then they should review ways that make modern tales different. Children are then ready to draw from their experiences with traditional as well as modern stories, in terms of structure and purpose to create their own imaginative versions of a contemporary folktale.

Using Tradebooks for Bibliotherapy

Jalongo (1983) recommends that teachers provide children with sensitive guidance to select the "right" book at the right time. Children who are under stress, who lack sufficient sensitivity toward their classmates, or who need to hear about how children like themselves resolved their problems, will probably profit from a bibliotherapeutic technique.

Jalongo points out that to be successful, you must plan carefully. First, consider what you expect to accomplish and how you might carry through after finding an appropriate book. The second step is to decide who will be involved. A book might be presented to one child, several children, or the entire class. The third step has to do with timing. Be sure the books you present are directed to classroom problems and are understandable to the children. The fourth step regards evaluation of your success in using this technique. For example, you might ask children whether the books influenced their thinking, feelings, and attitudes. Or you might have them rank order the value of a set of books.

Bibliotherapy is useful because children can profit from reading books about other people who shared their sentiments or experienced similar problems. From this type of book reading, children can be reassured that people make mistakes but can learn to change and be loved and accepted.

Utilizing Children's Books for Voluntary Reading

Many approaches have been devised to encourage students to read independently, as you will learn in Chapter 12. A key aspect of all of these approaches is motivating students to read. You will need many books, time set aside during the school day for voluntary reading, opportunities for students to borrow books for home use, and activities that acquaint students with interesting books and authors.

Voluntary reading is difficult to foster among students who are not particularly good readers. Most avoid it because it is hard, yet only by frequent reading and rereading will they become good readers. You will need to use clever ploys such as having reading take place for varying purposes, reading story introductions to students, and arranging for shared peer reading sessions. If funds are available, use taped books in your listening centers, along with filmstrips and videotapes. You can refer to reviews of these materials in reading journals (e.g., Naylor, 1988). Keep in mind that voluntary reading and listening should not be used as a reward for completing seatwork assignments, or else the very students you want to be reading won't read, because of their less well-organized work habits. Arranging book borrowing for reading takes time, and some books will be lost in the process, but if you put students in charge of monitoring the borrowing process and make individuals feel accountable for taking care of and returning books, you will manage the operation successfully.

One source of good beginner's books is a listing intended for a first-grade program described in Chapter 7 that features daily book reading and rereading (Pinnell, DeFord, & Lyons, 1988). The program contains several hundred books, ranging in difficulty from caption books and labeled pictures that children learn to read from picture clues to books that will challenge the best readers in first grade. Because many of the books were composed without restricting the vocabulary, children must figure out the words in the texts during the reading processs, that is, by reading in context. We have listed some examples in Figure 10.5, listed in an approximate order of difficulty from the easiest to the more difficult (Levels 1-20). Writing to the individual publisher would secure listings of many more books.

Key Concept 3

An integrated language arts approach can foster the development of reading and writing.

∎ INTEGRATING READING AND WRITING

James Britton (1987) offers a fitting introduction to the concept of an integration between reading and writing:

> It is in the course of conversational exchanges that young children learn, little by little, both to listen to and interpret what people say to them, and, at the same time, to put into words their own messages. It would be a perverse regime that attempted to prevail on them to separate those two achievements—focusing on listening in one context and on speaking in another. Yet precisely that dissociation marks the prevailing methods by which school children today are taught to write and read. (p. 1)

There has been an increasing demand in recent years to strengthen the teaching both of writing and of literature as well as to integrate writing with reading instruction. How might a reading program be combined with grammar and written usage exercises, literature, spelling, and handwriting? One approach, which was developed and tried out by Walmsley and Walp (1990) in an upstate New York school system, has successfully integrated these components in third and fourth grades. Another is to make effective use of computer software writing programs. The approach is congruent with the use of literature themes discussed in Chapter 3.

∎ Figure 10.5
∎ Examples of Children's Books
∎ for Voluntary Reading

Cat on the Mat (1983), by B. Wildsmith. Oxford.
In the Mirrow (1983), by J. Cowley. Rigby Education.
Kites, in Reading Unlimited Series. Scott, Foresman.
At School, in Instant Language Series. Wright Group.
Danny's Dollars (1986), by S. Green & S. Salmon, in Expressways II Series. Gage.
Dan the Flying Man (1983), by J. Cowley, in Storybox Series. Wright Group.
Bears in the Night (1971), by S. & J. Berenstain. Random House.
Monday, Monday, I Like Monday, by B. Martin. Holt.
Blue Bug's Book of Colors (1981), by V. Poulet. Children's Press.
Herman the Helper (1981), by R. Kraus. Windmill.
Katie Couldn't (1985), by B. McDaniel, in Rookie Reader Series. Children's Press.
Who Will Be My Mother? in Sunshine Series. Wright Group.
Cat and Dog (1960), by E. Minarik. Harper & Row.
Sue Likes Blue (1984), by B. Gregorich, in Start to Read Series. School Zone.
How Can You Hide an Elephant? in Magic Circle Series. Ginn.
Come On In (1983), in Series r. Macmillan.
Goodnight Moon (1977), by M. W. Brown. Harper & Row.
Enormous Watermelon, in Rigby Folktales Series. Rigby.
Green Eggs and Ham (1987), by Dr. Seuss. Random House.
Spot's Birthday Party (1982), by E. Hill. Putnam.
There's Something in My Attic (1988), by M. Mayer. Dial.
Clifford the Big Red Dog (1985), by N. Bridwell. Scholastic.
Monster at School, in Tadpole Monster Series. Bowmar.
The Surprise Party (1986), by P. Hutchins. Macmillan.
The Very Hungry Caterpillar (1981), by E. Carle. Putnam.
Caps for Sale (1984), by E. Slobodkina. Scholastic.

Figure 10.6
Weekly Schedule for Integrated
Language Arts Program

	Monday	Tuesday	Wednesday	Thursday	Friday
15 mins			Read-aloud		
35 mins	Directed Rdg (full-length book)	Ind. Rdg (incl. book conferences)	Reading Directed Rdg (full-length book)	Ind. Rdg (incl. book conferences)	Directed Rdg (short selections)
30 mins			Writing (Prewriting, composing, revision, and editing conferences)		
10 mins			Presentation (Sharing of reading and writing projects)		

Source (Figures 10.6, 10.7, 10.8, 10.9): From "Toward an Integrated Language Arts Curriculum in Elementary School: Philosophy, Practice and Implications" by S. Walmsley and T. Walp, *Elementary School Journal,* January 1990. Reprinted by permission of The University of Chicago Press.

Three principles guide an integrated reading and writing program:

- Genuine reading and composing are the primary language arts activities and should occupy the largest portion of the language arts period. This means that texts are read for their interest, not to "practice" reading, that reading can include listening and shared reading of books. It also means that composing involves a process writing approach and has classroom goals and shared presentations. This notion is depicted by Walmsley and Walp in Figure 10.6.
- A skills-through-application perspective is followed rather than a skills-first instruction. For example, students could learn about "getting main ideas" by reading several stories rather than studying contrived paragraphs in workbooks. They could write on a self-selected topic or one related to the reading. Similarly, conventional spelling patterns can be presented in the context of stories that students have written rather than through isolated word list drills. Walmsley and Walp show other ways to carry out these links in Figure 10.7.
- Listening and drama as well as reading and writing should be linked in the curriculum through content. A topic or text can be approached from different directions. Thus, students could read, write, listen to, and perform drama about the same themes or topics. To exemplify the approach, Walmsley and Walp suggest how the theme of "journeys" might be coordinated as seen in Figure 10.8.

Figure 10.7
Theme-Centered, Integrated Approach
to Language Arts

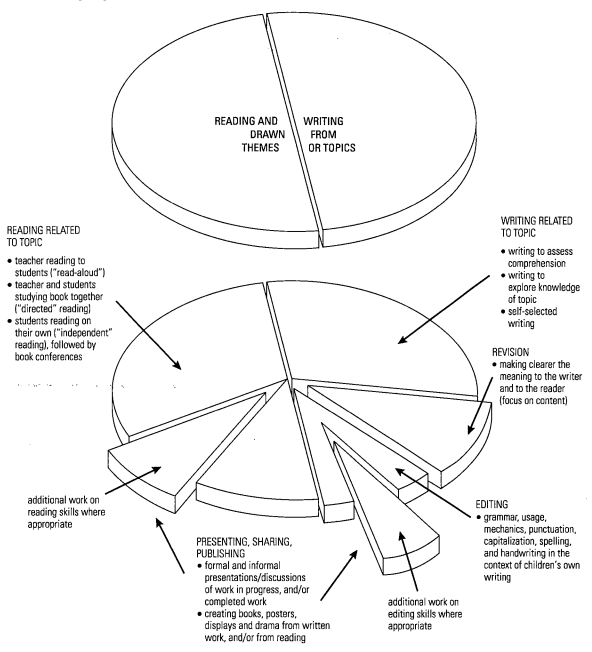

READING AND DRAWN THEMES

WRITING FROM OR TOPICS

READING RELATED
TO TOPIC

• teacher reading to
  students ("read-aloud")
• teacher and students
  studying book together
  ("directed" reading)
• students reading on
  their own ("independent"
  reading), followed by
  book conferences

WRITING RELATED
TO TOPIC

• writing to assess
  comprehension
• writing to
  explore knowledge
  of topic
• self-selected
  writing

REVISION
• making clearer the
  meaning to the writer
  and to the reader
  (focus on content)

additional work on
reading skills where
appropriate

PRESENTING, SHARING,
PUBLISHING
• formal and informal
  presentations/discussions
  of work in progress, and/or
  completed work
• creating books, posters,
  displays and drama from written
  work, and/or from reading

additional work on
editing skills where
appropriate

EDITING
• grammar, usage,
  mechanics, punctuation,
  capitalization, spelling,
  and handwriting in the
  context of children's own
  writing

▌ **Figure 10.8**
▌ **A Possible Web for the "Journeys"**
▌ **Theme**

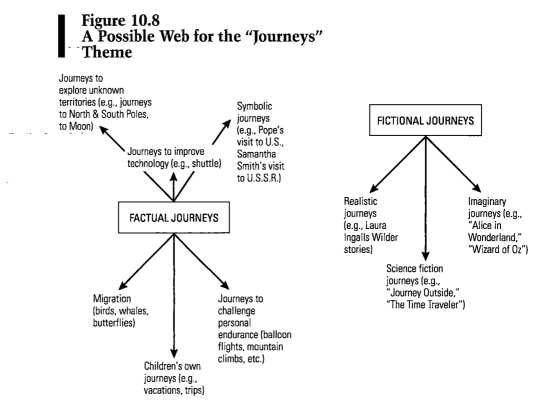

Integrating Reading with Writing Topically

There are two phases for the development of a program that is based on a theme (Walmsley & Walp, 1990). The first phase is to become knowledgeable about the themes you have chosen for integration and the reading materials that are related to it. This includes books intended for students to read as well as books for informing you. Extensive knowledge of children's literature is helpful. Also, opportunities to consult with subject matter experts, and released time to research the themes and topics in public libraries may be needed so that you can expand your background knowledge about the topics. When you have obtained greater knowledge about each, you can select books wisely, plan the organization of the materials, and guide students toward a deeper understanding of topics and individual books.

The second phase is preparing lesson plans and ordering student reading materials. Separate reading materials into three sets: "read-alouds" which are materials read by you to students, "directed reading materials" which are pieces that are read by the whole class in directed reading lessons, and "independent readings" which are full-length books to be read by students on their own. You will select these materials from a wide range of literature, taking into account students' interests, clarity and quality of writing, and the importance of sampling different text genres.

Read-aloud materials are aimed to introduce students to literature from the oral tradition. Walmsley and Walp (1990) recommend one full-length book per theme. Directed readings, which are central to the topic, should display complex literary style and.plot. Though generally too difficult for independent reading, the materials should be understood when studied with the teacher. The authors recommend selecting two to three books for a theme, although generally only one would be used for class reading. In addition, shorter expository pieces from magazine and newspaper articles, poetry, and reports can supplement the principal book. These materials will be expensive, since individual copies of directed readings will need to be purchased for the whole class.

Independent readings should vary in difficulty, from challenging to very easy, enabling all students to read and understand several materials. About ten pieces per theme are selected.

When planning the writing component, be sure to link writing with the themes in reading materials. Walmsley and Walp recommend that students write in three or more ways: short answers to questions about particular books, extended pieces that report on particular books, and extended pieces that are related broadly to the topic.

Finally, the language arts period as a whole is organized into a 90-minute schedule in which the parts of the program are allocated varying amounts of time (refer back to Figure 10.6). Teachers are free to rearrange or adjust the

Charts hung across this third-grade room remind students of what they have learned about the writing process and different forms of literacy. This teacher uses thematic units in both literature and content area instruction.

Figure 10.9
Language Arts Program Maintaining Separate Reading and Writing Instruction

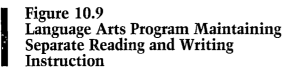

- comprehension
- vocabulary
- word attack
  (incl. phonics, -
  structural
  analysis, etc.)
- study skills

(Teach using Basal Reader
and supplementary
workbooks)

- reading to children
  (read-aloud)
- teachers and children
  studying books together
  ("directed" reading)
- children reading on
  their own ("independent"
  reading, in school and
  at home)

(Teach using techniques
presented in Figure 10.7)

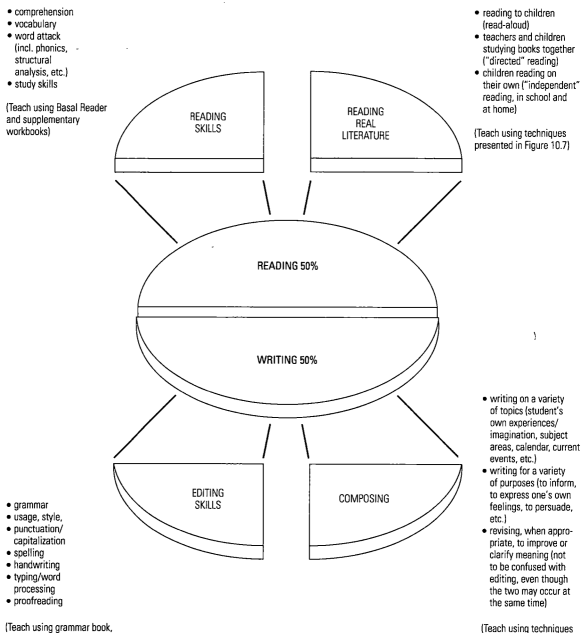

- grammar
- usage, style,
- punctuation/
  capitalization
- spelling
- handwriting
- typing/word
  processing
- proofreading

(Teach using grammar book,
spelling, and handwriting series)

- writing on a variety
  of topics (student's
  own experiences/
  imagination, subject
  areas, calendar, current
  events, etc.)
- writing for a variety
  of purposes (to inform,
  to express one's own
  feelings, to persuade,
  etc.)
- revising, when appro-
  priate, to improve or
  clarify meaning (not
  to be confused with
  editing, even though
  the two may occur at
  the same time)

(Teach using techniques
presented in Figure 10.7)

segments as the year progresses. Within the time frame of a topic and over a school year, for example, a teacher might gradually shift to providing more time for independent reading and less to directed reading.

The program offers a way for you to establish a coordinated language arts program in your classroom. The advantage is an opportunity to integrate thoroughly the aspects of language that have for years been disconnected in elementary school curricula. The principal disadvantage is that substantial planning and study are required to gather the requisite materials and organize the instruction. For that reason, Walmsley and Walp suggest that teachers initially integrate language through the use of basal reading materials. We offer this alternative to you, particularly since as a beginning teacher, it would be very difficult to organize a full-fledged integrated program in the first few years of teaching. This alternative is exemplified in Figure 10.9.

Key Concept 4

Teachers should establish instructional goals and guidelines for evaluating reading materials.

THE IMPORTANCE OF GOAL-SETTING

In the first part of this chapter we looked at how reading methods have changed. Then we described how reading can be taught and what kinds of materials can be used. It should be apparent now that because you have many methods and materials to choose from, you need to plan carefully before you begin teaching. Our purpose here is to give you a framework for thinking systematically about reading instruction. Ask yourself what you want to accomplish and then ask what kinds of materials will help your students do that kind of learning.

Setting Up Instructional Goals

The first thing to think about in setting up the classroom reading program is, what is it the students should be learning? Set clear goals for instruction, based on what you think your students need to learn. This is not easy to do. Many teachers begin, not with learning goals, but by thinking about their students and activities (Clark & Yinger, 1979). However, without setting goals, you may waste a lot of time on lessons and activities which do not advance students' reading achievement or enjoyment of reading in any particular way.

Many teachers rely primarily or even exclusively on commercial basal reading programs. Even if you do also, you should make a conscious decision to set overall goals for reading instruction. You need not slavishly follow the goals of any commercial program. Keep in mind that commercial programs are designed to attract as large a share of the market as possible. Thus, it is extremely unlikely that any commercial program will be tailored perfectly to the needs of your particular group of students.

You may also find that your school or district has "mandated" certain goals. Sometimes highly specific goals in reading are set and students tested to see how well they are progressing toward those goals. Often, though, goals for reading instruction stated in these mandates are sufficiently broad or generally worded to give the teacher considerable latitude in setting goals.

While it isn't necessary for you to invent your own goals, it *is* necessary to use your judgment in selecting appropriate goals from among the different sources of goals available. Two of the sources commonly used by teachers are (1) commercial programs, and (2) state or district curriculum guides. Throughout this book we have suggested a third source, your own knowledge derived from this book, other reading courses, and your understanding of students' needs. We explain next how ideas from these sources can be coordinated to guide your organization of lessons and materials.

Modifying a Basal Reading Program

Teachers in most schools rely upon a basal reader series when organizing their classroom reading program. You are likely to do the same, particularly when you begin teaching, but you will want to understand how to take advantage of good ideas while avoiding common problems in the way basals are typically used.

Many schools or districts "adopt" a particular basal reader series. This means that all classroom teachers at all grade levels are expected to use that series. However, you want to avoid the thoughtless approach of simply taking as many students as possible through the basal materials from the first to last page. Consult the teacher's guide for the program and read the sections giving an overview of the goals for student learning. Study the scope and sequence chart to determine how the major strands as well as substrands are represented at different reading levels. Then study the sequence for particular skills and how they are taught in the grade you teach or intend to teach.

Modifying the lessons in a basal program could be done by using the text materials but critically evaluating the skill lessons of the basal program against the suggestion we have made in the earlier chapters and your own analysis of what the students need. Often you may find a good match between the skills suggested for instruction and those you think ought to be taught at that time. At other times you will place more emphasis on some skills, rearrange lessons to match a particular story, or add lessons not present in the program. Examples of this approach appeared in the first key concept of this chapter.

Another way to modify a basal reading program is to use the goals listed in the scope and sequence chart but vary the text and worksheet practice materials from those recommended in the teacher's guide. This approach, which builds on ideas in the second and third key concepts, gives you a support system for teaching but allows you to modify what the children read and how they practice the skills. You could substitute language experience charts, tradebooks, or computer-presented text for the reader selections, and substitute independent reading or writing activities for some of the workbook pages. This way you can gradually adjust and enrich the menu provided by the basal program to better meet the needs of your students.

With either modified approach you can move systematically toward making sure that your major goals for classroom reading instruction are met. You are using the basal program as a foundation but not limiting students' learning to the opportunities that "by the book" use of the basal would provide. You avoid the main danger of using basals in the all-too-common practice of using them in an unthinking and inflexible way, without regard for students' needs. There are many more effective strategies for teaching reading than could be incorporated in any one commercial program. You will have knowledge of these strategies and know when they should be used.

EVALUATION OF READING MATERIALS AND METHODS

To become an effective teacher you need to learn how to choose the best materials from basal programs or other sources and how to adapt them to fit your children's interests and instructional needs. In so doing, you can accumulate a set of high quality materials and a repertoire of effective methods.

Evaluation of Textbooks

We described in the introduction to this chapter how children's reading materials have changed. In the 1940s and 1950s text writing began to be tailored to readability formulas. Lowered readability levels, it was argued, helped students more readily assimilate their lessons and increased motivation in the classroom. By the 1960s school officials had become aware of the concept of readability and began to use readability levels of textbooks as one criterion for textbook adoption.

As readability formulas became more widely used, publishers and authors came to produce materials to meet readability ranges for particular grade levels. Critics suggest, however, that texts produced in adherence to the formulas are not a solution to learning problems but a contributor to them. This is in part because the quality of writing, level of interest and challenge, and conceptual difficulty cannot be taken into account with readability formulas. Materials low in challenge may have low appeal. Materials consisting of short sentences and one-syllable words are not necessarily easy to understand, while some materials with long sentences are.

We recommend that you evaluate texts for children on more dimensions than the readability level. They could be analyzed in terms of their literary quality, their interest and appeal to children, or their content. We provide examples here of each of these other factors in evaluating text materials.

Evaluation of literary quality.   One way to evaluate stories your children might read is to compare the adapted text with the original. Many contemporary and classic children's stories are rewritten to be quite different from the original. Egan (1983) argues that current versions of classic folktales "usually contain poor versions of the old stories, giving prominence to incidental points, entirely missing others of far greater importance, and often finishing up with a new story that has only a superficial resemblance to the 'original'" (p. 228).

He suggests it is worth the effort to locate texts that are closer to the original language. These will represent more clearly the depth and richness of possible or intended meanings. Instead of projecting only innocence and light-heartedness, original fairy tales bring out evil as well as good, or tragedy as well as happiness. As Egan explains:

> In mythology and folktales, we are taken into a strange world which glitters with gold and precious stones, but which is also menacing. . . . Goodness wins out in the end, but it always remains interwoven with its darker side, and we cannot remove one without destroying the other as well.   (p. 230)

Evaluation of text interest.   Abrahamson and Shannon (1983) analyzed the 61 most popular picturebooks from 1982, based on the Children's Choices in *The Reading Teacher* for that year. Nearly three quarters of the children liked materials which had a conflict, opposing views, or several episodes. Less appealing were travel stories, nonfiction, and other types of writing. Their evaluation categories are listed here for you to use:

Stories in which characters must confront and resolve a problem;
Stories in which characters have opposing viewpoints, come from contrasting settings, or are involved in contrasting situations;
Stories featuring several episodes played out by the main characters;
Travel stories in which characters embark on a real or imaginary adventure away from home;
Nonfiction or biography or explanation of an observed phenomenon;
Poetry or verse;
Quest or aspiration stories;
Other: jokes, riddles, story collections, ABC books, counting books.

Evaluation of text content.   Schmidt, Caul, Byers, and Buchmann (1984) recommend that children's reading selections contain more *subject matter* content, *functional* content, or *ethos* content. They advise that texts without at least one of these contents ought to be considered deficient.

Subject matter is categorized as follows:

languge skills	music
fine arts and crafts	science
physical education	philosophy
mathematics	social science

The functional dimension has the following categories:

reasoning/problem-solving	initiative persistence
moral reasoning	absurdity/paradox
contemplation	humor in use of language
creativity	cunning/mother wit
feeling/catharsis	

The ethos dimension contains these categories:

humility	kindness/generosity
patience/forebearance	honesty
courage	hope

Expository Text Evaluation

Expository texts need a different sort of evaluation. Writing a perfect text for children to read and learn from is not easy. For example, after criticizing the quality of content area texts, Armbruster and Anderson (1984) attempted to write a good text. They discuss just how difficult this was to do. Be sure to evaluate the quality of the expository texts you plan to use. Because high quality texts are few and may be difficult to find, you may still end up using some inconsiderate (poorly written) texts. However, if you have carefully evaluated these texts, you will know where the problems lie and be able to compensate for weaknesses by providing students with extra instruction.

The following guidelines for evaluating the quality of an expository text are adapted from those formulated by Anderson and Armbruster (1984). The guidelines cover both the structure of the text and its topic:

1. The outline of the text should be apparent from reading the headings. The headings should be an accurate reflection of the most important ideas in each section.
2. The author's principal message should be coordinated with the structure of the text. For example, an author should not list facts when trying to express a cause and effect relationship.
3. The same text structure should be repeated, so the information on each subtopic can be presented in a parallel manner. For example, if the author is describing several countries, the same information (such as location, climate, history, and natural resources) should be presented for each, in about the same order.
4. The key relationships among ideas should be explicitly stated. Such relationships should not have to be inferred. For example, historical events

are often most clearly understood by children as problems that the people of that time met and resolved. In this case, the problem and its solution should be directly stated and related.

5. Events should be presented in their natural order, especially in texts written for younger children. This guideline applies both to descriptions of historical events and of processes or procedures.

6. A close reading should show that each idea in the text contributes to the author's stated purpose. Watch out for loosely written passages which simply list unrelated information.

7. Adequate information should be presented about each major concept. The information should be complete enough for a child to be able to grasp the underlying ideas.

8. Technical terms should be introduced only if they are important to an understanding of the topic. Clear and complete definitions should be included.

9. Figurative language, such as similes and metaphors, should be used only if their referents are likely to be known to most children.

Evaluation of Workbooks

Osborn (1984) notes that developers of workbooks do not always use research knowledge about instructional design, the giving of directions, or the sequencing and concentration of activities. Workbook practice pages seldom build upon students' reading of the basal selections, stories, or expository texts. Furthermore, the materials are seldom field-tested before being marketed.

As a result, workbook materials vary substantially in their quality. Whether you plan to use commercial practice materials or develop your own, you should be aware of how to evaluate their quality. We have grouped Osborn's suggestions for evaluation into three categories: tasks, format and language, and procedures.

Tasks. Workbook tasks should be related to other aspects of a reading lesson. A task should:

be related to lesson and text
provide review
have importance in the greater scope of a topic
provide practice for hard-to-teach children
have an obvious payoff for students

Format and language. A workbook practice page can be arranged in many different ways and use a variety of words, phrases, and illustrations to communicate what the task is and how it is to be done. A page should:

repeat language and concepts used in the lesson
use a small number of different response modes and task types

have a layout that helps, not interferes, with the task

highlight the text, not illustrations

Procedures. Workbook exercises are meant to provide guided and independent practice of skills taught in the lesson. They must be critically evaluated for quality of presentation, accuracy, and appropriateness. A procedure should:

provide clear, unambiguous, easy-to-follow instructions

use accurate information in both questions and answers

use a response mode that yields complete and meaningful information

use a response mode for reading and writing practice

make the purpose of the task clear

be part of a pattern of responses and a sequence of concepts

Evaluation of Teacher's Guide Materials

Teacher's guides may not explain how to teach comprehension, according to an analysis of materials by Durkin (1981). The guides often offer precise help with easy comprehension instructional issues but can be obscure or silent on difficult issues or when specific help is needed. Difficult-to-teach topics may often be mentioned rather than explained, and definitions of terms are substituted for instruction about the topic. Often, instruction in a concept is replaced by practice in doing a task. To make matters worse, guided practice may not be directly related to the concept being taught or the text being read.

If a teacher is relying on the guide and the guide does not give adequate advice about how to organize lessons or teach comprehension, then the teacher must improvise. Some teachers will be successful but others will not be. In the latter situation, story and expository text reading may be sacrificed or poorly taught while the more completely described workbook and skill instruction activities become overemphasized (Mason, 1983). To keep that from happening, you will need to develop a critical eye to distinguish good from not-so-good activities and the confidence to insert, replace, and modify lessons and practice materials.

Evaluate the teacher's guide to see if it has the weaknesses identified by Durkin. If you find serious weaknesses in the guide, use it selectively. That is, implement exactly only the activities you judge to be sound, and adapt or omit ones that are not adequately presented.

Here are some questions to ask when evaluating the quality of teaching guide materials.

1. Are the text materials at the center of instruction? It is hoped they are.
2. Is comprehension instruction adequately designed and explained? If not, review the concepts discussed in Chapters 2, 3, and 4 of this textbook.
3. Is there a good match between the activity and the text to be used? They should be connected.

4. Do the students have the opportunity to practice the skills taught? If not, provide practice materials.
5. Will the explanation for doing the workbook or other practice exercise take too much time or be too complex? If so, the exercise is flawed and should be omitted.
6. Will use of the workbook or other practice exercises take more time than the actual reading and writing of connected text? If so, the lesson needs to be refocused.

∎ SUMMARY

This chapter focused on the instructional approaches and materials used in teaching reading and connecting it with writing. In the perspective section we explained how reading instruction has changed over time in response to social needs. This background was provided to help you see how different instructional approaches that were meant to achieve different goals came about.

The first three key concepts covered the major reading approaches and materials. Basal reading programs were described in considerable detail and suggestions were given for using them in a flexible manner. Individualized reading approaches and integrated language arts were then described. Both have much to offer, especially if attention is paid to the careful organization of sequences of instruction. In the fourth key concept we emphasized the need for goal-directed instruction and covered various ways of evaluating reading materials.

From the classification and analysis of materials and methods in this chapter, we hope you have gained an understanding of the strengths and weaknesses of various reading methods and materials. Our aim was to help you learn to select appropriate methods and materials according to the needs of your students. In short, we believe the preferred approach will usually be an eclectic one, over a period of time, incorporating quite a variety of methods and materials.

∎ BIBLIOGRAPHY

References

Abrahamson, R., & Shannon, P. (1983). A plot structure analysis of favorite picture books. *The Reading Teacher, 37,* 44–50.

Anderson, T., & Armbruster, B. (1984). Content area textbooks. In R. Anderson, J. Osborn, & R. Tierney (Eds.), *Learning to read in American schools.* Hillsdale, NJ: Erlbaum.

Arbuthnot, M. (1957). *Children and books* (2nd ed.). Glenview, IL: Scott, Foresman.

Armbruster, B., & Anderson, T. (1984). Producing "considerate" expository text: or Easy reading is damned hard writing (Reading Education Report No. 46). Urbana, IL: University of Illinois, Center for the Study of Reading.

Barr, R., & Sadow, M. (1989). Influence of basal programs on fourth-grade reading instruction. *Reading Research Quarterly, 24,* 44–71.

Britton, J. (1987). *Writing and reading in the classroom* (Technical Report No. 8). Berkeley: University of California.

Burrows, A. (1952). *Teaching children in the middle grades.* Boston: Heath.

Clark, C., & Yinger, R. (1979). Teachers' thinking. In P. Peterson & H. Walberg (Eds.), *Research on teaching.* Berkeley, CA: McCutchan.

Dole, J., Rogers, T., & Osborn, J. (1987). Improving the selection of basal reading programs: A report of the textbook adoption guidelines project. *The Elementary School Journal, 87,* 283–298.

Durkin, D. (1981). Reading comprehension instruction in five basal reader series. *Reading Research Quarterly, 16,* 515–544.

Durkin, D. (1987). Influence on basal reader programs. *The Elementary School Journal, 87,* 332–341.

Egan, O. (1983). In defense of traditional language: Folktales and reading texts. *The Reading Teacher, 37,* 228–233.

The Elementary School Library Collection: A Guide to Books and Other Media (16th Edition). (1988). Williamsport, PA: Brodart Company.

Eliot, C. (1898). *Educational reform.* New York: Century.

Fisher, C., Berliner, D., Filby, N., Marliave, R., Cohen, R., Dishaw, M., & Moore, J. (1978). *Teaching and learning in elementary schools: A summary of the Beginning Teacher Evaluation Study.* San Francisco: Far West Regional Laboratory for Educational Research and Development.

Flood, J., & Lapp, D. (1986). Types of texts: The match between what students read in basals and what they encounter in tests. *Reading Research Quarterly, 21,* 284–297.

Galda, L. (1982). Playing about a story: Its impact on comprehension. *The Reading Teacher, 36,* 52–55.

Gourley, J. (1984). Discourse structure: Expectations of beginning readers and readability of text. *Journal of Reading Behavior, 16,* 169–188.

Jalongo, M. (1983). Bibliotherapy: Literature to promote socioemotional growth. *The Reading Teacher, 36,* 796–803.

Mason, J. (1983). An examination of reading in third and fourth grades. *The Reading Teacher, 36,* 906–913.

Mason, J., & Osborn, J. (1982). *When do children begin "Reading to learn"?: A survey of classroom reading instruction practices in grades two through five* (Technical Report No. 26). Urbana, IL: University of Illinois, Center for the Study of Reading.

Moss, J. (1982). Reading and discussing fairy tales—old and new. *The Reading Teacher, 35,* 656–659.

Naylor, K. (1988). Classroom materials. *The Reading Teacher, 42,* 84.

Osborn, J. (1984). The purposes, uses, and contents of workbooks and some guidelines for publishers. In R. C. Anderson, J. Osborn, & R. Tierney (Eds.), *Learning to read in American schools: Basal readers and content texts.* Hillsdale, NJ: Erlbaum.

Pinnell, G., DeFord, D., & Lyons, C. (1988). *Reading recovery: Early intervention for at-risk first graders.* Arlington, VA: Educational Research Service.

Schmidt, W., Caul, J., Byers, J., & Buchmann, M. (1984). Content of basal text selections: Implications for comprehension instruction. In G. Duffy, L. Roehler, & J. Mason (Eds.), *Comprehension instruction: Perspectives and suggestions.* New York: Longman.

Shannon, P. (1987). Commercial reading materials, a technological ideology, and the deskilling of teachers. *The Elementary School Journal, 87,* 307–331.

Smilansky, S. (1971). Can adults facilitate play in children? Theoretical and practical considerations. In *Play.* Washington, DC: National Association for the Education of Young Children.

Smith, N. (1926). *One hundred ways of teaching silent reading for all grades.* New York: World Book Company.

Smith, N. (1965). *American reading instruction.* Newark, DE: International Reading Association.

Stott, J. (1982). A structuralist approach to teaching novels in elementary grades. *The Reading Teacher, 36,* 136–143.

Sutherland, Z., & Livingston, M. (1984). *The Scott, Foresman anthology of children's literature.* Glenview, IL: Scott, Foresman.

Venezky, R. (1987). A history of the American reading textbook. *The Elementary School Journal, 87,* 247–266.

Walmsley, S., & Walp, T. (1990). Toward an integrated language arts curriculum in elementary school: Philosophy, practice, and implications. *The Elementary School Journal.*

West, R. (1964). *Individualized reading instruction.* Port Washington, NY: Kennikat Press.

Yamada, Y. (1983). How much can children learn from a single book? *The Reading Teacher, 36,* 880–883.

Children's Books Cited

Bloomfield, L., & Barnhart, C. (1961). *Let's read: A linguistic approach.* Detroit: Wayne State Press.

Bryce, C., & Spaulding, F. (1907, 1916). *The Aldine Readers: A primer.* New York: Newson.

Colman, H. (1963). *Peter's brownstone house.* New York: Morrow.

Foley, L. M. (1983). Somebody stole second. In I. E. Aaron & R. Koke (Eds.), *Hidden wonders.* Glenview, IL: Scott, Foresman.

Klein, L. (1983). *Old, older, oldest.* New York: Hastings House.

McCracken, G., & Walcutt, C. (1975). *Book A: Basic reading.* Philadelphia: Lippincott.

McGuffey's eclectic primer. Rev. ed. (1881). New York: American Book Company.

Williams, J. (1978). *The practical princess and other liberating fairy tales.* New York: Parents Magazine Press.

Further Readings

Abrahamson, R. J. (1981). An update on wordless picture books with an annotated bibliography. *The Reading Teacher, 34,* 417–421.

Baumann, J. F. (1984). How to expand a basal reading program. *The Reading Teacher, 37,* 604–607.

Blanchard, J., Mason, G., & Daniel, D. (1987). *Computer applications in reading* (3rd ed.). Newark, DE: International Reading Association.

Burris, N., & Lentz, K. (1983). Caption books in the classroom. *The Reading Teacher, 36,* 872–875.

Chall, J., & Conrad, S. Resources and their use for reading instruction. In A. C. Purves & O. Niles (Eds.), *Becoming readers in a complex society.* Part I, 83rd Yearbook of the National Society for the Study of Education. Chicago, IL: University of Chicago Press.

Copperman, P. (1986). *Taking books to heart: How to develop a love of reading in your child.* Reading, MA: Addison-Wesley.

Cox, J., & Wallis, B. (1982). Books for the Cajun child—Lagniappe or a little something extra for multicultural teaching. *The Reading Teacher, 36,* 263–266.

Dole, J., & Johnson, V. (1981). Beyond the textbook: Science literature for young people. *Journal of Reading, 24,* 579–582.

Greenlinger-Harless, C. S. (1984). Updated cross-referenced index to U.S. reading materials, grades K–8. *The Reading Teacher, 37,* 871.

Hansen, J. (1987). *When writers read.* Portsmouth, NH: Heinemann.

Jalongo, M., & Bromley, K. (1984). Developing linguistic competence through song picture books. *The Reading Teacher, 37,* 840–845.

Kitagawa, M., & Kitagawa, C. (1987). *Making connections with writing: An expressive writing model in Japanese schools.* Portsmouth, NH: Heinemann.

Koenke, K. (1981). The careful use of comic books. *The Reading Teacher, 34,* 529–595.

Miccinati, J., Sanford, J., & Hepner, G. (1983). Teaching reading through the arts: An annotated bibliography. *The Reading Teacher, 36,* 412–417.

Reimer, B. L. (1983). Recipes for language experience stories. *The Reading Teacher, 36,* 396–401.

Sharp, P. (1984). Teaching with picture books throughout the curriculum. *The Reading Teacher, 38,* 132–137.

Stauffer, R. (1970). *The language-experience approach to the teaching of reading.* New York: Harper & Row.

Storey, D. C. (1982). Reading in the content areas: Fictionalized biographies and diaries for social studies. *The Reading Teacher, 35,* 796–798.

Wagoner, S. (1982). Mexican-Americans in children's literature since 1970. *The Reading Teacher, 36,* 274–279.

Wood, K. (1983). A variation on an old theme: 4-way oral reading. *The Reading Teacher, 37,* 38–43.

Organizing and Managing the Classroom Reading Program

Because I had no sense of myself as a teacher, I took my cues from the people above and below me. I mimicked older teachers, when I wasn't arrogantly telling them how much I knew. I followed all the rules of the administrators and worried about my supervisor. If a student said, "But this is not the way we did it last year," I would change the procedure. Much of what I did was determined by fear that I would look like a fool in front of my students.

At the same time that I was filling everyone else's expectations, I was exhilarated by teaching. I loved interacting with so many students; I loved to think and write and talk about teaching; and I loved being in control. . . . I thought that I could control everyone's learning. If I prepared the perfect lesson, or devised the perfect exercise, every student would learn. I controlled discussions, tests, assignments, everything.

I enjoyed being the center of attention, and I worked hard at giving a good performance. Even when students worked in groups, I prided myself on my ability to "keep an eye on everyone" and squelch any "irrelevant" talk. . . .

Five years later, I began to feel competent, not just flashy, in a classroom. Because I was building a stronger sense of myself as a teacher (and as an adult outside of school), I could shed the external definitions of myself. I did not need student or administrative approval for what I did, and I could act and judge independently. As my competence grew, the loneliness and isolation of the classroom began to feel like an opportunity for freedom. . . .

As I returned to teaching [after having a baby], I carried with me a new understanding of what it meant to nurture others. Although I had less time to be obsessed about teaching, the time I spent thinking about classrooms was focused differently from before. I no longer thought so much about myself—what I would say, how I would appear, how I would judge and correct. Instead I thought about the students and what I could do to allow them to take more responsibility for their own learning. I wanted to accompany them through learning.
(Lightfoot, 1983, pp. 253–254)

▍ OVERVIEW

The purpose of this chapter is to provide information about how effective teachers organize and manage their classrooms for reading instruction. To prepare you for considering these ideas, the perspective section introduces a set of overriding principles of teaching and instructional decision-making. The key concepts that follow describe both classroom organization and management issues. Some relate specifically to the teaching of reading and others are an important component also for teaching other subjects.

The first key concept describes an appropriate learning environment. It sets out the more general classroom management issues and suggests how you might prepare for them. The second key concept provides advice about scheduling and organizing reading lessons in the school day. The third explains how the success of your reading program is complexly related to decisions you make about grouping children for instruction and to the climate for learning. The fourth presents alternative views about organizing your lessons. Each key concept describes what you need to consider and organize in order to create an effective instructional atmosphere.

Chapter 11 is organized around the following key concepts:

Key Concept 1: Teachers should have an understanding of classroom management principles, an essential background for effective reading instruction.

Key Concept 2: Reading should be scheduled at the most opportune time and in the most effective way possible.

Key Concept 3: Teachers need to understand the complex instructional and motivational issues involved in grouping children for instruction.

Key Concept 4: Teachers need to understand new ways of organizing their instructional content, methods, lesson sequences, and classroom settings.

▍ PERSPECTIVE
Establishing an Effective Setting for Reading Instruction

We know from the research on teacher effectiveness that there are many "ifs," "ands," and "buts" when it comes to organizing a classroom for effective teaching. There are no simple formulas or lists of procedures which you can follow. Rather, your effectiveness will depend on understanding some of the complexities of instruction. Three overriding principles, presented next, will help you establish an effective classroom environment. One is to pay attention to how class time is spent, a second is to learn to make instructional decisions while you are teaching, and a third is to understand how to construct simplified models of teaching.

Instructional Time and Its Efficient Use

An effective reading program obviously depends on there being adequate time for instruction. Students are not likely to progress well in learning to read unless there is enough time allocated to teaching and practicing reading. A beginning step is for you to arrange your schedule to allow enough time for reading on a daily and weekly basis.

The average amounts of time that elementary school teachers reported allocating to various subject areas were presented by Goodlad (1983). The times shown below are for hours per week. We consider this average time for reading, which in the early grades works out to about one hour and 45 minutes per day, to be the minimum amount of time you should set aside for reading and language arts. You might keep these average times in mind when you set up your schedule.

Early elementary	Hours per week
Reading-language arts	8.46
Mathematics	4.65
Social studies	2.09
Science	1.65
Art, music, drama, dance	2.97
Physical education, recess	1.49
Upper elementary	
Reading-language arts	7.41
Mathematics	5.12
Social studies	3.83
Science	2.93
Art, music, drama, dance	2.88
Physical education, recess	2.26

There is an average of 180 days in the school year, with approximately eight hours per week of reading and language arts instruction or about 288 hours per year. However, instructional time in school will be affected by child and teacher absences, snow days, and teacher strikes. Time for reading should also be considered beyond the classroom. For example, actual reading time is affected by outside-of-school reading opportunities. Some parents foster library book reading, enforce homework-reading, and send their children for academic after-school and summer camp lessons.

Of course, just setting aside *time* for reading is not sufficient. Rosenshine

(1979) pointed out that teachers need to distinguish between *allocated time* and *academic engaged time*. While allocated time is the amount of time scheduled, academic engaged time is the amount of time students spend working on academically relevant tasks. During the time allocated, students must be doing constructive work, work designed to encourage learning to read and reading to learn.

Finally, allocated and academic engaged time are usually affected by another factor, the reading group in which children are placed. Instruction given to low ability groups is typically of lower quality than that for high ability groups. There is less engaged time, a larger proportion of time is taken by management, the pace of instruction is slower, and there is an overemphasis on decoding and oral reading (Hiebert, 1983). This means that time and quality of instruction are often reduced for children assigned to low ability groups.

You can now see that thinking about time for instruction requires us to consider at least three dimensions: the number of hours available for instruction, children's attentiveness to the lesson, and the quality of the lesson for the group. Each dimension contributes to the amount that children learn. It is up to you to keep track of each so that you can provide maximum opportunities for reading and writing; keep children engaged with worthwhile literacy tasks, and develop higher quality instruction for children in low ability groups.

Making Good Decisions While Teaching

Effective reading instruction is an extremely complex process, and a teacher has to consider many factors at once. One solution is to sharpen your *decision-making* skills as you teach. This involves learning to make better on-the-spot instructional decisions and to adjust your plans in view of the immediate situation.

Taking appropriate action in an instructional situation requires you to understand *interactive decision-making*, or how to make decisions while teaching (Good, 1983; Clark & Yinger, 1979). In interactive decision-making, you begin by following a plan but, as the lesson moves forward, you see that the planned activities or topics may not be working. You adjust to the changes or new demands by modifying your lesson.

For example, we observed a reading lesson given to second graders who seemed unable to see cause-and-effect relationships in the basal story. Judging from the children's responses, the teacher identified the source of their confusion to be story events that had been presented in a flashback, a literary device unfamiliar to them. Although she hadn't planned to do so, the teacher decided to explain about flashbacks. She took the children through a review of story events, an exercise ending when they were able to tell her how to list the events on the chalkboard in sequential order. Only then did she resume the discussion of cause-and-effect relationships. Now the children were easily able to answer her questions.

As we see in this example, if you want your lesson to be a successful one, beneficial to the students' learning, you can't always stay with your original plan. Instead, you must make decisions about how to reorganize the lesson. In this example, if the teacher hadn't digressed from the discussion originally planned, her students probably would have learned very little. But because the teacher made a sound decision to modify the lesson, the students learned something about how to analyze stories with flashbacks, a comprehension ability likely to be useful in the future.

Situations similar to this will frequently arise; you will find you are not able to follow your original plan. Do not feel that you have failed. While it is true that more experienced teachers know better what to expect from their students and are less likely to have to depart radically from their plans, they also know that almost all lessons have moments when the unexpected happens. Among such unexpected occurrences may be the discovery that children know more about a certain topic than the teacher expected, or find uninteresting an activity that had been expected to capture their interest.

At times, these unexpected occurrences provide *teachable moments* for engaging children in learning and helping them recognize new ideas or make new connections among ideas. Teachable moments are those occasions when a child asks a question or makes a comment indicating a special readiness to learn something. More often than not, the teachable moment comes as a surprise to the teacher. For example, a teacher told us about giving a reading lesson during which a second grade student had a remarkable insight. One of the opening episodes in the basal story was about sighted children who wouldn't allow a blind boy to join in their game. The student commented that those children were actually "blind" in their own way. The teacher was then able to build upon this idea to develop the group's understanding of how the blind must sometimes cope with the mental blindness or ignorance of others, in addition to their physical handicap.

As you can see, given the many complexities in teaching effective reading lessons, it is not necessarily a good idea to map out in advance every detail of a lesson, and then stick rigidly to that plan. This kind of inflexibility could prevent you from taking advantage of the prime opportunities for learning provided by unexpected occurrences. While good planning is essential, it is equally important to learn how to make informed decisions in the course of teaching lessons. This line of reasoning led Brophy (1984) to suggest:

> . . . lessons that go entirely according to plan may be less successful at least in some respects, than lessons that go generally according to plan but that require some interactive decision making involving shifts to alternative strategies to respond to unforeseen developments. (p. 73)

As a decision-maker you will learn to take advantage of prime but unanticipated opportunities for learning as they arise, and to respond to cues from the children that they are understanding, or not understanding, the points you are trying to get across. You will try to provide instruction in a responsive manner, always keeping in touch with the students' thinking. A study by Peterson and Clark (1978) suggests that such responsive instruction may help students learn to think more reflectively.

Of course, making the proper "in-flight" adjustments to lessons is easier said than done. Brophy (1984) suggests that teachers go through three stages in developing their skills as decision-makers. Beginning teachers' earliest concerns are with "survival." They first address issues of classroom management and scheduling. Once these areas are under control, they turn to issues of instruction. In this second stage teachers are concerned with "procedure" or the mechanics of instruction. They generally rely on detailed written plans or the teacher's guide, referring to these materials frequently during the course of the lesson. This may cause them to behave somewhat too rigidly and not responsively enough. However, Brophy believes it wise for most beginning teachers to follow such scripts, because this practice allows them to deal with what they might otherwise find to be an overwhelmingly complex task.

In Brophy's view, teachers do not become good decision-makers, in the sense described above, until they reach the third stage. At this point they have gained enough experience and knowledge to feel comfortable and confident during lessons. Only then is it possible to adjust to unexpected occurrences, such as unplanned teachable moments.

We recommend that you set as a long-term, but not immediate goal, development of the ability to make sound in-flight decisions. As Brophy suggests, most beginning teachers will find themselves with immediate concerns for survival and procedure, and if so, these problems should be tackled first. Some of these techniques are described next and in the first two key concepts of this chapter. The use of scripts and routines, as well as simplified models, are possible and acceptable solutions. As you become a more effective manager, you will be more flexible and responsive to students' needs in learning to read, as shown in moment-to-moment interactions with them during lessons.

Using Simplified Models of Teaching

Although teaching is very complex and has far too many aspects for a beginning teacher to consider all at once, there are ways to simplify it. In fact, effective teachers do not try to attend to all aspects of instruction at one time. Instead, they construct simplified models of the classroom (Shulman, 1983). To simplify your own teaching, do not try at first to manage the children, create perfect lessons, set up smooth and meaningful interactions with students *and* understand what and how children are learning. No one can achieve instant and complete success on all aspects of teaching. According to Hawkins (1973): "It may be possible to learn in two or three years the kind of practice which then leads to another twenty years of learning" (p. 7).

In keeping with Brophy's notion of stages of teaching, at first simplify your instruction so that you can pay particular attention to classroom management. After all, children will not learn if they are inattentive to the lesson. Rely at first on clearly structured or even scripted lessons until the children are listening to you and to each other, working in groups and by themselves, and helping you maintain an orderly, smooth-running working environment. Then you can begin to experiment with your own instructional ideas.

Here are some examples of ways you can simplify the teaching situation in order to reduce its complexity:

1. For the first one or two weeks of the school year, imagine that all the children are "average-ability" students in reading. Use whole class instruction and have all the children read from the same textbook (perhaps a textbook meant for the grade you are teaching but no longer being used in your school), participate in the same skill lessons, and do the same writing activities and practice exercises. Listen to children as they read aloud together, in partners, or to you individually. Watch as they complete workbook exercises and look at their creative writing assignments. Notice which children answer your questions, talk to them about what they like to read, and ask what they find difficult about learning to read. Using this simplified, whole class model of instruction at the beginning of the year allows you the time to understand better how your students read, write, and learn. You will be able to make informal diagnoses of children's reading and gain information about how to group them for instruction.

2. Classroom discipline is the major problem faced by first year teachers, according to Veeman (1984). Since it takes time to establish appropriate lessons and effective management techniques, begin teaching reading by laying out a clear routine for reading lessons and setting up classroom rules for lessons, independent reading, and seatwork activity. Resolve discipline problems as quickly and quietly as possible. Eventually, you will learn to spot problem situations before they arise and will know how to keep children focused on their lessons or independent work.

3. As you teach a reading skill or concept, don't try to figure out whether all the children understand it. Instead pick out those children who are slightly below average as readers. Watch them as you teach and ask them questions to see if they understand. If they do, you are probably moving through the lesson at about the right pace, not so slow that most become bored and not so fast that too many become "lost" and stop trying to understand.

4. An idea for simplifying discipline problems, and which can lead to other ways to view grouped instruction, was suggested by an Indiana teacher of the year, Susan Talbot. When a group is about to begin a new story she announces the story name to the class and allows anyone else to join the group to read and discuss the story. Children from higher groups often

join because they want to read a story again, and children from lower groups often take part in reading a more difficult story. The approach allows children more story reading opportunities and gives the teacher a way of keeping hard-to-manage children working.

Using reasonable means such as these to reduce the number of different things you have to think about while teaching reading will help you to be more effective. When you are more experienced, you will know how to expand on these ideas and fit instruction more closely to your particular situation and the children you teach.

In summary, then, fulfilling the intent of these instructional principles means going beyond setting aside one hour a day to teach reading following preplanned lessons. It means making more efficient use of your students' lesson time, working toward proficiency in interactive decision-making, and using simplified teaching procedures.

Key Concept 1

Teachers should have an understanding of classroom management principles, an essential background for effective reading instruction.

█ CLASSROOM MANAGEMENT PRINCIPLES

Large-scale studies of schools and classrooms have led to the identification of a set of management characteristics that make a difference in learning. They show what teachers should do to improve their reading instruction. Rutter (1983) describes the following characteristics:

> Appropriate classroom management [characteristics] include a high proportion of lesson time spent on the subject matter of the lesson (as distinct from setting up equipment, handing out papers, dealing with disciplinary problems, etc.; a high proportion of teacher time spent interacting with the class as a whole, rather than with individuals; a minimum of disciplinary intervention; lessons beginning and ending on time; clear and unambiguous feedback to pupils on both their performance and what was expected of them; and ample use of praise for good performance. (p. 29)

Effective management involves gaining students' attention and providing an orderly environment for learning. Little time is wasted by distributing papers, making transitions from one activity to the next, or dealing with discipline problems. With group-based discipline standards, children know what is expected, and individuals are not singled out for criticism. Rule enforcement is carried out on the spot, with a minimum of lesson interference. Finally, criticism and physical punishment are avoided. As Rutter explained:

"In the long run good discipline is achieved by the majority of pupils *wanting* to participate in the educational process rather than doing so merely through fear of retribution" (p. 31).

Organization of the Classroom

Before you meet your students on the first day of class, many important decisions should already be made. We describe those decisions that have to do with organizing classroom spaces and setting up learning centers.

A well-organized classroom is usually one with a regular place for everything. Children know where to go for supplies and have a designated place for their own belongings. A well-organized classroom then can become a literacy-rich environment, filled with useful and interesting printed information. Children's work and art samples can decorate the walls. There can be displays including pictures and other materials related to topics being studied, notices about work activities and listings of child helpers, the classroom schedule, and new books.

Placement of desks, chairs, tables, learning centers, and materials should be determined before children arrive. Consider each in terms of the way you expect to work and how you want children grouped to work with you and to work independently.

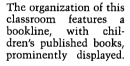

The organization of this classroom features a bookline, with children's published books, prominently displayed.

On graph paper, draw the floor plan of the way you would like to set up your classroom. Use a scale of one inch to represent four or five feet. Mark the likely location of chalkboards, bulletin boards, doors, windows, and coat and storage areas. Then show where you would place desks and learning centers. Indicate the areas you would use for large and small group activities. Draw arrows for the children's likely traffic patterns. Based on the way you expect to teach reading, write a brief explanation or justification for your plan.

Place your desk so that it serves a useful purpose. That is, decide how you will use it, whether as a place from which to watch children work, a place where children come for help, a center for correcting papers, or a storage place. If it is principally a place where individuals are helped, the desk ought to be at the back or side of the room. Then your interactions with children will be more private and less distracting to other children. If it is a place from which you monitor the class, place the desk at the front of the room. If you do not plan to use it except to store papers, put it in an out-of-the-way corner.

Your classroom is likely either to have separate desks for each child or tables where four to six children sit. If there are desks, you might place children in rows or in tablelike groups. The advantages to rows are twofold: Everyone can be facing you and see the blackboard as you conduct whole-class lessons. Children can see and hear you more easily and are less likely to talk to one another (especially if you place talkative and easily distracted children near the front of the room). One advantage to grouped desks is that you can foster cooperative learning by having children work together. The instruction we have recommended in this book slightly favors the grouped desk arrangement, although either could be used. You should make your decision based on whether you are going to emphasize teacher-directed or peer-supported activities.

Materials ought to be placed on shelves and labeled so that children can use them without help. Places need to be set up for children to hand in their completed work and to pick it up after it is corrected. Supplementary writing materials, learning games, and books need convenient and well-labeled places so that children can find and replace them without help. Tables for learning centers are often placed at the back or side of the classroom, away from your small group teaching area.

Setting Up Routines

Children need to know what they are supposed to do and when. Most want to learn and be cooperative. If you give them a chance to follow your rules, provided the rules are reasonable, most will be agreeable and will even help you monitor those who do not appreciate a regular, predictable structure. Prepare clear, simple rules for the whole class, small groups, and individual readers. Let children know how to conduct themselves in each learning setting and how to deal with problems without bothering you or others.

Children need to carry out routine activities without supervision. For example, they should know the rules for sharpening a pencil (some teachers have everyone check that they have two sharp pencils each day before school begins), leaving the room, lining up for recess, and waiting for class to begin or for groups to change. Children in orderly classrooms are responsive to the teacher's signaling, such as for reading groups to change places. They bring the correct materials with them to small group reading lessons, they have a serious attitude about reading, and they adapt to the established and predictable schedule.

Children need to know how to get help on independent work, when the teacher is working with other children. You should let children know how to signal their need for your help (e.g., raise their hands, come to your desk, write their names on the board), and how they might secure help from classmates. It is particularly important to establish these rules early in the school year. Otherwise great confusion will occur while you are trying to teach lessons to small groups or work with individuals.

Children should also know what to do when finished with assignments. Your solution will depend partly on the extra resources you have made available to children and also on children's ability to work without disturbing others. Ideally, children should look upon the time as an opportunity to do independent reading or writing, complete or correct back work, work on a long-term project, help other children, or work on supplementary science, math, or computer activities. As children become adept in working on their own, you can make more options available to them. At first, however, too many options could create confusion for the children and distract them from regular classroom tasks.

Setting Up Effective Instruction for Small Groups

Instructional research by Anderson, Evertson, and Brophy (1982) has led to a list of six general principles for teaching reading to small groups (p. 2). These are listed and explained below:

1. *Reading groups should be organized for efficient, sustained focus on the content to be learned.* Anderson et al. recommend that teacher time with each reading group average 25 to 30 minutes per day. Teach students to move into the reading group with their materials as soon as you give the signal. If appropriate for children from this cultural background, use an ordered turn arrangement to avoid wasting time waiting for volunteers and to allow all students to be prepared to respond. To maintain a focus on the academic task without having to deal with managerial problems, avoid letting children outside the reading group interrupt you. This can be accomplished in part by

positioning yourself so that you can monitor the rest of the class as you teach a reading group.

2. *All students should be not merely attentive, but actively involved in the lesson.* One way to do this is to begin lessons with an overview describing what students will learn and why it is important. Another way is to use questions, particularly those that require students to predict the content of the next segment of the story. Concentrate the discussion on the academic content and keep students focused on the topic, concept, or skill to be learned.

3. *Questions and tasks should be easy enough to enable the teacher to move the lesson along at a brisk pace.* They recommend about an 80 percent success rate for answers to your questions about new material and about a 95 percent success rate for review material.

4. *Students should receive frequent opportunities to read and respond to questions, and should get clear feedback about the correctness of their performance.* Choral responses and ordered turns give everyone the opportunity to answer. When they do answer, begin the lesson by acknowledging correctness briefly (nod, repeat what was said, or say "right"). Later in the lesson when children understand whether responses are correct or not, you can omit acknowledgments. Use praise sparingly unless you are trying to change the behavior of a problem student; for the most part, reserve it for particularly well phrased answers or answers to difficult questions. Avoid criticism; instead, help students correct their wrong answers. Use follow-up questions occasionally to help students integrate or better understand an important idea.

5. *Skills should be mastered to overlearning, with new ones gradually phased in while old ones are being mastered.* When presenting new information (such as new words), do not merely give the information and move on. Explain it, relate it to other work, or have students relate it to their knowledge or experience. Be sure that students know what to do and how to do it before they begin to work independently. One way to check is to have one of the slowest students in the group demonstrate how to accomplish the task. If necessary, give guided practice by doing the first two or three problems with the students.

6. *Although instruction takes place in the group setting for efficiency reasons, the teacher monitors the progress of each individual student and provides whatever specific instruction, feedback, or opportunities to practice each student requires.* Be sure everyone has opportunities to respond to your questions. You may need to keep children from calling out answers so that shy and slower children have an opportunity to answer. When using a choral reading approach, watch carefully that everyone responds together. If some children delay responding, give them individual chances to answer or coach them until they can answer. When asking individuals to respond, wait for answers (though not so long that others become impatient or the child being asked to respond becomes embarrassed). If a child cannot respond without help, give clues or simplify the question. If that does not work, give the an-

swer or call on another to answer. If part of the answer is given, rephrase it so that children hear the correct part. If you are not sure they understand, amplify on the answer or have someone explain why it is correct.

Responding to Different Types of Learners

Kedar-Voivodas (1983) reviewed research on teachers' attitudes toward their students. Teachers appear to distinguish three kinds of students:

1. *Pupils*—children who are "patient, docile, passive, orderly, conforming, obedient, and acquiescent to rules and regulations, receptive to and respectful of authority, easily controllable and socially adept" (p. 417).
2. *Receptive learners*—children who are able to "perform adequately in established curriculum areas, on prescribed measures, at set times, and by set criteria . . . [also] the ability to work independently and efficiently despite distractions. . . . Furthermore, related educational activities, such as homework and class assignments, have to be punctually and adequately performed" (p. 417).
3. *Active learners*—children who go beyond "the established academic curriculum both in terms of the content to be mastered and in the processes for gaining such mastery. . . . Scholarly traits include curiosity, active probing and exploring, challenging authority, an independent and questioning mind, an insistence on explanations, and a self-imposed discipline that serves the demands of scholarship rather than the wishes and desires of other people" (p. 418).

Children who fit the "active learner" description tend to be rejected more often by teachers than "pupils" or "receptive learners." This is because active learners are harder to discipline and work with. Furthermore, since more boys than girls seem to be active learners, a bias against those children can lead to a preference for instructing girls over boys.

We caution you to observe your own responses to active learners and avoid a bias in favor of "pupils" or "receptive learners." While active learners are undoubtedly more difficult to teach and will challenge and be more critical of your instruction, they have an attitude and approach toward learning that other children in the classroom would do well to emulate.

Fostering a Sense of Responsibility for Learning

An important long-term instructional goal is for children to take on the responsibility for their own learning. Children should read, study, and learn because they want to know about something or master a skill. They should strive to be more like *active learners.* Marshall and Weinstein (1984) reviewed the approaches that teachers can take to foster this attitude. From their work, we suggest the following guidelines:

Exercise

Observe, or watch a videotape of, an experienced teacher during the first ten minutes of the school day. When did children make the shift from talking to friends to getting ready to work? How long did it take? Did the teacher do anything to foster that shift, or was the routine so well established that the teacher did not need to signal the change? How did the teacher prepare for the first lesson (e.g., put work on the board, have children get out books, hand back papers, work with individuals)? Describe differences you saw in individuals' willingness to begin to work, and if the teacher had to encourage some individuals to begin working, how that was done.

Figure out ways to share the responsibility for learning with your students. To encourage students to be more involved in their reading lessons, offer them work choices, give them several things to do but let them choose what to do first, or let them choose whom to work with to get the task done.

Have students help you create the reading tasks and the goals. Discuss both short-term and long-term learning goals with them. Foster the concept of individually-determined goals.

Encourage students to check their own answers and evaluate their own performance. Give students opportunities to monitor their progress. Help them to understand how their performance on each assignment can foster a gradual improvement in their reading as well as mastery of different learning goals (such as reading fluency, word knowledge, problem solving, outlining, etc.).

▌ TASK ENVIRONMENTS

Teachers set up their classrooms so that students understand the task demands. However, teachers vary in the degree to which they are successful. Anderson, Stevens, Prawat, and Nickerson (1988) found two important dimensions of the more successful teachers, those whose classroom environments were more highly rated by the researchers. One dimension was the extent to which teachers structured classroom information to make it predictable and understandable to students. Highly rated teachers reduced the inferences students had to make, explicitly presenting information that would help students understand how to behave and how to respond to task demands. For example, they described not only procedural details and regular routines and patterns, but also how appropriate behavior could vary across tasks or lessons. One teacher said to students, "During morning work time, the rule for talking is quiet whispering if you are helping one another. During our silent reading time, you should be silent." Teachers gave reasons for exceptions and were consistent in following through on predictions and rules. They also explicitly linked ideas, relating specific rules to general principles, and by relating similar incidents to one another.

The second important dimension involved allowing students to use their knowledge to regulate their own task activity. Highly rated teachers allowed some choices within clearly defined limits, often building them into the regular routine. For example, one teacher scheduled independent work times during the afternoons in the fall, controlling their sequencing of work and monitoring their progress. By the spring, she allowed students to set their own priorities for accomplishing the tasks, and monitored their progress as they worked. This meant that the teacher was not the sole decision maker about what would be done and in what order.

Anderson et al. (1988) report the following observation of a successful teacher:

> Teacher A taught third grade in a school in which 23% of the students were from families receiving AFDC. Students were bused to this school from a wide variety of neighborhoods, including some rural areas and some public housing developments. The narratives revealed a classroom in which teachers and students respected one another, there was a great deal of humor, and students were frequently enthusiastic about a lesson presented by the teacher.
>
> The teacher provided a great deal of information to the students about the standards in the classroom and how, when, and why they applied. This information was "structured" in the sense that the teacher made explicit connections between events, their antecedents and consequences, and the expected student role, and she consistently followed through on her predictions, building credibility for her statements. This was especially evident during the first 3 weeks of school. For example, she said on the second morning of school, "Every morning when you come in, there will be math on the board for you to do," and then she followed through with this pattern throughout the year. Also on the second morning, she explained that the morning schedule would typically include movement between classes for reading, but that for 2 weeks they would be doing something different, thus communicating to students about an exception to a regular pattern rather than changing patterns after 2 weeks without warning. In several instances during the first few weeks, she noted students' progress and good behavior and linked their success to their own actions, making clear the links between cause and effect. Corrections or reminders were accompanied by explanations such as, "If you drop paste on the floor, please wipe it off well because someone could slip on it and get hurt."
>
> As the year progressed, the classroom ran fairly smoothly, with students adept at moving from one event to another quickly. The work accountability system was clearly in evidence, and its consistent use was another example of structuring of information for the students, in that consequences were predictable because the teacher enforced the system. For example, in one observation, students had a designated place to turn in certain assignments, and an aide immediately checked another assignment when completed. Before dismissal for lunch, the teacher collected all work and then called out the names of students who were finished and could leave for lunch. Throughout the year, the teacher provided a

great deal of information about time to the students, such as pointing out how many minutes were left in the period to finish up work, or saying to a student who appeared to be off-task that his reading group would begin in 5 minutes. These time references focused students' attention on the passing of time, thus providing information that went beyond a correction of off-task behavior.

Although opportunities for self-regulation on school tasks were not very evident early in the year, the fall observations did reveal that procedures for water, bathroom, and pencil sharpening were in place and running smoothly without teacher permission. The teacher did provide some choices in early fall assignments (e.g., names for a graph, symbols for class map) and commented on student self-regulation when it occurred (e.g., "Jennie, I like the way you use your time," to a girl who had chosen to keep working on an assignment when others took a bathroom break. On another occasion, when a girl finished a reading assignment and resumed work on an earlier math paper, the teacher noticed and said, "Good . . . you're getting that math done. That's a good idea too."). Sometimes, the teacher would cue students' behavior without explicitly telling them what to do, which might have been a way of easing students into more thinking for themselves (e.g., she held up a science book, saying, "If you see what I am holding up, you will know what to get ready for next.").

By mid-year and the spring observations, there was more direct evidence that students were making task-related decisions and functioning independently. For example, students spontaneously began their assigned classroom jobs. When doing morning math, students regularly chose where they wanted to sit and work. For some other assignments, students could make choices about where to work and were allowed to go into the hall when they wanted to work with partners. Apparently, no management problems resulted from this. Students also had the option of joining a more advanced math group for instruction when they finished their regular assignments. During afternoons, students sometimes had a period for finishing work, and they independently monitored what they needed to do and in what order.

Many of the teacher's messages to students, especially corrections, relayed the message that they had choices and could control themselves. For example, she said to a boy who had been inattentive in reading group, "Go to your seat and put your head down. When you really want to listen, you can come back." In several ways, the teacher conveyed expectations and opportunities for students to make informed choices about how they would meet task demands in her classroom. This occurred within an environment where relationships were warm, humor was frequent, and students were not at risk for failure on tasks (because the teacher provided them with adequate information about the tasks and the accountability system). (pp. 290–291)

Key Concept 2

Reading should be scheduled at the most opportune time and in the most effective way possible.

▌ SCHEDULING READING

Because elementary school reading is generally held to be highly important but difficult to teach, most teachers schedule reading for the first period in the day, every day of the week. Children are more likely at that time to be alert and willing to concentrate. Set aside as much as two hours a day for the lessons if the children you teach are from homes that do not provide much support for literacy development or if you are going to merge reading with the other language arts.

Setting Up Instructional Groups

When you teach reading, you will need to decide whether to group students, and if so, the basis on which groups will be formed (e.g., by ability or by interest), the size of the groups, and when and for how long each will be taught.

Although many variations are possible, we present these options for you to consider: (1) whole class instruction, (2) small group instruction, and (3) individualized instruction and peer work groups. You will probably use one of these approaches most of the time and rely on the others less often. Each requires a different type of schedule.

Whole class lesson schedule. Whole class lessons are appropriate when you want to teach skills that all the children can learn together and need to practice. These lessons might feature phonics, word analysis, comprehension and reading-to-learn strategies, or study skills. The sample schedule presented in Figure 11.1 is adapted from Good, Grouws, and Ebmeier (1983), who conducted instructional research on the teaching of mathematics.

This is a fast-paced whole class schedule. Other suggestions for whole class reading instruction are found in a study comparing American with Japanese instruction (Mason et al., 1989).

Small group lesson schedule. Small group lessons are appropriate when you want to teach certain skills or topics to some children but not others. In other words, you have found considerable diversity in the reading instructional needs and in the interests of the children in your class. Thus, whole class lessons may not be an effective way of furthering the learning to read of the majority of your students.

The following is an example of a small group plan, one used successfully in primary grade classrooms (Au & Kawakami, 1984; Tharp, 1982). The class is first divided into four or five instruction groups, with grouping being based on criterion-referenced test results. The assumption is that children in each group will benefit from receiving the same lessons and independent practice activities, because they are at about the same reading level. Each group is usu-

Figure 11.1
Sample Schedule
for Whole Class Instruction

Daily Review (first eight minutes except Monday)

1. Review the concepts and skills associated with the homework
2. Collect and deal with homework assignments

Development (about twenty minutes)

1. Briefly focus on prerequisite skills and concepts
2. Focus on meaning and promoting student understanding by using lively explanations, demonstrations, process explanations, illustrations, etc.
3. Assess student comprehension

Seatwork (about fifteen minutes)

1. Provide uninterrupted successful practice
2. Momentum—keep the ball rolling—get everyone involved, then sustain involvement
3. Alerting—let students know their work will be checked at end of period
4. Accountability—check the students' work

Homework assignment

1. Given on a regular basis at the end of each class except Fridays
2. Should involve about fifteen minutes of work to be done at home
3. Should include some review

Special Reviews

1. Weekly review/maintenance
   a. Conduct during the first twenty minutes each Wednesday
   b. Focus on skills and concepts covered during the previous week
2. Monthly review/maintenance
   a. Conduct every fourth Monday
   b. Focus on skills and concepts covered since the last monthly review

Source: From *Active Mathematics Teaching* by Thomas L. Good, Douglas A. Grouws, and Howard Ebmeier. Copyright © 1983 by Longman Inc. Reprinted by permission of Longman Inc.

ally composed of three to seven children. We recommend, however, that you try to place fewer children in the lowest ability group, because these children typically need the most teacher attention.

In this plan teachers meet with each group for 20 to 25 minutes every day. Usually they meet with one of the lower ability groups first. While each group is receiving direct instruction from the teacher, the remaining children are working independently at one of several learning centers set up around the room. At the signal for a change from the teacher, everyone moves, either to another learning center or to the center for teacher-directed instruction. By the end of the reading period every child has received instruction from the teacher and has worked at several different learning centers. A sample schedule is shown in Figure 11.2.

▮ **Figure 11.2**
▮ **Sample Daily Schedule**
▮ **for Small Group Instruction**

Introduction to day's activities (first five minutes)

Teacher explains to the whole class any new activities and reminds children about ongoing activities and projects. Children ask questions about the work.

Small group lessons (one hour and forty minutes)

Teacher signals that children should begin work. Teacher meets for twenty minutes with each of the five reading groups. Teacher gives lessons with an ETR or other systematic method of comprehension instruction and also teaches particular word identification or vocabulary skills.

Wrap-up (last five to ten minutes each day)

Completed assignments are handed in. Teacher discusses with the whole class their progress at learning centers. Teacher also asks for reactions to the work and for suggestions for future work. Occasionally, children present their completed work to the class.

Schedule for individualized instruction or peer work groups. Individualized instruction can be conducted by having children work on individual readings and other assignments, for example, as in the individualized reading approach discussed in Chapter 10. Recent investigations suggest, however, that student-led small group activities may lead to greater learning than individual activities where children work alone. The small group in this case is often called a "peer work group." There are three to four children in each group, one each of high and low reading ability and one or two of average ability. There is one task for every group to carry out with each member of the group contributing to the end product. For example, groups might be asked to read and write a brief summary of an expository text. To accomplish this task would require children first to read the text, perhaps aloud if one child in the group is a very poor reader, or perhaps silently but with the children helping one another with unknown words. Then the children discuss the text and compose a summary. The teacher circulates among the peer work groups, helping them negotiate who will do which tasks and advising them about the

Exercise

Observe, or watch a videotape of, the first five to ten minutes of time a class is organized for whole class instruction, small group instruction, and in peer work groups. Notice how each is set up, how the teacher organizes the work activities, and the nature of the work. Estimate how long it takes for everyone to begin working in each setting, how children who are confused get help, and how the teacher monitors the whole class while still working with groups or individuals.

▌ **Figure 11.3**
▌ **Sample Schedule for Individualized**
▌ **Instruction or Peer Work Groups**

Set up (five to ten minutes)

The teacher explains what children are to do for the day or week and gives deadlines for completion. Children ask questions about the work and materials are handed out. Children might work with those who select the same task or might be put into working groups by the teacher.

Worktime (sixty to seventy minutes)

The children work in small clusters at their desks or at learning centers. They might be discussing the tasks and figuring out how they should be done and who will work on each part. They might be reading or writing by themselves and giving help to one another as it is requested. The teacher circulates around the room instructing and providing information to individuals or groups.

Wrap-up (five to ten minutes)

The teacher might discuss with the children what they accomplished and learned, how or why it was important, and how it fits with their other work. Assignments might be collected or corrected, and children might share completed projects with the rest of the class.

assignment. The completed assignment is evaluated by the teacher or by the groups themselves.

An alternative, less structured approach is called a "multitask" organization. Here there are a number of possible tasks such as independent reading, writing, and research projects for children to carry out. These are chosen by the children to be carried out at their own pace in small groups at learning centers. Children are encouraged to help one another as they work on the same assignments, but they complete and hand in their own work. Again, the teacher works with the small groups for large portions of the reading period.

These two approaches have in common the reliance on students' taking the initiative, assuming responsibility for learning, and cooperating to accomplish tasks. In both, the teacher manages behavior problems on an individual basis, talking with children privately while others work. Lessons still need to be formulated by the teacher and taught either to small groups or to the whole class. What is unique is the use of groups in which students help one another and work together on projects.

A schedule for this type of classroom organization would be more flexible than the others we described. It is likely, however, to have a structure such as that shown in Figure 11.3.

Advantages of Various Arrangements for Reading Instruction

Decisions about how to organize your class into instructional groups are among the most difficult for beginning teachers to make. While grouping children into small, ability-defined groups (homogeneous grouping) is the most common approach, it may not be the best for your students, certainly

▌ **Figure 11.4**
▌ **Advantages of Different**
▌ **Instructional Arrangements**

Advantages of the whole class arrangement:

1. You can use one lesson and set of practice materials.
2. You can often give longer lessons.
3. You can supervise all children during practice activities.
4. You can give private help as children are working.
5. You can lessen problems of labeling, low expectations, elitism, and poor self-concepts because children of lower ability are less obviously identified.

Advantages of the small, homogeneous group arrangement:

1. Because children are more similar in ability, you can match instruction to ability.
2. You can provide individualized feedback for comprehension responses and oral reading.
3. You can monitor and hold the attention of all children in the group.
4. You can maintain an orderly instructional environment without having to depend on the children to do so on their own.
5. By varying the size of the groups, you can put fewer children in the low group and give lower achieving children somewhat more attention.

Advantages of the peer work group arrangement:

1. You can use mixed ability groups which allow grouping by interest, a reduction of elitism, and an opportunity for children to work cooperatively and learn from one another.
2. You can circulate among and work with all of the groups.
3. You can give children more choices of tasks and options in learning and perhaps improve motivation.
4. You can place responsibility for learning more directly on the children and perhaps improve their sense of control over their own learning.
5. Since children are helping one another, you can assign more difficult practice materials.

not on all occasions. You should consider the advantages and disadvantages of each alternative. A listing of some of the advantages is presented in Figure 11.4.

Matching Classroom Organization Tasks and Patterns to Students' Academic Needs and Attainments

Ideally, students should be assigned tasks that match their level of understanding and their learning needs. That is, teachers "must avoid the twin pitfalls of demanding too much and expecting too little" (Plowden Report, 1967, p. 311). However, as Bennett and Desforges (1988) report in a study of third through sixth grade classes, teachers typically assigned tasks that were too difficult for the low attaining students and consistently underestimated the capabilities of higher attaining students.

> Visible or not, mismatching caused problems, at least in the short term, for low attainers and wasted opportunities for high attainers. Low attainers produced very little work, concentrated on the production aspects of tasks, were slow to start, made extensive demands on the teacher, and consequently spent considerable time waiting for help. They had limited memory for the stimulus material

in writing tasks and limited comprehension of the procedures in mathematics tasks. In contrast, high attainers were often held up by the production features of tasks. (p. 227)

Individualizing instruction for groups of children so that mismatched instruction seldom occurs, as this research demonstrates, is not easy to do. How might you provide better-matched instruction? The suggestions we presented in the previous section indicate one way to improve instructional matching. You can use flexible grouping arrangements of whole class, small group, or individuals as benefitting the particular classroom situation and set of tasks. Bennett and Desforges (1988) also recommend that you not have students wait for help and that you make group instruction more sensitive to student abilities. If properly managed, "teaching to groups could hold advantages in terms of extended contact with students, more appropriate task demands, and better identification of students' problems through interaction" (p. 233). How this approach might be accomplished successfully is discussed in the next key concept.

Key Concept 3

Teachers need to understand the complex instructional and motivational issues involved in grouping children for instruction.

GROUPING CHILDREN

Children in most American elementary school classrooms are placed into groups for reading instruction. Three or four groups are common and placement in one or another group is almost always determined by reading ability. Instruction centers on the group, not on individuals. Moreover, grouping decisions are usually permanent arrangements, as few children are moved from one instructional group to another over the course of the school year.

These practices, while long-standing and based on reasonable ideas, can be detrimental to some students. Grouping sometimes has the effect of limiting opportunities for learning. Less effective instruction is often given to low-ability groups. Grouping can also reduce low-ability groups' interest in or motivation to work and learn and can lead to a low academic self-concept.

A study by Eder and Felmlee (1984) compared lessons given to the low and high ability groups in a first grade class. They found that the teacher set lower standards for conduct in the low groups and taught more structured lessons. The children in the low groups were less able to help the teacher maintain attention to the lesson. As a result, children in the low groups lost lesson time because the teacher had to spend more time on management.

All students have a chance to express ideas about their reading during small group discussions. Working with just a few students at a time gives the teacher the perfect opportunity to refine students' ability to think critically about text.

A study by Allington (1984) indicates in another way how ability grouping can affect reading lessons. High and low ability groups in grades one, three, and five read about the same amount orally but not silently. Low ability groups do much less silent reading, as much as a twenty-to-one difference. Most teachers have good readers read one story per session while poor readers often read only a few pages from a story. Good readers are paced at a faster rate and given more comprehension lessons; poor readers read fewer stories and are given more lesson drills and worksheets. While high ability learners can move at a faster pace, we believe the differences in instruction are often greater than necessary and tend to hold low ability children back.

Alternative Approaches

Considering the problems that can arise when children are taught in groups based on ability, an obvious question is whether it is necessary to use ability grouping for reading instruction, especially on all or most occasions. Here are four options you can consider:

1. Keep an ability grouping arrangement but foster a multidimensional concept of student ability, the view that everyone has different special abilities and that no one is best in every way.
2. Take special steps to give low ability students the chance to achieve higher status.
3. Use various types of heterogeneous (mixed ability) grouping.
4. Encourage cooperative learning by using different kinds of peer work groups.

Fostering a multidimensional concept of ability. Teachers should try to evaluate children on more than one dimension. In that way they find out that different children are "smart" in different areas. According to a review by Marshall and Weinstein (1984), when teachers foster a multiple- rather than single-ability concept of academic ability, children will begin to look for and talk about each other's different strengths. This means that no child will need to feel incompetent at everything, and everyone can be praised for some special ability. It could also help children see hard work and skill learning as undertakings that will increase their competence.

In your teaching you need not view children's ability only in terms of their overall reading scores. Instead, look for special reading talents such as an ability to act out the part of a story character, give good definitions of words, make interesting predictions about stories, remember information that was read, find important ideas in a text, or read with expression. Although children who are not fluent readers are less likely to be good in many other aspects of reading, you can help children find their special skill. Pointing out and making use of their special abilities will help children not only to differentiate aspects of their own reading but will encourage them to work on their deficiencies.

Improving the classroom status of low ability children. A serious problem of separating children by ability is the lowered sense of self-esteem and social status that children who are not in the "fast track" feel. Ability grouping can be detrimental to average- and lower-ability groups, particularly depressing achievement for students in low groups (Hallinan, 1984). Since, however, there are instructional advantages to ability grouping, a possible solution is for the teacher to enhance the status and self-esteem of lower-achieving children.

One approach for enhancing status was studied by Morine-Dershimer (1983). The basic idea is that children's academic status is influenced by their participation in classroom discussions. Teachers usually call on children who volunteer, and children volunteer if they know the answer. Because children who are called on become visible to their classmates, as *children-who-know*, they achieve a high status and become children that others turn to and learn from.

Morine-Dershimer studied how three teachers created or supported children-who-know. One teacher, who emphasized text content, factual information, and short answers, more often called on, and so supported, the best readers in the class. The other two teachers, who emphasized children's lesson-related experiences and problem-solving ideas, called on high, middle, and low-achieving readers about equally. The effect for these two teachers was the creation of high status children among low ability (and, originally, low status) children.

This means that high status can be given, even to low-achieving readers, if teachers encourage discussions that allow students to describe relevant experiences and ideas rather than only to remember and describe what they read. Possible additional advantages found by Morine-Dershimer are better attention among children to each other's answers and higher end-of-year gains in reading.

Heterogeneous grouping.   Instead of setting up ability-determined groups that remain stable over time, Marshall and Weinstein (1984) suggest using small groups, putting together children of differing abilities, and having them work together for many different purposes. With this procedure children have the chance to work with a larger number of their classmates. They have more opportunities to observe their own and others' strengths in a variety of tasks and situations. Also, lower achieving children may more often receive recognition for their work and effort.

Heterogeneous groups can be set up in reading even when a basal or other commercial reading program is being used and children are working with different readers. For example, while keeping ability groups for story reading, you could form other groups for writing, spelling, vocabulary development, and discussion of books read for recreation. You could group children interested in the same topic, such as rock collecting, and have them read tradebooks, magazines, and other materials. You could also group high, middle, and low readers together to work on reading-related projects, such as the presentation of a scene from a play.

Webb and Cullian (1983) studied the use of cooperative groups on children's social interactions and achievement. They successfully mixed children of high, middle, and low ability together in small groups of three and four. The teachers assigned tasks to be completed by the groups and emphasized cooperation, helpfulness, and coordination of effort. The teacher circulated among the groups, giving help as requested.

In another study (Webb & Kenderski, 1984), cooperative peer work groups were composed either of a mixture of high and middle or of middle and low ability children. The important result here was that the groups were more effective if children explained things to one another. This suggests that in order to promote helpfulness, a teacher should encourage children to explain their ideas and answers to one another.

Cooperative learning and flexible grouping.   Another way to organize the classroom is to form cooperative learning groups. Students work in small groups and are monitored and rewarded both for individual and group accomplishments. Stevens, Madden, Slavin, and Farnish (1987) describe how cooperative learning techniques can be effectively carried out for reading and writing lessons. The following cycle of activities provides a foundation for all cooperative lessons:

1. *Teacher instruction.* Initial instruction always comes from the teacher.
2. *Team practice.* Students work in four- to five-member, mixed-ability learning teams to master the material presented by the teacher, using worksheets or other practice materials. Depending on the content being studied, students may work on items and check answers with each other, drill one another, reach and discuss common answers, and so on. Students also assess one another to make certain that teammates will succeed on individual assessments.
3. *Individual assessments.* Students are individually assessed on their learning of the information or skills contained in the lesson.
4. *Team recognition.* Students' scores on individual assessments are summed to form team scores. Teams which meet certain preestablished criteria may earn certificates or other rewards (p. 435).

In one successful modification of this design, Stevens et al. (1987) had teachers create student partners. Each pair of students read books of similar levels of difficulty. Then teachers formed four-member teams by joining each pair with a team from a different reading ability level. Team members received points based on individual performance on quizzes, compositions, and book reports, which were summed to form a team score. Achieving a criterion of 90 percent on all activities gave a team "superteam" status; those achieving at a 80–89 percent criterion received a "greatteam" status.

The teachers had students read their basal stories in the regular ability-level reading groups (about 20 minutes a day). After stories were introduced, partner and team follow-up activities were assigned. When a student completed each of the activities, the partner initialed a student assignment form indicating successful completion of the work. After every three class periods students were given comprehension and vocabulary tests by the teacher.

a. *Partner reading.* After students read the story silently, they took turns reading aloud to their partner, reading a paragraph at a time. As one read, the listener followed and corrected any errors. Sometimes teachers circulated and listened to the oral reading to assess students' performance informally.
b. *Story-structure and story-related writing.* Grammar and story questions were given to students to answer half way through the story reading. At the end of the story reading, students answered questions about what

happened in the story resolution and wrote a few paragraphs about a pre-assigned aspect of the story.

c. *Words out loud.* Students practiced new and difficult words from the current story with their partner until they could read them smoothly and accurately.

d. *Word meaning.* Words new to their speaking vocabulary were studied, paraphrased, and written into meaningful sentences.

e. *Story retelling.* Students summarized the main points of their current story to their partner by paraphrasing.

f. *Spelling.* Students pretested each other on the weekly list of spelling words, helping one another to master the list.

g. *Whole class instruction.* One day a week students received instruction on a reading comprehension skill, after which teammates worked cooperatively on follow-up assignments. Three times a week students were involved in writing activities. After the teacher presented a 10–15-minute topic on some aspect of the writing process, students planned, drafted, reviewed, revised, edited, and published their pieces, using conferences both with teacher and with team members. The last 10 minutes of each workshop was spent sharing and discussing their writing with the entire class. The remaining two days of the language arts period were used for teacher-directed lessons on specific aspects of writing and language mechanics.

This elaborate cooperative learning plan was successfully implemented in 43 third and fourth grade suburban schools where 16 to 22 percent were minority students, and in the second study where 18 percent were from low-income families. The district allocated two hours per day for third grade reading, one hour for fourth grade reading, and one hour per day in each grade for language arts. This instructional plan helped students of all ability levels, improving particularly their decoding and comprehension skills. Writing and vocabulary skills were improved somewhat.

To put this complex plan into your classroom, study again the basic cycle of activities. Then we recommend that you devise your own instructional plan, using ideas from the second key concept and from earlier chapters about teaching comprehension, vocabulary, word identification, and writing. We believe that you can apply cooperative principles in ways that will help all of your students learn.

Key Concept 4

Teachers need to understand new ways of organizing their instructional content, methods, lesson sequences, and classroom settings.

COMPLEX CLASSROOM ORGANIZATIONAL PATTERNS

As you may have begun to realize from studying earlier chapters, especially Chapters 2 through 8, there are new trends in educators' thinking about classroom environments for learning. Educators once talked about the *content of instruction* in terms of skills, concepts, and procedures, but now the focus is on strategies used to learn, remember, and act in a self-directed manner. With respect to *instructional approaches and methods,* the terms have shifted from telling, explaining, and reviewing to modeling and coaching. Learning sequences, defined as subskills, were separated into manageable and teachable steps and involved drill and practice routines. Now, scaffolding and working within the student's zone of proximal development are described. Finally, *instructional settings* focused primarily on the task and product that individual students completed, usually in competition with one another. Now, it is realized that learning tasks are situated in a social setting, and if the setting is realistic, students can work in collaboration with one another under the support and guidance of the teacher. In this final key concept on classroom organization, we describe how each of these constructs is currently applied to classroom situations.

Instructional Content

Learning skills and procedures need to be placed within the perspective of the process of learning. That is, much of what you teach has an underlying *process* goal. For example, remembering facts and details from a lesson is often not as important as knowing how to choose what to remember and how to get the information into memory. Thus, strategies for learning, remembering, and solving problems and techniques for carrying out self-directed learning are the ultimate instructional goals. Much of the newer research involves the study of approaches for teaching students strategies that they can use to further their own learning.

In Chapter 1, we discussed the concept of teaching students how to benefit from comprehension monitoring strategies (e.g., Palincsar, 1984). We discussed evidence showing that students can comprehend the text content and learn strategies for comprehending as they read if you teach them to clarify when something does not make sense, ask themselves questions as a way of keeping track of important information, summarize what they just read, and make predictions about what the next text section might be about. The goal is to improve students' comprehension strategies for reading texts out of school as well as in school.

In Chapter 7, we discussed the concept of teaching students the value of self-monitoring their reading and self-checking words, sentences, text meaning, or pictures when their reading did not make sense (Clay, 1979; 1985). In her concluding chapter, Clay (1979) describes the centrality of strategy learning from the child's perspective:

> In the first two years of instruction the child learns how to teach himself to read. He learns the:
> • aspects of print to which he must attend
> • aspects of oral language that can be related to print
> • kinds of strategies that maintain fluency
> • kinds of strategies that explore detail
> • kinds of strategies that increase understanding
> • kinds of strategies that detect and correct errors.   (p. 269)

Learning to use strategies leads students to direct their own reading and learning from reading. Self-directed learning activities are activities wholly or partly under the control of the student. Students can use them when they are reading, studying materials for a test, writing, completing assignments, answering teachers' questions, and so on. Moreover, they can use them during any phase of in- or out-of-school reading and writing. Some are activities that help in the processing or learning of information. Others are self-management techniques that make learning more efficient and effective.

Thomas, Strage, and Curley (1988) propose a taxonomy of self-directed activities that are related to the completion of a reading assignment. This long list makes it quite apparent that there are many ways that you can teach students to understand and apply strategies as they read. The list also suggests activities that you might model when you are introducing new reading materials and tasks (see Figure 11.5).

Instructional Methods or Approaches

Instructional approaches that show students how to learn will help them become self-directed learners. We presented two approaches in Chapter 6, modeling and coaching. As you introduce a new topic or procedure, you can model the process that you want students to learn to use and then coach students as they try out the techniques of thinking about and monitoring the learning process. You also need to help students focus on their own mental operations so they can figure out how to think through the steps on their own.

In the following excerpt, Duffy and Roehler (1987) suggest how teachers' discussion questions and explanations could be used to help children to understand the process of thinking.

T: What do you think is going to happen next here? I mean, you're reading the story. What'll happen next? Candy?
S: [Gives a response]
T: Oh, okay. What do you think, Moss?
S: [Gives a response]
T: Interesting. Why do you think what you think? How can you make these

Figure 11.5
Classes of Self-Directed
Learning Activities

Cognitive activities:

Selection (activities that facilitate focusing selectively on material) —
- Seeking out criterion information
- Differentiating important from unimportant information
- Recording important information
- Organizing and highlighting information

Comprehension (activities that enhance understanding of the material) —
- Previewing the material
- Noting hard-to-understand points
- Using context cues
- Consulting resources and references

Memory enhancement (activities that enhance the memorability of the material) —
- Reviewing the material
- Using mnemonic strategies
- Using self-testing methods
- Making memory aids (charts, flashcards)
- Matching study strategies to memory demands of the test

Integration (activities that promote integration and the construction of relations) —
- Putting material in one's own words
- Constructing ideas/answers that go beyond the information given
- Using relational aids (diagrams, time lines)
- Relating information across sources
- Relating course content to prior knowledge

Cognitive monitoring (activities that serve to monitor learning and evaluate progress) —
- Knowing what you haven't yet mastered
- Keeping track of personal strengths and weaknesses in processing skill

Self-management activities:

Time management (activities that provide the opportunity to learn) —
- Establishing sufficient time to complete activities
- Keeping track of time
- Scheduling time
- Meeting time commitments
- Distributing time over tasks

Effort management (activities that serve to promote and maintain the disposition to learn) —
- Establishing a productive study environment
- Setting learning and achievement goals
- Initiating effort
- Securing the necessary materials
- Maintaining attention and avoiding distractions
- Providing incentives to learn

Volitional monitoring (activities that serve to monitor and evaluate the productivity of one's study habits) —
- Keeping track of the adequacy of time and effort management activities
- Monitoring attention
- Assessing strengths and weaknesses in study habits

Source: From "Improving Students' Self-directed Learning: Issues and Guidelines" by John W. Thomas, Amy Strage, and Robert Curley, *The Elementary School Journal*, vol. 88, no. 3, 1988. Reprinted by permission of The University of Chicago Press.

predictions like this? How can you predict what's going to happen next in the story?

S: I thought about the story and Roberto and his problem.

T: Yes, but how did you use that to predict? Did you use your own experience?

S: Yeah. I thought about what I thought would probably happen.

T: That's right. Because you've been thinking about the story and you've been thinking about Roberto and his problem. And that's part of what reading is. It's making predictions about what's going to happen next.

Another third grade teacher directed her low group students to what to think about when figuring out word meaning rather than just asking for what the word *down* meant in "My pillow is made from the *down* of geese."

T: What word is confusing in there?
S: *Down.*
T: *Down.* Okay, what are you going to do to figure that out?
S: It's like going down, or downstairs.
T: All right. Going downwards. You've already realized that that doesn't make sense. Now, what's next?
S: Look for clues.
T: All right. Are there any clues?
S: Pillow and geese.
T: All right. We looked for clues. Now we've got to think about what those clues tell us. The pillow is made from something of the geese. In your experience, what would a pillow be made of?
S: Feathers.
T: How are you going to know if you're right or wrong, George?
S: Read the sentence with that word in it.
T: All right. Try it, George.
S: My pillow is made from the feathers of the geese.
T: Would that make sense?
S: Yeah.
(p. 519)

Learning Sequence

Classrooms are workplaces where teachers and students are busy at many different tasks. In earlier chapters we described scaffolding (Chapters 1, 2, 4, and 6). There we showed how teachers introduce the task by modeling the learning activity, then coach students to participate in it, and then gradually release responsibility for the activity to the students. Those descriptions were particular examples of instructional sequencing. Here we present more general characteristics. The first focuses on the modeling phase, and the next shows how a task sequence can be linked to task demands. The basic concept of gradual movement from teacher responsibility to student responsibility remains as the central theme.

Teacher modeling is often the initial step of a learning sequence. The intention is to make instructional plans obvious to students so that they can carry out the activities successfully. Marx and Walsh (1988) recommend what they term "Participant-modeling instruction." By this, they mean instruction in which modeling how to plan the work task is featured, for often the plan, or process of the work task, is more important than the result, or product. For example, the process of researching a topic, organizing it into a written report, and editing the report may be more important than showing or reading the final piece.

We present an example of a three-step modeling process from Marx and Walsh's article:

The use of participant-modeling instruction to teach students cognitive plans is a threefold process. In the first phase, the teacher models aloud the approach or plan that students should use while solving classroom tasks. The teacher begins this modeled instruction by providing answers to two questions: What am I supposed to do in the task, and what do I already know about the task? Following this, the teacher models aloud the alternative strategies for completing the task and organizes these strategies into a coherent sequence. The aim of this part of instruction is to guide students' specific thinking about how they are going to solve the task. Last, the teacher considers aloud various contingency plans that may be used if the plan being modeled is not successful. This involves providing answers to two questions: How will I know that my plan is working, and what should I do if I run into trouble?

As an example, consider the following task: Compare and contrast plants and animals. A teacher might begin to model the plans for approaching this task by considering aloud what the task is asking (i.e., modeling a comprehension plan). "OK, I am supposed to compare and contrast animals and plants. This means that I have to find things that are the same between them and things that are different."

Next, the teacher models strategies for accomplishing the task. In the current example, she might say, "First, I need to think about all the things I know about animals and plants. One way to do this is to make a list of things I know about each. Animals: (a) are living things, (b) move around, and (c) need food to live. Plants: (a) don't move around, (b) are living things, and (c) need food to live. So to see what is the same and different about plants and animals, all I have to do is compare the two lists. Both lists mention that each is a living thing and needs food. So these are ways in which they are the same. Differences are present between the lists. Plants don't move around, while animals do."

Finally, the teacher might model various contingency plans that students might use if they have difficulty with the task. In our example, this may include various strategies for recalling information about characteristics of plants and animals. The teacher might say, "If I can't think of the general characteristics of plants, it might help if I think about specific examples of plants, say an oak tree, a rose, or a sunflower, and see how they are alike. I could imagine each in my mind and see how they are the same."

Modeling cognitive plans for students is a good start to providing them with a sound and predictable approach to classroom work. However, in order to master these plans, students require considerable practice. The last two phases of participant-modeling instruction address this need for practice. In the first practice phase, students are instructed to model aloud their cognitive plans for other students and the teacher. This occurs in much the same way that the teacher modeled the plan in the previous phase of instruction. As a particular student verbalizes his or her plan, the teacher and other students offer suggestions about the plan, point out errors, and generally provide feedback. The practice offered is thus heavily guided by the teacher and fellow students.

▌ Figure 11.6
▌ Cognitive Tasks and Task Demands

Task Type	Chief Demand Characteristics
Incremental	Introduces new ideas, procedures, or skills; demands recognition, discrimination.
Restructuring	Demands the invention or discovery of an idea, process, or pattern.
Enrichment	Demands application of familiar skills to new problems.
Practice	Demands the tuning of new skills on familiar problems.

Source: Table and excerpts from "Matching Classroom Tasks to Students' Attainments" by Melville Bennett and Charles Desforges, The Elementary School Journal, vol. 88, no. 3, 1988. Reprinted by permission of The University of Chicago Press.

During the last phase of participant-modeling instruction, students practice applying their newly acquired plans to tasks. This practice occurs without the explicit verbal guidance of other students or the teacher, although questions embedded in the task may remind students to execute parts of their plans (e.g., Did you restate the problem in your own words?). (pp. 213–214)

Usually we focus our attention on the end product, the work that students complete. The Marx and Walsh (1988) example explains how students' plans can be more important than the outcome, and how clear demonstrations by teachers help students to carry out their work effectively.

Bennett and Desforges (1987) suggest that the principle of scaffolding has four distinct phases and that each phase requires a different instructional focus. To understand this notion, assume you have already chosen the learning materials and you have decided on the learning goals or outcomes. Now, you are ready to plan the order of underlying cognitive tasks that utilize these materials and goals.

There is a four-part sequence of tasks, and each has a particular set of task demands (Figure 11.6). The introduction of new ideas, procedures, or skills leads students to recognize the important topics or procedural elements. You will highlight what is important and demonstrate the steps they need to employ, as Marx and Walsh (1988) outlined. Next, you will encourage students to restructure the information using students' terms, strategies, and processes. When students operate successfully at that level, you can arrange for an enrichment or transfer phase, which involves extending the familiar strategies they learned to new materials. Depending on the complexity of the task, these two phases may take several days or weeks (and the learning process for some tasks, such as report writing, can take years!). Finally, when students can easily extend familiar strategies to unfamiliar materials, you can set up opportunities for them to try out new strategies and approaches. This step allows students to refine the process of self-directed learning.

Instructional setting. The setting for learning can vary in its authenticity, that is, in its closeness to real-world tasks. This is termed *situated learning* (as described in Chapter 6), or learning in which tasks are embedded in everyday activities. When you have set a task in a realistic setting, such as having students learn words as part of reading a story or arranging for them to write to a pen pal, you can be more specific in modeling the task activity and explaining the learning goals than you can if the activity has been taken out of its natural context, such as having students decode or spell lists of words. You can assist them in identifying the problems and coach them to use effective strategies. As students gain more self-confidence and control of the concepts, they can collaborate (see Chapter 10), and solve problems by accomplishing a task together. Eventually, they can step back and reflect on their learning experience. Then they may even be able to see the more general characteristics, understand how tasks or procedures for carrying them out are related, and articulate underlying concepts. A model of this process is shown in Figure 11.7.

Now, learning has a more realistic framework because the importance of social interactions and the social construction of knowledge is recognized. Much learning can occur through collaborative or group problem solving activities. "Groups are not just a convenient way to accumulate the individual knowledge of their members. They give rise synergistically to insights and solutions that would not come about without them" (Brown, Collins, & Duguid, 1989, p. 40).

Collaboration among students offers opportunities to understand the different roles during the process of carrying out a task. When learning is the responsibility of a group and there are different roles to play, students can negotiate to do the parts of the group task that they can do well, and they can observe and learn from each other as they engage in joint problem solving. Collaboration requires discussions among students, revealing group thinking. Then, students will realize that the process of learning has many dimensions and approaches and what strategies for learning and remembering are effective. Misconceptions and inappropriate strategies can also be identified and corrected, and students can see other ways to solve problems and to learn.

▌ Figure 11.7
▌ A Model of Situated Learning

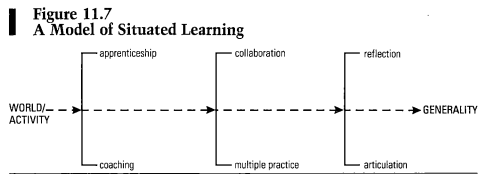

The learning process now allows students opportunities to develop cooperative working habits and become better prepared for the workplace, a place in which collaborative work situations are increasingly important.

To summarize, then, your planning and teaching operations will benefit from a multidimensional conception of instruction. Try to think of the content, process, learning demands, and sequence of the tasks which you arrange for students. Plan to work with students, modeling the process of thinking and doing a task, coaching students so that they begin to identify key characteristics, articulate the steps, and work on solutions that use their knowledge and skills. Then, organize the lesson over time so that students are led gradually from observing and trying out the ideas with simplified materials to operating the activities with minimal support from you. Finally, modify as needed the social organization and interaction patterns so that students have realistic examples of the learning tasks and can work in settings that invite cooperative role playing and joint problem solving.

▌ SUMMARY

In this chapter we presented information to help you understand how principles of classroom organization and management can be applied to enhance children's progress in learning to read. In the perspective we discussed three important areas of research contributing to our understanding of effective organization and management. These had to do with time and the efficiency of teaching, interactive decision-making, and simplified models of instruction.

We suggested in the first key concept that you prepare for the school year by establishing an orderly learning environment and relying on principles of effective classroom management. Among the procedures presented were those for establishing routines, setting up effective small group instruction, and giving attention to individual students.

We considered in the second key concept how reading instruction might be scheduled. A detailed discussion was provided for scheduling whole class instruction, the instruction of small groups formed on the basis of ability, and peer work groups.

In the third key concept, we explored the complex issues raised by grouping children for reading instruction on the basis of ability. The chief problem with this practice seems to be its detrimental effects on low ability children. We recommended that you consider remedying this problem by improving other children's opinions of low ability children, encouraging cooperative learning, and forming groups heterogeneous in ability.

In the fourth key concept we summarized the new views about organizing lessons based on emphasizing strategies, instructional methods such as modeling and coaching, a gradual release of responsibility, and realistic learning situations.

We covered many different ideas and procedures, more than you will be able to use right away. However, we hope you will eventually try the less widely used, but possibly more effective, alternatives presented in this chapter. As you experiment with ways to organize and manage your reading program and become more comfortable working with your class, you will gradually understand how to provide effective instruction for all your students.

∎ BIBLIOGRAPHY
References

Allington, R. (1984). Content coverage and contextual reading in reading groups. *Journal of Reading Behavior, 16*, 85–96.

Anderson, L., Evertson, C., & Brophy, J. (1982). *Principles of small-group instruction in elementary reading.* (Occasional Paper #58). East Lansing, MI: Institute for Research on Teaching, Michigan State University.

Anderson, L., Stevens, D., Prawat, R., & Nickerson, J. (1988). Classroom task environments and students' task-related beliefs. *The Elementary School Journal, 88,* 281–296.

Au, K., & Kawakami, A. (1984). Vygotskian perspectives on discussion processes in small-group reading-lessons. In P. Peterson, L. Wilkinson, & M. Hallinan (Eds.), *The social context of instruction: Group organization and group processes.* New York: Academic Press.

Bennett, N., & Desforges, C. (1988). Matching classroom tasks to students' attainments. *The Elementary School Journal, 88,* 221–234.

Brophy, J. (1984). The teacher as thinker: Implementing instruction. In G. Duffy, L. Roehler, & J. Mason (Eds.), *Comprehension instruction: Perspectives and suggestions.* New York: Longman.

Brown, J., Collins, A., & Duguid, P. (1989). Situated cognition and the culture of learning. *Educational Researcher, 18,* 32–42.

Clark, C., & Yinger, R. (1979). Teachers' thinking. In P. Peterson & H. Walberg (Eds.), *Research on teaching.* Berkeley, CA: McCutchan.

Clay, M. (1979). *Reading: The Patterning of Complex Behavior.* Portsmouth, NH: Heinemann.

Clay, M. (1985). *Early detection of reading difficulties* (3rd ed.). Portsmouth, NH: Heinemann.

Duffy, G., & Roehler, L. (1987). Improving reading instruction through the use of responsive elaboration. *The Reading Teacher, 40,* 514–520.

Eder, D., & Felmlee, D. (1984). The development of attention norms in ability groups. In P. Peterson, L. Wilkinson, & M. Hallinan (Eds.), *The social context of instruction: Group organization and group processes.* New York: Academic Press.

Good, T. (1983). Research on classroom teaching. In L. Shulman & G. Sykes (Eds.), *Handbook of teaching and policy.* New York: Longman.

Good, T., Grouws, D., & Ebmeier, H. (1983). *Active mathematics teaching.* New York: Longman.

Goodlad, J. (1983). *A place called school.* New York: Harper & Row.

Hallinan, M. (1984). Summary and conclusions. In P. Peterson, L. Wilkinson, & M. Hallinan (Eds.), *The social context of instruction: Group organization and group processes.* New York: Academic Press.

Hawkins, D. (1973). What it means to teach. *Teachers College Record, 75,* 7–16.

Hiebert, E. (1983). An examination of ability grouping for reading instruction. *Reading Research Quarterly, 18,* 231–255.

Kedar-Voivodas, G. (1983). Impact of elementary children's school roles and sex roles on teacher attitudes: An interactional analysis. *Review of Educational Research, 53,* 415–437.

Lightfoot, S. (1983). The lives of teachers. In L. Shulman & G. Sykes (Eds.), *Handbook of teaching and policy.* New York: Longman.

Marshall, H., & Weinstein, R. (1984). Classroom factors affecting students' self-evaluations: An interactional model. *Review of Educational Research, 54,* 301–326.

Marx, R., & Walsh, J. (1988). Learning from academic tasks. *The Elementary School Journal, 88,* 207–220.

Mason, J., Anderson, R., Omura, A., Uchida, N., & Imai, M. (1989). Learning to read in Japan. *Journal of Curriculum Studies, 21*(5), 389–407.

Morine-Dershimer, G. (1983). Instructional strategy and the "creation" of classroom status. *American Educational Research Journal, 20,* 645–662.

Palincsar, A. (1984). The quest for meaning from expository text: A teacher-guided journey. In G. Duffy, L. Roehler, & J. Mason (Eds.), *Comprehension instruction: Perspectives and suggestions.* New York: Longman.

Peterson, P., & Clark, C. (1978). Teachers' reports of their cognitive processes during teaching. *American Educational Research Journal, 15,* 555–565.

Plowden Report (1967). *Children and their primary schools. Report of the central advisory for education* (England). London: Her Majesty's Stationery Office.

Rosenshine, B. (1979). Content, time, and direct instruction. In P. Peterson & H. Walberg (Eds.), *Research on teaching: Concepts, findings, and implications.* Berkeley, CA: McCutchan.

Rutter, M. (1983). Complexities of schools and classrooms. In L. Shulman & G. Sykes (Eds.), *Handbook of teaching and policy.* New York: Longman.

Shulman, L. (1983). Autonomy and obligation: The remote control of teaching. In L. Shulman & G. Sykes (Eds.), *Handbook of teaching and policy.* New York: Longman.

Stevens, R., Madden, N., Slavin, R., & Farnish, A. (1987). Cooperative integrated reading and composition: Two field experiments. *Reading Research Quarterly, 22,* 433–454.

Tharp, R. (1982). The effective instruction of comprehension: Results and description of the Kamehameha Early Education Program. *Reading Research Quarterly, 17,* 503–527.

Thomas, J., Strage, A., & Curley, R. (1988). Improving students' self-directed learning: Issues and guidelines. *The Elementary School Journal, 88,* 313–326.

Veeman, S. (1984). Perceived problems of beginning teachers. *Review of Educational Research, 54,* 143–178.

Webb, N., & Cullian, L. (1983). Group interaction and achievement in small groups: Stability over time. *American Educational Research Journal, 20,* 411–423.

Webb, N., & Kenderski, C. (1984). Student interaction and learning in small-group and whole-class settings. In P. Peterson, L. Wilkinson & M. Hallinan (Eds.), *The social context of instruction: Group organization and group processes.* New York: Academic Press.

Further Readings

Anderson, L. M., Evertson, C. M., & Brophy, J. E. (1979). An experimental study of effective teaching in first-grade reading groups. *Elementary School Journal, 79,* 193–223.

Barr, R., & Sadow, M. (1989). Influence of basal programs on fourth-grade reading instruction. *Reading Research Quarterly, 24*(1), 44–71.

Brophy, J. E. (1982). Fostering student learning and motivation in the elementary school classroom (Occasional Paper #51). East Lansing, MI: Institute for Research on Teaching, Michigan State University.

Cazden, C. (1986). Classroom discourse. In M. Wittrock (Ed.), *Handbook of research on teaching* (3rd ed., pp. 432–463). New York: Macmillan.

Doyle, W. (1986). Classroom organization and management. In M. Wittrock (Ed.), *Handbook of research on teaching* (3rd ed., pp. 392–431). New York: Macmillan.

Dweck, C. S. (1986). Motivational processes affecting learning. *American Psychologist, 41* (10), 1040–1048.

Ellis, D. W., & Preston, F. W. (1984). Enhancing beginning reading using wordless picture books in a cross-age tutoring program. *The Reading Teacher, 37,* 692–698.

Guthrie, J. T. (1982). Effective teaching practices. *The Reading Teacher, 35,* 766–768.

Lave, J. (1988). *Cognition in practice.* Boston, MA: Cambridge.

Levine, D. U. (1982). Successful approaches for improving academic achievement in inner-city elementary schools. *Phi Delta Kappan, 63,* 523–526.

Mason, J. (1984). A question about reading comprehension instruction. In G. Duffy, L. Roehler, & J. Mason (Eds.), *Comprehension instruction: Perspectives and suggestions.* New York: Longman.

Palincsar, A. S. (1986). Metacognitive strategy instruction. *Exceptional Children, 53,* 118–124.

Resnick, L. (1988). Learning in school and out. *Educational Researcher, 16* (9), 13–20.

Rogoff, B., & Lave, J. (Eds.). (1984). *Everyday cognition: Its development in social context.* Cambridge, MA: Harvard University Press.

Walker, J., & Shea, T. (1988). *Behavior management: A practical approach for educators* (4th ed.). Columbus, OH: Charles E. Merrill.

Webb, N. (1982). Student interaction and learning in small groups. *Review of Educational Research, 52,* 421–445.

Chapter 12

Reading in the School, Home, and Community

When Ernie was fourteen his father died and the children were left to cope as best they could. Ernie talked of attending school until he was in the fifth grade, but he explained that he was never there long enough to understand what was going on. Similarly, Ernie's wife had never learned to read. She described how the school had been twelve miles from her home and therefore she had never managed to attend on a regular basis.

Among the difficulties Ernie spoke of were the problems he experienced when traveling. He spoke of coping with street names. He would have the word written on a piece of paper, and he would try to match it with the street name. With unmistakable sincerity, he added that it was no good if the first letter matched, that did not mean it was the right word. The whole word had to match. Another difficulty was being able to prove that the items he owned really belonged to him. He pointed to the ring I was wearing, and he repeated several times how important it was for me to be able to prove the ring was mine. Ernie went on to talk of the house he was buying; he had to rely on friends to tell him that the house was legally his.

Although Ernie faced these immense problems on a daily basis, they did not compare with the formidable task of finding employment. Ernie spoke of the application forms for his present job. He explained:

> I sat in school and the teacher helped me fill in the application. Well, it wasn't bad. Getting it was bad. But she showed me and it wasn't too bad. I filled it out at school and she showed me. So when I went to the job I filled it out again on my own and so I passed and so I got the job.
> (Taylor, 1983, pp. 85–86)

▮ OVERVIEW

We begin this chapter by taking a look at reading in the community. Given this perspective of how reading fits into the lives of many adults, you will have a picture of the wide variety of reading activities you will want your students to experience in school.

In the first key concept we discuss the importance of reading in the workplace. We show how literacy at work is quite different from literacy at school.

We suggest that it may be valuable for teachers to have children participate in some literacy activities similar in ways to those in the workplace.

The second key concept focuses on the steps teachers can take to promote students' independent application of reading and writing strategies. These include letting students choose their own independent assignments.

In the third key concept we look at recreational reading. We see that many adults engage in leisure time reading and look at children's patterns of reading outside of school. We present methods the teacher can use to promote children's reading of books, newspapers, and magazines.

The fourth key concept deals with bridging the gap between home and school and enlisting family support for children's literacy development. Among the topics covered are ongoing communication with parents and children's access to books at home.

Chapter 12 is organized around the following Key Concepts:

Key Concept 1: Teachers should prepare students to use literacy in many ways, including those likely to be useful in the workplace and community.

Key Concept 2: Teachers should guide students toward independence in literacy by gradually releasing responsibility to them.

Key Concept 3: Teachers should encourage voluntary reading, so students will choose to read independently for their own enjoyment and information.

Key Concept 4: Teachers should foster students' reading ability and interest by strengthening connections between reading at home and at school.

█ PERSPECTIVE
Profile of Reading Activities in a Community

Throughout this textbook, we have been making the assumption that reading is an important activity in the daily lives of many adults. In this section, we look more closely at the kinds of reading adults actually do, as shown in recent research. The purpose of providing this information is to make you more aware of how your students may eventually be using literacy, and of how the classroom reading program may be designed to prepare students for these uses.

Guthrie and Seifert (1983) conducted an extensive study of reading activity in a community. People in this community had somewhat more education than the average but were similar in occupational characteristics to people in the United States as a whole. Reading was defined as "gaining meaning from written messages," and adult wage earners were asked how

Exercise

In this exercise you will be comparing your own patterns of reading with those of two other people.

(1) Divide a blank sheet of paper into three columns, with headings as indicated below.

| Time | Types of Material | Setting |

(2) In the column labeled *Time*, record the times of the day in half-hour segments, beginning with the time you awaken on a typical weekday, to the nearest hour or half hour (e.g., 7:00 a.m., 7:30 a.m.). End with the last half hour before you go to sleep.

(3) For each of these half-hour segments, list in the second column the types of material you would normally read on a weekday. Use the following categories of material only: (1) newspapers, (2) books, (3) magazines (including comic books), and (4) brief documents. The category of brief documents includes labels, billboards, invoices, maps, forms, and similar items.

(4) Under setting, use the following categories to indicate where you did the reading: home, school, workplace, or other (while outdoors, for example, or in a store).

(5) Consider your list. In how many half-hour slots did your reading occur? What types of materials do you seem to spend the most time reading? In what setting is most of your reading done?

(6) Try to gather this same type of information on two other individuals, one an adult (preferably, one who is not a full-time student) and one an elementary school student. Prepare a form for each individual, as you did for yourself, and ask them to give you the information for each time segment, considering the kinds of reading they would do on a typical weekday.

(7) What similarities and differences do you observe between yourself and the other adult, in terms of time segments when reading occurred, types of materials read, and setting for reading? What similarities and differences do you find between the results for the adults and those for the child?

From this exercise you should have gained some sense of the differences which exist between children's reading patterns and those of adults. Possibly, you also discovered something about the reading patterns shown by different groups of adults. Keep these results in mind as you read of the findings of large-scale studies of the reading patterns of adults and children, and think of the factors which might explain the results you obtained.

much reading they did each month, while at home and at work, whether dealing with newspapers, books, magazines, or brief documents. Wage earners in this community were found to spend a considerable amount of time reading, an average of 157 minutes (between two and three hours) per day.

What kinds of reading material occupied these adults during the several hours they spent reading each day? Guthrie and Seifert discovered that adults most often dealt with brief documents. That is, they spent an average of 37 minutes reading such materials as newsletters, business correspondence, billboards, and directions. Guthrie and Seifert speculated that the use of literacy to read brief documents is important in urban settings where adults must deal with large organizations, such as businesses and government agencies.

The second most commonly read content was news and business, which was dealt with for an average of 17.8 minutes per day. According to Guthrie and Seifert, using literacy in this way points to a widespread interest in government and economic matters. Adults spent a similar amount of time, 17 minutes per day, reading about social issues, including topics such as health, psychology, and education. This kind of reading suggests that many people want to increase their knowledge in areas such as the physical, medical, and social sciences.

Reference materials (such as manuals, directories, and newspaper classified ads) were read for an average of 11.3 minutes per day. Guthrie and Seifert saw this kind of reading as serving a utilitarian function, aiding adults in accomplishing economic, domestic, and personal goals. Fiction (including literature, short stories, and humor found in books, magazines, and newspapers) was read for 7.4 minutes per day. When reading this type of content, adults seem to be using literacy primarily for an aesthetic function, enjoying the experience of reading as an end in itself. Finally, adults in this study read material with a sports and recreation content for 4.1 minutes per day. In short, adults read a range of different materials for a variety of purposes, spending much more time with some types of materials than with others.

Guthrie and Seifert also discovered that reading activities differed among occupational groups. For example, professionals and managers read about 224 minutes per day and spent more time than other workers reading brief documents and news and business content. They seemed highly oriented to institutions and politics. Another group, workers in unskilled occupations, read about 60 minutes per day, largely brief documents and reference materials. This suggests literacy being used for utilitarian benefits, as well as to support an orientation toward institutions. Guthrie and Seifert emphasize:

> The popular image that unskilled workers are nonreaders or are limited to the reading required by employment applications is contradicted by these findings. News and business, social issues, fiction, and sports were also read in moderation. In other words, political awareness, social development, aesthetic experience, and amusement were among the functions of reading in this group as well as others. (pp. 507–508)

There is an important practical implication growing from this study, which has given us a picture of how adults in a community use literacy. We see that people in different occupations will need or want to use literacy in different ways, and perhaps for somewhat different purposes. Teachers should be aware of the kinds of occupations and life-styles that their students have an interest in pursuing, and of the expectations for literacy that are likely to come from the home and community. But, while having this awareness, teachers will want to prepare students to use literacy for a wide variety of purposes, to make it possible for students to pursue a variety of life options.

Key Concept 1

Teachers should prepare students to use literacy in many ways, including those likely to be useful in the workplace and community.

▐ LITERACY IN THE WORKPLACE

Recent analyses of the job market in the United States suggest that employment opportunities are to be found largely in occupations requiring rather high levels of skill in reading and writing. Few occupations at present require little or no use of literacy, and these are quickly disappearing (Mikulecky, 1984).

If literacy is so important in the workplace, we need to know more about the kinds of reading skills workers actually use on the job. To find out, Diehl and Mikulecky (1980) studied people in 100 occupations, ranging from stonecutter to vice president of a large corporation. They looked at the reading tasks people faced, the different kinds of reading material encountered and the strategies used to complete tasks.

Diehl and Mikulecky's first major finding was that reading at work is an almost universal activity. Almost 99 percent of the people studied reported reading at work every day, for an average of almost two hours. These results suggest that, on most days, workers probably spend more time reading job-related materials than any other kind. Furthermore, reading seemed to be an important aspect of all kinds of jobs, blue-collar as well as white-collar. In general, workers seemed to think that reading helped them complete tasks more easily and efficiently.

What kinds of reading tasks did workers do? Tasks were placed in one of four categories (based on earlier work by Sticht, 1977):

"Reading-to-learn" in which the subject reads with the intention of remembering text information and applies some learning strategy to do so;

"Reading-to-do with no learning" in which the subject uses the material primarily as an aid to do something else (e.g., fix a machine) and later reports not remembering the information; these materials thus serve as "external memories";

"Reading-to-do with incidental learning" in which the subject uses the material primarily as an aid to do something else, but in the process learns (remembers) the information;

"Reading-to-assess" in which the subject quickly reads or skims material to determine its usefulness for some later task or for some other person; the material is then filed or passed on. (Diehl & Mikulecky, 1980, pp. 222–233)

Diehl and Mikulecky found that only 11 percent of the tasks involved reading-to-learn, 40 percent involved reading-to-do with no learning, 23 percent involved reading-to-do with incidental learning, and 26 percent involved reading-to-do tasks (63 percent of the time, when the categories of reading-to-do with no learning and reading-to-do with incidental learning are combined). This indicates that workers generally use reading material as a form of external memory, applying the information immediately and directly to complete the task. Workers did not usually learn the information and expected to refer to the same material when they faced the task again the next day.

How does reading at school match with this picture of reading in the workplace? There seem to be wide differences between the kinds of reading done by students and workers, as shown in a study by Mikulecky (1982). Students apparently spend much less time reading than workers. Also, students generally read textbooks, while workers deal with manuals, product directions, labels, computer printouts, and many other materials, often moving among formats. High school students reported reading-to-learn (66%) as the purpose of most of their tasks, with few tasks involving reading-to-do with no learning (2%) or reading-to-do with incidental learning (13%), and no tasks involving reading-to-assess (0%). The remaining 11 percent of the tasks fell into other categories, not discussed in Mikulecky's report.

Still another difference between reading at school versus on the job is in the degree to which the environment provides cues about how text information is to be applied. Many more of these cues are generally available in the workplace than at school. As Diehl and Mikulecky (1980) point out, much of the reading-to-do by workers is highly specific to a particular task and setting. For example, workers may be following a set of directions and diagrams to assemble a lathe, with its parts sitting right in front of them. Being able to refer to these physical objects helps the workers to read much more efficiently. Their task has become that of finding the match between the objects and their representation in the text.

On the other hand, students in school, who are often engaged in reading-to-learn tasks, usually do not have these physical cues in the environment. Thus, students must rely on the text and on their own background knowlege.

It seems, then, that school reading-to-learn tasks may require different kinds of problem-solving strategies from workplace reading-to-do tasks.

What are the practical implications of these analyses of the disparity between school and workplace literacy? The answer to this question is not a simple one. School should not be seen merely as a place to prepare students for the world of work, so the findings above should *not* be interpreted to mean that teachers should try to make school literacy activities identical to those of the workplace. Yet we wish students to have knowledge of the many different functions of literacy, including the functions of literacy in the workplace. Thus, we recommend that teachers at least introduce students to these functions.

▌ INSTRUCTIONAL GUIDELINES

The two kinds of reading tasks often faced by workers, but rarely by students, appear to be reading-to-do and reading-to-assess. Now that you are aware of this gap, you should look for opportunities to highlight these tasks, particularly when teaching content area lessons. For example, reading-to-do can be highlighted: During a science lesson students might be asked to carry out an experiment following written directions. Such directions are often found in science kits or textbooks, or the teacher may write them out on task cards. Primary grade students may carry out experiments to see which objects sink or float in a pan of water, while upper grade students may work with batteries and wires to create electrical circuits. Children can work either individually or in small groups, while the teacher circulates around the room to provide assistance.

Children could also be given written directions for a craft or cooking project. For example, written directions for making a mask out of a large paper sack and construction paper might be given to primary grade children. To make the task somewhat easier for younger children, drawings might be used to illustrate some of the steps. For cooking projects, recipes can be written on task cards for the children. Some foods can be prepared which do not require baking or frying, for example, snacks such as trail mix, sandwiches, jello, and lemonade. Cooking projects often go more smoothly if parents come to the classroom to help. Later, children can take copies of the recipes home.

Reading-to-assess might be highlighted when the children are doing research for reports in one of the content areas. For example, suppose that the children in a group are looking for information on different kinds of insects (i.e., one child is writing a report on ants, another on bees, another on grasshoppers, and so on). The children could be made aware of one another's topics and asked to pass along information about books or magazine articles other students might find useful. Or the teacher can lead the children in a discussion comparing the merits of various sources when one is seeking answers to particular questions (e.g., which provide detailed information, which are more general).

The teacher may also wish to acquaint students with certain practical uses of literacy that may be related to finding and keeping a job. These include being able to read the newspaper and notices, filling out application forms, using the telephone directory, using a building directory to locate a particular store or office, and reading a bus schedule. By the time they are in the upper elementary grades, some students may already have these skills. Others, however, could benefit from instruction in these areas. For example, the building directory could be pointed out, and information from it used when the children are visiting an office building.

The teacher should try to be aware of students' own personal uses for literacy and how to make reading functional for particular children. For example, a first grader may want to be able to read the information on a cereal box, in order to send away for an item. Some students make models, which requires the careful following of directions. Others may need to read bus schedules or maps in order to visit friends. Students may want to read the newspaper to find out the time for a movie or special show on television.

▌ INSTRUCTIONAL ACTIVITIES

Mikulecky (1984) suggests that classroom teachers can best prepare students to meet workplace demands for literacy by increasing the amount of reading and writing students do and involving them in activities which include real-world materials and problem-solving strategies similar to those workers use. Real-world materials include newspapers, advertisements, correspondence, and instruction manuals. The problem-solving strategies should center on the completion of a specific task in which reading and writing are absolutely necessary. Most activities should require students to work with others, since workplace literacy often involves the exchange of information and pooling of ideas among workers.

Realistic Literacy Experiences

To give elementary students realistic literacy experiences, Mikulecky (1984) recommends the following activities, which appear suitable for use with fourth through sixth graders:

1. The teacher makes the following suggestions: (a) Pretend you have just won a puppy in a raffle. How are you going to take care of your new pet? Find information by calling the veterinarian, reading pamphlets, finding library books. Make a schedule, based on your readings, to show what kinds of vaccinations your pet will need. Make a feeding timetable. What

types and how much exercise will the dog need? How big will it get and what size house will it need? (b) Plan to build a dog house. What materials would you use? Make a sketch or blueprint of the house you propose.

2. The children are to decide on a class mascot to be built life-size out of papier-maché. After choosing a character, the children research how to design and build the structures and how to make papier-maché. When enough information is gathered and plans written down, the children do the project.

3. Sooner or later most elementary schools have playground problems. Children can help solve them by gathering information, and considering alternative solutions. Groups of children can write, in their own words, what they see as major problems. Other groups can interview and write up opinions of teachers on playground duty. Still other students can read copies of school rules or books and pamphlets on playground and park safety. From this information, a selected group of students can compile a list of possible solutions, and how each could be employed. This list can serve as a basis for school discussion and decision making.

4. The teacher arranges for students to have pen pals from different countries. Over the school year, students can plan all the details of a trip to visit pen pals. This would include using an atlas, maps, travel schedules, and estimating accommodation and travel costs. Follow-up activities could include developing ways to fund such trips.

5. Students collect local restaurant menus and advertisements for restaurant discounts. Then they draw envelopes with differing amounts of pretend money. Each student must now decide what to order with the allotted money at each of five restaurants.   (pp. 256–257)

Group Tasks

Mikulecky also recommends having students work together on assignments, as workers often do on the job. Here are activities for upper grade students, which might be adapted for second and third graders:

Have students use telephone directories to find business addresses.
Appoint students to write and post instructions to absent students on how to do class assignments (the teacher can check these for accuracy).
Involve students in some classroom record-keeping and form-filling.
Have students skim current periodicals for articles on specific topics.
(pp. 255–256)

Problem-Solving Activities Using Several Types of Materials

In the following activities, students are required to read and write and collect information from more than one printed source. They also become involved in setting their own goals and in addressing an audience other than the teacher.

With guidance from the teacher, many fifth and sixth graders, and perhaps some fourth graders, will be able to carry out these activities.

> Students write a letter requesting information on a product.
>
> Students choose a place they wish to visit. They gather information on costs of travel, lodging, food, etc. for the trip. (Automobile association maps and booklets are particularly helpful.)
>
> Students interview three adults about the sorts of reading and writing they must do on their jobs. They write a letter to the principal, superintendent, or counselor explaining what one must learn to perform these jobs, or write a story for the class newspaper or magazine.
>
> Students summarize the main idea from several different materials they have read on a topic of their choice. They make the summary into a booklet or article a younger reader could understand.
>
> The teacher delegates authority. Students who have done well in class are allowed to determine what is needed to set up a terrarium, get a speaker to come to class and explain microcomputers, or whatever else is needed.
>
> Students plan to accomplish a goal or personal dream. This may involve writing letters and using catalogs, maps, advertising, price lists, and reference books. A final businesslike report can outline the resources needed and the steps required to make the dream come true. (Mikulecky, 1984, p. 256)

Key Concept 2

Teachers should guide students toward independence in literacy by gradually releasing responsibility to them.

▌ LEADING STUDENTS TOWARD INDEPENDENCE

In Chapter 1 of this textbook we described the overall goal of the classroom reading program as building a foundation for lifelong literacy. In Key Concept #1 of this chapter, we returned to this theme by looking at ways that teachers could provide students with functional literacy experiences similar in some ways to those in the workplace. Now in Key Concept #2, we will consider another means of building a foundation for lifelong literacy. This has to do with ensuring that students will be able to use literacy strategies on their own, when the teacher is not there to help them. We introduced this notion in Chapter 1 and returned to it periodically in later chapters.

The general idea is that teachers should take certain steps to help students gain independence in the use of reading and writing strategies they have been taught. We know that this aim has been accomplished if students can apply reading and writing strategies on their own in school, and also can use these strategies outside of school. For example, suppose that you are teaching students comprehension monitoring. Your end goal is to have students use comprehension monitoring whenever they read, not just during the lessons they have with you.

How will you help students to reach this goal of independence in the use of strategies? To increase students' ability to apply strategies on their own, teachers should think of gradually releasing responsibility for strategy use to them (Pearson, 1985). As discussed in Chapter 1, the idea is gradually to turn control of strategy use over to the students. The teacher should be doing less and less, while the students should be doing more and more.

Palincsar and Ransom (1988) believe that *guided practice* is a critical step for bringing strategies under full control of students. They see this step as especially critical for poor readers. According to Palincsar and Ransom, guided practice differs from ordinary practice because it involves collaboration between the teacher and student. In Pearson's model of the gradual release of responsibility, it is an intermediate step in leading students to independence in strategy use. The teacher and student carry out the strategy together, with the teacher tailoring the amount of assistance to the needs of the individual. The teacher gives just enough help, and no more, to enable the student to carry out the strategy successfully.

With reciprocal teaching, for example, Palincsar and Ransom point out that one child might need help in identifying the information to be addressed in the question, while another might need help only with phrasing the question. The teacher would adjust the level of support provided to each of these children, giving more to the first child and less to the second. In Chapter 2, Figure 2.2 (p. 61), we presented an example of teacher-student dialogue during reciprocal teaching lessons. In this dialogue you could see how the teacher gave more support in earlier lessons, and very little in later lessons, as the student became better able to ask questions about important information in the passages read.

After guided practice, Palincsar and Ransom recommend that students be given *independent practice*. That is, the teacher should give students the opportunity to execute the strategy on their own. Independent practice builds students' proficiency in using the strategy and encourages them to transfer use of the strategy to situations other than the original learning situation. This means having students extend use of the strategy to other settings and to other texts. For example, if the strategy was first learned in teacher-directed small group reading lessons, students could be given independent practice in using the strategy when reading with a partner. Students could be asked to carry out the strategy individually, while reading their science textbook. They might also be asked to use the strategy when completing homework.

Palincsar and Ransom stress the importance throughout strategy instruction of having students monitor their own success in learning and applying the strategy. One way to do this is to have students compare their performance during initial learning with their present performance. For example, in reciprocal teaching, students might reflect back on the difficulties they first experienced in identifying important passage information and in asking questions. They will be able to notice that these activities have now become much easier for them. The teacher could also have students discuss times when they used the strategy, other than during their reading lesson.

▌ INSTRUCTIONAL GUIDELINES

Johnston (1985) reminds us that the goal of strategy instruction is "to have students (a) recognize the strategy, (b) find it effective in attaining a desired goal, (c) adopt the strategy for their own use, and (d) generalize it to other situations" (p. 639). He makes several specific recommendations for meeting this goal.

1. *Have students describe the procedure in their own words.* This idea comes from the work on teaching students to make inferences about text, conducted by Hansen and Pearson (1983). After the students had participated in several systematic training lessons, they were asked, "What is it that we have been doing every time we meet to begin a new story?" Students gave answers such as, "We talk about our lives and we predict what will happen in the stories." By having students reflect upon what they had been doing, Hansen and Pearson made students aware of the procedures to be followed in the inference strategy.

Johnston believes that it is important to have students engage in this type of reflection, because students often are not aware of the procedures teachers are guiding them through. Students need to be made aware of these procedures, preferably through questions drawing out their own descriptions. If students cannot verbalize the procedures, they should be told about them. Johnston notes that this step strengthens strategy training because it promotes students' metacognition, or awareness of their own mental processes.

2. *Have students discuss why the strategy is useful.* Hansen and Pearson also asked students, "Why do we make these comparisons?" Students realized that it was because "they help us to understand the story." Johnston points out that questions like these help students to transfer or generalize the strategy, because they have come to an understanding of the overall goal of instruction and how it can be useful to them.

3. *Help students see how the strategy can be useful in a variety of situations.* Another kind of question teachers can ask is one promoting connection-making. Johnston gives the following example: "Last week I asked you to think about a social studies lesson on Japan. Today pretend that you are reading a science article about conservation. What might you be thinking about while you are reading the article?" (p. 639). Questions like these promote gen-

eralization by helping students to see how a strategy may be useful in a number of different situations, involving different kinds of texts.

4. *Promote self-monitoring.* Like Palincsar and Ransom, Johnston stresses the importance of having students monitor their own performance. He recommends that teachers teach self-monitoring by being careful about the kind of feedback they give students. Usually, teachers simply tell children if their answers are right or wrong. According to Johnston, this practice does little good because it teaches children to rely on the teacher, not on themselves.

To promote students' self-monitoring, teachers should respond with questions instead of right/wrong statements. For example, teachers might ask questions such as the following:

Do you think your answer is correct? How do you know?
Does that answer make sense to you? Why or why not?

Questions like these shift responsibility away from the teacher and over to the students. Students, rather than the teacher, become responsible for monitoring their own strategy use and comprehension.

Johnston adds that teachers need to remember to question students when they have responded successfully, as well as when they have been unsuccessful. If not, students will soon learn that "Does that answer make sense to you?" means "Wrong!" Students, especially poor readers, need to know when they are doing something correctly, as well as when they are experiencing difficulty.

▌ INSTRUCTIONAL ACTIVITIES
Independent Assignments

Another important step in leading students toward independence is to give them the opportunity to use their own judgment in independent assignments. For example, when students have finished reading a particular book or story, let them decide how they would like to respond to that piece of literature. If students do not have ideas of their own, you might suggest a number of options. Here are some possibilities students may find interesting (adapted from Harste, Short, and Burke, 1988, p. 306):

- Develop a commercial to sell classmates on a particular book.
- Create a work of art, such as a mural, diorama, mobile, or collage, based on the book.
- Write a new story using the same theme or involving the same characters.
- Put together a newspaper based on events in the book or showing aspects of life in that period of time.
- Invent a board game incorporating the book's characters or events.
- Interview another student about his or her response to the book.

- Conduct research on the setting of the story or on the author's life.
- Draw a comparison chart or web comparing books with similar themes or books on related topics.
- Organize a book party, in which students dress as book characters.

Taking the steps recommended in this key concept will strengthen your students' reading ability and independence. However, it is perfectly possible for students to be good readers and yet not be willing to do much recreational or voluntary reading. In the next key concept, we look at ways that you can round out the picture for your students by helping them develop an interest in voluntary reading.

Key Concept 3

Teachers should encourage voluntary reading, so students will choose to read independently for their own enjoyment and information.

█ ENCOURAGING VOLUNTARY READING

In this key concept, we turn to the kinds of reading people do in their leisure time, generally called *voluntary reading* or *recreational reading*. In voluntary reading the materials have been selected by the readers themselves, to be read either for information or for pleasure (Spiegel, 1981). This concept was introduced in Chapter 1 and discussed again in Chapter 3.

Some children and adults may spend several hours of leisure time a day reading, while others spend only a few minutes or no time at all (e.g., Greaney, 1980). Obviously, this is because reading is only one of many recreational activities available to people away from the workplace or the school. Competing activities include watching television, listening to music, participating in sports, attending religious activities, and socializing with friends. Yet both children and adults often choose to read, and older, literate adults indicate that reading is an activity to be valued across an entire lifetime (Ribovich & Erickson, 1980).

The goal of a teacher-initiated voluntary reading program is to bring students to enjoy reading and practice it as a leisure-time activity. A voluntary reading program can be justified on the grounds that reading for one's own information and pleasure has value in and of itself. For the developing elementary school reader, recreational reading has many other important benefits. For example, Spiegel (1981) suggests that voluntary reading helps students develop positive attitudes toward reading, expand their base of knowledge, develop automaticity in the use of word identification strategies, learn to use context cues, and increase their vocabulary.

Figure 12.1
Observation Checklist to Assess
Reading Attitudes

In the two-week period has the child:

	yes	no
1. Seemed happy when engaged in reading activities?		
2. Volunteered to read aloud in class?		
3. Read a book during free time?		
4. Mentioned reading a book at home?		
5. Chosen reading over other activities (playing games, coloring, talking, etc.)?		
6. Made requests to go to the library?		
7. Checked out books at the library?		
8. Talked about books he/she has read?		
9. Finished most of the books she/he has started?		
10. Mentioned books she/he has at home?		

Source: A child-based observation checklist to assess attitude toward reading," by Betty Heathington and J. E. Alexander, *The Reading Teacher,* April 1978. Copyright © 1978 International Reading Association, Inc. Reprinted with permission of Betty Heathington and the International Reading Association.

Teachers who wish to encourage children's voluntary reading will find it useful to know something about what motivates adults and children to read during their leisure time. They will also want to be aware of factors affecting people's reading of the different major print media. The adults surveyed by Guthrie and Seifert (1983) spent the most time reading newspapers, followed by books and then magazines. Children appear to spend more time reading books and magazines and less time reading the newspaper (Guthrie, 1981). Thus, the sections below include instructional guidelines and activities for encouraging children's voluntary reading of newspapers and magazines, as well as of books.

Checklist to Assess Attitudes Toward Reading

Children who develop a positive attitude toward reading are more likely to acquire a lifelong reading habit. For this reason, teachers want to be able to identify children who seem to dislike reading and need extra teacher attention to become involved in voluntary reading.

Heathington and Alexander (1978) present a simple checklist teachers can use to assess children's attitudes toward reading, as shown in Figure 12.1. They developed the checklist by interviewing sixty children in grades one through six. The children were asked about the behaviors of children who liked reading, as well as those of children who disliked it. The ten checklist items stemmed from their responses.

By using this checklist, teachers can identify children who appear to have negative attitudes toward particular types of reading activities, especially in the area of voluntary reading. Steps can then be taken to improve attitudes in problem areas. A two week period of observation should be sufficient, according to Heathington and Alexander. During this time, the teacher will usually have the opportunity to observe the child in both structured and free reading situations and at the library. In addition, the teacher will probably have spoken to the child about his or her voluntary reading and been able to note whether the child has finished reading any books.

▌ INSTRUCTIONAL ACTIVITIES
Helping Students Set Goals for Voluntary Reading

Reading for Pleasure: Guidelines, a booklet written by Spiegel (1981), provides many practical suggestions teachers can use to promote voluntary reading. Most of the ideas below are discussed in more detail in this booklet.

Spiegel recommends that teachers who wish to give a special emphasis to voluntary reading discuss with their classes the purposes for having a voluntary reading program. Teachers may establish goals for the class as a whole and have students react to these goals. Within this general framework, the students could also be asked to set their own personal goals. Figure 12.2 shows an example of some class and personal goals. In later group discussions, the teacher and children can assess how well the voluntary reading program is working, and the teacher can help the children arrive at new class and personal goals.

A slightly different approach is recommended by Indrisano (1978, cited in Spiegel, 1981). Each month, the teacher asks the students to list one goal they would like to meet through reading (see Figure 12.2). These goals can be as varied as the students' own interests and reading proficiency. For example, a primary grade child may set the goal of reading another book by Dr. Seuss, while an upper grade student may choose to read several magazine articles

▌ **Figure 12.2**
▌ **Class Goals Chart**

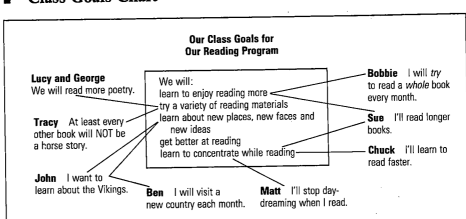

Our Class Goals for
Our Reading Program

Lucy and George
We will read more poetry.

Tracy At least every other book will NOT be a horse story.

John I want to learn about the Vikings.

We will:
learn to enjoy reading more
try a variety of reading materials
learn about new places, new faces and new ideas
get better at reading
learn to concentrate while reading

Bobbie I will *try* to read a *whole* book every month.

Sue I'll read longer books.

Chuck I'll learn to read faster.

Ben I will visit a new country each month.

Matt I'll stop day-dreaming when I read.

Source: From *Reading for pleasure: Guidelines* by D. L. Spiegel (Newark, DE: International Reading Association).

about computers. Once goals are set, the teacher aids the students in achieving their goals. The teacher may wish to encourage students to set different types of goals from one month to the next, so that they will develop a range of interests.

Initiating Voluntary Reading

Spiegel suggests that the teacher start voluntary reading by reading aloud to the class for a short period of time, perhaps ten minutes. Following this time, the children read on their own for a brief period (this time may be structured as sustained silent reading, as discussed in Chapter 3). Gradually, the period for the teacher's reading aloud may be shortened, while that for the students' silent reading is lengthened. It is recommended, however, that teachers always do some reading aloud to their classes.

A study conducted by Mendoza (1985) provides recommendations about elementary students' preferences when being read to by others. Teachers may wish to consider these points when reading aloud to their classes. Mendoza confirmed that most students, even in the upper elementary grades, enjoy having their teachers read aloud. Younger children, especially boys, may prefer being read to in a large group, while older students may prefer hearing books in a small group.

Mendoza observed that many teachers do not discuss books with children after they have been read aloud. Yet she found that 76 percent of primary children and 69 percent of upper grade students wanted to talk about the books they had heard. She strongly recommends that teachers allow time for such discussions.

According to Mendoza, "Apparently we make a mistake by thinking that once we have read a book to children, that should be the end of it" (p. 527). She found that almost all primary grade children want to look at a book themselves, especially to study the illustrations, and many older students want to read the book on their own. Teachers will want to make the book available to children, in multiple copies if possible.

Forming Groups to Encourage Voluntary Reading

In *jigsaw grouping* (Aronson, Blaney, Sikes, Stephan, & Snapp, 1975, cited in Spiegel, 1981) each student belongs to two different groups. The first group is based on interest. For example, a student might be interested in sports and so joins a group reading about the history of the Olympic games. Another student interested in popular music might join a group reading about recording stars. There might be four or five such groups in a classroom. The members of each interest group read independently to collect information on their topic. They then meet to discuss what they have learned and to generate a group outline organizing major pieces of information.

After the outlines have been produced, new groups are formed. These con-

Seeing their balloons move higher into the clouds on this chart reminds fourth graders of how much voluntary reading they have done. Setting up the chart is one of several means the teacher uses to promote voluntary reading.

sist of one member of each of the original interest groups (i.e., if there were four interest groups, each new group has four members). Children in the group share information following their interest group outline. This arrangement gives all children the opportunity to discuss their reading, as well as to learn information about another topic.

Interest groups might also be formed on an ad hoc basis, as two or more children seem to be interested in exploring the same topic. The volunteers meet in the group only as long as they want to, and the group can be dissolved at any time. At any given time, just one or two of these groups might be in existence in a classroom.

Another approach is to assign students to a "reading buddy" (Roeder & Lee, 1973, cited in Spiegel, 1981). The partners may read aloud to one another, present a book report prepared together, or help one another choose books for independent reading.

According to Spiegel, mixing children in different groups for the purposes of talking about their independent reading can also be a boon in classrooms with sustained silent reading. Having children meet and interact keeps interest high. Children can get ideas of what to read by talking to other children and be recognized for the reading they themselves are doing.

Voluntary Sharing

Spiegel argues convincingly that students *not* be required to share the reading they have done through book reports or other means. She believes the motivation for voluntary reading should be the students' own interest in reading, rather than external forces, such as teachers' requirements. On the other hand, she strongly recommends voluntary sharing, because many students enjoy sharing their reading experiences with other children and with adults. Encouraging voluntary sharing contributes to the development of a community of readers in the classroom.

Spiegel offers two sensible guidelines for voluntary sharing. According to the first guideline, teachers should be sure that the amount of time the student spends on a sharing project is much less than that spent on the original reading of the material. For example, if a child took about an hour to read a storybook, the sharing project should take up much less than an hour. Art projects such as murals or models frequently take up a great deal of time. Even though students often enjoy these projects, Spiegel points out that the projects may have more to do with artistic expression than with developing the habit of voluntary reading.

The second guideline is that teachers have children use techniques for sharing that promote the voluntary reading of other students. One way to do this is to have the children add pages to a catalogue of recommended books (Criscuolo, 1977, cited in Spiegel, 1981). When children have read a book they think will be interesting to their classmates, they write a synopsis or advertisement for it on a piece of 8″ × 10″ tagboard, perhaps including an illustration. The teacher makes sure the children include information such as the title, author, and where the book may be found (e.g., school or classroom library).

Sharing with Students in Other Classes

In Chapters 2 and 3 we mentioned how children in the classroom might form a *community of readers*, exchanging information about books they each enjoyed reading. This community can be extended beyond a single class, if the children share the joys of reading with students in other classes.

Children may be interested in giving *book talks*. During a book talk, a student tells about a book he or she especially enjoyed reading, with the aim of encouraging other students to read the book, too. A book talk might include reading a short portion of the book aloud. Begin by setting aside a time each week when your students can give book talks to their classmates. After they become familiar with this routine, arrange for them to give their book talks to another class.

Children can share the books they have written and published with students in other classes. For example, fourth and fifth graders might be allowed to read their own published books aloud to a class of first graders. After reading, they can receive comments and answer questions from the younger children. Experiences such as these help children to feel pride in their literary accomplishments. There can be benefits, too, for the younger children, who may be motivated to do more reading and writing on their own.

Children can serve as tutors to younger children, by reading their own writing aloud. The older children can also encourage the younger ones to read aloud and to write. Refer to Nevi (1983) for a discussion of how cross-age tutoring can be beneficial to the tutor.

Another method of sharing, which may boost the confidence and interest of a poor reader, is to have the student read aloud to younger children from a favorite book he or she has just finished. This method allows the student to read from an "easy" book that few classmates are likely to find appealing, while at the same time encouraging the reading interests of the younger children.

■ INSTRUCTIONAL ACTIVITIES
Encouraging Book Reading

On the average, American adults may spend only five minutes per day reading books (Guthrie, 1982). Older adults, however, appear to spend more time and read an average of almost a book a month (Ribovich & Erickson, 1980). Factors affecting the amount of book reading by adults include occupation, level of education, and leisure time available, as well as the individual's tastes and interests.

In reviewing studies of the extent of children's book reading, Greaney (1980) reports that children appear to do the greatest amount of reading near the end of elementary school. After this they seem to do less and less leisure reading, especially of books. Children from more privileged backgrounds, with better educated parents, seem to read books more than those from working class backgrounds. Children's level of reading proficiency also appears to affect how much they read books, with poor readers doing much less than good readers.

Children seem to spend surprisingly little time reading books in comparison to time spent on other leisure time activities. Fifty percent of the fifth graders studied by Fielding, Wilson, and Anderson (1986) read books for less than four minutes a day, while 30 percent read only two minutes a day or less and 10 percent reported never reading a book at all. A majority of the children spent 1 percent or less of their free time reading books.

The children were perfectly capable of reading books, for example, spending two hours or more reading when they had to prepare a book report. But on the average, children read books on only one day in five. "The problem," according to Fielding et al., "is not that students can't read, but that on most days they don't."

Fielding et al. suggest that substantial increases in reading achievement might be seen if children could be encouraged to read books for even ten minutes per day. Of all the children's leisure-time activities, book reading was found to be the single best predictor of reading achievement as measured by standardized tests, of size of vocabulary, and of gains in reading achievement from the second to fifth grade.

Why should book reading, in particular, be so strongly related to overall reading proficiency? First, according to Fielding et al., book reading can build background knowledge of many different topics. Second, it can acquaint children with the various structures of narrative and expository text. When reading tradebooks, children can gain experience with well-organized, well-written text, rich in information. This experience is not necessarily gained in work with basal readers and content area textbooks. Third, vocabulary growth is promoted in the manner discussed in Chapter 5. Finally, book reading serves as self-initiated practice, an opportunity for children to orchestrate all of the reading skills they have been taught, so that use of these skills becomes automatic. In a related report, Anderson, Wilson, and Fielding (1988) conclude that the case for book reading "is as strong as the case for any other practice in the field of reading, in or out of school" (p. 302).

Fielding et al. looked at the question of why some children become avid readers. They discovered that parents of avid readers created environments where reading would seem attractive to their children, but otherwise did not worry too much about it. For example, the parents made sure there were many books in the home and acted as models because they themselves enjoyed reading, but they did not have scheduled times for the children to read.

Interviews with the young avid readers themselves revealed other factors contributing to their interest in reading books.

Most interesting was that avid readers seemed to belong to *communities of readers*. They reported talking to peers, siblings, parents, or teachers about books they had read and getting recommendations for future reading from these same people. The avid readers never seemed to be at a loss for something to read. Though only a few of them read more than one book at a time, they all had plans for what they would read next.

The avid readers were more aware than their parents of past or present teachers' influence on their reading habits. They mentioned teachers having books available in the classroom, reading out loud to the class, recommending books to them, talking to them about books they had read, requiring them to read a certain number of books in a grading period, or just being such good teachers that children came to love reading by being in their classes. According to the children themselves, teachers can have a significant influence on the development of avid reading.

A noteworthy observation from the children's interviews is their admission that, except for one or two of them, reading is not always their number-one favorite way to spend free time. Watching television, playing video or computer games, and participating in sports were often favored over reading. But for these children, reading remained a frequent activity, perhaps because it is something they can do at any time, without involving anyone else. As one child put it, "It's always been there, and it always will be."

Making books accessible. In promoting children's independent reading of books, Fielding et al. suggest that the first step is to increase the children's access to books. Setting up a classroom library, as described in Chapter 3, can be a big help, particularly if the teacher gives brief talks to "sell" children on the books being placed there. "Flooding" classrooms with books is also a powerful technique (for more information about book floods, see Chapter 8).

Children may also gain access to books during visits to school or community libraries, but these do not offer the convenience of a classroom library. For example, as Fielding et al. point out, children may be absent on the day the class visits the library, or find that they are not really enjoying the books borrowed. With a classroom library, these problems do not arise because books can be borrowed or exchanged at any time.

If the school or community library is the primary source of books, special steps may have to be taken to be sure that less avid readers have suitable books. Spiegel (1981) points out that some children may benefit from extra time to browse among books in the school library. For these children, a brief, once-a-week class visit may not allow enough time for appropriate books to be located.

Helping children to build up a small home library may also increase book reading. Spiegel suggests that teachers look into ways that children can obtain books at little or no cost. The federally funded Reading Is Fundamental (RIF) program, which has the goal of distributing free books to children, operates in many communities. Also, children may order books inexpensively through book clubs. Some textbooks being discarded by the school may provide children with books for their home libraries. Teachers may organize sessions when the children may swap books with one another. Lowe (1977, cited in Spiegel) describes one method for conducting a book swap. The swapping is done in a single large room. The number of books each child brings to the room is recorded. He or she is then allowed to take that same number of books from the room.

Summer loss of reading proficiency is sometimes of concern to teachers, particularly those who work with children from low-income families. Crowell

Visiting the school library may be overwhelming to some young students. The teacher can help by showing children where a certain type of book may be found and by offering suggestions about specific books they might enjoy.

and Klein (1981) suggest that giving these children access to books over the summer vacation is one way to prevent a decline in reading proficiency. They designed a program which involved mailing paperback books to children who had just completed the first and second grades. Children received books at their own reading levels, which ranged from readiness to the third grade. One book was mailed each week for ten weeks during the summer vacation, and the children were allowed to keep the books. All of the children appeared to benefit from the program, but positive effects were greater for the first graders.

A procedure like the one used by Crowell and Klein is a good way to ensure that children have reading material over the summer, a natural extension to a recreational reading program carried out during the school year. Parents who ask what they can do to help their children over the summer could be told to take the children on regular visits to the library, help them select and purchase a number of paperback books, and otherwise make sure they have plenty of high-interest reading material.

Helping children find interesting books.   Some children may be doing little book reading because they are having trouble finding books they like. In this case, mechanisms should be used which allow the teacher and classmates to assist them in finding books they will enjoy. Spiegel suggests that teachers keep a folder where students can record the kind of reading material they would like to be able to find. Periodically, the teacher can give the child help in locating these materials or ask the librarian to do so.

The teacher could also have the children complete brief forms describing their reading interests, as recommended by Criscuolo (1977, cited in Spiegel) and shown in Figure 12.3. The forms can be posted so that the children will be aware of one another's interests and can let classmates know of relevant books. This method engages students in the task of "reading-to-assess" since they are deciding whether particular books match a classmate's interests. Children also become naturally involved in supporting one another's recreational reading.

Teachers should also be aware of books which can turn reluctant readers into avid readers. Being able to make suitable recommendations may be especially important for teachers working with upper elementary students who have had difficulty learning to read. Bennett and Bennett (1982) provide a bibliography of humorous children's books found to be favored by fourth, fifth and sixth graders. Other high-interest books are recommended by Cunningham (1983a, 1983b). In the first article she discusses books where children can choose their own adventures, while in the second she identifies books children can read for information, for carrying out projects, or for entertainment and escape.

Teachers are sometimes interested in expanding children's reading interests and leading them to read more challenging books. Spiegel (1981) takes the position that teachers' first priority should be to make sure that children *will* read. In her view, improving the quality of children's book reading is of less importance, in part because most children prefer choosing books for themselves and may become less motivated to read if teachers seem to be forcing specific books on them. To get around this problem, Spiegel recommends that the teacher use a group rather than individual approach. For example, the teacher can introduce the whole class to a variety of challenging books, differing in genre and topic from those most children are choosing to read. The teacher may give brief talks or read short sections of the new books

▌ **Figure 12.3**
▌ **Reading Interest Form**

Name _____

Hobbies _____

Favorite TV Program _____

Last Book I Read _____

Types of Books I Like _____

Age _____

out loud. By using procedures such as this one, the teacher can get around the problem of appearing to prescribe a certain book for a certain child.

Teachers interested in learning about new children's books may wish to read the book review columns in the following journals:

Horn Book Magazine
Language Arts
The New Advocate
The Reading Teacher

Also, children's librarians often are excellent sources of information about recently published children's books.

Encouraging Newspaper Reading

It is likely that almost all American adults read the newspaper, and according to Guthrie (1981), 60 to 70 percent of adults in the United States say they read the newspaper daily. By comparison, few children appear to read the newspaper every day: 5 percent of 6-year olds, 10 percent of 9-year olds, and 40 percent of 12-year olds. The newspaper content children choose to read changes as they grow older. Boys start by reading the comics, then add sports, and then the news. Girls begin with the comics, then add information relevant to personal and social development and the news.

According to Guthrie, teachers can increase children's newspaper reading by using the newspaper in classroom activities. Presumably, homework assignments which required use of the newspaper would have similar effects. Both school and home newspaper activities could be designed to promote children's interest in contents, such as national and local news, which they generally would not read on their own.

Stimulating interest in current events. Frequently, teachers are able to generate a great deal of interest in current events in classes from the third grade on up. An effective technique is to hold class discussions based on information in the newspaper and to allow children to share and post news articles. In almost every community, children's interest in local news can be stimulated by having them begin by reading about issues of concern to their families and neighbors. For example, a farming community may be experiencing a shortage of water, or a suburban community may be concerned about the lack of ambulance service to the nearest city hospital. At other times, the children's interest may be captured by the national news, for example, in the year of a presidential election. Older children may become involved in clipping newspaper articles on international news, perhaps for a particular country being covered in a social studies unit.

Children who do not have access to a newspaper at home may be encouraged to read the newspaper if one is delivered to the classroom. At the end of the school day, these children might be allowed to take sections home to read.

Following up a newspaper story.   A teacher might stimulate students' interest in newspapers by having them write a follow-up article. In this activity (developed by Nagel, in Watson, 1987) the teacher first has students read or listen to a story from a local newspaper likely to be of high interest to many students. The teacher leads students in a discussion of the story, and together the teacher and students develop a list of key questions. The teacher should explain that a follow-up story may appear in the newspaper, but that students will want to track down information on their own as well. The students then study the story to determine the sources they will want to reach for additional information and think about how these sources can be contacted, whether in person, by telephone, or by letter. Students will probably want to work in pairs to contact the sources.

The students should bring in the information obtained, even if the answer given was "no comment." The teacher can lead the group in a discussion of all information gathered. The discussion might include reasons for "no comment" responses or form letters. Finally, the students can use the information gathered as the basis for writing a follow-up article based on the original newspaper story. The students' article may be sent in to the local newspaper. If a follow-up article has already appeared, and the students received new or different information, they might write a letter to the editor.

Writing news stories from different points of view.   This activity developed by Holbrook (in Watson, 1987) may help students learn to read newspaper articles with a critical eye. It begins by having students read a newspaper article with a lot of human interest. Students are divided into small groups to read and discuss the article. The teacher then asks some groups to pretend that they were the people directly involved in the news event. The other groups are asked to pretend that they observed the event. Both groups write from their own perspective. When the groups have finished, students should have the opportunity to share their writing and to look at differences related to their particular points of view.

Homework assignments.   Criscuolo (1981) suggests a number of homework assignments which encourage children to read the newspaper. He recommends giving a newspaper assignment perhaps once a week, with about ten minutes of work for primary grade students and twenty minutes for sixth graders. Here are three ideas:

- *Sale items.* Ask children to select one of their possessions they would like to sell. As a homework assignment, have them read some classified ads under Merchandise for Sale to see what kind of information is given. Have them count the words in a four-line ad and write a four-line ad that will help sell their items. When the children turn in their ads, let them share them with each other.
- *Check the reviews.* Reviews of current books and movies are printed

in the newspaper. Ask the children to write a review of a recently published book they've read or a newly released movie they've seen. As a homework assignment, have them cut out the reviews published in their newspapers and compare them to their own written reviews.
- *Celebrities.* Ask children to select someone who is frequently in the news, e.g., an entertainer or a national figure. Ask them to keep a scrapbook of clippings on the exploits or experiences of the famous personality they select. As a follow-up activity, children can go to the library and write a biographical sketch of this famous person using a variety of reference aids. (pp. 921–922)

Encouraging Magazine Reading

Probably over 90 percent of American adults read magazines (e.g., Monteith, 1981; Ribovich & Erickson, 1980). In reviewing evidence of children's interests in magazines, Monteith (1981) reports that quite a number of magazines for young people are currently being published, and several are among the top 100 in the country in terms of subscriptions and newsstand sales. These include *Mad Magazine, Boy's Life, Seventeen Magazine,* and *Highlights for Children.* Children seem to be interested primarily in magazines containing either nonfiction or humor. Even poor readers appear to be motivated to read magazines, including those such as *Sports Illustrated* or *People,* which consist of text they are likely to find quite difficult. Monteith suggests that teachers should capitalize on children's interests in magazines as a natural way of developing motivation and encouraging the habit of recreational reading. Interests developed in reading magazine articles may also lead children to read books on the same topics.

Classroom use of magazines. Occasionally, the teacher may conduct either large or small group reading lessons based on high-interest magazine articles of basal reader selections or other texts. For examples, articles from the *Weekly Reader* may be read and discussed by the whole class. With a small group of proficient readers, even articles from magazines for adults, such as *Reader's Digest,* may be used. Often, magazine articles are suitable for content area reading lessons. For example, an article from *Ranger Rick* may fit well in a science unit.

Some children may not have access to magazines at home. If the teacher has subscriptions to children's magazines, copies of past issues could be sent home with these children. For a listing of children's magazines, refer to Watson (1987).

Homework assignments. Unlike most newspapers, many magazines are designed to appeal to readers with certain special interests. Thus, homework assignments involving magazines might serve the purpose of giving children time to become familiar with magazines they might enjoy reading. The teacher could introduce the homework assignment by having the children discuss interests, such as jokes, wild animals, fashion, or sports, which might be covered in magazine articles. Children can suggest magazines they already know of which contain such articles, and other magazines might be sought at the library. The children could then read one or two articles for homework and share the information learned with the class.

Key Concept 4

Teachers should foster students' reading ability and interest by strengthening connections between reading at home and at school.

❚ ENCOURAGING LITERACY BY MAKING CONNECTIONS TO THE HOME

As Taylor's (1983) work shows, the home provides many children with the foundation for becoming literate. Teachers should be aware of ways in which children's learning to read in school may interact with literacy experiences already available in the home. As pointed out in Chapter 1, it is important for the school to broaden children's literacy experiences and not to narrow them. For this reason, teachers should be sensitive to the fact that communication needs to flow in both directions. That is, information about children's school progress in learning to read needs to be sent to parents, but parents should also be encouraged to communicate with teachers about their knowledge of their children's progress. For example, children sometimes enter school already knowing how to read a number of storybooks. Asking parents for information like this may enable teachers to plan more challenging activities for certain children.

In general, the teacher should be sensitive to children's family circumstances and look for signs that parents are interested in encouraging their children's reading at home. Suggestions made in response to a parent's request are quite likely to be followed. On the other hand, in some instances parents may be put off by uninvited suggestions which they see as conflicting with family routines or values.

In some cases, too, the teacher may find that it is another family member, perhaps a grandparent or an older sister or brother, rather than a parent, who is willing and able to support the child's voluntary reading. Sometimes it is a neighbor, or the parent of another child in the class, who can be enlisted to take a child to the library. In some cases, however, the teacher should be aware that a high degree of home support for reading is not readily available to particular children. An extra dose of teacher attention may be the key to encouraging the voluntary reading of these children.

Discussed below are two major means that teachers can use to strengthen the connections between the home and school for the purpose of improving children's opportunities for learning to read. These have to do with communicating with parents and enlisting parents' help in encouraging children's voluntary reading by reading aloud to them, taking them to the library on a regular basis, and being involved in classroom activities. Many of the same ideas are easily adapted to situations where the teacher is trying to work with a family member other than the child's parents.

Communicating with Parents About Children's Learning to Read

Written communication. Schools generally rely on report cards as the chief means of communicating with parents about children's progress in learning to read, as well as in other academic and social areas. Because report cards are usually sent home only about four times a year, they generally can provide only a very broad overview of children's accomplishments. Thus, the teacher will probably wish to supplement report cards with other written reports to parents.

One option is *progress letters*, in which the teacher can describe in more detail the kinds of stories or expository selections the child is able to comprehend, some of the areas in which new vocabulary has been learned, and the kinds of books the child seems interested in reading on his or her own. Brief notes may be sent home with certain children on days when they have accomplished something special (for example, read their first published book to the class).

The teacher might also wish to send a letter home describing the goals of the classroom reading program and the types of activities planned for the children. Or the children themselves may write letters to their parents, describing their reading and writing activities and perhaps stapling to the letter a sample of work recently completed. Refer to Vukelich (1984) for further discussion of these and other ways of communicating with parents in writing.

Conferences, open houses, and classroom visits. While the work schedule of many parents makes it difficult for them to serve as classroom volunteers, they often are able to attend conferences and open houses. In many schools, parent conferences are scheduled at two times during the year (practical guidelines for scheduling and planning parent conferences are given by Granowsky, Rose, & Barton, 1983). On these occasions parents usually meet with the teacher to discuss their child's progress. The child's progress in learning to read, of course, should be an important part of this discussion. The teacher should be sure to give parents the chance to raise questions (for a listing of frequently asked questions and ideas for sensible responses, see Koppman, 1983).

Showing parents samples of the selections the child is reading and of the child's writing often gives them a better idea of how the child is progressing. Parents may be able to appreciate the progress a child has made if they are shown materials the child was working with earlier in the year, and then have the opportunity to contrast them with materials the child is presently using. The teacher should encourage parents to appreciate their children as individuals, with unique abilities and interests in reading and writing, and discourage what may be inappropriate comparisons with other children.

Open houses can serve as an occasion for the teacher to explain the classroom reading program to the parents as a group. The teacher may wish to display the children's reading materials, basal readers as well as content area textbooks and tradebooks, and have samples of the children's writing in folders for their parents to peruse.

Some schools hold "back to school" sessions when parents come to school and participate with their children in typical school activities. Or parents can be invited to visit the classroom during the school day to observe reading and writing activities. The teacher, principal, or reading specialist should try to be available to meet with the parents as the visit is being concluded to answer any questions.

Conferences, open houses, and other visits by parents may provide the teacher with opportunities to offer suggestions about ways that reading and writing can be encouraged at home. Figure 12.4 shows the suggestions most frequently made, according to Vukelich (1984).

∎ **Figure 12.4**
Suggestions Most Frequently Made for
Parent Reading Involvement

Activity or behavior	Number of times suggested, out of 24
Read to your child	22
Be a good literate model	14
Provide books, magazines, etc. for the child to read	13
Build a reading atmosphere at home (place, time, library area)	11
Talk and listen to your child	7
Exemplify a positive attitude toward reading, including praising your child for reading	7
Provide experiences for children that are reading related, e.g., library trips, or that can be used to stimulate interest in reading	7
Read environmental signs; capture reading opportunities in the environment	5
Provide contact with paper and pencils	4
Be aware of your child's interests	4
Point out similarity and differences in objects in the environment	4

Source: From Parents' role in the reading process by Carol Vukelich, *The Reading Teacher,* February 1984. Copyright © 1984 International Reading Association, Inc. Reprinted with permission of Carol Vukelich and the International Reading Association.

Parental Concerns

Homework.   Many parents want even their primary grade children to be given homework assignments and are happy to help with homework. Teachers should be certain to design homework to support the major goals of the classroom reading program, not to serve as busywork, and to help parents understand the reasons for giving certain kinds of homework assignments rather than others.

Homework will generally prove most valuable if it encourages children to use reading and writing in real-world ways. For example, independent reading of a book chosen by the child is a good substitute for paper-and-pencil activities. As mentioned earlier, another sound homework activity is to have the child read the newspaper for particular kinds of information. Corresponding with a pen pal is another example of a type of homework that teaches children about an important use of literacy. Parents could also help children write letters to relatives and friends. Still another possibility is to have children write in journals (refer to Chapter 8).

Television viewing.   Teachers may wish to alert concerned parents to the possibly negative effects of a great amount of television viewing on children's reading achievement. In a metaanalysis of 23 studies, Williams, Haertel, Haertel, and Walberg (1982) found a small but consistently negative relationship between hours of television viewing and school achievement. There seems to be no problem at all if children watch television for up to ten hours per week. However, watching television for longer amounts of time is related to lower levels of school achievement, especially for girls and for children of higher ability.

In general, the time children spend watching television is far greater than that spent reading books. The children studied by Fielding, Wilson, and Anderson (1986), for example, spent an average of two hours a day watching television, compared to only four minutes reading books.

Of course, the amount of time children spend watching television may reflect other home values and does not necessarily indicate a negative view toward reading and books. While teachers should handle the issue carefully, they might wish to encourage parents to monitor the amount of time their children spend watching television, to be sure that there is adequate time for recreational reading and homework. Telfer and Kann (1984) suggest that it may also be important for teachers and parents to be concerned about the amount of time students spend listening to the radio, records, and tapes.

Literate home environment.   The worries that some parents have about supporting their children's learning to read at home may be reduced if teachers help them understand that one of the best things they can do is simply continue modeling for their children the many uses of literacy in the home. Parents who read the newspaper, make shopping lists, write letters, or talk about favorite books are creating a literate home environment. In this perfectly natural way, they are giving their children the opportunity to see how valuable reading and writing can be in everyday life.

Involving Parents in a Voluntary Reading Program

Introducing the program. Spiegel (1981) reminds us that parents may need to be convinced of the value of a voluntary reading program. She warns that teachers may need to clarify for some parents the fact that voluntary reading is not a frill but a key component in a complete developmental reading program. To gain the support of parents, teachers may wish to send out a series of short newsletters explaining the reasons for having a voluntary reading program and how it will work. Spiegel offers the following suggestions:

Newsletter 1: Explanation of what a voluntary reading program is and how it will work in your class. Schedule of what information will be contained in subsequent newsletters.

This second grader works on a newsletter designed to keep her parents informed about her schoolwork. When completed, it will include comments from her teacher as well.

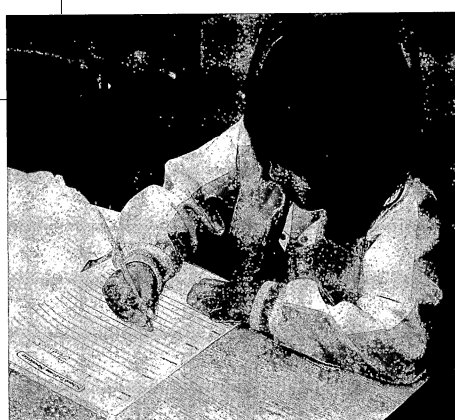

> *Newsletter 2* (two days later): Rationale for having a voluntary reading program, with emphasis on how it fits into the basic curriculum. Short statement of support from your principal and reading teacher.
> *Newsletter 3* (two days later): List of suggestions of ways parents can help support the program through their efforts at home.
> *Newsletter 4* (two days later): List of ways parents can volunteer their time in the classroom to support this program. (p. 58; *voluntary* substituted for the word *recreational*)

The voluntary reading program could also be discussed at an open house and during parent conferences. As Spiegel points out, asking parents to support voluntary reading gives them a positive, pleasant, and low-pressure way of helping their children at home.

Parents' reading aloud to children.   Judging from teachers' reports, having parents read aloud to their children, or listen to their children read, is probably the most common method of parent involvement (Epstein & Becker, 1982). For the purposes of promoting children's voluntary reading, this practice has much to recommend it. Many parents are reading aloud to their young children already, and others find that they can easily fit it into the family's routine. However, parents may differ in the way that they handle the reading aloud of storybooks. For example, research by Heath (1982) suggests that some parents may attempt to relate story ideas to the children's own experiences, while others do not. Heath also found that some parents expect their children to be able to answer questions about the story, while others do not. Findings such as these suggest that parents' reading aloud of storybooks may have a number of different effects on their children's learning to read (Teale, 1981).

Perhaps the best approach the teacher can take is to offer parents suggestions about books their children might especially enjoy hearing. This would seem preferable to recommending specific procedures that parents should follow in reading stories to their children, or a particular schedule or amount of reading to be done. As mentioned in Chapter 10, a good place to gather ideas is from the lists of Children's Choices published in *The Reading Teacher*. *Publishers Weekly* provides a monthly list of bestselling children's books.

Making use of the library.   Another step teachers can take is to encourage parents to take their children to the library. Specifically, teachers may be able to collect applications for library cards, provide parents with information on the location and hours of public libraries, and pass on announcements of special events (such as story hours). Teachers may also give parents ideas about books their children would enjoy borrowing. For example, parents of reluctant readers might appreciate knowing about books their children have enjoyed, so they can help them find other books by the same authors.

Little Books at Home

McCormick and Mason (1989) describe a program in which little books, with simple captions and clear pictures, were sent home for young children to keep. A teacher first introduced the books to the children in small groups. At home, the children's interest in the little books carried over to their parents. In many cases parents became actively involved in reading the little books with their children. Educationally at-risk children who received the little books made much better progress in learning to read than those who did not.

Many schools will not have programs to give children books to keep, but teachers can lend children easy, predictable books to take home. You will need to have an assortment of books available, preferably multiple copies of favorite titles. Be sure the books have strong picture cues and are of interest to the children. After you have read and discussed a book with the children, allow them to take it home.

Establish procedures for taking books home. For example, you might put the title of each book being borrowed on a list, and have children remind you to cross off the title when they have returned the book. Many teachers like to write the child's name on the outside of a manila envelope, and have children put books being borrowed in the envelope.

McCormick and Mason caution teachers and parents of children at the very earliest levels in learning to read to remember that children are just starting to get meaning from books. If children say their own words for the story, they should be encouraged in their attempts at meaning-making and not be made to call words accurately.

▌ SUMMARY

We opened this chapter with a profile of community reading activities. Studies of reading outside of school show us that most adults must do considerable reading as a part of their jobs.

In the first key concept we explained how workplace literacy differs from school literacy because it often involves "reading-to-do" rather than "reading-to-learn." We made suggestions for classroom activities involving students in realistic and problem-solving activities to give them a broader perspective on literacy.

In the second key concept we addressed the issue of how teachers can lead students toward greater independence in using reading and writing strategies. We described the concepts of guided and independent practice, and again mentioned the importance of teaching students to monitor their own comprehension.

In the third key concept we turned to voluntary reading and discussed approaches teachers might use to develop students' interest in books. We presented research suggesting that students' independent reading of books appears to have as powerful an effect on their achievement as any instructional practice. A classroom reading program is not complete if it does not have a strong voluntary reading component. While much attention should be given to books, teachers will probably want to foster students' voluntary reading of newspapers and magazines as well.

In essence, we returned in the fourth key concept to one of the themes introduced back in Chapter 1, that of the importance of the home in children's literacy development. We suggested that teachers keep parents informed about their children's learning to read and about classroom literacy activities. We looked at ways of increasing children's access to books while at home and of involving parents in a voluntary reading program. Students are well served when teachers can help them appreciate the value of literacy, not only in school but in the home and community.

▌ BIBLIOGRAPHY

References

Anderson, R. C., Wilson, P. T., & Fielding, L. G. (1988). Growth in reading and how children spend their time outside of school. *Reading Research Quarterly, 23* (3), 285–303.

Aronson, E., Blaney, N., Sikes, J., Stephan, C., & Snapp, M. (1975). The jigsaw route to learning and liking. *Psychology Today, 8,* 43–50. [cited in Spiegel, 1981]

Bennett, J. E., & Bennett, P. (1982). What's so funny? Action research and bibliography of humorous children's books—1975–1980. *The Reading Teacher, 35,* 924–927.

Criscuolo, N. (1977). Book reports: Twelve creative alternatives. *The Reading Teacher, 30* (8), 893–895.

Criscuolo, N. (1981). Creative homework with the newspaper. *The Reading Teacher, 34* (8), 921–922.

Crowell, D. C., & Klein, T. W. (1981). Preventing summer loss of reading skills among primary children. *The Reading Teacher, 34* (5), 561–564.

Cunningham, P. (1983a). The clip sheet: Adventures in reading and writing. *The Reading Teacher, 36* (6), 578–581.

Cunningham, P. (1983b). The clip sheet: Why should I read? *The Reading Teacher, 36* (7), 698–700.

Diehl, W. A., & Mikulecky, L. (1980). The nature of reading at work. *Journal of Reading, 24,* 221–227.

Epstein, J. L., & Becker, H. J. (1982). Teachers' reported practices of parent involvement: Problems and possibilities. *Elementary School Journal, 83* (2), 103–113.

Fielding, L., Wilson, P., & Anderson, R. C. (1986). A focus on free reading: The role of tradebooks in reading instruction. In T. E. Raphael (Ed.), *Contexts of school-based literacy.* New York: Random House.

Granowsky, A., Rose, A., & Barton, N. (1983). Parents as partners in education. Ginn Occasional Papers, Writings in reading and language arts, No. 2. Columbus, OH: Ginn.

Greaney, V. (1980). Factors related to amount and type of leisure reading. *Reading Research Quarterly, 15* (3), 337–357.

Guthrie, J. T. (1981). Acquisition of newspaper readership. *The Reading Teacher, 34,* 616–618.

Guthrie, J. T. (1982). Corporate education for the electronic culture. *Journal of Reading, 25,* 492–495.

Guthrie, J. T., & Seifert, M. (1983). Profiles of reading activity in a community. *Journal of Reading, 26* (6), 498–508.

Hansen, J., & Pearson, P. D. (1983). An instructional study: Improving the inferential comprehension of good and poor fourth-grade readers. *Journal of Educational Psychology, 75,* 821–829.

Harste, J. C., Short, K. G., & Burke, C. (1988). *Creating classrooms for authors: The reading-writing connection.* Portsmouth, NH: Heinemann.

Heath, S. B. (1982). What no bedtime story means: Narrative skills at home and school. *Language in Society, 11* (2), 49–76.

Heathington, B. S., & Alexander, J. E. (1978). A child-based observation checklist to assess attitudes toward reading. *The Reading Teacher, 31* (7), 769–771.

Indrisano, R. (1978). Reading: What about those who can read but don't? *Instructor, 87,* 94–98. [cited in Spiegel, 1981]

Johnston, P. (1985). Teaching students to apply strategies that improve reading comprehension. *Elementary School Journal, 85* (5), 635–645.

Koppman, P. S. (1983). Questions parents ask—Answers teachers give. Ginn Occasional Papers, Writings in reading and langue arts, No. 16. Columbus, OH: Ginn.

McCormick, C. E., & Mason, J. M. (1989). Fostering reading for Head Start children with little books. In J. Allen & J. Mason (Eds.), *Risk makers, risk takers, risk breakers: Reducing risks for young literacy learners.* Portsmouth, NH: Heinemann.

Mendoza, A. (1985). Reading to children: Their preferences. *The Reading Teacher, 38* (6), 522–527.

Mikulecky, L. (1982). Job literacy: The relationship between school preparation and workplace actuality. *Reading Research Quarterly, 17,* 400–417.

Mikulecky, L. (1984). Preparing students for workplace literacy demands. *Journal of Reading, 28* (3), 253–257.

Monteith, M. K. (1981). The magazine habit. *Language Arts, 58,* 965–969.

Nevi, C. N. (1983). Cross-age tutoring: Why does it help the tutors? *The Reading Teacher, 36* (9), 892–898.

Palincsar, A. S., & Ransom, K. (1988). From the mystery spot to the thoughtful spot: The instruction of metacognitive strategies. *The Reading Teacher, 41* (8), 784–789.

Pearson, P. D. (1985). Changing the face of reading comprehension instruction. *The Reading Teacher, 38* (6), 724–738.

Ribovich, J. K., & Erickson, L. (1980). A study of lifelong reading with implications for instructional programs. *Journal of Reading, 24,* 20–26.

Roeder, H. H., & Lee, N. (1973). Twenty-five teacher-tested ways to encourage voluntary reading. *The Reading Teacher, 27* (1), 48–50.

Spiegel, D. L. (1981). *Reading for pleasure: Guidelines.* Newark, DE: International Reading Association.

Sticht, T. G. (1977). Comprehending reading at work. In M. A. Just & P. A. Carpenter (Eds.), *Cognitive processes in comprehension.* Hillsdale, NJ: Erlbaum.

Taylor, D. (1983). *Family literacy: Young children learning to read and write.* Portsmouth, NH: Heinemann.

Teale, W. H. (1981). Parents reading to their children: What we know and need to know. *Language Arts, 58* (8), 902–912.

Telfer, R. J., & Kann, R. S. (1984). Reading achievement, free reading, watching TV, and listening to music. *Journal of Reading, 27* (6), 536–539.

Vukelich, C. (1984). Parents' role in the reading process: A review of practical suggestions and ways to communicate with parents. *The Reading Teacher, 37* (6), 472–477.

Watson, D. J. (Ed.) (1987). *Ideas and insights: Language arts in the elementary school.* Urbana, IL: National Council of Teachers of English.

Williams, P. A., Haertel, E. H., Haertel, G. D., & Walberg, H. J. (1982). The impact of leisure-time television on school learning. *American Educational Research Journal, 19*, 19–50.

Further Readings

Anderson, G., Higgins, D., & Wurster, S. R. (1985). Differences in the free-reading books selected by high, average, and low readers. *The Reading Teacher, 39* (3), 326–330.

Goldenberg, C. N. (1987). Low-income Hispanic parents' contributions to their first-grade children's word-recognition skills. *Anthropology and Education Quarterly, 18* (3), 149–179.

Janiuk, D. M., & Shanahan, T. (1988). Applying adult literacy practices to primary grade instruction. *The Reading Teacher, 41* (5), 880–886.

Neuman, S. B. (1986). The home environment and fifth-grade students' leisure reading. *Elementary School Journal, 86* (5), 335–343.

Razzano, B. W. (1985). Creating the library habit. *Library Journal, 110,* 111–114.

Scollon, R. (1988). Storytelling, reading, and the micropolitics of literacy. In J. E. Readence & R. S. Baldwin (Eds.), *Dialogues in literacy research.* Thirty-seventh Yearbook of the National Reading Conference, pp. 15–33.

■ ACKNOWLEDGMENTS

(p. 76) "The Sharks" by Denise Levertov: *Collected Earlier Poems, 1940–1960.* Copyright © 1959 by Denise Levertov. Reprinted by permission of New Directions Publishing Company.

(p. 105) Excerpts from "Writing to Clarify Thoughts About Literature" by Kathryn H. Au and Judith A. Scheu, paper for IRA Symposium, 1988. Reprinted by permission.

(p. 126) Excerpt from "Response and Responsibility: Reading, Writing, and Social Studies" by Ben F. Nelms, *The Elementary School Journal,* May 1987, vol. 87, no. 5. Copyright © 1987 by The University of Chicago. Reprinted by permission of The University of Chicago Press.

(p. 136) Figure and Excerpts from "K-W-L: A teaching model that develops active reading of expository text" by Donna M. Ogle, *The Reading Teacher,* February 1986, pp. 565, 567–569. Copyright © 1986 International Reading Association, Inc. Reprinted with permission of Donna M. Ogle and the International Reading Association.

(p. 148) Excerpt from "Balloons Not for All Arteries" by Lawrence K. Altman, *Reader's Digest,* December 1988. Originally appeared in *The New York Times,* August 2, 1988, "Experts Advise Caution on Using Balloons to Clear Arteries." Copyright © 1988 by The New York Times Company. Reprinted by permission.

(p. 164) Excerpts from "Teaching Students to Write Informational Reports" by John D. Beach, *Elementary School Journal,* 1983. Reprinted by permission of The University of Chicago Press.

(p. 183) "Night Comes" by Beatrice Schenk de Regniers from *A Bunch of Poems and Verses.* Copyright © 1977 by Beatrice Schenk de Regniers. Reprinted by permission of the author.

(p. 192) Excerpts from "Concept definition: A key to improving students' vocabulary" by Robert M. Schwartz and Taffy Raphael, *The Reading Teacher,* November 1985. Copyright © 1985 International Reading Association, Inc. Reprinted with permission of Robert M. Schwartz and the International Reading Association.

(p. 201) Excerpts from "Teaching elementary students to use word-part clues" by Thomas G. White et al., *The Reading Teacher,* January 1989. Copyright © 1989 International Reading Association, Inc. Reprinted with permission of Thomas G. White and the International Reading Association.

(p. 225) Excerpts from "Making Connections: Facilitating Literacy in Young Children" by Linda V. Beardsley and Miriam Marecek-Zeman, *Childhood Education,* February 1987, vol. 63, no. 3. Reprinted by permission of Linda V. Beardsley and Miriam Marecek-Zeman and the Association for Childhood Education International, 11141 Georgia Avenue, Suite 200, Wheaton, MD. Copyright © 1987 by the Association.

(p. 234) From "Reading to kindergarten children" by J. Mason, C. Petermann, and B. Kerr, *Emerging Literacy,* Strickland and Morrow, eds., 1988. Reprinted by permission of the International Reading Association.

(p. 435) Excerpt from "Classroom Task Environments and Students' Task-related Beliefs" by Linda M. Anderson et al., *The Elementary School Journal,* vol. 88, no. 3,

1988. Copyright © 1988 by The University of Chicago. Reprinted by permission of The University of Chicago.

(p. 450) Excerpt from "Improving reading instruction through the use of responsive elaboration" by G. Duffy and L. Roehler, *The Reading Teacher*, February 1987. Copyright © International Reading Association, Inc. Reprinted with permission of Gerald G. Duffy and the International Reading Association.

(p. 453) Excerpt from "Learning from Academic Tasks" by Ronald W. Marx and John Walsh, *The Elementary School Journal*, vol. 88, no. 3, 1988. Reprinted by permission of The University of Chicago Press.

(p. 467) Excerpts from "Preparing students for workplace literacy demands" by Larry Mikulecky, *Journal of Reading*, December 1984. Copyright © 1984 International Reading Association, Inc. Reprinted with permission of Larry Mikulecky and the International Reading Association.

Photo Credits

Cover: Superstock

Eugene Kam: pages 21, 34, 63, 68, 83, 85, 115, 129, 150, 167, 190, 209, 220, 246, 253, 272, 278, 336, 378, 409, 430, 444, 477, 482, 491

Elizabeth Crews: page 270

Jean-Claude Lejeune: page 362

All photos not credited are the property of Scott, Foresman and Company.

Index